XML Topic Maps

XML TOPIC MAPS

CREATING AND USING TOPIC MAPS FOR THE WEB

Jack Park, Editor
and
Sam Hunting, Technical Editor

✦Addison-Wesley

Boston • San Francisco • New York • Toronto • Montreal
London • Munich • Paris • Madrid
Capetown • Sydney • Tokyo • Singapore • Mexico City

The publisher offers discounts on this book when ordered in quantity for bulk purchases and special sales. For more information, please contact:

U.S. Corporate and Government Sales
(800) 382-3419
corpsales@pearsontechgroup.com

For sales outside of the U.S., please contact:

International Sales
(317) 581-3793
international@pearsontechgroup.com

Visit Addison-Wesley on the Web: www.awprofessional.com

Library of Congress Cataloging-in-Publication Data

Park, Jack.
  XML topic maps : creating and using topic maps for the Web / Jack Park and Sam Hunting.
      p.   cm.
Includes bibliographical references and index.
  ISBN 0-201-74960-2 (paperback)
  1. XML (Document markup language)   2. Metadata.   I. Hunting, Sam.   II. Title.
  QA76.76.H94 P376 2002
  005.7'2—dc21   2002003679

ISBN: 0-201-74960-2
Text printed on recycled paper
1 2 3 4 5 6 7 8 9 10—CRS—0605040302
First printing, July 2002

CONTENTS

Foreword xvii
Preface xix
Acknowledgments xxiii
Contributors xxv

Chapter 1:   Let There Be Light 1
Jack Park
   Opening Salvo 1
   Resources 8
      Topic Maps: General 8
      Topic Map Software: Commercial 9
      Topic Map Software: Open Source 9
   What's in Here? 9
      Historical and Background Chapters .10
      Technical Chapters 11
      Forward-Thinking Chapters 14

Chapter 2:   Introduction to the Topic Maps Paradigm 17
Michel Biezunski
   Managing Complex Knowledge Networks .17
   Primary Constructs 18
      Topics 18
      Associations 19
      Names 19
      Scopes and Namespaces 20
      Rules for Merging Topic Maps 21

The Big Picture: Merging Information and Knowledge 22

    A Step Toward Improved Interconnectivity .22

Design Principles for XTM 23

    Simplicity 23

    Neutrality 25

From ISO/IEC 13250 to XTM 25

Summary 30

Acknowledgments 30

Chapter 3:   **A Perspective on the Quest for Global**
               Knowledge Interchange **31**

Steven R. Newcomb

Information Is Interesting Stuff 32

Information and Structure Are Inseparable 34

Formal Languages Are Easier to Compute Than
    Natural Languages 34

Generic Markup Makes Natural Languages More Formal 35

A Brief History of the Topic Maps Paradigm 37

Data and Metadata: The Resource-Centric View 40

    Metametadata, Metametametadata 42

Subjects and Data: The Subject-Centric View .42

Understanding Sophisticated Markup Vocabularies 45

The Topic Maps Attitude 48

Summary 50

Chapter 4:   **The Rise and Rise of Topic Maps** **51**

Sam Hunting

Milestones in Standards and Specifications 53

    XTM 1.0 versus ISO 13250 54

    OASIS 55

    Current ISO Activities 55

Milestones in Software 64

The Future of Topic Maps 65

    The State of the Paradigm 65

    The Near Future 66

Chapter 5: **Topic Maps from Representation to Identity: Conversation, Names, and Published Subject Indicators** **67**

Bernard Vatant

What Is the Conversation About? .... .67

A Finger Pointing at a Planet .... .69

So What about Published Subject Indicators? .... .73

PSIs Are Binding Points for Subject Identity .... .74

PSIs Have to Meet High Quality Requirements .... .75

PSIs Are Good for Pragmatic Bottom-up Tasks .... .75

PSIs Cannot Pretend to Universality nor Strong Symbolic Signification .... .76

Back to the Conversation Subject .... .77

Addendum: A Note on the Figures .... .79

Chapter 6: **How to Start Topic Mapping Right Away with the XTM Specification** **81**

Sam Hunting

XTM Topic Mapping .... .81

Why Topic Maps? .... .82

Appetizer .... .83

Introducing <topic>, <baseName>, <scope>, <baseNameString>, and <occurrence> .... .84

Introducing <subjectIdentity> .... .85

Introducing <scope> .... .87

Main Course .... .88

Introducing <association>, <member>, and <roleSpec> .... .89

Introducing <instanceOf> .... .90

Dessert .... .93

Brandy, Cigars .... .97

Introducing <variant>, <variantName>, and <parameters> ...... .97

Introducing <resourceData> .... .98

Paying the Bill and Putting on Your Coat .... .98

Summary .... .99

Acknowledgments .... .100

Resources .... .100

Chapter 7: Knowledge Representation, Ontological Engineering, and Topic Maps **103**
Leo Obrst and Howard Liu

Knowledge as Interpretation 104

Data, Knowledge, and Information 104

Knowledge Issues: Acquisition, Representation,
and Manipulation 106

The Roots of Ontological Engineering: Knowledge Technologies 109

Root: Knowledge Representation 109

Root: Knowledge Engineering 112

Slightly Shriveled Root: Expert Systems
(and Their Deficiencies) 113

New Knowledge Technology Branches:
Toward Ontological Engineering 116

Branch: The Formalization of Semantic Networks
and the Rise of Description Logics 116

Branch: Constraint and Logic Programming 117

Ontological Engineering 119

Ontologies and Topic Maps 124

Ontologies 124

How Ontologies Relate to Topic Maps 125

How to Build an Ontology 126

Ontology-Driven Topic Maps 129

The Advantages of the Ontology-Driven
Topic Maps Approach 129

The Future of the Ontology-Driven
Topic Maps Approach 131

Summary 132

Acknowledgments 133

References 134

Selected Information and Research Sites 147

Chapter 8: Topic Maps in the Life Sciences **149**
John Park and Nefer Park

A Literature Review 149

The Need for Classification 150

The Five Kingdoms 151

Kingdom Animalia 152

Creating Topic Maps for a Web Site 155
    A First View 155
    Developing the XTM Document 155
    Where Are We Now? 163
Summary 165
Resources for More Information on the Life Sciences 166

**Chapter 9:   Creating and Maintaining Enterprise
                Web Sites with Topic Maps and XSLT** **167**
Nikita Ogievetsky
The XTM Framework for the Web 168
XTM as Source Code for Web Sites 171
HTML Visualization of Topic Map Constructs 173
Topics 174
    Special <topic> Elements: Root 174
    The Special Topic Map Website Ontology Layer 176
XSLT Layers 182
The XSLT Layout Layer 183
The XSLT Back-End and Presentation Layers 188
    Querying Topic Types 188
    Querying and Displaying Topic Names 190
    Querying and Displaying Topic Occurrences 192
    Querying and Displaying Topic Associations 195
Summary 197
Acknowledgments 197
References 198

Chapter 10:   Open Source Topic Map Software **199**
About Open Source Software 199
Four Projects 200

SemanText **204**
Eric Freese
Browsing Topic Maps 204
Creating and Modifying Topic Maps 204
Developing Inference Rules 208
Future Plans 209
Summary 210

XTM Programming with TM4J **211**
Kal Ahmed

The TM4J Core API 211
    File Organization and Packaging 211
    Package Dependencies 213
Getting Started 213
    Using the Basic API Features 213
    Loading a Topic Map 218
    Creating Implicit Topics 220
    Saving a Topic Map 221
    Using the Advanced API Features 223
    Property Change Listeners 225
TMP3—A Sample Topic Map Processing Application 228
    Defining the Topic Map Ontology 228
    Designing the Application 229
    Implementing the Application 230
    Extending the Application 243
TM4J Future Directions 244
Summary 244

Nexist Topic Map Testbed **244**
Jack Park

The Development of Nexist 245
    The Past 245
    The Present 245
Use Cases 245
Design Requirements 249
The Persistent XTM Engine 249
    The Persistent Store 249
    The XTM Engine 251
The User Interface 254
    The Server User Interface 254
    The Client User Interface 254
Summary 260
References 260

GooseWorks Toolkit 260
Sam Hunting
   Program Design 261
   GwTk's Omnivorous Nature 262
   ISO Compliance 263
   Use Cases 263
   Query Language 264
   Current Tools 265
   Summary 265

Chapter 11:   Topic Map Visualization 267
Bénédicte Le Grand
   Requirements for Topic Map Visualization 267
      Different Uses for Topic Maps 268
      Representation Requirements 268
      Navigation Requirements 269
   Visualization Techniques 270
      Current Topic Map Visualizations 270
      General Visualization Techniques 270
   Summary 281
   References 281

Chapter 12:   Topic Maps and RDF 283
Eric Freese
   A Sample Application: The Family Tree 283
   RDF and Topic Maps 284
      An Introduction to RDF 284
      The RDF Data Model 285
      RDF XML Syntax 288
      RDF Schema 291
      The Similarities 292
      The Differences 294
      Combining Topic Maps and RDF 295
   Modeling RDF Using Topic Map Syntax 296
      Example 1: Markup Schemes 299
      Example 2: Topic Reification 300
      Example 3: Associations 301

Example 4: Bag Data Structure 303
Example 5: Another Association 305
Example 6: Multiple Occurrences 307
Example 7: Another Bag Data Structure 309
Example 8: RDF 311
Example 9: Sorted Data Structures 315
Example 10: Aggregation 316
Example 11: Relational Data Structures 320
Example 12: Dublin Core Metadata 321
Summary 325
References 325

Chapter 13:   Topic Maps and Semantic Networks **327**
Eric Freese
Semantic Networks: The Basics 328
Comparing Topic Maps, RDF, and Semantic Networks 330
Building Semantic Networks from Topic Maps 330
Published Subject Indicators 331
Association Properties 332
Type Hierarchies 334
Topic Map Schemas 339
Harvesting the Knowledge Identified in Markup 353
Identifying and Interpreting the Knowledge Found
within Documents 353
Summary 354
References 355

**Chapter 14:   Topic Map Fundamentals for
                Knowledge Representation** **357**
H. Holger Rath
A Simple KR Example 357
A Quick Review of Concepts for Topic Maps and KR 359
Topic Map Templates 360
Class Hierarchies 362
Superclass–Subclass Relationship as Association 363
Class–Instance Relationship as Association 364
Association Properties 365

Inference Rules 366
   An Inference Rule Example 367
Consistency Contraints 373
   Constraint Patterns 374
   Topic Class Example 375
   Association Class Example 377
   Constraints and Class Hierarchies 379
Summary 380
References 380

Chapter 15:   Topic Maps in Knowledge Organization 383
Alexander Sigel
Suggestions for Reading This Chapter 383
   The Overlap between KO and TMs 384
   KO, Knowledge Structures, and TMs 385
   KOxTM: Impact Directions and Open Questions 386
What Is KO? 391
   Some Definitions: What Is and Does KO?
     To What End KO? 391
   Some Elements of KO Theory: On Problems
     and Principles 394
   KO in Practice 417
KO as a Use Case for TMs 424
   KO: A Primary Use Case for TMs 425
   Knowledge Networks in KM:
     A Typical KOxTM Use Case 425
   KO on Topic Map Core Concepts (the "T-A-O"
     and "I-F-S" of Topic Maps) 426
   The Potential Value of TMs for KO 427
   Temporary Impediments to TM Adoption: KO Prejudices 428
   KO Challenges That Recur with TMs 430
   Examples of KO Issues That Recur with TMs 431
Illustrative Examples 438
   Shorter Examples of Fruitful KO with TMs 439
   Toward a TM on KO Resources: First Experiences 447
A Look into the Future: Toward Innovative TM-Based
   Information Services 449

Summary 452
Acknowledgments 453
Selected Abbreviations 454
References 457

Chapter 16:   Prediction: A Profound Paradigm Shift **477**
Kathleen M. Fisher
Language 478
Transmitting the Word 479
Lightness of Being 480
A Brief History of Knowledge Representation and Education 484
The Ephemeral Nature of Many New Ideas 487
What the Research Suggests about Knowledge Representation
   and Learning 488
      Students Learn from Semantic Networks .488
      Students' Models Become Increasingly Similar
         to Instructors' Models 492
      Constructing Semantic Networks Alters the Ways
         We Think and Learn 492
      Semantic Network–Based Courses Teach, Not Just Tell 494
      Understanding Relations *Is* Understanding 496
A Paradigm Shift: Patterning Speech to Patterning Thought 498
Summary 500
Acknowledgments 500
References 500

Chapter 17:   Topic Maps, the Semantic Web, and Education **507**
Jack Park
What Is the Semantic Web? 508
How Can Topic Maps Play an Important Role
   in the Semantic Web? 511
What's Next? 511
      Education on the Web 512
      Constructivist Learning Theory 513
      Principles of Constructivist Learning 513
      Toward Constructivist Learning Environments 514
      IBIS 517
      Topic Maps 519

Toward an Implementation 521
An Application 526
Closing Salvo 526
References 527

Glossary **531**

Appendix A: Tomatoes Topic Map **543**

Appendix B: Topic Map for Chapter 9 ....**547**

Appendix C: XSLT Style Sheet for Chapter 9 ....**563**

Appendix D: Genealogical Topic Map **569**

Index **585**

FOREWORD

In 1962 I wrote a paper, "Augmenting Human Intellect: A Conceptual Framework," in which I laid out my vision for how humanity can tackle its most complex, urgent problems. I proposed a framework driven by a simple premise: As problems get harder, we need to get collectively smarter.

As I considered ways to increase our collective intellectual capabilities, I thought about language and the symbols that humans use to create conceptual models of the world. Our most basic conceptual structures have been evolving for thousands of years. Alphabets evolved from pictographs, followed by white space and punctuation. The introduction of the printing press led to conceptual structures such as paragraphs, page numbers, footnotes, concordance indices, and tables of contents.

I realized that computers offered radical new ways of portraying and manipulating conceptual structures, and that further evolving these symbols and techniques could greatly augment our capabilities.

Although one idea proposed in that paper—hypertext—has became pervasive today in simple form, I have been waiting for 40 years for the active exploration of concept mapping. As a result, I am delighted to see the work being done with Topic Maps, and I wholeheartedly support this book, which was edited by my friend and colleague Jack Park.

In order to achieve the full potential of Topic Maps, we need tools to integrate these conceptual maps with our vast repositories of documents and recorded dialog, as well as tools for manipulating and viewing these structures in different ways. I hope that this book is a first step in that direction, and that you, the reader, will help make these possibilities reality.

—Douglas C. Engelbart

PREFACE

In a former life, I built microprocessor-based data acquisition systems, originally for locating and monitoring wind and solar energy systems. I suppose it is fair to say that I have long been involved in roaming solution space. Along the way, farmers, on whose land the energy systems were often situated, discovered that my monitoring tools helped them form better predictions of fruit frost, irrigation needs, and pesticide needs. My program, which ran on an Apple II computer that had telephone access to the distributed monitoring stations, printed out large piles of data. Epiphany happened on the day that a manager of one of those monitoring systems came to me and asked, "What else is this data good for?" That was the day I entered the field of artificial intelligence, looking for ways to organize all that data and mine it for new knowledge.

A recent discussion on National Public Radio focused on the nature and future of literature. Listening to that conversation while navigating the perils of Palo Alto traffic, I heard two comments that I shall paraphrase, with emphasis placed according to my own whims, as follows: In the past, we turned to the *great works of literature* to ponder what is life. Today, we turn to the *great works of science* to ponder the same issues.

In some sense, the message I pulled out of that is that we (the really *big* we) tend to appeal to science and technology to find comfort and solutions to our daily needs. In that same sense, I found justification for this book and the vision I had when the book was conceived. Make no mistake here—I already had plenty of justification for the vision and the book. As is often pontificated by many, we are engulfed in a kind of information overload that threatens to choke off our ability to solve major problems that face all of humanity.

No, the vision is not an expression of doom and gloom. Rather, it is an expression of my own deep and optimistic belief that it is through education, through an enriched human intellect, that solutions will be found, or at least, the *solution space* will become a more productive environment in which to operate. The vision expressed here is well grounded in the need to organize and mine data, all part of the solution space.

While walking along a corridor at an XML conference in San Jose early in the year 2000, I noticed a sign that said "Topic Maps," with an arrow pointing to the right. I proceeded immediately to execute a personal "column right" command, entered a room, and met Steve Newcomb. The rest all makes sense. While in Paris later that year, I saw the need to take the XTM technology to the public. This book was then conceived at XML 2000 in Paris, and several authors signed on immediately. This book came with a larger vision than simply taking XTM to the public. I saw topic maps as an important tool in solution space. The vision included much more; topic maps are just one of *many* tools in that space. I wanted to start a book series, one that is thematically associated with my view of solution space.

This book is the first in that series, flying under the moniker *Open Knowledge Systems*. By using the word *open*, I am saying that the series is about making the tools and information required to operate in solution space completely open and available to all who would participate. *Open* implies that each book in the series intends to include an *Open Source Software* project, one that enables all readers to immediately "play in the sandbox" and, hopefully, go beyond by extending the software and contributing that new experience to solution space.

Each contribution to the *Open Knowledge Systems* series is intended to be a living document, meaning that each work will be available at *http://www.nexist.org*.[1] The entire contents of this Web site will be browsable and supported with an online forum so that topics discussed in the books can be further discussed online.

This book is about topic maps, particularly topic maps implemented in the XTM Version 1.0 specification format, as conceived by the XTM Authoring Group, which was started by an experienced group of individuals along with the vision and guidance of Steve Newcomb and Michel Biezunski, both contributing authors for this book. As with many new technologies, the XTM specification is, in most regards, not yet complete. In fact, a standard like XTM can *never* be complete simply because such standards must coevolve with the environment in which they are applied. In the same vein, a book such as this cannot be a coherent work simply because much of what is evolving now is subject to differing opinions, views, and so forth.

There are a few assumptions made by all of the authors who contributed to this book. Mostly, the assumptions presume some minimal familiarity with Extensible Markup Language (XML), Extensible Style Language (XSL and XSLT), and Resource Description Framework (RDF). Please keep in mind that the book presents many Web site references. Web sites occasionally disappear. While the links presented were tested during the writing phase and again during final manuscript editing, do not be surprised if some of them fail to remain in service. Since this book will remain a living document on the Web, we hope to keep all links up-to-date on the book's Web site.

---

[1] As this book is going into print, the Web site is going online.

Because of my view that solution space itself is coevolving along with the participants in that space, I have adopted an editorial management style that I suspect should be explained. My style is based on the understanding that I am combining contributions from many different individuals, each with a potentially different worldview and each with a different writing style. The content focus of this book is, of course, on topic maps, but I believe that it is not necessary to force a coherent worldview on the different authors—it is my hope that readers and, indeed, solution space will profit by way of exposure to differing views and opinions. There will, by the very nature of this policy, be controversy. Indeed, we are exploring the vast universe of discourse on the topic of *knowledge*, and there exists plenty of controversy just in that sandbox alone.

There is also the possibility of overlap. Some chapters are likely to offer the same or similar (or even differing) points of view on the same point. Case in point: knowledge representation. This book has several chapters on that topic: one on ontological engineering, one on knowledge representation, and one on knowledge organization. Two chapters talk in some detail about semantic networks, and other chapters discuss how people learn. It's awfully easy to see just how these can overlap, and they do. My management style has been that which falls out of research in chaos theory: use the least amount of central management, and let the authors sort it out for themselves. History will tell us whether this approach works.

ACKNOWLEDGMENTS

Producing this book turned out to be much harder than I expected. It's true, I was warned in advance that I was biting off more than I could chew, but such warnings never stopped me in the past. Let me tell you what was hard about the project.

It wasn't what people warned—that coordinating the efforts of many authors would be difficult. I chose some of the best authors in the world, and nobody let me down. I strongly believe that the results prove that. The difficulty was this: coordinating the manuscript with the rapidly changing technological landscape was a killer. Readers may also think I experienced difficulty in coordinating the various writing styles of a diverse authoring community. Actually, that was not a difficulty at all. I simply decided up front that the nature of this book would be "style permissive," and the result is a book with chapters of varying length and content. I decided very early that this book was not intended to be a "cookbook" for building topic maps. I believed that, given the rapidity with which the nature of topic maps technology might evolve, a "cookbook" approach would be premature.

This manuscript was first proposed in Paris during one of the earliest XTM Authoring Group meetings. Fat chance I had there to anticipate just how much our thinking would evolve over time. The manuscript was well developed by the time the first working version of XTM was made public. That's when the technological landscape started to evidence the massive convulsions of a magnitude-8 earthquake. Nevertheless, my team of coauthors persisted, and Sam Hunting jumped in recently and contributed an additional chapter (Chapter 4), which provides a bridge between the latest activities in the XTM community and the presentations of the other chapters. Sam and I gratefully acknowledge the assistance of Steve Newcomb and Michel Biezunski in developing the glossary. I gratefully acknowledge Sam's "hero's effort" in helping me to bring this book to completion. Working with Chrysta Meadowbrooke at Stillwater Publishing Services to massage this manuscript into shape was an enormous pleasure. I thank Kathy Glidden of Stratford Publishing Services for keeping this project on track.

Now, let me tell you what was, at once, easy and fun about this project. VerticalNet funded all of my early work on the XTM project, with the full and enthusiastic support of Hugo Daley and Adam Cheyer. I am very grateful for that support. The production of this book was made possible by the incredible enthusiasm and efforts of each of the coauthors who submitted a chapter for me to include and by the assistance of Mary T. O'Brien and Alicia Carey, both at Addison-Wesley. Mary O'Brien agreed with me that this book should be a "living document" with a Web presence and the ability to be kept up-to-date.

Perhaps, for me, the most profound influence on this project came from the two individuals who started topic maps in the first place, Steve Newcomb and Michel Biezunski. Along the way, by personal contact and by way of e-mail lists involved with topic maps, several other individuals have, in many ways, also contributed to this work. I am sure I will miss some names, but those who are pounding their way to visibility include Glen and Helen Haydon, Douglas Engelbart, Mary Keeler, Murray Altheim, Simon Buckingham Shum, Bernard Vatant, Mary Keeler, John Sowa, Robert Barta, Scott Tsao, Ann Wrightson, Steve Heckler, Sunthar Visuvalingam, Steve Pepper, Jeff Conklin, Kathleen Fisher, Alex Shapiro, Eugene Kim, Eric Armstrong, Rod Welch, and Peter Jones. I am also pleased to acknowledge and thank the reviewers of this manuscript who made many valuable comments and suggestions.

This book would not exist without the enthusiastic support of my wife, Helen, and the support of our children, John and Nefer, who also teamed up to contribute a chapter to the manuscript.

—Jack Park
  Brownsville, California
  March 2002

CONTRIBUTORS

Kal Ahmed

Founder, Techquila

Kal Ahmed is a consultant specializing in XML document and knowledge management solutions. He has long experience with XML and SGML document management systems and more recently has worked extensively with Topic Maps, both as a founding member of TopicMaps.org and as a contributor to the XTM 1.0 specification. Kal is the lead developer of the open source topic map toolkit TM4J and hosts other topic map and meta data processing tools on his site, *http://www.techquila.com*.

Michel Biezunski

Consultant, Coolheads Consulting

Michel Biezunski is an editor of the ISO/IEC Topic Maps standard. He holds a Ph.D. in the history of physics. He has been at the origin of the topic maps paradigm, together with Steven Newcomb, and is still actively involved in the design of its Reference Model. He is helping corporations and government agencies to implement topic map applications.

Kathleen M. Fisher

Professor of Biology and Director, Center for Research in Mathematics and Science Education, San Diego State University

Dr. Kathleen Fisher has worked in biology education research and development for 30 years. Her recent book with coauthors J. Wandersee and D. Moody, *Mapping Biology Knowledge*, is now available in paperback from Kluwer. She developed the

SemNet learning and knowledge construction tool with the SemNet Research Group. The Semantica software series knowledge transfer tools, successors to the SemNet software, are now being produced and marketed by Semantic Research, Inc., 1055 Shafter Street, San Diego, CA. The Semantica 2.1 authoring tool and the Semantica 3.0 Reader will be released in summer 2002.

Eric Freese

Senior Consultant, Chair, TopicMaps.org

Eric Freese has 15 years of experience in the area of information, document, and knowledge management. His experience includes research, analysis, specification, design, development, testing, implementation, integration, and management of database systems and computer technologies in business, education, and government environments. Eric is also the chief architect and developer of SemanText, an open source system that uses topic maps to build semantic networks through inference and data harvesting (*http://www.semantext.com*).

Sam Hunting

Principal, eTopicality, Inc.

Sam Hunting is the principal of eTopicality, Inc. (*http://www.etopicality.com*), a consultancy whose services include topic map creation, content analysis, and the development of document type definitions (DTDs). He is a founding member of TopicMaps.org, which developed the XML Topic Maps (XTM) specification. He is also a coauthor of the XTM 1.0 DTD. Cofounder of the GooseWorks project for creating open source topic map tools, he has been working with markup technology for over 10 years.

Bénédicte Le Grand

Assistant Professor, Laboratoire d'Informatique de Paris 6

Dr. Bénédicte Le Grand received her engineer diploma from the Institut National des Telecommunications in 1997. She received her Ph.D. in computer sciences from the Laboratoire d'Informatique de Paris 6. Her research deals with information retrieval and complex systems visualization, focusing on information retrieval and navigation on the Web. She has been working on topic maps characterization and visualization for several years. She is a founding member of TopicMaps.org.

Howard H. Liu

Principal, Confucius School

Howard Liu, an ontologist, a programmer, and a school principal, has coauthored research articles on ontological engineering and e-commerce. He actively pursues his interests in mathematics, music, languages, and ontology-driven information systems.

Steven R. Newcomb

Consultant, Coolheads Consulting (*http://www.coolheads.com*)

Dr. Steven Newcomb is a coeditor of the ISO 10744:1992 and 10744:1997 HyTime and 13250:2000 Topic Maps standards, cofounder of TopicMaps.org, and coeditor of the XTM specification. He originally developed the GroveMinder technology now owned by E-Premis Corporation. Steven is also the Founding Chair of the Extreme Markup Languages Conferences.

Leo Obrst

Lead Artificial Intelligence Scientist, MITRE

Dr. Leo Obrst works at the MITRE Artificial Intelligence Center in northern Virginia, where he is the Core Technical Area Coordinator for Knowledge Representation and Engineering (ontological engineering, semantics and formal methods, and constraint and logic technologies), focusing on context-based semantic interoperability, ontology-based modeling of complex decision making, natural language semantics, intelligent agents, and Internet knowledge brokering. Formerly, he was the Director of Ontological Engineering at VerticalNet.com, a department he formed to create ontologies in the product and service space to support business-to-business e-commerce. He is also a member of the W3C Web Ontology Working Group (*http://www.w3.org/2001/sw/WebOnt/*), a member of a number of working groups of OntoWeb (*http://www.ontoweb.org/*), and an active participant in the IEEE Standard Upper Ontology group, where he is an assistant technical editor for one proposed standard ontology candidate, the Information Flow Framework (*http://suo.ieee.org/*). He received his Ph.D. in theoretical linguistics from the University of Texas at Austin, focusing on aspects of the formal semantics of natural language.

Nikita Ogievetsky

Consultant; President, Cogitech, Inc.

Coming from Neutrino astrophysics, Nikita Ogievetsky devotes his time to research in the world of markup languages and knowledge management. He is a founding and participating member of TopicMaps.org and a frequent presenter at XML and SGML conferences. His company, Cogitech, Inc., provides training and consulting services.

Jack Park

Bootstrap Alliance, International Learning Consortium, Marysville Charter Academy for the Arts

Jack Park is a software developer, a "senior student" who teaches software development, and the father of two great kids. A founding member of TopicMaps.org, he is also the lead developer at *http://www.nexist.org*.

John L. Park

John Park is attending the 9th grade at a charter academy for the fine and performing arts. His interests drive him to practice and study computer graphics and computer gaming strategies. He is also studying software development.

Nefer L. Park

Nefer Park is attending the 11th grade at a charter academy for the fine and performing arts. Her work at school focuses on creative writing, singing, and sciences related to marine biology.

H. Holger Rath

Dr. Hans Holger Rath is Director Research & Development at empolis GmbH—a Germany based company providing premium products and services for content management and knowledge management. Holger started at STEP Electronic Publishing Solutions GmbH—a company acquired by empolis—in 1996 as senior consultant and project manager and headed the consulting department from 1998–2001. Prior to his work for STEP he was head of the Document Computing department at the Computer Graphics Center (ZGDV e.V.). Holger represents Germany in the ISO standards committee which is responsible for SGML, DSSSL, HyTime, and Topic Maps. He is co-editor of the new ISO standards initiative TMQL (Topic Map Query Language) and chair of the OASIS TC 'Vocabulary for XML Standards and Technologies'. He is a founding member of TopicMaps.org.

Alexander Sigel

Researcher in Knowledge Organization, Social Science Information Centre, Bonn, Germany

Alexander Sigel is Knowledge Manager and Knowledge Engineer for an information technology consultancy in Cologne, Germany, focusing on the insurance domain. In addition to managing sociocultural knowledge processes, he models conceptual knowledge structures in order to build sophisticated finding aids, currently in the context of a commercial Case-Based Reasoning system. Previously, he investigated methods and developed tools for improved conceptual knowledge organization and summarization of intellectual assets at the Social Science Information Centre in, Bonn. He holds an M.A. in information science. Alexander is an expert in knowledge organization, an active member of the International Society for Knowledge Organization, and a Perl enthusiast.

Bernard Vatant

Consultant, Mondeca

Bernard Vatant is a former high school mathematics teacher who graduated in 1975 from ENSET (Cachan, France). His research interests have long been in knowledge representation and organization, singularly applied to the popularization of astronomy. He has been working since the end of 2000 as a consultant for Mondeca (*http://www.mondeca.com*), where he participates in the development of topic maps and vocabularies and coordinates the Semantopic Map project. He has been a participating member in the XTM Authoring Group and is a founding member and current chair of the OASIS Topic Maps Published Subjects Technical Committee.

Chapter 1
LET THERE BE LIGHT

JACK PARK

Opening Salvo

We are smart enough to realize we are stupid, and stupid enough to make the problem of becoming smarter hard. —ANDERS SANDBERG[1]

I know; that's a heady, arrogant way to open a book. But this book is about heady stuff, and I'll try to prove it. To do so, I shall cast the information this book presents in a light far brighter than topic maps, computers, indeed, the Universe and Everything.[2] That's my intent, anyway.

David Weinberger had this to say about the Web:

> The world that we've carved for ourselves out of the rock and ice of the earth has always been a social world, one in which we share interests and presuppositions, and, most of all, a language. The sociality of the world has always been hemmed in by the fact of distance, a type of enforced intimacy that we take for granted. But there's no matter on the Web and thus no distance. It is a purely social realm; all we have are one another and what we've written. And what we've written has been written for others. The Web is a public place that we've built by doing public things.[3]

---

[1]From "Amplifying Cognition: Extending Memory and Intelligence," 1997. Accessed online at *http://www.extropy.org/ideas/journal/previous/1997/11-01.html.*

[2]With apologies to the late Douglas Adams. See his site at *http://www.douglasadams.com/.*

[3]From "Our Web," *JOHO (Journal of the Hyperlinked Organization)*, April 20, 2001. Accessed online at *http://www.hyperorg.com/backissues/joho-apr20-01.html#our.* A note on this quote: I first spotted it in the July 2001 issue of *Linux Journal*, and by way of Google I found it in *JOHO*.

It is not specifically topic maps that are heady stuff. Not even the new XTM specification. It's the World Wide Web, in particular, the *Semantic Web* aspect of it, that's heady stuff, together with all the stuff we've written.[4] Topic maps are part of the Semantic Web; of course, topic maps are not the whole story, but certainly XTM is destined to be an important tool in the vast and growing armamentarium emerging under the Semantic Web moniker. We have seen the Web grow from being a space where technical papers were shared to a space where just about everything humans think about is somehow covered by one or a zillion Web sites. And, in human interaction, we have experienced information overload. Indeed, information overload appears to be ubiquitous.

When I pick up a good technical book, I often hit the book's index first. Why? To see if my favorite scholar is mentioned, to see if my favorite topic is mentioned, and so forth. Indeed, many people use an index as a kind of filter to determine whether they want to go any further with the book. The big picture lies in the term *filter*. If you want to go somewhere in some territory, you choose to consult a map first rather than make SWAGs[5] and drive all over the place looking for what you want. That's where topic maps come in. They are *maps;* only maps, and not the territory itself.[6] And maps, being many things, are filters.

So, a topic map is just a map, and not the territory itself. How do I make a topic map more useful? What does *more useful* mean? Now that's a focus question if I ever saw one. It seems to me that if you want a map on which to plan the construction of, say, a new building, although you might start with a road map used to navigate the town in which you plan the construction, you would proceed with a topological map, perhaps one commissioned from a local surveyor. Thus I offer a response to the "What does *more useful* mean?" question as follows: the map must represent the territory in such a way that the application the map is intended to serve is best served.[7] You retort, "*Say what?*" to which I respond that there is, indeed, a semiotic aspect to this discussion— the words need to fit the problem space I have created. Let me explain.

This book discusses the application of topic maps in the service of knowledge representation. That's like uncovering an enormous snake pit.[8] First, there is the big question, "What is knowledge?" But why are we considering that when I'm just try-

---

[4]When I wrote this during March 2001, Google said it was searching 1,346,966,000 Web pages.

[5]Scientific wild ass guesses.

[6]The observation "The map is not the territory" has been attributed to Alfred Korzybski. See *http://www. gestalt.org/alfred.htm* for more information.

[7]I have always been a big fan of responses that don't say anything.

[8]Have you ever uncovered a snake pit? Trust me, you don't want to go there, but we do it here metaphorically anyway.

ing to justify the claim that a map must represent the territory in such a way as to be useful? I believe I am about to claim that a topic map is, indeed, a member of the set of objects that intentionally represent knowledge. Heady stuff, that. A semiotic stance dictates that we make sure that we do, indeed, represent that which needs to be represented. Representing less would result in ample insufficiency, and representing more would result in information overload. As my grandfather used to say, "You can't win for losing."

But as programmers we want to make sure we cover everything, which puts us at risk of generating information overload.[9] How do we cover everything without swamping ourselves with too much information? Hah! By making our topic maps more useful. Dang! Now we've gone full circle and must reask the question, "What does *more useful* mean?" That, my friend, is what topic maps are all about. Again, let me explain.

Topic maps are, indeed, automatically more useful—if done right. A topic map can be structured in such a way that information that lies on a user's critical path can be presented directly while peripheral information can be presented such that cognitive loads on the user are not increased by its presence. Figuring out how to "do topic maps right" is the focus of this book.

To animate what follows, let's revisit the map needed for the construction of a building located in some town. Starting with a road map, we can easily find the location of the building site. But with that map we cannot see what the terrain looks like in order to design the foundation for the building. Maybe the site is on a steeply sloping hill. Maybe it is on flat but marshy land. An online road map might give us hints by way of various signs, such as color gradients. Imagine that we find the location, click on it, and—presto!—another map appears. This time, it's a map drawn to a much larger scale; we have "zoomed in" on the location. Click again and we zoom in all the way to the particular plot of land. At this point, we notice along the margins of the map a few hypertext links. One of them says "Contour," and we click that. Now we have used what started out as an ordinary road map and navigated right down to the particular map we need in order to proceed. We found the right tool for the right job.

But topic maps are not just about navigating territories. We can easily repurpose them for use in the display or discovery of knowledge. Classrooms all over the world are using *concept maps* for this purpose. When concept maps begin to display lots of information in a relational way, they imply a new question: "Can concept maps be topic maps?" If we happen to implement a concept map engine on top of the XTM specification, those concept maps are converted to topic maps, which gain the ability

---

[9]Notice that I still haven't answered the question, "What is knowledge?"

to be shared, merged, and archived in a standard format for future use. Consider the concept map shown in Figure 1–1, which was constructed by my daughter, Nefer.[10]

She constructed this map by typing sentences into a text editor and feeding those sentences to a program I had written that was capable of parsing simple English-like sentences and building a knowledge base.[11] She wrote the following sentences.

> A animal is a livingthing.
>
> A mammal is a animal.
>
> A bird is a animal.
>
> A human is a mammal.
>
> Nefer is a particular human.

Of course, I had to coach her on how to type in a sentence: a *living thing* had to be represented as either a *livingthing* or a *living_thing* in my program. XML topic maps take us beyond all that. Her concept map, cast as an XTM document, contains several *topics* (the bubbles) and several *associations* (the arrows).

As maps or as representations of what we think we know, topic maps are just views into microworlds of knowledge. Figure 1–1 represents the view of a seven-year-old child. Consider the issue of view construction. A topic map, when built using the XTM specification, is just an XML document, meaning that it is a document comprised of a

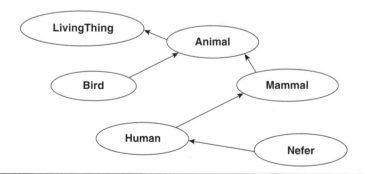

Figure 1–1   A simple taxonomic concept map

---

[10]She was seven years old at the time.

[11]The Scholar's Companion®.

bunch of named tags, like `<topic>` or `<association>`, and the data that fills in the space between tags. Here is the XTM document made from the diagram created by Nefer's sentences. The construction of this document is illustrated in the discussion of Nexist, my open source software project in Chapter 10.

```
<?xml version="1.0"?>
  <!DOCTYPE topicMap SYSTEM "xtm1.dtd">

  <!-- Topics -->
  <!-- Note: all topics are inferred from the relational statements
   that create the associations below -->

  <topicMap xmlns="http://www.topicmaps.org/xtm/1.0/"
      xmlns:xlink="http://www.w3.org/1999/xlink"
      id="NeferTree">

    <topic id="livingThing">
      <baseName>
        <baseNameString>Living Thing</baseNameString>
      </baseName>
    </topic>

    <topic id="animal">
      <baseName>
        <baseNameString>Animal</baseNameString>
      </baseName>
    </topic>

    <topic id="mammal">
      <baseName>
        <baseNameString>Mammal</baseNameString>
      </baseName>
    </topic>

    <topic id="bird">
      <baseName>
        <baseNameString>Bird</baseNameString>
      </baseName>
    </topic>

    <topic id="human">
      <baseName>
        <baseNameString>Human</baseNameString>
      </baseName>
    </topic>

    <topic id="nefer">
      <baseName>
        <baseNameString>Nefer</baseNameString>
```

```
    </baseName>
    <!-- nefer could have an <occurrence> here -->
  </topic>

  <!-- Note: topics which represent associations could include
    appropriate published subject indicators -->

  <topic id="isA">
    <baseName>
      <baseNameString>isA Association</baseNameString>
    </baseName>
  </topic>

  <topic id="isAParticular">
    <baseName>
      <baseNameString>isAParticular Association</baseNameString>
    </baseName>
  </topic>

  <!-- Associations -->

  <!-- "a animal is a livingthing" -->

  <association id="animalIsA">
    <instanceOf>
      <topicRef xlink:href="#isA"/>
    </instanceOf>
    <member>
      <topicRef xlink:href="#animal"/>
    </member>
    <member>
      <topicRef xlink:href="#livingThing"/>
    </member>
  </association>

  <!-- "a mammal is a animal" -->

  <association id="mammalIsA">
    <instanceOf>
      <topicRef xlink:href="#isA"/>
    </instanceOf>
    <member>
      <topicRef xlink:href="#mammal"/>
    </member>
    <member>
      <topicRef xlink:href="#animal"/>
    </member>
  </association>
```

```xml
<!-- "a bird is a animal" -->

<association id="birdIsA">
  <instanceOf>
    <topicRef xlink:href="#isA"/>
  </instanceOf>
  <member>
    <topicRef xlink:href="#bird"/>
  </member>
  <member>
    <topicRef xlink:href="#animal"/>
  </member>
</association>


<!-- "a human is a mammal" -->

<association id="humanIsA">
  <instanceOf>
    <topicRef xlink:href="#isA"/>
  </instanceOf>
  <member>
    <topicRef xlink:href="#human"/>
  </member>
  <member>
    <topicRef xlink:href="#mammal"/>
  </member>
</association>


<!-- "nefer is a particular human" -->

<association id="neferIsAParticular">
  <instanceOf>
    <topicRef xlink:href="#isAParticular"/>
  </instanceOf>
  <member>
    <topicRef xlink:href="#nefer"/>
  </member>
  <member>
    <topicRef xlink:href="#human"/>
  </member>
</association>

</topicMap>
```

How do you turn an XTM document into a view either on a computer screen or on paper at a printer? Among the many ways, there exists XSLT technology, which provides a tool for turning XML tags into HTML Web pages.

Combine topic maps with the other technologies that comprise the Semantic Web[12] and I imagine that lights will come on everywhere. How might that be so? Rather than casting in concrete any statements about combining topic maps with the Semantic Web, consider that many new and wonderful ideas are floating around, some of which are captured and discussed in this book. As such, this book was created to be a part of the evolution of the Semantic Web.

Resources

A good place to mention what's out there regarding topic maps is right up front.[13] Here is a brief listing of important Web sites. (Keep in mind that Web site addresses change from time to time.) After this list of resources, we'll talk more about what's in this book.

Topic Maps: General

http://www.topicmaps.org—the original XTM Web site.

http://www.topicmaps.net—a Web site created by Michel Biezunski and Steven Newcomb.

http://easytopicmaps.com—a WikiWiki (Hawaiian for "quick") Web site devoted to topic maps. Site visitors can add new information or update existing information at this Web site.

http://www.universimmedia.com—Bernard Vatant's "Semantopic Map" Web site.

http://www.oasis-open.org/committee/tm-pubsubj/—a Web site of the Published Subject Indicators committee led by Bernard Vatant.

http://topicmaps.bond.edu.au/—Robert Barta's topic maps Web site.

Professional XML Meta Data—a book by Kal Ahmed, Danny Ayers, Mark Birbeck, Jay Cousins, David Dodds, Josh Lubell, Miloslav Nic, Daniel Rivers-Moore, Andrew Watt, Robert Worden, and Ann Wrightson, published by Wrox Press (*http://www.wrox.com*), Birmingham, UK, 2001.[14]

---

[12]Discussed throughout this book, particularly in Chapters 13 (Topic Maps and Semantic Networks) and 17 (Topic Maps, Semantic Web, and Education), and at *http://www.semanticweb.org*.

[13]This list is not intended to be complete. Resources will be updated periodically at the book's official Web site: *http://www.nexist.org*. The Web being what it is, however, you should always be ready to use a good search engine.

[14]Many of the authors of this recent book are also founders of the XTM Authoring Group.

Topic Map Software: Commercial

http://www.ontopia.net—a site by participants in the XTM Authoring Group and creators of the Ontopia Knowledge Suite; free download available.

http://k42.empolis.co.uk—a site by participants in the XTM Authoring Group and creators of K42, a collaborative environment for capturing, expressing, and delivering knowledge; free download available.

http://www.mondeca.com—a site by participants in the XTM Authoring Group and creators of KIM, the Knowledge Index Manager.

Topic Map Software: Open Source

http://www.semantext.com—the site for the SemanText project discussed in Chapter 10.

http://tm4j.sourceforge.net—the site for the TM4J project discussed in Chapter 10.

http://nexist.sourceforge.net—the site for the Nexist project discussed in Chapter 10.

http://www.goose-works.org—the site for the GooseWorks graph project discussed in Chapter 10.

For other possibilities, check with *http://www.google.com* or search *http://sourceforge.net* for "topic map," "concept map," "mind map," and so on.

What's in Here?

This book covers an enormous range of topical information, and not all that information is expected (or even intended) to be of great value to everyone who opens these pages.[15]

It seems to me that topic maps can be viewed from more than one perspective. One perspective, which users experience, is the external view presented by a topic map. The internal structure of the topic map engine (the program that constructs a selected view) is another perspective. Another is data itself. This book discusses all perspectives. However, not all readers are expected to want or need to understand all perspectives. Let us, then, preview the book in such a way that you can get some idea of how to navigate it to best suit your individual needs.

---

[15] Well, I actually made it this far without answering the question, "What is knowledge?" In some sense, answering that question is left as an exercise for the reader, but I do touch on aspects of it in the closing chapter of this book.

I would like to think that the correct answer to "What's in here?" is this: whatever you want or need. But that is not the correct answer. That could never be a correct answer, so this book is intended to be a *living document*, one complete with one or more associated Web sites that keep the subjects presented here very much alive, evolving, and up-to-date. As a living document, this book aspires to *eventually* cover whatever you need or want within the domain of discourse known as topic maps. Eventually, we'll do topic maps right!

This book includes chapters arranged along three primary themes:

1. Historical and background information
2. Technical issues: how-to information, theory, and projects
3. Forward-thinking visions

Let's explore these themes in more detail.

Historical and Background Chapters

In the beginning, there was the topic map. No, wait! It's not like that. First, there was the invention of markup languages, followed by SGML and SGML topic maps. Then came XML and XML topic maps (named XTM). XTM is now a formal specification. First introduced to the world at the XML 2000 conference in Washington, DC, on December 4, 2000, XTM is now the subject of much discussion as it evolves to meet the changing needs of the Web community. Chapter 2, Introduction to the Topic Maps Paradigm, by Michel Biezunski lays out the history of XTM, particularly as it relates to the HyTime Topic Maps of the ISO 13250 standard. Michel, being a partner with Steven Newcomb in the quest for the platinum ring mentioned below, then describes the architectural elements of XTM itself. You will have the opportunity to come to grips with such concepts as *topic*, *association*, *name*, and so forth.

Beneath the XTM specification is a philosophical point of view. If you want to know what that is about and, perhaps, come to grips with the difference between a *shoe* and *shoe-ness*, then Chapter 3, A Perspective on the Quest for Global Knowledge Interchange, by Steven Newcomb is indicated. If you want to grab the platinum ring— global knowledge interchange—then you must look for some mechanism that not only structures exchanged information but also "puts everybody on the same page."[16]

---

[16]One should not read too much into this notion: given the heterogeneity of human thought and communication skills, it is generally thought that we will *never* find the *same page* for everyone. For the vast number of interesting use cases we can imagine for topic maps, however, it is likely that topic maps and the Semantic Web will provide useful augmentation of communication skills.

The need here is a way to find agreement on the semantics of the exchanged information. Otherwise, humans will likely exchange *noise* that is not easily processed into knowledge. XTM, the XML topic maps specification, is in a very important way a part of Steven's quest to make knowledge interchangeable. In fact, you will discover that there are two different topic map specifications, one an ISO standard (13250) and one an XML specification (XTM). Fitting alongside these are similar projects, such as NewsML,[17] which Ann Wrightson characterizes as being a "light" topic map syntax that also provides features in common with RDF.[18]

Since this book was conceived and first written, much has happened in the XTM field. In order to make the final draft of this book as complete as possible, Sam Hunting contributed Chapter 4, The Rise and Rise of Topic Maps: 1999–2002, which speaks to the many organizational and technical changes behind XTM and to the recent discussions about XTM itself.

An underlying theme of this book is that of *inquiry*. (Inquiring minds want to know. . . .) There is a rich and philosophical history of thinking that impacts the nature of inquiry. The process of inquiry should be conducted within events that result in the exchange of information that results in new knowledge. How, you might ask, can that occur when different participants in the exchange carry different notions of the meanings of topics being discussed? One response that fully anticipates this very question is the notion of Published Subject Indicators (PSIs) as prescribed in the XTM specification. Bernard Vatant contributed Chapter 5, Topic Maps from Representation to Identity, to illuminate XTM's approach to placing specific meanings on topics. As an example, consider the topic Nefer in the concept map illustrated earlier in Figure 1–1. We know that individuals with that particular name have existed throughout history. How can we *disambiguate* that topic? XTM tells us that we can append a specific reference to that particular topic (perhaps a Web page with a photograph of the individual)—a PSI. With that reference, any encounter with that particular topic will not carry any ambiguity regarding to whom the topic refers.

With the historical and requisite background views presented, it is time to go forth and build topic maps. The technical chapters in the book cover that.

Technical Chapters

The technical section opens with Sam Hunting's Chapter 6, How to Start Topic Mapping Right Away with the XTM Specification. This tutorial shows you how to

---

[17]See *http://www.newsml.org* for more information.

[18]Personal communication, August 2001.

construct an XTM 1.0 document. You will learn how and why to use all of the XML elements specified by the XTM document type definition as well as common pitfalls to avoid.

Following the tutorial, it is time to do some serious *knowledge engineering*—using XML topic maps to build knowledge repositories, including Web sites that provide knowledge-related services. We turn to the notion of *ontological engineering*, a term that was only recently coined.[19] Ontological engineering is now a mainstream activity practiced by some of the large e-commerce enterprises and dot-coms on the Web. This subject is important enough to warrant a chapter by Leo Obrst and Howard Liu, Knowledge Representation, Ontological Engineering, and Topic Maps (Chapter 7). The chapter presents a historical, theoretical, and practical sketch of the subject. An entire book-length treatment will eventually be needed, but a notion underlying this book's presentation is that ontological engineering is what you are doing when you construct XTM documents, and it is important to introduce that topic early. Bernard Vatant suggests in Chapter 5 that the use of PSIs is germane to the process of sharing knowledge, and constructing representations of knowledge is, at once, an art and a science, as explained in the Obrst and Liu chapter. Later in this book, we return to knowledge representation using semantic networks (in Chapter 13 by Eric Freese) and using topic map schemas (in Chapter 14 by Holger Rath).

But wait! There's more—ontological engineering just whets your appetite. So, we follow the gentle introduction to ontological engineering with a chapter that develops intermediate-level topic maps. For this, we turn to another notion that underlies this book: topic maps belong in the classroom. In fact, three different chapters speak to classroom issues—Chapter 8, Topic Maps in the Life Sciences; Chapter 16, Prediction: A Profound Paradigm Shift; and Chapter 17, Topic Maps, Semantic Web, and Education—where topic maps can add great value. John Lassen Park and Nefer Lin Park, with a bit of help from me, created Chapter 8, Topic Maps in the Life Sciences, which discusses the construction of several topic maps. Mind you, these are not simple topic maps. Rather, they form the beginnings of an extended kind of topic map, one that we call a *drill-down* topic map (that is, one that has the ability to reference an entire topic map from a topic in a different topic map). Building a drill-down topic map is a rather new enterprise, one not that well understood. Chapter 8 presents just one approach to an implementation of the drill-down feature.

---

[19]My first exposure to the term *ontological engineering* was in a book by Douglas Lenat and R.V. Guha, *Building Large Knowledge-Based Systems: Representation and Inference in the Cyc Project*, Addison-Wesley, Reading, MA, 1990. It is entirely possible that appropriate attribution should lie in sources much earlier than that.

In Chapter 8, one topic map serves as a very high level index into several other topic maps, each of which presents information in a more detailed fashion and serves as an index into even deeper presentations in the form of more topic maps. This application of topic maps satisfies part of what Kathleen Fisher (the author of Chapter 16) and I characterize as *constructivist learning*, a learning process in which children construct their own knowledge primarily by way of personal discovery during projects, some of which include the construction of concept maps and topic maps.

Chapter 8 begins the process of applying some of the ideas expressed in Chapter 7. In the final section of the book (see below), we pursue these knowledge representation ideas further.

You might be wondering, "How complex can a topic map be?" My immediate answer to that question is that we just don't know yet. We have intuitions, some backed up by some early observations, but, judging from efforts to surf Web sites that accumulate taxonomic information on living things, we already know that some sites, when fully downloaded, accumulate many tens of megabytes of information. Well, that's a huge download for kids in school, but for governmental agencies involved in large data management problems, that's small. As a small illustration of the complexity issue, the opening pages of Chapter 10, Open Source Topic Map Software, present two screen images of the TouchGraph program, one that shows a heavily populated image and one that renders a much simpler view. I am sure that as this book evolves we will be able to generate some heuristics about what constitutes a complex topic map.

Once you are familiar with XTM, you are ready to go out and build a Web site based on the topic maps paradigm. Concluding the technical section of this book, we have two chapters that present the "nuts and bolts" of topic maps. To build a Web site, you need to understand how to *transform* an XTM document into a Web page. Chapter 9 by Nikita Ogievetsky, Creating and Maintaining Enterprise Web Sites with Topic Maps and XSLT, serves as a virtual cookbook for building Web sites with XTM.

Building Web sites may require building topic map engines. For that, Chapter 10, Open Source Topic Map Software, provides an introduction to some software projects available to anyone who wants to download them from the Web and join in the fun known as *hacking software*. These projects are all *open source*, meaning that the source code is included in the download, and an accompanying license guarantees that those who play don't have to pay. Open source licenses also allow those who play to charge, that is, the software can be used in commercial projects. The chapter contains four subsections: (1) SemanText by Eric Freese, (2) TM4J by Kal Ahmed, (3) Nexist by myself, and (4) the GooseWorks toolkit by Sam Hunting and Jan Algermissen. All four projects are available on the Web; we expect more open source topic map projects to follow.

Forward-Thinking Chapters

Once you know what topic maps are and how to create them, it's time to think about what to do with them. The third section of the book presents material that is not mainstream today but just might become mainstream really soon. Some of the chapters discuss semantic networks and inference systems using XTM, things we can build today.

Bénédicte Le Grand, a computer scientist from Paris, contributed Chapter 11, Topic Map Visualization, which represents the kinds of technologies she uncovered in her Ph.D. dissertation research. If humans are social animals, as indicated by David Weinberger above, they are also, by and large, visual animals. Indeed, the visual theme recurs in later chapters when we wander into the classroom.

We now return to the knowledge representation theme introduced earlier with Chapters 7 and 8. Eric Freese contributed two chapters to this volume in addition to his section on SemanText in Chapter 10 mentioned above. Chapter 12, Topic Maps and RDF, presents the latest thinking on how XTM and RDF are both similar and different. The notion of combining XTM with RDF comes up in discussions often, so it makes sense to present as much about it as we know now. Chapter 13, Topic Maps and Semantic Networks, develops the logic behind a complete network that represents aspects of Eric's family. The entire XTM document that results is presented in Appendix D of this book.

To round out knowledge representation, Holger Rath contributed Chapter 14, Topic Map Fundamentals for Knowledge Representation. In this book, readers have the opportunity to sample many variations along the same theme, representing knowledge with topic maps. Holger's chapter ties together all the elements of XTM and PSIs at a level of detail that is different, perhaps deeper, than the other chapters.

To address aspects of topic maps that involve organization of knowledge, Alexander Sigel wrote Chapter 15, Topic Maps in Knowledge Organization. This is really a survey chapter that relates background and historical perspectives to approaches we might take in applying topic maps to the knowledge organization field.

I think the most "bang for the buck" will come as topic maps are moved into the classroom. Thus, the book closes with two chapters that focus on topic maps and pedagogy. The first is Kathleen Fisher's Chapter 16, Prediction: A Profound Paradigm Shift. She traces the history of concept mapping and relates concept maps to topic maps. Kathleen's chapter is the second of three chapters that discuss topic maps in the light of learning activities.

My final chapter—Topic Maps, Semantic Web, and Education (Chapter 17)—sketches notions of a constructivist learning environment coupled to the Semantic

Web, applying dialog-mapping technology to the problem of producing world-class, critical thinkers in classrooms everywhere. All that using XTM, as I show in my open source project, Nexist.

To summarize, this book presents the background, technology, and aspects of the future of topic maps and some important use cases for XTM. You can read the book in any way you wish, but I suggest that those not yet familiar with XTM read the entirety of the introductory section, Chapters 2 through 5, before launching off to explore the rest of the book.

Before I let you go, I should mention that there are some formatting conventions used throughout this book. Generally, we use a monospace font to denote syntax elements. In addition, we put XML element names between angle brackets (for example, `<association>`) and attributes between hyphens (for example, `-xlink:href-`). Finally, we use an italic monospace font when referring to `<topic>` elements by their `-id-` attributes (for example, *sea-star*).

Is the XTM specification work completed? Not by any stretch of the imagination. There remain a lot of details to take care of, and that work continues. But XTM is solid enough to begin using.

Happy reading.

Chapter 2

INTRODUCTION TO THE
TOPIC MAPS PARADIGM

MICHEL BIEZUNSKI

The World Wide Web enables us to create virtually unlimited quantities of information and to make it immediately available to the world. We do not suffer from lack of information availability, but we do have a hard time trying to locate the information we really need. Finding aids are therefore becoming highly desirable. Topic maps provide a standard approach to creating and interchanging finding aids.

There are two dimensions to accessing information: where the information is and how to interpret it. Finding aids help solve the first issue; the latter must be handled by applications.

Topic maps are opening a market for information assets presented as links, such as lists of terms, ontologies, and vocabularies. Topic maps do so by providing a standard way to represent and interchange these assets.

Managing Complex Knowledge Networks

Topic maps were originally designed to handle the construction of indexes, glossaries, thesauri, and tables of contents, but their applicability extends beyond that domain. Research is showing that topic maps—together with the Resource Description Framework (RDF)—can provide a foundation for the Semantic Web. They can serve to represent information currently stored as database schemas (relational and object). Where databases only capture the relations between information objects, topic maps also allow these objects to be connected to the various places where they occur. Knowledge bases can be designed that not only relate concepts together but also can point to the resources relevant to each concept.

This is possible because topic maps were originally designed as neutral envelopes, hospitable to any existing or future schema for knowledge representation. Therefore, all particular semantics for describing knowledge-bearing information have been carefully excluded from the topic map architecture. For example, the actual relations in existing thesauri, the types of objects described in given ontologies, the classifications used by librarians to separate domains of knowledge, and the various methods to provide dynamic delivery of structured information can be used to populate instances of user-defined topic maps because the neutral topic map envelope can manage them all.

Topic maps encompass a whole range of knowledge representation schemas, from very straightforward and unambiguous to quite complex and even ambiguous information. Ambiguity is not a bad thing. It is highly desirable for representing relationships that may be true or false, depending on circumstance. Legal information, which is highly nuanced, is an example of one such area of application.

Topic maps provide a common high-level backplane or framework for managing interconnected sets of information objects. Instead of having to create proprietary link-management systems, which are often extremely expensive, demanding, and costly to maintain, topic maps open a market for standard, more reliable, cheaper products that will accomplish the same types of tasks for the benefit of a significantly greater number of users. Topic maps render information assets independent of software applications. The high-level nature of topic maps makes them attractive to information architects, who need powerful means of representing a virtually unlimited number of relationship types between a virtually unlimited number of information types.

In that regard, topic maps have much in common with RDF. RDF also provides an abstract and powerful way to represent connections between information resources. The relationship between RDF and topic maps is currently being studied. Research has progressed far enough to show that there is a distinction between types of high-level models for information, in order, on the one hand, to provide to information owners a neutral language for knowledge representation and finding aids and, on the other hand, to provide a way for computers to run applications.

Primary Constructs

Topics

Topics are the main building blocks of topic maps. The word *topic* comes from the Greek word *topos*, which means both location and subject. A topic is a computer representation of a subject and may be applied to a set of locations. Each of these locations is a resource, called a *topic occurrence*. All occurrences of the same topic share the property of "being about" the subject represented by that topic. The subject of a topic is the primary characteristic of that topic, and the secondary characteristic resides in the topic occurrences. That subject can be expressed by pointing to a resource. Two cases are possible: either the resource itself *constitutes* the subject of the topic, or the resource merely *indicates* the subject. In the first case, the subject is addressable. In the latter case, it is not, and it can be only indicated by a resource. Chapter 5 discusses subject indicators.

Associations

Topics are connected to each other through *associations*. The definition of the association semantics is left to the designers of the topic map instance. Associations can be used to represent usual relations in thesauri (for example, narrower term, broader term, related term). They can express the relations used in relational database tables as well. Associations can also be used to overlay hierarchical structure upon existing information resources, and therefore associations are useful for building virtual tables of contents that serve to present information objects in a given order, regardless of the way they are actually stored.

Names

A topic usually has a *name*, but it can also have no name or several names. And each name can take several forms.

A topic with one name is the most common and straightforward case. However, if topics were allowed to have *only* one name, there would be nothing special about topic maps—just another schema for encoding ontologies, indexes, or vocabularies. Fortunately, a topic can have multiple names. This is a requirement for representing robust, scalable, interchangeable knowledge networks. For example, each animal, vegetable, and mineral has both a scientific name and a common language equivalent. Some terms have different spellings or aliases. A topic might be given different names in different languages or the same name in scientific nomenclature and several different natural language names. Topic maps do not connect names together; instead, they connect topics that may have multiple names.

A topic may have no name. This case may seem useless at first sight, but it is quite common. Any HTML link on the Web where an <A> element is used to express a link can be interpreted as an occurrence of a topic, the target of the link being another occurrence of the same topic. The topic exists because these two locations are about something shared, a subject they have in common, despite the fact that a computer cannot usually exploit this characteristic because HTML is not rich enough. For example, a sentence such as, "For more information about the product XYZ, go to . . ." is not exploitable because there is no regularity in the string used to express this idea. However, the mere fact that there is a reference to another location can be interpreted, in topic maps terms, as two distinct occurrences of the same topic. It is therefore possible to consider that simple links or cross-references are actually topics without names. Because of the aggregating character of a topic map, links can often be expressed as topic map constructs. Doing so not only makes construction and maintenance of topic maps simpler but also enables powerful management of the link information.

Furthermore, each name can be presented in a set of alternate forms that supplement the base name. In ISO topic maps, these are the display name and the name used as a sort key. This mechanism has been generalized with XTM, and all kinds of variant names can be used for purposes defined by users and are provided by topic map–compliant applications. For example, for a given base name, there can be several names used for display, depending on the medium. One variant can be for alternate text, and another for a graphic. A topic can have a variant name for display on a cell phone, on a computer screen, or on paper.

The fact that the name used for sorting is distinct from the base name is known by lexicographers and indexers. The default sort order used by computers is based on a simple algorithm that uses values assigned to each letter of the alphabet. Depending on the languages, sort algorithms may vary. In some languages, accented characters have the same value as their nonaccented equivalents. In other languages, it is different. For example, the German umlaut vowels are sorted as if they were followed by *e*, for example, *ä* is equivalent to *ae*. However, in French, *ä* is considered the equivalent of *a*.

Scopes and Namespaces

Information models are always relative to a certain perspective or are tuned to a given audience, depending on its language, expertise level, access rights, and so on. In a topic map, such perspectives are specified with *scopes*. Everything that characterizes a topic in the topic map can be scoped: topic names, topic occurrences, and roles played by topics in association with other topics. Scopes are themselves expressed as a set of topics (technically, as a set of references to topics).

Scopes represent a mechanism for fine-tuning the topic map until merging makes sense. When several topics have the same name, they don't automatically correspond to the same topic. But if they have the same name in the same scope, then there are reasons to think that they concern the same subject and therefore should be merged. Merging can occur between several topic elements in the same topic map or, more significantly, between topics coming from different topic maps. Scopes can be used to trigger merging or prevent merging from occurring. What happens to a topic map in the process of merging is not entirely defined by the standard; this allows application designers to create applications that interact very differently with their users. For example, a topic that has *New York* (the state) as one of its names is not the same topic as one named *New York* (the city). Only if a topic has one of its base names in a given scope identical to the base name of another topic within the same scope can they be considered the same topic. The name-based merging rule states that two different topics with the same name in the same namespace will be merged.

For that reason, scopes are *namespaces*. A namespace is defined here as a set of names that uniquely represents an object. In other words, within a given scope, uttering a name gives access to the object having that name (or no object, if no such object exists) but no more than one.

If scopes are used to distinguish names, then it becomes possible to filter what is displayed depending, for example, on the language scopes used for the topic map. Therefore, topic maps can help solve localization issues. Scopes can be used for many other purposes as well: access rights, expertise levels, validity limits, security, knowledge domains, product destinations, workflow management, and so on.

Rules for Merging Topic Maps

Topic maps are highly mergeable. According to the topic naming-constraint-based merging rule, two topics will be merged if they share one identical base name in the same scope. According to the subject-based merging rule, topics will be merged if they have the same subject identity, for example, their `<subjectIdentity>` subelement points to the same resource. The second merging rule is more reliable than the first, but it requires topics to point to the very same resource. This works only in a closed environment (which could be industry-wide) where the published subjects in use are widely known by the various topic map authors. See Chapter 5 for more on published subjects.

The subject-based merging rule is expected to encourage user communities that want to share ontologies to refer to these common subjects published on the Web. It is likely that competing ontologies will be created, but this is not a problem for topic maps since topic maps are neutral envelopes. On the contrary, it was the intent of the original designers of the topic map model to provide a way to connect information from various origins without requiring the whole world to refer to a unique worldview. Every attempt to reduce knowledge or ontologies to a single vision has failed miserably, and new attempts are also doomed to failure.

The Big Picture: Merging Information and Knowledge

Information management results from the unification of documents and data.

XML bridges a gap between two domains: documents and data. The gap was once considered unbridgeable. Documents were not highly structured, while databases were. By applying a database-like approach to documents, XML, following SGML, helps us to recognize that documents and databases are two sides of the same coin. A document, once structured, can be decomposed into a set of elementary fields (called *elements*). A database can be rendered as a document. The Web, as a platform for information interchange, does not enable us to determine the ultimate origin of an information source. A table in HTML can be produced by a document containing a table, or it may be delivered dynamically from a database.

Documents in XML and databases share a common property: they are more or less structured prior to processing. Processing structured information amounts to manipulating its structure, which is enabled by querying, extracting, and performing other operations.

Information is not always structured in a way that can be profitably used. Most information available today on the Web is simply not structured. Therefore, the methods previously discussed do not apply. Worse, this immense ocean of information may very well contain useful knowledge, but structuring it is simply impossible due to its sheer quantity. This is where technologies derived from artificial intelligence, natural language processing, linguistic analysis, and semantic recognition enter the picture. Finding aids such as search engines are based on these technologies.

The need to bridge the domain of information management with knowledge technologies exists. One of the problems that has slowed the penetration of technologies for managing knowledge is the absence of standards. Topic maps, together with RDF and new approaches now being explored, such as the DARPA Agent Markup Language (DAML), open a whole new area for the next generation of technology.

A Step Toward Improved Interconnectivity

Today's attempts to improve Web navigation use the *metadata approach:* structuring or qualifying the information in advance in order to make it navigable. But this presupposes that everybody in the world agrees on fields, terms, and so on. While this has already happened with the Dublin Core[1] for libraries, this goal cannot be achieved easily, and probably not at all for wider communities—especially when they are not aware of these issues (as opposed to librarians, who are).

Topic maps can prepare information to be navigated: to refer to external subjects available on the Web. By doing so, we do not impose any specific structure; we just use a term and point to a place on the Web where the term appears, possibly among a list of other terms, and where we know that everyone else using the term means the same thing we do. These terms can be (optionally) organized as a topic map and lead users to neighboring associated terms.

Topic maps improve navigation on the Web through a mechanism that uses these shared resources, which are called *published subjects*. For example, the published subject "New York" might be (if defined as such) the metropolitan area located in the state of New York and comprising the five boroughs of Manhattan, Brooklyn, Queens, the Bronx, and Staten Island. Therefore, anyone who wants to refer to this entity might point to the address where it is defined or simply use its name within a scope, hoping that this topic will merge with others coming from other topic maps.

Topic maps shared by communities of users having common interests use sets of published subjects. The whole topic map can be used as a template and simply imported into a local topic map.

Design Principles for XTM

Simplicity

Figure 2–1 sketches the developmental history of XTM. The roots lie in SGML. (Chapter 3 discusses the history of SGML in more detail.) XML was created because many users felt that SGML was too complicated. There was a need to simplify and limit its features to those that are essential for use in a Web context. XTM was designed with the same motivation: to simplify the ISO topic map specification for optimized use on the Web. (However, the development of XML shows that the eliminated complexity is returning in the associated specifications.)

Topic maps are intrinsically simple: they are made of topics. As mentioned earlier, topics express subjects and are related through associations. Topics can have several

---

[1] The Dublin Core is a metadata initiative found on the Web at *http://dublincore.org/*.

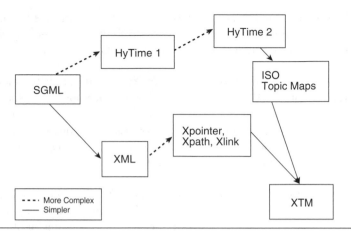

Figure 2–1   The history of XTM

names and occurrences, and scopes qualify the extent of validity of names, occurrences, and associations. And that's basically it.

It is a general law in the history of science and ideas that simplicity follows complexity and does not precede it. Theories and models are perceived as exceedingly complex at the time they are created and before they gain wide acceptance. After they're accepted, theories are simplified and reduced to their applicable cores. Only parts of them are used, and the underlying concepts become part of the shared, universal culture. Examples of this phenomenon include Newton's theory of gravity and Maxwell's theory of electrodynamics.

The development of the topic maps specification had to avoid two traps: the simplicity trap and the complexity trap. Simplicity might end up being a trap if the focus is on short-term applications, ignoring further developments in the future. Also, knowledge representation is sometimes far from being simple, and a simplistic approach not only misses much that needs to be captured but also can lead to false conclusions. Complexity might result from trying to accommodate too many inconsistent requirements. When the editors of a specification try to integrate many contributions, the choices made are likely to be inconsistent.

Creating a standard is the result of two opposing forces. If the technical experts lead the game, they might come up with a good solution but one that is not appealing to decision makers because it is too complex, and if decision makers implement a solution that is not technically correct, the standard will be adopted but will not be long-lived, and a new standard will need to be invented shortly thereafter. This tension explains why it takes a while to make a successful standard. The model underlying the ISO specification was developed over three years, between 1992 and 1995. Then the model stabilized, and the specification was processed into the ISO procedure for two more years, until 1997. Then the addition of scopes and facets provoked adjustments that resulted in two more years of work to make it all fit together. The fact that the specification is no more than 30 pages long after this substantial period of time accounts for its popularity.

Neutrality

A topic map represents a neutral envelope that allows any representation of knowledge to be encoded. Therefore, almost all information semantics have been removed from the XTM specification and left to the user. There are no provisions for choice of topics, topic types, occurrence types, association types, and so on. Such neutrality enables all existing models to be described in terms of topic maps. But the specification still retains the typing semantic, which has been preserved to facilitate interoperability of applications and to help leverage interest in topic maps in the database community as well as in the publishing industry, which uses topic types for specialized indexes.

Types applied to topics, associations, and occurrences are really a shortcut for a specific association whose semantic is "is an instance of." Saying, for example, that "New York is a topic of type City" amounts to saying that "New York is a topic that is connected to the topic City by the association whose semantic is 'is an instance of.'"

From ISO/IEC 13250 to XTM

This section describes the development effort undertaken to extend the ISO specification and add new features. It took one year to complete that task.

Addressing. One of the most obvious differences between the ISO topic maps specification and XTM is the fact that addressing in XTM is limited to Uniform Resource Indicators (URIs) while addressing in the ISO specification can be expressed with virtually any kind of notation. This restriction recognizes the central role played by the Web as a worldwide network used as a common, well-defined platform on which information can be interchanged.

In ISO/IEC 13250, HyTime (ISO/IEC 10744) is used as a base for addressing. HyTime contains a very powerful addressing model based on the paradigm of the bibliographic reference, which allows users to address anything, anywhere, at any time. It enables addressing objects that have not been prepared for being addressed. The HyTime addressing module supports all existing and future notations, the possibility of addressing by name or by position, and semantic addressing such as querying. The power of these addressing facilities should preserve the long-term addressability of information. However, the drawback to this approach is that unless software is equipped with a quasi-universal "Swiss Army knife" that enables addressing in virtually any notation, there is no guarantee that topic maps will become interchangeable in practice.

Another issue is that using HyTime requires declaration of the set of addressable objects, called the *bounded object set*, which is absent from the Web perspective. This constraint makes management of information possible. Without a bounded object set, there is no guarantee that an object that should be addressable by the topic map will actually be there. In XTM, instead of being guaranteed by the design of the addressing specification, this feature has to be resolved by applications. But this problem is not specific to topic map navigation—it is generic to the existence of an addressed object on all Web-based applications.

The Underlying Conceptual Model. Topic map concepts are expressed in the ISO specification purely as syntax. It's important to read the text in order to understand what the syntax actually means, and there are cases where the underlying conceptual model is not made explicit. There was an obvious need to clarify it and make it available in a more explicit way.

Architectural Forms versus Fixed DTDs. The ISO topic maps specification is a set of architectural forms[2] that express element type templates. Rather than being a fixed syntax, this mechanism, first introduced in HyTime (ISO/IEC 10744:1992), lets designers create their own element types by inheriting from a common template.

The inheritance mechanism is a two-level hierarchy in the ISO specification: topics, associations, and facets are three architectural forms that inherit from the HyTime varlink architectural forms. This solution is elegant, and it lets topic map users design their own local syntax for topic maps. Interchange is possible at the architectural level. However, the drawback of this solution is that each resulting DTD for topic maps is different. Several vendors have implemented topic maps, and they all ended up with different document structures, although the semantic value was all the same. In order to simplify interchange and align it on the usual methods used for XML, the XTM Authoring Group decided to publish a DTD rather than a set of architectural forms. Also, despite the fact that the DTD is now fixed, no flexibility in terms of knowledge representation semantics has been lost. Topic map designers still retain all the power they need to design topic map information the way they want.

---

[2]See, for example, *Structuring XML Documents* by David Megginson (Upper Saddle River, NJ: Prentice Hall, 1998).

Element Types Preferred to Attributes. The XTM DTD uses elements wherever possible, rather than attributes. This is possible because the number of primitives in XTM is very small and reading the syntax is intuitive. Here is an example of how the syntax has been transformed to be made more explicit. The following syntax in ISO/IEC 13250:

```
<topic types="city">
```

becomes in XTM:

```
<topic>
  <instanceOf><topicRef xlink:href="#city"/></instanceOf>
</topic>
```

This example makes it explicit that the instance of a topic is a reference to another topic. This is what the `instanceOf` and the `topicRef` element types mean. Note that the XTM syntax is more verbose than the corresponding syntax in ISO/IEC 13250. The syntax is only for interchange and is not likely to be used internally by applications to represent the topic map information.

The Generalization of Display Names/Sort Names into Variant Names. The ISO topic map specification has a provision to add to each name a variant form for display and another for sort keys. This mechanism has been expanded for XTM and is now available as a generic method to add variant names to topics for any processing context by defining parameters. Display and sort are in XTM only two specific cases of this feature. Also, variant names can now be considered in a hierarchy: variants nest. For example, where we choose a variant graphic for displaying a name, we might parameterize a choice between color and black-and-white versions and, further down in the hierarchy, a choice between various resolutions.

The Use of Simple Xlinks. When we were designing the ISO specification, topic maps were indistinguishable from independent linking. We had a choice of a series of links in HyTime: ilink, hylink, agglink, and varlink. We chose to go with varlink because this independent link form (whose name stands for "variable link") is easy to transform into the extended links then proposed for xlink. Also, the xlink specification has more to offer than what we needed for topic maps, and we didn't want to have to explain what to do with the unneeded characteristics of xlink, which have to do with link behavior. Another issue is that in topic maps everything is a topic even if it is not explicitly declared as such. For example, a role played in a link is treated as a topic in topic maps, not just as a simple string. One of the reasons why this is important is to allow for multilingual topic maps to express every single construct's semantics in a local language.

Emergent Topics: Mechanisms for Considering a Resource as a Topic. Sometimes resources are not expressed as topics but should be considered as topics. For example, an association between topics can only relate topics together. If one of the things that is connected through an association is not actually a topic, it can't play a role in the association—unless it automagically becomes a topic by virtue of the fact that it is used as if it were a topic. The mechanism whereby things become topics without requiring us to introduce supplementary markup with explicit topics is called *reification.*

Explicit Referencing. XTM has a mechanism to express explicitly the nature of the information being referenced. If it's a topic, then it's referenced using a `topicRef` element. However, if it's a resource, there are two options, as described below.

Studying the possibilities of convergence between topic maps and the RDF specification led us to the realization that when we are addressing a resource in topic maps, there are two cases that need to be distinguished: (1) the case where the resource itself *is* (or *constitutes*) the subject of a topic (for example, if a topic is a specific Web page) and (2) the case where the subject of the topic is *indicated* by the resource (for example, if the Web page is about a product that is the actual subject of the topic). Therefore, we introduced two different elements that make explicit which case is meant. If it's a resource *constituting* a subject, it's referenced using a `resourceRef` element. If it's a resource *indicating* a subject, it's referenced using a `subjectIndicatorRef` element.

This explicit referencing system provides a way for software application designers to set up the mechanisms to check whether the information contained in a topic map is consistent. It also makes the specification, and instances of the DTD, easier to understand.

The following example makes it clear that the instance of a topic is another topic (it refers to another topic).

```
<topic>
  <instanceOf><topicRef  xlink:href="#city"/></instanceOf>
  <baseName><baseNameString>New York</baseNameString></baseName>
</topic>
```

Here is another example:

```
<topic>
  <instanceOf>
    <subjectIndicatorRef xlink:href="doc1.htm#cityDescription"/>
  </instanceOf>
  <baseName><baseNameString>New York</baseNameString></baseName>
</topic>
```

Here there is no "city" topic but there is a chunk of information (for example, a paragraph of text) that describes what a city is. This is a case where we point to a resource that indicates the subject rather than constituting a subject. Eventually, when the topic map is processed, the result will be the same as if a topic had been explicitly created for that purpose.

The Lack of Facets in XTM. In ISO/IEC 13250, facets are qualifiers used to assign a property to an information object by providing a value for that property. Facets apply to absolutely anything and have no relationship with the topic map architecture. They have been removed from XTM because there are now ways to handle this requirement. The information object and the value of the property can now be considered as if they were two topics associated by the association whose semantic is "applies to." By virtue of this general reification mechanism, specific markup designed to support only facets is no longer needed in XTM.

The Notion of Published Subjects. The notion of public subjects has been kept in XTM but renamed as *published subjects* to emphasize the fact that when information is made addressable on the Web, that act is similar to the act of publishing, and published subjects should remain stable. For example, if a URL indicated the subject "USSR," the subject name should not have been updated even after the country changed its name because many documents are likely to refer to the "USSR" subject, even if the country name itself has changed.

An Explicit Processing Model. The processing model for topic maps is based on the observation that the syntax does not, and cannot, give a complete picture of what is going on in the heart of the topic map. When a topic map, in its interchange syntax, is processed by an application, it gets resolved into a graph. The graph contains nodes and arcs, and nodes have the properties of the constructs that are defined in the specification. There are three kinds of nodes: (1) t-nodes, which represent subjects; (2) a-nodes, which connect t-nodes; and (3) s-nodes, which qualify a-nodes. Roughly speaking, t-nodes correspond to topics, a-nodes correspond to associations, and s-nodes correspond to scopes. But this is not 100 percent exact, and the difference between the level of exactness and 100 percent accuracy is precisely what the processing model is about.

A topic resolves in a t-node in the topic map graph. But two topics might share the same subject. In that case, both of them resolve to one t-node in the graph. Thus, the processing model enforces the subject-based merging rule as topic map syntax alone cannot.

An association resolves in an a-node in the topic map graph. But a-nodes are connections that are more elementary than associations. Associations can only connect topics (or their surrogates). But there are a-nodes between a topic element and some of its characteristics. For example, there is an a-node between a topic and its base name, and there are a-nodes between a topic and each of its occurrences.

Summary

A topic map is composed of topics and associations between those topics. A topic typically is composed of two ingredients: (1) a reference to a subject and (2) references to occurrences of the topic. Following chapters take us much deeper into these and other elements of topic maps.

Acknowledgments

I would like to thank the members of the XTM Authoring Group and the current editors for the considerable amount of work they have accomplished. I would especially like to thank Steven R. Newcomb, who has played a key role in integrating concepts and envisioning the future of topic maps, as well as Sam Hunting and Murray Altheim, who coedited the original drafts with the strong spirit of a team. Working with them has been extremely productive. Finally, I would like to thank the reviewers for their comments and suggestions.

Chapter 3

A Perspective on the Quest for Global Knowledge Interchange

Steven R. Newcomb
(includes some material cowritten with Michel Biezunski)

In 1989, Yuri Rubinsky[1] made a video that he hoped would compel any viewer to grasp the importance of SGML, the ISO standard metalanguage from which has come much of the "Internet revolution," including HTML and XML. The intent of the video was to dramatize the enormous significance of a simple but revolutionary idea: any information—*any* information—can be marked up in such a way as to be parsable (understandable, in a certain basic sense) by a single, standard piece of software, by any computer application, and even by human readers using their eyes and brains.

In the video, aliens from outer space understand a message sent from Earth, because the message is encoded in SGML. This little drama occurs after the aliens first misunderstand a non-SGML message from Earth. (They have already eaten the first message, believing it to be a piece of toast.)

At the time, I was having great difficulty helping my colleagues understand the nature of my work, and I thought maybe Yuri's video would help. One of my colleagues, who had funding authority over my work, was surprised that I had never explained to him that the purpose of my work was to foster better communications between humans and aliens. He was quite serious.[2]

---

[1]Yuri Rubinsky (1952–1996) was not only a great wit and a Renaissance man; he was also a leader in thought whose words, deeds, dreams, and dedication continue to inspire people who work together to realize the promise of global knowledge interchange.

[2]Still attempting to make his point, Yuri made several more videos, one of which, with no alien subplot, was ultimately published as *SGML, The Movie*.

This experience and many others over the years have convinced me that, while the technical means whereby true global information interchange can be achieved are well within our grasp, there are significant anthropological obstacles. For one thing, it's very challenging to interchange information about information interchange. As human beings, we pride ourselves on our ability to communicate symbolically with each other, but comparatively few of us want to understand the details of the process. Communication about communication requires great precision on the part of the speaker and an unusually high level of effort on the part of the listener. I suspect that this is related to the fact that many people become uncomfortable or lost when the subject of conversation is at the top of a heap of abstractions that is many layers thick. It's an effort to climb to the top, and successful climbs usually follow one or more unsuccessful attempts.

When you have mastered the heap of abstractions that must be mastered in order to understand how global information interchange can be realized, the reward is very great. The view from the top is magnificent. From a technical point of view, the whole problem becomes simple. Very soon thereafter, however, successful climbers realize that they can't communicate with nonclimbers about their discoveries. This peculiar inability and its association with working atop a tall heap of abstractions are evocative of the biblical myth of the Tower of Babel. Successful abstraction-heap climbers soon find themselves wondering why their otherwise perfectly reasonable and intelligent conversational partners can't understand simple, carefully phrased sentences that say exactly what they're meant to say.

You have now been warned. This book is about the topic maps paradigm, which itself is a reflection of a specific set of attitudes about the nature of information, communication, and reality. Reading this book may be quite rewarding, but there may also be disturbing consequences. Your thinking, your communications with others, and even your grasp of reality may be affected.[3]

Information Is Interesting Stuff

Information is both more and less real than the material universe. It's more real because it will survive any physical change; it will outlast any physical manifestation of itself. It's less real because it's ineffable. For example, you can touch a shoe, but you can't touch the notion of "shoe-ness" (that is, what it means to be a shoe). The notion of shoe-ness is probably eternal, but every shoe is ephemeral.

---

[3]The writings of Plato, the ancient Greek philosopher who pioneered many of the basic philosophical ideas, have been having similar effects on their readers for thousands of years.

The relationship between information and reality is fascinating. (By *reality* here I mean "the reality of the material universe"—or what we think of as its reality.) We all behave as if we believe that there is a very strong, utterly reliable connection between information and reality. We ascribe moral significance to the idea that information can be *true* or *false*: we say that it's true when it reflects reality and false when it doesn't. However, there is no way to prove or disprove that there is any solid, objective connection between symbols and reality. Symbols are in one universe, reality is in another; human intuition, understanding, and belief form the only bridge across the gap between the two universes. The universe of symbols is a human invention, and our arts and sciences—the information resources that human civilization has accumulated—are the most compelling reflection of who and what we are.

Money, the "alienated essence of work" as some philosophers have put it, is also information. I once saw Jon Bosak[4] hold up a dollar bill in front of an XML-aware technical audience, saying, "This is an interesting document." The huge emphasis that our culture places on the acquisition of money is a powerful demonstration of our confidence in the power of information to reflect reality or, more accurately, in the power of information to *affect* reality. In the United States, we have a priesthood called the Federal Reserve Board, answerable to no one, whose responsibility is to protect and maximize the power of U.S. dollars to affect reality. The Fed seeks to control monetary inflation, for example, because inflation represents a diminishment of that power.

Thinking of money as a class of information suggests an illustration of the importance of context to the significance of information for individuals and communities: given the choice, most of us prefer money to be in the context of our own bank accounts. Thinking of money as information leads one to wonder whether information and money in some sense are the same thing. Some information commands a very large amount of money, and the visions of venture capitalists and futurists are often based on such intellectual property. In some circles, the term *information economy* has become a pious expression among those who are called upon to increase shareholder value. (On the other hand, the economic importance of information can be overstressed. Information when eaten is not nourishing, and when it is put into fuel tanks, it does not make engines run.)

Information has far too many strange and wonderful aspects to allow them all to be discussed here; I regret that I can only mention in passing the mind-boggling insights offered by recent research in quantum physics, for example.

For purposes of this writing, anyway, the most interesting aspect of information is the unfathomable relationship between information and the material universe, as well as

---

[4]Jon Bosak is widely regarded and admired as the father of XML.

the assumptions we all make about that relationship in order to maintain our global civilization and economy. That unfathomable relationship profoundly influenced the design of the topic maps paradigm. Those who would understand the topic maps paradigm must appreciate that there is some sort of chasm between the universe of information (that is, the world of human-interpretable expressions) and the universe of subjects that information is about—a chasm that is (today, anyway) bridgeable only by human intuition, not by computers. The topic maps paradigm recognizes, adapts itself to, and exploits this chasm. (We'll discuss this later.)

Information and Structure Are Inseparable

Excuse me for saying so, but there is no such thing as "unstructured information." Even the simplest kind of information has a sequence in which there is a beginning, a middle, and an end, some concept of unit, and, usually, several hierarchical levels of subunits. Information always has at least one intended mode of interpretation, and the interpretability of information is always utterly dependent on the interpreter's ability to detect structure.

Written and spoken natural languages have structures, although their structures are so subtle, variable, nuanced, and driven by human context that computers are still unable to understand natural languages reliably, despite many years of intense effort by many excellent minds. The fact that computers cannot reliably understand natural languages does not justify terming natural languages "unstructured." This strange term, *unstructured information*, was coined in order to distinguish information whose structure can be reliably detected and parsed by computers (*structured information*) from information, such as natural languages, that does not readily submit to computer processing given state-of-the-art technology (*unstructured information*).

Formal Languages Are Easier to Compute Than Natural Languages

Computers aren't reliable translators of human communication, but humans can translate simple aspects of their various affairs into the patois of computers. We call these expressively impoverished languages *formal languages*, which makes them sound a lot better than they are. Virtually everything that computers do for our civilization involves the use of formal languages.

If you think you are unfamiliar with formal languages, you are mistaken. Dialing a telephone number constitutes a kind of formal utterance; telephone numbers have a rigid syntax that constitutes a kind of formal language. Around the globe, different localities use different formal languages for controlling the behavior of telephone switches. In North America, for example, one of the syntactic rules of the local formal language for dialing telephone numbers is that, in order to reach a telephone whose number is outside the local area but still within North America, a *1* must be the first digit dialed when the dial tone is heard. This syntactic rule is not very expressive, but, like most of the features of most formal languages, it's simple, deterministic, and highly computable. It's so easily understood by machines, in fact, that this simple syntactic rule has been enforced by telephone switches in North America for decades.[5]

Generic Markup Makes Natural Languages More Formal

Starting in 1969, a research effort within IBM began to focus on generic markup in the context of integrated law office information systems.[6] By 1986, Charles Goldfarb had chaired an ANSI/ISO process that resulted in the adoption of Standard GML, also known as Standard Generalized Markup Language (SGML, ISO 8879:1986). Today, SGML is the gold standard for nonproprietary information representation and management; XML, the eXtensible Markup Language of the Web, corresponds closely to a Web-oriented ISO-standard profile of SGML called WebSGML. The Web's traditional language for Web pages, HTML, is basically a specific SGML tag set or markup vocabulary. XML, like SGML, allows users to define their own markup vocabularies.

SGML was based on the notion that natural language text could be marked up in a generalized fashion, so that different markup vocabularies (or tag sets) could be used to mark up different kinds of information in different ways, for different applications, and yet still be parsable using exactly the same software, regardless of the markup vocabulary. Since interchangeable information always takes the form of a sequence of characters, the ability to mark up sequences of characters in a way that is both standard (one piece of software works for everything) and user-specifiable (users can

---

[5]Less than ten years ago, the whole world was changed when the World Wide Web made it possible to give, in effect, telephone numbers to sources of information. These "telephone numbers" are known as Web addresses. For example, one such Web address, *http://www.w3.org*, is the most important source for information about the World Wide Web: it is the Web address of the World Wide Web Consortium. Needless to say, Web addresses are expressed by way of formal languages, one of which is known as the Hypertext Transport Protocol (HTTP).

[6]The team ultimately included Goldfarb, Mosher, and Lorie, whose initials became the name of the language: *GML*.

invent their own markup vocabularies) has turned out to be a key part of the answer to the question, "How can global knowledge interchange be supported?"

The SGML and XML languages that ultimately grew out of the early GML work now dominate most of the world's thinking about the problem of global information interchange. These languages represent an elegant and powerful solution to the problem of making the structure of *any* interchangeable information easily and cheaply detectable, processable, and validatable by *any* application.

Perhaps the most fundamental insight that led to the predominance of SGML and XML is the notion of *generic markup*, as opposed to *procedural markup*. Procedural markup is exemplified by tag sets that tell applications what to do with the characters that appear between any specific pair of tags (an element start tag and an element end tag). For example, imagine a start tag that says, in effect, "Render the following characters in italics," followed by the name of a ship, such as *Queen Mary*, followed by an end tag that says, in effect, "This is the end of the character string to be rendered in italics; stop using the italic font now." This set of instructions is indicated by the following syntax:

```
<italics>Queen Mary</italics>
```

These font-changing instructions are very helpful for a rendering application, but they are virtually useless for supporting applications that are looking for occurrences of the names of ships because many things are italicized for many reasons, not just the names of oceangoing ships. It turns out that generic markup offers significant economic benefits to the owners of information assets. For example, a start tag (for example, `"ship-name"`) that, in effect, says, "The next few characters are the name of a ship," that is, what *kind* of thing that character string is, is just as useful for rendering purposes as one that says, "Italics start here," but the generic tag can support many more kinds of applications, including applications that weren't even imagined when the information asset was originally created. Generic markup is not application-oriented; it is information-oriented. It provides information (*metadata*) about the information that is being marked up.

A start tag is a piece of formal, computer-understandable data that can appear in the midst of natural language data that the computer does not understand. Because of generic markup, we can now use computers to help us manage and interchange information in a hybrid fashion: the computer understands the computer-oriented formal information, and the rest is often explicitly rendered for human consumption.[7]

---

[7]The use of XML as a kind of communications protocol for business transactions between Web-connected business applications is probably less challenging. In such applications, XML is not necessarily chosen for its ability to represent hybrid resources. Instead, XML is chosen simply because "well-formed" XML is easily parsed by free software, and perhaps also because it is not difficult to debug problems in information that is represented in XML because XML is directly readable by human beings.

But problems remain.

- How, for example, are computers supposed to understand what the tags mean? The `"ship-name"` tag, by itself, could easily be misunderstood as indicating the beginning of the name of the recipient of some sort of shipment of merchandise, for example. Let's forget about computers for a moment and consider human beings instead. No matter which natural language you choose, most of the people on this planet can't read it. Even those who can read English may use a local dialect that may cause them to be misled as to the significance of a tag name. In general, how are human beings supposed to understand that this particular tag's intended purpose is limited to marking up the names of oceangoing ships? It is difficult to see how the dream of global knowledge interchange can be realized in the absence of a rigorous way to provide metadata about any kind of metadata, including markup.
- What about information that isn't marked up very well (or at all) to begin with?
- What about information whose structure is arguable or ambiguous? It can only be marked up one way at a time, unless you're willing to maintain two versions of the same source information—a strategy that can often be more than twice as expensive as maintaining a single source.
- What if you need to regard information as having a structure that is different from the structure its markup thrusts upon you, and you don't have the right or ability to change it, copy it, or reformat it?

As you can see, generic markup is only part of the answer to the problem of supporting global knowledge interchange. Much of the rest of the answer has to do with other kinds of metadata—kinds of metadata that are not internal to the information assets but are information assets in their own right. Although they are strikingly and subtly different from other kinds of metadata, topic maps are, among other things, just one of many kinds of such external metadata information assets.

A Brief History of the Topic Maps Paradigm

The work on topic maps began in 1991 when the Davenport Group was founded by UNIX system vendors (and others, including the publisher O'Reilly & Associates). The vendors were under customer pressure to improve consistency in their printed documentation. There was concern about the inconsistent use of terms in the documentation of systems and in published books on the same subjects. System vendors wished to include O'Reilly's independently created documentation on X-Windows, under license, seamlessly in their system manuals. One major problem was how to provide master indexes for independently maintained, constantly changing technical documentation aggregated into system manual sets by the vendors of such systems.

The first attempt at a solution to the problem was humorously called SOFABED (Standard Open Formal Architecture for Browsable Electronic Documents).

The problem of providing living master indexes was so fascinating that, in 1993, a new group was created, the Conventions for the Application of HyTime (CApH) group, which would apply the sophisticated hypertext facilities of the ISO 10744 HyTime standard. HyTime had been published in 1992 to provide SGML with multimedia and hyperlinking features. The CApH activity was hosted by the Graphic Communications Association Research Institute (GCARI, now called IDEAlliance). After an extensive review of the possibilities offered by extended hyperlink navigation, the CApH group elaborated the SOFABED model as topic maps. By 1995, the model was mature enough to be accepted by the ISO/JTC1/SC18/WG8 working group as a "new work item"—a basis for a new international standard. The topic maps specification was ultimately published as ISO/IEC 13250:2000.[8]

During the initial phase, the ISO/IEC 13250 model consisted of two constructs: (1) topics and (2) relationships between topics (later to be called *associations*). As the project developed, the need for a supplementary construct, one able to handle filtering based on domain, language, security, and version, emerged; as a result, a mechanism for filtering was added, called *facet*. This approach was soon replaced by a more powerful and elegant vision based on the notion of *scoping*. The notion of scope in topic maps is one of the key distinguishing features of the topic maps paradigm; scope makes it possible for topic maps to incorporate diverse world views, diverse languages, and diversity in general, without loss of usefulness to specific users in specific contexts and with no danger of irreducible "infoglut."

As an aside,[9] note that the scope and subject identity point aspects of the topic maps paradigm were first developed and articulated by Peter J. Newcomb and Victoria T. Newcomb during a 1997 breakfast conversation at the Whataburger restaurant in Plano, Texas. In our family, we still sometimes call those aspects the Whataburger model, although the Whataburger interchange syntax has not survived. The XTM conceptual model accurately reflects the Whataburger model, however; it has stood the test of time. It's interesting to note how the syntax of topic maps has evolved since Whataburger. The syntax that minimally and accurately reflected the Whataburger model turned out to be inexplicable to most people; it was a marketing fiasco. Michel Biezunski, who for many reasons is the primary hero of the story of topic maps, is not coincidentally also the origin of what I call Biezunski's Principle. Simply put, Biezunski's Principle is: *There is no point in creating a standard that nobody can understand.*

---

[8]For more information, see *http://www.y12.doe.gov/sgml/sc34/document/0129.pdf.*

[9]One far too verbose for a simple footnote!

(Another way he sometimes puts it is, "I'm not interested in convincing anyone that we are smarter than they are.") The whole idea of having a syntactic element type that corresponds to the notion of a topic is, in strictly technical terms, totally unnecessary baggage that actually obscures the deeper and beautifully simple structures that topic maps embody. Even so, the <topic> element type is the foundation of the syntax of topic maps, both in the ISO standard and in the XTM specification. This is because people intuitively and quickly grasp the notion of <topic> elements, and the whole idea that a topic can be represented syntactically as a kind of hyperlink is an inherently exciting one. For me, the popularity of the <topic> element type and the marketing success that the topic maps paradigm now represents are convincing demonstrations of the power of Biezunski's Principle. (I think Biezunski's Principle owes much to the work of Tim Berners-Lee and others, whose design for the World Wide Web succeeded in opening a whole frontier of human interaction and endeavor, where other designs, including more intellectually elegant and powerful ones, had failed to get serious global traction. But that's another story.)

The ISO 13250 standard was finalized in 1999 and published in January 2000. The syntax of ISO topic maps is at the same time very open and rigorously constrained, by virtue of the fact that the syntax is expressed as a set of *architectural forms*.[10] (Architectural forms are structured element templates; this templating facility is the subject of ISO/IEC 10744:1997 Annex A.3.[11]) Applications of ISO 13250 can freely subclass the element types provided by the element type definitions in the standard syntax, and they can freely rename the element type names, attribute names, and so on. Thus, ISO 13250 meets the requirements of publishers and other high-power users for the management of their source codes for finding information assets.

However, the advent of XML and XML's acceptance as the Web's *lingua franca* for communication between document-driven and database-driven information systems created a need for a less flexible, less daunting syntax for Web-centric applications and users. This goal, which was achieved without losing any of the expressive or federating power that the topic maps paradigm provides to topic map authors and users, is the purpose of the XTM (XML topic maps) specification.

The XTM initiative began as soon as the ISO 13250 topic maps specification was published. An independent organization called TopicMaps.Org,[12] hosted by IDEAlliance, was founded for the purpose of creating and publishing an XTM 1.0 specification as quickly as possible. In less than one year, TopicMaps.Org was chartered and

---

[10]Enabling technology for XML and SGML architectural forms is freely available at *http://www.hytime.org/SPt.*

[11]You can access the text of this annex at *http://www.ornl.gov/sgml/wg8/document/n1920/html/clause-A.3.html.*

[12]See the organization's Web site at *http://www.topicmaps.org.*

the core of the XTM 1.0 specification was delivered at the XML 2000 conference in Washington, DC, on December 4, 2000, with the final version of XTM 1.0 delivered on March 2, 2001.

Michel Biezunski (of InfoLoom) and I (of Coolheads Consulting) were the founding cochairs of TopicMaps.Org and coeditors of the Core Deliverables portion of the XTM specification as well as of the remaining portions of the Authoring Group Review version of the specification. In January 2001, Graham Moore (of Empolis) and Steve Pepper (of Ontopia) became the new coeditors, and Eric Freese (of ISO-GEN/DataChannel) became the chair of TopicMaps.Org. More recent events in the history of XTM and TopicMaps.Org are discussed in Chapter 4.

Data and Metadata:
The Resource-Centric View

Metadata is not only "about data"—it is also always data, itself. One person's data is another person's metadata. There is, in general, no difference between data and metadata; it's all a matter of perspective.

It is normal to think of metadata as being somehow "in orbit" around the data about which the metadata provides information. The existence of a *metadata* Web site that provides information about *data* Web sites affects global knowledge interchange in two ways.

1. When users are at the metadata Web site, their attention can be directed at one or more data Web sites, and users can know the reasons why.
2. When users are at the data Web site, they may derive more useful information if they also know about the availability of the metadata Web site and its reasons for expressing metadata about that data.

The idea that metadata can be externally and arbitrarily associated with data is a powerful one, but, by itself, this attractive and simple idea leads nowhere. When a single data Web site is associated with (that is, pointed at by) millions of metadata Web sites, the result can easily be "infoglut"—such a tidal wave of information that, as a practical matter, its overall utility is zero. There needs to be a way to use computers to determine the relevance of all this information to the user's specific situation and to show the relevant information while hiding the rest.

It is ironic that the recent huge improvement that information technology has brought to the accessibility of information—such as providing instant hyperlink traversal to any Web site, anywhere in the world—has itself made more and more information *inaccessible* due to the sheer quantity of it. The dream of global knowledge interchange recedes, even as it becomes real. Our power to filter out unwanted information must keep pace with the quantity of unwanted information. It's a race that we currently appear to be losing.

Although it may sound strange, it is imperative that we develop technical, economic, and business models that will allow businesses to make money by *hiding* information—by providing information that can be used to hide other information. It's also imperative that these models absolutely support and cherish diversity. This is because particular information filtration problems may, as a purely practical matter, require hiding information that emanates from a variety of sources and that reflects a variety of worldviews. These diverse sources may not even know about each other, much less deliberately design their products in such a way as to make them "federable" (that is, usable in concert) with one another. This is what the topic maps paradigm is all about: making diverse metadata sources more or less automatically federable.

One of the things that a metadata Web site may usefully provide is information as to which other Web sites have information on specific topics. Such metadata Web sites are often (and misleadingly) called search engines. But search engines do not usually provide topically organized information. Yahoo! is one notable exception, but it works only for a small number of topics and only in ways that are consistent with Yahoo!'s singular and necessarily self-serving view of the wide world of information. Instead, unlike Yahoo!'s topically oriented features, most search engines merely provide information about which other Web sites provide information that contains certain strings of characters. A user interested in information on a particular topic must be clever enough and lucky enough to be able to sneak up on relevant information on the basis of strings that he or she hopes will be found in such information—and not found in too much other information. The user must guess the language of the desired Web sites' information well enough to imagine which strings are relevant.

When a user attempts to find information, the user usually has a particular topic in mind about which he or she wishes to know more. The user is not interested in Web sites or specific information resources, except insofar as they offer information that is specifically relevant to that topic. The first order of business, then, really should be to allow the user and the computer to agree about exactly what topic the user wants to research. Once the computer has established the exact topic, the computer's task should be to hide all the information about the topic that, for one reason or another, the user should not be bothered with and to render only the remaining information. This kind of user interaction with the Web is supportable if topic maps are widely used because the topic maps paradigm explicitly permits and supports business models based on the development and exploitation of lists of topics that have names and occurrences in multiple languages for use in multiple contexts and that can themselves be found on the basis of their relationships with many other findable topics.

Still, there is an unbounded number of topics, there is an awful lot of information out there, and the sheer quantity is growing at a phenomenal rate. Many individual pieces of information can often be regarded as being relevant to many different topics simultaneously. Nobody will ever categorize everything, but many people will categorize some of it many times over, often in different and even conflicting ways.[13] The topic maps paradigm explicitly permits and supports business models that are based on the development and exploitation of categorizations of information resources. Every category can be represented as a topic. Similarly, every system of categorization can also be represented as a topic. In fact, there is nothing that can't be represented as a topic. The exploitation of preexisting categorizations is not only the key to hiding unwanted information; it's also the key to finding it in the first place, unless it happens to contain some string that you are lucky enough to guess and that doesn't also appear in more than a few other resources.

Metametadata, Metametametadata . . .

One way to federate metadata is to create metadata about the metadata. Then, of course, we may need to federate that metametadata with other metametadata, using metametametadata. The absurdity of this approach is obvious: there is little opportunity for benefit to be realized from standardization in a model that requires infinitely recursive metalevels. There must be a better way. And there is: the topic maps paradigm moves in the other direction by recognizing the existence of a single, implicit, *underlying* layer. It's the same underlying universe that is known in philosophical circles as *Platonic forms*[14] (so named for Plato, the ancient Greek philosopher mentioned earlier).

Subjects and Data: The Subject-Centric View

The notion of "shoe-ness" has already been mentioned as a notion that is eternal but ineffable, while any given shoe is ephemeral but concrete. As Plato might have pointed out, only our minds can sense shoe-ness, and only directly; we cannot sense shoe-ness with any of our five physical senses, even though we can certainly sense a given shoe in a variety of ways. We can be aware of shoe-ness—even the shoe-ness of

---

[13]Aristotle, who extended and applied Plato's ideas, proposed a very famous and influential system of categorization. Aristotle did not have to face the current situation in which many diverse, evolving, and useful worldviews—systems of categorization—must be allowed and encouraged to participate fully in a global civilization.

[14]The term Platonic form escapes simple description. A good Web page on the topic is *http://www. soci.niu.edu/~phildept/Dye/forms.html.*

a particular shoe— only with our minds. For Plato, shoe-ness exists in a plane of existence that is somehow more exalted, perhaps because it is more permanent than anything our five senses can sense. Plato's idea that there is a plane of existence that is accessible only by our minds is exploited by the topic maps paradigm in order to make data resources federable without endless layers of metadata upon metadata.

The topic maps paradigm recognizes that everything and anything can be a subject of conversation, and that every subject of conversation can be a hub around which data resources can orbit. Unlike the resource-centric view in which metadata orbits data resources, in the subject-centric view, data orbits subjects. If the subject itself happens to be a data resource, the orbiting data can, of course, be called metadata. But one of the essential lessons of the topic maps paradigm is that *all* data is *data about subjects*, but only some subjects are themselves data; most subjects are not information resources. When the problem of global knowledge interchange is approached with this subject-centric attitude, the solution becomes much simpler and easier. Indeed, for many people, and particularly for the people who have used it the most, the topic maps paradigm passes the most convincing test of all: the solution, once finally found, is obvious.

There is one problem: computers cannot access subjects unless those subjects happen to be information resources themselves. A computer cannot access the Statue of Liberty, for example, or love, or hot chocolate, or shoe-ness. There is no computer-processable pointer to any of these things. As a practical matter, there is no human-processable pointer to these things either—people can't wave their hands and produce these things out of thin air. However, people have another gift that makes it unnecessary to produce concrete things in order to discuss them: the ability to communicate symbolically, to understand each other on the basis of symbols. It's an everyday miracle that I can say to you the words, "Statue of Liberty," and you will immediately know I'm talking about a certain large greenish statue of a woman, created by Gustav Eiffel, that is situated on Liberty Island in New York Harbor, with a somewhat smaller prototype located in Paris, France. There is very little chance that you will misunderstand me (although it's possible that I could be referring to a certain unconventional pattern of play in American football).

If you've followed this discussion so far, you're ready to understand some imagery that was pivotal in the development of the topic maps paradigm. Imagine a chasm with two high cliffs, one on the left side of the chasm and one on the right. There is no physical bridge across the chasm. On the left-hand cliff is the universe of symbols and expressions. All written, pictorial, and other symbolic expressions exist on the left-hand cliff. On the right-hand cliff is the world of subjects of conversation. (The conversations themselves, since they are in the universe of symbolic expressions, are found only on the left-hand cliff.) On the right-hand cliff we find love, the Statue of Liberty, shoe-ness, the smell of hot chocolate, Minnie Mouse's high-heeled shoes, and every other thing that is or can ever be symbolized by the expressions found on the left-hand cliff: every actual and possible topic of conversation, without exception.

The first thing to realize about this imagery is that, while there is no bridge across the chasm, crossing it is the everyday miracle that our brains accomplish whenever we successfully understand any symbolic expression. We sense certain symbols, and somehow we intuit the corresponding thing on the right-hand cliff. Human intuition (the human brain, if you like) is the only transportation facility that can cross the chasm. This means that it must be true that it's possible for symbols to represent reality or, at least, that we constantly *assume* that symbols represent reality. (As engineers, we are compelled to admit that the fact that everybody assumes that it's true is good enough to get the job done.) As in the case of monetary information, for example, the validity of that assumption is what the high priests at the Federal Reserve Bank are supposed to ensure. Actually, civilization itself rests entirely on the unprovable assumption that information has some bearing on reality, so maybe we can afford to take a chance on it.

The second thing to realize about this imagery is that all data and all metadata are entirely on the left-hand cliff. The left-hand cliff has some reality, too, because information (expressions) do indeed exist. Wondrous to say, there is no "missing bridge to reality" problem on the left-hand cliff. When a subject happens to be an information resource, even an inanimate computing device can take us where we want to go by understanding and executing the symbols (Web addresses, for example) that uniquely identify that information resource. Indeed, history seems to show that the ease of accessing such addressable subjects—information resources—has in fact seduced us into thinking that only resources—symbolic expressions that can be addressed by computers—can be the hubs around which data can be organized.

And here is where the topic maps paradigm performs a bit of chicanery. Computers can't directly address the Statue of Liberty, for example, but they can address information about the Statue of Liberty. More to the point, they can address an information resource that serves as a surrogate for the Statue of Liberty. Since we're stuck with the limitations of computers (and the underlying limitations of symbolic expressions), the key is to allow anyone and everyone to establish conventions for such surrogates, according to their own needs and convenience, whereby arbitrary subjects can be uniquely represented by specific addressable information resources. The topic maps paradigm accomplishes this trick by taking the position that a certain specific kind of reference to an information resource must be interpreted not as a reference to that resource but rather as a reference to whatever subject of conversation is indicated by that information resource, when that information resource is perceived and understood by a properly qualified human being. In some sense, then, the topic maps paradigm lets the computer take a virtual journey across the chasm by riding on human perception and intuition.[15] The referenced resource becomes more than a resource: it becomes a symbolic surrogate, on the left-hand cliff, for something on the right-hand cliff, on the other side of the chasm, where only human intuition can reach.

Understanding Sophisticated Markup Vocabularies

If you want to understand the topic maps paradigm, you must understand something about markup vocabularies in general that is not yet widely understood: the structure of an interchangeable resource is not necessarily the same as the structure of the information that is being conveyed.

Back in 1986, SGML had just been adopted by the community of nations as the one-and-only markup language for everything and everybody. But Charles Goldfarb, its inventor and guardian, knew that much work remained to be done. He saw that many kinds of multimedia information and many business niches for such information would continue to be invented indefinitely. One of the things he wanted to do was to show that SGML could be used to encode multidimensional synchronizing information: to impose simultaneous, arbitrary temporal structures on arbitrary collections of information objects and their components.

Accordingly (and not coincidentally in order to have some fun), Dr. Goldfarb turned his attention to the problem of representing music abstractly.[16] Musical works are inherently multidimensional; to begin with, musical harmony is the result of multiple simultaneous melodies. Since an interchangeable document is necessarily a one-dimensional

---

[15]In a way, it's not very different from the insertion of formal, computer-processable tags into natural language data that the computer cannot understand. In the end, the utility of marked-up natural language information (and the utility of subject-indicating referenced information) is available only to human minds, but, because of the formality of the markup and the formality of the expression of reference to subject-indicating information, computers can be used to vastly enhance the productivity of the human minds to which the information is being made available.

[16]Dr. Goldfarb and I first met in July 1986 at the first meeting of the ANSI X3V1.8M committee, which he chaired. The mission of ANSI X3V1.8M was to create a Standard Music Description Language standard. We have been colleagues in the development of ANSI and ISO standards ever since, and we have both invested much of ourselves in our brainchildren. Ultimately, the music standard metamorphosed into the ultra-generalized ISO HyTime standard (ISO/IEC 10744:1997; see *http://www.ornl.gov/sgml/wg8/document/ n1920*), and the music standard became an application of HyTime. HyTime is a holistic solution to the question of how to create metadata assets that impose all kinds and combinations of arbitrary alternative structures on arbitrary sets of arbitrary information resources.

sequence of characters, the question immediately arises, in the case of a musical document, as to whether the concurrent melodies (or instrumental and/or vocal parts) should be expressed separately or whether all the notes that are supposed to sound synchronously in all of the concurrent melodies should appear adjacent to one another in the interchange file. Either way, the structure of the interchange syntax will be inconvenient for at least some applications. Either way, at least some of the basic structure of the information will be obscured by the interchange syntax. Therefore, for the sake of reliable information interchange, there must be a separate and distinct model of the information that is being conveyed by the music language, in addition to the syntactic model that governs the structure of that information while it is represented as an interchangeable document.

There are many kinds of information whose structure, like the structure of music information, must respond to one set of requirements when the information is being interchanged and to another, often contradictory set of requirements when the information is in ready-to-use form. Many decision makers are not yet ready to hear this message, for a variety of reasons.

Historically, the overwhelming majority of markup applications have been basically batch-typesetting jobs, which start at the beginning of the document and process each data segment in more or less the same sequence in which it appears in the document. The rendering of HTML documents by Web browsers is one example. The use of the word *document* to denote a class of information objects appears to have the connotation that all such information objects are intended to be rendered and used in the same order in which they are interchanged.

Currently, significant investments in the marketing of XML technology are directed at business-oriented information technology professionals. Such professionals are urged to regard XML as an opportunity to represent relational databases as interchangeable documents. All such documents, regardless of their schemas, are parsable by a single standard parsing technology, without reconfiguration. It's obvious that a relational table is exportable and importable as a sequence of named or numbered rows, each of which is itself a sequence of named or numbered fields.

The Document Object Model (DOM)[17] recommended by the World Wide Web Consortium (W3C) provides a convenient application programming interface (API) to the syntactic structure of information being interchanged in the form of XML documents. The DOM is extremely useful, but it has been oversold as the *ne plus ultra*

---

[17]The W3C DOM is not an object model; it's an API to a "DOM tree" whose exact nature is still being specified by a W3C working group. The task of this working group is to produce an object model (or at least a set of constraints on the structure of a DOM tree) called the XML InfoSet.

API to interchangeable information. The DOM does provide applications with random access to every part of an interchangeable document, so it makes many applications much easier to develop than they otherwise would be. However, the DOM cannot provide direct access to the semantic components of what a document *means*; it can only provide direct access to the syntactic components of how a document is represented for interchange.

Fortunately for the widespread acceptance of XML technology, which is basically a tremendous step toward global knowledge interchange, there are many popular kinds of information whose interchange is required for many kinds of economic reasons, including virtually all of the billboards on the information highway, for which the interchange structure can quite usefully be the same as the structure of the API. The DOM is a great all-purpose API for all of these kinds of information.

Topic maps are another matter, however. As in the case of music information, the structure of topic map information is not the same as the structure of interchangeable documents.

- Topic map documents can point to other topic map documents, saying, in effect, "The referenced topic map must be merged with the current one before the current one can be understood as its author intends." If any single subject is represented by `<topic>` elements in both topic maps, the topic maps paradigm requires that the result of processing the two documents must be, among other things, exactly one resulting topic (represented in some application-internal form) that has the union of the characteristics (the names, occurrences, and participations in associations with other topics) of the two `<topic>` elements. Therefore, the *only* way to understand an interchangeable topic map document is to process it fully, performing such merging and redundancy-elimination tasks as the paradigm requires.
- The element-containment structure of a topic map document, even in the absence of any requirement to merge it with another topic map document, bears no resemblance to the structure of the relationships between topics that are expressed by that document.

In other words, the API to topic map information is not, and can never be, the same as an interchangeable topic map that conveys that same information. From this interesting fact the question arises, "What is meant by an element type name, such as `<topic>`, in an interchange syntax like the interchange syntax of topic maps, in which there is no direct correspondence of the element structure to the structure of the information being interchanged?"

The answer is that the meaning of such a tag name is, like all other tag names, exactly what the designers of the interchange syntax intended it to mean. For example, for every <topic> element, a conforming topic map application must have an application-internal representation of that topic (that is, a topic whose subject is the same as that of the <topic> element). If there is no such internally represented topic, the application must create one; if there is already such an internally represented topic, the application must add to it (union it with) all the information about that topic that is represented by the <topic> element. The meaning of the <topic> tag name is still quite clear and rigorous; the only difference is that the meaning has to do with the creation of an application-internal form of the interchanged information—a form with its own API that must be used by conforming applications.

The Topic Maps Attitude

The topic maps paradigm is a step along the road to global knowledge interchange. It may well turn out to have been quite a significant step. Nonetheless, it is very obviously not the last step. If it successfully moves our species forward toward global knowledge interchange, the topic maps paradigm will owe much of its success to the fact that it is resolutely responsive to current technological, economic, and anthropological conditions, and just as resolutely responsive to certain philosophical values and attitudes. Some of these values came from the comparatively young traditions of the markup languages community.[18] Other values are derived from much older traditions. What follows is a summary of the values and perspectives that I find most remarkable.

- We must recognize that civilization is what makes it possible for us to have breakfast every morning, and civilization's increasing ability to develop and exploit information resources is generally correlated with the richness and quality of life available to each human individual living on our planet. Global knowledge interchange is important to every single living human being.
- We must cherish diversity by giving diverse worldviews the ability to be expressed and exploited alongside and in federated combination with all other worldviews. This includes respecting communities of interest, encouraging their formation, and not coincidentally causing them to provide themselves with usable interfaces for use by other communities of interest.
- We must understand that worldviews provide essential contexts for communication and that communication rests on our intuitive ability to cross the chasm between symbolic expressions and reality. We must work to provide

---

[18]The vanguard of the markup languages community still meets annually at a very lively conference called Extreme Markup Languages, where a significant portion of the history of topic maps has occurred in plain public view. See *http://www.idealliance.org* for details of the next conference.

computers with increasing sensitivity to (that is, apparent awareness of and ability to act upon) diverse human contexts.

- We must accept partial solutions and partial expressions, demanding neither comprehensiveness nor perfection. There never will be any such thing as a "complete" topic map, or one true ontology suitable for all contexts, or a holy grail of "knowledge." A single human being or organization can accomplish something only within some limited scope. Providing a way for incomplete, imperfect utterances to contribute, in some useful way, to the ongoing intellectual life of the human species is essential.

- We must understand and adapt to the fact that different subjects of conversation have different kinds of reality, for example, an information asset is real in one sense, the Statue of Liberty in another, shoe-ness in a third, and Minnie Mouse's high-heeled shoes in a fourth. At the same time, we must understand and exploit the fact that all subjects are, in some sense, the same, in that we humans seem to find them worthwhile to discuss.

- We must provide a way for ordinary people to quickly and easily gain a superficial understanding of global knowledge interchange—a way that does not compromise a deeper level of abstract simplicity and power.

- We must abandon "simplifying assumptions" that actually interfere with our ability to manage and maintain our increasingly complex civilization (for example, the resource-centric view of metadata and the idea that the interchange structure of information should always be the same as the structure of the information itself).

- We must provide technology that is suitable as a foundation for business models that, in the aggregate, make many significant contributions to global knowledge interchange and the general availability of knowledge.

- We must recognize infoglut as the single most formidable remaining enemy of global knowledge interchange in a world where the connectivity problem is already well on the way to being permanently solved.

- We must recognize that subjects of conversation are the true axis points of information, even though they are not addressable by computers. Creating addressable information resources to represent nonaddressable subjects allows the addressable resources to be used as public "hooks," called *published subject indicators* (see Chapter 5), on which topic relationships, names, and relevant information can be "hung."

- We must acknowledge that generic markup is the most natural and most economically conservative way to interchange and archive valuable information assets whose future exploitability cannot be completely predicted (that is, practically all information assets).

- We must accept that markup (whether generic or procedural) will always be too rigid or otherwise inadequate for all applications. Thus we must support the ability to impose arbitrary structure on arbitrary information by means of external, independently maintained metadata.

- We must understand the need for markup and other metadata to be described, even as they themselves describe other data.
- We must recognize that the federation of knowledge assets is an ongoing activity that must account for the evolution of the knowledge assets to be federated, without losing the value of investments in previous federating activities.

Summary

This chapter shows that topic maps provide us with two different and important views into an information space: (1) a resource-centric view, one in which we use metadata to describe the resources we reference with topics, and (2) a subject-centric view, in which topic maps provide the tools necessary to represent, to "talk about" subjects. These views, when coupled with the "topic map attitude" that topic maps, where possible, should be unified through merging, provide us with the opportunity for global knowledge interchange.

Chapter 4

THE RISE AND RISE OF TOPIC MAPS

SAM HUNTING

Following the success of TopicMaps.Org's crash program to release XTM 1.0, the topic map community entered a period of renewed technical activity. This chapter summarizes the milestones in the topic map space from the release of ISO standard 13250 to April 2002. Not mentioned, or mentioned only in passing, are papers (no matter how seminal), in-company efforts, allied though distinct fields (like conceptual graphs or RDF), and consulting services.

To begin, I present topic map milestones in standards and specifications as well as software (commercial and free). Then I give my own guesses for the near-term future of topic maps.

Figure 4–1 summarizes recent developments in standards, specifications, and software in the form of a time line that reveals four things:

1. The seminal character of ISO standard 13250
2. The rapid proliferation of software (commercial and open source) following a standards or specifications milestone
3. The rapid flowering of TopicMaps.Org and the scattering of its seeds into ISO (for standards work) and OASIS (for applications work)
4. The layered approach at ISO (the Reference Model and the Standard Application Model)

Most of the detail in Figure 4–1 is discussed in the following sections.

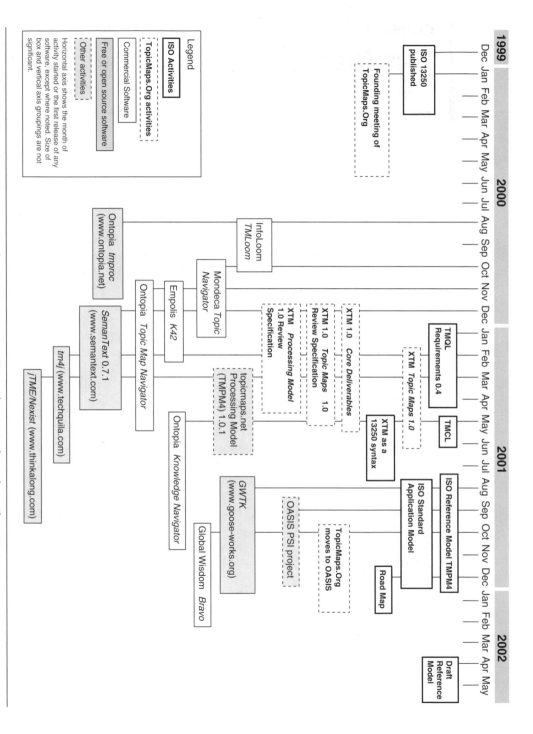

Figure 4–1   Time line of significant events for XML topic maps, December 1999 through April 2002

52

Milestones in Standards and Specifications

Topic map standards and specifications[1] have been written or are being written by the following organizations:

- ISO
- TopicMaps.Org
- OASIS

Our story begins with the ISO since a topic map interchange syntax was first formalized by ISO standard 13250 (now known by the catchy acronym HyTM, for HyTime Topic Maps) in December 1999. Soon after the release of HyTM, its editors and other interested parties formed TopicMaps.Org, with the objective of bringing the topic maps paradigm to the Web as XTM (for XML topic maps). From the perspective of the typical Web developer, HyTM suffered from a number of disabilities.

1. Although it was clearly implementable, as shown by the flurry of software development activity reflected in Figure 4–1, HyTM was specified in SGML—the kiss of death from the standpoint of adoption on the Internet, where even as long ago as 1999 XML was becoming the norm for serious advocates of bringing markup technology to new fields of endeavor.
2. Rather than defining a single syntax with a DTD, HyTM used a technique called SGML architectures,[2] which, while defining a formal syntax for information owners to derive their own element types from a meta-DTD. . . . Well, suffice it to say that the price for the power of architectures was considerable complexity, a price that most Web developers were unwilling to pay. (See Chapter 2 for a discussion of SGML architectures.)
3. There was a sense (however unfounded) that ISO and the Web were in some way foreign to each other.

Since the details of specifications development appeal only to standards wonks (and perhaps not even to them), I'll pass over the details of TopicMaps.Org's development of the XTM specification. To the credit of the XTM Authoring Group and the editors, the development and release of the XTM 1.0 DTD and its accompanying

---

[1] Standards wonks try to reserve the word *standard* for the work product of an international standards body, like ISO, reserving the word *specification* for the work products of other bodies. The distinction can be meaningful since standards have the force of law in certain jurisdictions.

[2] For more information, see ISO 10744:2 (1997), Annex 3, at *http://www.ornl.gov/sgml/wg8/docs/n1920/html/n1920.html*.

specification were accomplished in "Internet time," with drafts released in December 2000 and Version 1.0 in February 2001.[3]

XTM 1.0 versus ISO 13250

The XTM 1.0 specification is very accessible; it is distinguished by detailed examples and clear prose. From an implementer's perspective, it has presented only opportunities—all current versions (January 2002) of commercial topic map software can handle both HyTM and XTM syntax.[4] The specification clearly distinguishes between text to which applications are expected to conform (normative) and other (informative) text.[5] The fundamental nature of the topic maps paradigm is not changed: an XTM topic map remains an overlay on information resources as described by ISO 13250.

Differing from HyTM in some details, XTM 1.0

- Uses XML
- Defines a single DTD rather than an architecture
- Eliminates the `facet` element type of ISO 13250, since equivalent functionality can be gained with the `association` element type
- Generalizes the `sortName` and `dispName` of HyTM into `variant` while preserving the semantics of the HyTM element types through Published Subject Indicators (PSIs) on children of the variant name's `parameter` elements[6]
- Introduces the distinction between subject-indicating and subject-constituting resources[7]
- Uses XLink URI syntax, whereas HyTM permits arbitrary addressing schemes
- Uses pleasing XML-style long tag names (for example, `association` rather than `assoc`)
- Uses element types rather than attribute declarations where possible

---

[3]See *http://www.topicmaps.org/xtm*.

[4]An instance of HyTM's SGML can be transformed into XTM's XML using XSLT; see *http://www.cogx.com*.

[5]A standards wonk would take issue with defining application conformance in terms of an informative annex (see, for example, Section 4.5 of XTM 1.0), and with the specification's lack of definition for some often-used terms (for example, *ontology*).

[6]For a detailed discussion of these XTM element types, see Chapter 6. For PSIs, see Chapter 5.

[7]See Chapter 3.

OASIS

Having completed its work, TopicMaps.Org dissolved in October 2001 into OASIS (Organization for the Advancement of Structured Information Standards), which began work on applications of XTM 1.0. The first Technical Committee, chaired by Bernard Vatant, will produce recommendations for best practices for the publication, management, and use of published subjects, hopefully in 2002. The recommendations will cover not only syntax and structure for PSIs but also processes to ensure their wide and effective use by communities of interest and practice. Committee members have diverse backgrounds, including library science, intelligent agents, software engineering, agriculture (the United Nations Food and Agriculture Organization), Internet technologies, and the oil industry. Such diversity suggests that the topic maps paradigm is spreading to fields beyond its origin in the interchange of bibliographic information.

Current ISO Activities

While OASIS works at the application level, the topic map community has returned to its roots in ISO and started to refine the models that undergird the paradigm. Crucially, the XTM DTD has been stabilized[8] as the XML interchange syntax for topic maps (in addition to the original, SGML, interchange syntax, HyTM). Figure 4–2 shows the relationships among the various ISO efforts, as of April 2002.[9]

The topic map standards effort at ISO has three layers:

1. The modeling layer
2. The syntax layer
3. The constraints and queries layer

These layers are described below.

---

[8]The structured character of the ISO process is regarded by most as a sufficient guarantee of stability for the syntax specified by the XTM 1.0 DTD.

[9]Adapted from Lars Marius Garshol (who created the Norwegian submission to ISO), "Topic Maps: Road Map for Further Work," accessed on January 15, 2002, at *http://www.y12.doe.gov/sgml/sc34/document/ 0278.htm*. A caveat: the *only* document in Figure 4–2 that is normative is ISO 13250. In particular, the "Road Map" is only a submission. However, since the "Road Map" has met with acclaim, has a clear and coherent design, and gives every member of the topic map community a sandbox to play in, it seems reasonable to regard it as a product of community consensus and the basis on which topic map standards development will proceed.

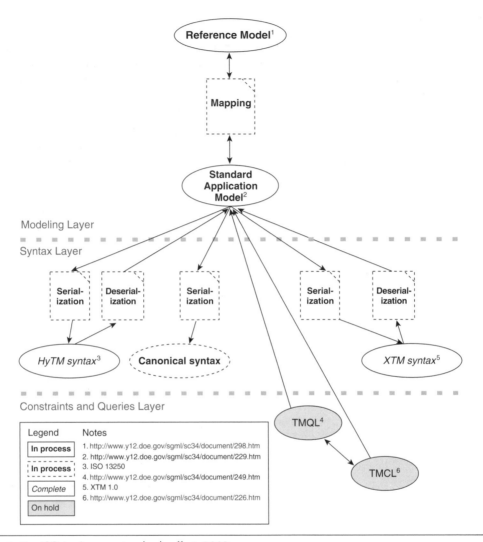

Figure 4–2   ISO topic map standards effort, 2002

The Modeling Layer

The modeling layer comprises a Reference Model (RM) and a Standard Application Model (SAM). The RM requires the minimum number of ontological commitments needed to merge knowledge about subjects, regardless of the diversity of the ontologies (sets of knowledge-bearing assertions) that govern the interpretation of such knowledge. The SAM's additional ontological commitments include familiar topic map features like topic names, occurrences, and scopes. The SAM is defined based on the conventions established by the Reference Model, in W3C XML InfoSet style.[10]

Because the thinking behind the RM is not familiar (unlike that for the SAM, which is discussed briefly after this section), I'll go into some detail about the RM and how it might work.

The Reference Model

The RM has now undergone two iterations. First came TMPM4, the topic map processing model left on the cutting-room floor during the development of XTM 1.0 and later submitted to ISO.[11] TMPM4 was superseded in April 2002 by the dRM.[12]

To define the essence of topic maps, the RM—informally, "the Graph"—turns to graph theory. The Graph permits implementers to adopt different application paradigms, whether object-oriented, relational, functional, or other, as discussed below. Further, the Graph can be interchanged in any number of serialization syntaxes, XTM and HyTM being the two standard ones.[13]

The Graph is not a mainstream, Graph Theory 101–style graph. It is not directed, connected, or symmetrical. Its arcs are typed; its nodes are characterized only insofar as they serve as the endpoints of arcs. Assertions are nodes connected with arcs. Graph construction rules determine which nodes can appear at the endpoints of which arcs. The Graph is implementable using a classical adjacency list representation, and its set of possible graph traversals yields a straightforward query language. (See Chapter 10 for a sample and brief discussion of sTMQL in the GooseWorks Toolkit.) TMPM4 and the dRM share these characteristics.

TMPM4 was characterized by simplicity. It had three types of nodes: a-node (association node), t-node (topic node), and s-node (scope node). It had four types of arcs: AM (a-node to member node, whether a-node or t-node), AX (a-node to templating t-node), AS (a-node to s-node), and SC (s-node to scope component, whether a-node

---

[10]For details, see *http://www.y12.doe.gov/sgml/sc34/document/0229.htm.*

[11]See Steven R. Newcomb and Michel Biezunski, "Topicmaps.net's Processing Model for XTM," accessible at *http://www.topicmaps.net* and *http://www.y12.doe.gov/sgml/sc34/document/0243.htm.*

[12]See Steven R. Newcomb and Michel Biezunski, "A High-Level Description of a Draft Reference Model for ISO 13250 Topic Maps," accessible at *http://www.y12.doe.gov/sgml/sc34/document/0298.htm.*

[13]For details, see *http://www.y12.doe.gov/sgml/sc34/document/0277.htm.* The GooseWorks Toolkit, which is based on TMPM4, represents Dublin Core HTML tags in the Graph. See *http://www.goose-works.org.* For a contract-based approach to interchanging the inherent topic map information of arbitrary syntaxes using the GooseWorks Toolkit, see also "The Omnivore" at *http://www.etopicality.com.*

or t-node). An AM arc could be optionally "labeled" with a t-node that specified the role played in the association by the node at the M (member) endpoint of the arc. This design effectively turned the AM arc into a three-ended arc—in graph jargon, a type of "hyperedge"—where one endpoint was the a-node, the second endpoint the member node, and the third endpoint the role-specifying "label." Though permitted by graph theory and implementable, the hyperedge proved controversial and was abandoned in the dRM.

The dRM is even simpler than TMPM4. It has only four arc types: AC, Cx, CR, and AP. Arc names are concatenations of their endpoints: AC (assertion to casting), Cx (casting to member, where any node can serve as the x endpoint of any number of Cx arcs), CR (casting to role specifier), and AP (association to pattern, where the pattern is not at the A endpoint of any arc, to avoid recursion). Like TMPM4, the dRM has construction rules: for example, a node that appears at the P endpoint of an AP arc may not appear at the A end of any other arc. (This design is identical to TMPM4's; the rule avoids an infinite regress.)

Figure 4–3 shows the components of an assertion.[14] Note especially that the hyperedge of TMPM4 has disappeared: instead of a single three-ended AM arc labeled with a role topic, we have three arcs with two endpoints—AC, Cx, CR—with the C (casting) endpoint in common. We say that the node at the x end of the Cx arc is cast in or plays the role at the R endpoint of the CR arc.

The dRM includes two "paradigmatic" assertion types. First, the topic-subjectIndicator assertion type is a two-role assertion type that is used to declare that subjects have subject indicators. (In TMPM4, the relation subject and subject indicator was left up to the application.) Second, the assertionPattern-role-rolePlayerConstraints

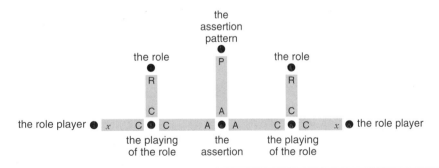

Figure 4–3   Components of an assertion in the draft Reference Model

assertion type is used to declare that assertion types (which, of course, are themselves subjects) specify the roles used in their instances. See the discussion of Figure 4–5, below, for an example of this assertion type.

Minor differences between the two versions of the RM include vocabulary changes. The dRM uses the word "assertion," reserving "association" for ontological commitments at the AM level. The dRM replaces TMPM4's "template" with "pattern," to avoid confusion with "topic map templates" at the AM level.

Now let's see how the Graph might work. Suppose (as in Figure 4–4) that our "working topic" (or focus, or hub topic) is the topic whose subject is "the person Robert",

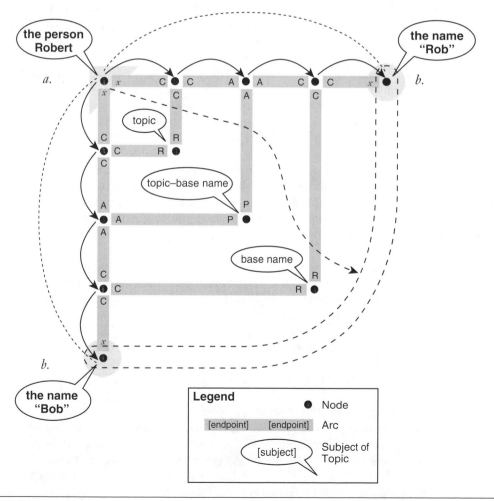

Figure 4–4   Sample assertion in the draft Reference Model

and we want to get all the base names for that topic (here, "Bob" and "Rob"). How do we get from point a to point b in the dRM?

An implementation that traversed all the arcs and nodes of the Graph would follow the path shown by the solid arrows in Figure 4–4. The implementation would start at point a (the topic marked with a grey triangle) and make two traversals to finish at both points b (the topics marked with grey circles), with each traversal proceeding along the following arcs: Cx_1, AC_2, AC_3, Cx_4, where an instance of an arc type is denoted with a superscript that shows the order of traversal. (Note that since the RM is not a directed graph, an arc of type Cx is an arc of type Cx whether traversed from C to x or from x to C.)

Starting its traversal at the x endpoint shared by the two Cx_1 arcs (point a), the implementation would arrive at the C endpoints and look upward along each CR arc to see that in each case topic "Robert" was playing the topic role. Next, traversing each AC_2 arc, the implementation would arrive at the A endpoints and look up each AP arc to see that the assertion was being patterned on the topic–base name assertion type. Then, traversing each AC_3 arc, it would arrive at the C endpoints and look up each CR arc to see that the topic ahead was cast in the base name role. Finally, traversing each Cx_4 arc, it would arrive at the x endpoints (point b) and collect the base name topics whose subject constituting resources are "Bob" and "Rob."

A less informative (or less naïve) implementation might leverage the known structure of the SAM and follow the path shown by the dotted arrows in Figure 4–4. This implementation would still start at point a and make two traversals to finish at both points b—but the intermediate traversals to the base name topics "Bob" and "Rob" would not be necessary.

Another implementation might apply even more leverage and follow the path shown by the dashed arrow in Figure 4–4. This implementation still starts at point a—but it would make a single traversal to the *set* of base name topics "Bob" and "Rob" (enclosed in a dashed outline).

Note that implementations, to demonstrate conformance, might expose, on demand, complete information for any traversal in a manner similar to ESIS output from James Clark's SGML parser nsgmls.

Like TMPM4, the dRM includes a typing mechanism for assertions. Figure 4–5 shows how the topic–base name assertions shown in Figure 4–4 are instantiated using patterns. To do this, let's set up two assertions, 1.0 and 2.0 (the shaded subgraphs in Figure 4–5). 1.0 and 2.0, we know, declare patterns because the subject at the end of each of their AP arcs is the "master pattern"—the assertionPattern-role-rolePlayer Constraints three-role assertion type built into the dRM (see node 0 in Figure 4–5):

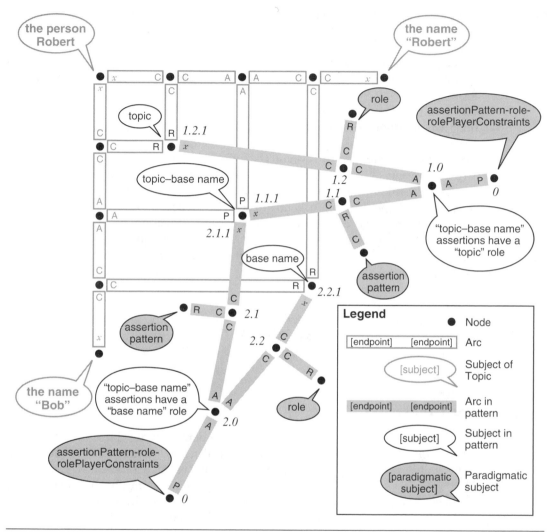

Figure 4–5 Sample pattern in the draft Reference Model

Note that to avoid overlap in the drawing, node 0 and the nodes with shaded paradigmatic subjects appear twice. In the real graph, each of these nodes must only appear once, by the subject based merging rule. Assertion 1.0 casts the topic whose subject is the topic-basename assertion (1.1.1) in the role of pattern (1.1), and the topic whose subject is topic (1.2.1) in the role of role (1.2); thus topic-basename assertions have a topic role. Assertion 2.0 casts the topic whose subject is the topic-basename assertion (2.1.1) in the role of pattern (2.1), and the topic whose subject is base name (2.2.1) in the role of role (2.2); thus topic-basename assertions have a basename role.

Note that the assertionPattern-role-rolePlayerConstraints assertion type declares a third role besides the assertionPattern and role roles described above: the rolePlayer-Constraints role. By design, the dRM says nothing about the nature of such role player constraints, how to assert them (though see TMCL, below), or how instances of assertions should be validated against them. All such decisions are made by designers of applications.

The Standard Application Model

The distinction between the RM and the SAM is like the distinction between chemistry and organic chemistry. Chemistry focuses on the nature of the chemical bond; the forces that bind atoms together into molecules are like the arcs that connect nodes in the Graph. In chemistry, no molecule is privileged over another, except as an object of study. However, organic chemistry privileges certain molecules, seeking to put them to industrial use; for example, the benzene ring is privileged when developing polycyclic organic compounds. Thus, the RM focuses on the nature of assertion itself, while the SAM takes assertion as given and focuses on defining the semantics of privileged assertion types.

To privilege the semantics of assertion types, the SAM defines information items with named and typed properties, as in W3C's XML InfoSet specification and in the Unified Modeling Language. This approach has the advantage of being more likely to gain immediate acceptance with developers.[15]

The Syntax Layer

The syntax layer comprises DTDs and documentation for HyTM's constructs, XTM's constructs, and constructs for a canonical syntax. Additional standards documents will show how to serialize the SAM into syntax and deserialize syntax into the SAM. Two instances of the SAM will be considered semantically equivalent if they produce instances of the canonical syntax that are byte-for-byte identical. (Because XTM 1.0 is designed to be useful to both humans and machines, there are sometimes several markup constructs that interchange the same knowledge. Order is not significant in some content models, for example. The canonical syntax will be optimized for machine-based identity comparisons, for example, in compliance testing.)

---

[15]As the SAM submission says, its approach does not have to be "learned" (that is, by developers; see *http://www.y12.doe.gov/sgml/sc34/document/0229.htm*). For example, the API to TM4J (*http://www.techquila. com*) is far more naturally expressed in SAM terms than in Reference Model terms. The reverse is true for GwTk (*http://www.goose-works.org*).

The Constraints and Queries Layer

The constraints and queries layer comprises Topic Map Query Language (TMQL) and Topic Map Constraint Language (TMCL). At the time of this writing, activities on this layer are on hold at the requirements-gathering phase, pending completion of work at the modeling layer. Following a thorough requirements-gathering phase, the TMQL Working Group summarized its general requirements, listed below.[16]

> TMQL shall have a concise and human-readable syntax.
>
> The execution of TMQL queries shall be defined in terms of operations on an abstract data model for topic maps and possibly also an environment. . . .
>
> TMQL query results shall be instances of an abstract TMQL data model.
>
> TMQL shall be independent of any particular interface between clients and the query processor.
>
> TMQL shall support all natural languages equally well. That is, TMQL shall be fully internationalized with respect to text representation, text ordering, etc.
>
> The TMQL standard shall be defined in two parts, first one with querying only, then one adding support for modifications.
>
> The TMQL standard shall not unduly constrain the form of implementations.
>
> The TMQL standard shall be formal, fully define the results of queries (so that any given query can only have one correct result in any given context) and, insofar as possible, be human-readable.
>
> TMQL shall be usable across a wide range of foreseeable platforms and applications over an extended lifetime (20–50 years).

TMCL is still in the early draft stage. User requirements are listed below.[17]

> TMCL shall permit the definition of classes of topic maps in order to:
>
> - enable the documentation of the structure and semantics of a class of topic maps;
> - provide a foundation for defining vertical or domain specific applications of topic maps;
> - provide means of validation to ensure consistency within a topic map or across a class of topic maps;

---

[16]Source: *http://www.y12.doe.gov/sgml/sc34/document/0229.htm*, accessed in April 2002.

[17]Source: *http://www.y12.doe.gov/sgml/sc34/document/0226.htm*, accessed in April 2002.

- enable applications to provide easier and more intuitive user interfaces for creating and maintaining topic maps;
- enable the separation of the tasks of modeling and populating topic maps.

TMCL shall be based on the Topic Map Data Model [now the RM] (and therefore support both XTM and ISO [HyTM] Topic Maps).

TMCL shall not attempt to cover every possible constraint.[18] Instead it should provide a solution for the most commonly required kinds of constraints and, at the same time, an extension mechanism to allow the expression of less common constraints by other means.

TMCL shall provide for modularization, and the ability to extend individual sets of constraints through reference to others.

TMCL shall be expressible as XML, using the topic map interchange syntax where applicable.

TMCL shall build on preexisting specifications and established best practice for knowledge representation and data modeling where possible. (Candidates for consideration include DAML/OIL, KIF, OKBC, OCL, PAL (Protégé Axiom Language), and XML Schema.)

TMCL shall be as concise and human-readable as possible within the terms of the preceding requirements.

Milestones in Software

Let's now look quickly at topic map software. Chapter 10 contains an extensive review of commercial and public domain topic map software. In this section, I am concerned only with showing the industrial strength of the commercial offerings and the diversity and originality of the free and/or open source efforts.

All commercial topic map software is written in Java and features topic map authoring and navigation. Acronym checklist compliance includes

- *Empolis K42:* application in Java using RMI, Jini, and SSL
- *Mondeca Knowledge Manager:* application in Java for J2EE using EJBs
- *Ontopia Knowledge Suite:* Java SDKs for J2EE using Java servlets and JSP

---

[18]Constraining the cardinality of the members of an association is not a requirement, for example.

In addition, Global Wisdom recently released Bravo, a collaboration tool based on Empolis's K42.

The free and/or open source software projects tend not to be checklist-compliant but focus on leading-edge problems for the topic map community.

The Future of Topic Maps

The State of the Paradigm

In the history of science, a paradigm associates a kind of problem, a theory for solving such problems, and a canonical example of solving the problem (often with a heroic figure as protagonist). Paradigms shift in historical time. For example, when Kepler calculated the elliptical orbits of the planets round the sun, this was a paradigm shift from Ptolemy, who calculated epicycles of the sun and planets round the Earth. Following paradigm shifts, the newly introduced problem-solving techniques are elaborated and formalized.

The topic map community has entered such a period of consolidation. As Michel Biezunski wrote in Chapter 2, topic maps originated in the problem of formalizing and interchanging finding aids like back-of-the-book indexes, glossaries, and thesauri. The solution was a markup language since that solved the interchange problem. (Our heroic figures came from the worlds of technical documentation and markup technology.) This classical approach is sometimes summed up as the "TAO" of topic maps, from the initials of the key constructs for representing finding aids: topics, associations, and occurrences.[19]

However, constructs that were important in marketing the topic maps paradigm to those initially most receptive to it no longer seem so compelling. For one thing, from work on the XTM conceptual model and the RM, we know that occurrences need not necessarily be privileged as an acronym's *O*. In RM terms, occurrences, base names, and variant names are all Assertions about Topic and Occurrence, Topic and Base name, and Base name and Variant name, respectively. ("ATOTBBV" lacks the resonance of "TAO," unfortunately.)

---

[19]Steve Pepper, in his XML Europe 2000 paper, "The TAO of Topic Maps: Finding the Way in the Age of Infoglut" (available at *http://www.gca.org/papers/xmleurope2000/papers/s11-01.html*), gives an excellent exposition of this view with historical and philosophical background.

The Near Future

Here are my personal guesses about what events will take place in the topic map space in the near future.

1. The topic maps paradigm will remain stable.
2. The XTM DTD 1.0 will become widely accepted.
3. The modeling work underpinning the HyTM and XTM interchange syntaxes will reinforce the paradigm, as will OASIS applications.
4. New levels of rigor based on models developed at ISO will enable
   a. Topic map queries and constraints
   b. Validation of associations against templates
   c. The extension of the paradigm across additional XML syntaxes
   d. The beginnings of knowledge federation
5. RDF and topic maps will attain a degree of convergence, enabled by the models, since:
   a. Both RDF and the Reference Model use a graph-based formalism.
   b. Convergence is "a simple matter" of mapping.

This is an exciting and gratifying time to be a topic mapper.

Chapter 5

Topic Maps from Representation to Identity

Conversation, Names, and Published Subject Indicators

Bernard Vatant

What Is the Conversation About?

What is the subject of this chapter? Very abruptly stated, it could be: *What is a subject?* This central identity question is indeed at the heart of all knowledge interchange issues, and the topic maps paradigm and specifications are about catching subjects in system representations. This fundamental process, referred to in topic maps terminology as *reification*, is at first sight as simple and straightforward as the basic language activity of catching the universe in words. Creating a new topic in a topic map is a process similar to the introduction of a new word in our vocabulary, representing a new subject in our knowledge. As a word or an image or an icon may be, a topic in a topic map is a *sign* both dreadfully simple and awfully complex. "A finger is pointing at the Moon," says the famous Zen aphorism; everybody can see the sign, but who understands what it is pointing at?

Two views of the world, grounded in different philosophical conceptions of what a subject is, are in competition here, and they support different methodologies for dealing with the subject identity question. The first viewpoint is referred to in this chapter as *naïve*, for it is an extension of an attitude we efficiently use when dealing with everyday individual objects. It considers individual objects and their classes to be living out there in the real world, just waiting for us to discover and choose the best possible representations and names for each of them. Was this naïve viewpoint in the minds of the founders of the topic maps paradigm? The naïve viewpoint could at first be considered as one of the main implicit axioms of the topic maps paradigm. Making the subject a binding point for all characteristics of a topic element is somehow assuming the absolute existence of this subject, before any representation of it and beyond all its characteristics: names, relationships (roles in associations), and occurrences. In many scopes, this viewpoint looks very sustainable indeed, just as naïve classification can be used in everyday life to handle and organize shopping lists, hardware catalogs, and address books. And the naïve viewpoint has led to very efficient systems of identification like ISBNs, license plates, and Social Security numbers. Note that these systems deal with individual objects classified into universally agreed-on classes: books, cars, people.

But extension of this naïve viewpoint to any kind of subject does not seem very sustainable, for many obvious reasons. The more conceptual and abstract the subjects get, the more ambiguity they gain. What are the real subjects, if any, represented by such words as *society* or *democracy* or *knowledge*? Assuming their absolute existence, independent of the social constructions around the words and concepts, would be both silly and dangerous. Hence the completely different viewpoint hereafter presented and referred to as *constructivist*. It assumes that except in the above ideal situations of well-defined individuals, subjects do not already exist but are emerging through a social constructive process, a "conversation around representation." The bottom line of the constructivist thesis is that most of the time, at least for abstract subjects, representations are put on the conversation table as a first stage for subject construction, before anyone clearly knows what subject they represent and whether they represent one or more subjects (or even any subject at all). So representations are considered here like tools for a subject-creation process. To sum it up, in the naïve viewpoint, representations are built out of or around preexisting subjects; in the constructivist viewpoint, subjects are emerging from a process involving representations as both raw materials and tools.

One interesting implementation of such a constructivist approach is found in the Wiki Web sites.[1] If while editing a Wiki page you write a new word in a given syntax (camel case with initial caps, like "NewSubject"), this action automatically creates a new page in the database (and a link to this page through that word), a page on which you will find the following invitation: "Discuss NewSubject here." If any other visitors step in and decide they have something to say about the concept of NewSubject, they can begin a conversation all about NewSubject.

Let's for the moment go back to more basic representations, keeping in mind natural language construction in childhood. A new word, to become an effective element in someone's language repertory, has to represent a new knowledge concept, which

---

[1] *WikiWiki* is Hawaiian for "quick." The Wiki Web sites were created by Ward Cunningham. See, for example, *http://c2.com/cgi/wiki*.

means it must acquire both distinctions from and connections to any preexisting vocabulary and knowledge, as well as some external authoritative reference in the outer world. This process occurs for every one of us and for every word and unique experience, as shown in the examples below. There are so many ways to connect a new word to an existing vocabulary and a new concept to existing knowledge, so many possible external references, and so many different personal backgrounds for any new word or subject that some consider it impossible for any two people to have the same comprehension of any subject—hence, in this view every communication is impossible or ambiguous.

Even if misunderstanding is a very "common place"[2] indeed to find ourselves, the above conclusion is certainly mostly wrong, considering the global efficiency of various languages: commands are executed, planes take off and land safely, mail is delivered correctly, and even the more subtle subjects addressed in music, poetry, and other fine arts seem to be communicated elegantly. So we must admit that there is a social process that somehow corrects for the variety of human experiences and makes for convergence on shared meanings. The thesis developed in this chapter states that ongoing conversation around the subject, involving a metalevel dialogue, is fundamental in this correction and convergence process. In fact, any efficient conversation is sustained by continuing control and feedback from each participant to ensure he or she stays tuned: "Do you really mean A is different from B?" "What do you mean exactly by X?" "Do you mean this Z or that Z?" All those kinds of questions, verbal and nonverbal, constantly redirecting the conversation and avoiding misunderstanding, are in fact all about subject identity. Without this metalevel communication, any conversation degenerates into parallel monologues.

A Finger Pointing at a Planet

Let's see now through a simple example how well-conducted conversation leads to subject emergence. Sarah and Jim have acquired some notion of what a planet is and looks like. One night Sarah points at Jupiter in the summer sky and asks her astronomer grandfather some questions.

SARAH: Do you know the name of that bright star over there?

GRANDFATHER: Of course, Sarah, but it's not a star, it's a planet. It's Jupiter, the biggest planet in the solar system. You've heard of it, of course. Looking great, isn't it?

---

[2]*Editor's note:* The author puns conceptually on the notion that, like the Greek *topos* from which the word *topic* derives, "common place" refers to both a subject of conversation (a cliché) and, taken literally, a location.

Sarah: Oh . . . I didn't think we could see Jupiter that bright! How come it looks like a star if it's a planet? Shouldn't it look round like Earth or the Moon?

Grandfather: It's very big, and the Sun lights it—that's why it shines, just as the Moon does. But it's also just a bit too far away to see its form with your naked eyes. With a little telescope you would see it *is* round. Maybe I'll show you one of these nights . . . but look carefully now. Does it really look like a star?

Sarah: There's something . . . it doesn't twinkle like the other stars.

Grandfather: There you are. That's a way you will know it's a planet . . . it does not twinkle . . .

The conversation goes on about stars and planets, under the Milky Way. Sarah's night encounter with the subject sets a strong mental representation of the planet concept in her mind, organizing it around her grandfather's authoritative and immediate introduction. Figure 5–1 presents the knowledge resulting from this conversation in terms of topics, associations, and roles.

Jim, Sarah's friend, has never closely observed the night sky and has been fed by environmental activist parents with concerns about our fragile little planet. (See a

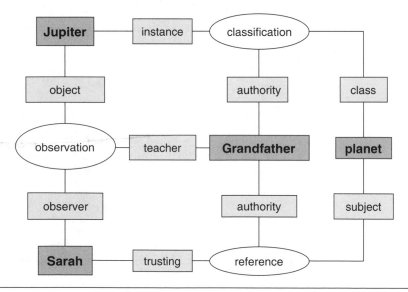

Figure 5–1   Sarah's view of the world after observing Jupiter with Grandfather[3]

---

[3]For an explanation of the shapes and lines used in the figures, see the Addendum at the end of this chapter.

representation of his acquired view in Figure 5–2.) Yet he has discovered that Jupiter is a planet and dreamed about Voyager's images in his private conversations with books (see Figure 5–3). He has not yet made a clearly consistent figure out of the various occurrences of *planet* in his mental universe. In fact, in Jim's mind, the word

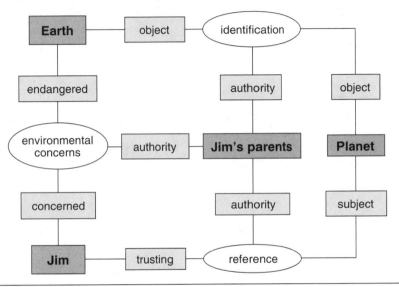

Figure 5–2   Jim's view of *Planet* as another name for endangered Earth

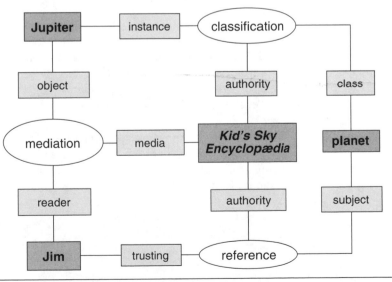

Figure 5–3   Jim's view of Jupiter as a planet

planet points to two different representations, two topics waiting to be merged; for him, *planet* doesn't really represent a single subject.

In Sarah's world representation, Grandfather's authoritative definition of a planet acts as a stable and external indicator of the subject. In her worldview, Grandfather is the paradigm of both authority and permanence. She knows she'll be able to refer to his paradigm for that matter and forever. She can refer to it both to sustain her inner mental representation and to exchange information with Jim so they can eventually settle the following debate.

SARAH: You know Jupiter, the planet?

JIM: Yes, I know it. What do you think?

SARAH: I saw it in the sky last summer with my grandfather.

JIM: You mean . . . your grandfather has a telescope?

SARAH: Yes, he does, but you don't need a telescope to see Jupiter, just your naked eyes.

JIM: You can't see it like that, it's too far away. You can see only stars at night, not planets!

SARAH: Sure you can. It's brighter than the brightest stars. And it's a planet just like Earth, but—

JIM: Wait! Jupiter is a planet, OK, but what do you mean "just like Earth"?

They begin to argue about what a planet is. How will they settle this argument? Perhaps Sarah will be declared an expert because of both Grandfather's authority and Jim's secret love, and that will settle the matter and yield a strong new reference for Jim, maybe changing forever his representation of planets to that shown in Figure 5–4. Or perhaps they will both agree to refer to some acknowledged expert as an external resource—maybe more of Grandfather's explanations.

Many things could be said about the above conversations. To pick only what is pertinent to the present thesis, it's clear that they are dealing with knowledge building and interchange, starting from an object's names and images and converging toward an agreement about the underlying subject.

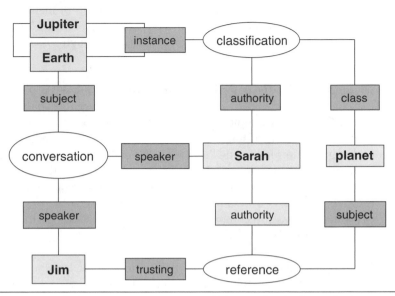

Figure 5–4   Jim's shift to a more consistent worldview under Sarah's authority

So What about Published Subject Indicators?

The above example, in the form of Sarah's reference to Grandfather, seems to yield at first sight an exact natural language equivalent of what Published Subject Indicators (PSIs) are about in the topic maps paradigm and of how they are built (through both acknowledged authority and the permanence of the authority's location). A PSI in the XTM 1.0 specification (*http://www.topicmaps.org/xtm*) is defined as follows:

> A subject indicator is a **resource** that is intended by the topic map author to provide a positive, unambiguous indication of the **identity of a subject** [emphasis added].

A published subject is any subject for which a subject indicator has been available for public use and is accessible via a URI. A PSI is therefore any resource that has been published in order to provide a positive, unambiguous indication of the identity of a subject for the purpose of facilitating topic map interchange and mergeability.

Had Sarah's grandfather put online, at a permanent address, his definition and description of a planet, it seems that would have made for Sarah a good PSI for the *planet* topic in her mental topic map: positive and unambiguous. Starting from that naïve viewpoint, and after a review of the reasons why PSIs are binding identity points (whereas names are representations carrying only a weak form of identity), we'll see what requirements apply to sustainable PSIs and, eventually, how PSIs can be built and managed to conform to the thesis of subject creation through conversation.

PSIs Are Binding Points for Subject Identity

The introductory example shows the role of an external authority in building subject identity between two human beings with different knowledge backgrounds. When exchanging information and knowledge through system representations in a so-called Semantic Web, one has to deal with one more constraint: the identity of subjects must be clear and unambiguous not only for human authors and users but also for computers exchanging the representations. Therefore this identity has to be defined in a way that both humans and computers can effectively use. Both names and PSIs are at first sight good candidates for that matter.

Names can be understood by human users and handled, exchanged, and compared by computers. PSIs have the same computability as names, and humans can use them to check what the subject is about. So the choice is between defining a topic subject by a name, "civilization," or by a (fictitious) PSI, "http://psi.socialsciences.org/civilization. html."

The XTM 1.0 topic maps specification claims that names and identities are clearly different notions, supported by different topic properties. In other words, the identity of a topic (the definition of its subject) is supported by names only in a relative form, valid only in a context (defined by a scope), whereas the absolute identity is supported by "subject identity," hopefully referring to the correct PSI. In the previous example, Sarah and Jim initially agree on a statement: "Jupiter is a planet." Had their conversation stopped at this first exchange, they would have agreed on that statement but would not have been aware they were giving quite different meanings to the word *planet* because they were using it in different scopes.

This simple example shows that agreement on names and even on statements—even in an apparently consistent context—does not mean there is shared understanding on the subject identity. Had this identity been defined by external reference, the topics would have been kept clearly distinct. The subject indicator for Sarah's *planet* is what she has seen and heard from her grandfather, whereas Jim's *planet* is in fact a dual word referring to different subjects, defined respectively in the Greenpeace Earth Charter and the *Kid's Sky Encyclopædia*. They will eventually merge when Jim gives up his fuzzy and inconsistent references for a more accurate and authoritative one. Consider *planet* as a unique subject in Sarah and Jim's conversation: it would be premature to merge the topic *planet* in Sarah's representation with the topic *planet* in Jim's representation, because Sarah and Jim have similar, but not identical, representations of *planet*. PSI comparison should avoid this kind of confusion, if the PSIs are of sufficient quality.

PSIs Have to Meet High Quality Requirements

PSIs must meet certain requirements for quality.

- **Stability:** The publisher must guarantee the permanence of the resource address.
- **Expertise:** The definition of subjects must be validated by authoritative sources.
- **Trust:** This evolves mainly as a consequence of the two previous requirements.

Note that these requirements do not concern the content of the published subject, neither its quality nor its permanence. An obvious case would be a PSI for "world population" that presents the most accurate and updated figures on that subject. Clearly the content would change frequently! The questions of what the content of a PSI should be and in what ways it can provide a positive and unambiguous indication of a subject's identity are very deep ones. Before that discussion, we'll explore what PSIs should be used for and what should not be expected from them.

PSIs Are Good for Pragmatic Bottom-up Tasks

Pulling toward Convergence of Ontologies

A topic map author may get carried away with the freedom allowed by the XTM specification when defining topics and associations. Even if it's completely right to do so in principle, such a total freedom of concept definition would lead to colorful, intelligent, but completely unsharable topic maps. Choosing topic references from among PSIs allows the author to anchor a representation in collective knowledge and perhaps push somehow to refine his or her (and the user's) reflection on the concepts. If the author considers that there is no available PSI fitting his or her notion of a subject, he or she should be given the ability to propose a new one, adding to the common knowledge.

Facilitating Information Exchange and Knowledge Construction Inside Communities

This may seem a kind of paradox: inside a community, there should be no ambiguity of terms since a community shares a common vocabulary and is often defined by this very sharing. But it turns out that working in a community requires generally more accuracy in the definition of terms than that needed for the exchange of general interest information. Moreover, there are always several stable, visible, and authoritative sets of URIs inside communities, which make potentially ideal candidates for PSI repositories. For example, language specifications and standards are de facto PSI repositories and are essential tools inside technical communities.

Creating Bottom-up Authority and Trust

PSIs can and should contain more than simple term definitions. A PSI repository maintained for the purpose of assistance in topic map authoring can itself be organized as a topic map, proposing PSIs for associations and role type definitions. One could imagine that such a PSI repository would propose also a list of its public users. That should make for a good part of the authority- and trust-building process. Authors and users will be empowered to use ontologies already developed by others in their community and even to participate in building those ontologies (thus creating a bottom-up bootstrapping process), rather than to adopt a single, top-down, "universal" ontology.[4]

PSIs Cannot Pretend to Universality nor Strong Symbolic Signification

The previous section speaks clearly and loudly for pragmatic, local, and community-grounded definition and use of PSIs. Attempts to define a unique set of universal concepts, once and for all, in so-called upper ontologies are clearly unsustainable from all human, conceptual, and technical viewpoints. Such attempts stand against all common sense, as well as historical evidence that they always lead to failure, as Michel Biezunski points out in Chapter 2. So a good PSI should be used inside a given context, the very context itself not being permanently defined to begin with but building itself following the constructivist bootstrapping process described in this chapter.

Defined that way, PSIs can't pretend to any strong symbolic signification for the representation of subjects. And in fact, as pointed out before, PSIs are not representations; they are only indications. They are used by authors to ensure consistency and grounding of their topic maps in a knowledge community, by computers to allow easy comparison and merging of topic maps, and maybe by technical middle or end users in a community. But PSIs will be of little or no use to average end users, who want to find subjects represented by familiar signs: words and statements, images and icons. Such an end user browsing a topic map directory is more likely to follow some inner

---

[4]See Chapter 7 by Leo Obrst and Howard Liu for more information on ontologies.

hunch of the meaning of topic names, based on interpretation of the topic context defined by its roles in associations, than to go and fetch a PSI to make sure that this understanding is tuned with the author's intention. If the topic map is semantically consistent, disambiguation by explicit reference to PSIs should not be necessary at the user's end, except for particularly controversial subjects that need very accurate definition. But there again it's more likely to happen in a specific technical context than in general interest navigation.

Back to the Conversation Subject

All of the above tells what PSIs should be good for and what they surely won't achieve. But the central question has been kept for the end: How should an effective PSI be built?

We've explored fundamental external properties: stability and validation by an authoritative expert, leading to trust. We've seen that building trust is a bootstrapping process. To start this process, we need some content and some authoritative expertise. Let's take another example of that: a good PSI for topic maps is at *http://www. topicmaps.org*. Why is it a good one? It's stable, and users find there a clear definition of topic maps, a discussion of their history, the vocabulary of topic maps, the XTM 1.0 specification, and validation by experts in the field. Moreover, it has a self-documenting domain name, it has gained visibility in search engines and directories, and a variety of sites in the Semantic Web community link to it.

Imagine you have just discovered topic maps and want to use a PSI to further explore this concept. What would make you choose TopicMaps.Org instead of another PSI? Are you going to check all the content? Surely not. The most important reason is that you trust it is the place where things are defined most accurately because all the experts you've read refer to it. But if you look carefully at the PSI from the inside, you enter the XTM community, and you see, as in any other community, ever-changing content, debates, and questions. You begin to wonder: What are topic maps *really*? Discovering that at the very heart lies anything but a permanent definition of the subject, will you for that reason give up TopicMaps.Org as a PSI for topic maps? Surely not; you will probably keep it for a better reason than ever: it's the place where the subject is more in question.

This leads us to a sweet paradox. The best PSI is the one that is most likely to change its content because it is maintained at the core of the community questioning the subject, and most subjects are moving targets. Coming back to the introductory example, imagine an ongoing conversation among Sarah, Jim, Grandfather, and Jim's parents in which they exchange and converge their various visions of what *planet* means for each of them (see Figure 5–5). Putting that conversation online, with all the view-points and properly linked documentation, yields a very nice collaborative PSI for *planet* in an educational topic map.

Let's take a last extreme but meaningful example. Imagine a repository of Buddhist PSIs. A central subject in Buddhism is emptiness. What would a user find as the content of a PSI for emptiness? A blank page is the only choice that makes sense. The permanent address of this blank page would be referred to by thousands of Buddhist topic maps. Clicking on this blank page would take users to the full list of these references, which they could browse. The best PSI ever . . . stable, authoritative, trustworthy. But no content?

That may seem strange (except to Zen adepts). As Steven Newcomb warned in Chapter 3, you can't learn about the topic maps paradigm without affecting your attitudes about information and communication. On the other hand, the example above could shed new light on his image of the unbridgeable chasm between conversation and its subject, which only our brains can bridge. Maybe there is neither a chasm nor a bridge problem because the conversation and its subject are on the same side after all—there is only conversation, outside and inside the subject, as the above examples show.

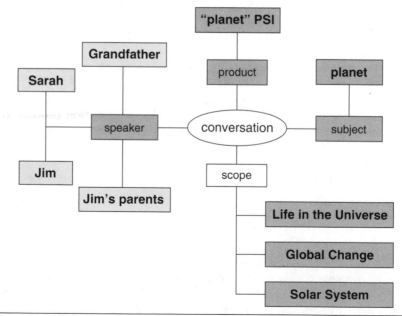

Figure 5–5 A subject indicator for *planet* emerging from ongoing conversation

And this book will be a good PSI for XTM ... if ongoing conversation keeps the subject alive!

Addendum: A Note on the Figures

Figures 5–1 through 5–5 are graphic representations of topic maps with two kinds of nodes.

1. Topics are represented by lightly shaded rectangles with the name of the topic (for example, Sarah, Jim, Grandfather, Jupiter, planet) inside.
2. Associations are represented by ovals with the name of the association type (for example, observation, reference) inside.

Associations are linked to topics playing a role in them by lines labeled by darkly shaded rectangles. The label is the name of the topic defining the role type (in topic map syntax, the *role specification*).

For example, Figure 5–1 conveys the following information.

Jupiter, Grandfather, and Sarah are members of an association.

The type of this association is *observation*.

Jupiter plays the role of *object*.

Grandfather plays the role of *teacher*.

Sarah plays the role of *observer*.

In Figure 5–5, a scoped association represents the ongoing conversation. The subject indicator is considered as a *product* of the conversation process. It's the only place where scope is used. But the topics with an *authority* role in the previous figures could have been considered as scopes as well; one typical use of scope is to document the source or provenance of an association.

Chapter 6

How to Start Topic Mapping Right Away with the XTM Specification

Sam Hunting

XTM Topic Mapping

XTM stands for "XML Topic Maps." By the end of this chapter, you will know 100 percent of what you need to know to start creating XML topic maps, even if you know 0 percent (or even less) now.

As for XML, all you need to know for now is that XML adds the angle brackets to words in documents that otherwise look like plain English (`<topic>`), that when these words have been "marked up" they are called *elements*, and that XML elements live in XML documents, one of which, an XML topic map, we are about to create. (You may choose to stop reading here and check the XML entry in the Resources section near the end of this chapter, or see Chapter 3 on markup.)

In this chapter, we will step through the creation of two topic maps. Because topic maps are simple and intuitive, we're going to start from the bottom up, with the angle brackets, and finish with theory, rather than working from the top down. By working through the examples you will understand

- All XTM elements
- How to merge XTM topic maps
- Some XTM pitfalls

To aid our understanding, we will avoid the following subjects: philosophy, history, politics, and theology (PHPT). Why would this be hard? Topic mapping jargon contains a lot of words that have been hijacked from PHPT; among them *subject*, *topic*, *associate*, *occur*, *resource*, *name*, and that hardy perennial, *is*. Also *indicates* and *identity*.

Fortunately, we can keep it simple by sticking to words in angle brackets like `<topic>`—they, at least, are clearly defined in the XTM specification, into which philosophy, religion, history, and politics do not enter.[1]

Why Topic Maps?

The purpose of topic maps is to interchange knowledge. Knowledge interchange may seem hard (knowledge is seen as subjective or as existing only in the mind), but in fact it can be approached pragmatically.

Let's make an analogy between tomato soup and topic maps.

Tomato Soup	Topic Maps
Taste	Knowledge
Can of tomato soup	Topic map document
Directions on the can	Processing methods

Thus, although "taste" is often regarded as very subjective, in fact we exchange it every day, via cans of tomato soup. Subjectivity holds as well for "knowledge," which we can exchange with topic maps. As the taste of tomato soup is interchanged in cans, so knowledge is interchanged in topic map documents. As you follow the directions on the side of the can to make (or at least reconstitute) tomato soup, so topic map software uses specified processing methods to make (or at least reconstitute) knowledge. (See Chapter 4.) If you pour two cans of soup into the same pan you might be said to merge them—but let's not get ahead of ourselves.

Inspired by the humble tomato, let's pick an area to actually map: *cuisine*. Why? It's a tradition of the XTM Authoring Group to share excellent meals. Cuisine also has a variety of rich relationships to express in topic map associations, like recipes and menus. Rationalizing further, cuisine requires the use of several human (in the jargon, *natural*) languages; meeting this requirement will exhibit a powerful feature of topic map applications called *scope*. A print representation of an occurrence of our topic occurs on the next page.

In developing our topic maps, let's imagine that we live in a world much like today's world, except that it is our topic map future, and topic maps are everywhere. Hundreds

---

[1]Any lie that occurs in this chapter is clearly indicated by a footnote marker associated with the (truthful) text, as seen in this footnote and many of the notes following.

of thousands of J. R. R. Tolkien fans have merged their shrines into a single representation of Middle Earth. Closer to home, it is possible to buy tomatoes via cell phone.

Appetizer

Topic map documents are very simple: there are only 19 XTM elements. So, when you finish this section, you will know 50 percent of what you need to know to start topic mapping. In this section, you'll learn about the following elements (listed alphabetically):

```
<baseName>
<baseNameString>
<occurrence>
<resourceRef>
<scope>
<subjectIdentity>
<subjectIndicatorRef>
<topic>
<topicRef>
```

Introducing `<topic>`, `<baseName>`, `<scope>`, `<baseNameString>`, and `<occurrence>`

Let's create a topic element and give it an ID in case we need to identify it later:

```
<topic id="myTomato">
```

(I lied about what you need to know about XML. XML elements also have attributes, like the -id- attribute in the example above.)

> **PITFALL:** An ID must be a string that is unique within the topic map document. It doesn't have to make sense, like *myTomato;* it just has to be unique.[2] In most examples, IDs are a pitfall because for teaching and readability we make the ID strings in tutorials and on whiteboards look like names that have a deeper meaning than mere uniqueness. They don't.

Since we want to talk about tomatoes, let's type in a base name[3] for our topic that reflects our intent: "tomato." Since we don't want these potentially shady characters wandering round the landscape,[4] we wrap them up in a `<baseNameString>` element like so:

```
<topic id="myTomato">
  <baseName>
    <baseNameString>tomato</baseNameString>
  </baseName>
</topic>
```

Just in case anyone doubts that what we're talking about really is a tomato, let's supply a little more information about the topic by adding an image of a tomato, suitably ripened for site display.

```
<topic id="myTomato">
  <baseName>
    <baseNameString>tomato</baseNameString>
  </baseName>
  <occurrence>
    <resourceRef xlink:href="tomato.gif"/>
  </occurrence>
</topic>
```

---

[2]Another lie. An ID does have to be unique (within an XTM document), but also it can't start with a number, and if you could use a character to simulate profanity in a comic strip or for punctuation, you probably can't use it in an ID. For more information see the XML listing in Resources near the end of this chapter.

[3]You'll see what the base name is the basis of when we talk about variants later in this chapter. Why didn't XTM just call the element *name*? Because that word is all mixed up with PHPT.

[4]This is a lie. We're just avoiding "mixed content." See the XML listing in Resources near the end of this chapter.

You can think of the -xlink:href- attribute as working just like the -href- attribute of an HTML <A> element: it points to a resource you want to get, in this case, the GIF file that is the occurrence of the tomato topic. That xlink: prefix means that the attribute also conforms to the XLink World Wide Web Consortium (W3C) specification (see the Resources section).

In a topic map, like any map, *the map is not the territory.*[5] Here the topic whose ID is *myTomato* is part of the map; the resource in the file tomato.gif is part of the territory. For this reason, topic maps are sometimes called *information overlays.* They are superimposed over resources without changing them, just as a road map is an information overlay for the road you are driving—not because it is draped over the steering wheel of your car but because the connections that images of roads make between images of cities on the map are useful when driving to real cities over real roads.

But wait a minute. Ultimately, in our topic map future I want to use a topic map to order my tomatoes from My Tomato Purveyor (MTP), Inc., using my cell phone. So I need to be 100 percent certain that when my cell phone sends "tomato," MTP's server knows I mean "tomato." The base name string "tomato" works fine for humans, but maybe machines need some help. I may need to say what the *subject* of my topic is more precisely.

Introducing <subjectIdentity>

In this section, you'll learn about the following elements (again listed in alphabetical order) and how to choose between them:

```
<resourceRef>
<subjectIdentity>
<subjectIndicatorRef>
<topicRef>
```

Let's give the "tomato" topic an identity that both machines and humans can understand. I know, MTP knows, and the computer can "understand" that the USDA specification for the kind of tomato I want lives at the following URI: *http://www.fed.gov/usda/doc/tomatogr.htm#gradeA.* Thus I can express our mutually agreed-upon knowledge and declare the subject of our topic in the following way.

```
<topic id="myTomato">
  <subjectIdentity>
  <subjectIndicatorRef xlink:href="http://www.fed.gov/usda/doc/
    tomatogr.htm#gradeA"/>
```

---

[5]This is a lie. In a topic map, sometimes the map *is* the territory, since a topic map (being electronic) can be an occurrence of a topic, just like our tomato GIF file. Since this feature (and it is a feature) of topic maps is littered with PHPT we, as beginners, will avoid it.

```
    </subjectIdentity>
    <baseName>
      <baseNameString>tomato</baseNameString>
    </baseName>
    <occurrence>
      <resourceRef xlink:href="tomato.gif"/>
    </occurrence>
</topic>
```

It turns out that all these years, although without knowing it, the USDA and governments in general have been creating rich sets of resources for topic mappers to point to when they want to agree that they are talking about the same subject, like grade A tomatoes. These resources are called *Published Subject Indicators* (PSIs) and are discussed further in Chapter 5.

Of course, the Canadian government has been grading tomatoes too, and to tell MTP that it's all one to me whether I get Canadian tomatoes or American tomatoes, I would add a second `<subjectIndicatorRef>` pointing to the Canadian PSI.

> **PITFALL:** If I used the subject identity for USDA grade A tomatoes for a topic with the `<baseName>` "potato," that would really confuse the humans, the machines, and/or both. So I won't do that.

We also could have defined the subject identity of our topic using `<resourceRef>`, as shown below.

```
<subjectIdentity>
  <resourceRef xlink:href="tomato.gif"/>
</subjectIdentity>
```

We and MTP would then agree that the file `tomato.gif` unambiguously specified our subject, instead of just being information relevant to it, which is what an occurrence is. We could define our subject this way, but we would be wrong to do so in this situation. Why? A resource specified with `<subjectIdentity>` *indicates* a subject (in our case, tomato). But a resource specified with `<resourceRef>` *constitutes* the subject, *is* the subject (in this case, the exact bits and bytes that make up that single image at the address given in the `<resourceRef>` element's -`xlink:href`- attribute value). If we were graphic artists, we might care about that. As cooks, or people who claim to be cooks, we don't.

Finally, we could have specified the subject identity of our topic using `<topicRef>`, as shown below.

```
<subjectIdentity>
  <topicRef xlink:href="#anotherTomato"/>
</subjectIdentity>
```

The `<topicRef>` element points to the `<topic>` element that in turn has a subject. (The `<topicRef>` element must point to a `<topic>` element.) We and MTP would then agree that the `<topic>` element with the ID *anotherTomato* specified our subject. We will see one reason we might want to point at a `<topic>` element that specifies our subject identity, rather than pointing at the subject directly, in the next section.

Introducing `<scope>`

Unlike an ID, a `<baseName>` might be required to make sense to at least some humans; unfortunately the `<baseName>` we have chosen makes sense only in English. Since cuisine is by definition French, let's give our topic a second name in that language, where FR stands for "French" and EN stands for "English."

```
<topic id="myTomato">
  <baseName>
    <scope>
      <topicRef xlink:href="#EN"/>
    </scope>
    <baseNameString>tomato</baseNameString>
  </baseName>
  <baseName>
    <scope>
      <topicRef xlink:href="#FR"/>
    </scope>
    <baseNameString>tomate</baseNameString>
  </baseName>
  <baseName>
    <baseNameString>tomato</baseNameString>
  </baseName>
  . . .
</topic>
```

Here we use `<scope>` to turn `<baseName>` elements on and off. *Tomate*, for example, will be the `<baseName>` data for the `<topic>` element from the point of view of humans who prefer to speak French. But what about the third `<baseName>`, the one with no `<scope>`? This is the default `<baseName>`—the one that is always on.[6] This is the `<baseName>` that a human who speaks neither English nor French should see.

Now, why did we use `<topicRef>` to make our first two `<scope>` elements? Let's set up the `<topic>` elements to point at and use PSIs to express their subject identities.

---

[6]More lies. First, some cuisine is Chinese. Second, in the jargon, "topic characteristics" are "valid" within scopes. Scopes don't really turn anything on or off—applications do that. The scope that is "always on" is called the *unconstrained scope*.

```
<topic id="EN">
  <subjectIdentity>
    <subjectIndicatorRef
    xlink:href="http://www.topicmaps.org/xtm/1.0/language.xtm#en"/>
  </subjectIdentity>
</topic>
<topic id="FR">
  <subjectIdentity>
    <subjectIndicatorRef
    xlink:href="http://www.topicmaps.org/xtm/1.0/language.xtm#fr"/>
  </subjectIdentity>
</topic>
```

Using this setup has several advantages. First, the topic map is easier to read (and to write). EN is a lot shorter than `http://www.topicmaps.org/xtm/1.0/language.xtm#en`.

Second, the topic map is easier to maintain. The subject indicated by the topic EN turns out to be one of the two-letter ISO codes for human languages. (ISO, the International Organization for Standardization, has, like governments, been publishing PSIs without knowing it was doing so for many years.) Better yet, it turns out that this ISO language list has been translated into a topic map and is available on the TopicMaps.org site. (Check the value of the `-href-` attribute.) Best of all, suppose that we discover that there is a better listing of language code PSIs somewhere (see *http://www.oasis-open.org/committees/tm-pubsubj/*), and MTP and we agree to use it. In that case, we need only update the two `-href-` attributes in the subject indicators of the `<topic>` elements EN and FR, and in the machine, all the `<topicRef>` elements that point to them will update too.

Main Course

In this section, you'll learn about the following elements:

```
<association>
<instanceOf>
<member>
<roleSpec>
```

Four more elements—so when you finish this section, you will know 70 percent of what you need to know to start topic mapping.

Of course, a tomato is no good in isolation. Well, it is, but we really care about tomatoes when they are associated with other things—in our case, with caramel—using menus and recipes.

Introducing `<association>`, `<member>`, and `<roleSpec>`

First, we'll set up the association between the tomato and the dish. Let's make a topic for a dish.[7]

```
<topic id="myConfite">
  <baseNameString>
    tomate confite farcie aux douze saveurs
  </baseNameString>
</topic>
```

Now let's associate our tomato and this dish by making them members of an `<association>`, using `<topicRef>` to define the `<member>` elements.[8]

```
<association id="tomate_confite_association">
  <member>
    <topicRef xlink:href="#myTomato"/>
  </member>
  <member>
    <topicRef xlink:href="#myConfite"/>
  </member>
</association>
```

That there is an association (some association) between *myConfite* and *myTomato* is not very informative, however. We need to explain what roles the two topics are playing in the association. So let's make some topics for roles.

```
<topic id="anIngredient">
  <baseName>
    <baseNameString>an ingredient</baseNameString>
  </baseName>
</topic>
```

---

[7] This dish is an occurrence of a subject whose topic is named "the crisis in French cooking" by Adam Gopnik in his book *Paris to the Moon* (Random House, 2000). In fact, its chef conceives of the dish as a proof by example (achieved with immense labor) that the topic, *tomato*, is properly associated with a dish in the scope of the dessert phase of a meal, since the tomato is an instance of the class *fruit* and not an instance of the class *vegetable*.

[8] Inside `<member>` we could also have used `<resourceRef>`, for something that *is* a subject. We could also have *indicated* a subject with `<subjectIndicatorRef>`—even used `<subjectIndicatorRef xlink:href= "#myTomato"/>`, which is equivalent to `<topicRef xlink:href="#myTomato"/>`. However, since we are pointing at something that we expect to create and manage as a `<topic>` in our topic map, it makes sense here to use `<topicRef>`.

(To keep the examples short, we'll leave the `<baseName>` elements out from now on. This is perfectly OK topic mapping—it's up to you whether your topics have `<baseName>` elements or not. In fact, the only thing that you must do with a `<topic>` element is give it an ID. We'll also tumble into the pitfall of giving elements IDs that look like names, purely for the sake of exposition.)

Here's another topic for another role.

```
<topic id="aDish"/>
```

Now we add the roles to our association using `<roleSpec>`.

```
<association id="tomate_confite_association">
  <member>
    <roleSpec>
      <topicRef xlink:href="#anIngredient"/>
    </roleSpec>
    <topicRef xlink:href="#myTomato"/>
  </member>
  <member>
    <roleSpec>
      <topicRef xlink:href="#aDish"/>
    </roleSpec>
    <topicRef xlink:href="#myConfite"/>
  </member>
</association>
```

Now we can interchange the knowledge that in this association, the tomato plays the ingredient role, and the confite plays the dish role.

Introducing `<instanceOf>`

Now we can distinguish the ingredient from the dish. But what about the association itself? What type of association is it? Let's make another topic.

```
<topic id="ingredient_of"/>
```

(Of course, in a real topic map, we could add a lot of detail to this topic—a PSI, one or more base names, and so on. Here, for purposes of exposition, we suggest all that robustness with the ID.)

Now let's revise our existing `<association>` element to say that the association `tomate_confite_association` is an association of the type `ingredient_of`.

```
<association id="tomate_confite_association">
  <instanceOf>
    <topicRef xlink:href="#ingredient_of"/>
  </instanceOf>
  <member>
    <roleSpec>
      <topicRef xlink:href="#anIngredient"/>
    </roleSpec>
    <topicRef xlink:href="#myTomato"/>
  </member>
  <member>
    <roleSpec>
      <topicRef xlink:href="#aDish"/>
    </roleSpec>
    <topicRef xlink:href="#myConfite"/>
  </member>
</association>
```

And in the same way, we can add other associations of the same type to our topic map.

```
<association id="caramels_confite">
  <instanceOf>
    <topicRef xlink:href="#ingredient_of"/>
  </instanceOf>
  <member>
    <roleSpec>
      <topicRef xlink:href="#anIngredient"/>
    </roleSpec>
    <topicRef xlink:href="#myCaramel"/>
  </member>
  <member>
    <roleSpec>
      <topicRef xlink:href="#aDish"/>
    </roleSpec>
    <topicRef xlink:href="#myConfite"/>
  </member>
</association>
```

Of course, for this markup we also have to add a new topic:

```
<topic id="myCaramel"/>
```

Caramel is one of the ingredients of the confite because the confite is in fact a dessert.

Now I can ask the topic map (using, in our topic map future, topic map software that understands the future topic map query language) for all the dishes that have tomatoes as ingredients, so I can consolidate my order to MTP when I finally flip open my cell phone and call them.

Back to the word *type*. This is one of those words that (among computer programmers at least) tends to generate the sort of heated PHPT-driven discussion I promised to avoid. We (and also computer programmers) say that "a tomato is a type of fruit," "2 is a type of number," "a lion is a type of animal," and so on. That means that fruits, numbers, and animals are all classes, and tomatoes, 2, and lions are all instances of each class.[9] Similarly, apples, 3, and aardvarks are also instances of the same three classes. Since we are in the topic map world, we make our classes with topics, but the same relationship between instance and class still holds.

Topic maps are fun to write, so once we get started making associations it's hard to stop. Let's make a menu.

```
<association id="entree_dessert">
  <instanceOf>
    <topicRef xlink:href="#menu"/>
  </instanceOf>
  <member>
    <roleSpec>
      <topicRef xlink:href="#dessert"/>
    </roleSpec>
    <topicRef xlink:href="#myConfite"/>
  </member>
  <member>
    <roleSpec>
      <topicRef xlink:href="#entrees"/>
    </roleSpec>
    <topicRef xlink:href="#myFoieGras"/>
  </member>
</association>
```

We also—as you may have predicted—have to make the following elements in our map.

```
<topic id="menu"/>
<topic id="dessert"/>
<topic id="entrees"/>
<topic id="myFoieGras"/>
```

And while we're thinking of typing, let's go back and type our confite, too.

```
<topic id="myConfite">
  <instanceOf>
    <topicRef xlink:href="#dessert"/>
```

---

[9] Typing is important for writing correct programs. Let's suppose that we feed a program an instance of class mineral (an instance whose type is mineral) when our program expects an instance of class animal (an instance whose type is animal)—a stone instead of a lion. The program should complain, and the programmer should figure out whether an instance of animal or mineral is required.

```
  </instanceOf>
  <baseName>
    <baseNameString>
      tomate confite farcie aux douze saveurs
    </baseNameString>
  </baseName>
</topic>
```

This way, if we want to ask our topic map for all the desserts, we'll get them. Better yet, since we know that there is a role on the menu called *dessert*, and we know that our confite is an instance of the class *dessert*, we can make sure that topics are playing sensible roles in our associations. The example below would not be sensible.

```
<member>
  <roleSpec>
    <topicRef xlink:href="#dessert"/>
  </roleSpec>
  <topicRef xlink:href="#myFoieGras"/>
</member>
```

> **PITFALL:** It's fair to say that in later versions of the topic map standard, there will be more sophisticated ways to say how members will play roles in associations. That is why I used the not-exactly-rigorous word *sensible* in the paragraph above.

Dessert

In this section, you'll learn about the following element:

`<mergeMap>`

This is only one more element, number 14 out of the 19 total elements, but it's a very important one. So let's say that when you finish this section, you will know 85 percent of what you need to know to start topic mapping.

The `<mergeMap>` element makes two or more topic maps into one topic map. In our topic map future, merging has allowed those Tolkien fans to merge their individual topic maps into a single giant shrine, with base names in English, Elvish, and so on.

Here, working on a smaller scale, we just need two topic maps to merge. Through a sophisticated analytical process we've made up another topic map that has the tomato topic in it—the actual recipe for the *tomate confite farcie aux douze saveurs*. Well . . . one step in the recipe, anyhow. The idea is that a step in a recipe is an association with the following members: an ingredient, an amount (of that ingredient), and a process. So, "take a case of tomatoes and peel them." Here is the topic map.

```
<topicMap>
  <association id="peel_case_tomatoes">
    <instanceOf>
      <topic id="classTopic" xlink:href="#step"/>
    </instanceOf>
    <member>
      <roleSpec>
        <topicRef xlink:href="#anotherIngredientTopic"/>
      </roleSpec>
      <topicRef xlink:href="#anotherTomatoTopic"/>
    </member>
    <member>
      <roleSpec>
        <topicRef xlink:href="#anAmount"/>
      </roleSpec>
      <topicRef xlink:href="#case"/>
    </member>
    <member>
      <roleSpec>
        <topicRef xlink:href="#aProcess"/>
      </roleSpec>
      <topicRef xlink:href="#peel"/>
    </member>
  </association>
  <topic id="anotherTomatoTopic">
    <subjectIdentity>
      <subjectIndicatorRef
          xlink:href="www.fed.goc/usda/doc/tomatogr.htm#gradeA"/>
    </subjectIdentity>
      <baseName>
        <scope>
          <topicRef xlink:href="#IT"/>
        </scope>
        <baseNameString>pomodoro</baseNameString>
      </baseName>
  </topic>
  <topic id="anotherIngredientTopic"/>
    <baseName>
      <baseNameString>an ingredient</baseNameString>
    </baseName>
  </topic>
  <topic id="anAmount"/>
  <topic id="step"/>
  <topic id="case"/>
  <topic id="aProcess"/>
  <topic id="peel"/>
  <topic id="IT">
    <subjectIdentity>
```

```
        <subjectIndicatorRef
        xlink:href="http://www.topicmaps.org/xtm/1.0/language.xtm#"/>
      </subjectIdentity>
    </topic>
</topicMap>
```

Here, for reference, are two topics from our original topic map. Compare them with the topics with IDs *anotherTomatoTopic* and *anotherIngredientTopic* in the topic map immediately above.

```
<topic id="myTomato">
    <subjectIndicatorRef
    xlink:href="www.fed.gov/usda/doc/tomatogr.htm#gradeA"/>
    </subjectIdentity>
<baseName>
    <scope>
      <topicRef xlink:href="#EN"/>
    </scope>
    <baseNameString>tomato</baseNameString>
  </baseName>
  <baseName>
    <scope>
      <topicRef xlink:href="#FR"/>
    </scope>
    <baseNameString>tomate</baseNameString>
  </baseName>
  <baseName>
    <baseNameString>tomato</baseNameString>
  </baseName>
</topic>
<topic id="anIngredient"/>
  <baseName>
    <baseNameString>an ingredient</baseNameString>
  </baseName>
</topic>
```

Watch closely! We now merge our topic maps, and somewhere in the computer the following magic happens.

- All topics with the same name in the same scope are merged (a *name-based merge*).
- All topics with the same subject identity are merged (a *subject-based merge*).

("Two things that are equal to the same thing are equal to each other."[10])

---

[10]Yet another lie. The merging requirements are more sophisticated and rigorous than this. See the XTM 1.0 specification at *http://www.topicmaps.org/xtmtm*.

In our two topic maps, two topics are merged. First, the topic with ID *anIngredient* is merged with the topic with ID *anotherIngredientTopic*. Why? They both have the same base name ("an ingredient") in the same scope (the unconstrained scope). Second, the topic with ID *myTomato* is merged with the topic with ID *anotherTomatoTopic*. Why? They both share a PSI, the USDA definition of a grade A tomato.

Now, what is the benefit of this merge? When two topics are merged into a single topic, that topic has all the topic characteristics of both topics—base names, occurrences, and roles played in associations—with any duplicate characteristics thrown away. The characteristics of our merged tomato topic become those listed below.

Base names:

- tomato in English (menu map)
- tomate in French (menu map)
- tomato in the unconstrained scope (both maps)
- pomodoro in Italian (recipe map)

Occurrences:

- tomato.gif, a resource (menu map)

Roles played in associations:

- ingredient in the *tomate_confite_association* association (menu map)
- ingredient in the *peel_case_tomatoes* association (recipe map)

Thus, by merging the two topic maps, we can get the quantity of tomatoes we need and the recipe we need them for. Using my cell phone in the topic map future, I merge our merged topic map with a third map (the price list for grade A USDA tomatoes available from MTP) and place an order. Shortly, our tomato salesman (Joe) merges the order with his sales projection topic map and smiles—at knowledge interchange in action.

> **PITFALL:** The interaction between the two merging rules explains why it's a bad idea for a topic with the base name potato to be given a subject identity of *tomato* (where other topics with that identity have the base name tomato). If we did this, under a name-based merge, topics named tomato and potato in the English scope would not be treated as one topic, but under a subject-based merge, they would! Thus, for example, all the recipes associated with tomato as an ingredient will also be associated with potato as an ingredient (conflating New York– and New England–style clam chowder, for example, not to mention Italian cuisine and vodka manufacture).

Is this a bug or is it a feature? It's a feature. If you choose to give topics that others think have different subjects the same name, it makes sense to merge them. Why give the same name to two different things? And if others think that topics to which you give different names have the same subjects, it makes sense to merge them. Why give two different names to the same thing?

If, in the merge process, your tomatoes get mixed with your potatoes, there are tricks to detect the situation using the children of <mergeMap>. If you get in trouble like this, you aren't a beginner anymore, so these tricks are out of the scope of this chapter. See the XTM 1.0 specification for more information.

Brandy, Cigars

In this section, you'll learn about the following elements:

```
<parameters>
<resourceData>
<variant>
<variantName>
```

When you finish this section, you will have covered 18 of the 19 topic map elements, so you will know almost everything you need to know to start topic mapping.

Introducing <variant>, <variantName>, and <parameters>

Some of our clients want to be able to display our menus on their Palm Pilots, and Joe at MTP wants to use his cell phone too. So, we pick a very short name suitable for use in wireless activities.

```
<topic id="myTomato">
  <baseName>
    <baseNameString>
      tomato
    </baseNameString>
    <variant>
      <variantName>
        <resourceData>
          TMT
        </resourceData>
      </variantName>
```

```
      <parameters>
        <topicRef xlink:href="#cell_phone"/>
      </parameters>
    </variant>
  </baseName>
</topic>
```

Thus, a cell phone user would see the short `TMT` instead of the longer `tomato`. (Of course we also need to add `<topic id="cell_phone"/>`. A more sophisticated topic map would use PSIs for the Motorola and Nokia product lines and might have variant names appropriate to each line, but since this example is in our topic map future, we don't have values for the `-href-` attributes yet.)

This example shows that a variant is a variant of a base name and that a base name is called *base* because it has variants.

Introducing `<resourceData>`

Finally, sometimes we want to embed a little bit of territory right in the topic map document. For this purpose, we have `<resourceData>`, which can occur in the `<variantName>` and `<occurrence>` elements.

The `<resourceData>` element is just a shortcut for `<resourceRef>`. It would be foolish to have to create a file and a URI for every tiny piece of text in the whole topic map, so with `<resourceData>` we allow text to be entered into the topic map document directly.

Paying the Bill and Putting on Your Coat

The `<topicMap>` element is our nineteenth and final element. We'll wrap up our example by putting our first topic map inside a `<topicMap>` element; see Appendix A in this book. (Note especially the XML plumbing at lines 1 through 4: the `xml` and `DOCTYPE` lines, as well as the namespace declarations that are attributes of the `<topicMap>` element.)

Note also that it is possible to have topic map tags that don't contain anything at all. In fact, `<topicMap>`, `<topic>`, and `<subjectIdentity>` all have this characteristic.

Is this a bug or a feature? It's a feature; the XTM specification is designed for interchange. It is descriptive, not prescriptive. You, as author, may wish to practice better informational hygiene. However, there are scenarios in which an author might wish to create such esoterica as the following:

- A `<topicMap>` with no children
- A `<topic>` element with no subject identity, base name, or occurrences
- A `<subjectIdentity>` element that refers to nothing
- A `<mergeMap>` element with no children

One obvious reason is the authoring process—put in an empty topic, link to it with the ID, and plan to circle back and add the rest later. The more philosophical reason is that sometimes knowledge of the world is partial, and so the interchange syntax requires that as little as possible be known.

Now you have 100 percent of the knowledge required to start topic mapping.

Summary

Here is what you learned in this chapter in a classic bottom-up rather than top-down approach.

- Topic maps consist mainly of topics and associations, as you saw when we created topic maps that associate the tomato topic with recipes and menus.
- A topic map is an overlay on information resources, as you saw when we created an occurrence for the tomato topic.
- A topic is a stand-in, proxy, or surrogate for a subject, as you saw when we discussed PSIs.
- Topics have characteristics (names, occurrences, and roles played in associations), as you saw when we gave our topics base and variant names, created an occurrence, and gave our associated topics role specifications.
- The author controls the meaning of a topic map through topic characteristics and choices of subject, as you saw when we controlled the merging process through our choice of base names and subject identity.
- Scopes in topic maps define the validity of associations and allow fine-tuning of merge operations,[11] as you saw when we scoped the base names of topics for the human languages English, French, and Italian.

Topic maps are about agreement. Even though I say *tomato*, and you say *tomate* or even *pomodoro*, we don't have to call *anything* off. Topic maps allow us to say what we mean and mean what we say.

---

[11]A terminological inexactitude. In truth, scopes define namespaces, and they do so in a more flexible and powerful way than colonized syntax. Synonyms are permitted, for example. The claim has been made that this namespace system can lead the way to the federation of global knowledge.

Since you now know 100 percent of what you need to know to start topic mapping—start topic mapping!

Acknowledgments

I would like the thank the founding coeditors of the XTM specification, Michel Biezunski and Steven R. Newcomb, and the members of the XTM Authoring Group, for the privilege of editing the original drafts of the XTM 1.0 specification and coauthoring the XTM 1.0 DTD. Also, I would like to thank Jean Delahousse of Mondeca for clearing the physical and conceptual space for me to write this chapter. Finally, my thanks to the reviewers for their comments and suggestions.

Resources

To learn more about topic maps, here are three good entry points.

> *http://www.topicmaps.org/*
>
> *http://www.topicmaps.net/*
>
> *http://www.oasis-open.org/cover/topicMaps.html*

And to show that topic maps are actual and not academic or theoretical, here are sites for topic map vendors and service providers, in no particular order.

> *http://www.infoloom.com/*
>
> *http://www.mondeca.com/*
>
> *http://www.ontopia.net/*
>
> *http://www.empolis.com/*
>
> *http://www.cogx.com/*
>
> *http://www.semantext.com/*
>
> *http://globalwisdom.org*
>
> *http://www.etopicality.com*

Other technical pieces related to topic maps are XML and XLink. XML is the W3C specification that says, among other things, that the tags we've discussed in this chapter are made from letters and angle brackets (`<tag>`) as opposed to being made, for example, with curly braces and nonletter characters ({_12^_}). XLink provides the way to perform semantic linking in XML. For more information, see these Web sites.

XML: *http://www.w3.org/XML/#dev*

XLink: *http://www.w3.org/XML/Linking*

For a nontechnical introduction to XML, see the following resources.

http://www.webreview.com/2000/06_23/webauthors/06_23_00_1.shtml
(parts 1 and 2)

http://www.webreview.com/2000/08_04/webauthors/08_04_00_4.shtml
(parts 1 and 2)

The draft ISO Reference Model for topic maps (see Chapter 4) uses a graph for its data model. For perspective on graph theory, see Randall Ripert, "The Mathematical Structure of the World: The World as Graph," available online at *http://neologic.net/ rd/Papers/Structure-J-20-Phil.html.*

Chapter 7

KNOWLEDGE REPRESENTATION, ONTOLOGICAL ENGINEERING, AND TOPIC MAPS

LEO OBRST AND HOWARD LIU

Consider the typical manner in which people currently use Web browsers. They click to link to a document for which they've either searched, using simple keywords, or which is already indexed on the page they are viewing. The document is then displayed before them. They must then read the document and, using their own internalized conceptual model of the world and that document's domain, interpret the meaning of the document. The knowledge in the document is not necessarily available to them: it may require extensive background information, long experience, or many years of formal education for users to understand what the document presents. For example, a retrieved document on the topic of interacting bosons in particle physics has knowledge that the average person cannot extract. The knowledge cannot be captured and transferred because the average person cannot interpret the words semantically, cannot decipher their intended meaning. Why? Because the person does not have a sufficiently rich conceptual model of that domain.

Today's applications (such as keyword-based search engines) require the individual human user to be their semantic interpreter, that is, the user must figure out the knowledge contained in a document without any computer software interpretation of the meaning of that document. This chapter will discuss ways to remedy that situation. By explicitly enabling the representation of semantics in ontologies and using these, tomorrow's applications can assist the user by performing some of the semantic interpretation automatically.

Knowledge as Interpretation

With the rise of the availability of information and its related traffic on the Internet comes a concomitant need to exploit and manage information flow and storage using more intelligent means. Because information actually forms an information continuum that ranges from completely unstructured data[1] to very structured knowledge, a variety of intelligent methods must be employed to filter, fuse, and represent data that ultimately becomes user- and institution-level knowledge.

This section briefly describes the interpretation process by which variously structured data gets transformed into usable knowledge, as well as some acquisition and representation issues concerning knowledge and its manipulation.

Data, Knowledge, and Information

The terms *data*, *knowledge*, and *information* are usually used in ill-defined ways, which is acceptable in colloquial conversations where only a rough, intuitive notion of their distinctive meanings are needed. There is a danger, however, that such usage may result in an obliteration of critical technical distinctions so that these terms in effect become synonyms, possibly with one term standing for all three in a watered-down fashion devoid of content.

In this chapter we do not try to give precise formal definitions to these three terms; instead, we try to informally delineate their meanings. By doing so, we hope to show that what we have called the *information continuum* above is actually better termed the *interpretation continuum*.

In this view, data and knowledge are simply end points on (for our purposes here) a linear continuum, as Figure 7–1 suggests. That which is nearer the left side of the continuum is termed *data*; that which is nearer the right side is termed *knowledge*, though in general the distinction between any two points on the line is more appropriately expressed in terms of their lesser or greater structure. But structure itself, though important, is not the crucial determining or characteristic factor for the continuum: interpretation is. Structure is a side effect of the degree of interpretation required. Knowledge is the relatively complex symbolic modeling (representation) of some aspect of a universe of discourse (that is, that which we can talk about as human

---

[1]Really, this is a misnomer or an actual misunderstanding, as Steven Newcomb points out in Chapter 3: there is no unstructured data. We concur. In the information continuum, which we discuss shortly, unstructured data is simply data that is *semantically interpreted* (solely) by the human being.

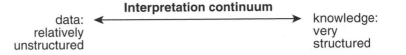

Figure 7–1   The interpretation continuum

beings); data is a relatively simple symbolic modeling. The following "equations" express the relationship between knowledge and data:

Knowledge = Data + Interpretation

Knowledge − Interpretation = Data

Information is used in this chapter in its more technical sense, as Frost derived from Shannon [1948]: information is "a measure of the extent to which a piece of knowledge tells you something which you did not previously know" [Frost 1986, p. 12]. Hence, the information contained in some piece of data depends on what a person already knows and in general will vary from individual to individual. Information represents change in knowledge:

New Knowledge = Old Knowledge + Information

But what now is interpretation and why is it important? Interpretation is the mapping between some structured subset of data and a model of some set of objects in a universe of discourse with respect to the intended meaning of those objects and the relationships among those objects.

Interpretation, therefore, is the mapping between notations (which we call *glyphs*), for example, strings of characters from some alphabet (for text) or some set of defined binary encodings (for graphics, video, and so on), and what those notations are intended to mean in a human-defined universe of discourse. Notations (or glyphs) are meaningless symbols unless they are given an interpretation, that is, mapped to objects in a model. Interpretation is semantics: it is interpreting the syntactic glyphs with respect to their intended semantics.

Typically the model lies in the mind of the human. We as humans "understand," which means we symbolically represent in some fashion the world, the objects of the world, and the relationships among those objects. We have the semantics of some part of the world in our minds: it is very structured and interpreted. When we view a textual document, we see glyphs on a page and interpret them with respect to what they mean in our mental model; that is, we supply the semantics (meaning). If we wish to assist in the dissemination of the knowledge embedded in a document, we make that document available to other human beings, expecting that they will provide the semantic interpreter (their mental models) that will make knowledge out of the notations (glyphs) on the document pages. However, there is no knowledge in that document without interpretation; interpretation makes knowledge out of squiggles on a page.

If we wish to have a computer assist in the dissemination of the knowledge embedded in a document, we need to partially automate the interpretation process, which means we need to construct and represent in a computer-usable way some portion of our mental model. What does that mean? We turn to this question in the next section.

Knowledge Issues: Acquisition, Representation, and Manipulation

Some of the data now being made accessible to individuals via the Internet is structured in relational databases. Most kinds of data exist as textual and graphical documents, video, speech, and other specialized data stores. All of these data sources, however, range from relatively unstructured to moderately structured. Relational databases, which have both an intensional database (the generic information or schema, that is, part of the metadata) and an extensional database (the instances or tuples of the schema), still greatly rely either on application code for the semantic interpretation of their data or, as is the case in general for documents and relatively less structured data, on human beings such as database administrators, users, and so on. The primary purpose of relational databases is for storage and ease of access to data, not complex use; software applications (with the data semantics embedded in nonreusable code via programmers) and human beings must focus on data use, manipulation, and transformation, all of which require a high degree of data interpretation.

To partially automate the interpretation process (that is, to shift some interpretation ability to the computer from the human), in recent years stochastic methods have been employed. These range from the data mining of statistically relevant patterns in relational databases to the use of statistical techniques in natural language processing, image processing, and so on. What most of these shallower (that is, interpretation-nonintensive) methods have in common is the attempt to discover statistically significant correlations of data, words, and relatively unstructured units and by those correlations to infer semantic significance. It is assumed that colocation or cooccurrence within some defined context signifies a semantic relation. What that semantic relation is, of course, must be conceived (interpreted) by a human being who inspects the statistically significant patterns. These methods, however, remove at least a portion of the noise from relatively unstructured data (thus performing a filtering function) and display before the interpreting human a subset of what can become knowledge once the human interprets it. Such methods attempt to bypass the knowledge bottleneck encountered by a previous generation of technologies epitomized by expert systems: capturing complex knowledge requires much work in elicitation from domain experts.

Prior to its redefinition by business, knowledge management was about managing structured knowledge in knowledge bases. This use is called *deep knowledge management* in today's lingo. Knowledge management today means approximately: "Enabling the employees of a corporation easy access, usually via a Web browser, to the knowledge represented as documents and data of the corporation." Deep knowledge management, it was thought by mainstream industry, requires time-consuming, responsible, and consistent knowledge acquisition; consistent (or at least partition-bound inconsistent), semantically correct, and expressive knowledge representation; tractable, semantically licensed, sound, but nonmonotonic reasoning; and ongoing knowledge maintenance. Such an effort was in general deemed too resource-intensive by industry. Coupled with extravagant claims made by a small set of researchers, and thus generative of unrealizably high expectations, this perception quashed or at least curtailed efforts toward deep representation. The need for such deep representation, however, continues and in fact has increased: to maximize the knowledge we can use, we must shift more of the burden of interpretation onto our computers. One way to do so is to annotate our data and documents with human-meaningful knowledge constructs, as the emerging topic map effort intends.

Figure 7–2 displays the interpretation continuum mentioned earlier, now annotated with additional information on methods and technologies (along the bottom) and types of knowledge (along the top) as the continuum progresses from data to knowledge.

If everyone agrees that shallow and deep methods and representations should be employed, that increased knowledge utility (hence increased computer-assisted interpretation) is desirable, then the question becomes: How might shallow and deep methods and representations be combined? Related questions then follow: Are there promising technologies that might help combine shallow and deep methods and representations? Are there technologies that can pave the way toward deep methods and representations? We believe that topic maps correlate well with ontological engineering.[2] In the next section, we look at the core knowledge technologies that have evolved into ontological engineering.

---

[2]Ontological engineering, as we shall describe shortly, is a relatively new discipline that seeks to apply the principles, methodologies, and rules of formal ontology to the design and implementation of knowledge-based information systems.

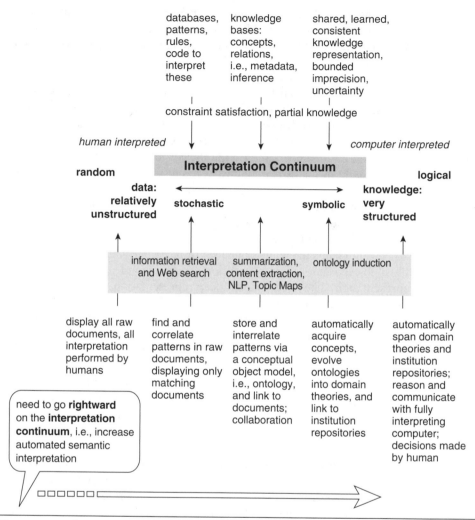

Figure 7–2   The annotated interpretation continuum

The Roots of Ontological Engineering: Knowledge Technologies

Root: Knowledge Representation

Knowledge representation technology addresses the structure and meaning of knowledge, answering the following questions.

- How is metadata, domain knowledge, or any other kind of knowledge to be represented? [Davis and Shrobe 1993]
- What mechanisms can be used to facilitate the acquisition, encoding, and storage of knowledge to allow both general access and rich expressivity? [Glaser 1996; Speel 1996a]
- What inference or other reasoning methods can be efficiently performed on that represented knowledge? How are they in turn represented to guarantee correctness and completeness? [Brewka 1996]
- Should general ontologies (vocabulary of the concepts, relations, and attributes, along with constraints on their meaning) and domain knowledge be represented logically, either in a first-order predicate logic, a modal logic, or a higher-order logic, that is, in either case as an axiomatic system in which knowledge represents theories? [Frost 1986]
- Should knowledge be represented as frames in a frame-based model (which can have a logical interpretation), that is, in terms of slots, facets, and methods defined over these? [Borgida and Patel-Schneider 1994; MacGregor 1991; Brachman and Schmolze 1985]
- Should probabilities be used in the representation, as in Bayesian networks? [Brewka 1996]
- What are the number, kinds, and levels of models needed to represent knowledge so that at the highest level users can interact with conceptually meaningful knowledge objects, yet at the lowest level, primitive data (such as structured or unstructured text, numbers, Booleans, graphic data, voice, video, and so on) is correctly and efficiently represented so that it can be accessed by and mapped to higher levels? [Lambrix and Padgham 1996]
- What are the special relations required to represent complex objects that have parts? [Artale et al. 1996; Borgo et al. 1996, 1997; Casati and Varzi 1999; Simons 1987]

Table 7–1 displays a refinement by Guarino [1994] of Brachman's [1979] original classification of the various primitives used by knowledge representation formalisms. The bottom five levels constitute "knowledge"; the topmost, the implementation of those knowledge levels for a given knowledge system. In this scheme, knowledge

Table 7–1 Classification of Knowledge Representation Levels

Level	Primitives	Primitive Concepts . . .	Main Feature	Interpretation
Implementational	Memory cells, pointers	Are implementation dependent	Formalization	Arbitrary
Logical	Propositions, predicates, functions, logical operators	Are predicates	Formalization	Arbitrary
Epistemological	Concept types, structuring relations	Are structuring primitives	Structure	Arbitrary
Ontological	Concept types, relations	Satisfy meaning postulates	Meaning	Constrained
Conceptual	Conceptual relations, primitive objects and actions	Are cognitive primitives	Conceptualization	Subjective
Linguistic	Linguistic terms	Are linguistic primitives	Language	Subjective

Source: *Reprinted with permission from Guarino [1994].*

spans from formalization (the logical constructs used) to natural language (how humans express the knowledge they possess, in speech and text; Lang 1991). Any knowledge management system in which computer software semantically interprets data (for example, in databases, on Web pages, in textual documents) to assist a human must similarly employ these levels of representation.

General issues in knowledge representation include the following: (1) expressivity versus performance tradeoffs, (2) the use of symbolic versus probabilistic or hybrid approaches, (3) the use of deductive versus inductive inference, and (4) approaches to knowledge composition (also called *knowledge fusion*; see Wiederhold [1994] and Gray et al. [1997])—how to combine syntactically and semantically heterogeneous knowledge fragments, the use of formal ontology and ontological engineering and their methodologies, efficient representation of subsumptive taxonomies and operations.[3] Other important issues include knowledge acquisition; extraction; discovery (how to capture knowledge from human experts, software, databases, and documents); the knowledge requirements of, and languages and implementations for, agents; the efficient representation and use of task knowledge and problem-solving methods; efficient operations in deductive databases; the uses of particular logics; and constraint programming systems.

A few commercial off-the-shelf products for knowledge representation of some complexity exist (excluding programming language systems). These include Cyc by Cycorps [Guha and Lenat 1990; Lenat and Guha 1990]; research tools such as PARKA by the University of Maryland [Andersen et al. 1995], Ontolingua/Chimaera by the Stanford University Knowledge Systems Laboratory [McGuinness et al. 2000], and Protégé-2000 by the Stanford University Medical Informatics Laboratory [Noy et al. 2000a)]; and description logic systems such as LOOM and PowerLOOM by the Information Systems Institute/University of Southern California (ISI/USC) [MacGregor 1991, 1994], and CLASSIC by AT&T/Lucent [Borgida and Patel-Schneider 1994]. In addition, logic and constraint programming systems enable users to represent knowledge deeply and reason about it. Some representative companies with logic and constraint programming systems include ILOG, Quintus, Sixtus, and Computational Logic, Inc. In addition, there are some knowledge-based tools commercially available that are mostly based on older technology such as expert systems. These are discussed in the next session on knowledge engineering.

The key issues faced by designers of knowledge representation technology include the following:

- Defining semantically rich and sufficiently correct models of knowledge domains to ensure meaningful and reasonable use of that knowledge by users at the levels they require
- Representing and encoding knowledge in information and knowledge management systems and knowledge bases efficiently and correctly
- Defining access and inference/reasoning methods to best use the knowledge

---

[3]A taxonomy based on subsumption is one in which classes or concepts are linked in a special class–subclass relation [Borgida and Patel-Schneider 1994]. This special relation is called the *is-a relation* in artificial intelligence, as in, for example, "a dog *is a* mammal, which in turn *is an* animate object". In taxonomies that are closed under the subsumption relation, efficient class-level reasoning is possible [Fall 1995a, 1995b, 1996]. In object-oriented programming terminology, a class subsumed by a parent class inherits the behavior and property of that parent class [Kim and Lochovsky 1989; Wand 1989; Rumbaugh et al. 1991; Graham 1994]. See also the literature on object-oriented databases [as in Zdonik and Maier 1990].

- Defining knowledge extraction, acquisition, and discovery methodologies to facilitate the capture of knowledge
- Defining mechanisms by which knowledge from disparate sources can be combined

Root: Knowledge Engineering

Knowledge engineering[4] and its new more formal variant, ontological engineering, is concerned with the creation and maintenance of knowledge bases. Knowledge bases are implementations of knowledge representation modeling schemes and their reasoning methods. As such, they can be considered applications of knowledge representation technology. This knowledge technology attempts to answer questions such as those listed below.

- What are efficient mechanisms for storing and accessing knowledge, ontologies, and metadata? [Bresciani et al. 1995]
- What inference and reasoning methods can be employed? How are these efficiently executed? [Speel 1996a, 1996b; Speel et al. 1995]
- How can differently structured, distributed, and dynamic knowledge bases interact with each other in sound ways, that is, by way of translation into a neutral knowledge representation or via mapping rules that link the different knowledge bases syntactically and semantically?
- What methodologies and mechanisms can be used to capture knowledge?

The issues that are important to this technology generally reflect the knowledge representation issues discussed in the previous section, with the emphasis on correct and efficient implementation. Crucial here are expressivity versus performance tradeoffs [Baader and Hollunder 1991], the kinds of inference and classification operations supported, the design and implementation of very large knowledge bases (greater than one million assertions) [Andersen et al. 1995], and knowledge capture and maintenance.

Many systems are called knowledge bases. Most are of proprietary, legacy, or specialized domain format (for example, CAD-CAM knowledge bases) or are based on older expert system technology (production rules using the Rete [Forgy 1982] or TREAT [Mirankar 1987, 1990] algorithms), among which are Brightware's (formerly Inference) ART-Enterprise, Gensym's G2, Teknowledge's M.4, IntelliCorp's KEE, and NASA's CLIPS. (See the "AI on the Web" site at *http://www.cs.berkeley.edu/~russell/ai.html* for more information.)

---

[4]In more specialized usage during the expert system era of the past, the term *knowledge engineering* focused on the solicitation of knowledge from domain experts by knowledge engineers. We are employing the more modern and general use of the term, which signifies the engineering discipline that applies the principles of knowledge representation and is concerned with the implementation of knowledge systems.

A common criticism of expert system technology, however, is that this approach to knowledge representation and reasoning is extremely brittle and very low level. A representation based only on one-level condition–action rules executing globally is inadequate with respect to granularity of meaning, the understanding it can provide to many different levels of users, and the ability to debug its reasoning chains.

The key issues faced in the realm of knowledge engineering include the following:

- Implementing and executing semantically rich and sufficiently correct models of knowledge domains to ensure meaningful and reasonable use of that knowledge by users at the levels they require
- Acquiring knowledge for knowledge bases, including processes by which knowledge can be automatically discovered and extracted from documents, document summaries, databases, Web sites, and other data sources
- Implementing and executing access and inference/reasoning methods to best use the knowledge and to provide users with the levels of detail and correctness they desire
- Implementing and executing mechanisms by which knowledge from disparate, distributed, and dynamic information sources can be combined

Setting off the real advances of the past 15 years in knowledge representation and knowledge engineering technology, which led to ontological engineering, entails first a short discussion of the deficiencies of the last (popularly conceived) high-water mark in knowledge representation research and development, the expert system era of the early to mid-1980s.

Slightly Shriveled Root: Expert Systems (and Their Deficiencies)

At their crest of popularity in the early 1980s, expert systems were widely perceived— including by some artificial intelligence (AI) practitioners who should have known better—as being what today would be called a "killer app," that is, an application so revolutionary it would sell AI as a primary technology whose day had come. What followed such hyperbole instead was "AI winter," a reaction against both the extravagant claims of some researchers and the equally extravagant premature embracing, by some managers, of an unproved technology. In effect, popular opinion underwent a sea change, from "these technologies are great and should be used everywhere" to "these technologies are terrible and should be used nowhere." AI researchers in general, of course, knew the strengths and weaknesses of these technologies and, for the most part, continued their research agendas as much as possible in such a funding-impoverished environment. Knowledge representation and knowledge engineering researchers in particular continued advancing the boundaries of sound and useful theory, formalisms, methods, and technologies.

In this section, we describe some of the benefits and deficiencies of expert systems, against which to better pose the subsequent 15 years of additional research into knowledge representation and knowledge engineering and the advantages of that research.

Expert systems were touted to be solid applications of symbolic AI based on the capture of domain knowledge from human domain experts, hence able to solve complex reasoning problems within those domains much as human experts would. Although expert systems ranged widely in representation and the types of reasoning and problem-solving methods employed, there are a few generalizations that are relatively accurate across that range. In general, for example, expert systems were production systems, that is, rule-based systems that supported backward and forward chaining with respect to reasoning. The rules of these systems were generally of the format <IF condition-set, THEN action-set>, that is, if the conditions in the antecedent currently held (or were true; this is the forward-chaining method) in the environment, then the actions of the consequent were executed, thereby changing the state of the environment and possibly enabling conditions on other rules in the entire domain rule set to become true, thus causing them to fire. Other common synonyms for *rule* were *demon* and *trigger*, the latter still being employed in database terminology, and another term of recent years (which partially overlaps the notion of agent, too), *sentinel.*

After an earlier phase of ad hoc experimentation in the late 1970s that included the development of some famous expert systems [Buchanan et al. 1977], for example, MYCIN and its expert system shell EMYCIN [Buchanan and Shortliffe 1985], later production systems were generally based on variations of the Rete algorithm [Forgy 1982]. Many commercial tools today (mentioned earlier) trace their ancestry to these early expert system shells, that is, general-purpose rule systems such as OPS5 [Forgy 1981; Cooper and Wolgrin 1988]. As mentioned previously, these rules could generally be executed in either of two modes, in forward- or backward-chaining fashion. Forward chaining (sometimes called *top-down, left-to-right inference*) was the prototypical expert system reasoning method; as described in the previous paragraph, it amounted to condition-testing of rules followed by action executions in a rule-forward fashion. This inference method was generally employed to transform or update a global state, based on some triggering new input in the environment. Backward chaining (or *bottom-up, right-to-left inference, goal-directed reasoning*) went the reverse direction; that is, if a rule's consequent goal states were to be considered true, then its conditions in the antecedent would generate new goals, with the new goals matching the consequents of other rules. The process continues until one of the goal states matches an initial state. This inference method was likely employed for queries on knowledge bases or to determine whether a theorem (the rule) was true with respect to the existing assertions and rules of the system.[5]

---

[5]Since this was prior to the formalization of knowledge representation, however, the use of terminology such as *assertion* and *theorem* was not predominant; instead, everything was just a *rule*.

Expert systems can be considered an advance over purely procedural code insofar as the rules for expert systems were more declarative in nature (stating "what," not "how," much as natural language, mathematics, and logic do) and thus more like so-called fourth-generation or higher-level programming languages, that is, specialized languages that had constructs closer to the level at which end users conceived the world. In addition, the reasoning methods in expert systems were not as arbitrary as those that could be implemented in third-generation procedural code, though often the reasoning methods actually used were not sound because, for example, they did permit arbitrary side effects on local and global states.

The primary deficiencies of expert systems thus were partially (and ironically) derived from their advantages and from the nature of the acquisition process used to obtain knowledge from domain experts for rules. The knowledge acquisition process is sometimes termed *the knowledge bottleneck* because it is so often a resource-intensive process on which all knowledge-based systems depend. This was particularly egregious in the expert system era because knowledge acquisition was generally the result of a distillation by specially trained knowledge engineers of knowledge gleaned via rigorous (and not so rigorous) protocols from human domain experts. The uncontested assumption was always that human experts indeed consciously knew what and how they did tasks, solved problems, and reasoned in their specific domains, an assumption that subsequently has been determined to be invalid.

The flip side of the so-called knowledge bottleneck argument against knowledge-based systems, and one not generally recognized sufficiently by detractors, is the *knowledge fragmentation, duplication, misconstrual, unmaintainability, and nonreusability programming morass* of ordinary procedural programming. In this scenario, every programmer is his or her own domain expert, and the encoded knowledge is in large part incorrect, insufficient, nonreusable, or unmaintainable except by methods equally as arduous as those employed by the programmer in the program's first encoding. The problem is compounded when such inaccessible knowledge is functionally duplicated across the world inconceivable numbers of times.

Expert systems ultimately failed as a panacea not only because there are no methods that are always and everywhere appropriate but also for a number of other reasons.

1. Expert systems, with few exceptions, were flat, that is, all knowledge was represented at the same global level: there were no major partitions or types of knowledge, either horizontally or vertically, and a change of knowledge state was always a global change.
2. Expert systems were brittle, that is, a slight modification in one or a few rules might have disproportionate ramifications across the entire system, invalidating or incorrectly validating knowledge apparently unrelated to the change.
3. The representation was inexpressive, that is, one could not express certain types of knowledge easily or at all.

4. The reasoning methods were not sound, consistent, or complete, or, much worse, their properties were not formally identifiable.

5. An expert system execution was nearly impossible to debug because of reasons 1 through 4 and because of the complexity and nondeterminism inherent in the structure of the expert system. Hence system execution was unpredictable. For example, with randomizing agendas (which just means that rules get ordered differently at different times for execution), the results of a system execution could be different each time, although the initial environment was the same.

However, much of the research performed for expert systems and especially production rule systems nowadays finds application in the technical area of active database systems, in which event–condition–action rules (sometimes called *triggers*) fire as a result of updating data and enforce a more coherent global semantics on the database. Prior to the emergence of active databases [Paton and Diaz 1999], a large portion of the semantics of databases was enforced in procedural code surrounding the database, which gives rise to underdetermined semantics (in addition to *representational imped-ance*, that is, the need to translate back and forth from one data representation to another, a source of inefficiency).

The deficiencies in expert systems prompted additional threads of research in AI into knowledge representation and reasoning. We briefly survey these threads from the last 15 years in the next section, culminating in ontological engineering.

New Knowledge Technology Branches: Toward Ontological Engineering

Branch: The Formalization of Semantic Networks and the Rise of Description Logics

The primary advances in knowledge representation technology over the last 15 years can be attributed to the increasing role of formal logic in representation and reasoning formalisms and to the development of theories based on logical and mathematical principles. During the heyday of expert systems, AI research and development were primarily focused on systems-based AI principles and algorithms, which tended to be either ad hoc and unsystematic or else founded on the informal notions of semantic networks; logic was relegated to a subsidiary role. Knowledge bases were conceived originally as semantic networks [Quillian 1969; Fahlman 1977, 1979] and only more recently began to be formalized [Brachman 1979]. The first logical formalization of a frame-based semantic network resulted in the seminal knowledge representation language KL-ONE [Brachman and Schmolze 1985], based on previous languages such as Krypton [Brachman and Levesque 1982; Brachman et al. 1983]. The success of KL-ONE inspired an entire subdiscipline in logical frame-based languages in AI called *terminological* or *description logics*, which thread continues to this day. KL-ONE and other description logics typically distinguish between an A-Box (for assertions) and a T-Box (for terminology). The T-Box is similar to an object-oriented subclass-based or AI isa-based subsumption hierarchy and serves the function of a schema (the intensional database) in relational database theory.[6] It represents the generic constructs of the knowledge representation system (entities, functions, relations, predicates, propositions, properties, attributes, values, rules, and constraints), sometimes called the *axioms* or the *ontology* of the knowledge base.[7] The A-Box is similar to instances in the object-oriented paradigm and related to tuples (the extensional database) in relational database theory. It represents the set of facts or instance-level assertions, which are built on the T-Box skeleton. Description logics attempted not only to formalize the notion of semantic networks but also to work out in some detail the nature of tractable automated reasoning.

In recent years, research in description logics has produced many formal results [Cadoli and Eiter 1998] and led to the construction of many automated systems, including LOOM [MacGregor 1991], CLASSIC [Borgida and Patel-Schneider 1994], and BACK [Hoppe et al. 1993].

Related to the research in semantic networks and description logics is the thread represented by truth maintenance systems, assumption- and justification-based systems, and evidential reasoning [Doyle 1979; de Kleer 1986; Forbus and de Kleer 1993; Kohlas 1994].

Branch: Constraint and Logic Programming

Although the field of logic programming was well established in the late 1960s, having enjoyed substantial interest dating from the discovery of the resolution principle [Robinson 1965] (which enabled much more efficient inference), the field was semi-independent from mainstream AI research and more closely aligned with the theorem-proving community. It was only after the introduction of Prolog in the late 1970s and

---

[6]For the relationship between databases and knowledge bases, see Ullman [1988, 1989]; Biller and Neuhold [1989]; Mylopoulos and Brodie [1989]; Reiter [1989]; and Gardarin and Valduriez [1989]. For an attempt at a unification of knowledge bases and database design, see Debenham [1998].

[7]Care must be taken, however, to distinguish the notion of ontology from the T-Box, insofar as, in some usage, an ontology may have both class-level and instance-level assertions. The notion of ontology is related to formal language theory; we'll say more about that later. By way of similarity, however, both an ontology and a T-Box represent primarily static or long-term knowledge, whereas an A-Box represents current, more dynamic knowledge.

early 1980s [Kowalski 1974, 1979a, 1979b; Warren 1977, 1979; Colmerauer et al. 1973; Clocksin and Mellish 1981; Lloyd 1984] that logic programming became much more solidly part of AI. With continuing work in improving the efficiencies of Prolog, including theoretical results on designing abstract machine models with potentially quick runtime implementations such as the Warren Abstract Machine (WAM) [Warren 1983; Aït-Kaci 1991] and abstract byte compilation, Prolog was embraced by much of the knowledge representation community. Further refinements during the late 1980s and early 1990s in global analyzing logic compilers and interpreters such as Berkeley's Mercury Prolog [Van Roy 1990, 1993a; Van Roy and Despain 1992] enabled Prolog implementations to achieve the efficiencies of standard C code [Van Roy 1993b].[8] In many cases, speedups were achieved by implementing the WAM in C. The result was that WAM-based logic programs underwent a two-step compilation process: first compilation into the WAM instruction set, usually implemented as C macros, then compilation of the resulting C code into machine object code, with C thus acting as a high-level assembly language.

Great headway was also made in algorithm development and research into the primary logic programming operation of unification [Knight 1989; Martelli and Montaneri 1982] and order-sorted unification [Aït-Kaci and Podelski 1991; Aït-Kaci et al. 1993], along with research into and implementations of constraint logic systems such as CHIP [Dincbas et al. 1988; Frühwirth et al. 1993] and ECLiPSe [Meier 1995; Wallace et al. 1997], parallel logic programming such as PARLOG [Clark and Gregory 1986], and parallel (concurrent) constraint logic programming [Saraswat 1989; Mudambi and Schimpf 1994; Herold 1995]. Also of note is the rise of synthesis or multiparadigm logic programming languages such as LIFE [Aït-Kaci and Podelski 1993], which synthesizes logic, functional, and object-oriented paradigms, and Oz [Smolka 1995; Haridi et al. 1997], which synthesizes logic, functional, constraint, and object-oriented paradigms and is a concurrent, distributed processing language. These later designs and implementations of logic and constraint programming languages incorporate research on continuations, coroutining, abstract machine models, feature logics, deep guards, preemptive and mobile threading, concurrency, and constructs from linear logic [Tarau et al. 1996; Tarau 1998].

A related technical thread is the field of deductive databases, which seeks to wed database technology with logic programming to provide the generality and efficiency of access of relational databases with the inference methods of logic programming [Das 1992; Minker 1988; Naqvi and Tsur 1989; Liu 1999].

---

[8]Van Roy [1993b] has stated, in fact, that Prolog implementations should be *faster* than C implementations, given the recent advances in Prolog compiler technology.

In recent years, the emergence of the Internet has generated a fusion between Web-based technologies and logic and constraint programming, including distributed inference engines and logic libraries [Tarau 1999; Cabeza and Hermenegildo 1996; Cabeza et al. 1996].

Ontological Engineering

One of the major challenges for modern Web technology, information retrieval, and high-performance knowledge bases is the realization of the premise of knowledge technologies: it takes a huge amount of foundational and domain knowledge to have content-based, highly precise, and human-meaningful data, documents, and robust problem solving. Human-meaningful categorization and annotation of Web pages ensures very precise retrieval of relevant items: documents, graphics, voice/music recordings, and video images. Topic maps address the issue of adding real content to the multimedia documents involved in Web technology and information—as does ontological engineering. In particular, in the realm of knowledge technologies, ontological engineering addresses these same issues, enabling the creation of human-meaningful, computer-interpretable, knowledge-based annotations to information products—while attempting, in addition, to enable robust problem solving in software systems.

The ontological engineering challenge can be viewed as having two requirements: the need to encode declarative domain knowledge and the need to encode problem-solving methods. Much research has focused on the latter, and powerful techniques have been developed for building complex problem-solving strategies from basic building blocks, for example, research on generic tasks [Chandrasekaran 1986; Chandrasekaran et al. 1998], function and behavior [Sasajima et al. 1995; Kitamura et al. 1997, 1998], components of expertise [Steels 1990], and problem-solving knowledge combined with domain knowledge within the ESPRIT CommonKADS project [Schreiber et al. 1993; Wielinga and Schreiber 1993; Wielinga et al. 1992; see also Speel 1996a, 1996b, and Benjamins 1993].

Encoding declarative (that is, nonprocedural, human-confirmable) domain knowledge in a modular, reusable fashion has also been addressed. In addition to the Cyc effort—perhaps the first attempt to codify ontological information or "commonsense knowledge," as two authors [Lenat and Guha 1990; Guha and Lenat 1990] characterized it—many other research efforts focused on developing foundational theories: for time [Hayes 1996; Kitamura et al. 1997; see also Hajnicz 1996 on time structures and their application]; space [Casati and Varzi 1999] and vague spatial concepts [Cohn and Gotts 1994; Varzi 2001]; events [Varzi and Pianesi 1996a, 1996b]; liquids [Hayes 1990]; physical objects [Borgo et al. 1996, 1997]; boundaries [Smith and Varzi 1997; Casati and Varzi 1995]; a general mereotopology for parts and wholes [Simons 1987;

Artale et al. 1996; Casati and Varzi 1995, 1999; Varzi 1998]; properties [Guarino and Welty 2000c]; and metaproperties of the privileged taxonomic/subclass relation [Guarino and Welty 2000a, 2000b].

Methods for encoding these ontologies in an operational and reusable fashion are relatively recent. These methods include contexts/microtheories [Guha 1991; Blair et al. 1992; McCarthy 1993; Buvac et al. 1995; McCarthy and Buvac 1997; Giunchiglia and Bouquet 1997, 1998; Giunchiglia and Ghidini 1998], compositional modeling [Falkenhainer and Forbus 1991], and reusable knowledge components [Clark and Porter 1997].[9] Related to these methods for reusing ontologies is technology for ontology and knowledge composition and merging [Wiederhold 1994; Maluf and Wiederhold 1997; Wiederhold and Jannink 1998; Mitra et al. 2000; McGuinness et al. 2000; Chalupsky 2000; Preece 1999; Noy and Musen 2000]. These methods typically encapsulate a theory as an independent data structure, define an interface for that theory, and then combine theories by defining mappings (sometimes called *lifting axioms, compositions, articulations,* or *image functors* [Liu et al. 2001]) between their interfaces. This entire knowledge discipline is called *ontological engineering.* In Figure 7–3, we display ontological engineering in its context.

Recent research on knowledge languages—for example, Knowledge Interchange Format (KIF), Ontolingua [Gruber 1993], Open Knowledge Base Connectivity (OKBC) language [Chaudhri et al. 1998], XML Ontology Exchange Language (XOL) [Karp et al. 1999], and Ontology Inference Layer (OIL) [Horrocks et al, 2000]—and techniques for knowledge sharing—for example, DARPA's Knowledge Sharing Effort [Neches et al. 1991], High Performance Knowledge Bases (HPKB) Project [Cohen et al. 1998; Pease et al. 2000], Rapid Knowledge Formation (RKF), the DARPA Agent Markup Language (DAML) [Bechhofer et al. 2000], and OIL [Horrocks et al. 2000]—offer a vehicle for enabling component-based knowledge to be represented and exchanged in a neutral form. In fact, the latter research efforts, for DAML and OIL (recently combined to DAML+OIL [Connolly et al. 2001]), are interesting in that they are parallel to the topic map effort in their concern for developing a Web-based XML language for expressing and interrelating ontologies:

> The Ontology Inference Layer (OIL) is a proposal for a Web-based representation and inference layer for ontologies, which combines the widely used modeling primitives from frame-based languages with the formal semantics and reasoning services provided by description logics. It is compatible with RDF Schema (RDFS), and includes a precise

---

[9]But see Lenat [1998] for a notion of context distinguished from microtheory. For additional discussion on the formalization of context, see Bouquet et al. [1999]; Brézillon et al. [1999]; Giunchiglia and Ghidini [1998]; and Obrst et al. [1999a, 1999b].

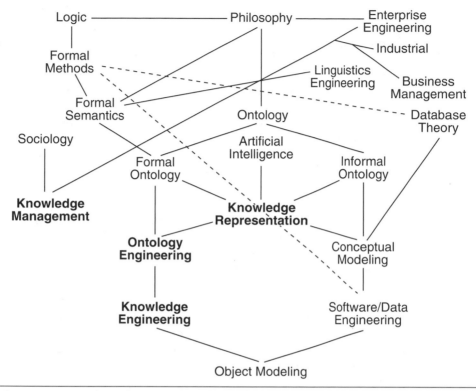

Figure 7–3   Ontological engineering and related disciplines

semantics for describing term meanings (and thus also for describing implied information).[10]

Ontological engineering's representations of foundational knowledge and problem-solving methods also provide a basis for constructing domain-specific knowledge acquisition tools, the basic representational components acting as templates for guiding the entry of domain-specific knowledge. Thus, knowledge engineers don't have to encode knowledge from scratch. This technique of generating and using domain-specific knowledge acquisition tools has been shown to be highly effective, for example in Protégé-2000 [Noy et al. 2000a], in the HPKB effort [Cohen et al. 1998; Pease et al. 2000], and in the current DARPA-sponsored RKF program.

---

[10]Source: *http://www.ontoknowledge.org/oil.*

In the technical view of ontological engineering, an ontology is the vocabulary for expressing the entities and relationships of a conceptual model for a general or particular domain, along with semantic constraints on that model which limit what that model means. Both the vocabulary and the semantic constraints are necessary in order to correlate that information model with the real-world domain it represents. To give substance to the notion of ontology, which has a well-defined and extensive technical tradition and a more recent computational research line that incorporates the results and methods of that tradition, we refer interested readers to Farquhar and Gruninger [1997]; Guarino [1998]; Uschold and Gruninger [1996]; Guarino and Giaretta [1995]; and Gruber [1993, 1995a]. More formally, we also recommend Burkhardt and Smith [1991]; Wiggins [1980]; Varzi [1998]; Cocchiarella [1991, 1995]; and Meixner [1997].

An ontology is thus both the vocabulary used to describe and represent an area of knowledge and the meaning of that vocabulary, that is, it is syntactically a language of types and terms that has a corresponding formal semantics which is the intended meaning of the constructs of the language and their composition. According to this notion, an ontology encompasses metadata and domain theories. Metadata is exactly that data which describes the semantics of the underlying simple (object-level) data. A domain theory is just a specialized ontology, that is, a vocabulary identifying the semantic entities, relationships, and attributes of the domain model, as well as the constraints on that domain. Hence, an ontology acts as the skeleton of a knowledge base and is comparable to the notion of schema in terminology.

Ontological engineering is the latest subdiscipline of knowledge representation in AI. It arose partially as a reaction against many of the recognized deficiencies in mainstream knowledge-based technologies, especially expert systems. These older AI technologies, though declarative in nature (that is, representing "what," not "how," as opposed to procedural representation, which algorithmically represents "how," not "what"), relied too heavily on all knowledge being represented at the same level, with one end result being that knowledge from one application could not be reused easily by another application. Knowledge was not as modular as it could be. Ontological engineering, borrowing from formal ontology and logic in philosophy and formal semantics in linguistics, addresses the problem of encoding declarative knowledge in a modular, reusable fashion by creating both foundational knowledge theories (general theories about entities, processes, time, agents, organizations, commercial products and services, and so on) and domain theories (theories about specific domains such as medicine, machine tooling, entertainment, electronic components, geopolitical crisis management, and so on). Ontological engineering usually characterizes an ontology (much like a logical theory) in terms of an axiomatic system, that is, a set of axioms and inference rules that together characterize a set of theorems (and their corresponding formal models), all of which constitute a theory.

Ontological engineering thus addresses the major challenge for computer-usable conceptual models and high-performance knowledge bases: encoding the massive amount of foundational and domain knowledge required specifically for robust problem solving.

The past 15 years of knowledge representation and engineering research threads and their convergence are displayed schematically in Figure 7–4. For a good recent overview of the state of the art in building ontologies, see Noy and Hafner [1997]. See also Guarino [1998] for papers on formal ontology as applied to information systems, ontological engineering, and some current problems in ontology representation. Ontological engineering is being applied to problems in areas such as knowledge management, information brokering, and e-commerce [Roddy et al. 2000; Obrst et al. 2001], and ontologies are explicitly considered a resource in intelligent agent technology (for more information, see the Federation for Intelligent Physical Agents site at *http://www.fipa.org/*).

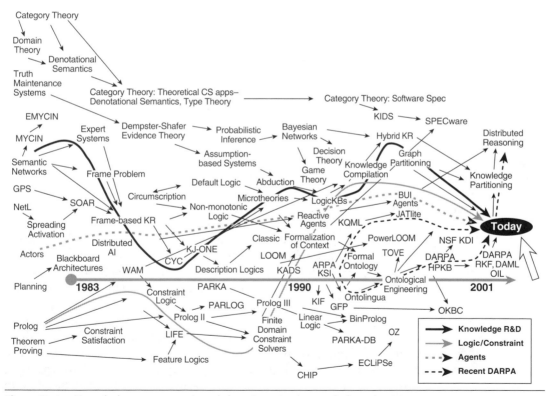

Figure 7–4   Knowledge representation and engineering research threads

Finally, with the emergence of the Internet and the rise of XML as a standard language focused on providing database-like structure to Web documents, ontological engineering has kept pace. In fact, most applications of ontological engineering now are Web-related, from information integration to semantic search and retrieval to electronic commerce. Because XML alone does not provide sufficient semantics for marked-up or annotated documents [Cover 1998], many semantic and ontological extensions to XML have been proposed. Among the extensions proposed are XOL [Karp et al. 1999]; Ontology Modeling Language/Conceptual Knowledge Markup Language (OML/CKML) [Kent 1999; Cover 2000], which has recently evolved into the IEEE Standard Upper Ontology candidate Information Flow Framework (IFF); Simple HTML Ontology Extension (SHOE) [Heflin et al. 1999]; and, as we have seen, very recent efforts such as DAML and OIL. In addition, Web-based systems such as Ontobroker [Fensel et al. 1998] and On2broker [Fensel et al. 1999]—antecedents of OIL that used the Web standard RDF and f-logic (a frame-based logic)—as well as OntoSeek [Guarino et al. 1999] have attempted to build ontological methods into Internet standards and usage. Many of these languages and systems constitute the contemporary effort known as the Semantic Web.

Ontologies and Topic Maps

Aside from their role as indexes to information resources, topic maps embody knowledge. It is a great advantage for a designer of topic maps to capitalize on this aspect. A semantically rich and correct knowledge representation enhances the value of a topic map. Because an ontology is a knowledge representation, we assert that it plays an important role in topic map design.

Ontologies

An ontology is a specification or "formalization of a conceptualization" [Gruber 1993, p. 199]. Alternatively, an ontology is a "logical theory which gives an explicit, partial account of a *conceptualization*, designed in order to be shared by more agents for various purposes" [Guarino and Giaretta 1995]. A conceptualization is a set of concepts and their relations to each other. For example, an ontology of PC repair may include such concepts as Hard Drive, Floppy Drive, Motherboard, CPU, and Fan. Such an ontology may also contain assertions, for example, a Technician Repairs a PC (where the capitalized words signify individual concepts). Thus, the concepts Technician, Repairs, and PC need to be contained in the ontology as well. In a corresponding topic map, all these concepts would translate easily into topics, and in addition Repairs would induce an association between the topics Technician and PC.

An ontology differs from other data models in that it is as concerned with the *relationships* among entities as with the entities themselves, and in the fact that the semantics of these relationships are applied uniformly. In a typical data structure, the relationships among data are ad hoc, and *all interpretation* is necessarily performed by a program accessing the data. In a typical database, the relationships among the data are partially represented by the data schema; nevertheless, *nearly all interpretation* is performed by a program accessing the data. A human, or another program, lacking knowledge of the specific semantics of a particular data structure or database is clueless as to what it means. In an ontology, relationships are defined more or less formally, and the semantics of a given relationship are consistently observed. If these relationships are given names that are appropriate to their meanings, a human viewing an ontology can understand it directly; and because a program can assume uniform semantics for a given relationship, it can act consistently across the whole ontology.

An ontology includes

- *Entities* (things)
- The *relationships* between those entities
- The *properties* (and property values) of those entities
- The *functions* and *processes* involving those entities
- *Constraints* on and *rules* about those entities

As depicted in Figure 7–5, what is considered an ontology can range from the simple notion of a taxonomy (knowledge with minimal hierarchic structure) to a vocabulary (machine-usable knowledge as standardized terminology with natural language definitions) and upward to a conceptual model (with more complex knowledge representation), finally culminating in the notion of an ontology as a logical domain theory (with very expressive, complex, consistent, and meaningful knowledge). The more complex notion of ontology (as a conceptual model and a logical theory) is what ontological engineers aspire to construct and use. Ontologies thus act as semantic conceptual models representing common knowledge in a well-defined, sound, consistent, extensible, reusable, and modular fashion.

How Ontologies Relate to Topic Maps

Historically, the topic map standard (ISO 13250) was defined to facilitate the merging of different indexing schemes. A common markup format used for indexing is a crucial step toward the goal of interoperability among indexing schemes. What is needed yet is *semantic* interoperability. Whereas the topic map specification ensures syntactic interoperability, ontologies provide semantic interoperability. If built from a

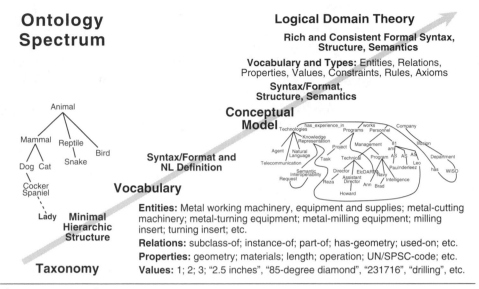

Figure 7–5   Ontology spectrum

sound ontology, topic maps can provide semantic interoperability not only among each other but among applications that use them as well.

The topic map specification provides a language to represent knowledge, in particular the conceptual knowledge with which one distinguishes information resources semantically. The ontological engineering discipline applied to building topic maps focuses precisely on this aspect. Ontological engineering emphasizes careful conceptual design and construction of topic maps to reflect correctly the semantics of the underlying knowledge. It provides principles and guidelines to ensure reusability, robustness, and even a wide range of applications. The design and construction of topic maps that provide meaningful expression of knowledge should be based on established principles of ontological engineering.

How to Build an Ontology

The process for building an ontology is similar to that used to build an object-oriented conceptual model [Booch et al. 1999] or an entity-relation database diagram [Teorey 1999]. The primary difference is that ontologies seek semantic expressiveness unconstrained by the various purposes the other models must fulfill. Here is a sequence of basic steps illustrated by an example.

1. Define a universe of discourse, which means simply that portion of the world you intend to model. Start this universe-of-discourse-defining process by listing the concepts you want to include in that universe, that is, the meaningful objects of that corner of the world, as far as you understand them. Many times, this can mean analyzing the documents that are "about" the corner of the world you want to model, down to the subjects, verbs, objects, adjectives, and relative clauses of the sentences of those documents. For example, in an author–work ontology/topic map, you may want to include such things as *Author*, *Person*, *Work*, *Play*, and *Wrote* on the schematic portion and *Shakespeare*, *Hamlet*, *Tempest*, *Goethe*, and *Faust* on the data portion. Indeed, the data portion can induce topics as well.

2. List how the various things relate to each other. Note that such things as *Wrote* are relations between two concepts. While doing this, you may discover things that you inadvertently left out in the first step. Well, add them in. In our example, *Author*, *Person*, *Work*, and *Play* are classes, where *Author* and *Play* are subclasses of *Person* and *Work*, respectively. The term *Wrote* is a slot, or a relationship, between *Author* and *Work*. We want to express the idea that an Author Wrote some Work.

3. Now build the ontology based on your analysis in steps 1-2 by using a knowledge representation engine (i.e., an ontology management tool such as Protégé) to create classes for the concepts and relations.

A simple guide by Gruber [1995a] on how to design an ontology is available on the Ontolingua site [Gruber 1995b]. It lists some key items to consider when developing an ontology:

- What the ontology is intended to be about (in general, plus assumptions)
- What you want to state in the ontology (in more detail)
- Concepts that should be included in the ontology (conceptualize the detail)
- Whether there are any ontologies in any set of available ontologies that may contain terms that can be used to develop the ontology
- What modifications you may want to make to the ontology over time

If you would like to build an ontology yourself, we suggest that you do so by using an ontology management tool. For example, download Protégé-2000 (see the Web site listing for Protégé-2000 at the end of this chapter), an open source ontology editor available to the public for free from Stanford Medical Informatics. Figure 7–6 shows an example of an author–work ontology built with Protégé-2000, based on an example given in the XTM 1.0 specification.

The same ideas are expressed in XTM in the code shown below, taken from the XTM 1.0 specification. Note that for simplicity's sake we haven't added such things as *Person* or *Play* to the ontology.

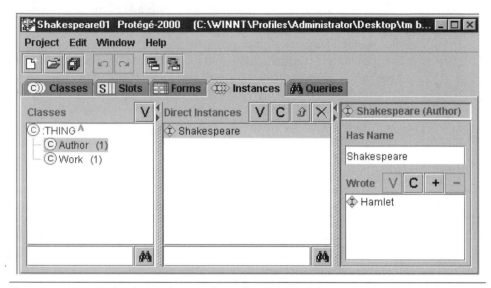

Figure 7–6   Example of an author–work ontology in Protégé-2000

```
<topic id="shakespeare">
  <instanceOf>
    <subjectIndicatorRef
      xlink:href="http://www.iptc.org/NewsML/topicsets/-
      topicset.iptc-topictype.xml#TopicTypes.Person"/>
  </instanceOf>
</topic>

<topic id="hamlet">
  <instanceOf>
    <subjectIndicatorRef
      xlink:href="http://www.shakespeare.org/plays.html"/>
  </instanceOf>
</topic>

<association>
  <instanceOf><topicRef xlink:href="#written-by"/></instanceOf>
  <member>
    <roleSpec><topicRef xlink:href="#author"/></roleSpec>
    <topicRef xlink:href="#shakespeare"/>
  </member>
  <member>
    <roleSpec><topicRef xlink:href="#work"/></roleSpec>
    <topicRef xlink:href="#hamlet"/>
  </member>
</association>
```

We'd like to give examples that illustrate knowledge representation problems and the guidelines to solve them, but the scope of this brief introduction to ontological engineering prohibits an adequate presentation. Please see the following references for examples of these problems: the ontological engineering papers in Guarino [1998] and a chapter titled "Mistakes Commonly Made When Knowledge Is Entered" in Lenat and Guha [1990]. Also, a tutorial on ontological engineering is available in Gómez-Pérez [1999].

Ontology-Driven Topic Maps

The main point in this subsection is the idea of ontology-driven topic maps. In the previous subsections we have talked about using ontological engineering as a discipline to guide the design and construction of topic maps. This subsection introduces the notion of ontology-driven topic maps: topic maps generated from ontologies. This approach is part of a growing trend to position ontologies at the heart of systems, whether an information system, a development process, or a database design [Guarino 1998]. This trend is fueled by the recognition that knowledge is a separate entity of foremost importance and that ontologies play a central role in the design and operation of information systems.

Topic maps can be generated from ontologies such as the one presented in the previous subsection. With the ontology-driven approach, the ontology is an explicit artifact distinct from the topic map it generates. We have advocated up to now the use of ontological engineering in building topic maps. At this point we further propose that an explicit ontology be created, which in turns induces the necessary topic map. At the time of this writing, no known mapping software exists to generate topic maps automatically from any standard knowledge representation language. We argue here the usefulness of this approach and expect that tools will become available to support it once the public recognizes the great potential in the knowledge aspect of topic maps.

The Advantages of the Ontology-Driven Topic Maps Approach

The ontology-driven topic maps approach offers several major advantages. An ontology-driven topic map is desirable for its maintainability. Producing the ontology first from which to generate the topic map separates the ontological design from the XTM implementation details. Moreover, as the XTM specification evolves, it naturally needs to change in order to fulfill purposes other than those strictly relevant to knowledge representation. As versioning of the specification occurs, if the ontology for a given topic map remains unchanged, then only the mapping from the ontology language to the XTM specification needs to be updated. Updating such a mapping for a given knowledge representation language relative to the new XTM version is preferable to updating all topic maps. For example, a change to the mapping may be occasioned by an update to the process requirements. Separating the ontology from the topic map enables conceptual changes to be explicitly recorded apart from all other changes. In this case, the ontology-driven topic maps approach offers the advantages of a typical loose coupling approach.

The ontology-driven topic maps approach makes available the use of numerous existing ontologies. Ontologies are the results of significant investment, as are topic maps. Taking the ontology-driven maps approach spares users the effort of building knowledge from scratch on domains for which considerable knowledge representation work has already been done. At the same time, this approach encourages an even greater reuse of knowledge on an ongoing basis by establishing the topic map community as an important part of the greater knowledge representation community. Both communities can reap the benefits of such a pool of shared knowledge.

Another benefit of using existing ontologies is that many of these ontologies have been tested and used successfully for various applications. Examples in the medical domain include such ontologies as those in the Unified Medical Language System (UMLS) project and the Generalised Architecture for Languages, Encyclopaedias and Nomenclatures in medicine (GALEN) project (see Web site listings for both at the end of the chapter). It makes sense to reuse a relevant portion of these ontologies to build topic maps about medicine.[11]

Yet another benefit of taking the ontology-driven topic maps approach is that applications exist or can be built to use the ontology for purposes besides those of topic maps. Ontologies are built using languages focused on knowledge representation, whereas topic maps are artifacts created specifically to organize Internet resources (by means of an overlay that leaves the original organization of the resources untouched). A single ontology may be used to serve multiple applications, among which can be inference engines and natural language applications, as well as to generate topic maps. It's advisable to leave the actual implementation to the topic map, allowing the conceptualization to be specified by the ontology.

We also note that, similar to the emerging XTM specification's considerations, ontological engineering already has a burgeoning research program in ontology merging and mapping, as previously discussed. And similar to topic maps, humans are the final

---

[11]As Sam Hunting points out elsewhere in this book, since ontologies themselves in their original form exist as documents, one can use topic maps to annotate them. In particular, one can use topic maps to annotate terms in an ontology with respect to those of another syntactically distinct ontology as means of documentation for a prospective merge or reuse.

arbiters of ontology merges, at least at this stage in the development of the technology, since merging two ontologies requires a human who understands the semantics of both to decide on the specific points of equivalence. However, having the same name—perhaps contrary to the implication in Chapter 2 on the difference between name-based merging and subject-based merging—is *not* a guarantee nor even a likelihood that two entities are semantically the same or similar, although the string identity of two nodes in distinct ontologies is a syntactic mechanism for proposing a semantic candidate for an ontology merger.

We've already shown how to build simple ontologies. Now we'd like to show how such an ontology can generate a topic map. As of this writing, software that generates a topic map from an ontology is not yet available for any knowledge representation language. Nevertheless, here is a start of one possible mapping from the Protégé-2000 knowledge model to the topic maps knowledge model. In the following, to the left of the arrow is the Protégé construct, and to the right of the arrow is the topic map construct.

Individual ➜ Topic

Class ➜ Topic

Individual-or-Class Instance-of ➜ Topic Instance-of

Subclass-of ➜ Subclass-of

Template-Slot ➜ Association-Type topic[12]

The Future of the Ontology-Driven Topic Maps Approach

In the future, we'd like to see many topic maps generated from ontologies so that the knowledge can be maintained by editing the ontologies. These ontologies would be published along with their topic maps. For those topic maps that aren't generated from ontologies, at least they should be designed with principles of ontological engineering to ensure semantic consistency of their terms.

---

[12]A discrepancy between slots and associations exists. One subtle difference is that a template-slot is applied to the type of an object in order to produce own-slots for the object, whereas associations in topic maps correspond to the own-slots themselves. (An own-slot is an assignment of a value of a given type to a given class or individual.) Another difference is that slots in general are strongly typed, whereas associations by themselves are not, but can be, strongly typed through the templating mechanism given in Published Subject Indicators.

We envision libraries of topic maps as well as libraries of ontologies that generate them. For a given ontology, there may be multiple topic maps, each an image of a distinct mapping. We hope that standard ontologies will become available for various domains of knowledge. As particular ontologies become public standards, we expect that some of the topic maps generated from these ontologies will become standards as well.

It is possible to create a topic map directly, especially if the topic map is small and expresses limited knowledge. After all, some topic maps don't need to offer much more than simple groupings of information resources. But whether you're building a simple index for a document or a sophisticated navigation map for a Web site, you are implicitly expressing knowledge. Thus, creating a semantically rich knowledge layer will add tremendous value to a topic map.

Summary

This chapter served as a brief introduction to ontologies and ontological engineering, the recent subdiscipline of computer and information science originating in knowledge representation and knowledge engineering research in AI. In this chapter we described the roots of ontological engineering, knowledge representation and knowledge engineering, and the lower branches which still help to support the emerging tree and feed sustenance into ontological engineering. We also provided a definition of ontology—actually, a set of definitions of ontology since, as we've seen, the real notion is of an ontology continuum, a range of what can be considered an ontology, from simple taxonomy to logical theory.

Ontological engineering has emerged from the past 15 years of research in knowledge technologies, which largely reacted against the deficiencies in expert systems and the lack of modular knowledge-based systems. Ontological engineering seeks to use ontologies as the formal encoding of human knowledge to make our software systems and Web technologies smarter, to shift the semantic interpretation burden onto our machines, thereby ensuring semantic interoperability of our systems and our documents. Helped greatly by advances in theoretical computer science, the rise of logic-based AI, and the methods and research interests of philosophy and theoretical and computational linguistics, ontological engineering has grown into a strong formal discipline that can assist the topic map community.

In addition, we described the relationship of ontological engineering to the emerging topic map specification, itself concerned with raising the human-meaningful, semantic standard of Web documents and artifacts. Like topic maps, ontologies can be used to attach conceptual and semantic information to Web documents and artifacts so that these are more conducive to human interpretation by being closer to what humans mean. But ontological engineering underscores the need for a true semantic representation for artifacts by providing semantic constraints—typically as axioms—to ensure that what an artifact actually means is what we intend it to mean. Both the ontological engineering and the topic map communities are directly interested in realizing the dream of the Semantic Web: that the Internet may someday become an extension of our animal (embodied, aware, and often conscious), sentient (fully self-aware), and epistemological (knowledge-bearing) understanding of our universe.

Is there one global Grand Ontology of Being, of Everything, of Data? No.[13] But we firmly believe that the quest for machine representation and interpretation of knowledge is a useful, inexorable, and absolutely necessary course. We envision linked ontologies, some of which represent their semantics in well-formed and sound ways and some of which don't (but those that don't can "borrow" soundness via the linkage from those that do), and contexts of interpretation that use those ontologies, to facilitate both human understanding of and machine support for semantic navigation of documents. We also hope for increased machine understanding of those documents, to shift more and more of the semantic interpretation burden[14] onto our eventual machine collaborators.

We invite you to explore further these fields—ontologies, knowledge representation, ontological engineering, and artificial intelligence. We think they will offer insight into your understanding and usage of topic maps. You may discover innovative uses for topic maps by focusing on the fact that they intrinsically *represent knowledge*. We hope that through this brief introduction we have achieved the goal of making you aware of an entire field devoted to representing knowledge, which is precisely what you are doing when you build a topic map. And, of course, we hope you will think of using our discipline, ontological engineering, which truly will propel you more readily to our common goal: the Semantic Web.

Acknowledgments

Portions of this chapter were conceived or written while both authors worked for VerticalNet, Inc., and also while one of the authors was at The MITRE Corporation. We acknowledge the support of both companies and express our appreciation for that support. We also thank Nicola Guarino for permission to display his classification of

---

[13]Although, as the insistent formal demons within us periodically remind us: "A finite grammar can generate an infinite number of sentences," and "A theory can describe/explain/predict an infinite range of phenomena."

[14]It may indeed be a joyful onus, as it is when two humans participate in a conversation, both semantically interpreting what the other says and evolving to a mutual understanding (model).

knowledge representation levels (Table 7–1) from his 1994 paper presented at the IV Wittgenstein Symposium. Finally, we thank the anonymous reviewers of this chapter for their comments and suggestions.

References

Aït-Kaci, Hassan. 1991. *Warren's Abstract Machine: A Tutorial Reconstruction*. Series in Logic Programming. Cambridge, MA: MIT Press.

Aït-Kaci, Hassan, and Andreas Podelski. 1993. Towards a Meaning of LIFE. *Journal of Logic Programming* 16(3–4):195–234. (Original version, 1991, PRL Research Report #11, June.)

Aït-Kaci, Hassan, Andreas Podelski, and Goldstein Seth Copen. 1993. Order-Sorted Feature Theory Unification. PRL Research Report #32, May.

Andersen, William, Kilian Stoffel, and James Hendler. 1995. Parka: Support for Extremely Large Knowledge Bases. In *Proceedings of International KRUSE Symposium: Knowledge Retrieval, Use, and Storage for Efficiency, Santa Cruz, CA, Aug. 11–13, 1995*; Gerard Ellis, Robert Levinson, Andrew Fall, and Veronica Dahl, eds., pp. 122–133.

Artale, A., E. Franconi, N. Guarino, and L. Pazzi. 1996. Part-Whole Relations in Object-Centered Systems: An Overview. *Data and Knowledge Engineering* 20(3): 347–383.

Baader, Franz, and Bernhard Hollunder. 1991. A Terminological Knowledge Representation System with Complete Inference Algorithms. In *International Workshop on Processing Declarative Knowledge (PDK'91), Kaiserslautern, Germany, July 1–3, 1991*; Harold Boley and Michael Richter, eds. Lecture Notes in Artificial Intelligence, Volume 567. Berlin: Springer-Verlag, pp. 67–86.

Bechhofer, Sean, et al. 2000. An Informal Description of Standard OIL and Instance OIL. Accessed in April 2002 at *http://www.ontoknowledge.org/oil/downl/oil-whitepaper. pdf*.

Benjamins, V. 1993. *Problem-Solving Methods for Diagnosis*. Ph.D. Thesis, University of Amsterdam, Netherlands.

Biller, H., and E. Neuhold. 1989. Semantics of Databases: The Semantics of Data Models. In *Readings in Artificial Intelligence and Databases*; J. Mylopoulos and M. L. Brodie, eds. San Mateo, CA: Morgan Kaufman, pp. 273–292.

Blair, Paul, R. V. Guha, and Wanda Pratt. 1992. *Microtheories: An Ontological Engineer's Guide*. Technical Report Cyc-050-92, March 5. Austin, TX: Cycorps. Accessed in April 2002 at *http://www.cyc.com/tech-reports/cyc-050-92/cyc-050-92.html*.

Booch, Grady, James Rumbaugh, and Ivar Jacobson. 1999. *The Unified Modeling Language User Guide.* Reading, MA: Addison-Wesley.

Borgida, A., and P. Patel-Schneider. 1994. A Semantics and Complete Algorithm for Subsumption in the CLASSIC description logic. *Journal of Artificial Intelligence Research* 1:277–308.

Borgo, S., N. Guarino, and C. Masolo. 1996. A Pointless Theory of Space Based on Strong Connection and Congruence. In *Principles of Knowledge Representation and Reasoning (KR96)*; L. Carlucci Aiello and J. Doyle, eds. Boston, MA: Morgan Kaufmann, pp. 220–229.

———. 1997. An Ontological Theory of Physical Objects. In *Proceedings of Qualitative Reasoning, 11th International Workshop, Cortona, Italy.* Published as Technical Report, Istituto di Analisi Numerica—CNR Pavia, Italy, pp. 223–231.

Bouquet, Paolo, et al., eds. 1999. *Modeling and Using Context. Second International and Interdisciplinary Conference (Context '99), Trento, Italy, September 1999.* Lecture Notes in Artificial Intelligence 1688. Berlin: Springer-Verlag.

Brachman, R. 1979. On the Epistemological Status of Semantic Networks. In *Associative Networks: Representation and Use of Knowledge by Computers*; N. V. Findler, ed. New York: Academic Press.

Brachman, R., and H. Levesque. 1982. In *Proceedings of the National Conference on Artificial Intelligence.* American Association for Artificial Intelligence, pp. 189–192.

Brachman, R., and J. G. Schmolze. 1985. An Overview of the KL-ONE Knowledge Representation System. *Cognitive Science* 9(2):171–216.

Brachman, R., et al. 1983. Krypton: A Functional Approach to Knowledge Representation. *IEEE Computer* (October):67–73.

Bresciani, P., E. Franconi, and S. Tessaris. 1995. Implementing and Testing Expressive Description Logics: A Preliminary Report. In *Proceedings of International KRUSE Symposium: Knowledge Retrieval, Use, and Storage for Efficiency, Santa Cruz, CA, Aug. 11–13, 1995*; Gerard Ellis, Robert Levinson, Andrew Fall, and Veronica Dahl, eds., pp. 28–39.

Brewka, Gerhard, ed. 1996. *Principles of Knowledge Representation.* Stanford, CA: Center for the Study of Language and Information (CSLI) and The European Association for Logic, Language, and Information (FoLLI).

Brézillon, Patrick, Roy Turner, Jean-Charles Pomerol, and Elise Turner, cochairs. 1999. *Workshop on Reasoning in Context for AI Applications, AAAI-99, Orlando, FL, July 1999.* Technical Report WS-99-14. Menlo Park, CA: AAAI Press.

Buchanan, Bruce, Randall Davis, and Edward Shortliffe. 1977. Production Rules as a Representation for a Knowledge-Based Consultation Program. *Artificial Intelligence* 8(1):15–45.

Buchanan, Bruce, and Edward Shortliffe. 1985. *Rule-Based Expert Systems: The MYCIN Experiments of the Stanford Heuristic Programming Project.* Reading, MA: Addison-Wesley.

Burkhardt, H., and B. Smith, eds. 1991. *Handbook of Metaphysics and Ontology.* Munich: Philosophia.

Buvac, Sasa, Vanja Buvac, and Ian A. Mason. 1995. Metamathematics of Contexts. *Fundamenta Informaticae* 23(3):263–301.

Cabeza, D., and M. Hermenegildo. 1996. html.pl: An HTML Package for (C)LP Systems. Accessed in April 2002 at *http://www.clip.dia.fi.upm.es/miscdocs/html_pl/html_pl_main.html.*

Cabeza, D., M. Hermenegildo, and S. Varmaa. 1996. The PiLLoW/CIAO Library for INTERNET/WWW Programming Using Computational Logic Systems. In *Proceedings of the First Workshop on Logic Programming Tools for INTERNET Applications, in Conjunction with JICSLP '96, Bonn, Germany, September 2–6, 1996.* Text and code accessed in April 2002 at *http://www.clip.dia.fi.upm.es/miscdocs/pillow/pillow.html.*

Cadoli, Marco, and Thomas Eiter. 1998. Computational Aspects of Knowledge Representations. Tutorial MP4, Fifteenth National Conference on Artificial Intelligence, Madison, WI, July 27, 1998.

Casati, Roberto, and Achilee C. Varzi. 1995. *Holes and Other Superficialities.* Cambridge, MA: MIT Press.

———. 1999. *Parts and Places: The Structures of Spatial Representation.* Cambridge, MA: MIT Press.

Chalupsky, Hans. 2000. OntoMorph: A Translation System for Symbolic Knowledge. In *Principles of Knowledge Representation and Reasoning: Proceedings of the Seventh International Conference (KR2000), San Francisco, CA, 2000*; A. G. Cohn, F. Giunchiglia, and B. Selman, eds. San Francisco, CA: Morgan Kaufmann. Also available at *http://www.isi.edu/~hans/publications/KR2000.pdf* (accessed in April 2002).

Chandrasekaran, B. 1986. Generic Tasks in Knowledge-Based Reasoning: High-Level Building Blocks for Expert System Design. *IEEE Expert* 1:23–30.

Chandrasekaran, B., J. R. Josephson, and V. Richard Benjamins. 1998. Ontology of Tasks and Methods. Laboratory for AI Research, Ohio State University. Appeared in 1998 Banff Knowledge Acquisition Workshop. The first part of the paper appears in What Are Ontologies and Why Do We Need Them?, *IEEE Intelligent Systems* 14(1):20–26, 1999. Accessed in April 2002 at *http://www.cis.ohio-state.edu/~chandra/Ontology-of-Tasks-Methods.PDF.*

Chaudhri, Vinay K., et al. 1998. Open Knowledge Base Connectivity Specification, V. 2.0.31. SRI, International and Knowledge Systems Laboratory, Stanford University, April 9. Accessed in April 2002 at *http://www.ai.sri.com/~okbc/spec.html.*

Clark, Keith, and Steve Gregory. 1986. PARLOG: Parallel Programming in Logic. *ACM Transactions on Programming Languages and Systems* 8(1):1–49.

Clark, Peter, and Bruce Porter. 1997. Building Concept Representations from Reusable Components. In *Proceedings of AAAI '97*. Menlo Park, CA: AAAI Press, pp. 369–376.

Clocksin, William F., and Christopher S. Mellish. 1981. *Programming in Prolog*. Berlin: Springer-Verlag.

Cocchiarella, N. B. 1991. Formal Ontology. In *Handbook of Metaphysics and Ontology*; H. Burkhardt and B. Smith, eds. Munich: Philosophia Verlag, pp. 640–647.

———. 1995. Knowledge Representation in Conceptual Realism. *International Journal of Human-Computer Studies* 43:697–721. A version appeared at the International Workshop on Formal Ontology in Conceptual Analysis and Knowledge Representation, Padova, Italy, January 1993.

Cohen, Paul R., et al. 1998. The DARPA High Performance Knowledge Bases Project. *Artificial Intelligence* 19(4):25–49. Also available at *http://reliant.teknowledge.com/HPKB/Publications/AImag.pdf* (accessed in April 2002).

Cohn, A. G., and N. M. Gotts. 1994. The "Egg-Yolk" Representation of Regions with Indeterminate Boundaries. In *Proceedings, GISDATA Specialist Meeting on Geographical Objects with Undetermined Boundaries*; P. Burrough and A. M. Frank, eds. London: Taylor and Francis, pp. 171–187.

Colmerauer, Alain, Henri Kanoui, Robert Pasero, and Phillipe Roussel. 1973. *Un Système de Communication Homme-Machine en Français*. Groupe d'Intelligence Artificielle, Faculté des Sciences de Luminy, Université d'Aix-Marseille II.

Connolly, Dan, et al. 2001. Annotated DAML+OIL Ontology Markup. W3C Note 18, December 2001. Accessed in April 2002 at *http://www.w3.org/TR/daml+oil-walkthru/*.

Cooper, Thomas, and Nancy Wogrin. 1988. *Rule-Based Programming with OPS5*. San Mateo, CA: Morgan Kaufmann.

Cover, Robin. 1998. XML and Semantic Transparency. Accessed in April 2002 at *http://www.oasis-open.org/cover/xmlAndSemantics.html*.

———. 2000. Ontology and Conceptual Knowledge Markup Languages (last modified November 25, 2000). Accessed in April 2002 at *http://www.oasis-open.org/cover/oml.html*.

Das, Subrata Kumar. 1992. *Deductive Databases and Logic Programming*. Reading, MA: Addison-Wesley.

Davis, R., H. Shrobe, and P. Szolovits. 1993. What Is in a Knowledge Representation? *AI Magazine* 14(1):17–33.

Debenham, John. 1998. *Knowledge Engineering: Unifying Knowledge Base and Database Design.* Berlin: Springer-Verlag.

de Kleer, J. 1986. An Assumption-Based Truth Maintenance System. *Artificial Intelligence* 28:127–162.

Dincbas, M., P. Van Hentenryck, H. Simonis, A. Aggoun, T. Graf, and F. Berthier. 1988. *The Constraint Logic Programming Language CHIP International Conference on FGCS 1988, Tokyo, November 1988.* Proceedings of the Fifth Generation Computer Systems Conference.

Doyle, Jon. 1979. A Truth Maintenance System. *Artificial Intelligence* 12:231–272.

Fahlman, Scott. 1977, 1979. *NETL: A System for Representing and Using Real-World Knowledge.* Cambridge, MA: MIT Press. (Originally, Ph.D thesis, 1977, MIT.)

Falkenhainer, B., and K. Forbus. 1991. Compositional Modeling: Finding the Right Model for the Job. *Artificial Intelligence* 51:95–143.

Fall, Andrew. 1995a. Heterogeneous Encoding. In *Proceedings of International KRUSE Symposium: Knowledge Retrieval, Use, and Storage for Efficiency, Santa Cruz, CA, Aug. 11–13, 1995*; Gerard Ellis, Robert Levinson, Andrew Fall, and Veronica Dahl, eds., pp. 134–146.

———. 1995b. An Abstract Framework for Taxonomic Encoding. In *Proceedings of International KRUSE Symposium: Knowledge Retrieval, Use, and Storage for Efficiency, Santa Cruz, CA, Aug. 11–13, 1995*; Gerard Ellis, Robert Levinson, Andrew Fall, and Veronica Dahl, eds., pp. 162–167.

———. 1996. *Reasoning with Taxonomies.* Ph.D. Thesis, Simon Fraser University, Canada.

Farquhar, Adam, and Gruninger, cochairs. 1997. *Ontological Engineering: Papers from the 1997 AAAI Symposium, March 24–26, Stanford, CA.* Technical Report SS-97-06. Menlo Park, CA: AAAI Press.

Fensel, Dieter, Michael Erdmann, and Rudi Studer. 1998. Ontobroker: The Very High Idea. In *Proceedings of the 11th International Flairs Conference (FLAIRS-98), Sanibal Island, Florida, May 1998.* AAAI Press. Accessed in April 2002 at *http://www.cs.vu.nl/~dieter/ftp/paper/flairs98.ps*.

Fensel, Dieter, et al. 1999. On2broker: Lessons Learned from Applying AI to the Web. Research Report, Institute AIFB. Accessed in April 2002 at *http://www.cs.vu.nl/~dieter/ftp/paper/on2broker.ps* .

Forbus, Kenneth D., and Johan de Kleer. 1993. *Building Problem Solvers.* Cambridge, MA: MIT Press.

Forgy, Charles. 1981. *OPS5 User's Manual.* Technical Report CMU-CS-81-135. Pittsburgh, PA: Carnegie Mellon University, School of Computer Science.

————. 1982. Rete: A Fast Algorithm for the Many Pattern/Many Object Pattern Match Problem. *Artificial Intelligence* 19:17–37.

Frost, Richard. 1986. *Introduction to Knowledge Base Systems.* New York: MacMillan Publishing.

Frühwirth, Thomas, et al. 1993. Constraint Logic Programming—An Informal Introduction. ECRC Technical Report ECRC-93-5. Accessed in April 2002 at *http://citeseer.nj.nec.com/30286.html.*

Gardarin, Georges, and Patrick Valduriez. 1989. *Relational Databases and Knowledge Bases.* Reading, MA: Addison-Wesley.

Giunchiglia, Fausto, and Paolo Bouquet. 1997. *Introduction to Contextual Reasoning: An Artificial Intelligence Perspective.* Technical Report 9705-19, May. Trento, Italy: Istituto per la Ricerca Scientifica e Tecnologica.

————. 1998. A Context-Based Framework for Mental Representation. Technical Report 9807-02, July. Trento, Italy: Istituto per la Ricerca Scientifica e Tecnologica.

Giunchiglia, Fausto, and Chiara Ghidini. 1998. Local Models Semantics, or Contextual Reasoning = Locality + Compatibility. In *Principles of Knowledge Representation and Reasoning (KR'98), Proceedings of the Sixth International Conference, Trento, Italy, June 2–5, 1998*; Anthony Cohn, Lenhart Schubert, and Stuart Shapiro, eds., pp. 282–289.

Glaser, Norbert. 1996. *Contribution to Knowledge Acquisition and Modelling in a Multi-Agent Framework (the CoMoMAS Approach).* Ph.D. Thesis, Doctorat de l'Université Henri Poincaré, Nancy, France.

Gómez-Pérez, Asunción. 1999. Tutorial on Ontological Engineering: IJCAI '99. Accessed in April 2002 at *http://www.ontology.org/main/presentations/madrid/theoretical.pdf.*

Graham, Ian. 1994. *Object Oriented Methods.* Reading, MA: Addison-Wesley.

Gray, P., et al. 1997. KRAFT: Knowledge Fusion from Distributed Databases and Knowledge Bases. Computing Science Dept., University of Aberdeen, UK. Accessed in April 2002 at *http://www.csc.liv.ac.uk/~mshave/NRIN.ps* and *http://www.csd.abdn.ac.uk/~apreece/Research/KRAFT/.*

Gruber, Thomas. 1993. A Translation Approach to Portable Ontology Specifications. *Knowledge Acquisition* 5:199–220.

————. 1995a. Towards Principles for the Design of Ontologies Used for Knowledge Sharing. *International Journal of Human and Computer Studies* 43(5/6):907–928.

————. 1995b. How to Design an Ontology. Web page as part of the Ontolingua guided tour. Accessed in April 2002 at *http://www-ksl-svc.stanford.edu:5915/doc/frame-editor/guided-tour/how-to-design-an-ontology.html.*

Guarino, N. 1994. The Ontological Level. (Invited paper presented at IV Wittgenstein Symposium, Kirchberg, Austria, 1993.) In *Philosophy and the Cognitive Sciences*; R. Casati, B. Smith, and G. White, eds. Vienna: Hölder-Pichler-Tempsky, pp. 443–456.

————. 1998. Formal Ontology in Information Systems. In *Proceedings of the First International Conference (FOIS'98), June 6–8, Trent, Italy*; N. Guarino, ed. Amsterdam: IOS Press, pp. 3–17.

Guarino, N., and P. Giaretta. 1995. Ontologies and Knowledge Bases: Towards a Terminological Clarification. In *Towards Very Large Knowledge Bases: Knowledge Building and Knowledge Sharing*; N. Mars, ed. Amsterdam: IOS Press, pp. 25–32.

Guarino, N., C. Masolo, and G. Vetere. 1999. OntoSeek: Content-Based Access to the Web. *IEEE Intelligent Systems* 14(3):70–80. Also available at *http://www.ladseb.pd.cnr.it/infor/Ontology/Papers/OntoSeek.pdf*.

Guarino, N., and C. Welty. 2000a. Ontological Analysis of Taxonomic Relationships. In *Proceedings of ER-2000: The 19th International Conference on Conceptual Modeling*; A. Laender and V. Storey, eds. New York: Springer-Verlag, pp. 21–224.

————. 2000b. Identity, Unity, and Individuation: Towards a Formal Toolkit for Ontological Analysis. In *Proceedings of ECAI-2000: The European Conference on Artificial Intelligence*; W. Horn, ed. Amsterdam: IOS Press. Also available at *http://www.ladseb.pd.cnr.it/infor/Ontology/Papers/LADSEB02-2000.pdf*.

————. 2000c. A Formal Ontology of Properties. In *Proceedings of 12th International Conference on Knowledge Engineering and Knowledge Management*; Rose Dieng, ed. Menlo Park, CA: AAAI Press. Also available at *http://www.ladseb.pd.cnr.it/infor/Ontology/Papers/EKAW-2000.pdf*.

Guha, R. V. 1991. *Contexts: A Formalization and Some Applications.* Ph.D. Thesis, Stanford University. Also published as Stanford University Technical Report STAN-CS-91-1399-Thesis, and Microelectronics and Computer Technology Corporation (MCC; Austin, TX) Technical Report ACT-CYC-423-91.

Guha, R. V., and Douglas Lenat. 1990. *Cyc: A Mid-Term Report.* Technical Report ACT-CYC-134-90. Austin, TX: Microelectronics and Computer Technology Corporation.

Hajnicz, Elzbieta. 1996. *Time Structures: Formal Description and Algorithmic Representation.* Lecture Notes in Artificial Intelligence 1047. Springer-Verlag.

Haridi, Seif, Peter Van Roy, and Gert Smolka. 1997. An Overview of the Design of Distributed Oz. Technical Report, Programming Systems Lab, Department of Computer Science, University of the Saarland. In *Proceedings of the Second International Symposium on Parallel Symbolic Computation (PASCO '97), July 1997, Maui, Hawaii.* ACM Press, pp. 176–187. Also available at *http://www.ps.uni-sb.de/Papers/abstracts/PASCO97.html*.

Hayes, P. 1990. Naive Physics I: An Ontology for Liquids. In *Readings in Qualitative Reasoning about Physical Systems*; Daniel S. Weld and Johan De Kleer, eds. San Mateo, CA: Morgan Kaufman, pp. 484–502.

———. 1996. *A Catalog of Temporal Theories.* Technical Report UIUC-BI-AI-96-01. Beckman Institute, University of Illinois at Urbana-Champaign.

Heflin, Jeff, Jim Hendler, and Sean Luke. 1999. Coping with Changing Ontologies in a Distributed Environment. Accessed in April 2002 at *http://www.cs.umd.edu/projects/plus/SHOE/pubs/#aaai99*.

Herold, Alexander, ed. 1995. *The Handbook of Parallel Constraint Logic Programming Applications.* (Final deliverable of the APPLAUSE ESPRIT project, November 1995.) Accessed in April 2002 at *http://www.clps.de/html/reports/book.ps.gz*.

Hoppe, T., et al. 1993. *BACK V5: Tutorial and Manual.* KIT-Report 100. Berlin: Technische Universität Berlin.

Horrocks, I., et al. 2000. The Ontology Inference Layer OIL. Accessed in April 2002 at *http://www.ontoknowledge.org/oil/TR/oil.long.html*.

Karp, Peter D., Vinay K. Chaudhri, and Jerome Thomere. 1999. XOL: An XML-Based Ontology Exchange Language. Pangaea Systems and SRI, International. Accessed in April 2002 at *http://www.ai.sri.com/~pkarp/xol/*.

Kent, Robert. 1999. Conceptual Markup Language: An Introduction. Accessed in April 2002 at *http://www.ontologos.org/Papers/Papers.html*.

Kim, Won, and Frederick Lochovsky, eds. 1989. *Object-Oriented Concepts, Databases, and Applications.* Reading, MA: Addison-Wesley.

Kitamura, Yoshinobu, Mitsuru Ikeda, and Riichiro Mizoguchi. 1997. A Causal Time Ontology for Qualitative Reasoning. In *Proceedings of IJCAI-97.* San Mateo, CA: AAAI Press, pp. 501–506. Also available at *http://www.ei.sanken.osaka-u.ac.jp/pub/kita/kita-ijcai97.pdf*.

———. 1998. Functional Ontology for Functional Understanding. In *Papers of Twelfth International Workshop on Qualitative Reasoning (QR-98), Cape Cod, USA, May 26–29* (AAAI Technical Report WS-98-01). San Mateo, CA: AAAI Press, pp.77–87. Also available at *http://www.ei.sanken.osaka-u.ac.jp/pub/kita/kita-pricai00.pdf* .

Knight, Kevin. 1989. Unification: A Multi-Disciplinary Survey. *ACM Computing Surveys* 21(1):93–124.

Kohlas, Jurg. 1994. Mathematical Foundations of Evidence Theory: A Theory of Reasoning with Uncertain Arguments. Conference on Mathematical Methods for Handling Partial Knowledge in Artificial Intelligence, Erice, Sicily, June 19–25, 1994. Appeared in *Mathematical Models for Handling Partial Knowledge in Artificial Intelligence*; G. Coletti, D. Dubois, and R. Scozzafava, eds. New York: Plenum Press, 1995.

Kowalski, Robert A. 1974. Logic for Problem Solving. DCL Memo 75. Edinburgh: Department of Artificial Intelligence, University of Edinburgh, Scotland.

———. 1979a. Algorithm = Logic + Control. *Communications of the ACM* 7:424–436.

———. 1979b. *Logic for Problem Solving*. New York: North-Holland.

Lambrix, Patrick, and Lin Padgham. 1996. A Description Logic for Composite Objects for Domain Modeling in an Agent-Oriented Application. In *Collected Papers of the 1996 Workshop on International Description Logics, Cambridge, MA, Nov. 2–4, 1996*; Lin Padgham et al., eds. AAAI Technical Report WS-96-05. Menlo Park, CA: AAAI Press, pp. 146–154.

Lang, E. 1991. The LILOG Ontology from a Linguistic Point of View. In *Text Understanding in LILOG*; O. Herzog and C. R. Rollinger, eds. Berlin: Springer-Verlag, pp. 464–481.

Lenat, D. 1998. *The Dimensions of Context-Space*. Technical Report, October 28. Austin, TX: Cycorp.

Lenat, D., and R. Guha. 1990. Building Large Knowledge-Based Systems. Reading, MA: Addison-Wesley.

Liu, Howard, Donald McKay, and Leo Obrst. 2001. Mapping Ontologies Via Image Functors: Formalizing Context. In preparation.

Liu, Mengchi. 1999. Deductive Database Languages: Problems and Solutions. *ACM Computing Surveys* 31(1):27–62.

Lloyd, John W. 1984. *Foundations of Logic Programming*. Berlin: Springer-Verlag.

MacGregor, Robert M. 1991. Inside the LOOM Description Classifier. *SIGART Bulletin* (Special Issue on Implemented Knowledge Representation and Reasoning Systems) 2(3):88–92.

———. 1994. A Description Classifier for the Predicate Calculus. *Proceedings of the AAAI 1994 National Conference*.

Maluf, David A., and Gio Wiederhold. 1997. Abstraction of Representation for Interoperation. In *Tenth International Symposium on Methodologies for Intelligent Systems*. Lecture Notes in Computer Science. New York: Springer-Verlag, pp. 441–455. Also available at *http://www-db.stanford.edu/pub/gio/paperlist.html*.

Martelli, A., and U. Montaneri. 1982. An Efficient Unification Algorithm. *ACM Transactions on Programming Languages and Systems* 4(2):258–282.

McCarthy, J. 1993. Notes on Formalizing Context. In *Proceedings of the 13th International Joint Conference on Artificial Intelligence (IJCAI)*. Los Altos, CA: Morgan Kauffman, pp. 550–560.

McCarthy, J, and Sasa Buvac. 1997. Formalizing Context (Expanded Notes). Stanford University Report STAN-CS-TN-94-13. Accessed in April 2002 at *http://www-formal.stanford.edu*.

McGuinness, Deborah L., Richard Fikes, James Rice, and Steve Wilder. 2000. An Environment for Merging and Testing Large Ontologies. In *Proceedings of the Seventh International Conference on Principles of Knowledge Representation and Reasoning (KR2000), Breckenridge, Colorado, USA, April 12–15, 2000*; A. G. Cohn, F. Giunchiglia, and B. Selman, eds. San Francisco, CA: Morgan Kaufmann, pp. 483–493. Also available at *http://www.ksl.stanford.edu/people/dlm/papers/kr00-abstract.html*.

Meier, Micha. 1995. *ECLiPSe 3.5 User Manual*. Munich: European Community Research Center (ECRC).

Meixner, Uwe. 1997. *Axiomatic Formal Ontology*. London: Kluwer Academic Publishers.

Minker, Jack, ed. 1988. *Foundations of Deductive Databases and Logic Programming*. Los Altos, CA: Morgan Kaufman.

Miranker, Daniel P. 1987. TREAT: A Better Match Algorithm for AI Production Systems. In *Proceedings of the Sixth National Conference on Artificial Intelligence (AAAI-87), August 1987*. Menlo Park, CA: AAAI Press, pp. 42–47.

———. 1990. *TREAT: A New and Efficient Match Algorithm for AI Production Systems*. San Mateo, CA: Morgan Kaufmann.

Mitra, Prasenjit, Gio Wiederhold, and Martin Kersten. 2000. A Graph-Oriented Model for Articulation of Ontology Interdependencies. Accepted for presentation at Extending DataBase Technologies, EDBT 2000, Konstanz, Germany, March 2000. Accessed in April 2002 at *http://www-db.stanford.edu/SKC/publications.html*.

Mudambi, Shyam, and Joachim Schimpf. 1994. Parallel CLP on Heterogeneous Networks. European Community Research Center (ECRC) Technical Report ECRC-94-17.

Mylopoulos, John, and Michael L. Brodie, eds. 1989. *Readings in Artificial Intelligence and Databases*. San Mateo, CA: Morgan Kaufman.

Naqvi, Shamim, and Shalom Tsur. 1989. *A Logical Language for Data and Knowledge Bases*. New York: Computer Science Press.

Neches, Robert, et al. 1991. Enabling Technology for Knowledge Sharing. *AI Magazine* 12(3):36–56. Also available at *http://www.isi.edu/isd/KRSharing/vision/AIMag.html*.

Noy, Natalya, and Carole Hafner. 1997. The State of the Art in Ontology Design: A Survey and Comparative Review. *AI Magazine* (Fall):53–74.

Noy, N. F., R. W. Fergerson, and M. A. Musen. 2000a. *The Knowledge Model of Protégé-2000: Combining Interoperability and Flexibility*. Technical Report SMI-2000-0830.

Stanford, CA: Stanford Medical Informatics, Stanford University. Also available at *http://smi-web.stanford.edu/pubs/SMI_Abstracts/SMI-2000-0830.html*.

Noy, N. F., and M. A. Musen. 2000b. PROMPT: Algorithm and Tool for Automated Ontology Merging and Alignment. Technical Report SMI-2000-0831. Stanford, CA: Stanford Medical Informatics, Stanford University. Also available at *http://smi-web.stanford.edu/pubs/SMI_Abstracts/SMI-2000-0831.html*.

Obrst, Leo, Greg Whittaker, and Alex Meng. 1999a. Semantic Context for Interoperable Distributed Object Systems. Accepted as poster for the Modeling and Using Context: Second International and Interdisciplinary Conference (Context'99), Trento, Italy, September 1999.

———. 1999b. Semantic Context for Object Exchange. In *Workshop on Reasoning in Context for AI Applications, AAAI-99, Orlando, FL, July 1999*; Patrick Brézillon, Roy Turner, Jean-Charles Pomerol, Elise Turner, cochairs. Technical Report WS-99-14. Menlo Park, CA: AAAI Press, pp. 80–85.

Obrst, Leo, Robert Wray, and Howard Liu. 2001. Ontological Engineering for E-Commerce. In *Proceedings of 2nd International Conference on Formal Ontologies in Information Systems (FOIS-01), October 17–19, 2001, Ogunquit, ME*.

Paton, Norman W., and Oscar Diaz. 1999. Active Database Systems. *ACM Computing Surveys* 31(1):63–103.

Pease, A., V. Chaudhri, F. Lehmann, and A. Farquhar. 2000. Practical Knowledge Representation and the DARPA High Performance Knowledge Bases Project. In *Proceedings of the Seventh International Conference on Principles of Knowledge Representation and Reasoning (KR2000), Breckenridge, Colorado, USA, April 12–15, 2000*; A. G. Cohn, F. Giunchiglia, and B. Selman, eds. San Francisco, CA: Morgan Kaufmann, pp. 25–49. Also available at *http://reliant.teknowledge.com/HPKB/Publications/KR-195.ps*.

Preece, Alun, et al. 1999. The KRAFT Architecture for Knowledge Fusion and Transformation. Presented at Expert Systems 1999 conference (winner of Best Technical Paper award). Accessed in April 2002 at *ftp://ftp.csd.abdn.ac.uk/pub/apreece/es99_final.ps*.

Quillian, M. R. 1968. Semantic Memory. In *Semantic Information Processing*; M. Minsky, ed. Cambridge, MA: MIT Press, pp. 216–270.

Reiter, R. 1989. Towards a Logical Reconstruction of Relational Database Theory. In *Readings in Artificial Intelligence and Databases*; J. Mylopoulos and M. Brodie, eds. San Mateo, CA: Morgan Kaufman, pp. 301–326.

Robinson, J.A. 1965. A Machine-Oriented Logic Based on the Resolution Principle. *Journal of the ACM* 12:33–34.

Roddy, David, Leo Obrst, and Adam Cheyer. 2000. Communication and Collaboration in a Landscape of B2B eMarketplaces. VerticalNet, Inc., white paper.

Rumbaugh, James, et al. 1991. *Object-Oriented Modeling and Design.* Englewood Cliffs, NJ: Prentice-Hall.

Saraswat, Vijay. 1989. *Concurrent Constraint Programming Languages.* Ph.D. Thesis, Carnegie Mellon University. Revised version published by MIT Press, 1992.

Sasajima, Munehiko, Yoshinobu Kitamura, Mitsuru Ikeda, and Riichiro Mizoguchi. 1995. FBRL: A Function and Behavior Representation Language. IJCAI'95. San Mateo, CA: Morgan Kauffman. Accessed in April 2002 at *http://www.ei.sanken.osaka-u. ac.jp/pub/sasa/1995.1.html.*

Schreiber, A., B. Wielinga, and J. Breuker. 1993. *KADS: A Principled Approach to Knowledge-Based System Development.* London: Academic Press.

Shannon, C. E. 1948. A Mathematical Theory of Communication. In *Key Papers in the Development of Information Theory*; D. Slepian, ed. New York: IEEE, 1974.

Simons, P. 1987. *Parts: A Study in Ontology.* Oxford: Clarendon Press.

Smith, Barry, and Achille C. Varzi. 1997. The Formal Ontology of Boundaries. *The Electronic Journal of Analytic Philosophy* 5(Spring).

Smolka, Gert. 1995. The Oz Programming Model. In *Computer Science Today*; Jan van Leeuwen, ed. Berlin: Springer-Verlag, pp. 324–343.

Speel, Piet-Hein. 1996a. *Selecting Knowledge Representation Systems.* Ph.D. Thesis, University Twente, Enschede, Netherlands.

———. 1996b. Can Description Logics Be Used in Real-Life Knowledge-Based Systems. In *Collected Papers of the 1996 Workshop on International Description Logics, Cambridge, MA, Nov. 2–4, 1996*; Lin Padgham et al., eds. AAAI Technical Report WS-96-05. Menlo Park, CA: AAAI Press, pp. 189–191.

Speel, Piet-Hein, Frank van Raalte, Paul van der Vet, and Nicolaas Mars. 1995. Runtime and Memory Usage Performance of Description Logics. In *Proceedings of International KRUSE Symposium: Knowledge Retrieval, Use, and Storage for Efficiency, Santa Cruz, CA, Aug. 11–13, 1995*; Gerard Ellis, Robert Levinson, Andrew Fall, and Veronica Dahl, eds., pp. 13–27.

Steels, L. 1990. Components of Expertise. *AI Magazine* 11(2):30–49.

Tarau, Paul. 1998. The BinProlog Experience: Implementing a High-Performance Continuation Passing Prolog Engine. Technical Report, BinNet Corporation.

———. 1999. Jinni: Intelligent Mobile Agent Programming at the Intersection of Java and Prolog. In *Proceedings of PAAM'99, London.*

Tarau, Paul, Veronica Dahl, and Andrew Fall. 1996. Backtrackable State with Linear Affine Implication and Assumption Grammars. In *Concurrency and Parallelism, Programming, Networking, and Security*; Joxan Jaffar and Roland H. C. Yap, eds. Lecture Notes in Computer Science 1179. Berlin: Springer-Verlag, pp. 53–64.

Teorey, Toby J. 1999. *Database Modeling and Design*, 3rd ed. San Francisco, CA: Morgan Kaufman.

Ullman, J. 1988, 1989. *Database and Knowledge Base Systems*, Volumes 1–2. New York: Computer Science Press.

Uschold, Michael, and Michael Gruninger. 1996. Ontologies: Principles, Methods, and Applications. *Knowledge Engineering Review* 11(2):93–136.

Van Roy, Peter. 1990. *Can Logic Programming Execute as Fast as Imperative Programming?* Ph.D. Thesis, Department of Computer Science, U.C. Berkeley.

———. 1993a. How to Get the Most Out of Aquarius Prolog. In *Aquarius Prolog 1.0 Documentation*. Digital Equipment Corporation, Paris Research Laboratory.

———. 1993b. *1983–1993: The Wonder Years of Sequential Prolog Implementation*. PRL Report #36, December.

Van Roy, Peter, and Alvin M. Despain. 1992. High-Performance Logic Programming with the Aquarius Prolog Compiler. *IEEE Computer* 25(1):54–68.

Varzi, Achille. 1998. Basic Problems of Mereotopology. In *Formal Ontology in Information Systems*; N. Guarino, ed. Amsterdam: IOS Press, pp. 29–38.

———. 2001. Vagueness in Geography. *Philosophy and Geography* 4(1):49–65. A version of this paper appeared as Vague Names for Sharp Objects in *Proceedings of the Workshop on Semantic Approximation, Granularity, and Vagueness: Principles of Knowledge Representation and Reasoning (KR-2000), April 12–16, Breckenridge, CO*; Leo Obrst and Inderjeet Mani, cochairs.

Varzi, Achille, and Fabio Pianesi. 1996a. Events, Topology, and Temporal Relations. *The Monist* 78(1):89–116.

———. 1996b. Refining Temporal Reference in Event Structures. *Notre Dame Journal of Formal Logic* 37(1):71–83.

Wallace, Mark, Stefano Novello, and Joachim Schimpf. 1997. ECLiPSe: A Platform for Constraint Logic Programming.

Wand, Yair. 1989. A Proposal for a Formal Model of Objects. In *Object-Oriented Concepts, Databases, and Applications*; Won Kim and Frederick Lochovsky, eds. Reading, MA: Addison-Wesley, pp. 537–559.

Warren, David H. D. 1977. *Applied Logic: Its Use and Implementation as Programming Tool*. Ph.D. Thesis, University of Edinburgh, Edinburgh, Scotland. Reprinted as Technical Note 290. Menlo Park, CA: Artificial Intelligence Center, SRI, International.

———. 1979. Prolog on the DECsystem-10. In *Expert Systems in the Micro-Electronic Age*; Donald Mitchie, ed. Edinburgh, Scotland: Edinburgh University Press.

———. 1983. An Abstract Prolog Instruction Set. Technical Note 309. Menlo Park, CA: Artificial Intelligence Center, SRI, International.

Wiederhold, Gio. 1994. An Algebra for Ontology Composition. In *Proceedings of 1994 Monterey Workshop on Formal Methods*. Monterey, CA: U.S. Naval Postgraduate School, pp. 56–61.

Wiederhold, Gio, and Jan Jannink. 1998. *Composing Diverse Ontologies*. Technical Report, August. Stanford, CA: Stanford University.

Wielinga, B., and A. Schreiber. 1993. Reusable and Shareable Knowledge Bases: A European Perspective. In *Proceedings International Conference on Building and Sharing of Very Large-Scaled Knowledge Bases '93, Tokyo, Japan, December 1993*. Japan Information Processing Development Center, pp. 103–115.

Wielinga, B., A. Schreiber, and J. Blenker. 1992. KADS: A Modeling Approach to Knowledge Engineering. *Knowledge Acquisition* 4(1):5–53.

Wiggins, D. 1980. *Sameness and Substance*. Oxford, U.K.: Blackwell.

Zdonik, Stanley B., and David Maier, eds. 1990. *Readings in Object-Oriented Database Systems*. San Mateo, CA: Morgan Kaufman.

Selected Information and Research Sites

AI on the Web: *http://www.cs.berkeley.edu/~russell/ai.html*

AT&T's CLASSIC: *http://www.research.att.com/sw/tools/classic/*

Brightware's Art-Enterprise: *http://www.brightware.com/products/art.html*

CLIPS: *http://www.ghg.net/clips/CLIPS.html*

Common KADS home page: *http://swi.psy.uva.nl/projects/CommonKADS/home.html*

DARPA Agent Markup Language (DAML): *http://www.daml.org/*

Federation for Intelligent Physical Agents (FIPA): *http://www.fipa.org/*

Formal Ontology in Information Technology, special issue of the *International Journal of Human-Computer Studies* 43(5/6), 1995, Nicola Guarino and Roberto Poli, eds.: *http://www.ladseb.pd.cnr.it/infor/Ontology/IJHCS/IJHCS.html*

GALEN project: *http://www.cs.man.ac.uk/mig/galen/*

Gensym's G2: *http://www.gensym.com/products/g2.htm*

Gio Wiederhold's Scalable Knowledge Composition Algebra: *http://www-db.stanford.edu/SKC/index.html*

High Performance Knowledge Bases (HPKB): *http://reliant.teknowledge.com/HPKB*

IRST Ontology page: *http://krr.irst.itc.it:1024/ontology.html*

ISI's LOOM home page: *http://www.isi.edu/isd/LOOM/*

Knowledge Engineering Methods and Languages: *ftp://swi.psy.uva.nl/pub/keml/keml.html*

Knowledge Interchange Format (KIF) Specification (draft proposed American National Standard [dpANS] NCITS.T2/98-004): *http://logic.stanford.edu/kif/dpans.html*

Knowledge Systems Laboratory, Stanford University: *http://ksl-web.stanford.edu/*

Ontological Foundations of Knowledge Engineering at Ladseb-CNR: *http://www.ladseb.pd.cnr.it/infor/Ontology/ontology.html*

Ontologies: What Are They, and Where's the Research? A panel held at KR'96, the Fifth International Conference on Principles of Knowledge Representation and Reasoning, November 5, 1996, Cambridge, Massachusetts: *http://www-ksl.stanford.edu/KR96/Panel.html*

Ontology Inference Layer: *http://www.ontoknowledge.org/oil/*

Peter Clark's Ontology Projects Site: *http://www.cs.utexas.edu/users/mfkb/related.html*

Protégé-2000: *http://protege.stanford.edu/*

Rapid Knowledge Formation (RKF): *http://reliant.teknowledge.com/RKF/*

Semantic Web: *http://www.w3.org/2001/sw/*

Teknowledge's M.4: *http://www.teknowledge.com/M4/index.html*

Toronto Ontologies for a Virtual Enterprise (TOVE): *http://www.ie.utoronto.ca/EIL/tove/toveont.html*

Unified Medical Language System (UMLS) project: *http://www.nlm.nih.gov/research/umls/umlsmain.html*

Chapter 8

TOPIC MAPS IN THE LIFE SCIENCES

JOHN PARK AND NEFER PARK

We have been asked to create a design for a new Web site that would allow learners all over the world to participate in the collection and representation of knowledge about the life sciences. Our goal is to develop a series of topic maps that will allow us to represent and navigate a large knowledge space. This chapter initiates a project that can be extended as a classroom exercise or a Web project or just studied as an illustration of how topic maps can be constructed. We begin with a literature review of life sciences concepts, then proceed to the design and construction of some basic topic maps that will provide a foundation for our Web site.

A Literature Review

This chapter explores many life sciences concepts that are widely used around the world. We cover the idea of the five kingdoms and go into some detail about the Animalia kingdom.[1]

We intend that our Web site will eventually be constructed so that people around the world can expand on the growing knowledge base there. Certainly, in the space of one chapter, we cannot cover everything learned in our research, but readers will be able to piece their knowledge and theories together with those of others and, perhaps, extend the work this chapter starts. This affords an opportunity for people to begin relating all of the life sciences together, linking them with math and other scientific domains, perhaps eventually linking to things artistic.

Our literature search was mostly conducted on the Web. Our research shows that if we are going to build a Web site where lots of different information can be captured using topic maps, it must begin with a knowledge structure that allows us to classify all living things. Such a knowledge structure has already been designed: it is called a

---

[1]Of course, we leave the rest of this taxonomic backbone as an exercise for interested readers.

taxonomy. There are lots of different opinions about how a life science taxonomy should be constructed, and the entire process of classification continues to evolve and change. For a long time, people have used a system that classifies living things into kingdoms. This chapter applies that system. (However, we believe that the Web site will allow for exploration of other taxonomic systems.) Now, let's explore the nature of classification.

The Need for Classification

Classification has been performed for as long as humans have been around. Throughout history humans have needed to group and separate things, putting those items into categories. Classification, as a subject of research, really begins with Aristotle and enters modern times with Carlous Linnaeus. However, as already mentioned, the process of classification remains a moving target.

Carlous Linnaeus, also known as Carl von Linné, is often called the Father of Taxonomy.[2] He was a Swedish biologist whose ambition was to catalog all known organisms. He used a polynomial[3] system to achieve his goal. In 1735 he published the first edition of his classification of living things, the *Systema Naturae*. His system (that is, the Linnaean system) of naming, grouping, and classifying organisms is used to this day. The highest level of classification is the kingdom, for example, the Animalia kingdom. Species are found as the last category in a list of classification terms, ordered from kingdom downward, that includes genus, family, order, class, and phylum. To see how the classification system works, we constructed two figures based on Web sites we visited. Figures 8–1 and 8–2 show where humans fit into the Linnaean system.

Figure 8–1 shows the taxonomy for humans, otherwise known as *Homo sapiens:* to what kingdom they belong and of what phylum, class, order, and family they are members. Figure 8–2 shows a more detailed view of how humans are classified. There are even more detailed levels of classification in the Animalia kingdom. We hope that our topic maps will reflect this detailed view.

We now turn to the five kingdoms and explore the levels of classification needed to describe animals in the Animalia kingdom.

---

[2]From *http://www.ucmp.berkeley.edu/history/linnaeus.html*, which is a page from the University of California at Berkeley's Museum of Paleontology Web site, accessed in April 2002.

[3]A polynomial, according to convention, is an algebraic equation with more than one term. Here, the word refers to the fact that we classify creatures with a series of names, as illustrated in Figure 8–1.

```
Linnaean System of Classification
Humans

Kingdom: Animalia
    Phylum: Chordata
        Class: Mammalia
            Order: Primates
                Family: Hominidae
                    Genus: Homo
                        Species: Sapiens
```

Figure 8–1   The Linnaean classification of humans. (Data used to create the figure was taken from two sources on the Web: Dennis O'Neil's Web site on Linnaean classification at *http://anthro.palomar.edu/animal/humans.htm*, and a Web site by Edward Goo on *Homo sapiens* at *http://www-classes.usc.edu/engr/ms/125/MDA125/living_files/frame.htm*, both accessed in April 2002.)

```
Linnaean System of Classification
Humans

Kingdom: Animalia
   Phylum: Chordata
 Subphylum: Vertebrata
    Class: Mammalia
  Subclass: Theria
 Infraclass: Eutheria
            Order: Primates
            Suborder: Anthropoidea
         Superfamily: Hominoidea
              Family: Hominidae
                 Genus: Homo
                   Species: Sapiens
```

Figure 8–2   A more detailed Linnaean classification of humans. (Data was taken from the sources listed for Figure 8–1.)

The Five Kingdoms

Every organism on Earth belongs to a kingdom. Originally, there were only two kingdoms: Animalia and Plantae. The five kingdoms classification system was proposed by R. H. Whittaker in 1969.[4] The five kingdoms now recognized are Monera, Protista,

---

[4]From *http://www.usoe.k12.ut.us/curr/science/sciber00/7th/classify/sciber/5king1.htm*, accessed in April 2002.

Table 8–1   The Five Kingdoms

Kingdom	Cell Organization	Method of Reproduction	Examples
Monera	Single or colony	Conjugation, fission	Bacteria, cyanobacteria
Protista	Single-celled (mostly), multicelled (some)	Conjugation, fission Asexual, sexual	Plankton, algae, amoeba, paramecium, diatoms
Fungi	Single-celled or multicelled	Spores, asexual, budding	Mushrooms, molds, mildews, yeast
Plantae	Multicelled	Propagation (grafting, budding, cutting, layering)	Angiosperms, gymnosperms, mosses, ferns
Animalia	Multicelled	Asexual, sexual	Sponges, worms, insects, mammals, reptiles, birds

Fungi, Plantae, and Animalia. Table 8–1 presents a composite of information about the five kingdoms based on the content of many of the Web sites (listed at the end of this chapter) we visited in our research.

Our research shows that the kingdoms are the largest and broadest classification unit[5]; each kingdom is composed of smaller classification units. Many Web sites and other sources state that there are 33 phyla in kingdom Animalia, while others state that there are 35 phyla.[6] We focus in this chapter on kingdom Animalia, and not the other kingdoms, because this chapter is intended to present only an example so that readers interested in the life sciences can think about, research, and develop their own ideas and theories and, perhaps, apply those ideas at our Web site.

Kingdom Animalia

The Animalia kingdom contains animals. Animals are defined as multicellular life forms (as compared to single-celled creatures such as bacteria, which are members of kingdom Monera). Animals are also *heterotrophic*, meaning they require complex organic compounds of nitrogen and oxygen typically found in other organisms to

---

[5]However, we will shortly mention that there exist *domains* based on cell type that reside above kingdoms.

[6]Differences in the number of phyla remind us that nothing in the life sciences can be "cast in concrete." Thus we expect our Web site will continue to change over time.

sustain life. Members of the Animalia kingdom reproduce sexually and inhabit many different environments. There are two subclassifications, called *subphyla*, into which animals are separated: invertebrates, which have no backbones, and vertebrates, which do have backbones. Invertebrates are simpler in form and function than vertebrates. Vertebrates are the most complex organisms in the animal kingdom.

The most well-known phyla of kingdom Animalia are the Mollusca, Porifera, Cnidaria, Platyhelminthes, Nematoda, Annelida, Arthropoda, Echinodermata, and Chordata, some of which are described in Table 8–2. As mentioned, there are 33 phyla (give or take a few), but, in terms of populations on Earth, these phyla named above make up the bulk of kingdom Animalia.

Table 8–2   Some of the Phyla for the Animalia Kingdom

Phylum	Attributes	Species
Chordata	Members of the Chordata phylum (chordates) include vertebrates and some invertebrates.	Humans and other mammals Birds Fish Reptiles Sea squirts Lancelets
Echinodermata	Members of the Echinodermata phylum (echinoderms) derive their name from their spiny skins. All creatures in this class are marine animals.	Starfish Sea cucumbers
Arthropoda	Members of the Arthropoda phylum (arthropods) constitute the largest population in the Animalia kingdom. An arthropod's body is covered with a hard, jointed skeleton.	Arachnids Insects Lobsters
Annelida	Members of the Annelida phylum (annelids) have soft bodies separated into segments. Each segment is used for crawling.	Earthworms Leeches Bristle worms
Mollusca	Members of the Mollusca phylum (mollusks) form the second largest population in the Animalia kingdom. Mollusks have hard shells and soft bodies	Squid Oysters Clams Snails

Source: *This table was constructed from data accessed in April 2002 at* http://encarta.msn.com. (Search for *Animalia*, then navigate to "Classification of Organisms.")

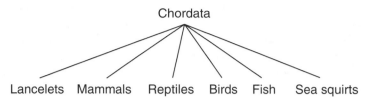

Figure 8–3   The Chordata phylum branching out into different classes

The *Chor* in *Chordata* refers to a spinal cord or backbone. Indeed, most of the classes in the Chordata phylum are vertebrates, as shown in Figure 8–3.

To keep this chapter simple enough to present, many of the details of the Linnaean classification system have been suppressed. To cite just one example, above kingdom there is the *domain* category. Domain Eukarya is of interest here because kingdom Animalia belongs to domain Eukarya, which means that members of kingdom Animalia are made of eukaryotic cells (described in Figure 8–4). Viruses are not part of any kingdom, due

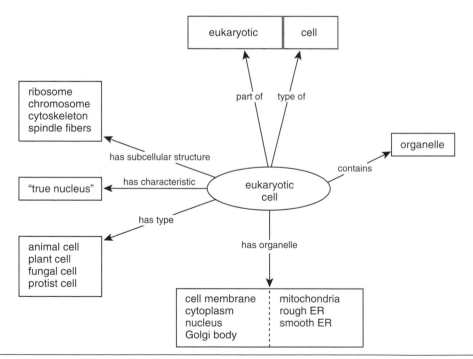

Figure 8–4   A concept map of a eukaryotic cell. (Reproduced with permission from Kathleen Fisher's Web site, *http://www.biologylessons.sdsu.edu/classes/lab7/semnet/ eukaryotic_cell.htm,* accessed in April 2002.)

to the fact that they are not cells and thus have nonliving characteristics. We hope that this kind of information will find its way into our topic maps eventually.

We now turn to the creation of our topic map, the design of which is based on our research and on some extended thinking about using XTM in a way not discussed elsewhere in this book: the drill-down pattern for topic map design.

Creating Topic Maps for a Web Site[7]

This section takes a designer's walk through the thought processes involved during the construction of the kind of topic map discussed here. We begin by sketching the design of several topic maps, each visualized as a layer that can be reached from another topic map by "drilling down" through a "higher" layer—a design pattern that could be as easy to implement as regular hyperlinks in a Web page.

A First View

Figure 8–5 is a big picture of the beginnings of our topic map. This first sketch presents our ideas about how a user might begin to navigate an imagined Web site by starting with the big picture, then drilling down to more detail by selecting topic maps that are, themselves, referenced as occurrences of some topic in the visible topic map. Figure 8–5 shows how two different typed occurrences will be used in the *Taxonomy* topic map; one is another topic map, and one is a book about the five kingdoms.

This is the method we visualize: a more detailed topic map is referenced as an occurrence of a particular topic in a less detailed topic map. We call this design pattern a *drill-down scheme*. Since XTM is a relatively new specification, it seems likely that other design patterns and methods for navigating between different topic maps will soon appear.

Creating the *FiveKingdoms* topic map means applying the same drill-down technique to each kingdom topic in the topic map, as shown in Figure 8–6.

Developing the XTM Document

Our plan is this: build the *Animalia* and *FiveKingdoms* topic maps so that they fit into the design structure sketched in Figures 8–5 and 8–6. Using Nexist, the open

---

[7]This section was created with a lot of help from our father, Jack Park. In fact, he used Nexist to create the XTM code presented here.

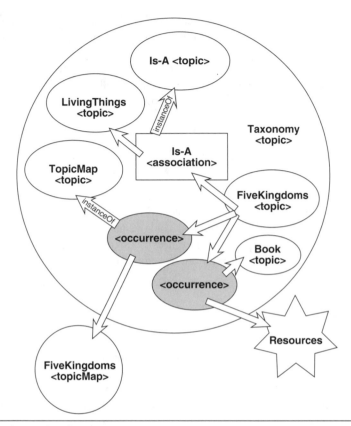

Figure 8–5   The top-level topic map

source software project discussed in Chapter 10 of this book, we will take a bottom-up approach. That is, we construct the *Animalia* topic map first. For now, the new topic map will remain empty. By creating it, we also create a database entry that we can reference later. Next, we construct the *FiveKingdoms* topic map. We take the bottom-up approach because, as we build the *FiveKingdoms* topic map, we'll make reference to the *Animalia topic map* when we construct an occurrence for the *Animalia topic*.[8] Similarly, for each of the other four kingdoms, before occurrences for each topic can be constructed, shell topic maps will be constructed.[9]

---

[8]Confusion alert: We are using the same word, *Animalia*, both to name a particular topic in one topic map and to provide a name for another topic map.

[9]The topic maps paradigm does not require a resource to exist before markup referencing it is created. See the proposed version of the ISO Reference Model, Section 11.2.5, at *http://www.y12.doe.gov/sgml/sc34/document/0243.htm*.

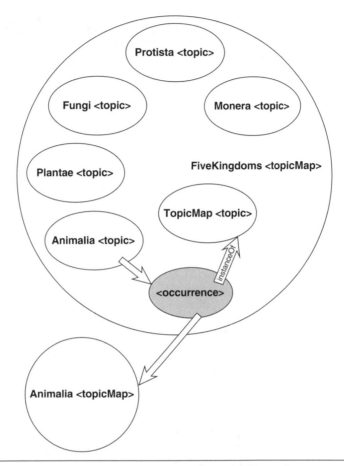

Figure 8–6   *FiveKingdoms* topic map pointing to the *Animalia* topic map

Let's follow the steps below, which use Nexist, to construct the project.

Step 1: Create a shell for the `Animalia` topic map.

Figure 8–7 shows how to make a shell topic map called *Animalia* that will later be used to represent the phyla of this kingdom. From there, further drilling down will eventually lead to genus and species levels.

Step 2: Create a shell for the `FiveKingdoms` topic map.

As shown in Figure 8–8, we next make the shell topic map that will contain topics that allow drilling down to topic maps for each of the five kingdoms.

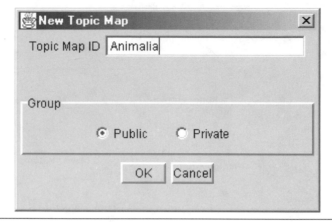

Figure 8–7   Creating the new *Animalia* topic map

Step 3: Create the TopicMap topic.

Now that we've created the *FiveKingdoms* topic map, it's time to begin the construction of the *Animalia* topic. Since one of its occurrences will be an instance of a topic map, the bottom-up design approach suggests that we first define the *TopicMap* topic. This particular topic must have a Published Subject Indicator (PSI), so we enter one while we construct the topic, as shown in Figure 8–9.[10]

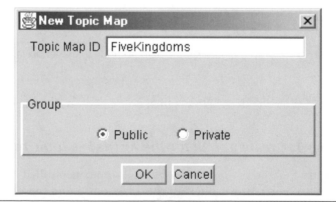

Figure 8–8   Creating the new *FiveKingdoms* topic map

---

[10]Development here called for a URI that is somewhat arbitrary. In the future, the specific PSI will, hopefully, reflect a URI that is a standard repository for PSIs.

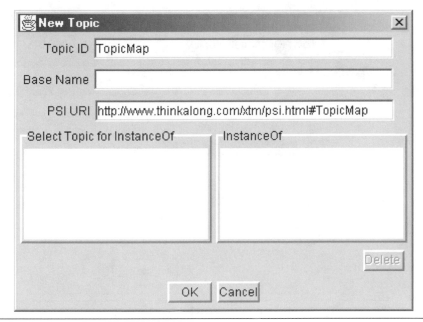

Figure 8–9   Creating the new *TopicMap* topic

Step 4: Create the `AnimaliaTopicMap` topic.

Our design anticipates that we will want to have each topic associated with a kingdom, and each occurrence will be an instance of the *TopicMap* topic. Suppose, however, that we might want to later add some associations to our occurrence. To do that, the occurrence must be *reified* [11] in a topic, so we insert a special topic, namely *AnimaliaTopicMap*, between the occurrence and the *TopicMap* topic. This means that our occurrence is an instance of *AnimaliaTopicMap*, which, itself, is an instance of *TopicMap*. A topic map engine that processes the XTM documents we are building here must be able to discover that our occurrence is, in fact, of type *TopicMap* and to present the occurrence according to the needs dictated by that occurrence type.

The new topic must be an instance of *TopicMap*, as illustrated in Figure 8–10.

Step 5: Create the `Animalia` topic.

Now we are ready to construct the topic that will serve as a container for one or more occurrences of type *TopicMap* and, perhaps, for other associated information.

---

[11] To *reify* is to make real. We do this by creating a topic that allows us to name the specific type of occurrence.

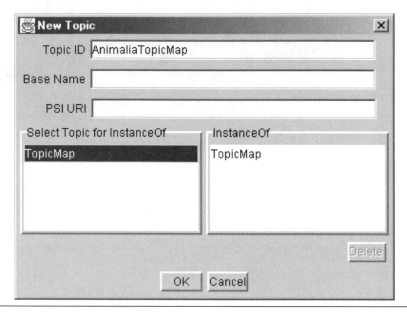

Figure 8–10   Creating the new *AnimaliaTopicMap* topic

This new topic is, at present, rather plain—not too much information, as shown in Figure 8–11.

With this topic, we are now able to construct an occurrence that links the *topic Animalia* with the *topic map Animalia*.

Step 6: Define an occurrence.

To construct an occurrence, we first select the *Animalia* topic in the TopicIDs pane in Nexist. Then we click the **New Occurrence** button. We begin occurrence construction by setting the InstanceOf parameter in the New Occurrence Editor window to *AnimaliaTopicMap*, as shown in Figure 8–12.

From there, we select the **Topic Map Occurrence** tab and select the *Animalia* topic map, as shown in Figure 8–13.

Selecting *Animalia* brings up the prompt shown in Figure 8–14.

Clicking the **Yes** button ends the New Occurrence session. We click the **Occurrences** button in Nexist and confirm that a new occurrence has been added. Since we

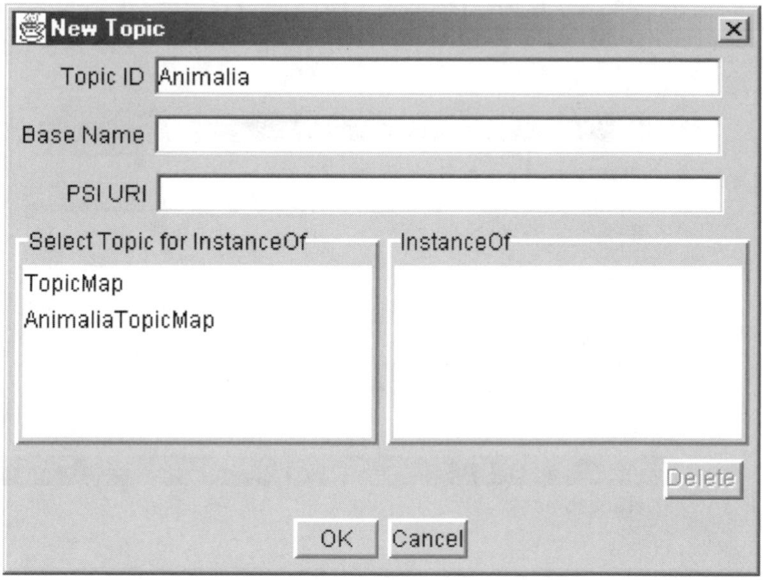

Figure 8–11 Creating the new *Animalia* topic

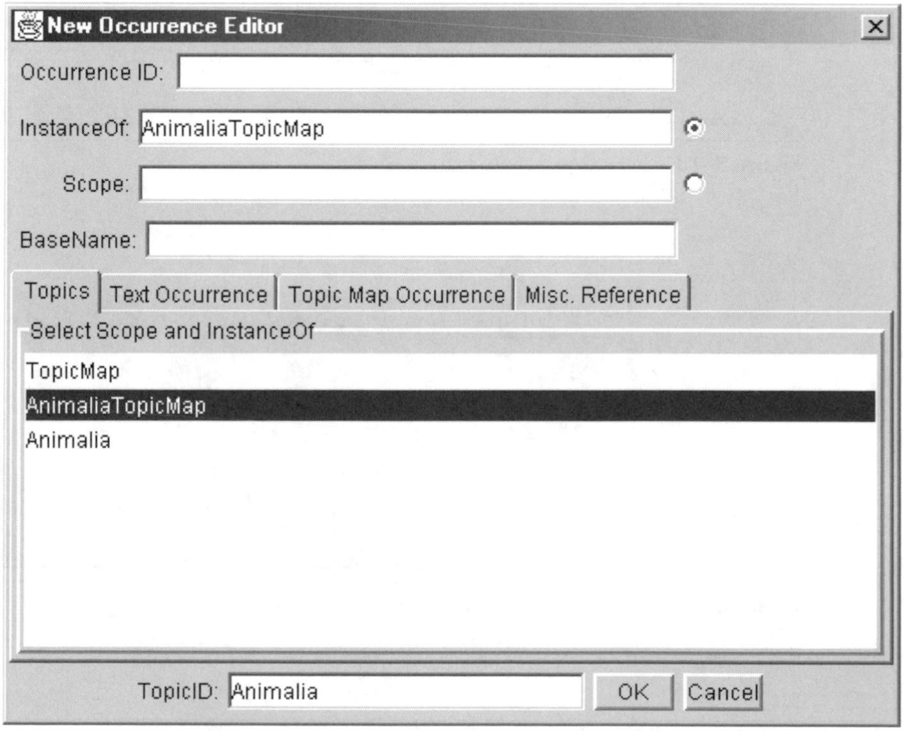

Figure 8–12 Setting the *InstanceOf* parameter in the New Occurrence Editor window

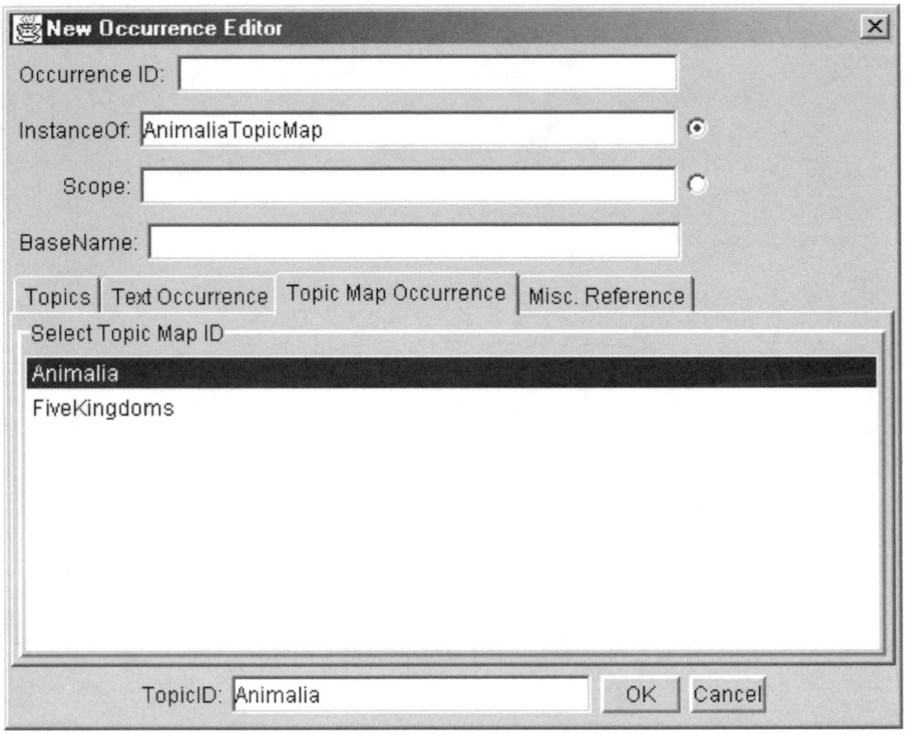

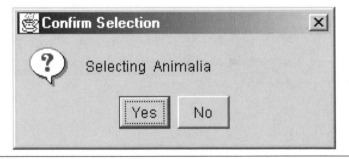

Figure 8–13   Selecting a topic map

Figure 8–14   The selection confirmation prompt

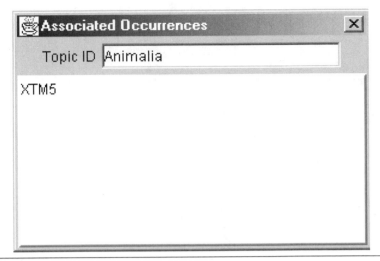

Figure 8–15   Viewing the new occurrence

did not define an OccurrenceID, Nexist has filled in one of its own: *XTM5*, as shown in Figure 8–15.

Where Are We Now?

Figure 8–16 shows precisely what we accomplished in steps 1–6.

We created two topic maps:

1. *Animalia*
2. *FiveKingdoms*

Within the *FiveKingdoms* topic map, we created three topics:

1. *TopicMap*
2. *AnimaliaTopicMap*
3. *Animalia*

Within the topic *Animalia*, we created an important occurrence, *XTM5*, which offers the topic map *Animalia* as its resource reference.

Here is the resulting XTM code for the topic map *Animalia*, which is just a shell for now.

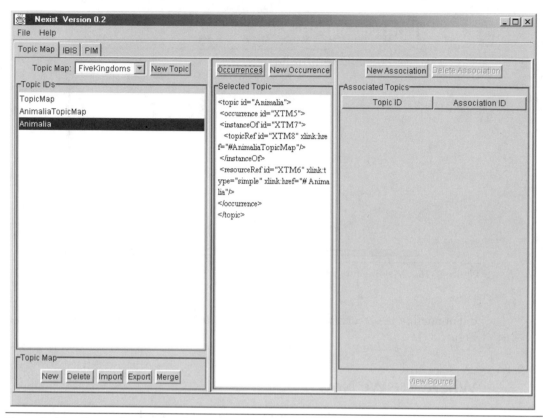

Figure 8–16   Our topic map thus far

```
<?xml version="1.0"?>
<!DOCTYPE topicMap SYSTEM "xtm1.dtd">
<topicMap xmlns="http://www.topicmaps.org/xtm/1.0/"
          xmlns:xlink="http://www.w3.org/1999/xlink"
          id="Animalia">

</topicMap>
```

The XTM code for the topic map *FiveKingdoms* is a bit more complex.

```
<?xml version="1.0"?>
<!DOCTYPE topicMap SYSTEM "xtm1.dtd">
<topicMap xmlns="http://www.topicmaps.org/xtm/1.0/"
          xmlns:xlink="http://www.w3.org/1999/xlink"
          id="FiveKingdoms">
```

```
<topic id="TopicMap">
  <subjectIdentity id="XTM1">
    <subjectIndicatorRef id="XTM2"
  xlink:href="http://www.thinkalong.com/xtm/psi.html#TopicMap"/>
  </subjectIdentity>
</topic>
<topic id="AnimaliaTopicMap">
  <instanceOf id="XTM3">
    <topicRef id="XTM4" xlink:href="#TopicMap"/>
  </instanceOf>
</topic>
<topic id="Animalia">
  <occurrence id="XTM5">
    <instanceOf id="XTM7">
      <topicRef id="XTM8" xlink:href="#AnimaliaTopicMap"/>
    </instanceOf>
    <resourceRef id="XTM6" xlink:type="simple" xlink:href="#Animalia"/>
  </occurrence>
</topic>
</topicMap>
```

Summary

In this chapter we constructed a topic map that is capable of referencing other topic maps using the drill-down design pattern. We created a resource reference aimed at a particular topic map, and we used that reference in an occurrence of a topic contained within another topic map. For this scheme to work, the topic map engine that presents our topic map must be capable of identifying the occurrence type. To permit identification of the occurrence type, we reified our occurrence in a topic, which, itself, is an instance of another topic (in our example, the *TopicMap* topic).[12]

The classification systems used in the life sciences are constantly evolving. This evolution tells us that any Web site applied to the representation of life sciences knowledge must, itself, be capable of sustaining evolutionary change. We believe that XML topic map applications will provide the ability to deal with change, perhaps by accommodating different versions of topic maps.

---

[12]Clearly, there may be other coding styles with which a drill-down capability can be generated. The style presented here was selected for its simplicity.

Resources for More Information on the Life Sciences

Some interesting Web sites are listed below.

http://www.perspective.com/nature/animalia

http://www.sidwell.edu/us/science/vlb5/Labs/Classification_Lab/classification_lab.html#background

http://animaldiversity.ummz.umich.edu/animalia.html

http://www.ucmp.berkeley.edu/history/linnaeus.html

http://www.kheper.auz.com/gaia/biosphere/kingdoms.htm

http://www.rmetzner-greenearth.org/geo_kingdoms.html

Chapter 9

CREATING AND MAINTAINING ENTERPRISE WEB SITES WITH TOPIC MAPS AND XSLT

NIKITA OGIEVETSKY

HTML offers excellent ways to deliver browsable information via the Web. A Web site is a "place" on the World Wide Web made up of one or more Web pages, often associated with a particular subject or theme. Examples of such Web sites are personal and business Web sites, online books, online stores, news portals, Web sites of online communities, and so on.

As a Web site grows and turns into a Web portal with a deeply interconnected Web site architecture in which users are provided a gateway to rich content—content with lots of links, images, and other types of information—its developers are faced with the growing challenges of enforcing link integrity and maintaining the enterprise look-and-feel standards and navigational order. Tasks that once were simple can turn into laborious and convoluted processes as the information resource base of the site expands.

However, enterprise Web site maintenance can be robust and straightforward. This chapter shows that using topic maps as the source code or site map of a Web site offers convenience, power, reliability, and rapid reconfigurability to the maintainers of large, complex Web sites.

Combining topic maps and XSLT technology opens fascinating new ways of using topic maps for the Web that facilitate the structuring of information and provide a consistent look and feel throughout entire Web sites. The Web design and implementation framework discussed here makes it almost impossible to break consistency, allowing Web masters to concentrate their efforts on delivering content while working with aggregation and syndication systems.[1]

---

[1]Here, the term *aggregation systems* refers to those Web sites that bring together content from many sources, while *syndication systems* are Web sites that either provide content syndicated by others or syndicate their own content for use on other Web sites.

In this chapter I assume that you are familiar with the XTM specification, as described in Chapter 2 by Michel Biezunski. I also assume that you have some familiarity with XSLT. XSLT can be used to transform XML documents into other XML documents and fragments, into HTML documents, and into plain text. (Ogievetsky [1999a] shows how to use XSLT to generate SQL scripts, JavaScript, Python, Java, and Perl.)

"An XSLT processor transforms a source document into a target document. An XSLT style sheet contains a set of template rules. A template rule has two parts: (1) a pattern, which is matched against nodes in the source tree, and (2) a template, which can be instantiated to form part of the result tree" [Ogievetsky 2001]. XSLT transformation is achieved by associating XPath patterns with XSLT templates. The processor seeks to match node patterns in the source document. For each match found, the processor applies an XSLT template to the matched XML source document and creates a fragment of transformed code (usually HTML) for the target document. When constructing the target document, elements from the source document can be filtered and reordered, and arbitrary structure can be added. More information on XSLT can be found in Kay [2001], Holman [2001], and other XSLT tutorials. Examples provided in this chapter work with Xalan and Saxon XSLT processors. These excellent processors are available free of charge from the *http://xml.apache.org/xalan-j/index.html* and *http://saxon.sourceforge.net/* Web sites.

The XTM Framework for the Web

The Cogitative Topic Map Websites (CTW) framework consists of three layers:

1. Topic map source code (markup) that controls Web site content and site maps
2. XSLT style sheets that control Web page layout and look-and-feel style
3. The whole Web universe of resources referenced by XTM topic `<occurrence>` resource locators

This framework was introduced for the first time in January 2000 at an XTM meeting in Alexandria, Virginia, and presented in August 2000 at the Extreme Technologies conference [Ogievetsky 2000]. The CTW framework is a further extension of the XML Web Applications Template Library (XWATL) [Ogievetsky 1999a, 1999b], which is built on XML Linking Language (XLink).

In the CTW framework, both the content and structure of an entire Web site are controlled by a single topic map document that provides for facilitated management of the site map and metadata in an undirected graph, as well as expedited maintenance of graphics, HTML fragments, and other external resources. In addition, the framework provides elegant solutions for natural language generation. Web sites built according to CTW are easily mergeable and dead link immune. XSLT brings a consistent look and feel as well as platform independence. XSLT style sheets can be shared among Web sites, providing even higher levels of consistency across the enterprise.

By default, Web pages in CTW are generated for every topic, with only one page per topic. Of course, this behavior can be easily customized based on topic types and other criteria. (See the XSLT Layout Layer section below.) Web page content is aggregated from topic characteristics. *Topic base names* and *name variants* are used for titles, hyperlink labels, and natural language generation. Different classes of *topic occurrences* are used to hold various types of HTML fragments, images, and so on. *Topic associations* control the site map and are transformed into navigational user interface elements such as hyperlinks, image maps, buttons, and so on.

Sounds great, doesn't it? Of course, nothing comes for free.

First, the CTW framework requires you to think of your content as a structured cognitive system. That is, when aggregating content you should be thinking in topic map terms. Thinking this way helps organize the knowledge represented on the Web site. (See Chapters 5 and 15 for more on knowledge representation and organization.)

Second, you have to design the look and feel of your pages in terms of *building blocks*. A building block in the XWATL framework is a visually, functionally, or semantically distinguishable page fragment. It can be as small as an individual image or as big as a news article. Thus, in the CTW framework, a Web page is composed of building blocks, each of which is a Web page fragment corresponding to a certain *topic characteristic* (a topic name, occurrence, or participation in an association). Different types of topic characteristics yield different types of page fragments, and different topic types yield different page layouts. In addition, pages and page fragments can be linked via explicit and implicit associations. Topic maps provide a very efficient way to maintain richly interlinked taxonomies of page types and page fragment types.

Thus, the building block requirement, which at first may seem to be an unnecessary constraint, in fact opens your mind to highly structured and even object-oriented thinking.

To optimize performance, CTW developers can identify static fragments and preprocess them at design or publishing time. Topic characteristics control whether corresponding building blocks are dynamic or should be preprocessed. In this chapter we are considering only static Web sites.[2]

---

[2]Additional material on this subject can be found at *http://www.cogx.com/ctw*.

But still . . . why do we need this intermediate knowledge repository in the form of a topic map? Why can't we just use something like Microsoft FrontPage to build nice Web pages filled with appropriate information?

Typically, an organization can cope with "nice Web pages" created with simple HTML editors while its Web site contains just a few pages. Problems arise as the amount of information resources increases and the user population grows more experienced and versatile. By then, the organization needs individual mechanisms for extracting information from each resource, merging that information with information from other resources, and rendering the results differently for different types of users. For n groups of users consuming information from m different information sources, you need at least $m*n$ different procedures—a combinatorial explosion (see Figure 9–1).

If you have an intermediate knowledge base only m extraction and n rendition procedures are required (see Figure 9–2). Obviously, maintenance is greatly facilitated when the combinatorial explosion is eliminated.

Maintaining source code for a Web site in a structured way significantly facilitates Web site architecture and maintenance. Topic maps were designed to facilitate navigating, searching, querying, filtering, customizing, and merging, and the CTW framework makes all these wonderful features available to Web developers. (Please refer to Chapter 2 for more on the history and design principles of the topic maps paradigm.)

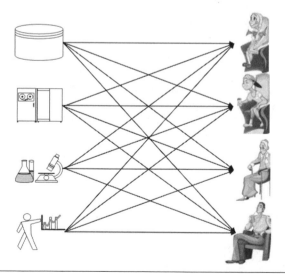

Figure 9–1   Separate extraction and rendition procedures needed for each information source and each group of users. (Images provided by arttoday.com.)

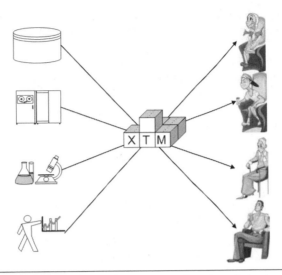

Figure 9–2   Facilitated maintenance with an intermediate knowledge base. (Images provided by arttoday.com.)

XTM as Source Code for Web Sites

There are presently several successfully implemented techniques for creating and using topic map documents as indexing layers on top of Web sites. In this approach, which provides powerful ways to facilitate navigation and visual comprehension of information, topic maps are created for existing knowledge bases (for example, books, conference proceedings, newsgroup postings, and other documents).

The CTW framework goes further, allowing use of XML topic maps as the source code for Web sites across the enterprise. A topic map can serve as the very foundation of Web site organization, a map fused into a territory. Authors start by devising their Web site ontology (see the Special Topic Map Website Ontology Layer section later in this chapter) and then populating the topic map according to the blueprinted rules. This also allows metadata to be maintained in a very structured way, at a higher level than that for a single site.

By default in the CTW framework, each topic can be rendered in the form of a Web page with topic characteristics yielding page content and classes of topics and topic characteristics controlling layout and rendition styles. The XSLT Layout Layer section below presents an example of how an XSLT processor can be instructed to generate Web pages only for certain types of topics. Note that in the case of a poorly constructed CTW topic map, some pages may be unreachable if their topics are not associated directly or indirectly with other topics in the source topic map document.

In other words, to make sense of the labyrinths of the information world, topic map authors collect and structure networks of pointers into the multidimensional information universe, distinguishing and classifying subjects they want to talk about by representing them as topics and assigning these topics categorized characteristics that presumably belong to, describe, relate to, and/or elucidate those subjects.

Thus a topic map document represents the view of its author on the information universe. As Michel Biezunski [2000] notes, topic maps are "style sheets for knowledge."

Indeed, style applies to more than just presentation and externals. We often say things like, "This is her style of thinking," or "He always sees things in his own way," or "from his perspective." A human being's comprehension is always influenced by a certain system of internal constraints; we unconsciously "style" information according to these constraints in order to categorize it comfortably, with minimal effort.

In the CTW framework, information is styled twice.

1. A human author styles information and organizes it in a topic map. He or she selects, classifies, and stores topics and their characteristics, including their associations with each other.
2. A program styles this topic map into a collection of interlinked Web pages (that is, a Web site) in order to present the accumulated knowledge to human readers in a convenient and friendly way. The program may apply XSLT style sheets to render the topic map on Web browsers in HTML, on wireless devices in Wireless Markup Language (WML), and so on.

In this chapter I assume that you have already learned how to accomplish the first step. Fitting your content into a cognitive schema and authoring topic maps are mentioned by Michel Biezunski (Chapter 2), Sam Hunting (Chapter 6), and John Park and Nefer Park (Chapter 8) in this book. These topics are also discussed on the TopicMaps.Org Web site (*http://www.topicmaps.org*), on the Web sites of topic map vendors, and in many other places.

Thus, let's move on to the design principles of the second step: designing your pages using building blocks. As an example, we will consider a very simple topic map of seashore creatures in Long Island, NY. This topic map is designed to provide an introductory approach to creating a topic map–driven Web site.

As a beginning scuba diver, I shot some pictures during my dives, learned some new information while talking with experienced scuba divers, and then went to a local library and collected more information from encyclopedias. I accumulated all these sources of information and organized them in a topic map that contains a representation of my knowledge about seashore creatures and my interpretation of the information I received. The next step is to create XSLT style sheets in order to share this knowledge with people via a Web site.

HTML Visualization of Topic Map Constructs

First, let's walk through the roles of various XTM elements and topic characteristics used to build XTM-driven Web sites. Table 9–1 shows a summary of the roles and HTML mappings in the CTW framework.

Now, let's look at the source topic map that represents my modest knowledge about local underwater life enhanced with images of the beautiful sea creatures captured on film.

Table 9–1   HTML Visualization and Styling of XTM Constructs

Topic Map Element	Rendered in HTML As
Topic map	Web site
Topic	Web page
Topic associations	Site map NLG text fragments*
Topic occurrences	Images, logo Text HTML fragments External links
Topic names	Page headers, titles Unordered and ordered lists Hyperlink titles NLG text fragments*

*Natural language–generated (NLG) text fragments are dynamic text fragments generated using topic characteristics as parameters and controlled by NLG templates—associations. This can be as simple as the common mail-merge function found in text editors and as complicated as a legal clause. NLG subsystem will be covered in one of the future volumes in this series. In the meantime you can read about it at *http://www.cogx.com/ctw*. NLG theory is covered in an excellent book *Building Natural Language Generation Systems* [Reiter and Dale 2000].

Topics

The `<topic>` elements in the topic map can be related explicitly by means of `<association>` and `<instanceOf>` elements and implicitly by means of scopes and characteristic assignments, thus providing many powerful ways to create and use an undirected graph of rich and deeply structured content.

Sometimes page content can embed the characteristics of more than one topic. This behavior can be specified for certain association classes or if the page content should reflect results of a topic map query expressed in XPath, or (in the future) in Topic Map Query Language (TMQL). Both cases go beyond the scope of this chapter and are not considered here. Now let's consider two special types of topics that play very important roles in our framework.

Special `<topic>` Elements: Root

A `<topicMap>` element is itself a resource. Any resource can indicate the subject of a topic. Therefore, a `<topicMap>` element can itself indicate the subject of a topic in any given topic map. A topic whose subject is indicated by the topic map document is called the *root topic*. It is said to reify the topic map.

The Web page generated for this root topic becomes the default page of the generated Web site. It is the first Web page (or WML card) that users see when entering the Web site. In the CTW framework all topic characteristics such as occurrences, topic names, and associations implicitly contain the root topic. This root topic will be added to the scopes of all characteristic assignments in its parent map when that map is merged with other maps. Thus, when we merge two CTW-based Web sites, we have a way to preserve individual styles and layouts when rendering topic characteristics brought from different merged documents.

Note that a base name or any other topic characteristic assignment with no explicitly specified scope is said to have an *unconstrained scope*. In the CTW implementation, the unconstrained scope is treated as if it contained the only the root topic. (See Sam Hunting's Chapter 6 and Kal Ahmed's XTM Programming with TM4J section of Chapter 10 in this book for general discussions on scopes and unconstrained scope.)

The code in Listing 9–1 shows the source code of the default topic (which in this code has the ID attribute *default*) of the Long Island Seashore Creatures Web page. Its `<subjectIndicatorRef>` child element points to the containing (parent) `<topicMap>` element.

Occurrence classes such as *landsc-img, description*, and others form the Special Topic Map Website Ontology Layer (STWOL), considered in the next section.

```
<topicMap xmlns:xlink="http://www.w3.org/1999/xlink" id="map">
  <topic id="default">
    <subjectIdentity>
      <subjectIndicatorRef xlink:href="#map"/>
    </subjectIdentity>
    <baseName>
      <baseNameString>Long Island Seashore
          Creatures</baseNameString>
    </baseName>
    <occurrence>
      <instanceOf>
        <topicRef xlink:href="#description"/>
      </instanceOf>
      <resourceData>As a beginning scuba diver, I shot some
          pictures during my dives, learned some new
          information while {. . .}
      </resourceData>
    </occurrence>
    <occurrence>
      <instanceOf>
        <topicRef xlink:href="#landsc-img"/>
      </instanceOf>
      <scope><topicRef xlink:href="#nikita"/></scope>
      <resourceRef xlink:href="ocean5.jpg"/>
    </occurrence>
    <occurrence>
      <instanceOf><topicRef xlink:href="#landsc-img"/></instanceOf>
      <scope><topicRef xlink:href="#nikita"/></scope>
      <resourceRef xlink:href="ocean14.jpg"/>
    </occurrence>
  </topic>
{. . .}
</topicMap>
```

Listing 9–1   Source code for the root topic

Figure 9–3 shows a page generated from the XTM source code presented above. It has the base name as the overall title, a list of animal taxonomy as the site map navigation bar on the left side (see the Querying and Displaying Topic Associations section), two photo image occurrences with credits for their photographers on the right, and an occurrence of descriptive type in the center. As a designer of the source code topic map, I decided to credit image authors via the scoping facility; scope is often used to indicate the source of an association.

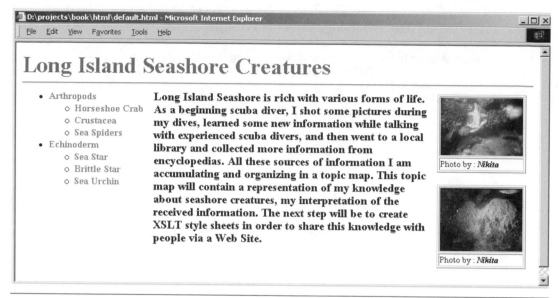

Figure 9–3   A Web page rendered for a root topic

The Special Topic Map Website Ontology Layer

A special category of topics mentioned above, the STWOL, has a very important role in the CTW rendition and publishing process. This layer consists of topic classes, classes of topic characteristics, and association templates, as well as association membership roles and scoping topics (also called *scoping themes*). Individual definitions of all these notions are covered elsewhere in this book and on the TopicMaps.Org Web site, so let's skip them to go directly to the application of the STWOL in the CTW publishing framework.

Note that STWOL is an imaginary subdivision, and any topic can become a part of it by virtue of being referenced by some other topic.[3] The concept of the STWOL is not XTM specific; however, most of the vendors and researchers working with topic maps came up with somewhat similar notions. For example, other publications may refer to "housekeeping topics," "the topic map kernel," "typing topics," "topic map schemas," and "the conceptual layer." In my original paper [Ogievetsky 2000] I called this category "system topics." It is also important to note that the ISO committee is

---

[3]*Editor's note:* Contrast this "late-binding" author-driven approach to ontological commitment with the approach outlined by Holger Rath in Chapter 14.

working on a topic map Reference Model, a Standard Application Model, and the Topic Map Constraint Language (TMCL), which together should embrace all of the above.

XSLT templates for page layout are dynamically chosen based on their corresponding topic types. XSLT templates for page fragment rendition and styling are chosen based on the types of corresponding topic characteristics. In other words, STWOL topics referenced as topic types control page layout, and STWOL topics referenced as types of topic characteristics control XSLT styling of Web page elements and building blocks. This is the main reason why STWOL topics are so important in the CTW framework.

The scoping themes of topic characteristics are used for querying and filtering. For example, scopes determine the name or resource appropriate in the current context. Another example of using scoping topics is presented in Ogievetsky and Rodygin [2000], where simile associations are used to build dynamic taxonomies.

Let's consider an example from the Long Island Seashore Creatures Web page mentioned earlier. The code in Listing 9–2 shows the <topic> element *sea-star*, an instance of *animal-class* (line 2). Besides the name *sea-star* (a base name in the unconstrained scope on line 7), this topic has a scientific name, *Asteroidea* (a base name in the *taxon* scope, lines 3–6), and is also called *starfish* (a base name in the *also-known-as* scope, lines 8–11).

```
1.   <topic id="sea-star">
2.   <instanceOf><topicRef xlink:href="#animal-class"></instanceOf>
3.    <baseName>
4.     <scope><topicRef xlink:href="#taxon"></scope>
5.     <baseNameString>Asteroidea</baseNameString>
6.    </baseName>
7.    <baseName><baseNameString>sea-star</baseNameString></baseName>
8.    <baseName>
9.     <scope><topicRef xlink:href="#also-known-as"/></scope>
10.    <baseNameString>starfish</baseNameString>
11.   </baseName>
12.  <occurrence>
13.   <instanceOf><topicRef xlink:href="#landsc-img"/></instanceOf>
14.   <scope><topicRef xlink:href="#nikita"/></scope>
15.   <resourceRef xlink:href="ocean6.jpg"/>
16.  </occurrence>
17.  <occurrence>
18.   <instanceOf><topicRef xlink:href="#landsc-img"/></instanceOf>
19.   <scope><topicRef xlink:href="#john"/></scope>
20.   <resourceRef xlink:href="ocean8.jpg"/>
21.  </occurrence>
22.  <occurrence>
23.   <instanceOf><topicRef xlink:href="#definition"/></instanceOf>
```

```
24.  <scope><topicRef xlink:href="#audubon"/></scope>
25.  <resourceData>The asteroid body has the form of a somewhat
         flattened star with arms (rays) usually numbering 5 or a
         multiple of 5{. . .}
26.  </resourceData>
27.  </occurrence>
28.  <occurrence>
29.  <instanceOf><topicRef xlink:href="#definition"/></instanceOf>
30.  <scope><topicRef xlink:href="#audubon"/></scope>
31.  <resourceData>The stars can regenerate lost arms{. . .}
32.  </resourceData>
33.  </occurrence>
34.  </topic>
35.  <association>
36.  <instanceOf><topicRef
         xlink:href="#class-subclass"/></instanceOf>
37.  <member>
38.  <roleSpec><topicRef xlink:href="#class"/></roleSpec>
39.  <topicRef xlink:href="#echinoderm"/>
40.  </member>
41.  <member>
42.  <roleSpec><topicRef xlink:href="#sub-class"/></roleSpec>
43.  <topicRef xlink:href="#sea-star"/>
44.  <topicRef xlink:href="#brittle-star"/>
45.  <topicRef xlink:href="#sea-urchin"/>
46.  </member>
47. </association>
```

Listing 9–2   Source code for the *sea-star* topic

I have several photos of sea stars. One taken by me (hence, in the scope of *nikita*) is represented by the <occurrence> element in lines 12–16, and one taken by my friend John (hence, in the scope of *john*) is represented by the <occurrence> element in lines 17–21. I also inserted descriptions of sea stars from the National Audubon Society [1981] and *The American Heritage Dictionary*, 1995 edition, represented by the <occurrence> elements in lines 22–33.

I learned from encyclopedias that class Asteroidea belongs to phylum Echinodermata, so these creatures fall in the category of echinoderms. So I used the *class-subclass* association to express the fact that the *sea-star*, *brittle-star*, and *sea-urchin* elements are subclasses of the *echinoderm* class. This fact is represented by the <association> element in lines 35–47.

Figure 9–4 shows a page generated from the XTM source code presented above. The page has the base name of the root topic as the overall title and the site map navigation bar on the left side. The main part of the page contains information directly

Figure 9–4   A Web page rendered for the `sea-star` topic

related to sea stars. The base name in the unconstrained scope is rendered in the largest font followed by the scientific name (in the *taxon* scope); the other name (in the *also-known-as* scope) is rendered in square brackets. Images are on the right, each in a two-row table: first row, the image itself; second row, the photographer's name. Descriptions of sea stars appear in the center with bibliographic references in square brackets underneath.

Note that in this example I made a design decision to express authorship via the scoping facility. In other words, the fact that a *definition* occurrence of *sea-star* in lines 22–27 is in the *audubon* scope can be read as, "In the context of the *National Audubon Society Field Guide of North American Seashore Creatures*, the definition of sea star is '*[text]*.'" Similarly, the fact that a *landsc-img* occurrence in lines 12–16 is in the scope of *nikita* can be read as, "This is a picture that Nikita claims is a photograph of a sea star that he took on the sea shore of Long Island."

The code for STWOL topics referenced by the *sea-star* topic is presented in Listing 9–3.

```
<topic id="animal-class">
  <instanceOf><topicRef xlink:href="#taxon"></instanceOf>
  <baseName><baseNameString>Class</baseNameString></baseName>
</topic>
<topic id="landsc-img">
  <instanceOf><topicRef xlink:href="#img"></instanceOf>
</topic>
<topic id="nikita">
  <instanceOf>
      <topicRef xlink:href="#underwater-photograph"></instanceOf>
  <subjectIdentity>
    <subjectIndicatorRef xlink:href="urn:padi-diver-no:9907571524">
  </subjectIdentity>
</topic>
<topic id="portr-img">
  <instanceOf><topicRef xlink:href="#img"></instanceOf>
</topic>
<topic id="john">
  <instanceOf>
      <topicRef xlink:href="#underwater-photograph"></instanceOf>
  <subjectIdentity>
    <subjectIndicatorRef xlink:href="urn:padi-diver-no:9999999999">
  </subjectIdentity>
</topic>
<topic id="definition">
  <instanceOf><topicRef xlink:href="#orole"></instanceOf>
</topic>
<topic id="description">
  <instanceOf><topicRef xlink:href="#orole"/></instanceOf>
</topic>
<topic id="orole">
  <subjectIdentity>
    <subjectIndicatorRef
      xlink:href="http://www.topicmaps.org/xtm/1.0/psi1.xtm#
          association-role">
  </subjectIdentity>
</topic>
<topic id="also-known-as">
  <baseName>
      <baseNameString>also known as</baseNameString></baseName>
</topic>
<topic id="taxon">
```

```
  <baseName><baseNameString >taxon</baseNameString></baseName>
  <occurrence>
    <instanceOf><topicRef xlink:href="#definition"/></instanceOf>
    <resourceData>Level or grouping in the animal
        hierarchy.<resourceData>
  </occurrence>
</topic>
<topic id="class-subclass">
  <subjectIdentity>
    <subjectIndicatorRef
      xlink:href="http://www.topicmaps.org/xtm/1.0/psi1.xtm#
          at-superclass-subclass"/>
  </subjectIdentity>
</topic>
<topic id="class">
  <subjectIdentity>
    <subjectIndicatorRef
      xlink:href="http://www.topicmaps.org/xtm/1.0/psi1.xtm#
          role-superclass"/>
  </subjectIdentity>
</topic>
<topic id="sub-class">
  <subjectIdentity>
    <subjectIndicatorRef
        xlink:href="http://www.topicmaps.org/xtm/1.0/psi1.xtm#
            role-subclass"/>
  </subjectIdentity>
</topic>
```

Listing 9–3   Source code for STWOL topics referenced by the *sea-star* topic

Note that there is an explicit referential constraint: any referenced topic should exist. In particular, if a topic element, a topic characteristic, or a topic association is pointing to another topic as a class or scoping theme, this second topic should exist explicitly in the form of a <topic> element, and by pure virtue of being pointed to it becomes a STWOL topic. In other words, the -xlink:href- attribute of the <topicRef> element imposes the same constraint as the -IDREF- attribute in XML except that -xlink:href- applies across multiple documents. You can also find similarity between this constraint and the referential integrity rule in relational database architecture by drawing an analogy between documents and tables and between -xlink:href- attributes and foreign keys. Surprisingly, this obvious rule is very fragile and can be easily broken.

Note that unlike <topicRef>, <resourceRef> and <subjectIndicatorRef> can address any XTM element by its ID. However, all three addressing mechanisms bear different semantics. For more information, please refer to Chapters 2 and 6.

The referential constraint obviously also applies to STWOL topics. Listing 9–4 defines the STWOL topics referenced by the STWOL topics in Listing 9–3.

```
<topic id="img">
  <instanceOf><topicRef xlink:href="#orole"/></instanceOf>
  <baseName><baseNameString>Image</baseNameString></baseName>
</topic>
<topic id="underwater-photograph">
  <instanceOf><topicRef xlink:href="#person"/></instanceOf>
  <baseName>
    <baseNameString>Underwater Photograph</baseNameString>
  </baseName>
</topic>
<topic id="person">
  <instanceOf><topicRef xlink:href="#animal"/></instanceOf>
  <baseName><baseNameString>Animal</baseNameString></baseName>
</topic>
```

Listing 9–4   Source code for STWOL `<topic>` elements

Note that sometimes the same STWOL topic can be both a topic class and a scoping topic. Thus, if a topic is an instance of several classes, it can have different names in the scopes of different classes. For example, in Listing 9–2, `taxon` is referenced as a scoping topic of the base name `Asteroidea`, and in Listing 9–3 `taxon` is referenced as a type of `animal-class` topic.

XSLT Layers

In CTW, following the framework introduced in XWATL [Ogievetsky 1999a, 1999b], XSLT style sheets are divided into three layers:

1. *The back-end or query layer.* This layer is responsible for extracting required information from the topic map, assembling natural language generation constructs, and building syntax that aggregation and syndication software agents can understand.
2. *The layout layer.* This layer controls how HTML elements are arranged on the Web page or WML card. It calls presentation-layer templates to style content.
3. *The presentation layer.* This layer contains XSLT templates responsible for the particular look and feel of the Web pages or WML cards. Note that the presentation and layout layers can be altered to build other presentations of the Web site, for example, WML or VoiceML.

The notions of the back-end (query), layout, and presentation layers are specific to the XWATL and CTW frameworks and do not belong to XSLT in general. Let's look in depth first at the XSLT layout layer. The back-end and presentation layers will be considered in the section after the next one.

The XSLT Layout Layer

Listing 9–5 shows an XSLT page generation and layout template.

```
1.  <xsl:template match="topicMap">
2.   <xsl:for-each select="topic">
3.    <xsl:document href="concat($out-dir,@id,'.html')">
4.    <!--In Xalan:
5.      <redirect:write select="concat($out-dir,@id,'.html')"-->
6.     <html>
7.      <header><style>{. . .}</style>
8.       <title><xsl:template name="name"/></title>
9.      </header>
10.     <body>
11.     <a href="default.html" class="h1">
12.      <xsl:call-template name="name">
13.       <xsl:with-param name="topic" select="$root"/>
14.      </xsl:call-template>
15.     </a>
16.     <hr/>
17.     <table width="800"><tr>
18.      <td valign="top" width="200">
19.       <xsl:call-template name="sitemap">
20.        <xsl:with-param name="classRef"
21.         select="'#animal-kingdom'"/>
22.        <xsl:with-param name="current" select="."/>
23.       </xsl:call-template>
24.      </td>
25.      <td valign="top">
26.       <xsl:call-template name="page-layout"/>
27.      </td>
28.     </tr></table>
29.     </body>
30.    </html>
31.   </xsl:document >
32.  </xsl:for-each>
33. </xsl:template>
```

Listing 9–5   An XSLT page generation and layout template

Let's look at what's happening in this code. Line 1 specifies that this template is to be instantiated for the `<topicMap>` element. Once inside the template, in line 2 we iterate over all `<topic>` elements in the topic map in order to create and output individual HTML pages. In line 3 we use XSLT 1.1 syntax to create multiple result documents. At the time of writing, this feature is available only in Saxon; other processors implementing XSLT 1.0 offer proprietary solutions (an example of Xalan syntax appears in the comments in lines 4-5). Output file names in lines 3 and 5 are formed by concatenating the output directory `$out-dir` path with the topic `-id-` and the `.html` suffix.

Note that in line 2 we could modify the default page-per-topic rule by specifying an XPath expression to filter topics based on certain criteria (for example, only topics of type *class* or *phylum*).

Now we start building actual HTML code. In line 8 we call the *name* XSLT template (discussed below in the Querying and Displaying Topic Names section) to extract the base name in the unconstrained scope and use it for the HTML header title. Then in line 10 we start creating the body of the HTML page. Across the top of the page we display the Web site title (lines 11–15) corresponding to the base name of the default topic in the unconstrained scope. (See Figures 9–3 and 9–4.) This title also serves as a hyperlink to the default page. The main part of the page is divided into two parts. On the left side, there is a site map navigation tree corresponding to the Long Island Seashore Creatures animal kingdom taxonomy. (See the Querying and Displaying Topic Associations section for more discussion on this.) For the center and right side of the page we call the *page-layout* template, which generates topic-specific layouts. Listing 9–6 presents this template.

```
1.   <xsl:template name="page-layout">
2.   <!--determine type of context topic-->
3.   <xsl:variable name="taxon">
4.    <xsl:call-template name="getTopicRef">
5.     <xsl:with-param name="topic" select="."/>
6.     <xsl:with-param name="ref">#taxon</xsl:with-param>
7.    </xsl:call-template>
8.   </xsl:variable>
9.   <xsl:choose>
10.   <xsl:when test="$taxon='phylum'">
11.    <xsl:call-template name="phylum-page-layout"/>
12.   </xsl:when>
13.   <xsl:when test="$taxon='class'">
14.    <xsl:call-template name="class-page-layout"/>
15.   </xsl:when>
16.   <xsl:otherwise>
17.    <xsl:call-template name="generic-page-layout"/>
18.   </xsl: otherwise>
```

```
19.  </xsl:choose>
20. </xsl:template>
```

Listing 9–6 The *page-layout* template, which generates topic-specific layouts

This code calls the *getTopicRef* template (lines 4–7) to determine whether the current topic is an instance of animal classification taxonomy *taxon* and, if so, to which classification group it belongs. (This template is discussed further in the Querying Topic Types section below.) If the current topic is an instance of the *taxon phylum*, the template calls the *phylum-page-layout* template designed to display information about a phylum (line 11); and if the current topic is an instance of the *class taxon*, the template calls the *class-page-layout* template designed to display information about animal classes (line 14). Otherwise, the template builds a generic page using the *generic-page-layout* template (line 17).

Listing 9–7 shows each of the referenced layouts. An HTML page generated by the *class-page-layout* template is shown in Figure 9–4, and an HTML page generated by the *generic-page-layout* template is shown in Figure 9–3.

```
1.  <xsl:template name="class-page-layout">
2.  <h1><xsl:call-template name="name"/></h1>
3.  <h3>Class
4.   <xsl:call-template name="name">
5.    <xsl:with-param name="scope">taxon</xsl:with-param>
6.   </xsl:call-template>
7.  </h3>
8.  [<xsl:call-template name="name">
9.    <xsl:with-param name="scope">also-known-as</xsl:with-param>
10. </xsl:call-template>]
11. <hr/>
12. <table align="right"><tr><td align="right">
13.  <xsl:apply-templates
14.      select="occurrence[instanceOf/topicRef/@xlink:href =
15.                                     '#landsc-img']"/>
16.  <xsl:apply-templates
17.      select="occurrence[instanceOf/topicRef/
18.         @xlink:href ='#portr-img']"/>
19. </td></tr></table>
20. <xsl:apply-templates
21.      select="occurrence[instanceOf/topicRef/
22.         @xlink:href =  '#definition']"/>
23. </xsl:template>
24. <xsl:template name="phylum-page-layout">
25. <h1><xsl:call-template name="name"/></h1>
26. <h2>Phylum
27.   <xsl:call-template name="name">
```

```
28.    <xsl:with-param name="scope">taxon</xsl:with-param>
29.   </xsl:call-template>
30.  </h2>
31.  <hr/>
32.  <xsl:apply-templates select="occurrence"/>
33.  <hr/>
34.  Classes of Phylum <xsl:call-template name="sitemap">
35.   <xsl:with-param name="classRef" select="concat('#',@id)"/>
36.   <xsl:with-param name="current" select="."/>
37.  </xsl:call-template>
38. </xsl:template>
39. <xsl:template name="generic-page-layout">
40.  <table align="right"><tr><td align="right">
41.   <xsl:apply-templates
42.        select="occurrence[instanceOf/topicRef/
43.           @xlink:href ='#landsc-img']"/>
44.   <xsl:apply-templates
45.        select="occurrence[instanceOf/topicRef/
46.           @xlink:href = '#portr-img']"/>
47.  </td></tr></table>
48.  <xsl:apply-templates
49.        select="occurrence[instanceOf/topicRef/@xlink:href =
50. '#description']"/>
51. </xsl:template>
```

Listing 9–7   Topic-specific page layout templates

Figure 9–5 shows a page generated using the *phylum-page-layout* template for phylum Arthropoda. The main part of the page contains the base name in the unconstrained scope rendered in the largest font; below is the scientific name (in the scope of *taxon*). Occurrences of type *definition* follow with definition sources presented as bibliographic references in square brackets. As mentioned before, in the CTW framework, an occurrence's scope indicates its source. On the very bottom of the page appears the fragment of the taxonomy tree corresponding to the children of the phylum.

A Note on Namespace Declaration. I want to bring your attention to the fact that for simplicity I omitted XTM namespace declarations in all XSLT fragments throughout this chapter. In order for the XSLT samples to work you should either strip off the default XTM namespace declaration or you should declare and use the XTM namespace in your XSLT style sheet as shown in Listing 9–8. (Line numbers are the same as those in Listing 9–7.) Appendixes B and C in the back of this book contain two source topic map documents and two corresponding style sheets for this chapter: one that omits the default namespace declaration and one that explicitly declares it.

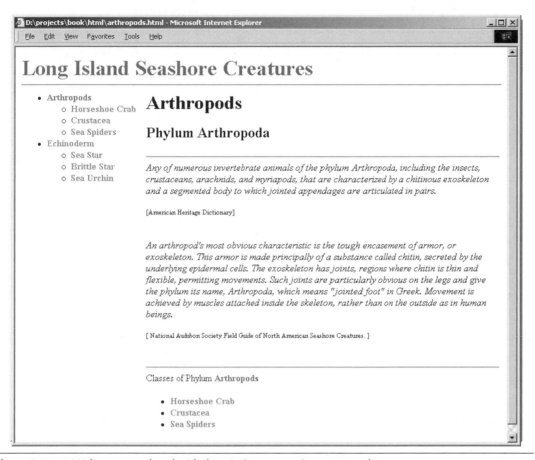

Figure 9–5   A Web page rendered with the *phylum-page-layout* template

```
<xsl:stylesheet  xmlns:xsl="http://www.w3.org/1999/XSL/Transform"
   xmlns:xlink="http://www.w3.org/1999/xlink"
   xmlns:xtm="http://www.topicmaps.org/xtm/1.0/"
   version="1.0">
. . .
32. <xsl:apply-templates select="xtm:occurrence"/>
. . .
44.  <xsl:apply-templates
45.    select="xtm:occurrence[xtm:instanceOf/
46.       xtm:topicRef/@xlink:href = '#portr-img']"/>
. . .
</xsl:stylesheet>
```

Listing 9–8   Modifications to Listing 9–7 if XTM namespace is declared

The XSLT Back-End and Presentation Layers

Now we will look at using XSLT templates from the back-end (query) and presentation layers to extract and visualize metadata and relationships.

Querying Topic Types

The templates in Listing 9–6 call the *getTopicRef* XSLT template to find instantiated ancestor *<topic>* elements along certain <instanceOf> *channels* (see below). In this section, as promised above, we examine how this works. Listing 9–9 shows a code fragment calling the *getTopicRef* template.

```
<xsl:call-template name="getTopicRef">
  <xsl:with-param name="topic"
    select="key('topic',instanceOf/topicRef/@xlink:href))"/>
  <xsl:with-param name="ref">#orole</xsl:with-param>
</xsl:call-template>
```

Listing 9–9   XSLT fragment calling the *getTopicRef* template

Let's look at what I call *channels*. This is where STWOL <topic> classes come into play. Sometimes you need to determine whether a given <topic>, <association>, association <member>, or <occurrence> element is an instance of a certain type. For example, you need to know this in order to determine the rendering style for a given topic characteristic or the content layout for a given <topic> element.

In the CTW framework, we distinguish several levels of abstraction. These levels can be thought of as *resolution levels*. *Resolution* here is used in the same way as it is used in geographical maps. (See also Chapter 11 for discussion on clustering and scaling in topic map visualization.) In the highest resolution mode all topics can be characterized as resources, key words, concepts, association member types, association types, occurrence types, and so forth. At the next level of abstraction we distinguish various flavors of the basic types mentioned above. In this context the basic types can be called *channels* or *bouquets* (from bouquet of fragrances) as introduced in Ogievetsky and Rodygin [2000].

A topic in XTM can be an instance of one or more topic classes. For example, topic *nikita* can be an instance of *scuba-diver* and *XTM-developer*.

Let's look at a typical topic characteristic assignment in Figure 9–6. It shows a connection between a topic, T, and a resource, R. This diagram establishes an occurrence of type O that is valid in scope S. Scope S is a set of scoping topics (themes): S1, S2,

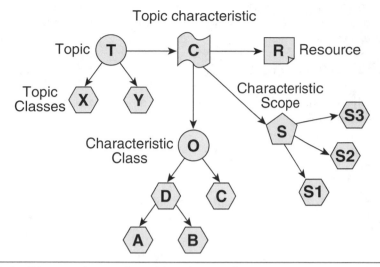

Figure 9–6   Diagram of a sample topic occurrence characteristic

and S3. Topic O, which is a class of occurrence C, is itself an instance of topics D and C (in other words, topics D and C are types of topic O). Topic D is an instance of topics A and B. Note that topics O, A, B, C, D, S1, S2, and S3 are all STWOL topics.

Now let's look at this diagram from another angle. A topic can be instantiated by a set of topics. For example, class squids and class snails are both instances of phylum Mollusca. (In other words, class squids and class snails are flavors of phylum Mollusca.) Also portrait image and landscape image occurrence roles are both instances of class image. (In other words, portrait image and landscape image are flavors of a more generic type, image).

You may ask how a class can be an instance of another class. Let's follow the way of thinking of a naïve researcher (me). At first I noticed these beautiful sea creatures: sea stars. I started shooting photos and collecting their pictures. I recorded them in my knowledge base as pretty invertebrates, instances of sea creatures with occurrences in many photos. Then I started reading about them. I learned that sea stars are part of the class known by the scientific name Asteroidea in the animal taxonomy and that they belong to the phylum Echinodermata along with sea urchins and sea lilies. And, in fact, there are nine orders within class Asteroidea (Platyasterida, Paxillosida, Valvatida, Spinulosida, Forcipulata, Notomyotida, Velatida, Brisingida, and Forcipulatida), but I did not want to get into that level of detail yet.

As another example, let's look at my oversimplified taxonomy of sea creatures as presented in Listing 9–2 and Appendix B: *sea star* is an instance of *animal-class* animal taxonomy classification grade and a subclass of *echinoderm*. *Echinoderm* in turn is an instance of *phylum* animal taxonomy classification grade and a subclass of *animal-kingdom*.

Listing 9–10 shows the XSLT template that determines whether the topic passed in the *$topic* parameter is an instance of the topic passed in the *$ref* parameter. It actually goes further and returns the flavor of the *$ref* class that the *$topic* parameter instantiates.

```
1.  <xsl:template name="getTopicRef">
2.  <xsl:param name="topic"/>
3.  <xsl:param name="ref"/>
4.  <xsl:choose>
5.  <xsl:when test="$topic/instanceOf/topicRef/@xlink:href=$ref">
6.   #<xsl:value-of select="$topic/@id"/>
7.  </xsl:when>
8.  <xsl:otherwise>
9.   <xsl:for-each select="key('topic',
10.      $topic/instanceOf/topicRef/@xlink:href])">
11.    <xsl:call-template name="getTopicRef">
12.     <xsl:with-param name="topic" select="."/>
13.     <xsl:with-param name="ref" select="$ref"/>
14.    </xsl:call-template>
15.   </xsl:for-each>
16.  </xsl:otherwise>
17.  </xsl:choose>
18.  </xsl:template>
```

Listing 9–10   Back-end XSLT *getTopicRef* template

Here's how it works. In line 5 we determine whether *$topic* is an instance of the *$ref* class. If it is, we return its -id- attribute; otherwise, we iterate over each class of *$topic* (line 9) and call the *getTopicRef* template (line 11) in an attempt to locate the *$topic* that is an instance of the *$ref>* class.

Note that the same approach can be generically applied to other association axes (such as *subclass-superclass*).

Querying and Displaying Topic Names

Now let's look at the <baseName> element extraction XSLT template shown in Listing 9–11. Its principle is very simple: it tries to find the base name of a topic passed in the *$topic* parameter whose scope contains the scoping topic specified in the *$scopic* parameter (lines 5–10). Note that the word *scopic* stands for "scoping topic" (a synonym of "scoping theme") and at one point was suggested as a topic maps neologism. If no base name has a matching scope or if the *$scopic* parameter is not specified, the template outputs the base name (if any) in the unconstrained scope.

```
1.   <xsl:template name="name">
2.    <xsl:param name="topic" select="."/>
3.    <xsl:param name="scopic"/>
4.    <xsl:choose>
5.     <xsl:when test="$topic/baseName/scope/topicRef/
6.         @xlink:href=concat('#',$scopic)">
7.      <xsl:value-of
8.         select="$topic/baseName[scope/topicRef/
9.            @xlink:href=concat('#',$scopic)]/baseNameString"/>
10.     </xsl:when>
11.     <xsl:otherwise>
12.      <xsl:value-of select=
13.         "$topic/baseName[not(scope)]/baseNameString"/>
14.     </xsl:otherwise>
15.    </xsl:choose>
16.   </xsl:template>
```

Listing 9–11   Back-end XSLT template for `<baseName>` element extraction

As an example, let's consider the use of this template in Listing 9–7 when it is applied to the `sea-star` topic (Listing 9–2) to render the Web page shown in Figure 9–4. Note that the default value of the `$topic` parameter is the current `<topic>` element (or current node in the XSLT sense). The first call to the name template in line 2 in Listing 9–7 does not specify the `$scopic` parameter and thus the return value is "sea-star"—the base name of the current topic in the unconstrained scope (line 7 in Listing 9–2). The second call (lines 4–6 in Listing 9–7) asks for the base name in the scope of `taxon` and returns "Asteroidea" (lines 3–6 in Listing 9–2). At last, the template call in lines 8–10 in Listing 9–7 returns "starfish"—a name in the `also-known-as` scope (lines 8–11 in Listing 9–2). Note that a call with the `$scopic` parameter equal to any other value, for example, *xyz*, would return "sea-star"—the base name in the unconstrained scope—because there is no name defined in Listing 9–2 for the *xyz* scope. Another detail to keep in mind is that according to XSLT processing rules, if multiple `<baseName>` elements are matched, only the value of the first one in the document order is returned by this template.

Real applications often require the use of more complicated templates, for example, to take care of situations when more then one `<baseName>` element is specified in the same scope or when the use of `<variantName>` elements is required. For the purposes of this chapter we explored only simple syntax examples. For advanced examples, visit *http://www.cogx.com*.

Querying and Displaying Topic Occurrences

The CTW framework uses topic occurrences to supply typed information about topics to be used as HTML or text fragments, images, or client- and server-side objects. You can instruct XSLT style sheets to use different rendition procedures and to apply different formatting styles for different occurrence role types. Thus occurrence classes control the rendering of referenced resources.

In the Long Island Seashore Creatures topic map, a topic (represented as a page) can have the following occurrence types: image with landscape proportions (*landsc-img*), image with portrait proportions *portr-img*), *definition*, and *description*. Other types of occurrences could be various specializations of the above as well as sound files, video, Scalable Vector Graphics (SVG) or Synchronized Multimedia Integration Language (SMIL) fragments, XPath expressions aggregating fragments from multiple documents or SQL queries, and so on.

A very simple occurrence layout and rendition template is shown in Listing 9–12. Here's what happens. First we determine the name of the scoping topic and hold it in a variable, *$scope-name* (lines 2–7). Next, for the *landsc-img* occurrence class, we build a two-row, single-column table and place the image in the upper cell and the byline in the bottom cell (lines 9–17). For the *portr-img* occurrence class, we build a single-row, two-column table and place the image in the left cell and the byline in the right cell (lines 20–25). The byline is determined from the *$scope-name* of the scoping topic of type *underwater-photograph*. In the case of the *definition* occurrence class, we print the definition text in italic type with the bibliographic reference in square brackets underneath (lines 30–31). Finally, for the *description* occurrence class, we simply print the text in a large font (lines 33–37).

```
1.   <xsl:template match="occurrence">
2.    <xsl:variable name="scope-name">
3.     <xsl:call-template name="name">
4.      <xsl:with-param name="topic" select="key('topic',
5.          scope/topicRef/@xlink:href)"/>
6.     </xsl:call-template>
7.    </xsl:variable>
8.    <xsl:choose>
9.     <xsl:when test="instanceOf/topicRef/
10.        @xlink:href='#landsc-img'">
11.     <table border="1" bgcolor="#ffffde"><tr><td>
12.      <img src="../images/{{resourceRef/@xlink:href }" width="130"/>
13.     </td></tr><tr><td>
14.      <font size="-1">Photo by :
15.      <i><b><xsl:value-of select="$scope-name"/></b></i></font>
16.     </td></tr></table>
17.    </xsl:when>
18.    <xsl:when test="instanceOf/topicRef/
```

```
19.        @xlink:href = '#portr-img'">
20.     <table border="1" bgcolor="#ffffde"><tr><td>
21.      <img src="../images/{{resourceRef/@xlink:href }" width="100"/>
22.     </td><td>
23.      <font size="-1">Photo by :<br/>
24.      <i><b><xsl:value-of select="$scope-name"/></b></i></font>
25.     </td></tr></table>
26.    </xsl:when>
27.    <xsl:when test="instanceOf/topicRef/
28.        @xlink:href = '#definition'">
29.     <i><xsl:value-of select="resourceData"/></i>
30.     <p class="bibitem">[<xsl:value-of
31.        select="$scope-name"/>]</p>
32.    </xsl:when>
33.    <xsl:when test="instanceOf/topicRef/
34.        @xlink:href = '#description'">
35.     <font size="+1"><b><xsl:value-of
36.        select="resourceData"/></b></font>
37.    </xsl:when>
38.    </xsl:choose>
39.    <br/>
40. </xsl:template>
```

Listing 9–12   XSLT Presentation layer template for occurrence rendition

Note that for simplicity we used only `<resourceData>` elements. If we had used a `<resourceRef>` element to point to an XML or HTML fragment, we could have taken several approaches. If we knew that the addressed document were a well-formed XML, and if we were not concerned with its volatility (that is, we were not concerned that the original might change after transformation), we could have used the XSLT `document()` function to insert a fragment during the transformation. Alternatively, we could have generated an `<xinclude:include>` instruction and resolved this fragment inclusion in a postprocessing phase or at runtime. Listing 9–13 shows what could have been used in place of line 29 in Listing 9–12.

```
<xsl:choose>
 <xsl:when test="resourceRef">
  <xinclude:include href="{resourceRef/@xlink:href}"
   xmlns:xinclude="http://www.w3.org/2001/XInclude"/>
 </xsl:when>
 <xsl:otherwise>
  <xsl:value-of select="resourceData"/>
 </xsl:otherwise>
</xsl:choose>
```

Listing 9–13   Optional `<resourceRef>` resolution

A brief note on `<xinclude:include>`: there exist several alternative mechanisms to resolve this instruction. To include non-XML fragments I usually use postprocessing procedures (with the help of regular expressions). Web browsers may become `xinclude`-aware in the near future. In the meantime, TalvaStudio (*http://www.talva. com*) and DOMXIncluder (*http://www.ibiblio.org/xml/XInclude/*) are examples of software systems that can provide these capabilities. For more information, please refer to the World Wide Web Consortium XML Inclusions (XInclude) Candidate Recommendation [World Wide Web Consortium 2002] that specifies a processing model and syntax for general-purpose inclusion. Postprocessing procedures for resolving `<xinclude:include>` are discussed at *http://www.cogx.com.*

Note also that the templates and XPath expressions discussed in this and other sections of this chapter are very generic and can be used for many other topic map processing tasks. In particular, they can be used for small-scale TMQL implementations (some of them are considered in the context of the query layer in this chapter). Sam Hunting's Chapter 4 in this book discusses the Topic Maps Query Language (TMQL).

The key() Function

The XSLT script of Listing 9–12 uses the `key()` function (line 4). Although I am trying to avoid going into the details of XSLT in this chapter, for this function I will make an exception because this subject is often not sufficiently covered elsewhere.

The XSLT `key()` function plays the role of a generalized ID: it finds nodes by testing XPath expressions against a given text string. "A key has a name as well as a value; each key name may be thought of as distinguishing a separate, independent space of identifiers. Keys are declared in the style sheet using `<xsl:key>` elements" [World Wide Web Consortium 1999b].

Proper use of `key()` functions dramatically improves performance and provides for more intuitive XSLT code. Listing 9–14 shows the definition of an `<xsl:key>` element with the name *topic* that provides a mechanism for matching `<topicRef>` elements to the corresponding `<topic>` elements.

```
1.  <xsl:key
2.    name = "topic"
3.    match = "topic"
4.    use = "concat('#',@id)" />
```

Listing 9–14   An `<xsl:key>` element indexing all topics in the topic map by their -@id- attributes

The function key('topic', '#*expression*') will match a <topic> element whose -id- is equal to the value of *expression*. For example, the function key('topic', '#abc') will match the topic whose -@id- is *abc*.

So, the XSLT key() function call in Listing 9–12 will return the referenced scoping topic.

If scope of the *baseName* contains more then one scoping topics, a node set containing all scoping topics will be returned. We can supply some additional criteria to filter only one of them for display. For example, we can specify that we are looking for the scoping topic that is an instance of *underwater-photographer*. Listing 9–15 shows the modified select expression.

```
1.  select="key('topic',scope/topicRef/@xlink:href)
2.  [instanceOf/topicRef/@xlink:href='#underwater-photographer']"
```

Listing 9–15   A select expression with filtering for topic type

In this case, the XSLT key() function in the first part (line 1) of the expression returns a node set of all scoping topics composing a given scope (the scope of the current occurrence in this case). In the second part (line 2), we are asking to give us only those topics that are instances of *underwater-photographer*.

Querying and Displaying Topic Associations

The site map (of the links between topic pages) is controlled by <association> elements. Different association types and association member roles are rendered with different styles. For example, association membership arcs between related topics can be rendered as buttons, text links, images, or generated text blocks with embedded textual links.

The Long Island Seashore Creatures topic map Web site uses only the simplest case: the *class-subclass* association class builds the localized animal taxonomy that is then rendered as the site map navigation tree. Other <association> classes that can be used in CTW topic maps are, for example, *containment*, *used-with*, *about*, and so on.

Listing 9–16 shows the *sitemap* tree rendition template. This template is called, for example, in line 19 in Listing 9–5.

```
1.  <xsl:template name="sitemap">
2.   <xsl:param name="classRef"/>
3.   <xsl:param name="current"/>
```

```
4.   <xsl:variable name="topic" select="key('topic',$classRef)"/>
5.   <xsl:choose>
6.    <xsl:when test="$topic=$current">
7.     <xsl:apply-templates select="$topic" mode="label"/>
8.    </xsl:when>
9.    <xsl:otherwise>
10.    <xsl:apply-templates select="$topic" mode="link"/>
11.   </xsl:otherwise>
12.  </xsl:choose>
13.  <xsl:variable name="aref"
14.      select="key('class-subclass-key',$classRef)"/>
15.  <xsl:if test="$aref">
16.   <ul>
17.    <xsl:for-each select="$aref/member[roleSpec/topicRef/
18.        @xlink:href='#sub-class']/topicRef">
19.     <li>
20.     <xsl:call-template name="sitemap">
21.      <xsl:with-param name="classRef" select="@xlink:href"/>
22.      <xsl:with-param name="current" select="$current"/>
23.     </xsl:call-template>
24.     </li>
25.    </xsl:for-each>
26.   </ul>
27.  </xsl:if>
28. </xsl:template>
```

Listing 9–16   The *sitemap* tree rendition template

In this code, parameter *$classRef* indicates the pointer into the current position in the site map, and parameter *$current* indicates the topic for which the current page is rendered. In line 4 we locate the topic referenced by *$classRef*, and if *$classRef* is equal to *$current*, we render a label (line 7); otherwise, we render a hyperlink pointing to the page generated for the *$classRef* topic.

In lines 13–14 we attempt to locate the *class-subclass* association in which the *$classRef* topic plays the role of a superclass. If such an association exists, the *sitemap* template calls itself for each topic playing the subclass role.

The XSLT key() function in lines 13–14 uses the *class-subclass-key* shown in Listing 9–17. It matches all associations of type *class-subclass* with the topics playing the superclass (*class*) role.

```
<xsl:key
  name = "classAssoc"
  match = "association
    [instanceOf/topicRef/@xlink:href='#class-subclass'] "
  use = "member[roleSpec/topicRef/@xlink:href='#class']
    /topicRef/@xlink:href"/>
```

Listing 9–17   The *classAssoc* *<xsl:key>* element

Summary

This chapter covers just some aspects of the CTW framework. I sketched the basics of applying the XSLT transform to topic map code to generate the HTML required for Web presentation. I discussed the three basic layers involved, the XTM code itself, the XSLT code required for transformation, and the universe of Web resources referenced by the topic map. We also looked at how a taxonomy of topic types and topic characteristics can be used to control Web pages presentation and layout. The chapter discussed querying topic maps with XPath and XSLT but just somewhat touched this subject. This and other very interesting subjects such as natural language generation, with topic maps and XSLT applying the CTW framework to Relational Database maintenance, building dynamic taxonomies with simile associations, and much more are discussed at *http://www.cogx.com* and may be published in future volumes of this series.

You can always find new and updated information at *http://www.cogx.com*, including downloadable sample applications and code.

Finally, I should mention that the design and implementation framework discussed in this chapter uses flat files for XML topic map documents repository. As such it scales up to several thousand topics. To go beyond that you should consider using Relational Database servers, XML databases, or native topic map engines.

Acknowledgments

Many thanks to Jack Park and Sam Hunting for great help and encouragement in reading and proofing the early drafts of this chapter, and to Steve Newcomb and Michel Biezunski for their support and advice. Also, I would like to thank the reviewers for their comments and suggestions.

References

Biezunski, Michel. 2000. Understanding Topic Maps. Accessed in April 2002 at *http://www.infoloom.com/whitepaper.htm*.

Devlin, Keith. 1991. *Logic and Information*. Cambridge, MA: Cambridge University Press.

Holman, Ken. 2001. *Practical Transformation Using XSLT and XPath*. Accessed in April 2002 at *http://www.cranesoftwrights.com/training/* and *http://www.cranesoftwrights.com/training/*; also published as *Definitive XSLT and XPATH* by Prentice Hall, 2001.

Kay, Michael. 2001. *XSLT Programmer's Reference: Second Edition*. UK: Wrox Press.

National Audubon Society. 1981. *National Audubon Society Field Guide of North American Seashore Creatures*. New York: Knopf.

Ogievetsky, Nikita. 1999a. Data Maintenance on the Web Made Easy with XML Templates. Accessed in April 2002 at *http://www.cogx.com/xml99/*.

———. 1999b. HTML Form Templates with XML. All in One and One for All. XSLT Template Library for WEB Applications. Accessed in April 2002 at *http://www.cogx.com/xwtl/*.

———. 2000. Dynamic Web Sites with Topic Maps and XSLT. Accessed in April 2002 at *http://www.cogx.com/Extreme2000*.

———. 2001. Harvesting Topic Maps with XSLT. Accessed in April 2002 at *http://www.cogx.com/kt2001/*.

Ogievetsky, Nikita, and Vladimir Rodygin. 2000. Building Adaptive Classificators with Topic Maps and XSLT. Accessed in April 2002 at *http://www.cogx.com/xml2000/*.

Reiter, Ehud, and Robert Dale. 2000. *Building Natural Language Generation Systems*. Cambridge, MA: Cambridge University Press.

World Wide Web Consortium. 1999a. XML Path Language (XPath) W3C Recommendation. Accessed in April 2002 at *http://www.w3c.org/tr/xpath*.

———. 1999b. XSL Transformations (XSLT) W3C Recommendation. Accessed in April 2002 at *http://www.w3c.org/tr/xslt*.

———. 2002. XML Inclusions (XInclude) Candidate Recommendation. Accessed in April 2002 at *http://www.w3.org/TR/xinclude/*.

Chapter 10

OPEN SOURCE TOPIC MAP SOFTWARE

Eric Freese, Kal Ahmed, Jack Park, and Sam Hunting

A specific goal of this book is to bring technology to the users. This chapter briefly reminds readers that there exist numerous commercial sources of topic map software— four of which, listed below, have been sponsors of TopicMaps.Org (*http://www. topicmaps.org*), the group that created the XTM specification. We expect more vendors to appear in the future.

Empolis: *http://k42.empolis.co.uk*

InfoLoom: *http://www.infoloom.com/*

Mondeca: *http://www.mondeca.com/*

Ontopia: *http://www.ontopia.net/*

We soon turn to the discussion of four open source projects. This chapter is thus a composite of project discussions by four authors: Eric Freese, Kal Ahmed, Jack Park, and Sam Hunting (with Jan Algermissen). First, however, a question: Just what is open source software?

About Open Source Software

The Open Source Initiative has this to say about open source software[1]:

> The basic idea behind open source is very simple. When programmers can read, redistribute, and modify the source code for a piece of software,

---

[1]From the front page of the Open Source Initiative Web site, accessed in May 2002 at *http://www. opensource.org*.

the software evolves. People improve it, people adapt it, people fix bugs. And this can happen at a speed that, if one is used to the slow pace of conventional software development, seems astonishing.

The operating system Linux (*http://www.linux.org/*) is perhaps the best-known open source project, but there are many, many more open source software projects. For instance, Sourceforge, just one of several open source project hosts, claims (as this is written) 39,248 projects, two of which are discussed in this chapter, and 416,546 registered users.[2]

Open source software projects come with a variety of licenses. Copyrights for the source code itself reside with the authors, who publish their source code along with some license to use that source code. Some licenses severely restrict users in what they can do with the software; others simply grant the right to do whatever users want with the code. Quite a few levels of restrictions are placed in between these extremes, again, depending on the license chosen. In most cases, licenses permit inclusion of software made from the source code in commercial products, without royalty fees returning to the author; thus, for the most part, open source software is also known as *free* software.

Four Projects

In this chapter we discuss four projects, each of which appears to be somewhat different than the others. Eric Freese's SemanText develops and demonstrates the ability to construct topic maps, to browse them, and to write rules and perform inferences on them. Kal Ahmed's TM4J started out without persistent store capability but has now added a database to the system. TM4J permits construction and browsing of topic maps. Nexist, by Jack Park, started out with the intent to offer persistence to XTM and to offer construction and browsing of XTM documents as well. When the Nexist project began, TM4J did not offer persistence, so Nexist began development of its own XTM engine. The GooseWorks project, started by Jan Algermissen and Sam Hunting, is developing a classic UNIX-style toolkit that implements the graph-based data model for topic maps described in the draft Reference Model for topic maps under development at ISO. The toolkit offers persistence, a query language, and association template validation.

---

[2]From the statistics section of the home page, accessed in May 2002 at *http://sourceforge.net.*

As these projects are maturing, we are seeing some blending of interests. For instance, inferencing and groves[3] as mentioned by Eric are of great interest to the Nexist project. Also, TM4J is easily coupled to Nexist, and this coupling has already begun.

Many other projects besides those discussed here exist. For instance, Figure 10–1 shows a screen shot of a project called MAK, which stands for Mind Map and Knowledge Management (*http://mak.sourceforge.net*).

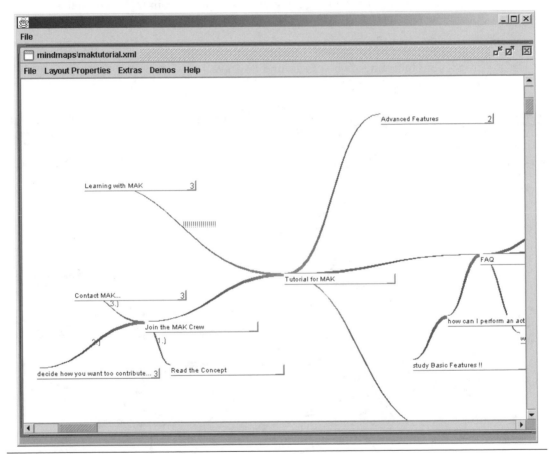

Figure 10–1   MAK (Mind Map and Knowledge Management) software, opened to a tutorial page that shows how MAK displays topical information

---

[3] A *grove* is a development of the SGML community, looking for a way to access and manipulate documents of many different types. A grove engine provides the ability to, for example, write reports that use components from a text editor, spreadsheet, and a relational database. It does so by providing a uniform API to the report writer. That is, it allows cells in a spreadsheet, paragraphs of text, and information in a relational database to be accessed in a uniform manner.

Figures 10–2 and 10–3 show two screen shots of TouchGraph (*http://touchgraph. sourceforge.net*), a Java application and applet that displays graph structures. These images are the TouchGraph applet serving as a site map for the open source Web collaboration tool called Lucid Fried Eggs (*http://www.memes.net*). In Figure 10–2, the screen displays a rather large number of nodes. Each node represents a Web page at the memes.net Web site. Pass the cursor over a node and a pop-up window displays some information about what is on that page. Click on the node and it migrates toward the center of the image. Click on the node again (or double-click) and the page itself opens in a new browser window.

These figures display several TouchGraph controls. The top-left slide bar controls the Zoom function, so you can zoom in or out. The slide bars at the bottom and the

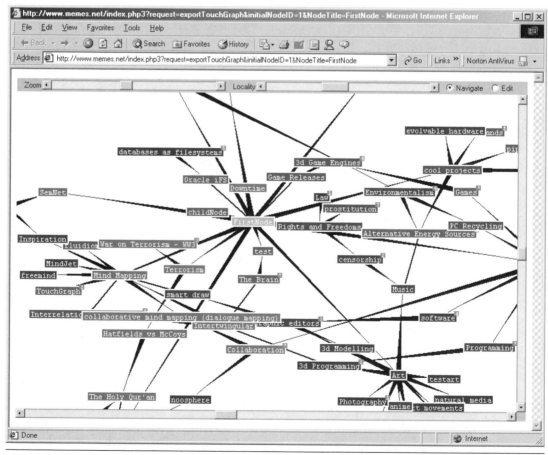

Figure 10–2   TouchGraph screen shot with a larger radius and thus more visible nodes

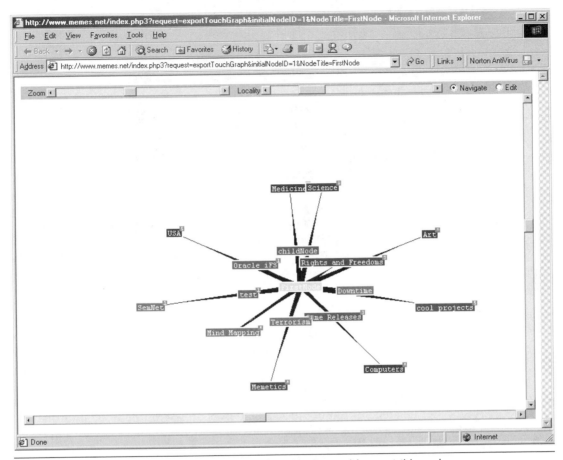

Figure 10–3   TouchGraph screen shot with a reduced radius and fewer visible nodes

right side give Pan functionality. The slide bar at the top right is titled Locality. It controls, essentially, the radius of the view presented. A larger radius makes more nodes visible. Figure 10–3 shows the same part of the graph as that shown in Figure 10–2 but with reduced radius.

Let's now look at four particular projects, each available on the Web.

SemanText

ERIC FREESE

The SemanText system is a demonstration topic map–based application written in Python that builds semantic networks from topic maps. As its developer, I first announced the SemanText system at the XML Europe 2000 conference. Semantic network nodes are created from topics and topic types. Links are created from associations between the topics. Additional rule-based information can be added to allow the semantic network processor to infer new knowledge beyond the class-instance relationship that is defined in the standard.

SemanText supports topic map creation, modification, and browsing. The current version of SemanText supports only the ISO 13250 (2000) topic map definition. Work is under way to support the XTM model now that the specification has been completed.

Browsing Topic Maps

SemanText uses a customized HTML browser interface that presents the topic map information in a manner that is familiar and intuitive for most users. Users can select a regular browser/hyperlink style of interface (Figure 10–4) or a button-based interface (Figure 10–5). A tree diagram interface was intentionally avoided so that circular links do not become a confusing issue when users browse through the information. When running in a Microsoft Windows environment, occurrence links are automatically displayed in the appropriate application. In other operating systems, occurrences are fed to a browser to handle in the most appropriate way.

Users begin browsing through the topic map by selecting a topic or topic type from the menu. All the information associated with the topic within a given scope is displayed, including any related topic and topic types, associations, and links to all occurrences. Users can select related topics by choosing them within this frame or by using the menu selections.

Creating and Modifying Topic Maps

SemanText can be used to create new topic maps. Existing topic maps can be read and modified. New topic maps created in SemanText contain a set of published subjects that enable all the functionality supported within the tool. Users can build topic maps by entering the information manually using a series of dialogs. Topics are created by completing input forms (Figure 10–6). Users can also create specialized type topics by

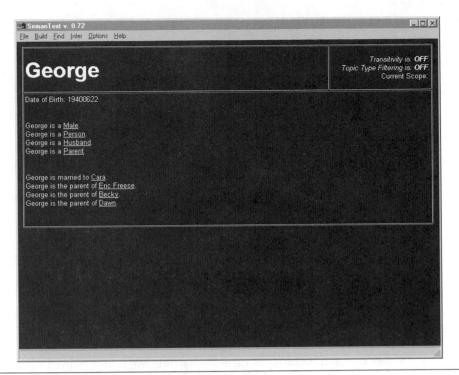

Figure 10–4 SemanText's browser-like user interface

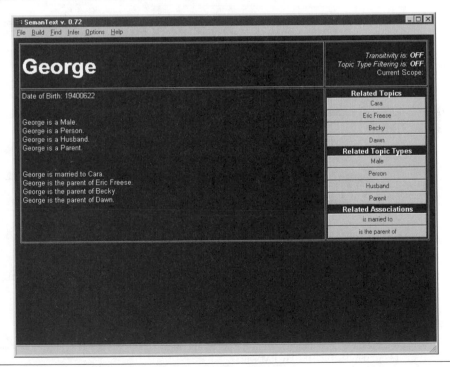

Figure 10–5 SemanText's button-based user interface

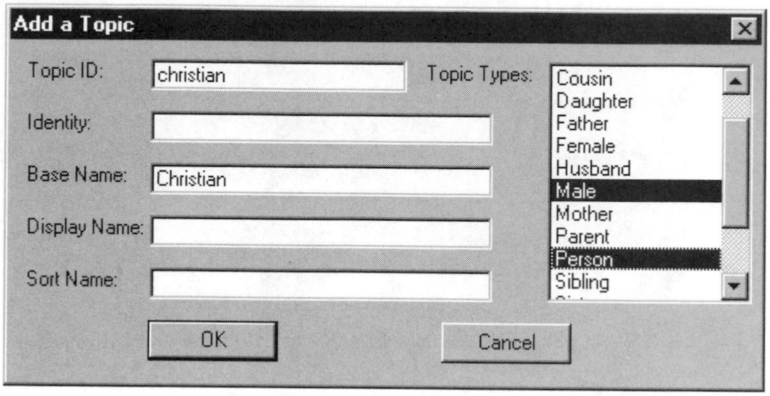

Figure 10–6   SemanText's topic input form

using similar input forms. Specialized dialogs also allow users to create associations (Figure 10–7), occurrences (Figure 10–8), and facets[4] (Figure 10–9).

Users can also build topic maps by parsing XML and SGML files and harvesting information from them into topics and associations. This automatic method uses a

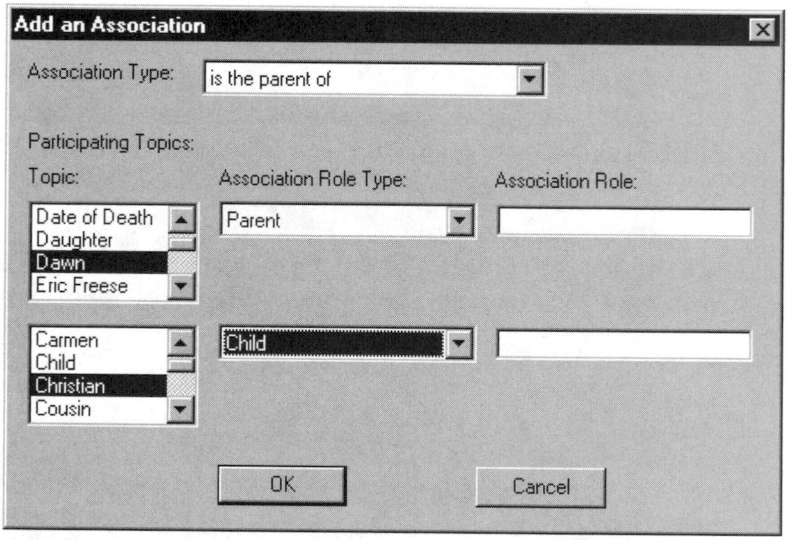

Figure 10–7   SemanText's association input form

---

[4]Facets have been dropped from the XTM specification and the XTM syntax. They remain in the ISO 13250 standard and the HyTM syntax.

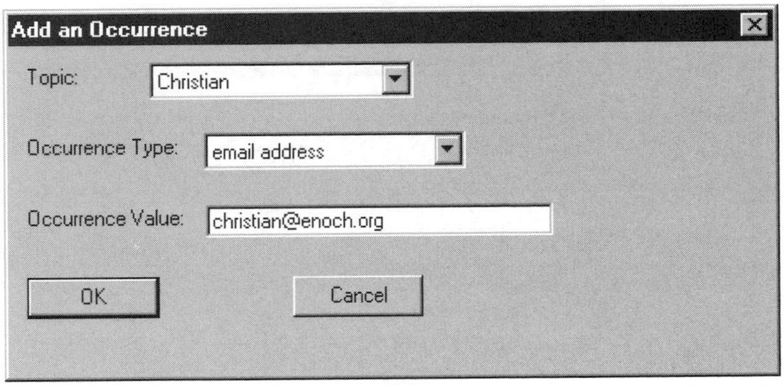

Figure 10–8   SemanText's occurrence input form

tree representation of the source file (Figure 10–10) that allows users to specify an element and how it and its contents should be added to the topic map (Figure 10–11). Users can select a single instance of an element or select all instances of an element within a given context.

Topic maps can be merged in two ways. A full merge combines two topic maps into one, connecting and resolving common topics with user intervention. Seman-Text also allows a different type of merge called a *reference merge*, in which the topic maps remain separate but links are made to common topics. This allows the base topic map to remain separate while still being able to reference one or more other topic maps.

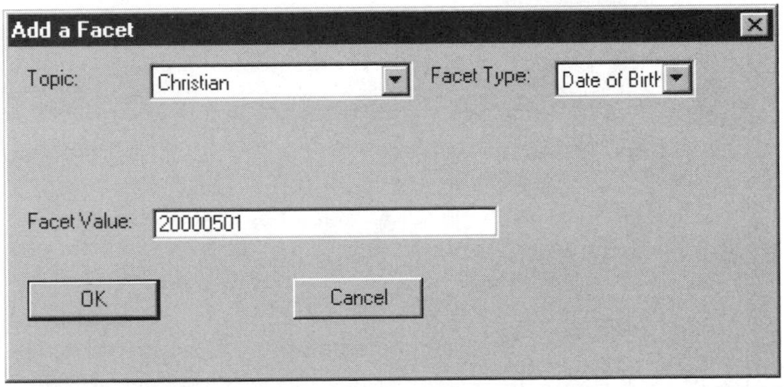

Figure 10–9   SemanText's facet input form

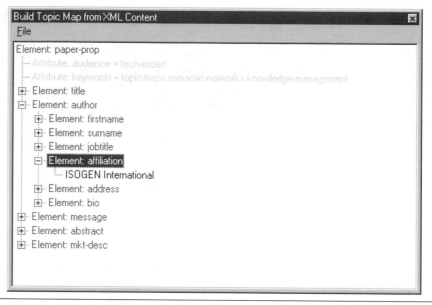

Figure 10–10   XML document tree in SemanText

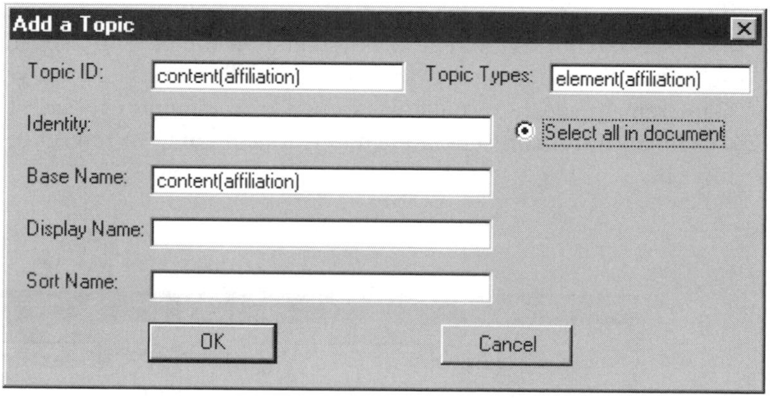

Figure 10–11   Harvesting data into a topic

Developing Inference Rules

SemanText includes a rules-based inference engine integrated with the topic map component. The inference engine interprets topic map structures to create facts in the form of a semantic network. These facts allow specialized queries to be made of the knowledge base in order to interpret the knowledge stored within the topic map.

Users can develop rules that interpret the facts within the knowledge base to infer new facts. At the same time, this process constructs new topic map structures that model the new facts. A form is used to add new rules for the inference engine. Users can construct rules using a set of proxy variables that can stand in place of any topic within a fact. This allows the development of generic rules that can process any topic based on the parameters within the rule. Figure 10–12 shows the process of defining a rule that tells the inference engine how to determine a cousin relationship within a genealogy topic map.

Future Plans

SemanText is still very much under development. As stated earlier, an XTM capability is forthcoming. Many other capabilities are being considered to demonstrate concepts and test theories.

Previous prototypes of the SemanText system used groves to represent the structure of the information. The current version of the system does not incorporate groves. Once the basic topic map capability has been completed and a suitable grove implementation can be identified, the grove paradigm can be included in the full system again. This will make non-SGML data accessible to the system, both for building topic maps and for browsing occurrences of topics.

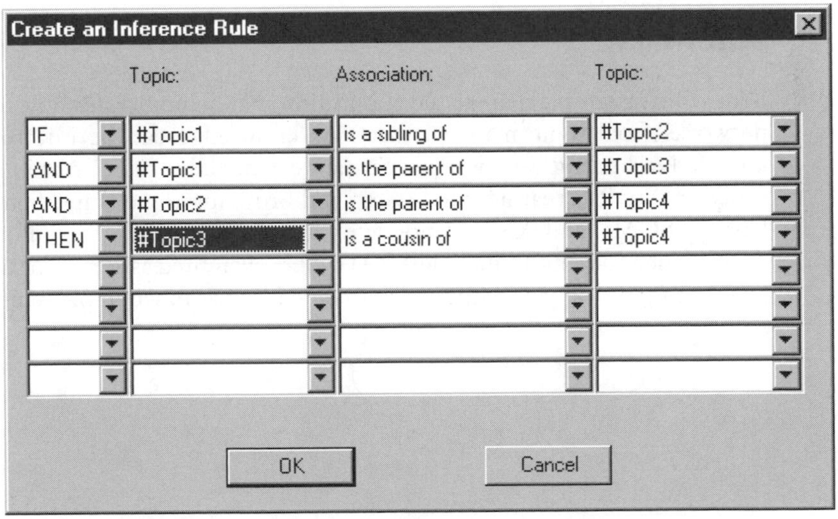

Figure 10–12   Creating an inference rule within SemanText

In many semantic network applications it is possible to assign weightings to the statements modeled in the nodes and links. These weightings tell the application the certainty value of a statement: the higher the value, the more factual or certain the statement. This allows the application to build inferences that can be weighted based on the information contained within the network. In the future, SemanText will include an inference engine that will be able to take confidence weighting into consideration. In addition, the inference engine will provide a mechanism for developing rules that will allow the semantic network to be automatically enhanced as users add new topics and associations. Work similar to this is currently taking place in the W3C's Semantic Web initiative.

A great deal of research has been done in the area of natural language processing. Hopefully a natural language input interface can be implemented so that SemanText can identify new topics and associations within flowing text in addition to the current harvesting capability.

Several output formats are being explored. Included among the possibilities are Open E-book, Virtual Reality Modeling Language (VRML) or Scalable Vector Graphics (SVG), audio input and output using Voice XML, and others. These various outputs will demonstrate new ways to access and view data.

The SemanText Web site (*http://www.semantext.com*) is the place to find the latest release of SemanText in addition to other information on topic maps, knowledge management, and similar applications.

Summary

SemanText is a topic map–based application that demonstrates how to build semantic networks from topic maps so that new knowledge can be inferred from existing knowledge-bearing associations. SemanText includes typical topic map application functionality for creating, modifying, and browsing topic maps. SemanText can also harvest SGML and XML content for its inherent topic map information. Future development directions include XTM syntax, weighted associations, natural language processing, a variety of output formats, and a grove-based implementation.

XTM Programming with TM4J

KAL AHMED

This section describes the practical aspects of creating topic map processing applications using an open source toolkit called TM4J (*http://tm4j.org/*). The core of TM4J is a set of Java APIs for parsing, manipulating, and writing topic maps in XTM 1.0 format. TM4J also contains a small number of command-line utilities for measuring various statistics about topic maps and for merging topic maps. In addition, the TM4J package supports storage of processed topic map information either in memory or in an Ozone object-oriented database system. The utility applications and the use of the Ozone database are beyond the scope of this chapter; however, you can find more information on using all of the applications in the TM4J documentation.

This section of Chapter 10 begins with a discussion of the core data model that TM4J exposes, focusing on how to read a file into TM4J, how to create and modify topic map constructs, and how to save the file again—the bread and butter, if you will, of topic map processing applications. Having covered the basics, we will look at the design and implementation of a simple processor that generates a topic map from a collection of MP3 tags.

In writing this section I have assumed that you have some familiarity both with the XTM 1.0 specification and with the principles of object-oriented programming languages and how they apply to the Java programming language.

The TM4J Core API

File Organization and Packaging

The TM4J distribution is organized as shown in Table 10–1.

TM4J is organized as a set of Java packages containing all of the interfaces and classes for the core API and the utility APIs and applications. The core API consists of two packages:

1. `org.tm4j.topicmap` contains the interfaces that define the core topic map constructs and the implementation of those interfaces. This package also contains factory and builder classes, which provide convenience functions

Table 10–1   Organization of the TM4J Distribution

Directory	File	Purpose of File
/		
bin/		Utility applications used to build the TM4J package (source distribution only).
docs/		Documentation.
	index.html	Documentation contents page.
	install.html	Instructions on getting and installing the third-party packages required by TM4J.
	Building.html	Instructions on compiling the source code yourself.
apiDocs/		Contains all the Javadoc documentation for the package. The file index.html should be your starting point.
tools/		Documentation of the command-line utilities. The file index.html is the starting point for this documentation.
devguide/		Developer's documentation. The file index.html is the starting point for this document.
lib/		The libraries used by TM4J. In the binary distribution of TM4J, this directory also contains the compiled TM4J libraries.
src/		Source code (source distribution only).
resource/		A collection of test files and other resources used for testing TM4J.
	LICENSE.TXT	License information for the TM4J package.
	README.TXT	Release information. This file may contain information and warnings not yet included in any other documentation.
	build.xml	The Jakarta Ant makefile for compiling the sources (source distribution only).

for the creation of topic map objects. The interfaces defined by this package are implemented by the packages org.tm4j.topicmap.memory and org.tm4j.topicmap.ozone. The former package provides an implementation in which the processed topic map information is stored in memory. The latter provides the facility to persist processed topic map information in the Ozone object-oriented database. Although this chapter focuses on the in-memory implementation, by design almost all the code shown here can be used with the Ozone implementation without any change.

2. org.tm4j.topicmap.utils contains the utility classes for importing, walking, and exporting topic maps.

In addition to these core packages, there is also a package called org.tm4j.topicmap.cmd, which is the home for command-line utilities; a further (undocumented) package `org.tm4j.topicmap.tests`, which contains unit tests for various features of the core API; and `org.tm4j.net`, which is a small framework package for defining and processing generic network addresses.

Package Dependencies

Both the binary and the source distributions of TM4J come with all the libraries needed to both compile and run applications. This means that to compile and/or run applications built using TM4J, you must have all these files specified in the CLASS-PATH of your Java compiler/interpreter.

Getting Started

Once you've downloaded and installed TM4J and its dependent packages, you're ready to start coding. This section guides you through some of the basic and advanced features of the TM4J API and the processes of loading and saving topic maps in XTM format as well as creating implicit topics.

Using the Basic API Features

The Topic Map Object Classes

The core TM4J API consists of a number of interfaces that represent the basic constructs of a topic map,[5] plus implementations of those interfaces that are held either in memory or in an Ozone database. You will find the interfaces defined in the package `org.tm4j.topicmap` and the implementations provided in the packages `org.tm4j.topicmap.memory` and `org.tm4j.topicmap.ozone`. However, not all constructs of the XTM 1.0 specification map directly to an interface and implementation in the core API. Table 10–2 shows which elements of the XTM 1.0 interchange DTD map to interfaces and implementations in the API.

Some of the other constructs found in the XTM DTD are represented as properties of these core classes. For example, `<instanceOf>` is represented by the `type` property of the `Association` and `Occurrence` interfaces and the `types` property of the `Topic` interface; it can be accessed using the functions `getType(s)` and `setType(s)` on these objects.

---

[5]*Editor's note:* These constructs relate closely to those regarded as basic by the Standard Application Model for topic maps; see Chapter 4.

Table 10–2 TM4J Topic Map Object Interfaces and Implementations

XTM 1.0 DTD Element	TM4J Interface	TM4J In-Memory Implementation
`<topic>`	Topic	TopicImpl
`<scope>`	Scope	ScopeImpl
`<topicMap>`	TopicMap	TopicMapImpl
`<baseName>`	BaseName	BaseNameImpl
`<variant>`	Variant	VariantImpl
`<variantName>`	VariantName	VariantNameImpl
`<parameters>`	Scope	ScopeImpl
`<association>`	Association	AssociationImpl
`<member>`	Member	MemberImpl
`<occurrence>`	Occurrence	OccurrenceImpl

The `TopicMapObject` Interface

All the interfaces that define topic map constructs are derived from the interface `org.tm4j.topicmap.TopicMapObject`. This interface and its implementation, `org.tm4j.topicmap.TopicMapObjectImpl`, provide the following features:

- Access to the `ID` property of the object
- Access to the `resourceID` property of the object
- An interface for registering one or more property change listeners

The `ID` property is a session-unique identifier for the object. Typically, this property is set by the parser, but applications that create topic map objects must provide a value for this property. The default parser assigns a pseudo-unique identifier string to this property for all objects it creates.

The `resourceID` property represents the URI of the topic map document element represented by the topic map object. This value is typically set only by a parsing application. The default parser assigns this property a value that is normalized from the value of the –id– attribute of the XTM element to a full URL, using the source document's base URL as the root.

The property change listener interface is dealt with in more detail in the Using the Advanced API Features section.

Creating Topic Maps and Topic Map Objects

You can create topic map objects in two ways with TM4J. The most basic way uses the constructor of the appropriate class directly. This is the least flexible method of object creation—it requires that the application be fixed to one specific implementation of the TM4J interfaces.

The TopicMapProviderFactory and TopicMapFactory interfaces add flexibility by hiding the specific implementation used behind a generic topic map object creation API. The TopicMapProviderFactory and its related interface TopicMapProvider hide implementation-specific details of connecting to the source of topic map information. The TopicMapProvider object is responsible for managing a collection of one or more TopicMap objects and also for providing the facility to create or import a new topic map into the store. For the in-memory implementation, the TopicMapProvider implementation provides a simple way to initialize TM4J with one or more topic maps loaded from XTM files. For implementations that rely on database connections (such as the Ozone implementation), this interface allows the database connection to be established and managed in a manner that is completely transparent to the programmer.

The TopicMapFactory interface provides a createXXX() function for each of the topic map object types shown in Table 10–2 and it guarantees to return objects conforming to the expected interfaces, but the precise implementation of those interfaces depends on the implementation of the TopicMapFactory interface used. The implementation org.tm4j.topicmap.memory.TopicMapFactoryImpl returns the default in-memory implementations of the interfaces, but by using the interface (rather than any specific implementation of it), the code you write can be quickly and easily converted to use the persistent Ozone database implementation or any future implementations of the TM4J interfaces.

Utilities

So far, we have examined only TM4J's heart—the implementation of the core objects of a data model for XTM. However, TM4J also contains a number of utility classes that provide higher-level services. Most important of these are the TopicMapUtils interface, the WalkerHandler interface and TopicMapWalker class, the IDGenerator interface, and the IDGeneratorFactory class.

`TopicMapUtils`. The interface `org.tm4j.topicmap.TopicMapUtils` defines a set of indexes and utility functions for manipulating the topic map objects in a single topic map. Among these are functions for retrieving all objects of a specific type, retrieving all objects in a specific scope, and extracting a name from a topic suitable for either display or sorting. Every implementation of the `TopicMap` interface must provide access to an object implementing the `TopicMapUtils` interface through the function `getUtils()`. The default implementation of the `TopicMapUtils` interface is suitable for use with any implementation of the `TopicMap` interface, building all the necessary indexes in memory on creation. Alternate implementations of the TM4J interfaces are free to also provide alternate implementations of the `TopicMapUtils` interface; however, you can use the default implementation with any implementation of the `TopicMap` interface.

`WalkerHandler` and `TopicMapWalker`. The `TopicMapWalker` class is a utility class that enumerates the contents of a `TopicMap` object held in memory. The walker visits each topic and association in the topic map in turn, generating element start and end events to represent the topic map. These events are delivered through the `Topic MapHandler` interface. The `WalkerHandler` interface defines a simple event-driven interface that receives notification of the start and end of different topic map document constructs during the course of a parse or walk of a topic map document's structure. Readers familiar with the Simple API for XML (SAX) API will recognize this architecture. A class that implements this interface and then connects to a parser or walker object receives the structure of the topic map document as a stream of element start and end notifications, or simple event notifications (the `onXXX()` methods) for elements that do not contain other topic map objects.

`IDGenerator` and `IDGeneratorFactory`. In working with topic maps, it is often necessary to generate unique identifiers—especially when creating topics (which require the assignment of values to their `resourceID` properties). The API for generation of identifiers is defined by the interface `org.tm4j.topicmap.utils.IDGenerator`, and a default implementation is provided by the class `org.tm4j.topicmap.utils.IDGeneratorImpl`. The default implementation generates an identifier based on the current system time (in milliseconds). Both the `XTMParser` and `TopicMapFactoryImpl` classes use an `IDGenerator` for creating IDs of the topics and associations that are "implicit" in the topic map (see the Creating Implicit Topics and Implementing the Application sections that follow for more details). You may provide your own implementation of this very simple interface and make it the default by setting the system property `org.tm4j.topcimap.idGenerator` to the name of the class that implements an `IDGenerator` interface—the default parser and the implicit object creation routines will then use an instance of this new class for generating new IDs.

The `IDGeneratorFactory` class provides an easy way to retrieve the implementation of the `IDGenerator` interface that has been specified by the system property. Calling the function `newIDGenerator()` returns a new instance of the class specified by the system property settings. If no value was specified for the system property settings, or if the class specified was not found or could not be instantiated, then the factory returns a new instance of the default `org.tm4j.topicmap.utils.IDGeneratorImpl` class.

Error Handling

TM4J defines a number of exception classes. Table 10–3 shows the exceptions subclassed from `org.tm4j.topicmap.TopicMapProcessingException` and the conditions under which they are raised.

In addition to these exceptions, there is the `TopicMapRuntimeException`, which is subclassed from the Java `RuntimeException` class. This exception class is used to wrap other exceptions and system errors and pass them out of a function without requiring that the exception be explicitly handled in the calling code. The `TopicMapRuntime Exception` is especially of use when parsing XTM files or handling property change events. However, you should be sure that some outer layer of your application must catch and handle these exceptions.

The other exception class worth mentioning at this point is the `TopicMapProvider Exception` class. Exceptions of this class are raised only when creating new topic maps or retrieving existing topic maps from a `TopicMapProvider`. These exceptions are raised to indicate system errors such as a failure to connect to a database or to locate a file to be loaded.

Table 10–3 Exceptions Subclassed from `TopicMapProcessingException`

Exception	When Raised
`DuplicateObjectIDException`	When an attempt is made to create a topic object with an ID that is already assigned to some other object
`MergedTopicSubjectClashException`	When the merging process attempts to merge two topics but finds they have different subject resources
`TopicNotFoundException`	When an attempt is made to remove a topic from a topic map when that topic is not part of the topic map

Handling Network Addresses

Any topic map processing system is required to handle network addresses and network address resolution. This facility is provided by the package org.tm4j.net. The core of this package is the Locator and LocatorFactory interfaces. A locator is simply an address string in a specific notation. A notation defines how the address string is processed. The most common form of address string notation, and the only one currently supported by TM4J, is the URI notation.

As with topic map objects, you should not create instances of the classes implementing the Locator interface directly. Instead you should use the LocatorFactory interface's createLocator() method, passing in the name of the address notation being used and the address string itself.

The TM4J address-parsing and resolution framework is fully extensible, allowing you to register your own specific address notations with customized processing and resolution services.

Loading a Topic Map

The steps of loading a topic map from an XTM file into memory are fairly simple but involve a number of separate classes, so they are worth describing in detail. The steps are as follows.

1. Get the TopicMapProviderFactory implementation for the storage mechanism you intend to use for the parsed file. For an in-memory storage of the parsed topic map information, create a new instance of the class org.tm4j.topicmap.memory.TopicMapProviderFactoryImpl.

2. Use the TopicMapProviderFactory interface to create a new TopicMap Provider. This is achieved by calling the createTopicMapProvider() method of the TopicMapProviderFactory interface. This method requires a Java Properties object which specifies any options to be used by the TopicMapProviderFactory in constructing the TopicMapProvider. For a database storage mechanism, these options might include the address of the database server, the user name and password, and so on. For the in-memory implementation, the property set is currently ignored.

3. Get the LocatorFactory provided by the TopicMapProvider. This factory object will be used to construct notation-independent address objects. The method getLocatorFactory() returns the LocatorFactory object appropriate for the TopicMapProvider.

4. Create a base locator for the topic map. The topic map's base locator is used to resolve any addresses contained within the topic map which refer to other resources and is also used as a unique identifier for the topic map in the

TopicMapProvider. Typically, you will use a base address generated from the address of the input file. Locators are constructed by calling the create Locator() method of the LocatorFactory interface. This method takes two parameters—the notation of the locator address and the address string itself. TM4J currently handles only addresses using standard URI notation, so you should always specify the string "URI" for the notation and use a valid URI string for the address.

5. Create the topic map object itself. To create an empty topic map, simply call the createTopicMap() method of the TopicMapProvider interface, passing the base locator created in step 4 as a parameter. To create a topic map from an XTM source file, call the addTopicMap() method. This latter method takes a Java InputStream object as the source to be parsed, the base locator of the source (as created in step 4), and optionally the existing topic map with which the source is to be merged. If this last, optional parameter is not null, then rather than create a new topic map, the source will be parsed and the topic map information will be merged with the specified topic map.

6. Retrieve the topic map from the TopicMapProvider. This step is not necessary if you used the methods in step 5 since each of these methods actually returns the TopicMap object created or updated by the method call. However, a topic map managed by a TopicMapProvider can be retrieved by using its base address as the key—to retrieve a topic map, simply call the getTopicMap() method, passing in the base address (as a Locator object).

It looks like a lot of work when written down in prose, but the code is far more compact. See Listing 10–1 for an example. Notice that about two-thirds of the code is error handling!

```
protected TopicMap readTopicMap(File tmFile)
{
  TopicMapProviderFactory providerFactory =
    new TopicMapProviderFactoryImpl();
  try
  {
    TopicMapProvider provider =
  providerFactory.createTopicMapProvider(System.getProperties());
    LocatorFactory locFactory = provider.getLocatorFactory();
    Locator baseLoc = locFactory.createLocator("URI",
                                  tmFile.toURL().toString());
    TopicMap tm = provider.addTopicMap(new FileInputStream(tmFile),
                               baseLoc,
                               null);
    return tm;
  }
  catch(TopicMapProviderException ex)
  {
    System.out.println("Error in opening topic map provider: "
      + ex.getMessage());
```

```
    }
    catch(MalformedURLException ex)
    {
      System.out.println("Could not convert file path to a
        valid URL");
    }
    catch(LocatorFactoryException ex)
    {
      System.out.println("Error constructing base locator. "
        + ex.getMessage());
    }
    catch(FileNotFoundException ex)
    {
      System.out.println("Error opening input file. "
        + ex.getMessage());
    }
    return null;
}
```

Listing 10–1   Loading a topic map with TM4J

Creating Implicit Topics

An XTM file may contain more topics and associations than are defined by `<topic>` and `<association>` elements. In TM4J, these are called *implicit* topics and associations. TM4J implements the creation of implicit topics under certain circumstances.

If the parser encounters a `<subjectIndicatorRef>` element within any element other than a `<subjectIdentity>` element, it creates a new topic, which represents the subject indicated by the resource to which the `<subjectIndicatorRef>` element points. This new topic has only a single subject indicator (using the URL value provided by the `<subjectIndicatorRef>` element). The reference in the XTM file is then converted to a reference to the newly created topic.

For example, consider the following simple topic map (the name-space declarations in the root `<topicMap>` element have been omitted for clarity).

```
<?xml version="1.0"?>
<topicMap . . .>
   <topic id="foo">
     <instanceOf>
       <subjectIndicatorRef xlink:href=
           http://www.techquila.com/PSI/music.html#album/>
     </instanceOf>
   </topic>
</topicMap>
```

When this XTM file is parsed, the parser will create two <topic> objects: one with an ID of "http://www.techquila.com/default#foo", which represents the <topic> element in the XTM file, and the other with an ID of "http://www.techquila. com/default#xxxxx", where xxxxx is a pseudo-unique identifier generated by the system IDGenerator. This second <topic> element has no other characteristics except for a single value in its subjectIndicators property, which will be "http://www. techquila.com/PSI/album.html".[6]

Saving a Topic Map

Figure 10–13 shows the architecture of the process of writing a topic map to an XTM file. The export process is split between three interoperating objects.

1. The TopicMapWalker object is responsible for enumerating the objects contained in the topic map being written. Access to the topic map is provided through the TopicMap interface, which is implemented by the TopicMapImpl class. It passes the results of the enumeration as topic map object start and end events using the WalkerHandler interface.
2. The XTMWriter object implements the WalkerHandler interface, translates the start and end of the topic map objects encountered by the walker into XTM syntax, and passes them to the ContentHandler interface.
3. The XMLSerializer object implements the ContentHandler interface and formats and outputs the text of the XTM file.

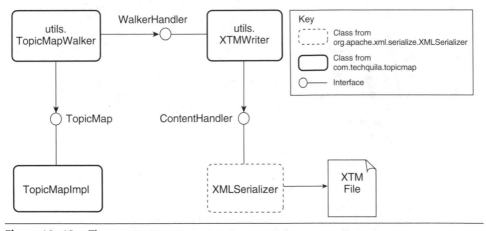

Figure 10–13   The export process

---

[6]*Editor's note:* Compare this approach to the Node Demander Is a Subject Indicator Rule in the processing model for topic maps at *http://www.topicmaps.net*; see Chapter 4.

This means you have to take several steps to save a topic map.

1. Create a serialization object.

   Figure 10–13 shows the use of the class org.apache.xml.serialize.
   XMLSerializer, but you can use any class that implements the org.xml.
   sax.ContentHandler interface. Depending on the actual implementation
   used, there may be some steps required to initialize the serializer, such as
   specifying the output format and the file to be written.

2. Create an XTMWriter object.

   The XTMWriter is connected to the serializer by calling the setContent
   Handler() function, passing the serializer as a parameter.

3. Create a TopicMapWalker object.

   The TopicMapWalker object is connected to the XTMWriter object by calling the setHandler() function and passing the XTMWriter object as a
   parameter.

4. Start the walk.

   Do this by calling the walk() function on the TopicMapWalker object and
   passing the topic map to be saved as a parameter.

See Listing 10–2 for sample source code.

```
public void writeTopicMap(TopicMap tm, File tmFile)
  {
    // Create the writer
    XTMWriter tmWriter = new XTMWriter();
    try
    {
      if (!tmFile.exists())
      {
        tmFile.createNewFile();
      }
      // Create and initialize the output serializer.
      XMLSerializer serial = new XMLSerializer();
      serial.setOutputByteStream(new FileOutputStream(tmFile));
      OutputFormat of = new OutputFormat();
      of.setEncoding("UTF-8");
      of.setMethod("xml");
      of.setIndent(2);
      of.setIndenting(true);
      serial.setOutputFormat(of);

      // Link the serializer to the writer
      tmWriter.setContentHandler(serial.asContentHandler());

      // Create the walker
      TopicMapWalker tmWalker = new TopicMapWalker();
```

```
    // Link the writer to the walker and walk the topic map.
    tmWalker.setHandler(tmWriter);
    tmWalker.walk(tm);
}
catch(IOException ex2)
{
  System.out.println("IO Exception while serializing topic map:
      " + ex2.getMessage());
}
catch(TopicMapProcessingException ex)
{
  System.out.println("TopicMapProcessingException while
      serializing topic map: " + ex.getMessage());
}
}
```

Listing 10–2   Saving a topic map with TM4J

Using the Advanced API Features

Topic Merging

TM4J implements both subject-based and name-based topic merging. Merging requires that a topic exhibit its own characteristics (names, occurrences, and roles played in associations) plus the characteristics of all topics merged with it. This requirement is implemented in TM4J using a "soft" approach to merging which does not actually assign characteristics to a topic as a result of merging. A TopicImpl object has a mergedTopics property, which is a collection of the other topics that have been merged with it. In TM4J, the topic that contains such a list is known as the *base topic* of the merged set. When a topic characteristic is requested from the base topic, the union of the characteristics of that object and all its merged topics is returned.

Regardless of which of the merged topics is addressed, the access of topic characteristic properties is delegated to the base topic, thus ensuring that all the merged characteristics are correctly returned. However, if desired, you can also access only the property values of the object, without regard to its merging. This is achieved through the getXXX() functions, which take a boolean parameter—passing in "false" will return only the characteristics of the addressed <topic> object.

TM4J's default implementation of merging is highly dynamic. Altering a characteristic of a topic may cause it to be instantly merged with another topic or to be unmerged. The event of a topic being merged or unmerged may be trapped by listening for changes to the baseTopic property of the <topic> object.

When merging takes place, if the merge causes the merged set of characteristics for the <topic> object to include more than one value for its subject property (this is the URI of the addressable subject that constitutes the topic), a MergedTopicSubject ClashException will be raised. It is the responsibility of the client application to handle this exception.

Scope

XTM defines a scope as a set of subjects, described either by references to topics (using a <topicRef> element) or by references to subject indicators (using a <subject IndicatorRef> element). You can then apply this scope to any of the topic characteristic assignments of name, membership in an association, and occurrence. TM4J models scope as a first-class object as defined by the interface org.tm4j.topicmap. Scope, which contains a collection of <topic> objects that are either the topics referenced from the <topicRef> elements in the <scope> element or implicit topics created to represent the subjects indicated by the resources specified in the <subject IndicatorRef> elements in the <scope> element. A single instance of the Scope interface may in turn be shared between any number of objects that implement the interface org.tm4j.topicmap.ScopedObject.

Both the Scope interface and the ScopedObject interface provide a means of manipulating the set of topics that form the scope; however, the effect of using each of these interfaces is different. If the alteration is made directly on the Scope object, then the change will affect all ScopedObject objects sharing that Scope—in other words, the change is made, as would be expected, to the Scope object directly. If, on the other hand, the alteration is made through the ScopedObject interface, this causes a new Scope object to be created. The newly created Scope object is a copy of the Scope object that the ScopedObject object is currently referencing with the changes requested by the function call applied—this new Scope object then becomes the one referenced by the ScopedObject object through which the alteration was made. In other words, altering the scope of an object through its ScopedObject interface causes it to split away from the other ScopedObject objects that share the same scope and defines a new, unique scope for that object.

In addition to managing the topics that form the scope, the Scope interface provides utility functions that enable you to determine whether or not the object is in a specified scope. This operation is provided by the inScope() functions and returns true if the Topic object or collection of Topic objects passed as parameters to the function form a subset of those contained in the Scope object itself.

The XTM concept of the unconstrained scope is supported by TM4J. Any scope containing no topics is defined as being in the unconstrained scope, which is defined as the set of all topics in the topic map—so if a scope represents the unconstrained scope, then the `inScope()` functions will always return "true". Notice that this approach to the unconstrained scope effectively prevents the creation of an "empty" scope (a scope with no topics in it) since such a `Scope` object will instead represent the unconstrained scope. However, the uses of an empty scope are so limited that this is not currently regarded as a major problem.

Property Change Listeners

TM4J provides a generic way for any client application to detect changes made in a topic map. This architecture enables TM4J to act as a Model in the popular Model-View-Controller (MVC) application architecture. This facility is provided by allowing client objects to register themselves with any core topic map object as a *property change listener.* A property change listener is simply a class that implements the `java.beans.PropertyChangeListener` interface. As the name suggests, it may be registered to listen for changes made to a named property of the object or for changes made to any of the properties of the object. Each class that implements the `TopicMapObject` interface defines a number of named properties, which are shown in Table 10–4.

Table 10–4   Properties of TM4J Objects

Interface	Property Name	Description
`TopicMapObject`	`resourceID`	The URI of the element from which this topic map object was generated
`Topic`	`subject`	The URI of the addressable subject that is the subject of the topic
	`subjectIndicators`	A collection of URIs of descriptors of the subject of the topic
	`types`	The topics that define the class(es) to which this topic belongs
	`names`	The set of base names for this topic
	`occurrences`	The set of occurrences of this topic
	`rolesPlayed`	The set of members of which this topic is a part
	`baseTopic`	The topic with which this topic is merged

(continued)

Table 10–4   Properties of TM4J Objects (*continued*)

Interface	Property Name	Description
Scope	scopeString	A string encoding of the topics that make up the scope
BaseName	string	The string value of the name
	variants	The set of child variants of this base name
	scopeString	A string encoding of the scope and the name string of this base name
Variant	string	The string value of the name
	variants	The set of child variants of this variant
	variantNames	The set of child variant names of this variant
VariantName	resourceRef	The resource that is the value of the variant name
	resource	The string that is the value of the variant name
Association	members	The members of this association
	type	The topic that defines the class to which this association belongs
Member	parent	The association of which this member is a part
	roleSpec	The topic that defines the role this member plays in its parent association
	players	The set of topics that are playing the role defined by this member in its parent association
Occurrence	type	The topic that defines the class of occurrence to which this occurrence belongs
	resourceRef	The address of the resource that is the value of this occurrence
	resource	The string resource that is the value of this occurrence

When a property of an object is altered, the `propertyChange()` function is called on each listener registered against that property (or against all properties) of the object. The `propertyChange()` function receives a single parameter—a `Property-ChangeEvent` object. From this object, the listener may determine which object was changed (the "source" of the property change event), which property was changed, the value of that property prior to its alteration, and the property's value after the alteration has been made.

Some limitations to the current implementation of the property change listeners are worth noting here.

- The notifications are generated after the alteration to the object is made, and as a result the listener is not allowed to veto the change (although enough information is provided to allow the listener to change the value of the object back to its original setting).
- The order in which multiple listeners on the same property are invoked is arbitrary and is not even guaranteed to be the same from one property change notification to the next.
- The notification takes place in the same thread as the property change. This last detail has two implications. First, it means that code that makes the change is blocked until all listeners have received and processed the notification. Second, it means that if you implement change listeners you must ensure that a live-lock situation is not caused by a series of property change listeners altering properties of the same object.

Multivalued Properties

All multivalued properties follow a specific pattern of accessors. There is always a `getXXX()` function, which returns a collection; a `setXXX()` function, which takes an array of the type of value to be assigned to the property; and an `addXXX()` function, which takes a single instance of the type of value to be assigned to the property. The `setXXX()` function may be invoked with a null parameter, which causes the property value to be cleared.

The TM4J API guarantees to never return a null value for the `getXXX()` accessor of a multivalued property—if the object has no values at all for that property, an empty collection is returned. This means that code such as the following will execute correctly.

```
Iterator typesIt = topic.getTypes().iterator();
```

Note: This guarantee of no null return values does not apply to properties that have only a single value—in those cases, the null return value indicates that the property is not set for that object.

TMP3—A Sample Topic Map Processing Application

TMP3 is a sample application of TM4J. Its purpose is to create a topic map of a collection of MP3 files. Actually, it has two purposes—to serve as sample code for topic map creation and manipulation and to provide a way to quickly generate some sample XTM files for use in other applications.

In this section we go through the design process for the application, beginning with the design of the ontology for the information we're going to store in the topic map.

Defining the Topic Map Ontology

In TM4J, a topic map "ontology" defines what classes of entities and relationships are modeled in the topic map. (See Chapter 14 for a similar approach to topic map ontologies.) In syntactic terms, the topic map ontology is the set of classes of topics, associations, members, and occurrences in the topic map. These classes are themselves defined by topics. The application processes only a small subset of the ID3v2 tags that are typically found in MP3 files. (You can find the full details of the ID3v2 tag set at *http://www.id3.org*.) TMP3 will process only the tags for album name (TALB), performer (TPE1), and song name (TTT2).

The analysis process used to determine the topic map ontology from this set of metadata is beyond the scope of this chapter. The UML diagram in Figure 10–14 shows the results of the analysis. The important feature of the results of the analysis is that the MP3 track itself is considered to be an occurrence of a *song* topic and is represented as a typed property of the Song class. The associations between the classes of topics are shown as classes themselves, and the roles played in the associations are shown as text over or under the line representing the association.

As well as defining the classes of topics that occur in the data set, it is important to decide what form of identity to assign to each class of topic to uniquely establish the subject that the topic represents. The identities chosen for this application are shown in Table 10–5. The song name is considered a sufficiently unique identity for a *song* topic, since we would like all different versions of the same song to be merged into the same topic, regardless of the performer. In most cases, a performer's name is unique; this is not always true, but it will be sufficient for the purposes of this application. Finally, an album's name is not considered to be a sufficient identity by itself—consider the number of albums called "Best of" or "Greatest Hits"—and so the added context of the performer's name is required to make the identity of an album sufficiently unique. In implementation, this context may be represented either by defining a scope on the name of the topic representing the album or by combining the album name and performer name into a single name string in the unconstrained scope.

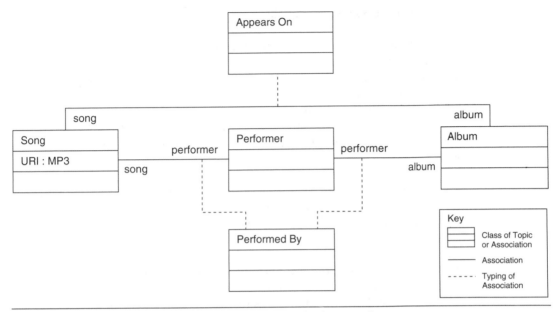

Figure 10–14   UML diagram of topics and associations for the MP3 data set

Table 10–5   Identities for TMP3 Topic Classes

Topic Type	Identity
Song	Song name
Performer	Performer name
Album	Album name in the context of Performer

Designing the Application

Having designed the classes of topics, associations, and occurrences we will be creating and manipulating, we can continue to design the application. For simplicity, and to avoid obscuring the topic map code with processing for the graphical user interface, TMP3 is a command-line application. It simply examines all files contained within a specified directory and extracts metadata from all identified MP3 files. Since MP3 files contain no consistent identity information for the songs, performers, and albums, the application makes extensive use of TM4J's merging capabilities to identify and merge duplicates automatically.

The Metadata Processing Framework

This application makes use of a reusable and extensible metadata processing framework, called MDF. The framework allows an application to process data by passing it down a chain of (possibly interacting) modules. Each module receives and may update a map of metadata properties and values. The modules also all have access to the topic map and may use the results of metadata processing to update the topic map. All modules implement the same, simple interface, allowing the modules to be chained together in any order. The metadata processing framework defines the following kinds of modules.

- **Producer modules** do not process the metadata received on the input but instead evaluate some other source of data and extract metadata values from the data source. Producer modules are typically located at the start of a chain of modules.
- **Translator** and **Converter modules** process entries in the metadata map into new entries in the map. Translator modules copy the values of particular properties into new properties with different names. Translator modules enable downstream modules to locate and make use of metadata values. Converter modules locate particular properties in the map and convert the values from one data type to another. Converter modules also enable downstream modules to make use of properties by ensuring that the data type is that expected by the downstream module.
- **Mapper modules** take values from the metadata map and create structures reflecting this data in the shared data store (in this case, the topic map).

The metadata processing framework defines extensible classes for all of these types of modules as well as an interface for creating new kinds of metadata processing modules. Going into detail about the metadata processing framework is beyond the scope of this book, but you can read more about MDF and download the complete application from *http://www.techquila.com/mdf.html*.

Our topic map application uses two modules—a Producer, which extracts MP3 metadata from a file, and a Mapper, which converts that metadata into topics and associations in the topic map.

Implementing the Application

The basic architecture of this application is shown in Figure 10–15. The Directory Scanner is a simple class that enumerates through the contents of a directory, feeding the files found in the directory (and each of its subdirectories) into the FileListener interface of the TMP3Extractor class. The TMP3Extractor class is a Producer module

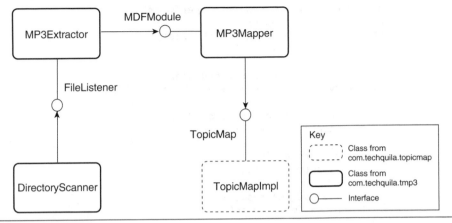

Figure 10–15   The metadata processing architecture of TMP3

that examines the ID3 tags of the file received from the `DirectoryScanner`. The values found are added to the metadata map and passed on to the chained `MP3Mapper` module. One map of metadata is created for each of the MP3 files located by the `DirectoryScanner`.

The `MP3Mapper` module interacts with the topic map and creates topics and associations representing the metadata discovered. The `MP3Mapper` creates a set of topics and associations for each set of metadata received from the `TMP3Extractor`.

Listing 10–3 shows the main processing function of the application.

```
public void run()
{
  System.out.println("Generating MP3 topic map from directory: "
      + m_mp3Dir.toString() + " to topic map:
      + m_tmFile.toString());
    //Either read an existing XTM file or else create
    // a new topic map.
  if (m_tmFile.exists())
  {
    m_tm = readTopicMap(m_tmFile);
  }
  else
  {
    m_tm = createTopicMap();
  }

    // Create the processing chain
  TMP3Extractor extractor = new TMP3Extractor(null, null);
```

```
MP3Mapper mapper = new MP3Mapper(m_tm);
extractor.chain(mapper);
Hashtable initInfo = new Hashtable();
extractor.init(initInfo);

   // Initialise the directory scanner
DirectoryScanner scanner = new DirectoryScanner(null);

   // Link the scanner to the MP3 extractor
scanner.addListener(extractor);

   // Start processing
scanner.scan(m_mp3Dir);

   // Write out the results
writeTopicMap(m_tm, m_tmFile);
}
```

Listing 10–3 Main processing function of TMP3

The main processing function first attempts to locate the topic map file specified on the command line. If it exists, the topic map is opened and updated; if it does not exist, a new topic map is created. The code for reading a topic map appeared earlier in this chapter (Listing 10–1). Creating a new topic map uses almost exactly the same code—the only difference is that the call to addTopicMap() is replaced with a call to createTopicMap() to get a new, empty TopicMap object.

Once the topic map document is read or created, the processing chain is created. First, new instances of the TMP3Extractor and MP3Mapper classes are created with the MP3Mapper being chained onto the end of the TMP3Extractor. Then, these are initialized with an empty map of values (neither class requires any parameters for initialization). Finally, the DirectoryScanner is created and the TMP3Extractor is added as a listener. The TMP3Extractor will now be notified as the DirectoryScanner finds files in the directory hierarchy. The null parameter in the DirectoryScanner constructor specifies the FileFilter to be used. You can use a FileFilter to prevent the DirectoryScanner from passing certain files to the listener. The default (which we have opted for here) is to pass all found files to the listener.

The processing is started by calling the scan() function of the DirectoryScanner, passing the directory to be scanned.

Listing 10–4 shows the initialization functions of the MP3Mapper class.

```
public class MP3Mapper extends BasicMDFModuleAdapter
{
```

```java
// Default typing topic ids
private static final String TT_ALBUM = "tt-album";
private static final String TT_SONG = "tt-song";
private static final String TT_PERFORMER = "tt-performer";
private static final String OT_MP3 = "mp3";
private static final String AT_PERFORMED_BY = "at-performed-by";
private static final String AT_APPEARS_ON = "at-appears-on";


// Default typing topic PSIs
// These PSIs are used if not overridden in the initialization
private static final String PSI_BASE =
   "http://www.techquila.com/psi/music.html";
private String PSI_ALBUM = PSI_BASE + "#album";
private String PSI_SONG  = PSI_BASE + "#song";
private String PSI_PERFORMER = PSI_BASE + "#performer";
private String PSI_MP3 = PSI_BASE + "#mp3";
private String PSI_PERFORMED_BY = PSI_BASE
  + "#assoc-performer-performance";
private String PSI_APPEARS_ON = PSI_BASE
  + "#assoc-recording-song";


   // Typing topic PSIs as Locator objects
private Locator m_psiAlbum;
private Locator m_psiSong;
private Locator m_psiPerformer;
private Locator m_psiMP3;
private Locator m_psiPerformedBy;
private Locator m_psiAppearsOn;


// Initialization input keys
// The values for these keys if found in the initialization
// hashtable will define the PSIs for the typing topics.
private static final String KEY_PSI_ALBUM = "PSI_ALBUM";
private static final String KEY_PSI_SONG  = "PSI_SONG";
private static final String KEY_PSI_PERFORMER = "PSI_PERFORMER";
private static final String KEY_PSI_MP3 = "PSI_MP3";
private static final String KEY_PSI_PERFORMED_BY
  = "PSI_PERFORMED_BY";
private static final String KEY_PSI_APPEARS_ON
  = "PSI_APPEARS_ON";


// Info output keys
public static final String ALBUM_TOPIC = "albumTopic";
public static final String PERFORMER_TOPIC = "performerTopic";
public static final String SONG_TOPIC = "songTopic";

TopicMap m_tm;
TopicBuilder m_builder;
TopicMapFactory m_factory;
TopicMapUtils m_utils;
```

```
// Cache of the infrastructure topics
protected Topic m_tAlbum;
protected Topic m_tPerformer;
protected Topic m_tSong;
protected Topic m_tMP3;
protected Topic m_tPerformedBy;
protected Topic m_tAppearsOn;

public MP3Mapper(TopicMap tm)
{
  m_tm = tm;
  m_builder = new TopicBuilder(tm);
  m_factory = tm.getFactory();
  m_utils = tm.getUtils();
}

public void initialise(Hashtable info)
{
  setPSIs(info);
  createInfrastructure();
  super.initialise(info);
}

/**
 * Overrides the default PSIs with those specified in the
 * hashtable.
 */
public void setPSIs(Hashtable info)
{
  if (info.containsKey(KEY_PSI_ALBUM))
    PSI_ALBUM = (String) info.get(KEY_PSI_ALBUM);

  if (info.containsKey(KEY_PSI_SONG))
    PSI_SONG = (String) info.get(KEY_PSI_SONG);

  if (info.containsKey(KEY_PSI_PERFORMER))
    PSI_PERFORMER = (String) info.get(KEY_PSI_PERFORMER);

  if (info.containsKey(KEY_PSI_MP3))
    PSI_MP3 = (String) info.get(KEY_PSI_MP3);

  if (info.containsKey(KEY_PSI_PERFORMED_BY))
    PSI_PERFORMED_BY = (String) info.get(KEY_PSI_PERFORMED_BY);

  if (info.containsKey(KEY_PSI_APPEARS_ON))
    PSI_APPEARS_ON = (String) info.get(KEY_PSI_APPEARS_ON);
}

public void createInfrastructure()
{
  makePSILocators();
```

```
    makeTopicTypes();
    makeAssociationTypes();
}

protected void makePSILocators()
{
    m_psiAlbum = m_builder.makeURILocator(PSI_ALBUM);
    m_psiSong = m_builder.makeURILocator(PSI_SONG);
    m_psiPerformer = m_builder.makeURILocator(PSI_PERFORMER);
    m_psiMP3 = m_builder.makeURILocator(PSI_MP3);
    m_psiPerformedBy = m_builder.makeURILocator(PSI_PERFORMED_BY);
    m_psiAppearsOn = m_builder.makeURILocator(PSI_APPEARS_ON);
}

    protected void makeTopicTypes()
    {
        m_tAlbum = m_builder.createTopic(TT_ALBUM, "Album");
        m_tAlbum.addSubjectIndicator(m_psiAlbum);

        m_tSong =  m_builder.createTopic(TT_SONG, "Song");
        m_tSong.addSubjectIndicator(m_psiSong);

        m_tPerformer = m_builder.createTopic(
                        TT_PERFORMER, "Performer");
        m_tPerformer.addSubjectIndicator(m_psiPerformer);

        m_tMP3 = m_builder.createTopic(OT_MP3, "MP3 File");
        m_tMP3.addSubjectIndicator(m_psiMP3);
    }

    protected void makeAssociationTypes()
    {
        try
        {
            m_tPerformedBy = m_builder.createTopic(
                            AT_PERFORMED_BY, "performed by");
            BaseName bn = m_factory.createBaseName(null);
            bn.setData("performs");
            bn.addTheme(m_tPerformer);
            m_tPerformedBy.addName(bn);
            m_tPerformedBy.addSubjectIndicator(m_psiPerformedBy);

            m_tAppearsOn = m_builder.createTopic(
                            AT_APPEARS_ON, "appears on");
            bn = m_factory.createBaseName(null);
            bn.setData("includes");
            bn.addTheme(m_tAlbum);
            m_tAppearsOn.addName(bn);
            m_tAppearsOn.addSubjectIndicator(m_psiAppearsOn);
        }
        catch(DuplicateObjectIDException ex)
```

```
            {
                throw new RuntimeException("Unexpected
                    DuplicateObjectIDException while initializing
                    association types.");
            }
        }


    . . .


    }
```

Listing 10–4   Initialization functions of the MP3Mapper class

During initialization, the infrastructure topics required to represent our classes of entities and relationships are created and added to the topic map. Note that in the makeAssociationTypes() function the BaseName objects are created with a null value specified for the first parameter. This parameter defines the resource ID parameter of the BaseName objects; since an -id- attribute is not required for a <baseName> element in the XTM syntax, the null value is allowed in this constructor. Passing a null for the ID parameter of a Topic constructor is not allowed and will result in an IllegalArgumentException being thrown from the constructor function.

Listing 10–4 does not show the actual creation of topics since this function is delegated to another class—the TopicBuilder (Listing 10–5). Note that the MP3Mapper class uses overridable PSI strings for the infrastructure topics but will use a fixed default value if no override is specified. Using PSIs to define the subjects of *song*, *album*, and so on means that the topic map thus created will be mergeable with any topic maps using the same PSIs (especially any topic maps created with the same application).

```
public class TopicBuilder
{
  protected TopicMap m_tm;
  protected TopicMapUtils m_utils;
  protected TopicMapFactory m_factory;
  protected LocatorFactory  m_locatorFactory;
  protected IDGenerator m_idGenerator;

  public TopicBuilder(TopicMap tm)
  {
    m_tm = tm;
    m_utils = tm.getUtils();
    m_factory = tm.getFactory();
    m_locatorFactory = tm.getLocatorFactory();
    m_idGenerator = IDGeneratorFactory.newIDGenerator();
```

```
}

/**
 * Creates a new topic in the topic map with an ID
 * and a name in the unconstrained scope. The new
 * topic is not typed.
 * @param id: the unique ID to be assigned to the topic
 * @param baseName: a name string which will be added to the
 *                  new topic
 * @returns: the new Topic object created
 */
public Topic createTopic(String id, String baseName)
{
  return createTopic(id, null, baseName, null);
}


/**
 * Creates a new topic in the topic map with an ID, a type,
 * and a name in the unconstrained scope.
 * @param id: the unique ID to be assigned to the topic
 * @param type: the type of the new topic
 * @param baseName: a name string which will be added to the
 *                  new topic
 * @returns: the new Topic object created
 */
public Topic createTopic(String id, Topic type, String baseName)
{
  return createTopic(id, type, baseName, null);
}


/**
 * Creates a new topic in the topic map with an ID, a type, and a
 * name in a specific scope.
 * @param id: the unique ID to be assigned to the topic
 * @param type: the type of the new topic
 * @param baseName: a name string which will be added to
 *                  the new topic
 * @param baseNameScope: the scope in which the name will be
 *                       added
 * @returns: the new Topic object created
 */
public Topic createTopic(String id, Topic type,
                         String baseName, Scope baseNameScope)
{
  try
  {
    Topic ret = m_tm.getTopicByID(id);
    if (ret != null) return ret;

    // Create the topic
    ret = m_factory.createTopic(id);
```

```
      // Set the type (if defined)
      if (type != null) ret.addType(type);

      // Create the baseName & set its string value
      BaseName bn  = m_factory.createBaseName(null);
      bn.setData(baseName);

      // Add a scope to the baseName (if defined)
      if (baseNameScope != null) bn.setScope(baseNameScope);

      // Add the baseName to the topic
      ret.addName(bn);

      // Return the topic or the topic it merged with.
      return ret.getBaseTopic();
    }
    catch(TopicMapProcessingException ex)
    {
      System.out.println(
              "Error in creating topic: " + ex.getMessage());
      ex.printStackTrace();

      throw new TopicMapRuntimeException(ex);
    }
  }

  /**
   * Creates a "binary" association between two topics.
   * @param assocType: the type of the new association
   * @param role1Type: the type (or roleSpec) of the first role
   * @param role1Player: the topic playing the first role
   * @param role2Type: the type of the second role
   * @param role2Player: the topic playing the second role
   * @returns: the new association created
   */
  public Association createAssociation(Topic assocType,
                        Topic role1Type, Topic role1Player,
                        Topic role2Type, Topic role2Player)
  {
    try
    {
      Association assoc =
            m_factory.createAssociation(m_idGenerator.getID());
      if (assocType != null) assoc.setType(assocType);

      Member m1 = m_factory.createMember(assoc, null);
      if (role1Type != null) m1.setRoleSpec(role1Type);
      m1.addPlayer(role1Player);

      Member m2 = m_factory.createMember(assoc, null);
      if (role2Type != null) m2.setRoleSpec(role2Type);
      m2.addPlayer(role2Player);
```

```
      return assoc;
    }
    catch(DuplicateObjectIDException ex)
    {
      // This should not happen since we are using
      // the IDGenerator for all our IDs
      throw new RuntimeException(
              "Unexpected DuplicateObjectIDException!");
    }
}


/**
 * Creates a new occurrence for a topic.
 * @param parent: the topic to receive the new occurrence
 * @param occursType: the type of the new occurrence
 * @param address: the locator address the new occurrence points to
 * @returns: the newly created occurrence
 */
public Occurrence createOccurrence(Topic parent,
                    Topic occursType, String address)
{
  try
  {
    Occurrence occ = m_factory.createOccurrence(null);
    if (occursType != null) occ.setType(occursType);
    try
    {
      Locator locator = m_locatorFactory.createLocator("URI",
                                                address);
      occ.setDataLocator(locator);
    }
    catch(LocatorFactoryException ex)
    {
      // This is not a fatal error - just
      // log a message and continue
      System.out.println("WARNING: Failed to create a valid URI
              locator for occurrence address: " + address);
    }

    parent.addOccurrence(occ);
    return occ;
  }
  catch(DuplicateObjectIDException ex)
  {
    throw new RuntimeException("Unexpected
                          DuplicateObjectIDException!");
  }
}


/**
 * Creates a new URI notation locator with the specified address.
 * @param address: the URI address for the locator
```

```
 * @returns: the newly created Locator object
 */
public Locator makeURILocator(String address)
{
  try
  {
    Locator locator = m_locatorFactory.createLocator("URI",
                                            address);
    return locator;
  }
  catch(LocatorFactoryException ex)
  {
    throw new RuntimeException("Failed to create URI locator
                              for address: " + address);
  }
 }
}
```

Listing 10–5   Functions of the `TopicBuilder` class

For each file that the `DirectoryScanner` encounters, the file name is added into a hashtable which is passed to the `rcv()` function of the first module in the chain, the `TMP3Extractor`. This function is implemented in the base class provided by the MDF framework. The `rcv()` function calls the `process()` function of the `TMP3Extractor` class, which extracts the album name, song name, and performer name and stores them in the map. The `rcv()` function then passes the updated map to the `rcv()` function of the next module in the chain, the `MP3Mapper`.

The code for the `MP3Mapper`'s `process()` function is shown in Listing 10–6. This function creates topics to represent the performer, album, and song that are identified by the metadata. The metadata values are used as names for the *performer* and *song* topics, but the *album* topic is assigned a name generated from both the metadata value for the album name and the performer name. As well as creating the topics, the `process()` function also creates associations between the topics and a single occurrence for the *song* topic. The code for creating associations and topics is implemented in the `TopicBuilder` class as the functions `createAssociation()` and `createOccurrence()`, which are shown in Listing 10–5.

```
public class MP3Mapper extends BasicMDFModuleAdapter
{
  public void process(Hashtable info)
  {
    String albumName = (String)info.get(TMP3Extractor.ALBUM_NAME);
    String performerName =
        (String)info.get(TMP3Extractor.PERFORMER_NAME);
```

```
String songName = (String)info.get(TMP3Extractor.SONG_NAME);

try
{
  // First create a topic for the performer
  Topic performer =  mapPerformer(performerName);
  info.put(PERFORMER_TOPIC, performer);

  // Create a scope for the album name
  Scope nameScope = m_factory.createScope(null);
  nameScope.addTheme(performer);

  // Create a topic for the album
  String nName = normalize(albumName);
  Topic  album = m_builder.createTopic(toId("album-", albumName),
                    m_tAlbum,
                    albumName,
                    nameScope);

  // Add an unscoped base name
  BaseName bn = m_factory.createBaseName(null);
  bn.setString("'" + albumName + "' by " + performerName);
  album.addName(bn);
  info.put(ALBUM_TOPIC, album);

  // Create an association between album and performer
  Association assoc;
  assoc = m_builder.createAssociation(m_tPerformedBy,
                    m_tAlbum, album,
                    m_tPerformer, performer);
  m_tm.addAssociation(assoc);

  // Create a topic for the song
  nName = normalize(songName);
  Topic song = m_builder.createTopic(toId("track-", songName),
                    m_tSong,
                    songName);
  info.put(SONG_TOPIC, song);

  // Create an association between song and album
  assoc = m_builder.createAssociation(m_tAppearsOn,
                    m_tSong, song,
                    m_tAlbum, album);

  // Create an association between song and performer
  assoc = m_builder.createAssociation(m_tPerformedBy,
                    m_tSong, song,
                    m_tPerformer, performer);

  // Create an occurrence of the song
  String songLoc = (String)info.get(TMP3Extractor.MP3_URI);
```

```
      if (songLoc != null) m_builder.createOccurrence(song, m_tMP3,
          songLoc);
    }
    catch(DuplicateObjectIDException ex)
    {
      System.out.println("WARNING: Error while processing
                          MP3 tag - " + ex.toString());
    }
  }

  /**
   * Creates a topic to represent the performer.
   * The performer's name is used in a normalized form as the
   * ID of the topic.
   */
  public Topic mapPerformer(String performerName)
  {
    String normName = normalize(performerName);
    Topic ret = m_builder.createTopic(toId("performer-",
        performerName),
                      m_tPerformer,performerName);
    return ret;
  }

  /**
   * Naive string normalization.
   * This function simply forces the input string to lowercase.
   * @return The normalized form of the input string.
   */
  public String normalize(String in)
  {
    return in.toLowerCase();
  }

  /**
   * Naive string to ID value normalization.
   * This function replaces spaces with underscore characters
   * and ampersands with plus-signs in an attempt to generate
   * a valid ID string.
   *
   * @return The normalized version of the input string with
   *     the specified prefix.
   */
  public String toId(String prefix, String in)
  {
    String ret = normalize(in);
    ret = ret.replace(' ', '_');
        return prefix+ret.replace("&", "+");
  }
}
```

Listing 10–6   The process() function

Note: To make the resulting XTM file easier for a human to read, the `MP3Mapper` class uses the titles of songs and albums and the names of performers to generate the ID for the topic representing that entity. For example, the topic representing the performer "The Clash" gets the ID *performer-the_clash*, and the topic representing their eponymous album gets the ID *album-the_clash*. In a more robust application, this form of ID generation would not be acceptable since you could end up with two different topics being assigned the same ID.

Extending the Application

Below are some suggestions for using the topic maps generated by TMP3.

- Create a graphical user interface to navigate around the topic map and create playlists of MP3 files.
- Create (as a separate topic map) topics for each of the bands in the mapped MP3 collection. These topics could include occurrences that point to fan sites, associations with topics representing other performers who have influenced the bands, and so on. Using the TM4J command-line merge application makes it possible to merge this topic map with your MP3 topic map, creating a much richer source of information.

The TMP3 application packaged with TM4J is a convenient way to quickly generate a topic map from a collection of MP3 files. This topic map by itself has organizational functions similar to those in many commercial and noncommercial MP3 management applications, but TMP3 manages only a very limited subset of the metadata found in an MP3 file. However, the topic map can be easily extended, as suggested below.

Handle more of the tags in the ID3v2 specification. This would probably require additions to the TMP3 ontology as well as extra code. The additional code could be added to the source for `TMP3Extractor` and `MP3Mapper`, but a more modular approach would be to create new modules and simply chain them on to the existing ones.

Improve the name handling of `TMP3Extractor`. You may find that your MP3 files are not consistently tagged, for example, you may find you have "The Clash", "the clash", and "Clash, the" as performer names. By normalizing the name string in some way you can ensure more successful merging of topics that represent the same performer.

You can also tackle this problem by hand-creating a separate topic map file that lists each performer as a `<topic>` element with all variants of the performer's name listed as separate `<baseName>` elements. By merging the automatically generated topic map with this *names* topic map, all of the different topics representing the same performer will get merged. For example, the following topic map solves the tagging problem with The Clash mentioned above.

```
<?xml version="1.0"?>
<topicMap . . .> <!-namespace declarations omitted ->
  <topic>
    <baseName>
      <baseNameString>The Clash</baseNameString>
    </baseName>
    <baseName>
      <baseNameString>the clash</baseNameString>
    </baseName>
    <baseName>
      <baseNameString>Clash, The</baseNameString>
    </baseName>
    <baseName>
      <baseNameString>clash, the</baseNameString>
    </baseName>
  </topic>
</topicMap>
```

TM4J Future Directions

TM4J is constantly under active development. This chapter dealt with the current stable release (0.6.2) of the software. The plans for the next release of TM4J include an extended indexing system and basic querying capabilities. In addition, the TM4J project is planning to host a small number of add-on applications, including a topic map editing environment and a tool for generating Web pages from topic map information. In addition, recent developments of a standard formal model for XTM and proposals for a common topic map programming API will also influence future developments of the software.

Summary

TM4J is an open source set of Java APIs for processing topic map documents in XTM 1.0 format. In this section, I used TM4J to show the practical aspects of creating a topic map ontology, designing and implementing an application, and extending that application, using a topic map for a collection of MP3 files as a test bed.

Nexist Topic Map Testbed

JACK PARK

This section provides a greatly simplified look at what's inside the Nexist Topic Map Testbed. This discussion is intended for those who would enter the domain of the code hacker who loves to get down and dirty with the Java programming language.

For other readers, there's not much here, other than pretty screen shots (and I know how we all love those screen shots). Nexist is available with both source code and compiled Java classes (for users) at *http://nexist.sourceforge.net*; the screen shots give you some idea of Nexist's capabilities.

The Development of Nexist

The Past

Nexist started out as a combination of several projects. Originally, I built a topic map engine by combining two existing open source projects, Jext (*http://www.jext.org/*), and GraphMaker (*http://www.bluemarsh.com/java/graph/*). Jext provides a powerful text editor environment that is already XML-literate. GraphMaker provides a user interface that serves as an editor and display for graph structures.

Figure 10–16 shows the nature of Jext. The program allows users to maintain a set of XML elements. As illustrated, there are elements for DocBook and for XTM. Users can construct XTM or DocBook documents at will. When users construct a topic map document, they can copy and paste them into GraphMaker, as illustrated in Figure 10–17.

Users can also construct topic map documents in GraphMaker and, similarly, copy and paste them into Jext, where the documents are translated back to their serialization syntax. This project predates XTM, and writes ISO 13250 documents.

The Present

The current project, Nexist, is a project very much in progress. It started out as a combination of the prior projects mentioned above and recently morphed into a lone project that combines aspects of both Jext and GraphMaker, but now with the added features of SemanText, as described by Eric Freese earlier in this chapter. Going one step further, Nexist adds a persistence engine, comprised of the Java relational database engine HypersonicSQL (HSQL) (*http://sourceforge.net/projects/hsqldb*). HSQL allows for configuration as either an in-memory database engine or as a cached-on-disk database engine. I have chosen to cache XTM tables on disk. Figure 10–18 shows Nexist in one of its many early stages of development.

Use Cases

This section enumerates the use cases that Nexist must satisfy at present. These use cases are based on experience with the Jext/GraphMaker project, with SemanText,

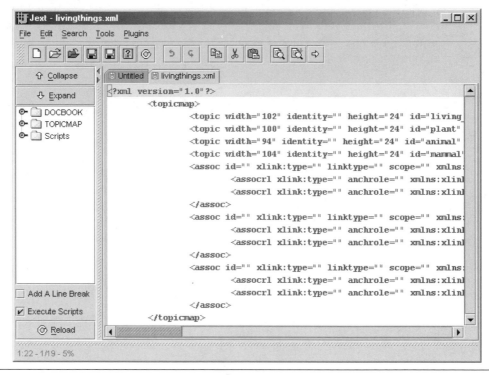

Figure 10–16   Jext serving as a topic map editor[7]

and with XTM itself. In the very beginning, the use cases for the Jext/GraphMaker version were those listed below.

- User accesses Nexist from a local application.
- User creates a topic map with nodes and arcs graphically.
- User creates a topic map with textual display and XML tags.
- User adds a topic.
- User deletes a topic.
- User edits a topic.
- User adds an association.
- User deletes an association.
- User edits an association.
- User adds a `mergeMap`

---

[7]*Note:* This project was built prior to the XTM specification; the XML code shown is not XTM code.

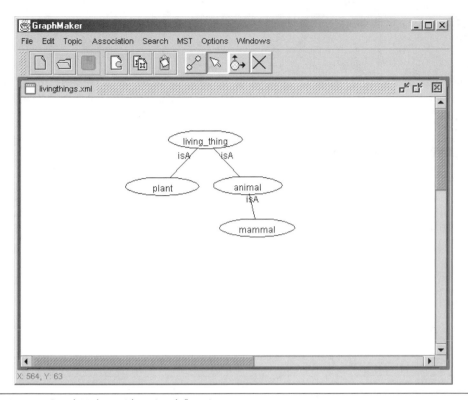

Figure 10–17   GraphMaker with a simple[8] topic map

- User deletes a `mergeMap`
- User edits a `mergeMap`
- User edits a topic map graphically.
- User edits a topic map in textual display.
- User exports a topic map from graphical to textual display.
- User exports a topic map from textual to graphical display.
- User exports a topic map to a text file from either textual or graphical display.
- User imports a topic map to textual or graphical display from a text file.
- User views a selected topic.
- User views topics related to a selected topic.

---

[8]"Simple" graphs are easy to lay out. As the screen shots of TouchGraph at the beginning of this chapter illustrate, the more nodes you have to display, the harder it is to lay out the graph so that it is easy to read.

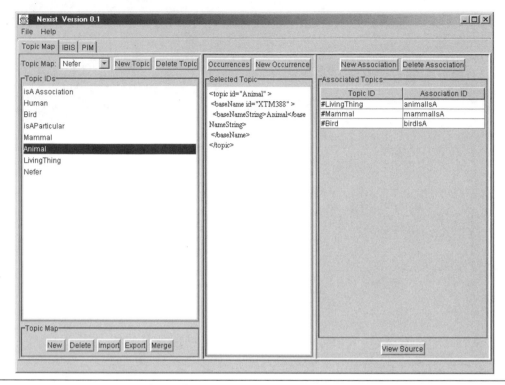

Figure 10–18   Nexist in one of its early stages

Working with SemanText added a few more use cases.

- User creates meta–topic map graphically or textually.
- Meta–topic map creates new topics derived from an imported general topic map by inference.
- User finds topics with the Search function.

Working with the XTM standard added the following use cases.

- User merges different topic maps.
- Nexist parses an XTM document.
- Nexist creates an XTM document.

The following use cases relate to a persistent store for topic maps.

- Nexist saves XTM documents in a persistent store.
- Nexist retrieves XTM documents from a persistent store.

Future plans include the consideration of the following additional use cases.

- Users collaborate from different locations to construct a topic map.
- Users access Nexist from a Web browser.
- Users register as change listeners for selected topics and associations.
- Users can perform only allowed editing operations.
- Nexist controls versions of topic maps.

Design Requirements

The current version of Nexist strives to meet the following requirements.

- Nexist shall store XTM documents in a persistent store.
- Nexist shall support the creation and maintenance of XTM documents by means of a textual user interface.
- Nexist shall allow users to browse various topics in a selected XTM document.

Once these requirements are satisfied, the next version will add further requirements and implement the required functionality.

The Persistent XTM Engine

The persistent XTM engine has been the focus of this project. The discussion of this engine appears in two parts: (1) the persistent store and (2) the engine itself.

The Persistent Store

The solution space includes open source projects available for Java applications. I elected[9] to apply the HSQL database to Nexist because it is relatively lightweight and offers the opportunity to get started with relational tables right away. The code can easily be modified to run with more sophisticated database systems such as MySQL or PostgreSQL.

Given the XTM DTD, we see an XTM `<topicMap>` element as a *container* for one[10] or more `<topic>`, `<association>`, or `<mergeMap>` elements. We also see the `<topic>`, `<association>`, and `<mergeMap>` elements as containers for other elements.

---

[9]This relates to what has been done so far. As this is written, I am considering importing Kal Ahmed's TM4J as an optional XTM implementation, which will give access to a different database system.

[10]*Editor's note:* More accurately, zero or more, but a topic map with no topics, or with topics but no associations, is uninteresting.

In the relational database arena, the game is to take objects you have out here in viewer land and break them up so they can be stored in tables much like those in a spreadsheet, where columns represent various things, and rows represent instances of those things. So, let us digress for a moment and examine just what we need to do. We have <topicMap> elements, which contain perhaps many <topic> elements and many <association> elements. Right away, we find that we probably want a table to keep track of <topicMap> instances, a table for <topic> instances, a table for <association> instances, and a table for each of the other elements in the DTD.

Relational databases use a language called SQL (often pronounced "Sequel") as a way to configure and access databases. For instance, we already know that we want a table for the <topicMap> element, so we use the following SQL statement to do that. (Remember that a <topicMap> element needs an identifier, an -id- attribute in the XTM ontology.)

```
CREATE CACHED TABLE
    TOPICMAP(TOPICMAPID VARCHAR PRIMARY KEY,BASE VARCHAR)
```

This particular statement is required by HSQL to create a table in a file saved to disk storage. Leave out CACHED and the table is created in memory. In either case, this statement says to create a new table named TOPICMAP and to give it two columns, one named TOPICMAPID and one called BASE, and then to set the datatype in those two columns to variable length characters (VARCHAR).

Let's look at a slightly more complex table, one for a particular contained object, an <occurrence> element.

```
CREATE CACHED TABLE
    OCCURRENCE (OCCURRENCEID VARCHAR PRIMARY KEY,
TMID VARCHAR, TOPICID VARCHAR, SCOPEID VARCHAR,
BASENAMEID VARCHAR, INSTANCEOFID VARCHAR,
    RESOURCEREFID VARCHAR, RESOURCEDATAID VARCHAR)
```

What do we know about <occurrence> elements? First, we know that any given <occurrence> element is contained by a <topic> element, which is itself contained by a <topicMap> element. So, for every instance (row) in the OCCURRENCE table, we are very interested in that row's owners. For that, our OCCURRENCE table has one column called TMID, the -id- attribute of the <topicMap> element that contains the <topic> element that contains this <occurrence> element, and we have a column called TOPICID for the <topic> element that contains this <occurrence> element. With those, we can now retrieve any particular <occurrence> element we need, typically with an SQL statement that looks like this.

```
SELECT * FROM OCCURRENCE WHERE TMID='xxx' AND TOPICID='yyy'
```

Now, consider the problem of using a huge number of SELECT statements combined with another SQL operation, JOIN, and you can see that in order to fill up all the containers of a large topic map, there will be a lot of SQL action. We would like to keep the amount of work done by SQL to a minimum. This thinking allows us to consider the opportunity for two improvements in performance.

1. We need to retrieve only those topics or associations we need at any particular time.
2. We can code our own joins for improved database performance.

We begin by comparing our goals to those satisfied by the Enterprise JavaBean (EJB) specification. EJBs were created to manage projects that need persistent store, so we find them interesting right away. We notice that the EJB specification calls for two kinds of EJB beans: Entity and Session beans [Jubin and Freidrichs 1999; Monson-Haefel 1999]. Session beans manage transactions. We don't have any specific requirement for transaction management at this time,[11] so, for simplicity, we skip session management. An open question is, of course, "Can we get away with skipping session management?"[12]

Entity beans come in two varieties associated with persistent storage: container-managed and bean-managed persistence. We compare the two strategies and see that the bean-managed strategy fits our desire to hand-code our database join operations. But we do not plan to use the entire EJB suite, so we decide to construct our own EJB-like XTM element classes. Thus begins the discussion of the engine itself.

The XTM Engine

As the UML diagram in Figure 10–19 shows, the XTM engine turns out to be rather simple (written while suppressing a large grin).

Actually, it really is simple. There are a bunch of Java classes intended to serve the entire needs of the XTM elements. Let's consider one such class, XTMTopic. UML diagrams basically provide a way to design and illustrate the relationships between objects in a software project using a graphical syntax. I am using UML diagrams here to illustrate a couple of important points for readers who intend to download the source code and play with Nexist. Figure 10–20 splits its own tiny universe of the XTMTopic class into two parts:

1. Data
2. Methods

---

[11] Transaction management will become extremely important as Nexist evolves toward participation in a Web portal for knowledge activities.

[12] As it turns out, we implemented our own session manager. Each user who logs into the Nexist server gets an individual session.

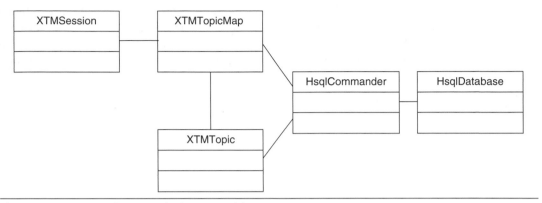

Figure 10–19   UML diagram of a fragment of the XTM engine in Nexist

The diagram is that of a Java class, an object that serves as a container to hold data and to hold the methods used to perform operations on that data. By providing a class to contain these items, object-oriented software offers a uniform approach for constructing and maintaining large programs that manipulate data. In Figure 10–20, data is listed in the upper portion of the box, while methods are listed below the data.

The points I want to illustrate with this diagram are the following.

- XTMTopic is a container for individual objects, such as the <subjectIdentity> element and the –id– attribute of the <topicMap> element that contains this <topic> element.
- XTMTopic is a container for lists of objects, such as <instanceOf>, <baseName>, and <occurrence>.
- XTMTopic serves as an interface to provide the ability to add objects to the container and to manipulate the lists held by the container.
- XTMTopic serves as its own database interface, by means of the insertSelf, restoreSelf, updateSelf, and deleteSelf methods.

The thrust of the Nexist project has been to test the following working hypothesis:

> XTM provides a sufficient API for constructing knowledge management systems.

Each of the use cases and requirements listed earlier form the context in which this working hypothesis is tested.

```
┌─────────────────────────────────────────────────┐
│                    XTMTopic                       │
├─────────────────────────────────────────────────┤
│ # id  : String  = null                            │
│ # subjectIdentity  : XTMSubjectIdentity  = null   │
│ # instanceOfList  : ArrayList  = null             │
│ # baseNameList  : ArrayList  = null               │
│ # occurrencesList  : ArrayList  = null            │
│ # isDirty  : boolean  = false                     │
│ # tmID  : String  = null                          │
├─────────────────────────────────────────────────┤
│ + XTMTopic ( String id, String tmID, boolean isRestore ) :│
│ + XTMTopic ( String id ) :                        │
│ + getID ( ) : String                              │
│ + setSubjectIdentity ( XTMSubjectIdentity id ) : void │
│ + getSubjectIdentity ( ) : XTMSubjectIdentity     │
│ + addInstanceOf ( XTMInstanceOf io ) : void       │
│ + addOccurrence ( XTMOccurrence xo ) : void       │
│ + addBaseName ( XTMBaseName bo ) : void           │
│ + getInstanceOfList ( ) : ArrayList               │
│ + setInstanceOfList ( ArrayList al ) : void       │
│ + getOccurrencesList ( ) : ArrayList              │
│ + setOccurrencesList ( ArrayList ol ) : void      │
│ + getBaseNameList ( ) : ArrayList                 │
│ + setBaseNameList ( ArrayList bl ) : void         │
│ + toString ( ) : String                           │
│ + insertSelf ( ) : void                           │
│   restoreSelf ( ) : void                          │
│ + updateSelf ( ) : void                           │
│ + deleteSelf ( ) : void                           │
└─────────────────────────────────────────────────┘
```

Figure 10–20   UML diagram of the XTMTopic class

A design requirement for Nexist is to construct a persistent XTM engine. This engine is greatly similar to TM4J created by Kal Ahmed (discussed earlier in this chapter). The primary differences reside solely in implementing the persistent store,[13] providing version control, and maintaining a permission-based access control

---

[13]As this is written, TM4J has moved to *http://sourceforge.net/projects/tm4j* and now uses the open source Java object database Ozone (*http://www.ozone-db.org*). The primary difference now is that Nexist uses a relational database as compared to TM4J's object database. Indeed, Nexist sessions can plug TM4J directly into Nexist.

system. In order to develop this engine, a user interface has been developed concurrently. The next section discusses that user interface.

The User Interface

Nexist is designed as a client–server system. The client has a complex user interface, while the server has a simple, utilitarian user interface. Let's first look at the server user interface.

The Server User Interface

When the Nexist server (NEXServer) is booted, the first screen (Figure 10–21) provides a simple set of menu selections for managing the server. Selecting the HSQL Manager menu item provides a database manager (Figure 10–22).

The primary capability provided here is the ability to examine elements of topic maps. This feature is most useful when debugging Nexist source code.

The Client User Interface

The client user interface is the workstation where users interact with Nexist. As shown in Figure 10–23, Nexist uses a tab-based design. The program is an engineering

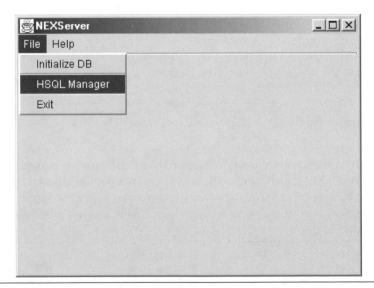

Figure 10–21   Nexist server with menu selections

HSQL Manager   [x]

File   View   Command   Options

Prop   ┌Command──┐
        │ select * from topic   [Execute] │
        └──┘
        ┌Result───┐

TOPICID	TMID	CHILDID	PSI	AUTHOR	EDATE
Animalia	FiveKingdoms	(null)	(null)	(null)	(null)
Test Issue	Test Issue	(null)	(null)	(null)	(null)
Offer a Quest...	Test Issue	(null)	(null)	(null)	(null)
Test Issue	Test Issue	Offer a Quest...	(null)	(null)	(null)
For Offer a Q...	Test Issue	(null)	(null)	(null)	(null)
Offer a Quest...	Test Issue	For Offer a Q...	(null)	(null)	(null)
Against Offer ...	Test Issue	(null)	(null)	(null)	(null)
Offer a Quest...	Test Issue	Against Offer ...	(null)	(null)	(null)
Offer a Conje...	Test Issue	(null)	(null)	(null)	(null)
Test Issue	Test Issue	Offer a Conje...	(null)	(null)	(null)
For Offer a C...	Test Issue	(null)	(null)	(null)	(null)
Offer a Conje...	Test Issue	For Offer a C...	(null)	(null)	(null)
Against Offer ...	Test Issue	(null)	(null)	(null)	(null)
Offer a Conje...	Test Issue	Against Offer ...	(null)	(null)	(null)
A focus quest...	Test Issue	(null)	(null)	(null)	(null)
For Offer a Q...	Test Issue	A focus quest...	(null)	(null)	(null)
For A focus q...	Test Issue	(null)	(null)	(null)	(null)
A focus quest...	Test Issue	For A focus q...	(null)	(null)	(null)
Against A foc...	Test Issue	(null)	(null)	(null)	(null)
A focus quest...	Test Issue	Against A foc...	(null)	(null)	(null)

Figure 10–22   Database manager

prototype on which many different knowledge management and collaboration ideas can be built and tested, so it turns out to be rather simple to design a tab-based system. Users simply write code for a new tab, drop that code into a particular directory, and tell Nexist the tab exists by adding a line of code to an XML properties file.

Nexist, as an open source project, now consists of a core set of three functional tabs: the Topic Map tab and two added features, an Issue-Based Information System (IBIS) tab and a Personal Information Manager (PIM) tab. Chapter 17 discusses the IBIS feature.

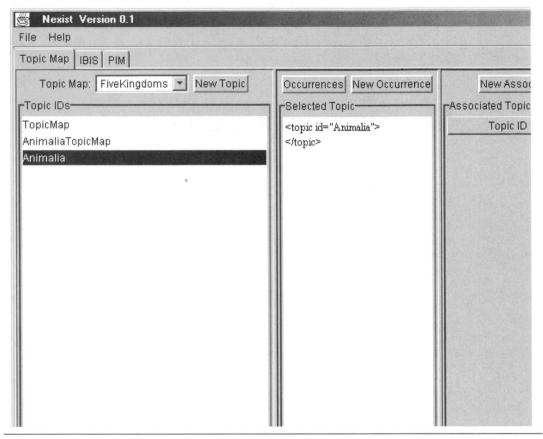

Figure 10–23   Nexist screen showing three feature tabs

Let's walk through a few of the screens available in Nexist to examine some of the system's capabilities. First, we need the ability to create a new topic map (Figure 10–24). Group buttons are not yet implemented.[14]

Once we have a new topic map, we need to add topics. In Figure 10–25 the new topic is declared to be an instance of another topic.

The new topic shown in Figure 10–26 has a PSI.

---

[14]In a collaboration environment, it may prove useful to declare topic maps as either public—available for others to see—or private.

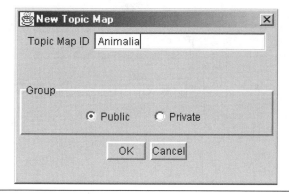

Figure 10–24   New Topic Map dialog

A topic might need an occurrence. Occurrences can be of two primary types:

1. Simple text notes
2. Resource-based occurrences

Simple text notes might describe, say, a book with its title, author, ISBN, and so forth. Resource-based occurrences are those that point to objects, which are either outside the topic map itself or inside the topic map (for example, another topic). The next

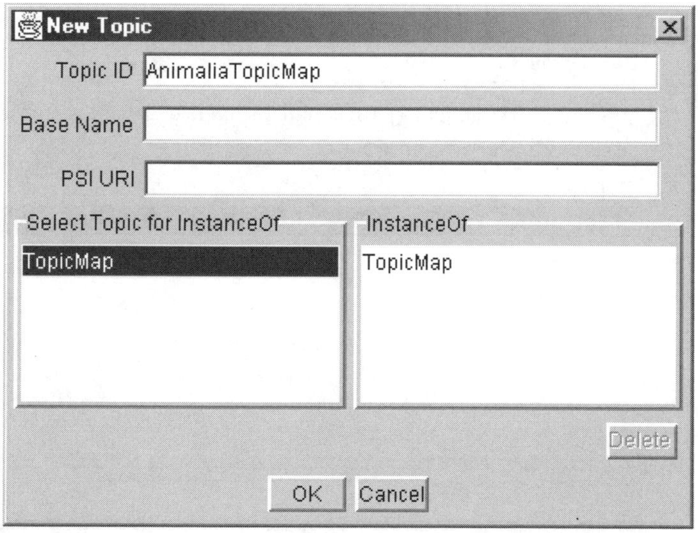

Figure 10–25   New topic with `instanceOf` declared

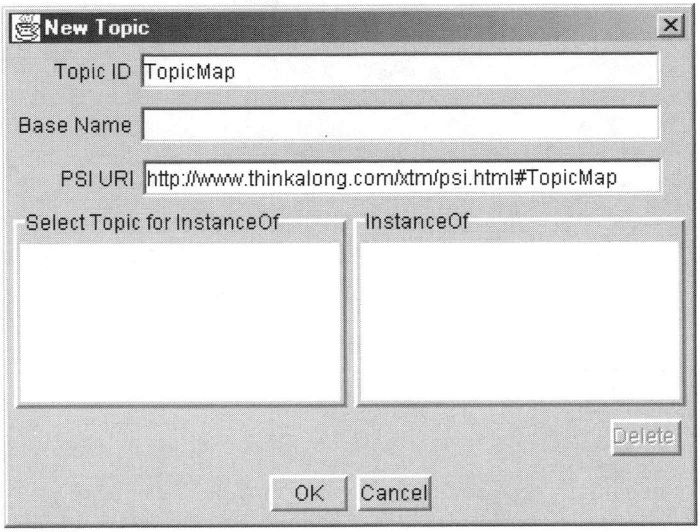

Figure 10–26   New topic with a PSI specified

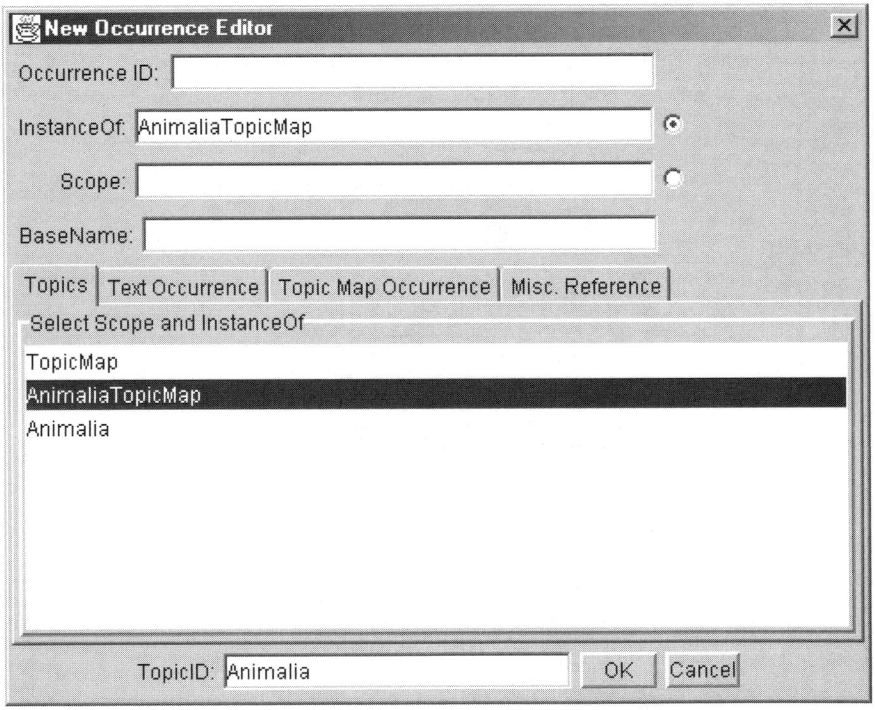

Figure 10–27   Resource-based occurrence: declaring a resource type

three screen shots show how a resource-based occurrence is constructed in Nexist. First, we declare the type of this resource[15]; the reference is to a resource of type topic map (Figure 10–27).

Next, we select the resource itself by providing a URI for it. Nexist provides a list of available topic maps stored in its database (Figure 10–28).

Now, we want to view the occurrences for a selected topic. Examine the figures above and compare them with Figure 10–29. Notice that, if the user does not specify an ID for any XTM object, Nexist provides one itself. In this case, Nexist provides XTM5[16] as an ID for the occurrence we made and illustrated above.

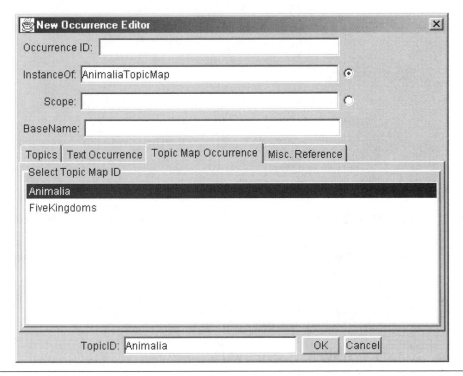

Figure 10–28   Resource-based occurrence: selecting a topic map

[15]*Important note:* Occurrences are not required to be declared an instance of anything, but in the example being developed here, we are, indeed, declaring a *type* for this occurrence.

[16]The Nexist persistent XTM engine supplies a unique ID value for each element in the database, if one is not found in imported XTM documents or supplied by the user while creating elements at the user interface.

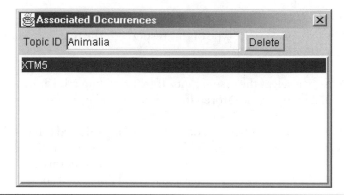

Figure 10–29   Occurrences for the topic `Animalia`

Summary

The Nexist project, as an open source project, provides many ways for new users and developers to develop or apply it to suit their own needs. Indeed, the same point should be made in relation to each of the open source projects discussed in this book.

References

Jubin, Henri, and Jurgen Freidrichs. 1999. *Enterprise JavaBeans by Example.* Upper Saddle River, NJ: Prentice Hall.

Monson-Haefel, Richard. 1999. *Enterprise JavaBeans.* Sebastapol, CA: O'Reilly.

GooseWorks Toolkit

SAM HUNTING

This section briefly describes the GooseWorks Toolkit (GwTk), a free, open source, Apache-licensed implementation of the graph-based data model for topic maps specified in the draft Reference Model (dRM) for topic maps under development at ISO (informally, the Graph). GwTk implements the version of the dRM also known as TMPM4. (See Chapter 4 for a discussion of the dRM.[17])

GwTk, written in C by Jan Algermissen (*http://www.topicmapping.com*), provides the major building blocks to assemble topic map applications of various kinds, such as command-line tools, CGI applications, Web browser plug-ins, and large-scale editing and processing applications. GwTk can be easily used as an extension to common scripting languages, such as Python, Ruby, and Perl. Currently a Python extension module is included in the distribution.

You can download GwTk from *http://www.goose-works.org*. There you will also find more complete documentation than this brief section provides, including

- Programmer's Guide (Python)
- Introduction to sTMQL (discussed below)
- C API Documentation
- Python API Documentation

Program Design

GwTk decouples the markup processor from the Graph builder. In the world of GwTk's topic map graph representation, any assertion interchanged by a topic map document can be expressed in terms of just four event types:

1. `subjectEquivalence`
2. `associationMembership`
3. `associationTemplating`
4. `associationScoping`

The markup processor maps SAX parsing events generated by a topic map document to these four Graph builder events. The *tm2gwe* tool, included with the distribution, prints out an XML serialization of the Graph builder's event stream.

Here is some detail on how these event types are handled.

---

[17]For TMPM4, see Steven R. Newcomb and Michel Biezunski, Topicmaps.net's Processing Model for XTM, accessible at *http://www.topicmaps.net* and *http://www.y12.doe.gov/sgml/sc34/document/0243.htm*. For the dRM, see Steven R. Newcomb and Michel Biezunski, A High-Level Description of a Draft Reference Model for ISO 13250 Topic Maps, accessible at *http://www.y12.doe.gov/sgml/sc34/document/0298.htm*. As of this writing (April 2002), a revised version of GwTk that conforms to the current dRM is in development but has not yet been released.

subjectEquivalence(SIRset, SCR)

This event handler is called when the processor encounters markup that expresses the equivalence of subjects. The SIRset parameter is a set of resources that indicates one and the same subject. SIRset is never empty. The SCR parameter is a single optional resource that is the subject constituted by any of the resources in SIRset.

associationMembership(Ra, Rp, Rm)

This event handler is called when the processor encounters markup that expresses an association membership. It is called with resources that indicate the subjects of the association (the Ra parameter), role played (the Rp parameter), and member (the Rm parameter).

associationTemplating(Ra, Rx)

This event handler is called when the processor encounters markup that expresses the templating of an association (as opposed to the templating of a topic map, as described in Chapter 14). It is called with the two resources that indicate the subjects of the association (the Ra parameter) and the template (the Rx parameter). (See Chapter 4 for a discussion of association templates, now called *patterns* in the dRM.)

associationScoping(Ra, [set of component resources])

This event handler is called when the processor encounters markup that expresses the scoping of an association. It is called with the resource that indicates the subject of the association (the Ra parameter) and with a set of resources each of which indicates a subject that is a scope component of the association's set.

GwTk's Omnivorous Nature

The serialization of a topic map Graph may be interchanged between systems using not just two syntaxes (XTM and HyTM) but any number of syntaxes.[18] XTM tags are not necessarily the only tags that an application could deem capable of making an assertion that two subjects are equivalent, for example. GwTk's design and the four event handlers above enable it to react to markup events in HTML with Dublin Core metadata to create a topic map Graph (which can then be exported in XTM syntax

---

[18]For example, one can imagine an application of the dRM that privileges markup representing only super-type and subtype associations, as opposed to privileging class–instance and topic–base name associations (through the `<instanceOf>` and `<baseName>` markup constructs).

using another GwTk tool, *gwxtm*). NewsML is another candidate for the same treatment, as some RDF syntaxes may be.[19]

ISO Compliance

GwTk complies with the rules for topic map integrity laid down in the dRM, including

- The name-based merging rule
- The subject-based merging rule
- The rule that a node demander is a subject indicator
- All rules prohibiting redundancies

These rules are all expressions of the simple idea that there should be one node for one subject in a topic map Graph.

Note that at GooseWorks we expect that handling transitions between versions of the dRM will be reasonably simple. First, the Graph is itself quite simple, whatever its version, and its documentation is short and lucid. Second, revisions to the dRM do not affect XTM syntax, so GwTks markup processor module is as stable as that syntax, at least on the input side. Finally, it is unlikely that any new Graph building events will be required, although one, `associationScoping`, may need to be rethought. (See Chapter 4 for a discussion of the dRM.)

Use Cases

GwTk was designed for compliance (therefore, from the top down), and it is driven by use cases to the extent that the topic maps paradigm is driven by use cases. One interesting potential approach—though not one capable of generating interesting screen shots—would be to create a command line for navigating topic maps, as an intuitive replacement for navigating the Linux file system. You would then use the console not to manage files but to manage your intellectual property as represented in the form of topics, associations, and scopes. Here, `ls` would list the current subject identity, `cs` would change subjects, `cm` would change maps (as opposed to `cd` to change directories), and so on. You could even administer the map by setting privileges for traversals, perhaps by using an ontology along the lines of those suggested by Holger Rath in Chapter 14.[20]

---

[19]See *http://www.topicmapping.com/dc.*

[20]A prototype for such a tool is available for download at *http//www.etopicality.com/gwsh.*

Query Language

GwTk allows the topic map Graph to be queried with its subject-based Topic Map Query Language (sTMQL) module.[21] sTMQL queries traverse the Graph and return sets of subject-indicating or subject-constituting resources. Here is the simple BNF for sTMQL.

```
stmql          ::= query ['AS' type]
query          ::= ['BASE' uri] 'FROM' set pathPattern
set            ::= 'ALL' | query | '{' uri_list '}'
pathPattern    ::= 'DO' (traveExpr | checkExpr)+ 'DONE'
travExpr       ::= 'TRAVERSE' (AX | AM)
checkExpr      ::= 'CHECK'
AM             ::= ( 'mAMa' | 'mAMr' | 'aAMm' | 'aAMr'
                   |'rAMa' |'rAMm') '(' (set | ANYROLE) ')'
AX             ::= 'aAXx' | 'xAXa'
uri_list       ::= uri | uri ',' uri_list
uri            ::= ''' (any valid URI character)+ '''
type           ::= 'SUBJECTS' | 'URIS' | 'STRINGS'
```

The AM and AX productions deserve some explanation. They represent graph traversals in the dRM version corresponding to TMPM4. Lowercase letters represent node types; uppercase letter pairs represent arc types. A traversal always begins at a node and ends at a node. Here is an example of an sTMQL session (from *gwq*, included with the toolkit).

```
gwq> \N
FROM {'... psi1.xtm#at-topic-basename'}
DO
TRAVERSE xAXa
TRAVERSE aAMm({'... psi1.xtm#role-basename'})
DONE AS STRINGS
-----------------------------------------------------
Napoleon the Emperor
Napoleon the pastry
-----------------------------------------------------
Count: 2
gwq>
```

In the above example, we want to get all the base names from a topic map. Since this is a topic map Graph representation, the PSIs from its association templates are available to us. Therefore, we know that every base name is a topic that plays the base

---

[21]Although sTMQL is not and does not claim to be TMQL, it was written very much to meet the requirements for TMQL. See *http://www.y12.doe.gov/sgml/sc34/document/0229.htm.*

name role in a topic–base name association (that is, one that is templated by a topic whose PSI is `...  psil.xtm#at-topic-basename`). So, with `FROM` (line 2), we make that template node the starting point for the query.

From that node, we want to traverse to the set of association nodes that are templated by it; line 4 (`TRAVERSE xAXa`) does this. From each one of those association nodes, we want to traverse out to the member nodes that play the base name role. Line 5 (`TRAVERSE aAMm`) does this—the URI parameter restricts this traversal to arcs labeled by topics that have the PSI `...psil.xtm#role-basename` as a subject-indicating resource. That is, we traverse only to nodes that play the base name role.

In line 6 (`DONE AS STRINGS`) we collect the results of our query. (Here, we return the base name strings, although we could also return the URIs of the `<baseNameString>` elements that demanded the node playing the base name role, or GwTk objects to be queried further.)

Of course, this particular query could and probably should be packaged into a single API call for typical topic map applications, such as those supported by the Standard Application Model. Recall, however, that a goal of the Reference Model is to be omnivorous with respect to markup, and so we must allow traversals to all forms of association without privileging any.

Current Tools

The following GwTk tools (source code and binaries) are included in the distribution:

- *gwa:* counts associations, topic name–based merges, and subject identity merges
- *gwq:* an interactive shell that demonstrates sTMQL
- *gwv:* an association validator
- *gwtree:* prints a merge tree from merges specified by the `<mergeMap>` element
- *gwxtm:* outputs a single topic map document from the graph of merged topic maps
- *tm2gwe:* shows the event stream as an XTM document is processed
- *tm2html:* creates an HTML representation of a topic map

Summary

I hope that GwTk provides many happy hours of development for topic mappers, in addition to proving that the ISO Reference Model is easy both to understand and implement.

Chapter 11

TOPIC MAP VISUALIZATION

BÉNÉDICTE LE GRAND

Topic maps provide a bridge between the domains of knowledge representation and information management. Topics and associations build a networked information overlay above information resources that allows users to navigate at a higher level of abstraction. However, this information overlay may contain millions of topics and associations, and users may still have problems finding relevant information. Therefore, the issue of topic map visualization and navigation is essential.

A topic map defines a multidimensional topic space. A topic has one or more names within a scope, may also have occurrences, and may play a role as a member of zero or more associations. Topics, associations, and occurrences may have a type that is a topic; for example, a particular occurrence might be a book, in which case the <occurrence> element in a topic map would be linked to a <topic> element for which the subject is that book. A topic map is actually a multidimensional knowledge base, one typically associated with multidimensional databases.

In this chapter we first discuss topic map visualization requirements. Then we explore existing visualization techniques and study whether (and how) they can be applied to topic map representation.

Requirements for Topic Map Visualization

Topic maps are very powerful in their ability to organize information, but they may be very large. Intuitive visual user interfaces may significantly reduce users' cognitive load when working with these complex structures. Visualization is a promising technique for both enhancing users' perceptions of structure in large information spaces and providing navigation facilities. It also enables people to use natural tools of observation and processing—their eyes as well as their brains—to extract knowledge more efficiently and to find insights [Gershon and Eick 1995].

Users' needs must be clearly identified in order to design useful visualizations. Before presenting visualization requirements, we need to study how topic maps are used.

Different Uses for Topic Maps

There are two basic uses for topic maps, as described below.

1. If the user has a specific question, query languages (such as the Topic Map Query Language [Ksiezyk 2000]) are well suited. They consider the relationships among objects, thus allowing query languages to find more accurate answers than do traditional search engines, which seek only the occurrences of words.
2. If the user wants to simply explore a Web site, a topic map can provide an overview so the user can decide where to start her or his exploration.

The first type of information retrieval does not require specific visualizations; textual interfaces usually suffice. The second type of information retrieval is more complex since the subject of interest is not clearly defined. In this case, users may be compared to tourists in a city they're visiting for the first time. They need to know what they should see and how to get to these different places quickly. They may want either to follow a guide or to explore by themselves.

We can see from this example that there are two kinds of requirements users have when retrieving information: *representation* and *navigation*. Good representation helps users identify interesting sources, whereas efficient navigation is essential for accessing information rapidly. Both representation and navigation are essential in a good visualization. According to Schneiderman [1996], "the visual information-seeking mantra is: overview first, zoom and filter, then details on-demand."

Representation Requirements

First of all, we need to provide users with an overview of the topic map. This overview must show the main features of the structure in order to allow users to deduce the topic map's main characteristics at a glance. Visual representations are particularly fitted to these needs since they exploit human abilities to detect patterns.

Users need to know what are the main subjects of the topic map. Once those are identified, users need more structural information, such as the generality or specificity of the topic map. This kind of information should appear clearly on the representation to help users compare different topic maps quickly; this way users can choose to explore in detail only the most relevant ones. The position of topics on the visual display should reflect their semantic proximity. These properties can be deduced from the computation of metrics on the topic map [Le Grand and Soto 2001].

Topic maps are multidimensional knowledge bases. Thus we need to represent topics and the relationships among these topics (associations). Topics have many characteristics, such as names, occurrences, and roles as members of associations, all of which depend on a context (scope). All these characteristics should appear in the visualization.

However, the stated requirements are incompatible—it is neither possible nor relevant to display simultaneously both general information and details. Think of a geographic map: a map of the world cannot—and should not—be precise. If users want details, they must narrow their interest, for example, choose a specific country. As in geographical maps, we need to provide different scales in topic map representations.

Moreover, visualizations should be dynamic to adapt to users' needs in real time. Combinations of time and space can help ground visual images in users' experiences of the real world and so tap into their knowledge bases and inherent structures.

To sum up the visual display requirements, we need to represent the whole topic map in order to help users understand it globally. This overview should reflect the main properties of the structure. However, users should be able to focus on any part of the topic map and see all the dimensions they need. Providing these several scales requires the use of different levels of detail. Finally, the representation should be updated in real time to enable user interaction.

Navigation Requirements

A good navigation system allows users to explore the topic map and access information quickly. Free navigation should be kept for small structures or expert users since the probability of getting lost is very high. For beginners, predefined navigation paths are preferable until topics of interest are identified.

Navigation should be intuitive so that it is easy to get from one place to another. Several metaphors are possible: users may travel by car, by plane, by metro, or simply by "teleportation"—as on the Web—to their destination. The differences lie in what they see during their journey. From a car, they see details; from a plane, they have an overview of the city. . . . Navigation is essential because it helps users build their own cognitive maps (maplike cognitive representations of an environment), and it helps increase the rate at which users can assimilate and understand information.

To sum up the navigation requirements, navigation needs to be intuitive, and there should be constraints for beginning users, whereas expert users should be allowed to explore the structure freely.

Visualization Techniques

This section examines which visualization techniques meet the representation and navigation requirements described above and thus may be used to represent topic maps. First we consider current topic map visualizations; then we explore visualization techniques used for more general complex structures.

Current Topic Map Visualizations

Several topic map engines provide visualizations of topic maps. Most of them display lists or indexes from which users can select a topic and see related information. This representation is very convenient when users' needs are clearly identified. The navigation is usually the same as that on Web sites: users click on a link to open a new topic or association. The Ontopia Navigator (omnigator), shown in Figure 11–1, provides an example of such a visualization.

Apart from this browser-based navigation, other types of visualizations are currently available. The empolis K42[1] application displays topic maps as hyperbolic trees (Figure 11–2); Mondeca's Topic Navigator[2] builds graph representations in real time, according to what users are allowed or need to see (Figure 11–3). A three-dimensional interactive topic map visualization tool, UNIVIT (Universal Interactive Visualization Tool), is proposed in Le Grand and Soto [2000]. The example shown in Figure 11–4 was drawn with UNIVIT, which uses virtual reality techniques such as three dimensions, interaction, and different levels of detail.

General Visualization Techniques

Most of the graphical representations described earlier are based on graphs or trees. The advantages and drawbacks of this type of representation are presented in this section, as well as other visualization techniques—currently used in other contexts—that may be adapted to topic maps.

---

[1] See *http://k42.empolis.co.uk/*.

[2] See *http://www.mondeca.com/site/products/products.html*.

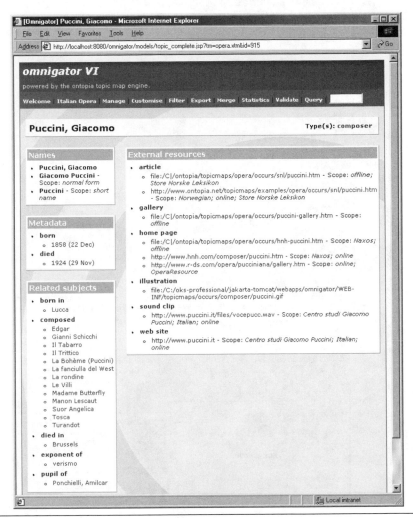

Figure 11–1   The omnigator (courtesy of Steve Pepper, Ontopia)

Graphs and Trees

Topic maps can be seen as a network of topics, so network and graph visualizations techniques are interesting to the topic map community.

Graphs and trees are suitable for representing the global structure of topic maps. Humans better understand trees, which are hierarchical and easy to interpret. Topic maps are not hierarchies and thus cannot be—directly—represented as trees. However,

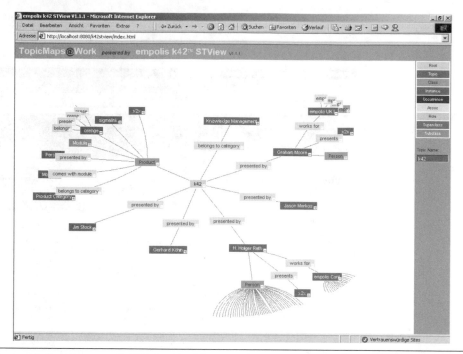

Figure 11–2   The empolis K42 StarTreeView application (courtesy of Hans Holger Rath, empolis)

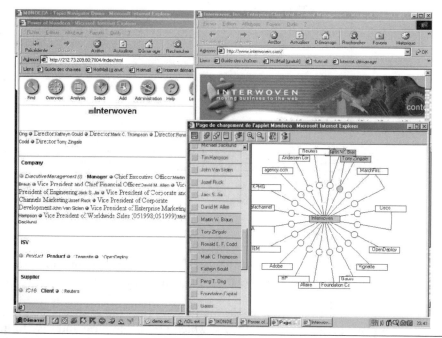

Figure 11–3   Mondeca's Topic Navigator (courtesy of Jean Delahousse, Mondeca)

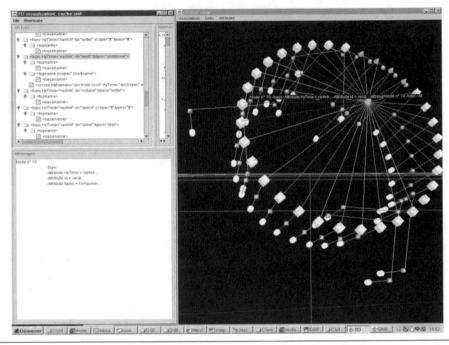

Figure 11–4   Three-dimensional interactive topic map visualization with UNIVIT (reprinted with permission from Le Grand and Soto [2000])

it can be interesting to transform small parts of a topic map into trees. By doing so with a little part of a topic map (to avoid clutter), we may benefit from the advantages of trees.

Techniques such as hyperbolic geometry [Munzner 1997] allow the display of a very large number of nodes in a graph, as shown in Figure 11–5. Efficient node positioning makes it possible to intuitively derive information from the distance between nodes. For instance:

- Topics linked together by an association can be represented close to each other in the graph.
- Topics of the same type or pointing to the same occurrences can be clustered.

Graphs and trees meet the representation requirement since they can represent the whole topic map. However, the representation may become cluttered rapidly as the number of topics and associations increases.

The second requirement, facilitating navigation by representing all the different parameters of a topic map (name, type, scope, and so on), can be really challenging.

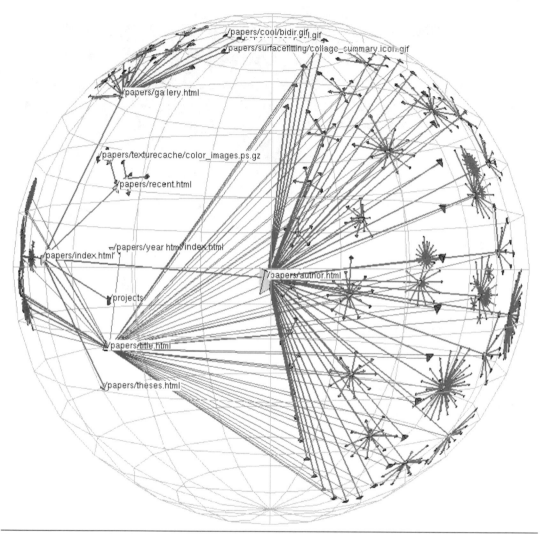

Figure 11–5 Example of a graph in three-dimensional hyperbolic space (courtesy of Tamara Munzner)

Figure 11–6 is a graph obtained with GraphVisualizer3D (now NV3D) [Nvision 1994]. Different shapes and colors are used to symbolize various dimensions of nodes and arcs on the graph. This kind of graph may be used to visualize a topic map; topics would be nodes, and associations would be arcs. However, the number of different shapes, colors, icons, and textures is limited. This representation is not suited for a topic map containing millions of topics and associations.

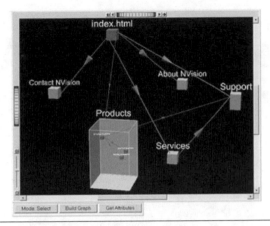

Figure 11–6   GraphVisualizer 3D (courtesy of Nvision)

The MineSet Tree Visualizer [Silicon Graphics 1999] displays hierarchical data structures in a three-dimensional landscape, revealing quantitative and multidimensiona characteristics of data. Using a fly-through technique, users view data as visual representations of hierarchical nodes and associations. Users explore data with any level of detail or summary, from a bird's-eye perspective down to detailed displays of source data.

Maps

Topic maps are designed to enhance navigation in complex information systems; therefore, representing topic maps as maps seems natural.

NicheWorks [Wills 1997] provides a schematic representation, as illustrated in Figure 11–7.

This visualization technique can show the global structure of a topic map, but it seems impossible to display details on such a representation.

ET-Maps [Chen et al. 1996] are used for Internet home page categorization and searches. They illustrate the relative importance of each page according to the size of the corresponding zone on the map (Figure 11–8). They may be used to represent topics and associations instead of Web pages.

Finding structures in vast multidimensional data sets, be they measurement data, statistics, or textual documents, is difficult and time-consuming. Interesting, novel relations among the data items may be hidden in the data. The self-organizing map (SOM)

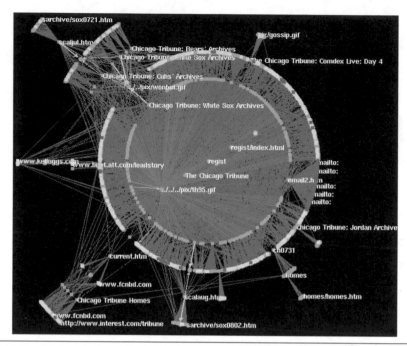

Figure 11–7 NicheWorks map of the *Chicago Tribune* Web site (reprinted with permission from Wills [1997])

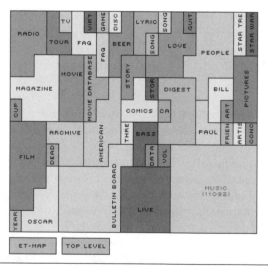

Figure 11–8 ET-Map (courtesy of Hsinchun Chen)

algorithm of Kohonen [Kaski et al. 1998] can be used to aid the exploration: the structures in the data sets can be illustrated on special map displays. When applied to the mapping of documents, this algorithm automatically organizes the documents onto a two-dimensional grid so that related documents appear close to each other, as shown in Figure 11–9. This representation is suited for reflecting the structure through efficient node positioning, but it fails at displaying associations and topic maps in multiple dimensions.

ThemeScape [Aurigin 2000] provides different types of maps. They look like topographical maps with mountains and valleys, as shown in Figure 11–10. The concept of the layout is simple: documents with similar content are placed closer together, and peaks appear where there is a concentration of documents about a similar topic. Higher numbers of documents create higher peaks. The valleys between peaks can be interesting because they contain fewer documents and more unique content.

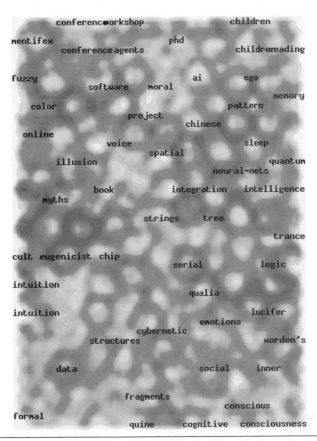

Figure 11–9 Self-organizing map (courtesy of Teuvo Kohonen)

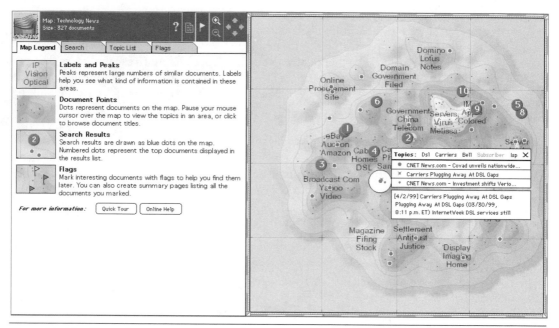

Figure 11–10   ThemeScape map (courtesy of Aurigin)

Topic labels reflect the major two or three topics represented in a given area of the map, providing a quick indication of the documents' subjects. Additional labels often appear when users zoom into the map for greater detail; different levels of magnification can declutter the map and reveal additional documents and labels.

This visualization technique is very interesting since it combines different representations in several windows. Users may choose one of them according to the type of information selected.

Virtual Worlds and Multidimensional Representations

Visual data-mining tools depict original data or resulting models using three-dimensional visualizations, enabling users to interactively explore data and quickly discover meaningful new patterns, trends, and relationships.

Visual tools may use animated three-dimensional landscapes that take advantage of humans' abilities to navigate in three-dimensional space, recognize patterns, track movement, and compare objects of different sizes and colors. Users may have complete control over the data's appearance.

The concept of Populated Information Terrains (PITs) [Benford and Mariani 1994] aims at extending database technology with key ideas from the new fields of virtual reality and Computer-Supported Cooperative Work. A PIT is defined as a virtual data space that may be inhabited by multiple users. The underlying philosophy of PITs is that they should support people in *working together within data* as opposed to merely *with* data. PITs may be seen both as a means of improving the way in which users browse and interact with data and as a means of actively supporting cooperative sharing. Users may appear on the visualization, as shown in Figure 11–11; their representations are called *avatars*.

Figure 11–12 illustrates the use of a city metaphor; this visualization was developed by Planet 9 Studios [1999]. Topic maps may be represented as cities in which topics are buildings and associations are streets, bridges, and so on. Topics and associations related to the same scope can belong to the same neighborhood. Multiple dimensions of a topic map can be represented with this technique.

Figure 11–11   Virtual world featuring several avatars (courtesy of Daniel Thalmann, designed by Mireille Clavien, Laboratoire d'Infographie, Ecole Polytechnique Federale de Lausann)

Figure 11–12   Example of a virtual city (courtesy of Planet 9 Studios; copyright 2002, Planet 9 Studios, Inc., San Francisco, CA)

One representation of topic maps as virtual cities [Le Grand and Soto 2001] is shown in Figure 11–13. Topics are represented as buildings, the coordinates of which are computed from a matrix of similarities between topics. Users may navigate freely or follow a guided tour through the city; they may also choose to walk or fly. The properties of topics are symbolized by the characteristics of the corresponding buildings, such as name, color, height, width, depth, and so on. Occurrences and associated topics are displayed in two windows at the bottom of the screen. Since humans are used to two dimensions, a traditional two-dimensional map is also provided. The two views—the map and the virtual city—are always consistent with each other.

Representing topic maps as populated virtual worlds may help users work collectively. Virtual reality techniques include interactivity and the use of different levels of detail. The level of detail makes it possible to display many scales: details appear only when the user is close to the subject of interest. Immersion in virtual worlds makes users feel more involved in the visualization. They may explore the world and interact with data. However, they may get lost in the virtual world. In order to avoid these problems, predefined navigation paths should be proposed.

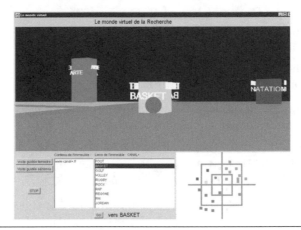

Figure 11–13   Virtual city and a two-dimensional map (reprinted with permission from Le Grand and Soto [2001])

Summary

This chapter briefly reviewed several types of information visualization techniques. Some efficiently represent the global structure of a topic map while others are better at displaying details or providing interaction with data. The ultimate topic map visualization tool should benefit from all these advantages by combining several techniques. This can be done by displaying several windows or by selecting the most appropriate representation for a given level of detail.

Information visualization is an important topic, given the high-dimensional nature of the data we must process on a continual basis. Visualization techniques are rich with opportunity to improve; topic maps provide a way to tap into that opportunity.

References

Aurigin. 2000. ThemeScape Product Suite. Accessed in April 2002 at *http://www.aurigin.com/aureka_online.html#themescape.*

Benford, S., and J. A. Mariani. 1994. Populated Information Terrains: Virtual Environments for Sharing Data. Accessed in April 2002 at *http://www.crg.cs.nott.ac.uk/research/applications/pits/.*

Chen, H., C. Schuffels, and R. Orwig. 1996. Internet Categorization and Search: A Self-Organizing Approach. *Journal of Visual Communication and Image Representation* (Special Issue on Digital Libraries) 7(1):88–102.

Gershon, N., and S. G. Eick. 1995. Visualization's New Tack: Making Sense of Information. *IEEE Spectrum* (Nov.):38–56.

Kaski, S., T. Honkela, K. Lagus, and T. Kohonen. 1998. WEBSOM—Self-Organizing Maps of Document Collections. *Neurocomputing* 21:101–117.

Ksiezyk, R. 2000. Answer Is Just a Question [of Matching Topic Maps]. Paper presented at XML Europe 2000, Paris, France, June 2000. Accessed in April 2002 at *http://www.gca.org/papers/xmleurope2000/papers/s22-03.html*.

Le Grand, B., and M. Soto. 2000. Information Management—Topic Maps Visualization. Paper presented at XML Europe 2000, Paris, France, June 2000. Accessed in April 2002 at *http://www.gca.org/papers/xmleurope2000/papers/s29-03.html*.

Le Grand, B., and M. Soto. 2001. Topic Maps Metrics. Paper presented at Knowledge Technologies 2001, Austin, TX, March 2001. Accessed in April 2002 at *http://www2.gca.org/knowledgetechnologies/2001/proceedings/LeGrand%20Slides.pdf*.

Munzner, T. 1997. H3: Laying Out Large Directed Graphs in 3D Hyperbolic Space. Paper presented at IEEE Symposium on Information Visualization, Phoenix, AZ, October 1997. Accessed in April 2002 at *http://graphics.stanford.edu/papers/h3/*.

Nvision Software Systems, Inc. 1994. NV3D Technical Capabilities Overview. Accessed in April 2002 at *http://www.nv3d.com/html/tco.pdf*.

Planet 9 Studios. 1999. Animation for the Expansion of San Francisco International Airport. Accessed in April 2002 at *http://www.planet9.com/worlds/sfo/*.

Schneiderman, Ben. 1996. Information Visualization: Dynamic Queries, Starfield Displays, and LifeLines. Department of Computer Science, University of Maryland. Accessed in April 2002 at *http://www.cs.umd.edu/hcil/members/bshneiderman/ivwp.html*.

Silicon Graphics, Inc. 1999. MineSet 3.0 Datasheet. Accessed in April 2002 at *http://www.tgs.com/pro_div/solution/Mineset3_0.pdf (checked 4/5/02)*

Wills, G. J. 1997. NicheWorks—Interactive Visualization of Very Large Graphs. Paper presented at GraphDrawing 97, Rome, Italy, September 1997. Accessed in April 2002 at *http://www.dia.uniroma3.it/calendar/gd97/*.

Chapter 12

TOPIC MAPS AND RDF

ERIC FREESE

This chapter introduces the Resource Description Framework (RDF). RDF is a W3C recommendation that enables the encoding, exchange, and reuse of structured metadata, based on XML. RDF is often seen as a competing technology to topic maps. However, recent experience has shown that these two metadata models may have much more in common than originally appears at the surface.

A Sample Application: The Family Tree

For illustration purposes throughout this chapter (as well as Chapter 13 on topic maps and semantic networks), a genealogical chart (that is, a family tree) is used to explain the concepts presented. Family trees express relationships between people, whereas topic maps, RDF, and semantic networks describe relationships between data items. Knowledge can be inferred by examining and compiling the relationships between the nodes of any of these networks. For example, in Figure 12–1, Eric, Becky, and Dawn are siblings because they share the same parents. Keri and Olivia are cousins because their parents are siblings. Cara is Carmen's grandparent because Carmen's parent is Cara's child.

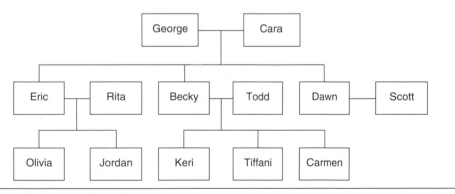

Figure 12–1 Genealogical chart

In topic map terms, each item within a box can be considered a topic. The names within the boxes can be considered unique identifier values and possibly base names. The horizontal lines between the boxes represent marriage associations. The horizontal lines connecting boxes from above represent sibling associations. The vertical lines represent parent–child associations.

A family tree provides a familiar baseline for many possible applications. In fact, many data sets that can be modeled as trees or networks are possible candidates for modeling as a topic map.

Consider a parts breakdown or parts list. The systems, assemblies, subassemblies, and parts could be considered topics or resources. The fact that an assembly is used within a specific system could be one type of association. A schematic of an assembly could be an occurrence of a topic.

A corporate organizational chart is another example. Each person, organization, or position could be modeled as a topic. Staff members at lower levels have a "reports to" association with the higher levels. Further associations could be developed within the same levels of the organization. Persons matrixed between organizations (dotted-line relationships) could also be modeled. Metadata such as employee ID and salary level could be stored about each topic within the chart.

RDF and Topic Maps

Very similar claims are made for both RDF/RDFS (RDF Schema, the W3C RDF-related specifications) and topic maps. Both are promoted as methods for associating arbitrary metadata with arbitrary content. Both claim to support an unbounded variety of information-finding and other functions. Indeed, both have been openly described as panaceas for every kind of information management woe. This section compares the merits of topic maps and RDF.

An Introduction to RDF

The Internet affords everyone access to distributed information on a global scale. However, this information is often difficult to find. Metadata, or structured data about data, improves discovery of and access to such information. While metadata will help in this direction, it is still up to applications to interpret the metadata. For various applications to work consistently on the metadata, common conventions about semantics, syntax, and structure must be developed. Individual groups and communities have their own jargon, which in turn defines the semantics, or meaning, of metadata that addresses their particular needs. Syntax facilitates the exchange and use of metadata among multiple applications by arranging data elements for machine processing. The structure of the information acts as a formal constraint on the syntax for the consistent representation of semantics, thus making machine processing easier. RDF uses XML formalisms (elements, attributes, namespaces) to define the structure of the information so that an XML parser can assist in identifying specific pieces of information.

RDF is an infrastructure that enables the encoding, exchange, and reuse of structured metadata. This infrastructure enables metadata interoperability through the design of mechanisms that support common conventions of semantics, syntax, and structure. RDF does not stipulate semantics for each resource description community, but rather provides the ability for each of these communities to define its own metadata elements as needed. RDF, like XTM, uses XML as the common syntax for the exchange and processing of metadata. By exploiting features of XML, RDF imposes structure that provides for the unambiguous expression of semantics and, as such, enables consistent encoding, exchange, and machine processing of standardized metadata.

RDF provides standard mechanisms for representing semantics that are grounded in a simple yet powerful set of XML constructs. It also provides a way to publish both human-readable and machine-processable vocabularies. Vocabularies are the set of properties, or metadata elements and/or attributes, defined by groups or communities. The ability to standardize the declaration of vocabularies enables the reuse and extension of semantics among disparate information communities. For example, the Dublin Core Metadata Initiative, an international resource description community focusing on simple resource description for discovery, has adopted RDF. Several other communities have adopted the Dublin Core and extended it based on their own unique requirements. RDF is designed to support semantic modularity by creating an infrastructure that supports the combination of distributed attribute registries. This permits communities to declare vocabularies that may be reused, extended, and/or refined to address application- or domain-specific descriptive requirements.

The RDF Data Model

RDF provides a model for describing resources. Resources have properties (attributes or characteristics). RDF defines a *resource* as any object that is uniquely identifiable by a URI. A URI can represent something that is addressable on the Web, such as the White House Web site. URIs can also represent things that are not addressable, such as the building called the White House. The properties associated with resources are identified by *property types*, and property types have corresponding *values*. Property types express the relationships of values associated with resources. In RDF, values may be atomic in nature (text strings, numbers, and so on) or other resources, which in turn may have their own properties. A collection of these properties that refers to the same resource is called a *description*. At the core of RDF is a syntax-independent model for representing resources and their corresponding descriptions. Figure 12–2 illustrates a generic RDF description. Within the graphs shown in this chapter, boxes represents resources, labeled arrows represent property types, and strings at the ends of arcs or lines represent values. The arrows denote the direction in which the properties relate the resources.

Consider the following statements:

> The parent of Eric is George.
>
> George is a parent of Eric.

To the human reader, the above statements convey the same meaning. To a computer, however, the statements are merely different strings. The human's ability to extract meaning from varied syntax is much different from the capabilities of the computer. RDF uses a three-valued model of resources, property types, and corresponding values to express the semantics.

In order to enable machine processing, RDF expresses semantic information by associating properties with resources. So, before anything about Eric or George can be said, the data model requires the declaration of a resource representing the main subject, in this case, Eric. Thus, the data model corresponding to the statement "The parent of Eric is George" has a single resource ("Eric"), a property type ("parent"), and a corresponding value ("George"). The RDF Model and Syntax Specification [Lassila and Swick 1999] represents the relationships among resources, property types, and values in a directed labeled graph, shown in Figure 12–3.

If additional descriptive information about George were desired, for example, his birthplace and date of birth, an elaboration on the previous example would be required. As discussed earlier, before descriptive properties can be expressed about the *person* George, there needs to be a unique identifiable resource *representing* him.

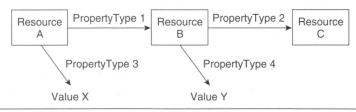

Figure 12–2   Generic RDF description

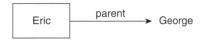

Figure 12–3   Example of an RDF statement

Given the previous example, Figure 12–4 graphically represents the data model corresponding to this description.

In this case, "George" the value is replaced at the end of the arc by a uniquely identified resource denoted by "Person_A". This new resource has associated property types "name", "birthplace", and "DOB" with their respective values at the ends of a new set of arcs. The use of unique identifiers for resources allows for the unambiguous association of properties. This is an important point since the person George may be the value of several different property types. George may be not only the parent of Eric but also a member of a set of current employees within a particular company. The unambiguous identification of resources provides for the reuse of explicit, descriptive information.

In the previous example, the unique identifiable resource for the person was created, but not for the person's name, birthplace, or birth date. The RDF model allows for the creation of resources at multiple levels of detail, based on the needs of the community defining the semantics to be modeled. In order to represent personal names, for example, the creation of a resource representing the person's name could have additionally been described using "first name", "middle name", and "surname" property types. Clearly, this iterative descriptive process could continue down many levels. Are there practical and logical limits of these iterations?

There is no one right answer to this question. The answer depends on the domain requirements. These issues must be addressed and decided upon in the standard practice of individual resource description communities. In short, experience and

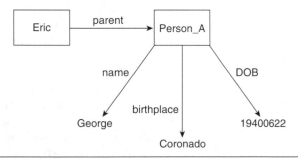

Figure 12–4   Extended RDF statement

knowledge of the domain dictate the level of detail that should be captured and reflected in the data model.

The RDF data model additionally provides for the description of other descriptions. For instance, often it is important to assess the credibility of a particular description, for example, "A birth certificate shows that George was born on June 22, 1940." In this case the description tells us something about the statement "George was born on June 22, 1940"; that a birth certificate asserts this to be true. Similar constructs are useful for the description of collections of resources. For instance, "George is the parent of Eric, Becky, and Dawn." While this statement is more complex, the same data model applies. More detailed discussion of these issues is available in the RDF Model and Syntax Specification [Lassila and Swick 1999].

Describing Figure 12–1 in RDF terms, each item within a box can be considered a resource. The names within the boxes can be considered a "name" property value. Each horizontal line between the boxes represents a "marriage" property type between two resources. Each horizontal line connecting boxes from above represents a "sibling" property type between two or more resources. Each vertical line represents a "parent" or "child" property type between two resources.

RDF XML Syntax

RDF defines a simple yet powerful model for describing resources using XML-based syntax. The syntax representing this model is used to store instances of this model into machine-readable files and to communicate these instances among applications.

RDF provides the ability for communities to define semantics. It is important, however, to disambiguate these semantics among communities. The property type "parent", for example, may have broader or narrower meaning depending on different community needs. If multiple communities use the same property type to mean very different things, problems may occur. To prevent this, RDF uniquely identifies property types by using the XML namespace mechanism to provide a method for unambiguously identifying the semantics and conventions governing the particular use of property types. This is done by creating an XML namespace that uniquely identifies the governing authority of the vocabulary.

For example, the property type "parent" can be defined by some genealogical community as "one who has begotten offspring or one who occupies the role of mother or father" and specified by the <Parent> element. An XML namespace is used to identify the schema for this genealogical vocabulary by pointing to the definitive resource, as defined by the community, that defines the corresponding semantics. (Additional information on RDFS is discussed later.) For example, assuming the genealogy XML

Figure 12–5   Sample RDF statement using namespaces

namespace as the namespace prefix "GEN:", the data model representation for Figure 12–3 would be as shown in Figure 12–5.

This more explicit declaration identifies a resource "Eric" with the semantic of property type "Parent" unambiguously defined in the context of "GEN" (some genealogical vocabulary). The value of this property type is "George".

The code below shows the corresponding syntactic way of expressing this statement using XML namespaces to identify the use of the genealogy schema.

```
<RDF:RDF xmlns:RDF="http://www.w3.org/RDF/RDF/"
         xmlns:GEN="http://www.mygenealogy.com/" >
  <RDF:Description RDF:about = "http://uri-of-Eric">
    <GEN:Parent>George</GEN:Parent>
  </RDF:Description>
</RDF:RDF>
```

In this case, the RDF and genealogy schemas are declared and abbreviated as RDF and GEN, respectively. The RDF Schema is declared as a boot-strapping mechanism for the declaration of the necessary vocabulary needed for expressing the RDF data model. The GEN schema is declared in order to use the vocabulary defined by this community. The URI associated with the namespace declaration references the corresponding schema. The element <RDF:RDF> (which can be interpreted as the element <RDF> within the RDF namespace) is a simple wrapper that marks the boundaries in an XML document where the content is explicitly intended to be mappable into an RDF data model instance. The element <RDF:Description> (the element Description within the RDF namespace) is correspondingly used to denote or instantiate a resource with the corresponding URI http://uri-of-Eric. The element <GEN:Parent> in the context of the <RDF:Description> tag represents a property type "GEN:Parent" and the content of the element represents a value of "George". The syntactic representation is designed to reflect the corresponding data model.

In Figure 12–4, where additional descriptive information regarding the parent is required, similar syntactic constructs are used. In this case, while it may still be desirable to use the "Parent" property type to represent the person responsible for the creation of the intellectual content, additional property types—"name", "birthplace", and "date of birth"—are required. For this case, since the semantics for these elements are not defined in the genealogy schema that has been constructed in this chapter, an additional resource description may be used. It is reasonable to assume the creation of an RDF schema (call it "GDC", a namespace identifier) with semantics similar to GEDCOM (GEnealogical Data COMmunications[1]) could be introduced to describe the parent of Eric. The data model representation for this example is shown in Figure 12–6.

This, in turn, could be syntactically represented as shown in the code below.

```
<RDF:RDF xmlns:RDF="http://www.w3.org/RDF/RDF/"
         xmlns:GEN="http://www.mygenealogy.com/"
         xmlns:GDC="http://www.gedcom.com/" >
  <RDF:Description RDF:about="http://uri-of-Eric">
    <GEN:Parent RDF:resource="#Person_A"/>
  </RDF:Description>

  <RDF:Description RDF:ID="Person_A">
    <GDC:Name>George</GDC:Name>
    <GDC:Birthplace>Coronado</GDC:Birthplace>
    <GDC:DOB>19400622</GDC:DOB>
  </RDF:Description>
</RDF:RDF>
```

The RDF, genealogy, and GEDCOM schemas are declared and abbreviated as RDF, GEN, and GDC, respectively. In this case, the value associated with the property type "GEN:parent" is now a resource. While the reference to the resource is an internal identifier, an external URI, for example, to a controlled authority of names, could have been used as well. Additionally, in this example, the semantics of the <Parent> element have been further defined by the semantics defined by the schema referenced by GDC. The structural constraints (predefined elements and attributes plus

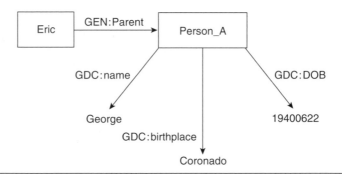

Figure 12–6   Extended RDF statement using namespaces

---

[1]See, for example, *http://www.genserv.com/gs/genged1.htm.*

the predefined semantics for these elements and attributes) RDF imposes to support the consistent encoding and exchange of standardized metadata provide for the interchangeability of separate packages of metadata defined by different resource description communities. In other words, between RDF applications, an element with the name <RDF:Description> will always mean the same thing. This does not guarantee that RDF software will be able to process the semantics represented by markup defined by different communities.

RDF Schema

The RDF Schema (RDFS) candidate recommendation [Brickley and Guha 2000] is a companion standard to RDF that provides information about interpretation of the statements given in an RDF data model. It also specifies constraints that should be followed by the RDF statements.

Descriptions used by RDF applications can be modeled as relationships among Web resources. As stated previously, the RDF data model provides a simple model for describing relationships among resources in terms of named properties and values. You can think of RDF properties as attributes of resources that thus correspond to traditional attribute–value pairs. RDF properties also represent relationships between resources. As such, the RDF data model can resemble an entity-relationship diagram. The RDF data model does not provide a mechanism for declaring these properties. It also does not provide any mechanisms for defining the relationships between these properties and other resources. That is the role of RDFS.

Resource description communities require the ability to say certain things about certain kinds of resources. In describing genealogical resources, for example, descriptive attributes including "birthplace", "surname", and "maiden name" are common. The declaration of these properties (attributes) and their corresponding semantics are defined in the context of RDF as an RDF schema. A schema not only defines the properties of the resource (for example, title, author, subject, size, color, and so on) but also may define the kinds of resources being described (books, Web pages, people, companies, and so on).

The RDFS candidate recommendation does not specify a vocabulary of descriptive elements such as "parent". Instead, it specifies the mechanisms needed to:

- Define such elements
- Define the classes of resources with which they may be used
- Restrict possible combinations of classes and relationships
- Detect violations of those restrictions

RDFS defines a *schema specification language*. It provides a basic *type system* for use in RDF models. It defines resources and properties such as `rdfs:Class` and `rdfs:subClassOf` that are used to specify application-specific schemas.

The typing system is specified in terms of the basic RDF data model—as resources and properties. The resources within the typing system become part of the RDF model of any description that uses them. The schema specification language is a declarative representation language influenced by ideas from knowledge representation (for example, semantic nets, frames, predicate logic) as well as database schema specification languages and graph data models. The RDFS specification language is considered to be less expressive, but much simpler to implement, than full predicate calculus languages.

In RDF, all vocabularies are expressed within a single well-defined model. This allows for a finer-grained mixing of machine-processable vocabularies and addresses the need to create metadata in which statements can draw upon multiple vocabularies managed in a decentralized fashion by independent communities of expertise.

You can find further discussion of RDFS on the W3C Web site (*http://www.w3.org*).

The Similarities

Topic maps and RDF are similar in that they both attempt to alleviate the same problem of findability in the mass of data on the Internet. They both do so by annotating information resources. Both can provide annotations by reference or within the items being described. Greater strength is gained when the annotations are done through reference, however.

Both models are very simple and elegant at one level, but because of the use of referencing both are also extremely powerful. In topic maps, most things are topics (not just those items marked up with the `<topic>` element). In RDF, the value of a resource's property may itself be a resource that in turn has properties.

Both markup schemes can be extended. ISO topic maps in HyTM syntax are based on HyTime architectures that allow an implementer to use whatever markup scheme is most appropriate. This customized scheme can still be processed by a topic map application via the architectures. Interchangeability of some of these extensions can be accomplished by published subjects, which may be implemented as standardized topics and associations where the semantics represented are documented and publicly accepted. RDF expressions can be extended via RDF schemas that describe the use of property types and objects. RDF schemas developed by user communities also define a set of publicly accepted semantics. XTM does not currently provide as much flexibility and extensibility as either the ISO model or RDF because its element names are fixed. The use of Published Subject Indicators (PSIs) does provide one method for extending XTM. Topic map templates and association templates are another possible method for extending XTM.

In both cases, the extension mechanism for the model uses the base syntax of the model. RDFS uses RDF syntax to define the structures contained within. You can define templates and PSIs for XTM using the topic map syntax defined in the XTM specification.

You can use both models to build semantic networks of information. A semantic network is a knowledge representation technique (discussed in more detail in Chapter 13). It applies a link with a specified semantic between two nodes that represent objects or concepts. Several applications have demonstrated how this can be accomplished. Tim Berners-Lee's concept of the Semantic Web (discussed in Chapter 17) is based on this ability to model the semantics of the information being described. The use of RDFS also allows the modeling of semantic information contained within the RDF properties.

Because RDF is fundamentally a framework for metadata, that is, for attaching property–value pairs to information resources, it can do the same job as facets or occurrences in ISO topic maps in HyTM syntax or occurrences in XTM. RDF could be used instead of facets and would arguably provide more power (because of the recursive model and the fact that more metadata semantics, such as data types, are predefined).

Topics (as syntactically expressed by topic links and topic associations) are like RDFS, in that both establish relationships between things. The RDFS candidate recommendation establishes a certain set of relationships. An unbounded number of relationship types can be expressed using topic associations. The topic map standard and specifications very deliberately steer clear of establishing a list of relationship types, leaving that question for users and implementers to decide.

Topics can have topic occurrences—arbitrary information objects considered relevant to the subjects of the topics in user-definable ways. This bears some resemblance to the idea that information object structures can be characterized by RDFS expressions; they are in some sense instances of a model expressed in RDFS.

Topic maps take a topic-centric view, whereas RDF takes a resource-centric view. This may seem to be a difference. Topic maps start from topics and model a network of relationships layered above the information resources; they even have the capability of modeling knowledge without any reference to the underlying resources. However, RDF can work in essentially the same way using resources.

The Differences

The topic map model is commonly considered more abstract than RDF. However, it can be simplified by providing templates that allow topic maps to be built without the up-front design cost that RDFS's more rigid design already obviates. ISO is currently considering the development of a Topic Map Constraint Language (TMCL) that could then be used to create such templates. (TMCL is discussed in Chapter 4.) When it does, topic maps will be at least as easy to create as RDF schemas.

In RDFS, RDF has something topic maps don't have (yet), that is, a standardized way to express an ontology *and* the constraints upon it. Further discussions on issues such as this are contained in Chapters 4, 7, 13, and 14 of this book.

Neither ISO 13250 nor XTM 1.0 have concepts that parallel bags, sequences, and alternatives as they are defined within RDF. Applications may define these structures. Published subjects for these concepts, referenced by associations, roleSpecs, and scopes, can be created. By defining them as published subjects, the concepts will survive even when topic maps that use them are merged with other topic maps.

The chief differentiator between topic maps and RDF is the notion of the scope within which topic characteristics are considered valid. It is the ability to define topics and associations within a scope that gives topic maps a greater ability to model knowledge.

When you ignore the syntax of topic maps, every topic has basically three kinds of characteristics:

1. Topic names
2. Topic occurrences
3. Roles played by the topic in relationships with other topics

For example, a particular topic name ("New York City") may be one characteristic of a topic whose subject is a certain metropolis known to us all. The same topic can also have the name "Nieuw Amsterdam" as a second characteristic of the topic. The second characteristic is validly a characteristic of the same topic within a different scope—the scope of a particular historical period very early in the life of the city. The same topic may have an occurrence that is a map of the city, another occurrence that is an expression of the geographical location of the city, yet another occurrence that is a set of laws governing the municipality, and so on. Each of these occurrences may also have a distinct scope.

The topic that has the name characteristic "New York City" may participate in a variety of relationships with other topics. It may be an instance of a topic whose subject is the abstract notion of "city"; this is a class–instance relationship. It may be contained in the

"New York State", and this relationship can be expressed as a "container/contained" association between the "New York City" topic and the "New York State" topic. Each such relationship is valid within some scope, such as the scope of "geography".

Because of the notion that topics have their characteristics within scopes, topic maps afford the capability of ignoring irrelevant or unwanted characteristics. This turns out to be crucial when information objects participate in many knowledge-bearing structures simultaneously—a normal situation in any serious Semantic Web. RDF offers no such capability out of the box, absent some standard definitions using RDFS. As of this writing, these standard definitions do not exist.

It seems possible to model most of the concepts within topic maps using RDF. However, some of the semantics contained within a topic map will be lost, specifically any information described using scope. If a topic were to be regarded as an RDF resource, then an association between two topics could be an RDF triple, in which the property stands for the association type (for example, "written-by") and its value is another resource representing the other topic. An occurrence could be modeled by another RDF triple, in which either the resource or the value of its property would be a real information resource as opposed to a topic. (In this case, the property would represent the occurrence role, for example, "defined".)

Combining Topic Maps and RDF

Topics within the topic map model can be considered as a collection of resources (that is, a collection of anchors). A topic can also be the target or anchor of a link. This implies that a topic can be perceived both as part of a link and as a collection of resources. A topic map interpreter can interpret an element as a topic, while a link interpreter can interpret the same element as a link.

A strong point for RDF is the ability to easily create a frame-based notation for a resource or a topic. Thus, RDF is a very efficient way to express a set of properties attached to a particular resource or topic. A property can even be a complete script since a property is also an element (that is, the element could be set to CDATA). The frame concept of RDF is very powerful when it is time to attach a set of properties to a topic or a resource.

The RDF notation's strength is its ability to define a particular resource set of properties, whereas the topic map model is superior in its ability to express a collection of resources related to a topic. Topic maps have the ability to define associations between topics (that is, links or collections of resources). RDF has the ability to define a schema for an RDF frame. Thus, a set of properties can be formally defined by combining the models.

A possible scenario for combining topic maps and RDF might be something like the following.

```
<topic xlink:type="extended" . . . and so on . . .>
  <resource xlink:type="locator" xlink:href=". . . and so on . . ."
  rdf:type="dublinCore">
    <dc:creator>Dr Livingstone</dc:creator>
    <dc:language>English</dc:language>
      . . . and so on . .
  </resource>
</topic>
```

By picking the best features of both models it might be possible to attach a set of properties to a locator (that is, to express an RDF frame for each locator) and have each topic be a link. It is also possible to envision that the link (that is, the topic) could also be an RDF frame and then contain any kind of property even if a property's value could be as complex as a script. However, in the current XTM specification this kind of integration is impossible since the XTM tag set and content model definitions are fixed and all children of the <topicMap> element must use the XTM namespace. This makes it nearly impossible to mix and match markup between the different schemes.

Delcambre and Bowers [2000] have worked on representing topic maps, as well as other forms of what they call "superimposed information," in a generic way. Using RDF with RDFS as the underlying representation, their approach is to use a meta-model and then describe the metamodel, the model of interest (for example, the topic map model), the schema (for example, the topic map definition), and the instances (for example, the topics, topic relations, and so on).

One example developed by Delcambre and Bowers represents a topic map (with topic types, topic association types, occurrence roles, topics, topic relation instances, and occurrences) using RDF/RDFS representation. Neither facets, themes, nor scopes have been incorporated into their work thus far and are not currently planned for inclusion. If Delcambre and Bowers were able to incorporate these features in their work, they would bridge many of the differences between the topic map and RDF communities.

Modeling RDF Using Topic Map Syntax

This section uses several of the examples found within the RDF family of specifications and applies topic map concepts and syntax to model the concepts in RDF. This is for illustration only and does not necessarily constitute the only or best method for mapping between the two models. Each model is a fully tagged example that can stand alone.

The XTM specification defines a set of commonly used constructs. The constructs are modeled using PSIs. Many of the main constructs of RDF can also be modeled using PSIs as shown below.

Examination of the different examples reveals that XTM markup tends to be much more verbose than RDF. One reason for this is that XTM was developed as an interchange syntax where data relationships are specifically marked up. RDF was designed for transmission of information on the Web and thus needed to be more compact. Unlike XTM, RDF does not have a fixed tag set. This allows you to develop specialized tags in RDF that model specific semantics for a user community. XTM's fixed tag set forces users to work within a generic model. For example, an RDF schema might define a tag for *city*, whereas XTM would need markup resembling the following to model the topic *city*.

```
<topic id="T001">
  <instanceOf>
    <topicRef xlink:href="#city"/>
  </instanceOf>
</topic>
```

Once the model is understood, it is fairly easy to develop topic maps. One benefit of the fixed markup is that the development of applications is simpler since the known element types are known for any valid topic map. Another benefit is the ease in which topic maps can be merged. Here is a simple example of a complete topic map listing.

```
<topicMap>
 <topic id="rdf-statement">
  <subjectIdentity>
   <subjectIndicatorRef xlink:href=
      "http://www.w3.org/1999/02/22-rdf-syntax-ns#Statement"/>
  </subjectIdentity>
  <baseName>
   <baseNameString>RDF statement</baseNameString>
  </baseName>
 </topic>

 <topic id="rdf-resource">
  <subjectIdentity>
   <subjectIndicatorRef xlink:href=
      "http://www.w3.org/2000/01/schema#Resource"/>
  </subjectIdentity>
  <baseName>
   <baseNameString>RDF resource</baseNameString>
  </baseName>
 </topic>

 <topic id="rdf-subject">
  <subjectIdentity>
```

```
  <subjectIndicatorRef xlink:href=
      "http://www.w3.org/1999/02/22-rdf-syntax-ns#subject"/>
 </subjectIdentity>
 <baseName>
  <baseNameString>RDF subject</baseNameString>
 </baseName>
</topic>

<topic id="rdf-predicate">
 <subjectIdentity>
  <subjectIndicatorRef xlink:href=
      "http://www.w3.org/1999/02/22-rdf-syntax-ns#predicate"/>
 </subjectIdentity>
 <baseName>
  <baseNameString>RDF predicate</baseNameString>
 </baseName>
</topic>

<topic id="rdf-property">
 <subjectIdentity>
  <subjectIndicatorRef xlink:href=
     "http://www.w3.org/1999/02/22-rdf-syntax-ns#Property"/>
 </subjectIdentity>
 <baseName>
  <baseNameString>RDF property</baseNameString>
 </baseName>
</topic>

<topic id="rdf-bag">
 <subjectIdentity>
  <subjectIndicatorRef xlink:href
     ="http://www.w3.org/1999/02/22-rdf-syntax-ns#Bag"/>
 </subjectIdentity>
 <baseName>
  <baseNameString>RDF bag</baseNameString>
 </baseName>
</topic>

<topic id="rdf-alt-bag">
 <instanceOf>
  <topicRef xlink:href="#rdf-bag"/>
 </instanceOf>
 <subjectIdentity>
  <subjectIndicatorRef xlink:href=
     "http://www.w3.org/1999/02/22-rdf-syntax-ns#Alt"/>
 </subjectIdentity>
 <baseName>
  <baseNameString>RDF alternative bag</baseNameString>
 </baseName>
</topic>
```

```
<topic id="rdf-sequence">
 <instanceOf>
  <topicRef xlink:href="#rdf-bag"/>
 </instanceOf>
 <subjectIdentity>
  <subjectIndicatorRef xlink:href=
      "http://www.w3.org/1999/02/22-rdf-syntax-ns#Seq"/>
 </subjectIdentity>
 <baseName>
  <baseNameString>RDF sequence</baseNameString>
 </baseName>
</topic>

<topic id="rdf-list-item">
 <subjectIdentity>
  <subjectIndicatorRef xlink:href=
      "http://www.w3.org/1999/02/22-rdf-syntax-ns#li"/>
 </subjectIdentity>
 <baseName>
  <baseNameString>RDF list item</baseNameString>
 </baseName>
 </topic>
</topicMap>
```

Example 1: Markup Schemes

The first example comparing the markup schemes is from Figure 1 in the RDF specification. The RDF markup models the statement, "Ora Lassila is the creator of the
resource http://www.w3.org/Home/Lassila."

```
<?xml version="1.0"?>
<rdf:RDF xmlns:RDF="http://www.w3.org/1999/02/22-rdf-syntax-ns#"
         xmlns:s="http://description.org/schema/" >
  <rdf:Description RDF:about="http://www.w3.org/Home/Lassila">
    <s:Creator>Ora Lassila</s:Creator>
  </rdf:Description>
</rdf:RDF>
```

You could use various methods to model the same statement using XTM syntax. For
example, you could use a minimalist method in which no topics are created, only
associations. The roles and members within each association would point to URIs
using the <subjectIndicatorRef> element as shown below.

```
<?xml version="1.0"?>
<!DOCTYPE topicMap SYSTEM "xtm1.dtd">
<topicMap xmlns="http://www.topicmaps.org/xtm/1.0/"
          xmlns:xlink="http://www.w3.org/1999/xlink">
 <association>
```

```
  <instanceOf>
   <subjectIndicatorRef xlink:href=
     "http://www.w3.org/1999/02/22-rdf-syntax-ns#Statement"/>
  </instanceOf>
  <member>
   <roleSpec>
    <subjectIndicatorRef xlink:href=
      "http://description.org/schema/Creator"/>
   </roleSpec>
   <subjectIndicatorRef xlink:href=
     "http://www.bogus.org/Ora%20Lassila"/>
  </member>
  <member>
   <roleSpec>
    <subjectIndicatorRef xlink:href=
      "http://www.w3.org/2000/01/schema#Resource"/>
   </roleSpec>
   <resourceRef xlink:href="http://www.w3.org/Home/Lassila"/>
  </member>
 </association>
</topicMap>
```

Example 2: Topic Reification

The example above accurately models the statement, but it doesn't really take advantage of the full power of the topic maps paradigm. In order to model knowledge, you must define topics that reify the subjects being discussed. Consider the example below, which models the same statement as the previous XTM example.

```
<?xml version="1.0"?>
<!DOCTYPE topicMap SYSTEM "xtm1.dtd">
<topicMap xmlns="http://www.topicmaps.org/xtm/1.0/"
          xmlns:xlink="http://www.w3.org/1999/xlink">
 <topic id="rdf-resource">
  <subjectIdentity>
   <subjectIndicatorRef xlink:href=
     "http://www.w3.org/2000/01/schema#Resource"/>
  </subjectIdentity>
 </topic>
 <topic id="rdf-statement">
  <subjectIdentity>
   <subjectIndicatorRef xlink:href=
     "http://www.w3.org/1999/02/22-rdf-syntax-ns#Statement"/>
  </subjectIdentity>
 </topic>
 <topic id="creator">
  <subjectIdentity>
   <subjectIndicatorRef xlink:href=
     "http://description.org/schema/Creator"/>
```

```
   </subjectIdentity>
  </topic>
  <topic id="ora.lassila">
   <subjectIdentity>
    <subjectIndicatorRef xlink:href=
        "http://www.bogus.org/Ora%20Lassila"/>
   </subjectIdentity>
   <baseName>
    <baseNameString>Ora Lassila</baseNameString>
   </baseName>
  </topic>

  <association>
   <instanceOf>
    <topicRef xlink:href="#rdf-statement"/>
   </instanceOf>
   <member>
    <roleSpec>
     <topicRef xlink:href="#creator"/>
    </roleSpec>
    <topicRef xlink:href="#ora.lassila"/>
   </member>
   <member>
    <roleSpec>
     <topicRef xlink:href="#rdf-resource"/>
    </roleSpec>
    <resourceRef xlink:href="http://www.w3.org/Home/Lassila"/>
   </member>
  </association>
</topicMap>
```

In the topic map example above, topics have been defined for some of the concepts contained in the statement. PSIs define base RDF items such as *rdf-resource* and *rdf-statement*. An association of type *rdf-statement* sets up the RDF triple. In this example, the topics *creator* and *Ora.Lassila* are also created so that additional information can be connected to them, for example, through occurrences. These could remain as resources, however. That is part of the flexibility the topic map model provides. The association uses two `<member>` elements to contain the subject and object of the RDF triple. The first `<roleSpec>` element in the first member holds the predicate within the triple.

Example 3: Associations

The next example is based on Figures 2 and 3 in the RDF specification, which model the statements, "The individual referred to by `employeeID85740` is named Ora Lassila and has the e-mail address lassila@w3.org. The resource http://www.w3.org/Home/Lassila was created by this individual." Here is the RDF markup.

```
<?xml version="1.0"?>
<rdf:RDF xmlns:rdf="http://www.w3.org/1999/02/22-rdf-syntax-ns#"
         xmlns:s="http://description.org/schema/"
         xmlns:v="http://description.org/vcard/">
  <rdf:Description rdf:about="http://www.w3.org/Home/Lassila">
    <s:Creator rdf:resource="http://www.w3.org/staffId/85740"/>
  </rdf:Description>

  <rdf:Description rdf:about="http://www.w3.org/staffId/85740">
    <v:Name>Ora Lassila</v:Name>
    <v:Email>lassila@w3.org</v:Email>
  </rdf:Description>
</rdf:RDF>
```

The following topic map models the same statement. Topics are created for some of the resources in the RDF; others are defined as resources. In addition, topics are created for the Creator property type, while occurrences represent the Email property. We define the Name property using a <baseName> element.

```
<?xml version="1.0"?>
<!DOCTYPE topicMap SYSTEM "xtm1.dtd">
<topicMap xmlns="http://www.topicmaps.org/xtm/1.0/"
          xmlns:xlink="http://www.w3.org/1999/xlink">
 <topic id="rdf-statement">
  <subjectIdentity>
   <subjectIndicatorRef xlink:href=
      "http://www.w3.org/1999/02/22-rdf-syntax-ns#Statement"/>
  </subjectIdentity>
 </topic>
 <topic id="rdf-resource">
  <subjectIdentity>
   <subjectIndicatorRef xlink:href=
      "http://www.w3.org/2000/01/schema#Resource"/>
  </subjectIdentity>
 </topic>
 <topic id="creator">
  <subjectIdentity>
   <subjectIndicatorRef xlink:href=
      "http://description.org/schema/Creator"/>
  </subjectIdentity>
 </topic>
<topic id="email">
  <subjectIdentity>
   <subjectIndicatorRef xlink:href=
      "http://description.org/vcard/email"/>
  </subjectIdentity>
 </topic>
 <topic id="ora.lassila">
  <subjectIdentity>
```

```
    <subjectIndicatorRef xlink:href=
        "http://www.w3.org/staffId/85740"/>
   </subjectIdentity>
   <baseName>
    <baseNameString>Ora Lassila</baseNameString>
   </baseName>
   <occurrence>
    <instanceOf>
     <topicRef xlink:href="#email"/>
    </instanceOf>
    <resourceData>lassila@w3.org</resourceData>
   </occurrence>
  </topic>

  <association>
   <instanceOf>
    <topicRef xlink:href="#rdf-statement"/>
   </instanceOf>
   <member>
    <roleSpec>
     <topicRef xlink:href="#creator"/>
    </roleSpec>
    <topicRef xlink:href="#ora.lassila"/>
   </member>
   <member>
    <roleSpec>
     <topicRef xlink:href="#rdf-resource"/>
    </roleSpec>
    <resourceRef xlink:href="http://www.w3.org/Home/Lassila"/>
   </member>
  </association>
 </topicMap>
```

Example 4: Bag Data Structure

The next example models the RDF bag structure illustrated in Figure 4 of the RDF recommendation. A *bag* is essentially a list of items. The order of occurrence within a bag is not significant, and duplicates are allowed. RDF defines several types of containers with different semantics attached to each.

An Alt is a special form of container: the list of items is treated as a choice group in which only one item is selected. A Sequence is another type of container for which the order is significant.

The examples use the Alt container to model the statement, "The source code for X11 may be found at ftp.x.org, ftp.cs.purdue.edu, or ftp.eu.net."

```
<?xml version="1.0"?>
<rdf:RDF xmlns:rdf="http://www.w3.org/1999/02/22-rdf-syntax-ns#"
         xmlns:s="http://description.org/schema/">
  <rdf:Description rdf:about="http://x.org/packages/X11">
    <s:DistributionSite>
      <rdf:Alt>
        <rdf:li rdf:resource="ftp://ftp.x.org"/>
        <rdf:li rdf:resource="ftp://ftp.cs.purdue.edu"/>
        <rdf:li rdf:resource="ftp://ftp.eu.net"/>
      </rdf:Alt>
    </s:DistributionSite>
  </rdf:Description>
</rdf:RDF>
```

In the topic map below, we define a different topic type that has the semantic of the RDF Alt attached to it. The definition of PSIs and the explanation of how they are to be processed make the uniform processing of the container possible. We define an association to build the container. A topic is created for the association in order to reify it. The reifying topic is included in another association linking the container to the creator.

```
<?xml version="1.0"?>
<!DOCTYPE topicMap SYSTEM "xtm1.dtd">
<topicMap xmlns="http://www.topicmaps.org/xtm/1.0/"
          xmlns:xlink="http://www.w3.org/1999/xlink">
 <topic id="material"/>
 <topic id="site"/>
 <topic id="alt">
  <subjectIdentity>
   <subjectIndicatorRef xlink:href=
      "http://www.w3.org/1999/02/22-rdf-syntax-ns#Alt"/>
  </subjectIdentity>
 </topic>
 <topic id="li">
  <subjectIdentity>
   <subjectIndicatorRef xlink:href=
      "http://www.w3.org/1999/02/22-rdf-syntax-ns#li"/>
  </subjectIdentity>
 </topic>
 <topic id="distribution-sites">
  <subjectIdentity>
   <subjectIndicatorRef xlink:href="#sites"/>
  </subjectIdentity>
 </topic>

 <association>
  <member>
   <roleSpec>
    <topicRef xlink:href="#material"/>
   </roleSpec>
   <resourceRef xlink:href="http://x.org/packages/X11"/>
```

```
    </member>
    <member>
     <roleSpec>
      <topicRef xlink:href="#site"/>
     </roleSpec>
     <topicRef xlink:href="#distribution-sites"/>
    </member>
   </association>

   <association id="#sites"/>
    <instanceOf>
     <topicRef xlink:href="#alt"/>
    </instanceOf>
    <member>
     <roleSpec>
      <topicRef xlink:href="#li"/>
     </roleSpec>
     <resourceRef xlink:href="ftp://ftp.x.org"/>
     <resourceRef xlink:href="ftp://ftp.cs.purdue.edu"/>
     <resourceRef xlink:href="ftp://ftp.eu.net"/>
    </member>
   </association>
</topicMap>
```

Example 5: Another Association

Section 3.3 of the RDF recommendation explains the about capability. This ability provides a mechanism for referencing resources that are being described. The aboutEach capability defines a bag as a resource to which a set of properties can be applied. Any properties are applied to each member of the bag, not to the bag in general. The aboutEachPrefix capability declares that there is a bag whose members are all the resources whose resource identifiers begin with the character string given as the value of the attribute. Each of the statements in the description has the attribute applied individually to each of the members of the bag.

The RDF example below demonstrates the about capability. It expresses that Ora Lassila is the creator of the bag *pages*. It does not, however, say anything about the individual pages, the members of the bag. The object referred to is the container, not its members.

```
<?xml version="1.0"?>
<rdf:RDF xmlns:rdf="http://www.w3.org/1999/02/22-rdf-syntax-ns#"
         xmlns:s="http://description.org/schema/">
  <rdf:Bag rdf:ID="pages">
    <rdf:li rdf:resource="http://foo.org/foo.html" />
    <rdf:li rdf:resource="http://bar.org/bar.html" />
  </rdf:Bag>
```

```
  <rdf:Description rdf:about="#pages">
    <s:Creator>Ora Lassila</s:Creator>
  </rdf:Description>
</rdf>
```

The topic map version below provides a combination of the bag and demonstrates the association of the instance of the *creator* topic with the bag. We define the bag using an association that is then included as a member of another association using the <resourceRef> element.

```
<?xml version="1.0"?>
<!DOCTYPE topicMap SYSTEM "xtm1.dtd">
<topicMap xmlns="http://www.topicmaps.org/xtm/1.0/"
          xmlns:xlink="http://www.w3.org/1999/xlink">
 <topic id="resource">
  <subjectIdentity>
   <subjectIndicatorRef xlink:href=
       "http://www.w3.org/2000/01/schema#Resource"/>
  </subjectIdentity>
 </topic>
 <topic id="rdf-statement">
  <subjectIdentity>
   <subjectIndicatorRef xlink:href=
       "http://www.w3.org/1999/02/22-rdf-syntax-ns#Statement"/>
  </subjectIdentity>
 </topic>
 <topic id="bag">
  <subjectIdentity>
   <subjectIndicatorRef xlink:href=
       "http://www.w3.org/1999/02/22-rdf-syntax-ns#Bag"/>
  </subjectIdentity>
 </topic>
 <topic id="li">
  <subjectIdentity>
   <subjectIndicatorRef xlink:href=
       "http://www.w3.org/1999/02/22-rdf-syntax-ns#li"/>
  </subjectIdentity>
 </topic>
 <topic id="creator">
  <subjectIdentity>
   <subjectIndicatorRef xlink:href=
       "http://description.org/schema/Creator"/>
  </subjectIdentity>
 </topic>
 <topic id="ora.lassila">
  <subjectIdentity>
   <subjectIndicatorRef xlink:href=
       "http://www.bogus.org/Ora%20Lassila"/>
  </subjectIdentity>
  <baseName>
```

```
    <baseNameString>Ora Lassila</baseNameString>
   </baseName>
 </topic>
 <topic id="page.list">
  <subjectIdentity>
   <subjectIndicatorRef xlink:href="#pages.a"/>
  </subjectIdentity>
 </topic>

 <association id="pages.a">
  <instanceOf>
   <topicRef xlink:href="#bag"/>
  </instanceOf>
  <member>
   <roleSpec>
    <topicRef xlink:href="#li"/>
   </roleSpec>
   <resourceRef xlink:href="http://foo.org/foo.html"/>
   <resourceRef xlink:href="http://bar.org/bar.html"/>
  </member>
 </association>

 <association>
  <instanceOf>
   <topicRef xlink:href="#rdf-statement"/>
  </instanceOf>
  <member>
   <roleSpec>
    <topicRef xlink:href="#creator"/>
   </roleSpec>
   <topicRef xlink:href="#ora.lassila"/>
  </member>
  <member>
   <roleSpec>
    <topicRef xlink:href="#resource"/>
   </roleSpec>
   <topicRef xlink:href="#page.list"/>
  </member>
 </association>
</topicMap>
```

Example 6: Multiple Occurrences

The next example models Figure 6 of the RDF recommendation. The example models the statement, "Sue has written 'Anthology of Time', 'Zoological Reasoning', 'Gravitational Reflections'." In this statement the resource has multiple statements using the same property. This is different than having a single statement whose object is a bag containing multiple members.

```
<?xml version="1.0"?>
<rdf:RDF xmlns:rdf="http://www.w3.org/1999/02/22-rdf-syntax-ns#"
         xmlns:dc="http://purl.org/dc/elements/1.1/"
         xmlns:s="http://description.org/schema/">
  <rdf:Description rdf:about=
      "http://www.books.org/books/AnthologyOfTime">
    <dc:creator rdf:Resource="http://www.writers.org/people/Sue" />
    <dc:title>Anthology of Time</dc:title>
  </rdf:Description>
  <rdf:Description rdf:about=
      "http://www.books.org/books/ZoologicalReasoning">
    <dc:creator rdf:Resource="http://www.writers.org/people/Sue" />
    <dc:title>Zoological Reasoning</dc:title>
  </rdf:Description>
  <rdf:Description rdf:about=
      "http://www.books.org/books/GravitationalReflections">
    <dc:creator rdf:Resource="http://www.writers.org/people/Sue"/>
    <dc:title>Gravitational Reflections</dc:Title>
  </rdf:Description>
  <rdf:Description rdf:about="http://www.writers.org/people/Sue">
    <s:Name>Sue</s:Name>
  </rdf:Description>
</rdf:RDF>
```

This example uses metadata items from the Dublin Core. The Dublin Core defines metadata specifically about publications. This topic map has been set up to specifically model the RDF statements more or less verbatim.

```
<?xml version="1.0"?>
<!DOCTYPE topicMap SYSTEM "xtm1.dtd">
<topicMap xmlns="http://www.topicmaps.org/xtm/1.0/"
          xmlns:xlink="http://www.w3.org/1999/xlink">
 <topic id="author">
  <subjectIdentity>
   <subjectIndicatorRef xlink:href=
      "http://purl.org/dc/elements/1.1/creator"/>
  </subjectIdentity>
 </topic>
 <topic id="sue">
  <subjectIdentity>
   <subjectIndicatorRef xlink:href=
      "http://www.writers.org/people/Sue"/>
  </subjectIdentity>
  <baseName>
   <baseNameString>Sue</baseNameString>
  </baseName>
 </topic>
 <topic id="anthology.of.time">
  <subjectIdentity>
   <subjectIndicatorRef xlink:href=
```

```
        "http://www.books.org/books/AnthologyOfTime"/>
   </subjectIdentity>
   <baseName>
    <baseNameString>Anthology of Time</baseNameString>
   </baseName>
   <occurrence>
    <instanceOf>
     <topicRef xlink:href="#author"/>
    </instanceOf>
    <resourceRef xlink:href="#http://www.writers.org/people/Sue"/>
   </occurrence>
  </topic>
  <topic id="zoological.reasoning">
   <subjectIdentity>
    <subjectIndicatorRef xlink:href=
       "http://www.books.org/books/ZoologicalReasoning"/>
   </subjectIdentity>
   <baseName>
    <baseNameString>Zoological Reasoning</baseNameString>
   </baseName>
   <occurrence>
    <instanceOf>
     <topicRef xlink:href="#author"/>
    </instanceOf>
    <resourceRef xlink:href="#http://www.writers.org/people/Sue"/>
   </occurrence>
  </topic>
  <topic id="gravitational.reflections">
   <subjectIdentity>
    <subjectIndicatorRef xlink:href=
       "http://www.books.org/books/GravitationalReflections"/>
   </subjectIdentity>
   <baseName>
    <baseNameString>Gravitational Reflections</baseNameString>
   </baseName>
   <occurrence>
    <instanceOf>
     <topicRef xlink:href="#author"/>
    </instanceOf>
    <resourceRef xlink:href="#http://www.writers.org/people/Sue"/>
   </occurrence>
  </topic>
</topicMap>
```

Example 7: Another Bag Data Structure

The next example models Figure 7 of the RDF specification: the statement, "The committee of Fred, Wilma, and Dino approved the resolution." The statement says that the committee members as a whole voted in a certain manner; it does not

necessarily state that each committee member voted in favor of the article. It would
be incorrect to model this sentence as three separate `approvedBy` statements, one for
each committee member, since this would state the vote of each individual member.
Rather, it is more appropriate to model this as a single `approvedBy` statement whose
object is a bag containing the committee members' identities.

```xml
<?xml version="1.0"?>
<rdf:RDF xmlns:rdf="http://www.w3.org/1999/02/22-rdf-syntax-ns#"
         xmlns:s="http://description.org/schema/">
  <rdf:Description rdf:about="http://bogus.org/resolution">
    <s:approvedBy>
      <rdf:Bag>
        <rdf:li rdf:resource="http://bogus.org/members/Fred"/>
        <rdf:li rdf:resource="http://bogus.org/members/Wilma"/>
        <rdf:li rdf:resource="http://bogus.org/members/Dino"/>
      </rdf:Bag>
    </s:approvedBy>
  </rdf:Description>
</rdf:RDF>
```

In the associated topic map, an association defines the bag (the committee members).
We then define another association, which links the bag with the resolution.

```xml
<?xml version="1.0"?>
<!DOCTYPE topicMap SYSTEM "xtm1.dtd">
<topicMap xmlns="http://www.topicmaps.org/xtm/1.0/"
          xmlns:xlink="http://www.w3.org/1999/xlink">
 <topic id="resolution.being.considered">
  <subjectIdentity>
   <subjectIndicatorRef xlink:href="http://bogus.org/resolution"/>
  </subjectIdentity>
 </topic>
 <topic id="bag">
  <subjectIdentity>
   <subjectIndicatorRef xlink:href=
      "http://www.w3.org/1999/02/22-rdf-syntax-ns#Bag"/>
  </subjectIdentity>
 </topic>
 <topic id="li">
  <subjectIdentity>
   <subjectIndicatorRef xlink:href=
      "http://www.w3.org/1999/02/22-rdf-syntax-ns#li"/>
  </subjectIdentity>
 </topic>
 <topic id="approvedBy">
  <subjectIdentity>
   <subjectIndicatorRef xlink:href=
      "http://description.org/schema/approvedby"/>
  </subjectIdentity>
 </topic>
```

```
<topic id="committee">
 <subjectIdentity>
  <subjectIndicatorRef xlink:href="#N21"/>
 </subjectIdentity>
</topic>
<topic id="resolution"></topic>

<association id="N21">
 <instanceOf>
  <topicRef xlink:href="#bag"/>
 </instanceOf>
 <member>
  <roleSpec>
   <topicRef xlink:href="#li"/>
  </roleSpec>
  <resourceRef xlink:href="http://bogus.org/members/Fred"/>
  <resourceRef xlink:href="http://bogus.org/members/Wilma"/>
  <resourceRef xlink:href="http://bogus.org/members/Dino"/>
 </member>
</association>

<association>
 <instanceOf>
  <topicRef xlink:href="#approvedBy"/>
 </instanceOf>
 <member>
  <roleSpec>
   <topicRef xlink:href="#resolution"/>
  </roleSpec>
  <topicRef xlink:href="#resolution.being.considered"/>
 </member>
 <member>
  <roleSpec>
   <topicRef xlink:href="#resource"/>
  </roleSpec>
  <topicRef xlink:href="#committee"/>
 </member>
</association>
</topicMap>
```

Example 8: RDF

RDF has the capability to make statements about RDF statements. For example, consider the sentence, "Ora Lassila is the creator of the resource http://www.w3.org/Home/Lassila." RDF would regard this sentence as a regular RDF statement. If, instead, the sentence is written, "Ralph Swick says that Ora Lassila is the creator of the resource http://www.w3.org/Home/Lassila," nothing has been said about the resource http://www.w3.org/Home/Lassila; instead, a fact has been expressed about a statement Ralph has made. In order to express this fact in RDF, the original statement is modeled as a resource with five properties. This process is formally called *reification*. A model of a statement is called a *reified statement*.

```
<?xml version="1.0"?>
<rdf:RDF xmlns:rdf="http://www.w3.org/1999/02/22-rdf-syntax-ns#"
         xmlns:s="http://description.org/schema/">
  <rdf:Description>
    <rdf:subject rdf:resource="http://www.w3.org/Home/Lassila" />
    <rdf:predicate rdf:resource=
      "http://description.org/schema/Creator" />
    <rdf:object>Ora Lassila</rdf:object>
    <rdf:type rdf:resource=
      "http://www.w3.org/1999/02/22-rdf-syntax-ns#Statement" />
    <s:attributedTo>Ralph Swick</s:attributedTo>
  </rdf:Description>
</rdf:RDF>
```

In topic maps, reification is done by defining topics for items to be reified. The initial statement is modeled as an association. In order to reify the association a new topic must be defined for it (id="rdf-statement.a"). The topic's subject identity is then defined as the ID of the association.

```
<?xml version="1.0"?>
<!DOCTYPE topicMap SYSTEM "xtm1.dtd">
<topicMap xmlns="http://www.topicmaps.org/xtm/1.0/"
          xmlns:xlink="http://www.w3.org/1999/xlink">
 <topic id="resource">
  <subjectIdentity>
   <subjectIndicatorRef xlink:href=
     "http://www.w3.org/2000/01/schema#Resource"/>
  </subjectIdentity>
 </topic>
 <topic id="subject">
  <subjectIdentity>
   <subjectIndicatorRef xlink:href=
     "http://www.w3.org/1999/02/22-rdf-syntax-ns#subject"/>
  </subjectIdentity>
 </topic>
 <topic id="predicate">
  <subjectIdentity>
   <subjectIndicatorRef xlink:href=
     "http://www.w3.org/1999/02/22-rdf-syntax-ns#predicate"/>
  </subjectIdentity>
 </topic>
 <topic id="object">
  <subjectIdentity>
   <subjectIndicatorRef xlink:href=
     "http://www.w3.org/1999/02/22-rdf-syntax-ns#object"/>
```

```
   </subjectIdentity>
  </topic>
  <topic id="rdf-statement">
   <subjectIdentity>
    <subjectIndicatorRef xlink:href=
       "http://www.w3.org/1999/02/22-rdf-syntax-ns#Statement"/>
   </subjectIdentity>
  </topic>
  <topic id="subject.a">
   <instanceOf>
    <topicRef xlink:href="#subject"/>
   </instanceOf>
   <subjectIdentity>
    <subjectIndicatorRef xlink:href=
       "http://www.w3.org/Home/Lassila"/>
   </subjectIdentity>
  </topic>
  <topic id="predicate.a">
   <instanceOf>
    <topicRef xlink:href="#predicate"/>
   </instanceOf>
   <subjectIdentity>
    <subjectIndicatorRef xlink:href=
       "http://description.org/schema/Creator"/>
   </subjectIdentity>
  </topic>
  <topic id="object.a">
   <instanceOf>
    <topicRef xlink:href="#object"/>
   </instanceOf>
   <subjectIdentity>
    <subjectIndicatorRef xlink:href=
       "http://www.bogus.org/Ora%20Lassila"/>
   </subjectIdentity>
   <baseName>
    <baseNameString>Ora Lassila</baseNameString>
   </baseName>
  </topic>
  <topic id="ralph.swick">
   <subjectIdentity>
    <subjectIndicatorRef xlink:href=
       "http://www.bogus.org/Ralph%20Swick"/>
   </subjectIdentity>
   <baseName>
    <baseNameString>Ralph Swick</baseNameString>
   </baseName>
  </topic>
  <topic id="attributedto">
   <subjectIdentity>
```

```
     <subjectIndicatorRef xlink:href=
         "http://description.org/schema/attributedTo"/>
    </subjectIdentity>
   </topic>

   <topic id="rdf-statement.a">
    <subjectIdentity>
     <subjectIndicatorRef xlink:href="#statement.a"/>
    </subjectIdentity>
   </topic>

   <association id="statement.a">
    <instanceOf>
     <topicRef xlink:href="#rdf-statement"/>
    </instanceOf>
    <member>
     <roleSpec>
      <topicRef xlink:href="#predicate.a"/>
     </roleSpec>
     <topicRef xlink:href="#subject.a"/>
    </member>
    <member>
     <roleSpec>
      <topicRef xlink:href="#resource"/>
     </roleSpec>
     <topicRef xlink:href="#object.a"/>
    </member>
   </association>

   <association>
    <instanceOf>
     <topicRef xlink:href="#rdf-statement"/>
    </instanceOf>
    <member>
     <roleSpec>
      <topicRef xlink:href="#attributedTo"/>
     </roleSpec>
     <topicRef xlink:href="#ralph.swick"/>
    </member>
    <member>
     <roleSpec>
      <topicRef xlink:href="#resource"/>
     </roleSpec>
     <topicRef xlink:href="#rdf-statement.a"/>
    </member>
   </association>
  </topicMap>
```

Example 9: Sorted Data Structures

Figure 13 of the RDF recommendation brings up the possibility of sharing resources between statements. A single resource can be the value of more than one property; that is, it can be the object of more than one statement and therefore pointed to by more than one arc. For example, a single Web page might be shared between several documents and might then be referenced more than once in a site map. Or two different (ordered) sequences of the same resources may be given.

The following example specifies the collected works of an author, sorted once by publication date and then sorted again alphabetically by subject.

```
<rdf:RDF xmlns:rdf=http://www.w3.org/1999/02/22-rdf-syntax-ns#>
  <rdf:Seq rdf:ID="JSPapersByDate">
    <rdf:li rdf:resource="http://www.dogworld.com/Aug96.doc"/>
    <rdf:li rdf:resource="http://www.webnuts.net/Jan97.html"/>
    <rdf:li rdf:resource="http://www.carchat.com/Sept97.html"/>
  </rdf:Seq>
  <rdf:Seq rdf:ID="JSPapersBySubj">
    <rdf:li rdf:resource="http://www.carchat.com/Sept97.html"/>
    <rdf:li rdf:resource="http://www.dogworld.com/Aug96.doc"/>
    <rdf:li rdf:resource="http://www.webnuts.net/Jan97.html"/>
  </rdf:Seq>
</rdf:RDF>
```

The topic map equivalent defines a special sort of RDF bag for handling sequences and sets up a PSI for it. Associations set up the bags referring to the appropriate resources in the appropriate order.

```
<?xml version="1.0"?>
<!DOCTYPE topicMap SYSTEM "xtm1.dtd">
<topicMap xmlns="http://www.topicmaps.org/xtm/1.0/"
          xmlns:xlink="http://www.w3.org/1999/xlink">
 <topic id="seq">
  <subjectIdentity>
   <subjectIndicatorRef xlink:href=
      "http://www.w3.org/1999/02/22-rdf-syntax-ns#Seq"/>
  </subjectIdentity>
 </topic>
 <topic id="li">
  <subjectIdentity>
   <subjectIndicatorRef xlink:href=
      "http://www.w3.org/1999/02/22-rdf-syntax-ns#li"/>
  </subjectIdentity>
 </topic>

 <association id="JSPapersByDate">
  <instanceOf>
```

```
    <topicRef xlink:href="#seq"/>
   </instanceOf>
   <member>
    <roleSpec>
     <topicRef xlink:href="#li"/>
    </roleSpec>
    <resourceRef xlink:href="http://www.dogworld.com/Aug96.doc"/>
    <resourceRef xlink:href="http://www.webnuts.net/Jan97.html"/>
    <resourceRef xlink:href="http://www.carchat.com/Sept97.html"/>
   </member>
  </association>

  <association id="JSPapersBySubj">
   <instanceOf>
    <topicRef xlink:href="seq"/>
   </instanceOf>
   <member>
    <roleSpec>
     <topicRef xlink:href="#li"/>
    </roleSpec>
    <resourceRef xlink:href="http://www.carchat.com/Sept97.html"/>
    <resourceRef xlink:href="http://www.dogworld.com/Aug96.doc"/>
    <resourceRef xlink:href="http://www.webnuts.net/Jan97.html"/>
   </member>
  </association>
</topicMap>
```

Example 10: Aggregation

The RDF example in Section 7.2 of the RDF recommendation takes aggregation a bit further. In this example a single resource has statements concerning its creators, other sites, and different titles.

```
<rdf:RDF xmlns:rdf="http://www.w3.org/1999/02/22-rdf-syntax-ns#"
         xmlns:dc="http://purl.org/dc/elements/1.1/">
  <rdf:Description rdf:about="http://www.foo.com/cool.html">
    <dc:creator>
      <rdf:Seq rdf:ID="CreatorsAlphabeticalBySurname">
        <rdf:li>Mary Andrew</rdf:li>
        <rdf:li>Jacky Crystal</rdf:li>
      </rdf:Seq>
    </dc:creator>

    <dc:identifier>
      <rdf:Bag rdf:ID="MirroredSites">
        <rdf:li rdf:resource="http://www.foo.com.au/cool.html"/>
        <rdf:li rdf:resource="http://www.foo.com.it/cool.html"/>
      </rdf:Bag>
    </dc:identifier>
```

```
        <dc:title>
          <rdf:Alt>
            <rdf:li xml:lang="en">The Coolest Web Page</rdf:li>
            <rdf:li xml:lang="it">Il Pagio di Web Fuba</rdf:li>
          </rdf:Alt>
        </dc:title>
      </rdf:Description>
</rdf:RDF>
```

The topic map version demonstrates several topic map features at the same time. Each of the property types is declared as a topic. These topics then appear as classes within <instanceOf> elements. The *identifier* and *title* topics are modeled as occurrences of the main topic. Scopes are used to differentiate between the English and the Italian versions.

```
<?xml version="1.0"?>
<!DOCTYPE topicMap SYSTEM "xtm1.dtd">
<topicMap xmlns="http://www.topicmaps.org/xtm/1.0/"
          xmlns:xlink="http://www.w3.org/1999/xlink">
 <topic id="resource">
  <subjectIdentity>
   <subjectIndicatorRef xlink:href=
      "http://www.w3.org/2000/01/rdf-schema#Resource"/>
  </subjectIdentity>
 </topic>
 <topic id="seq">
  <subjectIdentity>
   <subjectIndicatorRef xlink:href=
      "http://www.w3.org/1999/02/22-rdf-syntax-ns#Seq"/>
  </subjectIdentity>
 </topic>
 <topic id="li">
  <subjectIdentity>
   <subjectIndicatorRef xlink:href=
      "http://www.w3.org/1999/02/22-rdf-syntax-ns#li"/>
  </subjectIdentity>
 </topic>
 <topic id="creator">
  <subjectIdentity>
   <subjectIndicatorRef xlink:href=
       "http://purl.org/dc/elements/1.1/creator"/>
  </subjectIdentity>
 </topic>
 <topic id="identifier">
  <subjectIdentity>
   <subjectIndicatorRef xlink:href=
       "http://purl.org/dc/elements/1.1/identifier"/>
  </subjectIdentity>
 </topic>
 <topic id="title">
```

```
  <subjectIdentity>
   <subjectIndicatorRef xlink:href=
      "http://purl.org/dc/elements/1.1/title"/>
  </subjectIdentity>
</topic>
<topic id="mary.andrew">
 <subjectIdentity>
  <subjectIndicatorRef xlink:href=
     "http://www.bogus.org/Mary%20Andrew"/>
 </subjectIdentity>
 <baseName>
  <baseNameString>Mary Andrew</baseNameString>
 </baseName>
</topic>
<topic id="jacky.crystal">
 <subjectIdentity>
  <subjectIndicatorRef xlink:href=
     "http://www.bogus.org/Jacky%20Crystal"/>
 </subjectIdentity>
 <baseName>
  <baseNameString>Jacky Crystal</baseNameString>
 </baseName>
</topic>
<topic id="creators.list">
 <subjectIdentity>
  <subjectIndicatorRef xlink:href=
     "#CreatorsAlphabeticalBySurname"/>
 </subjectIdentity>
</topic>

<association id="CreatorsAlphabeticalBySurname">
 <instanceOf>
  <topicRef xlink:href="#seq"/>
 </instanceOf>
 <member>
  <roleSpec>
   <topicRef xlink:href="#li"/>
  </roleSpec>
  <topicRef xlink:href="#mary.andrew"/>
  <topicRef xlink:href="#jacky.crystal"/>
 </member>
</association>

<topic id="cool.html">
 <subjectIdentity>
  <subjectIndicatorRef xlink:href="http://www.foo.com/cool.html"/>
 </subjectIdentity>
 <occurrence>
  <instanceOf>
   <topicRef xlink:href="#identifier"/>
  </instanceOf>
  <scope>
```

```
      <subjectIndicatorRef xlink:href=
        "http://www.topicmaps.org/xtm/1.0/language.xtm#en"/>
    </scope>
    <resourceRef xlink:href="http://www.foo.com.au/cool.html"/>
   </occurrence>
   <occurrence>
    <instanceOf>
     <topicRef xlink:href="#identifier"/>
    </instanceOf>
    <scope>
     <subjectIndicatorRef xlink:href=
        "http://www.topicmaps.org/xtm/1.0/language.xtm#it"/>
    </scope>
    <resourceRef xlink:href="http://www.foo.com.it/cool.html"/>
   </occurrence>
   <occurrence>
    <instanceOf>
     <topicRef xlink:href="#title"/>
    </instanceOf>
    <scope>
     <subjectIndicatorRef xlink:href=
        "http://www.topicmaps.org/xtm/1.0/language.xtm#en"/>
    </scope>
    <resourceData>The Coolest Web Page</resourceData>
   </occurrence>
   <occurrence>
    <instanceOf>
     <topicRef xlink:href="#title"/>
    </instanceOf>
    <scope>
     <subjectIndicatorRef xlink:href=
        "http://www.topicmaps.org/xtm/1.0/language.xtm#it"/>
    </scope>
    <resourceData>Il Pagio di Web Fuba</resourceData>
   </occurrence>
  </topic>


  <association>
   <member>
    <roleSpec>
     <topicRef xlink:href="#creator"/>
    </roleSpec>
    <topicRef xlink:href="#creators.list"/>
   </member>
   <member>
    <roleSpec>
     <topicRef xlink:href="#resource"/>
    </roleSpec>
    <topicRef xlink:href="#cool.html"/>
   </member>
  </association>
 </topicMap>
```

Example 11: Relational Data Structures

RDF's data model supports only binary relations; in other words, statements specify relationships between two resources. The following example shows a possible way to represent higher arity relations in RDF using just binary relations. The technique uses an intermediate resource with additional properties of this resource giving the remaining relations. In the example, consider the subject of one of John Smith's recent articles—library science. The Dewey Decimal Code is the classification method used to categorize that article. Dewey Decimal Codes are far from the only subject categorization scheme, so to hold the classification system relation we identify an additional resource as the value of the subject property and annotate this resource with an additional property that identifies the categorization scheme used.

```
<rdf:RDF xmlns:rdf="http://www.w3.org/1999/02/22-rdf-syntax-ns#"
         xmlns:dc="http://purl.org/dc/element/1.1/"
         xmlns:l="http://mycorp.com/schemas/my-schema#">
  <rdf:Description rdf:about="http://www.webnuts.net/Jan97.html">
    <dc:subject rdf:value="020 - Library Science"
           l:Classification="Dewey Decimal Code"/>
  </rdf:Description>
</rdf:RDF>
```

In the topic map version, the classification code is associated directly with the Dewey Decimal Code topic. The optional -id- attribute on the <occurrence> element allows the occurrence of the code to be referenced when used to describe the subject of the publication.

```
<?xml version="1.0"?>
<!DOCTYPE topicMap SYSTEM "xtm1.dtd">
<topicMap xmlns=http://www.topicmaps.org/xtm/1.0/
      xmlns:xlink="http://www.w3.org/1999/xlink">
 <topic id="subject">
  <subjectIdentity>
   <subjectIndicatorRef xlink:href=
       "http://purl.org/dc/elements/1.1/subject"/>
  </subjectIdentity>
 </topic>
 <topic id="dewey">
  <baseName>
   <baseNameString>Dewey Decimal Code</baseNameString>
  </baseName>
  <occurrence id="dewey.020">
   <resourceData>020 - Library Science</resourceData>
  </occurrence>
 </topic>

 <topic id="webnuts.org.Jan97">
  <subjectIdentity>
```

```
      <subjectIndicatorRef xlink:href=
         "http://www.webnuts.net/Jan97.html"/>
   </subjectIdentity>
   <occurrence>
    <instanceOf>
     <topicRef xlink:href="#subject"/>
    </instanceOf>
    <resourceRef xlink:href="#dewey.020"/>
   </occurrence>
  </topic>
<topicMap>
```

Example 12: Dublin Core Metadata

The Dublin Core metadata is designed to facilitate discovery of electronic resources in a manner similar to a library card catalog. The vocabularies defined by the Dublin Core Initiative use RDF as the specification language. The following example illustrates the Digital Libraries program and metadata about that program expressed in the Dublin Core syntax.

```
<rdf:RDF xmlns:rdf="http://www.w3.org/1999/02/22-rdf-syntax-ns#"
         xmlns:dc="http://purl.org/dc/elements/1.1/" >
  <rdf:Description rdf:about="http://www.dlib.org/">
    <dc:title>D-Lib Program - Research in Digital
        Libraries</dc:title>
    <dc:description>The D-Lib program supports the community of people
     with research interests in digital libraries and electronic
     publishing.</dc:description>
    <dc:Publisher>Corporation for National Research
        Initiatives</dc:publisher>
    <dc:date>1995-01-07</dc:date>
    <dc:subject>
      <rdf:Bag>
      <rdf:li>Research; statistical methods</rdf:li>
      <rdf:li>Education, research, related topics</rdf:li>
      <rdf:li>Library use studies</rdf:li>
      </rdf:Bag>
    </dc:subject>
    <dc:type>World Wide Web Home Page</dc:type>
    <dc:format>text/html</dc:format>
    <dc:language>en</dc:language>
  </rdf:Description>
</rdf:RDF>
```

Dublin Core data can also be modeled using topic map syntax. We define each classification of data as a topic. Each use of a classification type can be modeled using occurrences.

```
<?xml version="1.0"?>
<!DOCTYPE topicMap SYSTEM "xtm1.dtd">
<topicMap xmlns="http://www.topicmaps.org/xtm/1.0/"
          xmlns:xlink="http://www.w3.org/1999/xlink">
 <topic id="bag">
  <subjectIdentity>
   <subjectIndicatorRef xlink:href=
      "http://www.w3.org/1999/02/22-rdf-syntax-ns#Bag"/>
  </subjectIdentity>
 </topic>
 <topic id="li">
  <subjectIdentity>
   <subjectIndicatorRef xlink:href=
      "http://www.w3.org/1999/02/22-rdf-syntax-ns#li"/>
  </subjectIdentity>
 </topic>
 <topic id="title">
  <subjectIdentity>
   <subjectIndicatorRef xlink:href=
       "http://purl.org/dc/elements/1.1/title"/>
  </subjectIdentity>
 </topic>
 <topic id="description">
  <subjectIdentity>
   <subjectIndicatorRef xlink:href=
      "http://purl.org/dc/elements/1.1/description"/>
  </subjectIdentity>
 </topic>
 <topic id="publisher">
  <subjectIdentity>
   <subjectIndicatorRef xlink:href=
      "http://purl.org/dc/elements/1.1/publisher"/>
  </subjectIdentity>
 </topic>
 <topic id="date">
  <subjectIdentity>
   <subjectIndicatorRef xlink:href=
      "http://purl.org/dc/elements/1.1/date"/>
  </subjectIdentity>
 </topic>
 <topic id="subject">
  <subjectIdentity>
   <subjectIndicatorRef xlink:href=
      "http://purl.org/dc/elements/1.1/subject"/>
  </subjectIdentity>
 </topic>
 <topic id="subject.research">
  <instanceOf>
    <topicRef xlink:href="#subject"/>
```

```
 </instanceOf>
 <baseName>
  <baseNameString>Research; statistical methods</baseNameString>
 </baseName>
</topic>
<topic id="subject.education">
 <instanceOf>
   <topicRef xlink:href="#subject"/>
 </instanceOf>
 <baseName>
  <baseNameString>Education, research, related
     topics</baseNameString>
 </baseName>
</topic>
<topic id="subject.library">
 <instanceOf>
  <topicRef xlink:href="#subject"/>
 </instanceOf>
 <baseName>
  <baseNameString>Library use studies</baseNameString>
 </baseName>
</topic>
<topic id="type">
 <subjectIdentity>
  <subjectIndicatorRef xlink:href=
      "http://purl.org/dc/elements/1.1/type"/>
 </subjectIdentity>
</topic>
<topic id="format">
 <subjectIdentity>
  <subjectIndicatorRef xlink:href=
      "http://purl.org/dc/elements/1.1/format"/>
 </subjectIdentity>
</topic>
<topic id="language">
 <subjectIdentity>
  <subjectIndicatorRef xlink:href=
      "http://purl.org/dc/elements/1.1/language"/>
 </subjectIdentity>
</topic>

<topic id="dlib.org">
 <subjectIdentity>
  <subjectIndicatorRef xlink:href="http://www.dlib.org"/>
 </subjectIdentity>
 <occurrence>
  <instanceOf>
   <topicRef xlink:href="#title"/>
  </instanceOf>
```

```
    <resourceData>D-Lib Program - Research in Digital
      Libraries</resourceData>
  </occurrence>
  <occurrence>
   <instanceOf>
    <topicRef xlink:href="#description"/>
   </instanceOf>
   <resourceData>The D-Lib program supports the community of people
      with research interests in digital libraries and electronic
      publishing.</resourceData>
  </occurrence>
  <occurrence>
   <instanceOf>
    <topicRef xlink:href="#publisher"/>
   </instanceOf>
   <resourceData>Corporation for National Research
      Initiatives</resourceData>
  </occurrence>
  <occurrence>
   <instanceOf>
    <topicRef xlink:href="#date"/>
   </instanceOf>
   <resourceData>1995-01-07</resourceData>
  </occurrence>
  <occurrence>
   <instanceOf>
    <topicRef xlink:href="#subject"/>
   </instanceOf>
   <resourceRef xlink:href="#subject.research"/>
  </occurrence>
  <occurrence>
   <instanceOf>
    <topicRef xlink:href="#subject"/>
   </instanceOf>
   <resourceRef xlink:href="#subject.education"/>
  </occurrence>
  <occurrence>
   <instanceOf>
    <topicRef xlink:href="#subject"/>
   </instanceOf>
   <resourceRef xlink:href="#subject.library"/>
  </occurrence>
  <occurrence>
   <instanceOf>
    <topicRef xlink:href="#type"/>
   </instanceOf>
   <resourceData>World Wide Web Home Page</resourceData>
  </occurrence>
  <occurrence>
   <instanceOf>
```

```
   <topicRef xlink:href="#format"/>
  </instanceOf>
  <resourceData>text/html</resourceData>
 </occurrence>
 <occurrence>
  <instanceOf>
   <topicRef xlink:href="#language"/>
  </instanceOf>
  <resourceRef xlink:href=
     "http://www.topicmaps.org/xtm/1.0/language.xtm#en"/>
 </occurrence>
 </topic>
</topicMap>
```

Summary

As you can see in the examples presented in this chapter, it is possible to model most RDF structures using topic map syntax. In fact, it may be possible to combine the two models. Work has begun that may lead to a possible unification of the models. Representatives from the RDF community and the topic map community have been discussing the best path for possibly unifying the two models. At the very least, it seems possible to further demonstrate interoperability between the models.

In the development of the XTM specification, the XTM Authoring Group has taken a great deal of care in considering RDF capabilities. The ability to handle resources is an excellent example of the bridging of the two models.

References

Brickley, Dan, and R. V. Guha. 2000. Resource Description Framework (RDF) Schema Specification 1.0. Accessed in April 2002 at *http://www.w3.org/TR/2000/CR-rdf-schema-20000327/*.

Delcambre, Lois, and Shawn Bowers. 2000. A Generic Approach for Representing Model-Based Superimposed Information. Accessed in April 2002 at *http://www.cse.ogi.edu/~shawn/rpe/bowersrpe.pdf*.

Lassila, Ora, and Ralph Swick. 1999. Resource Description Framework (RDF) Model and Syntax Specification. Accessed in April 2002 at *http://www.w3.org/TR/1999/REC-rdf-syntax-19990222/*.

Miller, Eric. 1998. An Introduction to the Resource Description Framework. *D-Lib Magazine*, May. Accessed in April 2002 at *http://www.dlib.org/dlib/may98/miller/05miller.htm*.

Chapter 13
TOPIC MAPS AND SEMANTIC NETWORKS

ERIC FREESE

In science fiction movies and television shows, past and present, humans of the future often interact with computers to receive information built from a vast database of knowledge somewhere. The computers can quickly locate and assemble, from a galaxy's worth of data, the precise information needed at the time by the user. But how was that data organized? What mechanisms were used to aggregate the information from what must have been millions of documents generated from thousands of sources, including human writers and databases?

How far off is this futuristic scenario? The future is, in fact, now—and it is no longer fiction. Standards, specifications, and techniques now exist that allow the grouping and organization of data so that it can be retrieved and processed quickly and efficiently. The standards include the XML family of specifications as well as the topic map standard (ISO 13250) and specification (XTM 1.0). The techniques include semantic networks and inferencing engines.

In this chapter we'll build an entire topic map that models the relationships shown in Figure 13–1, which is from the family tree example introduced in Chapter 12. The entire XTM document developed in this chapter appears in Appendix D.

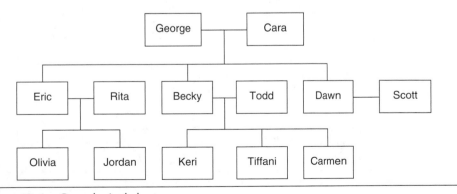

Figure 13–1   Genealogical chart

Semantic Networks: The Basics

The *semantic network* is a representation formalism that has been used for many years in artificial intelligence (AI) research. Semantic networks consist of *nodes* and *links*. Nodes usually represent objects, concepts, or situations within a specific domain. Links represent relationships between the nodes that have a semantic meaning to them. Both the nodes and the links can have labels. Continuing with the genealogical chart, it is possible to represent a simple fact such as "Eric is a descendant of George" in a semantic network by creating two nodes—one to represent a person named "Eric" and another to represent a person named "George." We then create a link specifying an "is-a-descendant-of" relationship between the nodes (Figure 13–2).

If we want to add another person to the pedigree, we could add a node for Olivia to the network, as shown in Figure 13–3.

Notice that in Figure 13–3, two initial facts ("Olivia is a descendant of Eric" and "Eric is a descendant of George") have been represented. However, it is possible to deduce a third fact, "Olivia is a descendant of George," by simply following the links. The ability to deduce new facts based on semantic relationships of the same type is called *transitivity*. Transitive relationships allow new relationships to be derived by simply creating new links by following relationships of the same type. Generally, the semantic of a link applies in only one direction. So it is correct to say that "Eric is a descendant of George" but incorrect to imply that "George is a descendant of Eric." It is possible, though, to create links that do flow in the opposite direction. Based on this, we could establish a new link that says, "George is an ancestor of Eric" and thus "George is an ancestor of Olivia." This allows the transitivity to apply in both directions.

Reflexive relationships occur when the link can be applied in all directions within a set of nodes being related and the nodes are of the same type. Within the genealogy chart a statement such as "Spouse1 is married to Spouse2" can be considered reflexive.

Figure 13–2   Diagram of a simple fact

Figure 13–3   Diagram of an inherited (transitive) fact

Thus both of the following statements are true: "Eric is married to Rita" and "Rita is married to Eric." Thus the "is-married-to" link is reflexive when both nodes are instances of "Spouse."

Symmetric relationships occur when the positioning of the nodes within the relationship does not affect the truthfulness of the resulting statement and the nodes types are different. Using the marriage example in a slightly different way, the following can be said: "Husband is married to Wife" and "Wife is married to Husband." Here the "is-married-to" link is symmetrical because the nodes are instances of different types ("Husband" and "Wife").

This illustrates the careful attention that must be given when defining the semantics to be used within a set of information. If you want a link to be both symmetrical and reflexive, you might be able to use transitivity on the nodes to accomplish this. Within the "is-married-to" link, "Husband" and "Wife" could be defined as subclasses of "Spouse." "Eric" and "Rita" could then be defined as "Husband" and "Wife", respectively, but each could still be "Spouse" since "Husband" and "Wife" can be subclasses of the topic "Spouse." In doing so, the "is-married-to" link is now both reflexive and symmetrical.

Semantic networks make it easy to model inheritance hierarchies and thus assert facts based on these hierarchies. By tracing through the hierarchy and applying the relationship types, facts asserted in higher nodes can be asserted about the lower ones without having to represent these assertions explicitly.

Computer languages such as Prolog can model and process the logic contained within a semantic network. They allow the programmer to define the meanings of links programmatically so that a computer can understand and process the links and make inferences about the nodes based on the links between the nodes in the network.

Semantic networks are frequently used to model the knowledge stored within expert systems. Expert systems use facts and rules to analyze complex sets of data and make inferences based on the data within the semantic network and other inputs. The bits of knowledge that are stored within the semantic network are combined in such a way that a computer program can infer information about a node by following the links within the network.

Semantic networks represent binary relations between nodes. In other words, a relationship generally connects only two nodes. This may seem to be a shortcoming, but research has shown that any *n*-ary relation can be decomposed into a set of binary relations. The use of binary relations does have some effect on the representation of the information. This is due to the decomposition process required in order to represent a concept. For example, a statement such as "Washington, D.C., is a city in the

United States" is fairly simple in human language. However, in a semantic network it would need to be decomposed into several binary relations, including: "Washington, D.C., is a city" and "United States is a country." These statements model the information in the sentence, but in order for the statement to be fully understood, the semantic network would also need to include general knowledge facts such as, "city is located in country." It is this general knowledge that can have the greatest impact on the overall quality of the knowledge contained within the semantic network.

Comparing Topic Maps, RDF, and Semantic Networks

Interesting structural commonalities exist between topic maps, RDF, and semantic networks.

- Topic maps, RDF, and semantic networks are organized into a network of information nodes or modules.
- Topic maps, RDF, and semantic networks allow the user to model links between the nodes.
- Topic maps, RDF, and semantic networks allow the user to attach semantic information to the nodes and the links.

A basic difference also exists. The topic map concept focuses more on the navigation between topics than on the processing of associations between topics, and any linking, while worthwhile, is still considered in some applications to be of secondary importance. Semantic networks focus on the links between the nodes and the knowledge that is represented by the linked sets of nodes. The links within a semantic network are also directional, whereas they are not in the topic maps paradigm.

Building Semantic Networks from Topic Maps

This section walks through the development of a topic map that can be used to build a semantic network. We continue to use the genealogical example as we discuss some of the issues and how we can overcome them. You can find all the examples below within the complete topic map found in Appendix D.

Published Subject Indicators

As stated earlier, almost all objects within a topic map are topics. However, it would be useful to define a set of objects that declare specific processing semantics within the topic map. We can use such declarative parts to define classes of topic maps that share a common set of topics types with predefined semantics. Examples of declarative constructs include topic classes, association type classes, occurrence type classes, and themes. The XTM 1.0 specification uses Published Subject Indicators (PSIs), as discussed in Chapter 5 in this book, to define a minimal set of topics that have specific meanings attached to them. We can use PSIs to define more topics on an application-by-application basis.

As part of the development of the sample topic map, we define a set of PSIs that will be used to assign specific semantics to the topics within our topic map.

```
<topic id="topic.class">
  <instanceOf>
   <topicRef xlink:href=
      "http://www.topicmaps.org/xtm/1.0/core.xtm#class"/>
  </instanceOf>
  <subjectIdentity>
   <subjectIndicatorRef xlink:href=
      "http://www.semantext.com/psi/topic-class"/>
  </subjectIdentity>
  <baseName>
   <baseNameString>topic class</baseNameString>
  </baseName>
 </topic>

<topic id="association.class">
  <instanceOf>
   <topicRef xlink:href=
      "http://www.topicmaps.org/xtm/1.0/core.xtm#class"/>
  </instanceOf>
  <subjectIdentity>
   <subjectIndicatorRef xlink:href=
      "http://www.semantext.com/psi/association-class"/>
  </subjectIdentity>
  <baseName>
   <baseNameString>association class</baseNameString>
  </baseName>
 </topic>

<topic id="occurrence.class">
  <instanceOf>
   <topicRef xlink:href=
      "http://www.topicmaps.org/xtm/1.0/core.xtm#class"/>
  </instanceOf>
  <subjectIdentity>
```

```
    <subjectIndicatorRef xlink:href=
        "http://www.semantext.com/psi/occurrence-class"/>
   </subjectIdentity>
   <baseName>
    <baseNameString>occurrence class</baseNameString>
   </baseName>
  </topic>

  <topic id="theme.class">
   <instanceOf>
    <topicRef xlink:href=
        "http://www.topicmaps.org/xtm/1.0/core.xtm#class"/>
   </instanceOf>
   <subjectIdentity>
    <subjectIndicatorRef xlink:href=
        "http://www.semantext.com/psi/theme-class"/>
   </subjectIdentity>
   <baseName>
    <baseNameString>theme class</baseNameString>
   </baseName>
  </topic>
```

These PSIs define exactly what roles within our sample topic map a particular topic may play. This is particularly important because many of the main building blocks within a topic map are topics. By specifying an exact semantic under which a topic may be used, the topic map designer can convey to users (either human or machine) exactly how he or she intended a topic to be used or processed.

Association Properties

The properties described previously—transitivity, reflexivity, and symmetry—are necessary for using topic maps to model semantic networks. Since associations can be seen as relationships between topics, there needs to be a way to model the semantics that these properties carry with them in topic maps. This can also be done through PSIs.

The examples below define the properties mentioned above that associations can have.

```
<topic id="association.property">
  <instanceOf>
   <topicRef xlink:href=
       "http://www.semantext.com/psi/occurrence-class"/>
  </instanceOf>
  <subjectIdentity>
   <subjectIndicatorRef xlink:href=
       "http://www.semantext.com/psi/association-property"/>
  </subjectIdentity>
  <baseName>
```

```
     <baseNameString>association property</baseNameString>
    </baseName>
 </topic>

 <topic id="transitive">
  <instanceOf>
   <topicRef xlink:href="#association.property"/>
  </instanceOf>
  <subjectIdentity>
   <subjectIndicatorRef xlink:href=
      "http://www.semantext.com/psi/transitive-association"/>
  </subjectIdentity>
  <baseName>
   <baseNameString>transitive association</baseNameString>
  </baseName>
 </topic>

 <topic id="reflexive">
  <instanceOf>
   <topicRef xlink:href="#association.property"/>
  </instanceOf>
  <subjectIdentity>
   <subjectIndicatorRef xlink:href=
      "http://www.semantext.com/psi/reflexive-association"/>
  </subjectIdentity>
  <baseName>
   <baseNameString>reflexive association</baseNameString>
  </baseName>
 </topic>

 <topic id="symmetrical">
  <instanceOf>
   <topicRef xlink:href="#association.property"/>
  </instanceOf>
  <subjectIdentity>
   <subjectIndicatorRef xlink:href=
      "http://www.semantext.com/psi/symmetrical-association"/>
  </subjectIdentity>
  <baseName>
   <baseNameString>symmetrical association</baseNameString>
  </baseName>
 </topic>
```

The topics defined above define the specific association properties that can be used within our sample topic map. The *association.property* topic itself will be used as a class of occurrence, while the others are instances of that occurrence. These properties will be used as occurrences of the topics that are instances of the occurrence class. They are essentially metadata about how these associations are intended to be interpreted and processed. When the association class is used, these properties will be attached to each occurrence of the association class.

Type Hierarchies

All topics, occurrences, and associations can be modeled as instances of a set of classes (types). The classes themselves are expressed as topics. The XTM specification defines a set of association classes for building topic hierarchies or ontologies. Class–instance is a class of association that expresses class–instance relationships between topics that play the roles of class and instance, respectively. The subjects *class–instance*, *class*, and *instance* are all defined by PSIs in the XTM specification. Superclass–subclass is a class of association that expresses superclass–subclass relationships between topics that play the roles of superclass and subclass, respectively. The subjects *superclass–subclass*, *superclass*, and *subclass* are all defined by PSIs published in the specification. It is possible for a topic to be a superclass or subclass in one association and a class or instance in another within the same topic map.

Many people get confused about class–instance relationships and superclass–subclass relationships. Within this chapter, a *class* is used to describe other objects; an *instance* is a specific occurrence of that class. Classes are anything that can be subdivided; instances cannot. Superclass–subclass relationships exist only between classes.

So what constitutes a class or an instance? It depends on the application of the knowledge being modeled. If the application is a topic map of generic familial relationships, the topic "Wife" could be an instance of the topic "Spouse" since it will not be broken down any further. However, in the application being described in this chapter, the topic "Wife" is not an instance of the class "Spouse" but a subclass of the superclass "Spouse." The topic "Rita" is an instance of the class "Wife." The topic "Rita" is not a subclass of anything since it will not be subdivided any further.

The superclass–subclass relationship is transitive by default. However, it is possible to infer additional transitive associations from the instance topic within a class–instance association to any superclasses of which the class topic is a subclass. This enables inferences beyond those explicitly present in the topic map document, to be made automatically as the hierarchy is built by a processor. For example, assume an association where "Husband" and "Wife" are subclasses of the superclass "Spouse." Assume another association in which "Eric" is an instance of the class "Husband." Based on these two associations, it would be possible to infer that "Eric" is also an instance of the class "Spouse."

In addition to the type hierarchies described above, there are several association types that can be modeled in much the same way, which would be useful in other applications. These relationships include:

- Component–object (wing/airplane)
- Member–collection (tree/forest)

- Portion–mass (slice/loaf)
- Stuff–object (air/atmosphere)
- Feature–activity (eating/picnic)
- Place–area (city/country)
- Phase–process (assembly/manufacturing)

The declarations below define some basic topics and begin the construction of the topic hierarchy or ontology contained within a genealogy topic map. These declarations begin to build the relationships between the classes that topics within the topic map might take and how the topics themselves could be related.

```
<topic id="person">
 <instanceOf>
  <topicRef xlink:href="#topic.class"/>
 </instanceOf>
 <baseName>
  <baseNameString>Person</baseNameString>
 </baseName>
</topic>

<topic id="male">
 <instanceOf>
  <topicRef xlink:href="#topic.class"/>
 </instanceOf>
 <baseName>
  <baseNameString>Male</baseNameString>
 </baseName>
</topic>

<topic id="female">
 <instanceOf>
  <topicRef xlink:href="#topic.class"/>
 </instanceOf>
 <baseName>
  <baseNameString>Female</baseNameString>
 </baseName>
</topic>

<topic id="parent">
 <instanceOf>
  <topicRef xlink:href="#topic.class"/>
 </instanceOf>
 <baseName>
  <baseNameString>Parent</baseNameString>
 </baseName>
</topic>

<topic id="mother">
 <instanceOf>
```

```
    <topicRef xlink:href="#topic.class"/>
   </instanceOf>
   <baseName>
    <baseNameString>Mother</baseNameString>
   </baseName>
  </topic>

  <topic id="father">
   <instanceOf>
    <topicRef xlink:href="#topic.class"/>
   </instanceOf>
   <baseName>
    <baseNameString>Father</baseNameString>
   </baseName>
  </topic>
```

The code above defines several topics for several concepts or roles that appear in a genealogy. Several other basic topics, including spouse, wife, husband, child, daughter, son, sibling, sister, and brother, are defined within the family tree but are not listed here in the interest of space (see Appendix D for the full listing).

```
  <association>
   <instanceOf>
    <subjectIndicatorRef xlink:href=
       "http://www.topicmaps.org/xtm/1.0/core.xtm
          #superclass-subclass"/>
   </instanceOf>
   <member>
    <roleSpec>
     <subjectIndicatorRef xlink:href=
        "http://www.topicmaps.org/xtm/1.0/core.xtm
           #superclass"/>
    </roleSpec>
    <topicRef xlink:href="#parent"/>
   </member>
   <member>
    <roleSpec>
     <subjectIndicatorRef xlink:href=
        "http://www.topicmaps.org/xtm/1.0/core.xtm#subclass"/>
    </roleSpec>
    <topicRef xlink:href="#mother"/>
    <topicRef xlink:href="#father"/>
   </member>
  </association>
```

We can build a hierarchy by using the superclass–subclass and the class–instance relationships. The use of the `<instanceOf>` element is equivalent to defining a class–instance association. As stated before, the superclass–subclass relationship is used to subdivide classes. For example, the *parent* topic can be subdivided into *mother* and *father*.

At this point in our topic map it is possible to infer that if someone is a father, that person is also a male and a parent. This is due to the transitivity property exhibited by the class–instance and superclass–subclass associations. None of the items in the blocks shown in the genealogical chart have been defined. The example below starts to define those items. (Only a subset of the possible topics has been defined for illustration purposes.)

```
<topic id="eric">
  <instanceOf>
   <topicRef xlink:href="#male"/>
  </instanceOf>
  <instanceOf>
   <topicRef xlink:href="#person"/>
  </instanceOf>
  <baseName>
   <baseNameString>Eric</baseNameString>
  </baseName>
 </topic>

 <topic id="rita">
  <instanceOf>
   <topicRef xlink:href="#female"/>
  </instanceOf>
  <instanceOf>
   <topicRef xlink:href="#person"/>
  </instanceOf>
  <baseName>
   <baseNameString>Rita</baseNameString>
  </baseName>
 </topic>

 <topic id="olivia">
  <instanceOf>
   <topicRef xlink:href="#female"/>
  </instanceOf>
  <instanceOf>
   <topicRef xlink:href="#person"/>
  </instanceOf>
  <baseName>
   <baseNameString>Olivia</baseNameString>
  </baseName>
 </topic>

 <topic id="jordan">
  <instanceOf>
   <topicRef xlink:href="#male"/>
  </instanceOf>
  <instanceOf>
   <topicRef xlink:href="#person"/>
  </instanceOf>
```

```
<baseName>
 <baseNameString>Jordan</baseNameString>
</baseName>
</topic>
```

One challenge in defining a topic map is determining the methodology to be used for defining what should be a topic and how the topic hierarchy is to be defined. It is important to use a consistent method to ensure that the topic map structures are interpreted in the same way. One possible method is to provide as much information as possible for each topic. For instance, for the topic named *Eric*, it might be possible to also add `<instanceOf>` elements for *husband*, *father*, *son*, *child*, and so on. Another method is to define a minimal set of types and use other topic map structures such as associations to define the additional information. This method allows us to place knowledge in the context in which it occurs. An additional advantage to this second method is that scopes can be used to control when specific information is in effect.

The next step is to define some associations between the topics.

```
<topic id="marriage">
 <instanceOf>
  <topicRef xlink:href="#association.class"/>
 </instanceOf>
 <baseName>
  <baseNameString>Marriage</baseNameString>
 </baseName>
</topic>

<association>
 <instanceOf>
  <topicRef xlink:href="#marriage"/>
 </instanceOf>
 <member>
  <roleSpec>
   <topicRef xlink:href="#husband"/>
  </roleSpec>
  <topicRef xlink:href="#eric"/>
 </member>
 <member>
  <roleSpec>
   <topicRef xlink:href="#wife"/>
  </roleSpec>
  <topicRef xlink:href="#rita"/>
 </member>
</association>

<topic id="family">
 <instanceOf>
  <topicRef xlink:href="#association.class"/>
```

```
  </instanceOf>
  <baseName>
   <baseNameString>Family</baseNameString>
  </baseName>
 </topic>

 <association>
  <instanceOf>
   <topicRef xlink:href="#family"/>
  </instanceOf>
  <member>
   <roleSpec>
    <topicRef xlink:href="#husband"/>
   </roleSpec>
   <topicRef xlink:href="#eric"/>
  </member>
  <member>
   <roleSpec>
    <topicRef xlink:href="#mother"/>
   </roleSpec>
   <topicRef xlink:href="#rita"/>
  </member>
  <member>
   <roleSpec>
    <topicRef xlink:href="#child"/>
   </roleSpec>
   <topicRef xlink:href="#olivia"/>
   <topicRef xlink:href="#jordan"/>
  </member>
 </association>
```

Now that we've covered the basics of laying out a semantic network using XTM constructs, we turn to the issues of the validity and consistency of the network we have created.

Topic Map Schemas

The XTM specification says almost nothing about validation and consistency. Instead, the conformance section focuses on the understanding of the defined constructs, the interchange syntax, and the import and export of topic maps.

However, the implementer of a topic map needs some degree of support when designing and creating a map potentially consisting of millions of topics and associations. The question of consistency within the topic map becomes a key issue because it is nearly impossible to check a map of that size manually. Chapter 14 discusses topic map schemas and consistency constraints in more depth.

The constraints used in this example are defined using a set of topic, occurrence, and association patterns declared in a template using topic map syntax. These patterns declare the possible parameters and their combinations. The patterns are defined as topics and associations. A predefined theme "schema" used to scope an association signals that the association and its members have a special meaning—they are constraints for topics/associations of the given type.

Work has begun on a Topic Map Constraint Language (TMCL) to address some of the issues raised in this section. The examples shown below will most likely not be in accordance with TMCL since it did not exist at the time this chapter was written. Note that current proposals for TMCL explicitly do not address issues of cardinality, a shortcoming in my view. (See Chapter 4 for a discussion of TMCL.)

The associations defined above exist between the members of a particular family. They define the types of relationship and the roles played by each member. However, there is no indication of how each member topic relates to the others. A human reader can probably figure out how the relationships work. However, the specification provides no guidance or mechanism on how such relationships are to be programmatically validated. Using the schema approach, a pattern can be defined that specifies the required and valid topics within the association. The pattern would include information such as:

- The member topic types of the association
- How many of each type can occur within the association

```
<topic id="minimum.occurrences">
 <instanceOf>
  <topicRef xlink:href="#occurrence.class"/>
 </instanceOf>
 <subjectIdentity>
  <subjectIndicatorRef xlink:href=
     "http://www.semantext.com/psi/minimum-occurences"/>
 </subjectIdentity>
 <baseName>
  <baseNameString>minimum occurrences</baseNameString>
 </baseName>
</topic>

<topic id="maximum.occurrences">
 <instanceOf>
  <topicRef xlink:href="#occurrence.class"/>
 </instanceOf>
 <subjectIdentity>
  <subjectIndicatorRef xlink:href=
     "http://www.semantext.com/psi/maximum-occurrences"/>
 </subjectIdentity>
```

```xml
 <baseName>
  <baseNameString>maximum occurrences</baseNameString>
 </baseName>
</topic>

<topic id="schema">
 <instanceOf>
  <topicRef xlink:href="#theme.class"/>
 </instanceOf>
 <subjectIdentity>
  <subjectIndicatorRef xlink:href=
     "http://www.semantext.com/psi/schema"/>
 </subjectIdentity>
 <baseName>
  <baseNameString>topic map schema</baseNameString>
 </baseName>
</topic>

<topic id="marriage.schema">
 <instanceOf>
  <topicRef xlink:href="#association.class"/>
 </instanceOf>
 <baseName>
  <baseNameString>Marriage</baseNameString>
 </baseName>
 <occurrence>
  <instanceOf>
   <topicRef xlink:href="#association.property"/>
  </instanceOf>
  <resourceRef xlink:href="#reflexive"/>
 </occurrence>
 <occurrence id="minimum.spouses">
  <instanceOf>
   <topicRef xlink:href="#minimum.occurrences"/>
  </instanceOf>
  <resourceData>2</resourceData>
 </occurrence>
 <occurrence id="maximum.spouses">
  <instanceOf>
   <topicRef xlink:href="#maximum.occurrences"/>
  </instanceOf>
  <resourceData>2</resourceData>
 </occurrence>
</topic>

<association>
 <instanceOf>
  <topicRef xlink:href="#marriage.schema"/>
 </instanceOf>
 <scope>
  <topicRef xlink:href="#schema"/>
```

```
   </scope>
   <member>
    <roleSpec>
     <topicRef xlink:href="#spouse"/>
    </roleSpec>
    <resourceRef xlink:href="#minimum.spouses"/>
    <resourceRef xlink:href="#maximum.spouses"/>
   </member>
  </association>

  <topic id="family.schema">
   <instanceOf>
    <topicRef xlink:href="#association.class"/>
   </instanceOf>
   <baseName>
    <baseNameString>Family</baseNameString>
   </baseName>
   <occurrence id="maximum.parents">
    <instanceOf>
     <topicRef xlink:href="#maximum.occurrences"/>
    </instanceOf>
    <resourceData>2</resourceData>
   </occurrence>
  </topic>

  <association>
   <instanceOf>
    <topicRef xlink:href="#family.schema"/>
   </instanceOf>
   <scope>
    <topicRef xlink:href="#schema"/>
   </scope>
   <member>
    <roleSpec>
     <topicRef xlink:href="#parent"/>
    </roleSpec>
    <resourceRef xlink:href="#maximum.parents"/>
   </member>
   <member>
    <roleSpec>
     <topicRef xlink:href="#child"/>
    </roleSpec>
   </member>
  </association>
```

The section of code above defines two new topics that define the number of times members can occur within an association. Occurrence declarations within the topics state that a minimum and a maximum of two persons are required for an association following *marriage.schema* to validly exist within this application. In a topic map under construction, each instance of a marriage association built using this schema can then be checked to make sure that the marriage does in fact consist of two persons. These two persons listed must be of type *spouse* due to the transitivity property of the superclass–subclass relationship. Another occurrence states that an association following the *marriage* association schema is reflexive. The *family* association establishes that a family can be made up of zero, one, or two parents and any number of children.

While the description of the *marriage* association is fairly straightforward, as stated before, it is not so clear how the topics within the *family* association relate to each other. Assuming that topics are given human-understandable base names, it might be possible for a person reading the topic map to determine the interactions between the members of an association. We know that *Eric* has the role of *husband* within the family, *Rita* the role of *mother*, and *Olivia* and *Jordan* the role of *child*. However, there is nothing that explicitly states the relationships between *Eric*, *Rita*, *Olivia*, and *Jordan*.

It would be helpful to have a mechanism to define how *n*-ary relationships can be interpreted. In such a model it would be possible to define:

- The associations between the different topic, in all directions
- The properties of the associations (reflexive, transitive, symmetrical)
- The types of the associations
- The roles each topic plays within the associations

The topic map template model proposed here can be extended to model inference rules that are then used to infer the additional information stored in the *n*-ary associations. This is done by first defining a set of PSIs for the building blocks' inference rules.

```
<topic id="inference.rule.schema">
 <instanceOf>
  <topicRef xlink:href="#theme.class"/>
 </instanceOf>
 <subjectIdentity>
  <subjectIndicatorRef xlink:href=
     "http://www.semantext.com/psi/inference-rule-schema"/>
 </subjectIdentity>
 <baseName>
  <baseNameString>inference rule schema</baseNameString>
 </baseName>
</topic>

<topic id="inference.rule.variable">
 <instanceOf>
  <topicRef xlink:href="#topic.class"/>
 </instanceOf>
 <subjectIdentity>
```

```
    <subjectIndicatorRef xlink:href=
       "http://www.semantext.com/psi/inference-rule-variable"/>
   </subjectIdentity>
   <baseName>
    <baseNameString>inference rule topic variable</baseNameString>
   </baseName>
  </topic>

  <topic id="inference.rule">
   <instanceOf>
    <topicRef xlink:href="#association.class"/>
   </instanceOf>
   <subjectIdentity>
    <subjectIndicatorRef xlink:href=
       "http://www.semantext.com/psi/inference-rule"/>
   </subjectIdentity>
   <baseName>
    <baseNameString>inference rule</baseNameString>
   </baseName>
   <occurrence id="minimum.conditions">
    <instanceOf>
     <topicRef xlink:href="#minimum.occurrences"/>
    </instanceOf>
    <resourceData>1</resourceData>
   </occurrence>
   <occurrence id="minimum.statements">
    <instanceOf>
     <topicRef xlink:href="#minimum.occurrences"/>
    </instanceOf>
    <resourceData>1</resourceData>
   </occurrence>
  </topic>

  <topic id="inference.rule.condition">
   <instanceOf>
    <topicRef xlink:href="#topic.class"/>
   </instanceOf>
   <baseName>
    <baseNameString>inference rule condition</baseNameString>
   </baseName>
  </topic>

  <topic id="inference.rule.statement">
   <instanceOf>
    <topicRef xlink:href="#topic.class"/>
   </instanceOf>
   <baseName>
    <baseNameString>inference rule statement</baseNameString>
   </baseName>
  </topic>
```

```
<association>
 <instanceOf>
  <topicRef xlink:href="#inference.rule"/>
 </instanceOf>
 <scope>
  <topicRef xlink:href="#inference.rule.schema"/>
 </scope>
 <member>
  <roleSpec>
   <topicRef xlink:href="#inference.rule.condition"/>
  </roleSpec>
  <resourceRef xlink:href="#minimum.conditions"/>
 </member>
 <member>
  <roleSpec>
   <topicRef xlink:href="#inference.rule.statement"/>
  </roleSpec>
  <resourceRef xlink:href="#minimum.statements"/>
 </member>
</association>
```

These structures are then combined to build inference rules that when processed can build additional associations between topics. An inference rule consists of one or more conditions and one or more statements. In logical terms, the conditions equate to "if" clauses and the statements equate to "then" clauses. The `inference.rule.variable` topic type has special meaning in this application. It represents a placeholder for any topic that matches the conditions specified in the inference rule construct being used.

For example, to infer the relationships between members within a *family* association, we could define the following topics.

```
<topic id="anytopic.1">
 <instanceOf>
  <topicRef xlink:href="#inference.rule.variable"/>
 </instanceOf>
 <baseName>
  <baseNameString>any topic #1</baseNameString>
 </baseName>
</topic>

<topic id="anytopic.2">
 <instanceOf>
  <topicRef xlink:href="#inference.rule.variable"/>
 </instanceOf>
 <baseName>
  <baseNameString>any topic #2</baseNameString>
 </baseName>
</topic>
```

```
<topic id="is.sibling.schema">
 <instanceOf>
  <topicRef xlink:href="#association.class"/>
 </instanceOf>
 <baseName>
  <baseNameString>is sibling of</baseNameString>
 </baseName>
 <occurrence id="minimum.children">
  <instanceOf>
   <topicRef xlink:href="#minimum.occurrences"/>
  </instanceOf>
  <resourceData>2</resourceData>
 </occurrence>
</topic>

<association>
 <instanceOf>
  <topicRef xlink:href="#is.sibling.schema"/>
 </instanceOf>
 <scope>
  <topicRef xlink:href="#schema"/>
 </scope>
 <member>
  <roleSpec>
   <topicRef xlink:href="#child"/>
  </roleSpec>
  <resourceRef xlink:href="#minimum.children.sibling"/>
 </member>
</association>

<topic id="ir.sibling.in.family.1-2">
 <subjectIdentity>
  <subjectIndicatorRef xlink:href="#N123"/>
 </subjectIdentity>
</topic>

<association id="N123">
 <instanceOf>
  <topicRef xlink:href="#is.sibling.schema"/>
 </instanceOf>
 <scope>
  <topicRef xlink:href="#inference.rule.schema"/>
 </scope>
 <member>
  <roleSpec>
   <topicRef xlink:href="#sibling"/>
  </roleSpec>
  <topicRef xlink:href="#anytopic.1"/>
  <topicRef xlink:href="#anytopic.2"/>
 </member>
</association>
```

```
<topic id="ir.sibling.1-2">
 <subjectIdentity>
  <subjectIndicatorRef xlink:href="#N234"/>
 </subjectIdentity>
</topic>

<association id="N234">
 <instanceOf>
  <topicRef xlink:href="#family.schema"/>
 </instanceOf>
 <scope>
  <topicRef xlink:href="#inference.rule.schema"/>
 </scope>
 <member>
  <roleSpec>
   <topicRef xlink:href="#child"/>
  </roleSpec>
  <topicRef xlink:href="#anytopic.1"/>
  <topicRef xlink:href="#anytopic.2"/>
 </member>
</association>

<association>
 <instanceOf>
  <topicRef xlink:href="#inference.rule"/>
 </instanceOf>
 <scope>
  <topicRef xlink:href="#inference.rule.schema"/>
 </scope>
 <member>
  <roleSpec>
   <topicRef xlink:href="#inference.rule.condition"/>
  </roleSpec>
  <topicRef xlink:href="#ir.sibling.in.family.1-2"/>
 </member>
 <member>
  <roleSpec>
   <topicRef xlink:href="#inference.rule.statement"/>
  </roleSpec>
  <topicRef xlink:href="#ir.sibling.1-2"/>
 </member>
</association>
```

Essentially, in the inference rule above we are defining the sibling relationship between any two children within a family. In English prose the rule could be stated, "*If* two persons within a family both have the role of child, *then* both persons can be considered siblings." The processing model for inferencing in this proposal states that in an association of type inference-rule, when all the premises are true, then the inferences are made. In effect, the result of processing this rule is the creation of the association shown below. The accompanying topic declaration and association schema set the rules for how the association is controlled.

```
<association>
 <instanceOf>
  <topicRef xlink:href="#sibling.schema"/>
 </instanceOf>
 <member>
  <roleSpec>
   <topicRef xlink:href="#sibling"/>
  </roleSpec>
  <topicRef xlink:href="#olivia"/>
  <topicRef xlink:href="#jordan"/>
 </member>
</association>

<topic id="sibling.schema">
 <instanceOf>
  <topicRef xlink:href="#association.class"/>
 </instanceOf>
 <baseName>
  <baseNameString>Sibling</baseNameString>
 </baseName>
 <occurrence>
  <instanceOf>
   <topicRef xlink:href="#association.property"/>
  </instanceOf>
  <resourceRef xlink:href="#reflexive"/>
 </occurrence>
 <occurrence id="minimum.siblings">
  <instanceOf>
   <topicRef xlink:href="#minimum.occurrences"/>
  </instanceOf>
  <resourceData>2</resourceData>
 </occurrence>
</topic>

<association>
 <instanceOf>
  <topicRef xlink:href="#sibling.schema"/>
 </instanceOf>
 <scope>
  <topicRef xlink:href="#schema"/>
 </scope>
 <member>
  <roleSpec>
   <topicRef xlink:href="#sibling"/>
  </roleSpec>
  <resourceRef xlink:href="#minimum.siblings"/>
 </member>
</association>
```

A more complex example is defining the rule for determining whether two people are cousins within the family tree. We can do this by extending the example above. This new rule requires several premises to be true before other facts can be determined.

```
<topic id="anytopic.3">
 <instanceOf>
  <topicRef xlink:href="#inference.rule.variable"/>
 </instanceOf>
 <baseName>
  <baseNameString>any topic #3</baseNameString>
 </baseName>
</topic>

<topic id="anytopic.4">
 <instanceOf>
  <topicRef xlink:href="#inference.rule.variable"/>
 </instanceOf>
 <baseName>
  <baseNameString>any topic #4</baseNameString>
 </baseName>
</topic>

<topic id="is.parent.schema">
 <instanceOf>
  <topicRef xlink:href="#association.class"/>
 </instanceOf>
 <baseName>
  <baseNameString>is parent of</baseNameString>
 </baseName>
</topic>

<topic id="ir.parent.in.family.N345">
 <subjectIdentity>
  <subjectIndicatorRef xlink:href="#N345"/>
 </subjectIdentity>
</topic>

<association id="N345">
 <instanceOf>
  <topicRef xlink:href="#is.parent.schema"/>
 </instanceOf>
 <scope>
  <topicRef xlink:href="#inference.rule.schema"/>
 </scope>
 <member>
  <roleSpec>
   <topicRef xlink:href="#parent"/>
  </roleSpec>
  <topicRef xlink:href="#anytopic.1"/>
 </member>
 <member>
```

```
   <roleSpec>
    <topicRef xlink:href="#child"/>
   </roleSpec>
   <topicRef xlink:href="#anytopic.2"/>
  </member>
 </association>

 <topic id="ir.parent.in.family.N456">
  <subjectIdentity>
   <subjectIndicatorRef xlink:href="#N456"/>
  </subjectIdentity>
 </topic>

 <association id="N456">
  <instanceOf>
   <topicRef xlink:href="#is.parent.schema"/>
  </instanceOf>
  <scope>
   <topicRef xlink:href="#inference.rule.schema"/>
  </scope>
  <member>
   <roleSpec>
    <topicRef xlink:href="#parent"/>
   </roleSpec>
   <topicRef xlink:href="#anytopic.3"/>
  </member>
  <member>
   <roleSpec>
    <topicRef xlink:href="#child"/>
   </roleSpec>
   <topicRef xlink:href="#anytopic.4"/>
  </member>
 </association>

 <topic id="ir.sibling.in.family.N567">
  <subjectIdentity>
   <subjectIndicatorRef xlink:href="#N567"/>
  </subjectIdentity>
 </topic>

 <association id="N567">
  <instanceOf>
   <topicRef xlink:href="#is.sibling.schema"/>
  </instanceOf>
  <scope>
   <topicRef xlink:href="#inference.rule.schema"/>
  </scope>
  <member>
   <roleSpec>
    <topicRef xlink:href="#child"/>
   </roleSpec>
```

```xml
   <topicRef xlink:href="#anytopic.1"/>
   <topicRef xlink:href="#anytopic.3"/>
 </member>
</association>

<topic id="cousin.schema">
 <instanceOf>
  <topicRef xlink:href="#association.class"/>
 </instanceOf>
 <baseName>
  <baseNameString>is cousin of</baseNameString>
 </baseName>
 <occurrence id="minimum.children.cousin">
  <instanceOf>
   <topicRef xlink:href="#minimum.occurrences"/>
  </instanceOf>
  <resourceData>2</resourceData>
 </occurrence>
</topic>

<topic id="ir.cousin.N678">
 <subjectIdentity>
  <subjectIndicatorRef xlink:href="#N678"/>
 </subjectIdentity>
</topic>

<association id="N678">
 <instanceOf>
  <topicRef xlink:href="#cousin.schema"/>
 </instanceOf>
 <scope>
  <topicRef xlink:href="#inference.rule.schema"/>
 </scope>
 <member>
  <roleSpec>
   <topicRef xlink:href="#cousin"/>
  </roleSpec>
  <topicRef xlink:href="#anytopic.2"/>
  <topicRef xlink:href="#anytopic.4"/>
 </member>
</association>

<association>
 <instanceOf>
  <topicRef xlink:href="#inference.rule"/>
 </instanceOf>
 <scope>
  <topicRef xlink:href="#inference.rule.schema"/>
 </scope>
 <member>
  <roleSpec>
```

```
   <topicRef xlink:href="#inference.rule.condition"/>
  </roleSpec>
  <topicRef xlink:href="#ir.parent.in.family.N345"/>
  <topicRef xlink:href="#ir.parent.in.family.N456"/>
  <topicRef xlink:href="#ir.sibling.in.family.N567"/>
 </member>
 <member>
  <roleSpec>
   <topicRef xlink:href="#inference.rule.statement"/>
  </roleSpec>
  <topicRef xlink:href="#ir.cousin.N678"/>
 </member>
</association>
```

This second rule can be restated in English as, *"If* a first person is the parent of a second person within a family, *and* a third person is the parent of a fourth person within a family, *and* the first person and third person are siblings within a family, *then* the second person and the fourth person are cousins." The processing of this rule on the entire family tree results in the generation of the following association, among others.

```
<association>
 <instanceOf>
  <topicRef xlink:href="#cousin.schema"/>
 </instanceOf>
 <member>
  <roleSpec>
   <topicRef xlink:href="#cousin"/>
  </roleSpec>
  <topicRef xlink:href="#olivia"/>
  <topicRef xlink:href="#keri"/>
 </member>
</association>
```

Although not shown in these examples, when a set of premises is true, it is possible to infer several associations at the same time. This increases the power of the inference rule mechanism by reducing the number of times a premise must be examined before making any inference. This also reduces the processing required to build the semantic network. The inference rules can be stored and managed separately and applied to topic maps as appropriate. Since they are topic maps themselves, application of the rules is a matter of merging the topic maps and processing the rules.

This template now provides all the information necessary for a system, or a human reader unfamiliar with the subject matter, to establish the relationships between the topics within the association. It also clarifies the items and the associations among them and allows new associations to be built automatically.

Harvesting the Knowledge Identified in Markup

One of the benefits of XML is the ability to define a set of markup tags that explicitly label the content of a data set rather than using formatting tags such as those in HTML. By using content tagging, you can develop programs that identify certain topics within the information and harvest them to populate a topic map or semantic network. In many cases, the associations or relationships between the topics may not be explicitly stated in the markup. Tools can be developed that allow the user to define associations and topic types so that data extracted from documents can be placed into the topic map and interpreted by the computer. In fact, the inference rule model discussed above could be extended to include the ability to define extraction rules. These rules could operate just like inference rules and exist independently from the topic map being built. They could be applied to several source documents by merging them into the topic map under construction.

Infoloom, Inc. (*http://www.infoloom.com*) uses an example of this process to create the topic maps for conferences of the Graphics Communication Association (GCA), now IDEAlliance. Presenters submit papers using a standard document type definition (DTD) that contains several content tags such as author name, affiliation, city, state/province, country, key word, and acronym. Based on the specific tags, topic maps can be built on the associations between the marked items. For example, within the United States, a city occurs within a state, so topics can be defined for each city and state and associations can be built between each city/state pair. A more detailed topic map might also include counties, such that a particular city can occur within one or more counties (as when city and county boundaries overlap within the same geographic area) and each county occurs within a state.

Identifying and Interpreting the Knowledge Found within Documents

The field of knowledge management has been gathering momentum over the past year or so. Current world events are causing organizations worldwide to rethink their knowledge management strategies and tools. As new requirements for knowledge bases are developed, systems will need to keep pace with the new requirements. The definition of knowledge management depends on the individual doing the defining. In general, it is an attempt to classify and organize information within an enterprise so that this information can be located and used. Developers have introduced several tools and systems they claim perform some sort of knowledge management. However, these systems range from simple document management systems to advanced repositories that purport to process the meaning contained within the text to classify the information.

Many mechanisms are used within these systems to classify and organize the information. Some simply match key words and phrases; others use statistical theories to match patterns of terms and contextual relationships that represent an idea.

Whether topic maps can be used to model the knowledge managed by these systems remains to be seen. At this time, no developers of commercially available tools or systems advertise the ability to use a topic map to interchange the knowledge contained within, nor do they advertise that these tools or systems can export a topic map for interchange of the information.

This, however, does not mean that the extraction of knowledge from within documents cannot be done. Several methods exist for identifying the structures found within natural language. Tools capable of using the harvesting rules may be able to process the markup based on natural language to build topic maps, but the engine underneath would need to be very powerful in order to work with the large amounts of granular information that would be generated.

Summary

With the advent of the Web, the amount of easily available information has exploded. Methodologies such as RDF and topic maps were developed because of the need to separate the good information from all the junk.

The XTM specification has gathered a great deal of support, as discussed in Chapter 4. Early adopters have shown that it is indeed a useful specification and have also identified areas in which it can be extended or improved. One of the signs of the true power of topic maps is that many of the extensions can be accomplished using the topic maps paradigm.

The ability to construct semantic networks from topic maps provides an exciting possibility of having a standard by which knowledge can be stored *and* interchanged. In the past, knowledge storage and management schemes have come and gone. However, most of them provided no way to interchange the data between systems and applications. Topic maps can interchange the gathered knowledge of an organization.

In the near future more topic map–based systems will appear. As more topic maps are created, many of them will be made publicly available. As topic maps are shared and combined, the large knowledge bases we see in those science fiction shows could well become a reality.

References

Barr, Avron, and Edward A. Feigenbaum. 1981. *The Handbook of Artificial Intelligence.* Reading, MA: Addison-Wesley.

Biezunski, Michel. 1999. Topic Maps at a Glance. Paper presented at XML Europe '99, Granada, Spain, May 1999. Accessed in April 2002 at *http://www.infoloom.com/ gcaconfs/WEB/TOC/t0301_.HTM.*

Dewdney, A. K. 1989. *The Turing Omnibus.* Rockville, MD: Computer Science Press.

Freese, Eric. 2000. Using Topic Maps: For the Representation, Management and Discovery of Knowledge. Paper presented at the XML Europe 2000 Conference, Paris, June 2000. Accessed in April 2002 at *http://www.gca.org/papers/xmleurope2000/ papers/s22-01.html.*

Harmon, Paul, and David King. 1985. *Expert Systems: Artificial Intelligence in Business.* New York: John Wiley & Sons.

Pepper, Steve. 1999. Euler, Topic Maps and Revolution. Paper presented at XML Europe '99, Granada, Spain, May 1999. Accessed in April 2002 at *http://www.ontopia. net/topicmaps/materials/euler.pdf.*

Rath, Hans Holger. 2000. Topic Maps Self-Control. Paper presented at Extreme Markup Languages 2000, Montreal, Canada, 2000. Accessed in April 2002 at *http:// www.gca.org/attend/2000_conferences/Extreme_2000/Papers/Rath/tom-hhr.PDF.*

Rath, Hans Holger, and Steve Pepper. 1999. Topic Maps: Introduction and Allegro. Paper presented at XML '99, Philadelphia, PA, 1999. Accessed in April 2002 at *http:// www.ontopia.net/topicmaps/materials/allegro.pdf.*

Sowa, John F. 2000. Knowledge Representation—Logical, Philosophical and Computational Foundations. Pacific Grove, CA: Brooks/Cole.

Chapter 14

TOPIC MAP FUNDAMENTALS FOR KNOWLEDGE REPRESENTATION

H. HOLGER RATH

Topic maps offer flexible and powerful techniques for knowledge representation (KR). They define the general concepts and provide—with intention—just the necessary minimum of semantics. But KR requires more semantic to model ontologies, class hierarchies, association properties, inference rules, and constraint-based validation.

This chapter explains why these semantics are needed, gives some examples of applications, and presents an approach to a technical solution. The solution itself will make use of the topic maps paradigm.

KR is already well understood within the field of artificial intelligence (AI) research. Concepts like semantic networks and conceptual graphs were developed to model knowledge. The general approach of the topic maps paradigm defines the basic constructs for KR with topic maps, but supporting this particular application domain was not a design goal of the topic map standardization effort. Therefore, the required semantics must be defined as a kind of application profile.

A Simple KR Example

KR is a key issue in enterprise knowledge management applications, for example, a corporate memory. Thus, the example used throughout this chapter comes from this application domain.

Here's the scenario. A company runs a couple of projects they provide to customers. The project team members, one of whom is the project manager, have certain technical skills. Every project uses a couple of technologies, for example, specific products or standards. Based on this information, the topic map will contain the following classes.

Topic classes (all defined as topics):

- Company
- Owner
- Employee
- Customer
- Project
- Project manager
- Team member
- Technology
- Product
- Standard

Association classes and their roles (all defined as topics):

- Ownership (owner, company)
- Employment (company, employee)
- Personal skill (employee, technology)
- Project membership (project, team member)
- Project leadership (project, project manager)
- Project technology (project, technology)
- Project customer (project, customer)
- Company customer (company, customer)

Occurrence classes (all defined as topics):

- Business plan
- Contract
- Résumé
- Project plan
- Status report
- Product description
- Standard text

Topic instances and their classes:

- Bertelsmann MOHN Media (company)
- empolis (company)
- eCOM (company)
- Peter (employee)
- Mike (employee)
- Marisa (employee)
- WK (customer)
- LEX (project)
- LLM (project)

- SL (technology)
- SGML (standard)

Association instances, their classes, and their roles:

- Ownership: Bertelsmann MOHN Media (owner), empolis (company)
- Ownership: empolis (owner), eCOM (company)
- Employment: eCOM (company), Peter (employee), Mike (employee), Marisa (employee)
- Personal skill: Peter (employee), SGML (technology), SL (technology)
- Personal skill: Mike (employee), SL (technology)
- Personal skill: Marisa (employee), SGML (technology)
- Project membership: LEX (project), Peter (team member), Mike (team member)
- Project leadership: LEX (project), Peter (project manager)
- Project technology: LEX (project), SL (technology), SGML (technology)
- Project customer: LEX (project), WK (customer)
- Project customer: LLM (project), WK (customer)
- Company customer: eCOM (company), WK (customer)

This chapter discusses the various drawbacks of this modeling approach and presents solutions for them. Note, for example, that no employees have been assigned to the LLM project, and Marisa, though an employee, isn't assigned to any projects. These facts present management issues that a topic system using KR could assist with.

A Quick Review of Concepts for Topic Maps and KR

Listed below are some brief definitions of important concepts we'll use in this chapter.

- *Topic map templates:* the ontology part of a map containing topics that are candidates for classes or scopes
- *Class hierarchies:* the super- and subclass associations of a map
- *Association properties:* mathematically defined properties for binary associations, like transitivity
- *Inference rules:* the rules that define the possible deduction of knowledge not explicitly coded
- *Constraints:* constraining conditions that support guided editing and semantic validation of topic maps

The sum of the listed concepts plus the superclass–subclass concept—specified in XTM 1.0 for the definition of *class hierarchies*—results in what we call a *topic map schema*. The schema itself can be expressed as a topic map. Thus, the schema map controls the "real" map and defines the semantic needed by topic map tools. This chapter gives examples for every conceptual part of the schema.

All concepts rely on the use of *Published Subject Indicators* (PSIs). All the PSIs in this chapter are either already declared in the XTM specification,[1] using the domain name *topicmaps.org*, or are introduced for the purposes explained in this chapter, using the domain name *topicmaps.com* (owned by empolis GmbH).

Additional concepts like the Topic Map Query Language (TMQL) and user profiling [Ksiezyk 2000] are not in the scope of this chapter, but both could also be expressed as topic maps. (See Chapter 4 for a discussion of TMQL.)

Topic Map Templates

Most of the objects that declare a topic map ontology are topics: namely, scoping topics, classes (topics, occurrences, and associations all may be instances of classes), and roles (that topics play in an association). But neither ISO 13250 nor the XTM specification provides a mechanism for identifying a map's ontology objects before they have been referenced by instances—and this can lead to some confusion. Users often mix up *ontology* topics and *regular* topics during discussions. In addition to that, the different tasks of topic map design, creation, and maintenance are hard to distinguish and separate.

The same is true for the control of user access rights: as long as there is no distinction between parts of the map, different rights cannot be assigned to the different parts of the map. A separate ontology part could also be used for defining categories of topic maps that share a common set of classes with predefined semantics.

The ISO working group has already responded to the need to separate the ontology part of a topic map. It coined the term *topic map template* (here, informally, "template") for all ontology topics of a map, as mentioned above. At the present time this term is only "semi-official" since the concept has not yet been refined and added to the standard.[2]

---

[1]See *http://www.topicmaps.org/xtm/index.html#psi-mandatory* for a list of those PSIs included in the XTM 1.0 document.

[2]The templating ontology proposed here should be distinguished from the association templates mentioned in the first draft of the ISO Reference Model (*http://www.y12.doe.gov/sgml/sc34/document/0243.htm*). There, an association template is "a topic whose subject is a set of constraints used to validate instances of a given association type" and is defined in terms of topic map graph constructs.

We define a template as a topic map that consists of scoping topics, classes, and roles. As discussed later in this chapter, it also consists of consistency constraints and inference rules. Table 14–1 lists a set of PSIs for the basic classes.

These PSIs serve as subject indicator references for the classes of the classes of the application domain.

Let's return to our company scenario. The ontology topics for the example are company, employee, customer, project, technology, product, standard, ownership, owner, employment, personal skill, project membership, team member, project leadership, project manager, project technology, company customer, and project customer.

The code below shows the definition of the ontology topic *tc-company* as a topic class and an association role class.

```
<topic id="tc-company">
  <instanceOf>
    <subjectIndicatorRef xlink:href=
        "http://www.topicmaps.com/xtm/1.0/template.xtm
          #topic-class"/>
  </instanceOf>
  <instanceOf>
    <subjectIndicatorRef xlink:href=
        "http://www.topicmaps.com/xtm/1.0/template.xtm
          #association-role-class"/>
  </instanceOf>
  <baseName><baseNameString>company</baseNameString></baseName>
</topic>
```

Table 14–1 PSIs for Basic Classes

Description	PSI
Topic class	*http://www.topicmaps.com/xtm/1.0/template.xtm#topic-class*
Occurrence class	*http://www.topicmaps.com/xtm/1.0/template.xtm#occurrence-class*
Association class	*http://www.topicmaps.com/xtm/1.0/template.xtm#association-class*
Association role class	*http://www.topicmaps.com/xtm/1.0/template.xtm#association-role-class*
Scoping topic class	*http://www.topicmaps.com/xtm/1.0/template.xtm#scoping-topic-class*

The topic *tc-company* is an instance of a class that is identified by the subject indicator references *http://www.topicmaps.com/xtm/1.0/template.xtm#topic-class* and *http://www.topicmaps.com/xtm/1.0/template.xtm#association-role-class*. Because of these references, the topic map software can be aware that *tc-company* is a topic class and an association role class—even before the class is referenced by a topic instance or used as an association role.

The definition of further ontology topics representing occurrence classes, association classes, association role classes, and scoping topic classes is done in a similar way. The "real" topic map uses the domain-specific classes.

The code below shows the definition of the topic *t-ecom* to represent the company eCOM.

```
<topic id="t-ecom">
  <instanceOf>
    <topicRef xlink:href="#tc-company"/>
  </instanceOf>
  <baseName><baseNameString>eCOM</baseNameString></baseName>
</topic>
```

The application designer can choose what to call the -id- attributes and the base names. Only the PSIs are predefined.

Class Hierarchies

In our approach to topic map schemas, all topics, occurrences, and associations are instances of classes. The classes themselves are expressed as topics. The class–instance relationship declared by the <instanceOf> element is in fact merely a syntactically privileged association class defined in the text of the XTM 1.0 specification. If we are looking at the class–instance relation from an ontology/taxonomy view, then there is a justifiable demand for a superclass–subclass relationship as well.

Our example contains some superclass–subclass relationships:

- Company → customer, owner
- Employee → team member
- Team member → project manager
- Technology → product, standard

The XTM specification predefines PSIs that specify both superclass–subclass and class–instance relationships.

Note: Even if it might be possible that a topic class is also an instance of another topic class, users must understand that this expresses not a superclass–subclass relationship but only the class–instance relationship.

Superclass–Subclass Relationship as Association

Both class hierarchies and association properties (see the Association Properties section below) are the basis for compact topic maps, efficient creation and maintenance efforts, and a reduction of coding errors. Real-life ontologies and taxonomies could not be defined without extensive use of superclass–subclass relationships.

Our approach again makes use of PSIs, now predefined by the XTM specification (see Table 14–2). We need them for the superclass–subclass association, superclass association role, and subclass association role.

The code below shows an example of a class hierarchy in our application domain. (The topic classes *tc-company*, *tc-customer*, and *tc-owner* form a superclass–subclass relationship: *tc-company* → *tc-customer*, *tc-owner*.)

```
<association id="a-spclss-sbclss-company-customer-owner">
  <instanceOf>
    <subjectIndicatorRef xlink:href=
        "http://www.topicmaps.org/xtm/1.0/psi1.xtm
            #superclass-subclass"/>
  </instanceOf>
  <member>
    <roleSpec>
      <subjectIndicatorRef xlink:href=
          "http://www.topicmaps.org/xtm/1.0/psi1.xtm,
              #superclass"/>
    </roleSpec>
    <topicRef xlink:href="#tc-company"/>
  </member>
  <member>
```

Table 14–2   PSIs for Superclass–Subclass Associations

Description	XTM PSI
Association class *superclass-subclass*	*http://www.topicmaps.org/xtm/1.0/psi1.xtm#superclass-subclass*
Association role *superclass*	*http://www.topicmaps.org/xtm/1.0/psi1.xtm#superclass*
Association role *subclass*	*http://www.topicmaps.org/xtm/1.0/psi1.xtm#subclass*

```
      <roleSpec>
        <subjectIndicatorRef xlink:href=
            "http://www.topicmaps.org/xtm/1.0/psi1.xtm
                #subclass"/>
      </roleSpec>
      <topicRef xlink:href="#tc-customer"/>
    </member>
    <member>
      <roleSpec>
        <subjectIndicatorRef xlink:href=
            "http://www.topicmaps.org/xtm/1.0/psi1.xtm
                #subclass"/>
      </roleSpec>
      <topicRef xlink:href="#tc-owner"/>
    </member>
</association>
```

Class–Instance Relationship as Association

The XTM also permits the class–instance relationship (syntactically privileged by the `<instanceOf>` element) to be declared using the `<association>` element. This allows the assignment of a scope to the expressed class–instance relationship, which is not possible when using the `<instanceOf>` element. The technical solution again makes use of XTM PSIs, listed in Table 14–3.

Table 14–3   PSIs for Class–Instance Associations

Description	XTM PSI
Association class `class-instance`	*http://www.topicmaps.org/xtm/1.0/psi1.xtm#class-instance*
Association role `class`	*http://www.topicmaps.org/xtm/1.0/psi1.xtm#class*
Association role `instance`	*http://www.topicmaps.org/xtm/1.0/psi1.xtm#instance*

Here's an example of an alternative definition of topic `t-ecom` as an instance of class `tc-company`.

```
<topic id="t-ecom">
  <baseName>
    <baseNameString>eCOM</baseNameString>
  </baseName>
</topic>
<association id="a-clss-inst-company-bmm">
  <instanceOf>
    <subjectIndicatorRef xlink:href=
        "http://www.topicmaps.org/xtm/1.0/psi1.xtm
```

```
            #class-instance"/>
    </instanceOf>
    <member>
      <roleSpec>
        <subjectIndicatorRef xlink:href=
            "http://www.topicmaps.org/xtm/1.0/psi1.xtm
              #class"/>
      </roleSpec>
      <topicRef xlink:href="#tc-company"/>
    </member>
    <member>
      <roleSpec>
        <subjectIndicatorRef xlink:href=
            "http://www.topicmaps.org/xtm/1.0/psi1.xtm
              #instance"/>
      </roleSpec>
      <topicRef xlink:href="#t-ecom"/>
    </member>
</association>
```

Association Properties

Mathematics defines the reflexive, symmetric, transitive, antireflexive, and antisymmetric properties for binary relationships. Because associations can be seen as relationships, we can apply these properties to associations that connect two topics.

Taking a closer look at the benefits of each property shows that only transitivity is of real value for topic map purposes. In our approach, transitivity allows the deduction of information from the map that is not explicitly part of it.

Returning to our sample scenario, the ownership association is transitive because if Bertelsmann MOHN Media owns empolis and empolis owns eCOM, then we can derive that Bertelsmann MOHN Media owns eCOM.

Assigning properties to objects is the task of facets in an ISO topic map. With XTM, a functional equivalent for facets can be expressed using specialized occurrences. Therefore, we define a PSI for an occurrence class and a PSI to which the `<resourceRef>` element points (Table 14–4).

Table 14–4   PSIs for the Association Property *transitive*

Description	PSI
Occurrence class *property*	*http://www.topicmaps.com/xtm/1.0/template.xtm#assoc-property*
Association property *transitive*	*http://www.topicmaps.com/xtm/1.0/template.xtm#assoc-prop-transitive*

Here's an example of code stating that the association class *ac-ownership* is transitive.

```
<topic id="ac-ownership">
  <instanceOf>
    <subjectIndicatorRef xlink:href=
        "http://www.topicmaps.com/xtm/1.0/template.xtm
            #association-class"/>
  </instanceOf>
  <baseName><baseNameString>Ownership</baseNameString></baseName>
  <occurrence>
    <instanceOf>
      <subjectIndicatorRef xlink:href=
          "http://www.topicmaps.com/xtm/1.0/template.xtm
              #assoc-property"/>
    </instanceOf>
    <resourceRef xlink:href=
        "http://www.topicmaps.com/xtm/1.0/template.xtm
            #assoc-prop-transitive"/>
  </occurrence>
</topic>
```

Inference Rules

The definitions of superclass–subclass relationships between classes and of transitivity properties for associations already allow powerful inferencing of knowledge not coded in the topic map. But a topic map may contain further knowledge that could be inferred if we specify the inference rules.

Below is an inference rule for our example, assuming that projects are run only by employees and not by freelancers (where *$employee* is an instance of the class *employee*).

> If *$employee* is a team member in project *$project*
>
> And *$employee* works for company *$company*
>
> And *$project* has customer *$customer*
>
> Then *$company* has customer *$customer.*

Here's the rule in a more verbose form, which is closer to the topic map constructs.

> If topic *$employee* plays role *team member* in association *project membership* together with topic *$project* playing role *project*
>
> And topic *$employee* plays role *employee* in association *employment* together with topic *$company* playing role *company*

And topic *$project* plays role *project* in association *project customer* together with topic *$customer* playing role *customer*

Then topic *$company* plays role *company* in association *company customer* together with topic *$customer* playing role *customer*.

This quite simple rule is analyzed further below.

- The "if [condition] then [inference]" structure defines the inference rule. The condition might be built by several subconditions connected by the logical (Boolean) connector AND.
- The variables *$employee*, *$project*, *$company*, and *$customer* have to be instantiated when the rule is evaluated (that is, matched against the concrete topic map).
- In the *project membership*, *employment*, and *project customer* associations, instances of the topic variables have to play the appropriate roles.
- The *company customer* association is inferred, and the instances of the topic variables play the roles *company* and *customer*.

An elegant solution makes use of the *reification* of an association as a topic which can then be used as a member of another association.

An Inference Rule Example

The code in this section defines the inference rules for the team member role, as described above.

Here we define our topic variables.

```
<topic id="ir-t-AN-EMPLOYEE">
  <instanceOf>
    <subjectIndicatorRef xlink:href=
        "http://www.topicmaps.com/xtm/1.0/template.xtm
            #inference-variable"/>
  </instanceOf>
  <baseName>
    <scope>
      <subjectIndicatorRef xlink:href=
          "http://www.topicmaps.com/xtm/1.0/template.xtm
            #inference-rule-schema"/>
    </scope>
    <baseNameString>AN EMPLOYEE</baseNameString>
  </baseName>
</topic>
<topic id="ir-t-A-PROJECT">
```

```
      <instanceOf>
        <subjectIndicatorRef xlink:ref=
            "http://www.topicmaps.com/xtm/1.0/template.xtm
                #inference-variable"/>
      </instanceOf>
      <baseName>
        <scope>
          <subjectIndicatorRef xlink:href=
              "http://www.topicmaps.com/xtm/1.0/template.xtm
                  #inference-rule-schema"/>
        </scope>
        <baseNameString>A PROJECT</baseNameString>
      </baseName>
    </topic>
    <topic id="ir-t-A-COMPANY">
      <instanceOf>
        <subjectIndicatorRef xlink:href=
            "http://www.topicmaps.com/xtm/1.0/template.xtm
                #inference-variable"/>
      </instanceOf>
      <baseName>
        <scope>
          <subjectIndicatorRef xlink:href=
              "http://www.topicmaps.com/xtm/1.0/template.xtm
                  #inference-rule-schema"/>
        </scope>
        <baseNameString>A COMPANY</baseNameString>
      </baseName>
    </topic>
    <topic id="ir-t-A-CUSTOMER">
      <instanceOf>
        <subjectIndicatorRef xlink:href=
            "http://www.topicmaps.com/xtm/1.0/template.xtm
                #inference-variable"/>
      </instanceOf>
      <baseName>
        <scope>
          <subjectIndicatorRef xlink:href=
              "http://www.topicmaps.com/xtm/1.0/template.xtm
                  #inference-rule-schema"/>
        </scope>
        <baseNameString>A CUSTOMER</baseNameString>
      </baseName>
    </topic>
```

The *ir-project-membership* association pattern uses two topic variables with the base names *AN EMPLOYEE* (and ID *ir-t-AN-EMPLOYEE*) and *A PROJECT* (and ID *ir-t-A-PROJECT*), respectively.

```
<association id="ir-project-membership">
  <instanceOf>
```

```
      <topicRef xlink:href="#at-project-membership"/>
    </instanceOf>
    <scope>
      <subjectIndicatorRef xlink:href=
          "http://www.topicmaps.com/xtm/1.0/template.xtm
              #inference-rule-schema"/>
    </scope>
    <member>
      <roleSpec>
        <subjectIndicatorRef xlink:href=
            "http://www.topicmaps.com/xtm/1.0/template.xtm
                #t-employee"/>
      </roleSpec>
      <topicRef xlink:href="#ir-t-AN-EMPLOYEE"/>
    </member>
    <member>
      <roleSpec>
        <subjectIndicatorRef xlink:href=
            "http://www.topicmaps.com/xtm/1.0/template.xtm
                #t-project"/>
      </roleSpec>
      <topicRef xlink:href="#ir-t-A-PROJECT"/>
    </member>
</association>
```

The *ir-employment* association pattern relates two topic variables with the base names *A COMPANY* and *AN EMPLOYEE*, respectively.

```
<association id="ir-employment">
  <instanceOf>
    <topicRef xlink:href="#at-employment"/>
  </instanceOf>
  <scope>
    <subjectIndicatorRef xlink:href=
        "http://www.topicmaps.com/xtm/1.0/template.xtm
            #inference-rule-schema"/>
  </scope>
  <member>
    <roleSpec>
      <subjectIndicatorRef xlink:href=
          "http://www.topicmaps.com/xtm/1.0/template.xtm
              #t-company"/>
    </roleSpec>
    <topicRef xlink:href="#ir-t-A-COMPANY"/>
  </member>
  <member>
    <roleSpec>
      <subjectIndicatorRef xlink:href=
          "http://www.topicmaps.com/xtm/1.0/template.xtm
              #t-employee"/>
    </roleSpec>
  </roleSpec>
```

```
    <topicRef xlink:href="#ir-t-AN-EMPLOYEE"/>
  </member>
</association>
```

The *ir-project-customer* association pattern relates two topic variables with the base names *A PROJECT* and *A CUSTOMER*, respectively.

```
<association id="ir-project-customer">
  <instanceOf>
    <topicRef xlink:href="#at-project-customer"/>
  </instanceOf>
  <scope>
    <subjectIndicatorRef xlink:href=
        "http://www.topicmaps.com/xtm/1.0/template.xtm
            #inference-rule-schema"/>
  </scope>
  <member>
    <roleSpec>
      <subjectIndicatorRef xlink:href=
          "http://www.topicmaps.com/xtm/1.0/template.xtm
              #t-project"/>
    </roleSpec>
    <topicRef xlink:href="#ir-t-A-PROJECT"/>
  </member>
  <member>
    <roleSpec>
      <subjectIndicatorRef xlink:href=
          "http://www.topicmaps.com/xtm/1.0/template.xtm
              #t-customer"/>
    </roleSpec>
    <topicRef xlink:href="#ir-t-A-CUSTOMER"/>
  </member>
</association>
```

The *ir-company-customer* association pattern relates two topic variables with the base names *A COMPANY* with *A CUSTOMER*, respectively.

```
<association id="ir-company-customer">
  <instanceOf>
    <topicRef xlink:href="#at-company-customer"/>
  </instanceOf>
  <scope>
    <subjectIndicatorRef xlink:href=
        "http://www.topicmaps.com/xtm/1.0/template.xtm
            #inference-rule-schema"/>
  </scope>
  <member>
    <roleSpec>
      <subjectIndicatorRef xlink:href=
```

```
          "http://www.topicmaps.com/xtm/1.0/template.xtm
                #t-company"/>
      </roleSpec>
      <topicRef xlink:href="#ir-t-A-COMPANY"/>
    </member>
    <member>
      <roleSpec>
        <subjectIndicatorRef xlink:href=
            "http://www.topicmaps.com/xtm/1.0/template.xtm
                #t-customer"/>
      </roleSpec>
      <topicRef xlink:href="#ir-t-A-CUSTOMER"/>
    </member>
</association>
```

Before the associations can be used as role players in the inference role association, they have to be reified by topics.

```
<topic id="t-reified-ir-project-membership">
  <subjectIdentity>
    <resourceRef xlink:href="#ir-project-membership"/>
  </subjectIdentity>
</topic>
<topic id="t-reified-ir-employment">
  <subjectIdentity>
    <resourceRef xlink:href="#ir-employment"/>
  </subjectIdentity>
</topic>
<topic id="t-reified-ir-project-customer">
  <subjectIdentity>
    <resourceRef xlink:href="#ir-project-customer"/>
  </subjectIdentity>
</topic>
<topic id="t-reified-ir-company-customer">
  <subjectIdentity>
    <resourceRef xlink:href="#ir-company-customer"/>
  </subjectIdentity>
</topic>
```

The association of class *inference-rule* refers to the four other associations and assigns them the appropriate roles. The reified *ir-project-membership*, *ir-employment*, and *ir-project-customer* association patterns become conditions—implicitly connected by Boolean AND operators[3]—and the reified *ir-company-customer* association pattern becomes the THEN of the inference rule.

---

[3] A Boolean OR could be modeled by further inference rule associations. More complex Boolean operator combinations could be modeled with OR and NOT associations that combine the conditions accordingly—but this might lead to quite complex association hierarchies and would probably be better solved with a programming language.

```
<association id="ir-1">
  <instanceOf>
    <subjectIndicatorRef xlink:href=
        "http://www.topicmaps.com/xtm/1.0/template.xtm
            #inference-rule"/>
  </instanceOf>
  <scope>
    <subjectIndicatorRef xlink:href=
        "http://www.topicmaps.com/xtm/1.0/template.xtm
            #inference-rule-schema"/>
  </scope>
  <member>
    <roleSpec>
      <subjectIndicatorRef xlink:href=
          "http://www.topicmaps.com/xtm/1.0/template.xtm
              #inference-condition"/>
    </roleSpec>
    <topicRef xlink:href="#t-reified-ir-project-membership"/>
  </member>
  <member>
    <roleSpec>
      <subjectIndicatorRef xlink:href=
          "http://www.topicmaps.com/xtm/1.0/template.xtm
              #inference-condition"/>
    </roleSpec>
    <topicRef xlink:href="#t-reified-ir-employment"/>
  </member>
  <member>
    <roleSpec>
      <subjectIndicatorRef xlink:href=
          "http://www.topicmaps.com/xtm/1.0/template.xtm
              #inference-condition"/>
    </roleSpec>
    <topicRef xlink:href="#t-reified-ir-project-customer"/>
  </member>
  <member>
    <roleSpec>
      <subjectIndicatorRef xlink:href=
          "http://www.topicmaps.com/xtm/1.0/template.xtm
              #inference-statement"/>
    </roleSpec>
    <topicRef xlink:href="#t-reified-ir-company-customer"/>
  </member>
</association>
```

Table 14–5 lists all the necessary PSIs for the inference rule code.

The *any* topic is used in a condition association if an association class, topic, or role could be any topic—it is a variable that is not instantiated.

Table 14–5 PSIs for Inference Rules

Description	PSI
Topic map *object*, part of inference rule *schema*, which is identified by a scoping topic*	*http://www.topicmaps.com/xtm/1.0/template.xtm#inference-rule-schema*
Topic class *inference variable*	*http://www.topicmaps.com/xtm/1.0/template.xtm#inference-variable*
Association class *inference rule*	*http://www.topicmaps.com/xtm/1.0/template.xtm#inference-rule*
Association role *inference condition*	*http://www.topicmaps.com/xtm/1.0/template.xtm#inference-condition*
Association role *inference statement*	*http://www.topicmaps.com/xtm/1.0/template.xtm#inference-statement*
The *any* topic	*http://www.topicmaps.com/xtm/1.0/template.xtm#any-topic*

* The inference rule patterns must be distinguishable from the constraint patterns. Therefore, a separate scoping topic is needed.

Consistency Constraints

ISO 13250 and the XTM specification cover the subjects of validation and consistency only slightly. The Conformance section of ISO 13250 focuses on the understanding of the defined constructs, the interchange syntax, and the import/export of topic maps.

Both the designer and the editor of topic maps need system support when designing and creating a map that will consist of millions of topics and associations. The question of the consistency of the map becomes a key issue because it is nearly impossible to check a map of that size manually. For that reason we need concepts to declare consistency constraints and to validate that those constraints have been obeyed [Rath 1999; Grønmo 2000].

Consequently, a separate schema is needed that contains all the information necessary for the validation process. We call such constructs *consistency constraints* or just *constraints.* The validation is the task of the topic map development environment (for example, an editor or an editorial system). It should be performed permanently or on demand—like structure validation in an SGML/XML editor.

In our approach the constraints are either declared in the template as a set of topic, occurrence, and association patterns or implemented with a programming language using the API of the topic map editor/engine. The latter option gives more freedom, but for the price of a lot of effort. The first option is probably sufficient for most applications.

- Here are examples of a topic constraint and an association constraint, respectively.
- A topic of class *project* has to have at least one English name, one project plan, and between one and ten status reports, and it has to be associated with a project manager.
- An association of class *project membership* has to have exactly one project that has one or more project team members.

Constraint Patterns

The constraints are defined as patterns to which topics and associations must conform in order to be valid against a topic map schema. These patterns declare the possible parameters and their combinations. The patterns are defined as topics and associations. A predefined scoping topic schema which is used as the scope signals that these topics and associations have a special meaning—they are constraints for topics/associations of the given class.

The *any* topic introduced earlier will be used if the pattern needs a wild card for topics. A predefined scoping topic is assigned to the association as the scope if some topics must participate (playing the specified role) in the association.

The declaration of minimum and maximum numbers of objects in a pattern (like names, occurrences, and association roles) is accomplished indirectly through `<resourceData>` occurrences assigned to a topic reifying the appropriate object.

The PSIs shown in Table 14–6 define the "constraint schema" scoping topic, the "required association role" scoping topic, and both the "minimum" and "maximum" occurrence classes.

Table 14–6   PSIs for Constraints

Description	PSI
Topic map *object* is part of constraint *schema*, which is identified by a scoping topic.	*http://www.topicmaps.com/xtm/1.0/template.xtm#constraint-schema*
The topic has to be used in the association that is identified by a scoping topic.	*http://www.topicmaps.com/xtm/1.0/template.xtm#topic-role-requirement*
This occurrence class indicates the minimum number of reified *object*.	*http://www.topicmaps.com/xtm/1.0/template.xtm#min-number*
This occurrence class indicates the maximum number of reified *object*.	*http://www.topicmaps.com/xtm/1.0/template.xtm#max-number*

Topic Class Example

The example below shows a pattern that constrains the topic class *tc-project*.

```
<topic id="X">
  <instanceOf>
    <topicRef xlink:href="#tc-project"/>
  </instanceOf>
  <baseName id="bn-project-english">
    <scope>
      <subjectIndicatorRef xlink:href=
          "http://www.topicmaps.com/xtm/1.0/template.xtm
              #constraint-schema"/>
      <topicRef xlink:href=
          "http://www.topicmaps.org/xtm/1.0/language.xtm
              #en"/>
    </scope>
    <baseNameString>X</baseNameString>
  </baseName>
  <occurrence id="o-project-plan">
    <instanceOf>
      <topicRef xlink:href="#oc-project-plan"/>
    </instanceOf>
    <scope>
      <subjectIndicatorRef xlink:href=
          "http://www.topicmaps.com/xtm/1.0/template.xtm
              #constraint-schema"/>
```

```
      </scope>
      <resourceData>X</resourceData>
    </occurrence>
    <occurrence id="o-status-report">
      <instanceOf>
        <topicRef xlink:href="#oc-status-report"/>
      </instanceOf>
      <scope>
        <subjectIndicatorRef xlink:href=
            "http://www.topicmaps.com/xtm/1.0/template.xtm
                #constraint-schema"/>
      </scope>
      <resourceData>X</resourceData>
    </occurrence>
  </topic>
  <topic id="t-reified-bn-project-english">
    <subjectIdentity>
      <resourceRef xlink:href="#bn-project-english"/>
    </subjectIdentity>
    <occurrence>
      <instanceOf>
        <subjectIndicatorRef xlink:href=
            "http://www.topicmaps.com/xtm/1.0/template.xtm
                #min-number"/>
      </instanceOf>
      <scope>
        <subjectIndicatorRef xlink:href=
            "http://www.topicmaps.com/xtm/1.0/template.xtm
                #constraint-schema"/>
      </scope>
      <resourceData>1</resourceData>
    </occurrence>
  </topic>
  <topic id="t-reified-o-status-report">
    <subjectIdentity>
      <resourceRef xlink:href="#o-status-report"/>
    </subjectIdentity>
    <occurrence>
      <instanceOf>
        <subjectIndicatorRef xlink:href=
            "http://www.topicmaps.com/xtm/1.0/template.xtm
                #min-number"/>
      </instanceOf>
      <scope>
        <subjectIndicatorRef xlink:href=
            "http://www.topicmaps.com/xtm/1.0/template.xtm
                #constraint-schema"/>
      </scope>
      <resourceData>1</resourceData>
    </occurrence>
```

```
<occurrence>
  <instanceOf>
    <subjectIndicatorRef xlink:href=
      "http://www.topicmaps.com/xtm/1.0/template.xtm
         #max-number"/>
  </instanceOf>
  <scope>
    <subjectIndicatorRef xlink:href=
      "http://www.topicmaps.com/xtm/1.0/template.xtm
         #constraint-schema"/>
  </scope>
  <resourceData>10</resourceData>
</occurrence>
</topic>
```

Here's an explanation of the constraint for topics of class *tc-project*, as expressed above.

By convention, a data value of capital X means *any value*. Thus, attributes of type -id-, elements of type <baseNameString>, and occurrences may have any value.

The topics that are instances of the PSI *[...]#min-number* declare that there must be a minimum number of instances of the reified element in the topic map—but more instances than the minimum are allowed. Thus, there may be 1–n elements of type <baseName> with scope English. (The XTM PSI for the English language is used here).

The topics that are instances of the PSI *[...]#max-number* declare that there may be a maximum number of instances of the reified element in the topic map—but fewer instances than the maximum are allowed. Thus, there may be 1–10 occurrences of class *oc-status-report*.

If no topic for minimum or maximum number reifies an element, the same number of that element in the pattern must be in the topic map. Thus, there must be one occurrence of role class *oc-project-plan*.

Association Class Example

There is also a pattern for association classes that controls the scope, the combination of valid association roles using *min-number*/*max-number* topics, and the valid topic classes for every role.

The code below shows an example of a pattern that constrains the association class *ac-project-membership*.

```
<association id="X">
  <instanceOf>
    <topicRef xlink:href="#ac-project-membership"/>
  </instanceOf>
  <scope>
    <subjectIndicatorRef xlink:href=
        "http://www.topicmaps.com/xtm/1.0/template.xtm
            #constraint-schema"/>
  </scope>
  <member>
    <roleSpec>
      <topicRef xlink:href="#tc-project"/>
    </roleSpec>
    <topicRef xlink:href="#tc-project"/>
  </member>
  <member id="m-team-member">
    <roleSpec>
      <topicRef xlink:href="#tc-team-member"/>
    </roleSpec>
    <topicRef xlink:href="#tc-employee"/>
  </member>
</association>
<association id="X">
  <instanceOf>
    <topicRef xlink:href="#ac-project-membership"/>
  </instanceOf>
  <scope>
    <subjectIndicatorRef xlink:href=
        "http://www.topicmaps.com/xtm/1.0/template.xtm
            #constraint-schema"/>
    <subjectIndicatorRef xlink:href=
        "http://www.topicmaps.com/xtm/1.0/template.xtm
            #topic-role-requirement">
  </scope>
  <member>
    <roleSpec>
      <subjectIndicatorRef xlink:href=
        "http://www.topicmaps.com/xtm/1.0/template.xtm
            #any-topic"/>
    </roleSpec>
    <subjectIndicatorRef xlink:href=
        "http://www.topicmaps.com/xtm/1.0/template.xtm
            #any-topic"/>
  </member>
  <member>
    <roleSpec>
      <topicRef xlink:href="#tc-project"/>
    </roleSpec>
    <topicRef xlink:href="#tc-project"/>
  </member>
</association>
```

```
<topic id="t-reified-m-team-member">
  <subjectIdentity>
    <resourceRef xlink:href="#m-team-member"/>
  </subjectIdentity>
  <occurrence>
    <instanceOf>
      <subjectIndicatorRef xlink:href=
         "http://www.topicmaps.com/xtm/1.0/template.xtm
            #min-number"/>
    </instanceOf>
    <scope>
      <subjectIndicatorRef xlink:href=
         "http://www.topicmaps.com/xtm/1.0/template.xtm
            #constraint-schema"/>
    </scope>
    <resourceData>1</resourceData>
  </occurrence>
</topic>
```

Here's the explanation of the constraint for associations of class `ac-project-membership`.

The listed association roles are mandatory because the `<member>` elements are not reified by a `min-number` topic.

All `ac-project-membership` associations have to have the one association role `tc-project`.

The schema `[…]#topic-role-requirement` signals that every topic of an explicitly given class has to play the listed role in at least one association of the given class. Every topic of class `tc-project` has to play the role `tc-project` in at least one association of class `ac-project-membership`.

The `min-number` topic means that there has to be a minimum number of the reified association members in the topic map, but more than that number are allowed. The `max-number` topic means that there could be a maximum number of the reified association members in the topic map, but fewer than that number are allowed.

An association of class `ac-project-membership` consists of at least one team member.

Constraints and Class Hierarchies

The defined constraints are automatically valid for all subclasses of the topic class or the association class. Subclasses of the defined association roles and topic classes playing that role are automatically valid as well.

The declaration of class hierarchies (for example, class `tc-product` is a subclass of `tc-technology`) simplifies the declaration of constraints. Declaring the constraint for a general superclass automatically declares the same constraint for all its subclasses. An example would be SGML, which, if a topic of class `tc-standard`, could be allowed to play the role `tc-technology` in an `ac-project-technology` association.

Summary

Topic maps provide a powerful paradigm for defining intelligent link networks over continually growing information pools. Real-world topic maps consist of a large number of objects that require validation to assure the quality of the map. The following concepts help with quality assurance or make implicitly coded knowledge explicit.

- Topic map templates define the ontology of the application domain.
- Class hierarchies express the superclass–subclass relationships.
- Association properties assign transitivity to binary associations.
- Inference rules declare how to derive implicit knowledge.
- Constraints are the validation rules.

The sum of these concepts describes the topic map schema.

As discussed in this chapter, the topic map schema can be modeled as a topic map. Using the topic maps paradigm also for the definition of the listed control structures allows self-control of topic maps and simple handling by topic map tools. PSIs distinguish the schema objects from the objects of a "regular" topic map.

References

Freese, E. 2000. Using Topic Maps for the Representation, Management and Discovery of Knowledge. Paper presented at XML Europe 2000 Conference, Paris, June 2000. Accessed in April 2002 at *http://www.gca.org/papers/xmleurope2000/papers/s22-01.html*.

Grønmo, G. O. 2000. Creating Semantically Valid Topic Maps. Paper presented at XML Europe 2000 Conference, Paris, June 2000. Accessed in April 2002 at *http://www.gca.org/papers/xmleurope2000/papers/s29-02.html*.

Ksiezyk, R. 1999. Trying Not to Get Lost with a Topic Map. Paper presented at XML Europe 1999 Conference, Granada, May 1999. Accessed in April 2002 at *http://www.infoloom.com/gcaconfs/WEB/TOC/t0331.HTM*.

————. 2000. Answer Is Just a Question [of Matching Topic Maps]. Paper presented at XML Europe 2000 Conference, Paris, June 2000. Accessed in April 2002 at *http:// www.gca.org/papers/xmleurope2000/papers/s22-03.html*.

Pepper, S. 1999. Navigating Haystacks and Discovering Needles. In *Markup Languages: Theory and Practice*, 1.4; C. M. Sperberg-McQueen and B. T. Usdin, eds. Boston: MIT Press.

Rath, H. H. 1999. Technical Issues on Topic Maps. Paper presented at MetaStructures '99 Conference, Montreal. Accessed in April 2002 at *http://www.infoloom.com/ montreal99/metastruct/tom-hhr-paper.pdf*.

————. 2000. Topic Maps: Templates, Topology, and Type Hierarchies. In *Markup Languages: Theory and Practice*, 2.1; C. M. Sperberg-McQueen and B. T. Usdin, eds. Boston: MIT Press.

Rath, H. H., and S. Pepper. 2000. Topic Maps: Knowledge Navigation Aids. In *The XML Handbook*, 3rd ed.; C. F. Goldfarb and P. Prescod, eds. Upper Saddle River, NJ: Prentice Hall.

Sowa, J. F. 2000. *Knowledge Representation—Logical, Philosophical and Computational Foundations*. New York: Brooks/Cole.

Chapter 15

TOPIC MAPS IN KNOWLEDGE ORGANIZATION[1]

ALEXANDER SIGEL

Suggestions for Reading This Chapter

Reading Prerequisites. Because knowledge organization (KO) is a broader and more abstract context for topic maps (TMs), before reading on, make sure you have acquainted yourself with the basic topic map concepts and technology as presented in this book (for example, Chapters 2, 6, and 14) so that you understand the core concepts of TMs and have worked through some examples.

Suggested Reading Path for Practitioners. I recommend that you read through the following parts of this chapter first:

- The beginning of this section, through to the end of the KO, Knowledge Structures, and TMs subsection
- The entire subsection, Some Definitions: What Is and Does KO? To What End KO?
- The example in the Key Ingredients of KO Theory and an Introductory Example subsection
- The in-text summary in the Overview: Problems and Principles subsection
- The KO in Practice subsection
- From the KO as a Use Case for TMs section to the end of the chapter

Since the What Is KO? section discusses relevant elements of KO theory of potential value for a TM methodology on a rather abstract level, you may want to skip most of it until a second, in-depth reading. (Everyone is invited to reread it.) The KO as a Use Case for TMs section reads more easily since there the relationship between TMs

---

[1]This chapter elaborates on ideas I first presented in earlier papers [Sigel 1999, 2000a, 2000b].

and KO is worked out in more practical terms. Note that this chapter uses several abbreviations; you may wish to refer to the list of abbreviations at the end of this chapter as you're reading.

The Overlap between KO and TMs

There is a natural overlap and complement between KO and TMs. I am convinced that KO, with its relevant knowledge of and experiences in concept organization, can strongly contribute in this area. Since this idea impacts both the KO and TM communities, this chapter offers an invitation to anyone interested in TMs to draw from the KO background and to KO experts to include the case of KO with TMs in their research.[2]

KO is about organizing objects of thought (and associated carriers of information) so that humans can work with them more easily. The central aim is improved access, more sophisticated finding aids, and a clearer overview. To this end, KO deals with structured metadata (for example, indexing). KO expresses and orders statements about subject matter, which are comprised of *concepts* and *relations*. TMs allow us to express, reuse, find, or merge such statements of complex knowledge networks on a new level. In a nutshell, KO knows about the methodological issue of how to organize assertions, and TMs, in their assertion-centric view [Newcomb 2001a], are ideal tools for managing such organized assertions, even during the very process of organizing them.

Presumably you now want to know just *how* KO can help to get your job done better. Most likely, your job is to improve the organization of a body of knowledge in your application domain.[3] That's why you're interested in TMs as a technology and tool. You need a methodology to build future-proof TMs or an interoperable PSI infrastructure. Probably you are expecting to find here the ultimate answers to the following questions.

- What is the essence of KO? How is KO applied? Who applies KO to what end?
- How could the main issues in KO inform my understanding of TMs such that I can apply TMs more efficiently?
- How can KO methodology and techniques help me design and construct better TMs and TM infrastructures?
- How can I profit from KO experiences for my task? Which problems has KO surmounted? Which problem is KO tackling now?

---

[2] KO experts are interested in how TMs might aid the process of organizing knowledge, what this might mean in practice, and which consequences this might have for indexing theory.

[3] You might also be a TM expert, seeking to improve TM methodology, architecture, and applications.

I would have liked to write such a how-to tutorial, with lots of practical examples, scenarios, and concrete recommendations, so that TM adepts could draw from lessons learned in KO. However, I must ask you to lower your expectations. What I did accomplish, albeit with the notable bias of a researcher in conceptual KO, is to chart the territory, to discuss selected issues of mutual interest, and to illustrate them with examples, thereby focusing on KO as a TM use case. I consider this chapter a first step in an ongoing effort to close the gaps between both communities by actively adapting and transferring knowledge.[4] Although the exploration of the intellectual crossover between both communities (KOxTM) has already begun, there is still a long way to go. KO researchers have had their first experiences with TM tools but still lack experience with large-scale application projects. Therefore, not much can be said definitively, and a systematic and comprehensive treatment remains a desideratum. A next step would be to further explore the central issues in practice and come up with a best-practice document.[5]

Remember: the basic problem is that we are dealing here with human thought and social processes. This very nature makes it difficult to provide sound advice on how to do something (for example, how to automate indexing, how to best design a TM). Perhaps more than elsewhere, there exists no silver bullet, and advice depends much on the individual case. In the following pages, I have *italicized* some important recommendations.

With such a recent and rapidly evolving area as TMs, I can only set the scene and stimulate open dialogue and exchange in order to learn more. In the spirit of this book, I encourage you to share your suggestions with me at the Web site for this book, so that I can improve this chapter.

KO, Knowledge Structures, and TMs

KO is the interdisciplinary field that theoretically reflects the practical activity of organizing knowledge for specific purposes and discourse communities. Let's begin by considering *knowledge* as an intellectual construction by a cognitive subject, mediated by a sign system such as language, which is the result of an interpretative process with regard to circumstances, or knowledge objects, in the "real" world. Of paramount interest are intersubjectively validated knowledge structures, that is, social or cultural constructs:

---

[4] I am not aware of much other significant work on transferring KO expertise to TMs, except by Svenonius [2001], Vizine-Goetz [2001], and the Networked Knowledge Organization Systems/Services group (NKOS; see *http://nkos.slis.kent.edu/*). Unfortunately, I could not attend Elaine Svenonius's Extreme Markup 2001 keynote address, but Ann Wrightson remarked [personal communication via e-mail, August 2001] that she was "well received, and will I guess become a 'marker' for topic map folks in KO, much as John Sowa has become a 'marker' in KR [knowledge representation]."

[5] Not unlike what Murray Altheim started; see *http://www.infoloom.com/pipermail/topicmapmail/2001q3/003001.html*.

the view (conceptualization) a discourse community shares on relevant objects of discourse and how such a community thinks those objects are interrelated.[6] In this sense, KO is about finding such conceptualizations and modeling them as ontologies analyzing language-mediated discourse (in particular in its presence in documents and information needs) according to the deep structures involved, representing their essence in the form of normalized subject metadata assigned to information resources.

A certain normalization of knowledge structures (as, for example, in vocabulary control) is a necessary means to achieve predictability in indexing and searching, such that like phenomena are grouped together as much as possible, independent from their unlimited variety of surface structures. KO ultimately aids *inquiry*—human understanding and problem solving[7]—in two ways: (1) by collocating like subjects (and information resources "about" like subjects) and (2) by summarizing the contribution and potential usefulness of information resources with respect to such subjects, according to different views, and in varying selectivity and depth.

TMs allow knowledge structures to be expressed as structured link networks, shared, and merged. TMs can be employed to express both contradictory discourse community views and subject metadata for knowledge repositories.

KO, therefore, is about how to arrive at and represent appropriate conceptual access structures to aid working with knowledge (knowledge networks or knowledge spaces). TMs are a special paradigm and technology to handle such networks, particularly to model (represent, explicate) knowledge structures. Thus with TMs you can create sophisticated finding aids that allow semantic searching and visual browsing of those complex knowledge structures.

KOxTM: Impact Directions and Open Questions

In this section, I briefly sketch KOxTM areas in general and raise important questions. Since they are open research questions, my main concern is to raise awareness of them, not to answer them.

Given there exists exploitable, fruitful overlap at all, what kinds of interrelations might be interesting? Basically, we can consider two cases.

1. We can apply principles, methods, and experiences from KO to TM authoring and usage, including merging. When KO challenges inevitably haunt us also in their new TM disguise, some KO background will certainly be of help.

---

[6] Compare with the figures in Chapter 5 by Bernard Vatant on the coevolution of a shared conceptualization.

[7] Compare with Jaenecke [1994].

2. We can investigate the effect of the TM paradigm on the ease of use and quality of practical KO and KO theory. (TMs are a valuable KO tool, thus anyone interested in KO should have a closer look at them).

Respectively, I have called those impact directions (1) *KO for TMs* (KO practice and research as a quarry for TMs) and (2) *KO with TMs* or *TMs in KO* (the title of this chapter).

I also have come up with two basic questions.

1. How can we, with principled KO, prepare for better semantic interoperability between independently authored TMs and between independently operated PSI registries?
2. How could TM-based services alleviate pressing KO problems, in particular, how to reorganize, enhance, and semantically integrate heterogeneous subject data?

My response to these two questions is to enumerate two simple beliefs: (1) It is possible to apply KO experiences in a PSI architecture such that unnecessary scattering of like topics (and PSIs) is diminished, and (2) TMs can help with some KO problems (for example, through flexible indexing views, scope filtering, semantic retrieval, or ontology-based modeling of a more formal semantics in order to achieve semantic interoperability).

In my view, the most important of the several crucial issues discussed within both the TM and the KO communities is to arrange for *semantic interoperability* of the resulting interlinked knowledge network, which is also a hot topic for the Semantic Web.[8] The message is that KO has some stake in this area [ISKO et al. 1996].

KO strives to virtually integrate knowledge organization systems (KOSs) and subject metadata. This allows transparent switching and intermediating between diverging expressions of conceptualizations.

As examples of semantic interoperability problems in the design of knowledge networks, consider the following:

■ The interpretation of what a resource (for example, a Web page) is about
■ What a given metadata entry (for example, a descriptor or a class) means to different actors
■ How a brokering system can decide that two classes from different classification systems are about the same subject

---

[8]See *http://www.semanticweb.org/*. See also the coverage of Semantic Web within the Electronic Transactions on Artificial Intelligence (ETAI) site, *http://www.etaij.org/seweb/*; several workshops, for example, *http://semanticweb2001.aifb.uni-karlsruhe.de/*; and Fensel et al. [2000].

Semantic interoperability becomes even more important if we are interested in knowledge structures rather than their carriers (knowledge sources; for example, documents). Just as RDF is said to be rather resource-centric and TMs to be rather topic-centric, KO sees a shift from the document-oriented to the predication-oriented paradigm. Bibliographic reference systems deal with bibliographic entities like books and papers, but not with predications made in or attributable to such entities. Modern KO, formal semantics in knowledge representation (KR), and the Semantic Web meet in the issue of semantic interoperability both because ontologies help to achieve this interoperability and because a larger indexing depth leads toward KR of selected predications. Primarily, we are interested in relationships between predications, and only secondarily in relationships between documents. The separation of the knowledge structure level from the document level in TMs aids semantic interoperability: it becomes possible to model views of different social worlds on how to express subject matter in language. Interoperability is achieved by flexibly keeping such interpretation contexts apart, or by combining them, as needed. With TMs we can represent the usage of terminologies in different language worlds.

KR and related fields need semantic interoperability for information fusion, intelligent information integration [IJCAI 1999], and the cooperation between information agents who have to exchange and negotiate their ontological commitments. Let me give some examples of current work in semantic interoperability of relevance to KO.

Heflin and Hendler [2000] discuss why semantic interoperability is not solved by XML, why Resource Description Framework (RDF) is only a partial solution, and how Simple HTML Ontology Extension (SHOE) might help.[9] Amann and Fundulaki [1999, p. 249] interpret the RDF schema resulting from their integration of ontologies and thesauri as the domain model in mediation-based systems playing "an essential role in achieving *semantic interoperability* between the sources."

Hunter [2001] is an example for modern KO and its utmost importance for the organization of digitized and digital document-like objects.[10] She stresses that metadata interoperability is a fundamental requirement for access to information within Networked KOSs (NKOS) and concludes that using XSLT to map between metadata descriptions originating from different domains is good only for syntactical and structural mapping; you have to hard-code semantic mappings. In her view, the only possibility for providing flexible semantic mappings is with the employment of semantic knowledge bases (ontologies, thesauri).

---

[9]This should apply all the more to Ontology Inference Layer (OIL) and now DARPA Agent Markup Language + OIL (DAML+OIL) since SHOE is a kind of precursor.

[10]See also the NKOS Web site, *http://nkos.slis.kent.edu/* (including the participants' page, *http://nkos.slis.kent.edu/NKOS_participants.html*), and proceedings from two workshops [NKOS 2000, 2001].

What Are Useful KO Principles? What Is Principled KO?[11]

Principled KO refers to principles and criteria sought in KO theory: that it is desirable to be able to appeal to some guideline in order to decide how to organize a large knowledge structure and how to evaluate its design. In the ideal case, these principles would have certain explanatory power and could predict what "sound"[12] KO is and why, or could even help to generate and evaluate "sound" KOSs. Such principles, meant to aid in quality assurance, must necessarily be linked to the purpose and goal of KO; hence they are always epistemologically bound to users and embedded in usage contexts. They are also linked to a healthy scientific approach, but our interest is more in their utility than the ethics involved. Principled KO asks, for example, the following questions.

- What constitutes "good" or "sound" (ecologically valid or grounded) KOSs?
- Why does this KOS or indexing constitute "good" or "bad" indexing? For which users and usage contexts?
- Under which circumstances (and why) is KO *A* a better overview or conceptual access structure for user *U* than KO *B*?

From this we see that evaluation and judgment of KO are not that easy. At least in part, the quality of a KOS depends on the context of its application. Therefore, absolute rules that you could follow might not even exist. Keep this in mind during your search for indexing rules and principles. KO introductions, manuals, and textbooks[13] or the ISO standards for documentation and information science[14] may transmit the notion that such rules exist (for example, that there exists a foolproof recipe for how to make a thesaurus). However, critics claim that while much effort has been devoted to how to technically express recognized conceptual structures in concrete KOSs, we still know little about the most interesting (and most challenging) part of intellectual KO: how to reliably recognize and construct such structures. Of minor importance are the more numerous abstract rules on how to represent a

---

[11] I'm always looking for ways to improve this section. Use the book's Web site to comment.

[12] My use of "sound" here is inspired by "sound inferencing" and decidability in mathematics. However, since KO deals with soft factors (people and social phenomena), no context-free formal system or algorithm for "good" KO exists.

[13] See, for example, Soergel [1985], Fugmann [1993, 1999], Iyer [1995], Lancaster [1998], Svenonius [2000], Craven [1997–2002], and Aitchison et al. [2001]. Concerning Svenonius, I heard criticisms by an NKOS proponent that while her book is very valuable, it unfortunately does not cover more modern KO approaches. This is a pity, given the lack of good textbooks in this area.

[14] See ISO [1999] (for example, on abstracting, mono- and multilingual thesauri, and documentary languages).

conceptualization in a concrete KOS (for example, in thesaurus construction). In the words of Mai:

> What becomes much more important is the interpretative processes in knowledge organization and the cultural and social context of which the knowledge organization is a part. . . . [The technical approach to KO] often ignores the most difficult part of creating a knowledge organization, namely the application of these rules and guidelines in specific domains.[15] [Mai 1999, pp. 547, 555]

In my view, KO principles do exist but are only partially discovered. It is important to adapt abstract principles already recognized in concrete situations to TM design in order to avoid fundamental mistakes.

What Are Pressing KO Problems?

There exist quite a few *pressing KO problems*, as reflected in reviews of KO conferences and the corresponding sections of the bibliography of the literature on KO [*KO* 1999]. There exists the longstanding KO problem of the comparability and compatibility between KOSs, that is, semantic interoperability. For illustrative purposes I quote some of the special challenges formulated by Green, which in my view are also part of the challenges in TM design.

> Is there a universal set of relationship types applicable across all contexts?
>
> How can we build integrated knowledge organization schemes that reflect a multiplicity of relational views?
>
> Is the incorporation of a relational approach to retrieval feasible, given the volume and diversity of material online?
>
> How could we evaluate the impact of incorporating a relational approach to online retrieval? [Green 1998]

The first question Green poses is part of the question asking which set of basic concepts and relations we should use. The second is related to view-based indexing. The third and fourth ask for the feasibility and evaluation of indexing with many semantic relations (and hence of semantic retrieval along those relations). We still know little about principles for sound ontology design, about how to determine the quality of

---

[15] "In specific domains" may be misleading. What is meant is that instead of searching for abstract rules, KO should be more informed by context-dependent methods like activity-theoretical domain analysis.

concrete KOSs and subject metadata for an information resource,[16] about limitations of subject analysis (with the tension between relativism and objectivism), about the relative merits and problems of universal versus special KOSs (and the balance between universals and cultural multiplicity), or about the implications of the trend from decentralized provision and control over KOSs and subject metadata to a more decentralized model.

What Is KO?[17]

Some Definitions: What Is and Does KO?
To What End KO?

The field of KO is certainly not new. It is rooted in thousands of years of experience, mostly in the library and information science (LIS) area. Likewise, the need for systematic representation of knowledge was recognized long ago.[18] KO began to flourish in the last quarter of the nineteenth century with universal classification systems like the Dewey Decimal Classification (DDC) published in 1876 and the Universal Decimal Classification (UDC) published in 1899. Bliss [1929, 1933], who early used the term *organization of knowledge*, inspired the baptism of the whole field. The specific term *knowledge organization* was coined upon the foundation of ISKO (July 22, 1989) and was soon widely adopted.

---

[16] This would have to include qualitative explanations of indexing reasons, as stated from the viewpoint of the information needs of the communities for which the indexing is done.

[17] If you want to learn more about KO, I strongly recommend resources related to the International Society for Knowledge Organization (ISKO). The organization's Web site is at *http://www.isko.org/*. ISKO holds an international conference every two years, and regional ISKO chapters have their own conferences. ISKO runs the journal *KO—Knowledge Organization*. An excellent classified bibliography covering the last ten years of ISKO is available [*KO* 1999], although up to now only on paper, and a three-volume bibliography for earlier periods exists [Dahlberg 1982a, 1984, 1985]. There are several book series. Unfortunately, the volume about ten years of ISKO Festschrift containing reprints of important KO articles (edited by Schmitz-Esser) has not yet appeared. The most recent international ISKO conference was held in 2000 in Toronto. The proceedings volume [Beghtol et al. 2000] contains several papers of relevance for TMs (some are also cited in this chapter). Excellent reports on this conference (which communicate insights about current KO directions and views) appeared in the *KO* journal [Green 2000b; Mai 2000b]. Proceedings volumes of previous ISKO conferences also exist [Ohly et al. 2000; El Hadi et al. 1998; Green 1996a; Meder et al. 1995; Albrechtsen and Örnager 1994; Fugmann 1990]. As of this writing, the next international ISKO conference will be held in July 2002 in Granada.

[18] See, for example, Barth [1996] on 5,000 years of libraries (particularly Chapter 3 on Mesopotamia and Egypt and Chapter 4 on Greek and Roman civilization).

Anderson defines KO as if it were centered around documents only, instead of around knowledge structures. According to him, KO is

> the description of documents, their content, features and purposes, and the organization of these descriptions so as to make these documents and their parts accessible to persons seeking them or the messages that they contain. Knowledge organization encompasses every type and method of indexing, abstracting, cataloguing, classification, records management, bibliography and the creation of textual or bibliographic databases for information retrieval. [Anderson 1997, p. 336]

Before I quote Dahlberg's important systematic and differential definition, I have to introduce her "Systematifier," based on her Syndisciplinarity theory [Dahlberg 1994], on which McInerney [1997] writes, "The Systematifier looks at the facets of any knowledge field to represent concepts embedded within it and can be applied to multidisciplinary, transdisciplinary and other forms of interdisciplinary endeavors."

Dahlberg's own Information Coding Classification (ICC) [Dahlberg 1982a, 1982b, 1996a][19] applies those principles, as does her definition of KO reprinted below (translated by me from the original German). For clarity's sake, in the following I have added her nine Systematifier facets in square brackets. (In items 5 and 6, the facet used under item 4 continues.)

> [Knowledge Organization is a] subject field concerned with the organization of
>
> a. Knowledge items (concepts) and
>
> b. Objects of all types (minerals, plants, animals, documents, images, objects in museums, etc.) which one relates to corresponding concepts or concept classes in order to capture the knowledge about the world of the known in an ordered form and to be able to disseminate this knowledge for utilization.
>
> Knowledge Organization embraces the following nine subfields:
>
> 1. [Theories, Principles] The suppositions from epistemology, mathematics, system theory, cognitive sciences and science of science for the organization of concepts, as well as their historical background;
>
> 2. [Object, Component] The knowledge about the elements and structures of concept systems;

---

[19] See also *http://index.bonn.iz-soz.de/~sigel/ISKO/ICC/*.

3. [Activity, Process] The methodology for intellectual creation, maintenance and revision of these systems and their computerization, including issues of the paradigmatic and syntagmatic relationing of its element and items, as well as making these systems compatible and evaluating them;

4. [Property, Attribute] The methodology of intellectual and automatic application of these systems by classification and indexing,

5. [Property, Attribute continued] the knowledge about the existing universal and

6. [Property, Attribute continued] the special taxonomies and classification systems as well as documentation languages (thesauri);

7. [Concepts influencing or coming from outside fields] The issues that result from influences of the linguistic and terminology areas, including the problems of retrieval, especially online retrieval;

8. [Application and Determination] The applications of subject analysis and representation of all types of documents in all subject areas;

9. [Distribution and Synthesis: Actuosciences and Professional Aspects] The complete environment of knowledge organization at the working place, in single centers, societies, countries and in the international area, as well as issues of education, economics, users, etc. [Dahlberg 1998, pp. 966–967]

The interdisciplinarity of KO becomes clear from what Jaenecke formulates:

Knowledge organization comprises activities carried out in single branches of science in the form of disciplines engaged in the production, representation, processing, and utilization of knowledge, including those rendering assistance to this end; in addition to these it comprises methodical themes transcending the boundaries between disciplines, as well as connections to epistemology and the cognitive sciences. [Jaenecke 1994, p. 11]

I want to add that practical KO is a cultural activity that intends to enable user groups to better accomplish their tasks when working with knowledge present (mainly) in document repositories. KO adds subject access points to items, targeted to the needs of those groups. It thus creates an improved conceptual access structure (overlay) that exhibits an informational value (asset) of its own. Of course, this is inherently coupled with ontological foundations and representational aspects. Nevertheless, the specific purpose for which a KOS is made implies its own requirements and constraints.

"Important" is not only what KO is but what the *purpose* of KO is. Summarizing some of Jaenecke's points, the aim of KO is to order knowledge, to make it accessible. Since resources for survival, including intellectual resources, are scarce, KO has the urgent task (of great social importance) to contribute to processing the store of knowledge in such a way that it becomes once more overseeable for humans with our physical limitations. This will allow people to inform themselves in order to stay competent and to dispose of the right knowledge for action.[20]

Kiel [1994], in his reply to Jaenecke, argues for an epistemologically open conception of KO that should support users instead of controlling them.

Some Elements of KO Theory: On Problems and Principles

The organization of knowledge is always dependent on purpose and context. Hence, there necessarily exist a variety of different KO forms and views. With the rise of Digital Libraries (DLs) and the increased needs for KO in business contexts, KO has become relevant and mainstream in ontology engineering and knowledge management (KM), albeit under different names. Although the actual wording is no longer fashionable, part of the conceptual framework of a KO work dating 20 and more years back[21] may still be highly relevant, if reread with TM glasses. It has become apparent how indispensable KO expertise is wherever information assets have to be organized by subject for target groups [Campbell 2000].

Key Ingredients of KO Theory and an Introductory Example

While there is not yet a "KO recipes for TM design" cookbook, reflecting KO principles as TM hands-on dos and don'ts, I can select key ingredients needed for such a dish, namely answers to questions like the following.

- What is a document about? How is a document relevant for whom?
- Under which circumstances can two documents be regarded as alike or, better, functionally equivalent? (The same holds for descriptors!)
- What are basic building blocks of conceptual structures? Which categories, concepts, and relations do we want to employ?

---

[20] Isn't that closely related to the purpose of Engelbart's Open Hypertext System (OHS; *http://www. bootstrap.org*), in accordance with Berners-Lee's Semantic Web initiative (*http://www.semanticweb.org*) and Jack Park's vision of amplifying human intellect by creating tools to solve problems (as exemplified by this book)?

[21] See, for example, Wersig & Wersig [1985], originally published in 1978, on principles of thesaurus construction and maintenance.

- Is there a methodology to arrive at a normalized deep structure and to isomorphically represent it, independent of the form in which it appeared? How far can formal KR be of help here?
- To which shared constructions do we ontologically commit ourselves? Semantics: How can we convey meaning and understand each other?
- How can we encourage authors and users to semantically mark up recognized conceptual structures? Can an adequate KOS registry architecture help us avoid wasting intellectual effort? We are interested in semantically interoperable structures (shared understanding), not in a multitude of knowledge islands.
- What intellectual markup is necessary to aid powerful Semantic Retrieval?
- Under which circumstances do multiple indexing views improve indexing quality? When are they worth the higher cost?

Let me present an introductory example of how aspects of such key ingredients of KO theory might be applied. Imagine the following socially shared deep conceptual structure, expressed at the surface as this nominal phrase: the oral inoculation of foxes against rabies by way of baits laid out by a hunter.

A fox is a wild forest animal, susceptible to canine madness if not vaccinated. A fox can be hunted by a hunter. A hunter is a human who hunts forest animals for pleasure or ecological reasons, using a rifle to shoot, or who takes care of those animals, for example, by laying out inoculation bait. Canine madness (or rabies, or hydrophobia) is an illness caused by . . . that causes . . . , with which foxes can be afflicted. The illness can be prevented with an antirabies inoculation. Inoculation is the prevention of certain diseases by immunization. A bait, an instrument to attract animals, can be employed as an instrument, for example, to apply oral inoculation, for example, to foxes.

Mentioning *fox, inoculation, rabies*, and so on, in a joint context, can activate this deep conceptual structure. Concepts (fox, rabies, and inoculation) are positioned in a polyhierarchical ontology (fox is-a forest animal, which is-an animal, which is animated, but also: fox is-an object being hunted, is-a provider of fur, and so on). A concept can have several names (for example, rabies, hydrophobia). Analyzing the common upper concepts of many concepts, we arrive at shared categories (process, animated agent). Between the concepts, many relations hold (hunter—hunted—hunting instrument—inoculation—active agent—passive agent—causing agent—disease). For practical purposes, such *n*-ary relations are often factorized into several binary relations. Imagine, further, that we have several documents that examine different aspects of this complex concept and that we have several users (a doctor, a bait manufacturer, a hunter, someone just bitten by a mad fox), with their respective information needs. Finally, imagine[22] a contest in which several indexers assign descriptors to those

---

[22] In the spirit of Cooper's Indexing Documents by Gedanken Experimentation [Cooper 1978].

documents, and juries, one for each target user group, award points to each indexer, depending on how well she or he has managed to make relevant documents more accessible for those target groups. I hold that the indexing results and the scores in such a contest partially depend on the operationalization a jury sets up, that is, the epistemological stance the jury takes. The search for KO principles is the search for criteria that allow a just judging in this contest.

Robert Fugmann kindly extended the above example.[23] He provided me with suggestions on how we might index documents using relational indicators (see below) as a conceptual syntactic device: We take for granted a hierarchically structured vocabulary (for example, bait, foxes) that also includes all relevant process concepts, for example, inoculation, luring, eating, and rabies formation (disease as process). The organizing principle is that every topic of importance to the targeted users has to be named, as well as every participation of this topic in a crucial process. Subject matter not relevant to users is not to be described. The function of so-called pseudodescriptors is to organize "real" descriptors, that is, to allow the retrieval of descriptors (and statements) by logical groups of the descriptors involved. We can define arbitrary pseudodescriptors. Fugmann provides examples of two pseudodescriptor types: `matter – matter attribute` (MA) and `matter – virus` (MV). Squared brackets delimit segments. Also, +*n* (where *n* is a number) appended to a process descriptor denotes the type of the family member (positive evidence), and -*n* the type of negative evidence. The following statements may hold in documents and queries.

> Foxes are subjected to inoculation: `[foxes; inoculation+3; MA]`

> Foxes are the agents of eating: `[foxes; eating+2; MA]`

> Baits are subjected to eating, that is, a substance is a luring agent, and it is subjected to eating: `[bait; eating+3; MA]`; alternatively: `[luring+2; eating+3; MA]`

If available, a lexicalized natural language expression like "baits" can be used. A systematic expression (`luring+2`) is particularly helpful if no lexicalization exists. Here, `luring+2` is less precise because it can mean any attractant, for example, a flower's odor.

> Foxes do not form rabies: `[foxes; rabies formation-1; MA]`

> Foxes are subjected to luring: `[foxes; luring+3; MA]`

Only if the luring process and the inoculation are *explicitly* described in the document to be indexed should luring and inoculation be additionally indexed.

---

[23] Personal communication, August 9, 2001. See also Fugmann [1999, p. 88f., paragraph 258].

A bait contains a form of rhabdovirus (for passive immunization): [bait; rhabdovirus; MV]

Exercise: How would you represent such statements in a TM?

Overview: Problems and Principles

A field of inquiry is often defined by its problems, how the problems are approached, and which principles have been found to explain observed phenomena and regularities (allowing solutions). To prepare us for the later discussion on how KO problems and principles recur with TMs, this section jointly treats pressing KO problems and a few principles in KO.

Via the KO bibliography [*KO* 1999] you can of course locate literature on (abstract) KO principles.[24] Unfortunately, most principles or rules in KO assume the possibility of objective KO, are of a technical nature, concern the easier task of essence expression, or are tied to specific KOSs.

KO is about aiding people in their knowledge work by organizing knowledge through (virtual or overlaid) conceptual access structures. Such structures allow us, in addition to providing easier access to documents as a core function in an Information Retrieval System (IRS), to gain overview and understanding (compare with Chapter 16).

Summarizing this section, we first get to know the object of knowledge work, that is, fundamentals about knowledge, *knowledge structures*, and their social construction within domains. Next we briefly encounter established processes and forms of knowledge structuring in KO and their function. Because knowledge results from interpretation, we position ourselves with regard to epistemology (what we can know and how this is limited) and hermeneutics (how we can interpret and understand manifestations of culture). The estimation of the epistemological potential of an information resource leads to a discussion of the dual character of *aboutness* and *relevance*, and then to *likeness* and the *collocation principle*. The next logical step is to ask for basic building blocks for knowledge structures. We encounter *categories, concepts,* and *relations*. Which manifestations of those are universal and which context-dependent? Which set should we agree upon, use, or even standardize? The introduction of relations opens the door to *semantic indexing* (indexing with a variety of semantic relations) and to *semantic retrieval* (fine-grained searching along semantic relations). The question arises of what constitutes sound KO? What are principles guiding sound ontology design? How can we prepare

---

[24]Examples of such basic principles are collocation and facet analysis into basic categories with citation order. See also, for example, Fugmann's Five-Axiom Theory of Indexing [Fugmann 1985] and Hjørland's Nine Principles of KO [Hjørland 1994].

today for the interoperability needed tomorrow? One answer lies in *a theory of categories* and in *facet analysis.* When is a conceptual access structure optimal? How can the quality of a KOS and associated metadata be evaluated? This is usage- and context-dependent. Allowing conflicting multiple conceptualizations introduces indexing views, or *view-based indexing.* This leads to the idea, adapted from user-oriented indexing, that the different viewpoints of user groups must be modeled in an ontology-based relevance model, and the indexing must consist of qualitative argumentations (relevance reasons) why a certain document is relevant from this special viewpoint. The next section on KO theory deals with KOSs, that is, with *ontologies,* thesauri, and the like. I argue that registries of KOSs as a whole but also of their entries are urgently needed,[25] and I sketch some basic requirements any future *registry architecture* would have to meet. The aim with such registries (and services) is to early on forestall the *arbitrary* proliferation of unrelated but maybe similar topics. I then deal with KR or more *formal semantics.* Finally, I resume the challenge of *semantic compatibility and interoperability of KOSs* and outline some approaches to transfer (map, bridge, merge) between different conceptualizations of like subjects, particularly in the light of the prevailing trend to decentralized provision of metainformation.

Exercise: Brainstorm (with pencil and paper) how such issues might be relevant to TMs and your work, and compare your ideas now with your view after a detailed reading of this section.

Knowledge, Knowledge Structures, and KOSs as Social Constructions

This section takes a look at what knowledge might be (how knowledge structures and their materialization in KOSs are dynamic because they result from social construction in an open interpretation process) and relates this to TMs.

Dahlberg [1974] defined *knowledge elements (concepts)*; later [1978b] she introduced the term *knowledge unit* for concept and redefined *knowledge element* to stand for *characteristic.*

Jaenecke, who has published on the KR approach taken by Leibniz [Jaenecke 2002] and who works on a theory of knowledge modules or building blocks,[26] holds that *knowledge is not a definable concept,* but that a general generative schema (signified by the neologism *karakteristik*) can be provided for the definition of single types of knowledge that adhere to such a schema [Jaenecke 2000a].

---

[25]This need is similar to the need for registries of PSIs.

[26]And whether knowledge can be represented according to this theory with TMs [Jaenecke 2001].

Thus knowledge is not a concept but a *category* that can be reduced to other categories, as defined in this *karakteristik* of knowledge (my translation):

> Knowledge is a product of the human spirit, mediated by language, that is distinguishable from other brainchildren by certain quality attributes, defined in a *delimitation criterion*. It always occurs in closed *knowledge building blocks* (which are available in a *linguistic representation*), and refers to *knowledge objects*. The *relation between knowledge and knowledge object* governs the reference between knowledge, mediated by language, and the reality. Via certain *rules for the combination of knowledge building blocks* it is possible to construct more complex units. [Jaenecke 2000a, p. 73, emphasis in the original]

We will reencounter these ideas on the organization of concepts in knowledge systems in the sections on KR and formal semantics. We have already seen above that knowledge is an active internal construction of a thinking subject. It can be externalized, and by sharing and adapting extends to social constructs within discourse communities. As Jack Park (in Chapter 17 of this book) argues for constructivist epistemology, citing the radical constructivists Maturana and Verela, I want to direct readers to Ernst von Glasersfeld's [1998] *radical-constructivist knowledge theory* and its critical discussion.

Capurro, philosopher and teacher in information science and KM, has written much about the *relation between hermeneutics and knowledge* [Capurro 2000a, 2000b, 1997, 1986/1989]. Summarizing one of his central points, knowledge is the result of an interpretation or understanding process with regard to circumstance by language (involving a semiotic process with interpreter, object, and sign). KM is the management of understanding and/or (scientific) explanation processes.

This leads me to conclude that knowledge structures as represented in TMs should be sources and results of shared understanding processes. Since understanding is open-ended, it is a requirement that we can also represent incomplete or partial knowledge.

Mai [1999] developed a *postmodern theory of KO*. He sees KOSs as "a common platform for communication between authors and users" and writes:

> A postmodern theory of knowledge organization . . . regards knowledge organizations as active constructions of a perceived conception of the particular discourse communities in the company, organization or knowledge fields for which the knowledge organization was intended. [Mai 1999, p. 547]

And later:

> To create an organization of knowledge in a particular company, organization or any other information center or library, one needs to start with the discourse in the organization or domain. [Mai 1999, p. 554]

Indeed, a KO is a shared conceptualization of knowledge, and it serves in effect the same function for humans as an ontology does for information agents. While a realistic epistemology (universal approaches) assumes that it is possible to describe in a KO the world as it is, that is, to find a neutral and objective representation of the universe of knowledge already there, postmodern KO is an active construction of a reality and a particular worldview. Each social praxis leads to its own KO.

Green counterbalances both positions:

> In moving from earlier assumptions of culturally neutral, universally applicable classification schemes to assumptions of culturally biased, non-universal schemes, we may have overreacted. [Green 2000b, p. 57]

And in the end:

> Here no extreme answer will be suitable. Therefore there is the need for further exploration to determine where the most realistic in-between position is. [Green 2000b, p. 58]

Mai emphasizes that we should work toward a better understanding of the conditions that create the dynamism of KO "so that we can build theories and knowledge organizations that are based on insight and not on some dream about an objective universe of knowledge that is out there waiting to be discovered and displayed" [Mai 2000b, p. 61].

Solomon [2000], in reviewing contextualization strategies[27] whose strengths lie in attempting to situate KO schemes in the work interactions of people and artifacts, summarizes the *dimensions of knowledge* as given by Blackler [1995], a paper heavily cited in KM. Solomon is convinced that Blackler's dimensions provide keys to what a KO scheme must be and do in order to facilitate human activity. The *dependence on context* means also that "there is no one best KO approach for any situation" [Solomon 2000, p. 260]. Blackler's abstract in part reads:

> Knowledge is analyzed as an active process that is mediated, situated, provisional, pragmatic and contested. The approach suggests that attention

---

[27]Inter alia domain analysis; compare with Hjørland & Albrechtsen [1995] and Lykke Nielsen [2000].

should be focused on the systems through which people achieve their knowledge and on the processes through which new knowledge may be generated. [Blackler 1995]

This is also related to activity-theory, as discussed by Hjørland [1997].[28]

Ontology-Bound Conceptual Access Structures and Corresponding Subject Metadata Assigned to Information Resources

At the core of KO is the aim to provide (for target groups) the best intellectual access structures by subject over (or above) information resources. Applied KO[29] is intended to optimize the intellectual organization layer (that is, the conceptual access and navigation structure) of knowledge repositories in order to better support user communities in working with knowledge to fulfill their tasks. Working with knowledge comprises among other things the retrieval, creation, and sharing of knowledge. It is well known that KO is at the very heart of retrieval: as Svenonius [2000, p. ix] writes, "But technology is not enough. The effectiveness of a system for accessing information is a direct function of the intelligence put into organizing it."[30]

KOSs consist of concepts interlinked with typed relations (in practice, only a fairly small set of typed relations). Such structures or models can take the form of full-fledged ontologies, apt for automatic reasoning, but the traditional KO forms of thesauri and classifications, which are less explicit and formal, still prevail.

Universal KOSs[31] subdivide all knowledge. As a consequence of trying to be a universally accepted compromise, single disciplines and fields typically regard universal KOSs as not always fully apt, up-to-date, or detailed enough for their purposes. Therefore, many special KOSs exist in addition to universal KOSs.[32] To serve the information needs of users, information resources (classically books and journal articles, but now also images, dynamic Internet documents, and so on) are summarized

---

[28] Already in 1994 Hjørland had stated his view of knowledge as a historically developed product in which principles of organization are tied to domain-specific criteria [Hjørland 1994].

[29] In part this also comprises applied KM.

[30] See also the keynote address for the Extreme Markup 2001 conference [Svenonius 2001].

[31] For example, universal classifications like UDC, DDC, LCC, Colon, Bliss, BBK/LBC, and RVK. (See the Selected Abbreviations section for full names.)

[32] At this point it should be noted that, for example, based on Dahlberg [1974], the history of the failure of some universal and special KOSs should be reviewed again in order to improve today's efforts. Lack of acceptance may often go back to the inflexibility of such KOSs to accommodate different viewpoints in the same instrument, now overcome by modern KOSs.

(abstracted, classified, indexed) [Endres-Niggemeyer 1998]. This results in subject metadata associated with ontology-bound conceptual access structures.

In order to arrive at the "best" conceptual access structure, one has to empirically analyze how information needs and knowledge structures are conceptualized in domains (*domain analysis*). This involves a certain hermeneutic stance.

The Role of Epistemology in Subject Analysis and Representation

We have learned that since knowledge results from interpretation, semiotic processes are always involved. This is true not only for knowledge structures and KOSs. An interpretation act also takes place when an indexer tries to ascertain which subjects a resource is about.[33] Those subjects are in both the document and its context (similarly, in text interpretation there is an immanent and an external viewpoint).[34] The context is determined by the role the subject plays in discourse, that is, by its purpose and usage. Thus an indexer has to estimate the potential usefulness from the viewpoint(s) of users' needs. To avoid extremes, in determining relevance a balance must be achieved between what authors express and what users see in documents. In nontechnical domains[35] a mere extraction of words (full-text extractive indexing) does not help that much to collocate like subjects. The assignment of reconstructed contexts to resources in the form of subject metadata is needed.[36] Mai [2000c] heavily bases his work on the subject indexing process on Peircean semiotics.

Interpretation necessarily introduces variance and some loss of control,[37] but it also has the potential to better collate like subjects. Unfortunately, even the value of human indexing is quite limited since hermeneutics is a never-ending open process. (For background information, please compare with the concept of unlimited semiosis in semiotics.[38]) In my view, the main reasons for intra- and inter-indexer inconsisten-

---

[33] I touched on the duality of aboutness and relevance earlier and will revisit them below.

[34] Compare this with Heinz von Foerster's constructivistic saying: "The hearer and not the speaker determines the meaning of an utterance" (in German: "Der Hörer, nicht der Sprecher bestimmt die Bedeutung einer Aussage") [von Foerster and Pörksen 2001, p. 100].

[35] That is, mainly in the humanities, arts, social sciences, and so on.

[36] Epistemological limitations of this process are treated in, for example, Hjørland [1997] and Mai [2000c]. There you will encounter discussions on subjectivity versus objectivity, relativism, pragmatism versus empiricism, and so on.

[37] This is the reason why automated indexing is sometimes more consistent.

[38] A hypothetically infinite process by which one sign or set of signs can take the place of another sign or set of signs which in turn can be replaced by yet another sign or set of signs, and so on. Without such polysemy, artists and poets would soon run out of figurative images like tropes. The inexhaustible production of new meanings that results is a key concept in the semiotics of Umberto Eco.

cies are insufficient instruction and training and the mentioned epistemological openness, even on the conceptual level (not only on the terminological level).

Aboutness and Relevance, Collocation and Functional Equivalence

The basic functions of IRSs and finding aids are

1. To present only those documents that are relevant to the subject sought
2. To collocate like subjects (or concepts), that is, to cluster or organize subjects such that documents on similar subjects can be found closer together and documents on different subjects have larger distances between them—the cluster hypothesis in information retrieval (IR)

Both concepts (relevance and similarity) are strongly related. Mai [2000a, p. 26] wrote, "If it is impossible to give a precise description of a document's subject matter, it makes little sense to claim that documents are arranged according to likeness in subject matter."

Much has been written in information science (IS) about the concept of aboutness (topicality and so on) and how to determine and measure it. Aboutness and relevance[39] can be said to be two sides of the same coin.[40] Hjørland [2000] suggests the concepts of *nonrelevance* and *epistemological relevance*. Hjørland, inspired by the impressive review of relevance research by Mizzaro [1998], wrote a letter to the editor of *JASIS*. According to Hjørland, nonrelevance is much easier to define than relevance. He relates (non)relevance to motivations to cite and postulates, "A theory of relevance should concentrate on what can be regarded as healthy, scientific criteria, and thus contain some norms corresponding to good scientific practice" [Hjørland 2000, p. 209]. In addition, Hjørland prefers to regard relevance as an epistemological rather than a psychological concept, "to investigate underlying theoretical assumptions and epistemologies both in the queries and in the documents in the databases" because "relevance is a function of theoretical assumptions" [Hjørland 2000, p. 210].

To understand which subjects a document is about means also to understand its epistemological function within a discourse community, that is, qualitative reasons for its relevance in discourse. To collocate like subjects, one must first understand *likeness*. For an update of his view, see [Hjørland 2001].

---

[39] Not to be confused with pertinence.

[40] See, for example, Greisdorf [2000] and Bruza and Huibers [1996]. For a thorough review of relevance, see Mizzaro [1997, 1998].

Hjørland writes about his second of nine principles in KO:

> No advanced indexing, subject analysis, categorization or classification can therefore be based on common properties or similarities, but should be interpreted in the light of the theoretical context! "Similarity" is therefore an unfruitful concept. What should be grouped together are documents with identical or related functions for the purpose of the subject analysis. The concept of "similarity" therefore should be replaced by the concept of "functional equivalence" (or "isomorphism"). [Hjørland 1994, p. 93]

Mai [2000a] argues that likeness has not been adequately defined in classification theory and suggests an alternative understanding, based on domain analysis and pragmatism. Functional equivalence also includes defining flexible criteria for equivalence classes of documents, for example, works by the same author, on the same story, from the same school of thought, and so on.

Conceptology, Terminology, Concepts, and Relations

This section briefly examines the nature of categories, concepts (including facets of basic categories), and relations over concepts. This is the realm of conceptology and terminology in KO.[41] I strongly advise you to consult the references since the treatment here is very short and simplified.

Categories. The study of categories goes back to Aristotle. Dahlberg [1978a, 1978b, 1995] described his categories and made them fertile for KO. Recently, Barité [2000b] has drawn attention to the neglected theoretical study of categories, which is essential for understanding how sound KOSs can be built. Although categories are basically simple, the concept of categories is difficult to understand and not consistently used in the literature.

Categories are abstractions used to understand the regularities of objects for representing notions. An example of a category is *properties*. Another example is S. R. Ranganathan's [1965] "PMEST" (his postulated fundamental categories: Personality (Entity or Thing), Matter, Energy, Space, and Time).

In KO, categories are interesting as "levels or dimensions of analysis applied to the interior structuring of human knowledge and their most representative abstractions: concepts" [Barité 2000b, p. 5].

---

[41] Compare with Pathak [2000].

Barité [2000b, p. 7–9] finds seven characters of categories, for example, mutual exclusiveness, and that we have reached agreement only on a limited set of them. The idea of basic categories is strongly linked to facet analysis (see below).

Concepts. From terminology[42] we know the differences between *concept*, *term*, and *designation*. Those concepts have been standardized by ISO/TC 37.[43] Fortunately, several selections of definitions are readily accessible,[44] so I omit the mere repetition of definitions here. For the purpose of this chapter let's roughly understand *concept* as a language-independent unit of knowledge[45] that is defined by the totality of necessary (essential) predications that can be made about an object of thought, that is, about its properties. The concepts are said to be identical if they share the same properties (characteristics).

Facet Analysis or Semantic Factoring and the Value of an Indexing Language Grammar. Of direct importance for the design of sound KOSs is the application of semantic factoring of concepts into basic categories (facet theory and classification) [Ranganathan 1962; Vickery 1965; Priss and Jacob 1999]. Avoid enumerative systems wherever possible! Instead, construct arbitrarily complex items out of categories that are used as elementary building blocks. Thus complex concepts can be factorized into basic concepts, and more detailed concepts can be synthesized out of basic concepts. (Hence this is also called the *analytico-synthetic method*.) Unfortunately, in practice it is not always very clear how to analyze a concept into facets. An ontology is said to be complete if all relevant complex entities in a domain can be sufficiently expressed (described) with a combination of basic categories. Often a combination of facets and subfacets must have only one normalized order (to have a fixed classification, for example, for classified bibliographies or book shelving). This is the function of citation order.[46]

---

[42] For a core bibliography, see Nuopponen [2001].

[43] See *http://korterm.or.kr/isotc37/isomain.htm* for the home page of ISO TC 37. An excerpt of the standard ISO 1087:1990 Terminology—Vocabulary can be found at *http://www.medinf.mu-luebeck.de/~ingenerf/ pg_term/iso1087.htm*. The standard is under revision and will become DIS 1087-1 Terminology Work—Vocabulary—Part 1: Theory and Application; see *http://linux.infoterm.org/iso/standards.htm*.

[44] Compare the following Web sites for glossary information on the terminology of terminology, based on ISO/DIS 1087 and ISO/DIS 5127: *http://gift.irmkant.rm.cnr.it/def/tc37.htm*, *http://www.c-l.com/emu/te/ glos-iso/b_iso_en.htm*, *http://www.dit-online.com/termi/main.htm*, and *http://www.schmalenbach.com/termi/begrif/ main.htm*.

[45] Independent of a specific language but not independent of linguistic expression in language. Relevant in this context is the work by Fred W. Riggs on Onomantics [Riggs 1996–1997] and in particular his current interest in TMs as one technology to leverage Electronic Nomenclators for analyzing concepts (personal communication, October 2001).

[46] Compare with the canon of principles like PMEST or "wall-picture" (for example, Ranganathan [1989]).

Fugmann [1999, Section 5.3] has repeatedly pointed out the value of an indexing language grammar.[47] In his Figure 5 he shows how an indexing language with a strong grammar makes precombined descriptors[48] superfluous: instead of precombined terms (or enumerative classifications), arcs connect simple concepts (which could be organized in facets) to form the more complex ones. For indexing languages, Fugmann advocates syntactic tools such as relational indicators, related to frames,[49] and topological approaches, related to semantic and graphical retrieval.[50]

Relations and Framelike Gestalt Knowledge Structures. Now that we have concepts, we want to interconnect them with relations. For example, for a chemical process we want to connect the reagents, any catalysts, the auxiliary conditions, and the result; for a medical process we want to link diagnosis with treatment. The importance of such Gestalt structures within knowledge-based searching is well known.[51]

There is a long debate in KO but no consensus about which types of relations between concepts are most useful. Clearly, the common thesaurus relations[52] are not sufficient but constitute a domain-independent minimum.

In Chapter 16, Kathleen M. Fisher discusses the nature of relations and their elusiveness. She also summarizes 30 years of research in KO when she states on relations that "there is no universal, parsimonious set of relations for describing all knowledge, although people looked for such a set for many years."

Despite the diversity of relations and our lack of consensus on them, relations are essential in understanding: they put concepts into contexts. For a thorough treatment of relations in KO, see Perreault [1994]. Rahmstorf, based on his 1983 dissertation and his experiences since then, has suggested 41 binary relations.[53] Examples of his relations are causal, conditional, concessive, thematic, and so on. The results of longstanding work by Schmitz-Esser [1999, 2000a, 2000b, 2000c] on thesaurus relations were at one time documented in TM PSI registry format.[54]

---

[47] Compare with Section 3.2 in Supper [1978].

[48] See Fugmann's Figure 5, in particular the precombined descriptors on the right-hand side.

[49] See Fugmann's Sections 5.3.3 and 5.3.4. See also the earlier example.

[50] See Fugmann's Section 5.3.6.

[51] See Shute and Smith [1993]. The most relevant passage is on p. 32, where the authors describe the conceptual framework underlying their third hypothesis, also citing Humphrey's MedIndEx.

[52] Broader term (BT), narrower term (NT), and the catch-all related term (RT).

[53] The list is part of the Concepto software documentation (distributed by Antje Rahmstorf Sprachsysteme, Heidelberg).

[54] Previously found at *http://psi.seruba.com/core-associations.html*. Unfortunately, the company Seruba is no longer active. The Web site was active until approximately July 2001.

Some of those relations seem to resemble relations developed in Rhetorical Structure Theory (RST)[55] [Nicholas 1994; Hovy 1990]. As in RST, in KO the question of which criteria to apply to avoid arbitrary proliferation of relations remains open. If in doubt, we should be rather reluctant and parsimonious when introducing new relations, in order to ease later merging of relation types. In any case, relations, like concepts, should be organized in polyhierarchies.

Relational and Frame-Based Indexing and Semantic Retrieval. BIOSIS uses the term *relational indexing* to denote that terms can be located in context and that relationships between terms are preserved, shown, and used for searching in order to ensure more accurate search results.[56] I use it in a similar way here to indicate the explicit usage of typed relations in the indexing language to specify the roles the descriptors play in relations. No postcoordination (not even with proximity operators) can help later in always discerning hits when the concepts play different roles in one or several semantic relations.

Relational indexing[57] therefore is a way to keep contexts apart and to allow more precise retrieval in order to help us when many hits are involved. The simplest form to separate contexts is to employ links or to segment (with shared running index numbers behind groups of descriptors that belong together). This at least prevents the ambiguity that results from a mixture between completely unrelated descriptors. It is more sophisticated to explicitly name the roles played by the participants of an association. When talking about relational indicators (with reference to Fillmore's deep case), Fugmann [1999] cites the example of the roles of agents in corrosion: causes of corrosion, active and passive substances sustaining corrosion, substances accelerating and retarding corrosion, results of corrosion, and so on. Similarly, van der Vet and Mars [1999] have suggested a method that is capable of discerning between documents in which, for example, aspirin is mentioned as a cure versus as a cause for headache.

Relations can also be organized themselves, for example, by hierarchical relations. For example, the "cures" relation may be a form of an abstract "causation" relation. Organizing relations helps tremendously to improve the quality of KOSs and to protect against arbitrary proliferation of relations.

If we organize many contextual relations around a concept, we effectively arrive at a frame structure. Green has worked on relational indexing with such structures. Since her 1989 dissertation, she has published often on this topic [Green 1996b, 1997, 2000a].

---

[55] See the RST home page, maintained by William C. Mann, at *http://www.sil.org/linguistics/rst/*.

[56] See *http://www.biosis.org/products_services/relational_indexing.html*.

[57] Going back to Farradane's work [for example, 1967, 1977, 1980].

The idea of indexing with relators is quite old, but has for various reasons not (yet) really taken off.[58] Only when relations come into play (that is, implicit contextual information went into the markup) will the full power of semantic retrieval be at our disposal. My understanding of semantic retrieval is closely related to that of Rahmstorf [1994a, 1994b, 2001] except that I mean fine-grained retrieval along semantic relations.[59] It is clear that such semantic retrieval is needed only in special application domains, but it seems to me that there people are willing to pay higher indexing costs.

Multiple and Adaptable Indexing Views and Their Potential Effect on Indexing Quality

We are led to believe that the need for epistemological openness; a certain dependence on domains, cultures, and contexts (in contrast to purely objective universality); and the multiplicity of existing and possible worldviews requires any KO approach to provide ways to express and handle multiple, typically conflicting conceptualizations. This is the requirement that suggests introducing indexing views (view-based indexing or perspectives), into KO. If we take seriously the idea that different discourse communities conceptualize differently, the goal is no longer to find a universal classification as a compromise but to maximize the utility for both by separating both contexts and maximizing locally to the needs of each community. We can have two different views about the aboutness of a document, and we thus can conceptually adapt the subject representation of a document to the user communities. The better (more ecologically valid) we are able to model domain conceptualizations, the better our qualitative relevance reasons can be, and the better our principles to check the quality of KOSs and indexing. In this sense, multiple and adaptable indexing views may have a positive effect on indexing and hence on retrieval quality [Sigel 2000c].

KOSs: Ontologies, Thesauri, Classifications

Ontologies in KO and Ontological Engineering. Ontologies are a major issue in KO since they are the formalization of the conceptualization of knowledge structures. This is not the place for a metadiscussion on ontologies in general. Chapter 7 by Leo Obrst and Howard Liu treats ontologies in depth from the viewpoint of ontological engineering. My discussion here briefly focuses on the important points for KO.

Modern KO is fairly compatible with ontological engineering. A difference might be that the interest of KO in ontologies is in the possibility of enabling people to work

---

[58] Because, for example, it is very costly indeed and thus only applicable in certain niches, it was not supported by older retrieval systems, and it was not well presented to users.

[59] As popularly described, for example, in Schmidt and Müller [2000], Rath [1999], and, to a lesser extent, Gerick [2000].

with knowledge rather than the aspect of formal representation for knowledge-based systems. But for epistemological reasons, KR has to investigate which concepts and relations are appropriate for a given task.

While elsewhere finer distinctions may be necessary,[60] for the purpose of this chapter I take a somewhat simplified perspective. Here I am interested in what *unifies* classifications, thesauri, ontologies, taxonomies, category systems, terminological knowledge bases, intellectual access structures, and the like—not what separates them. Anyhow, differences are often blurred.[61] There is currently no terminological consistency between different areas working on such concepts. Therefore I subsume them for the moment under KOSs and will sometimes even refer to them under the umbrella of ontology.

Ontology, understood in philosophy as the area of knowledge about the most universal structures of being, about the condition of being and existence, goes back to Aristotle. There are already several good resources in the DMOZ open directory project.[62] Philosophical ontology may be related to relevance and artificial intelligence (AI) ontologies thus: Schmidt, in connecting AI and metaphysics, states, "A far better way to describe metaphysics is to call it the study of aboutness" [Schmidt 2001]. In lay terms, an ontology lists the kinds of things that the users of the ontology chose to regard as relevant, about which they want to discourse.[63] Ontology is also a fashionable term in KM and business-related brokering of products of services (product ontology).

Without diving into many details, I just claim that the understanding of ontology in KO is not too far away from that in mainstream AI/KR. A concrete example is Endres-Niggemeyer [2000], who is currently working on modeling the domain of bone marrow transplantation as an ontology in order to improve summarization. I follow Stuckenschmidt and colleagues [1999] who, in describing their research program (development concepts for reusing uncertain knowledge models), devote attention also to ontologies and to a process model for their structured development (ontology engineering).

---

[60] For example, Amann and Fundulaki [1999] on orthogonality of ontologies versus thesauri, or Amann et al. [2000] on the integration of ontologies and thesauri, applied to RDF schema creation and metadata querying.

[61] For example, with a classified thesaurus (thesaurus entries grouped in classes), a classification with a systematic entry vocabulary; in short, a *classaurus* or *thesaurofacet* [Aitchison 1969].

[62] See under Society: Philosophy: Metaphysics: Ontology (at *http://www.dmoz.org/Society/Philosophy/ Metaphysics/Ontology/*), cross-referenced to Computers: Artificial Intelligence: Knowledge Representation (at *http://www.dmoz.org/Computers/Artificial_Intelligence/Knowledge_Representation/*), for example, the Corazzon [2000–2002] ontology.

[63] See also the short discussion in the Aboutness and Relevance, Collocation and Functional Equivalence section in this chapter (above), as well as the slides of the tutorial by Guarino and Velty [2000] on conceptual modeling and ontological analysis.

Though there are differences in the wording and not all definitions are very concrete or substantial, I believe on a general level that the following statement is compatible with the KO view on ontologies: "An ontology consists of a set of concepts, axioms, and relationships that describe a domain of interest."[64]

Sowa [2000a, p. 492] gives a definition in his glossary, Mädche and Staab [1999] formulate one in their material on ontology modeling and acquisition for text mining, and Viezzer [2000] summarizes papers from the European Conference on Artificial Intelligence 2000 ontology workshops. A readable definition is also provided by Denham Grey [2001]. Two widely recognized KO textbook authors and experts in classification and thesauri have published their views on ontologies [Soergel 1999; Vickery 1997].

Hodge [2000b], in her KOSs taxonomy, lists ontologies with thesauri and semantic networks under "relationship groups." KO expert Schmitz-Esser [1999, 2000a, 2000b, 2000c] worked out a concrete proposal for the construction of new, highly interconnected semantic-linguistic structures and now applies it in practice.[65]

To conclude this section, I provide here a rough working explanation of how I currently understand ontology. A subjective observer recognizes, interprets, and evaluates subjects or topics of potential relevance for a given information need. The analysis of domains results in a certain conceptualization of the things in the world about which certain discourse communities converse. As far as necessary for the task, implicit assumptions of the conceptualization are explicitly expressed (modeled or specified). Thus an ontology is a specification of such entities that are subjectively relevant for user groups, and the conceptualization reflects the viewpoints of the groups. Since the relevance differs for different user groups, ontologies must be flexible and allow views.

The Need and Basic Requirements for Registries of KOSs and Their Entries. Resources in DLs (for example, Web pages) are now commonly described by subject metadata. Current best practice in KO has adopted Dublin Core (DC) metadata,[66] wrapped in RDF.[67] Of primary interest is the field DC.subject, because this holds the entries from KOSs (classes, descriptors, terms) that characterize the content of such

---

[64]From the announcement of the SUO workshop at IJCAI 2001, August 4–6, 2001; see *http://reliant.teknowledge.com/IJCAI01/.* However, Robert Barta, in a review of the draft of this chapter, pointed out that an axiom-based ontology is not the same as an ontology as simple type system.

[65]See also the literature cited in Schmitz-Esser [2000a].

[66]See the home page of the Dublin Core Metadata Initiative at *http://dublincore.org/.*

[67]For example, Hirsch [2000] describes RDF/XML for use in specialized information systems; see also the Current Cites Bibliography: Metadades, XML, RDF, at *http://www.bib.ub.es/ee/metabibl.htm.*

Internet resources. A substantial share of such subject metadata consists of uncontrolled free terms.

One quality of the Internet is that in general no control is possible. For subject metadata this has the consequence that no one can be expected (let alone be forced) to use a certain controlled vocabulary according to given rules. Everything depends on voluntary cooperation. A different experience with the Internet is this: if a useful service is offered, many people will use it. An author wanting to self-describe his or her own pages is much more willing to use controlled vocabulary (which may stem from several KOSs) if there is a service that supports the author in:

- Finding freely available[68] and generally accepted KOSs
- Selecting the appropriate ones for the purpose at hand
- Selecting appropriate categories and entries from one or more such KOSs

This is the basis for the idea of a registry and service of freely usable KOSs on the Internet to describe electronic resources.

Back in 1998 I proposed that an organization in KO (for example, ISKO) maintain a searchable registry of machine-readable, publicly available KOSs whose metadata can be used on the Web without restrictions. My rationale was that more authors voluntarily using metadata with controlled vocabularies will increase acceptance of metadata and make semantic interoperability easier. I had then collected a first list by hand [Sigel 1998b]; nowadays better efforts exist. Most link lists are still maintained only by hand and on an irregular basis. In addition, they lack the necessary architecture to provide a brokering infrastructure for categories and relations.

Hodge [2000a] very briefly reported on NKOS efforts to describe KOSs with a DTD. Although attributes for such a registry have been collected,[69] this would be only metadata for KOSs, not for their contents! Several workshops have been held,[70] and there exists an ongoing project funded by the European Union.[71]

When we envisage a better architecture for such registries, we have to take into account that, as Michel Biezunski writes in Chapter 2, "it is likely that competing

---

[68] If good-quality KOSs are freely available, the rate of acceptance is much higher, of course.

[69] See the NKOS home page, *http://nkos.slis.kent.edu/*.

[70] For example, the breakout session at the 8th DC Metadata Initiative Workshop, October 2000 in Ottawa, Canada, on DC-Registry, chaired by Rachel Heery. See the home page of the DCMI Registry Working Group at *http://dublincore.org/groups/registry/*.

[71] SCHEMAS—Forum for Metadata Implementers. See the home page of this project at *http://www.schemas-forum.org/*.

ontologies will be created." In a project on mapping and brokering product and phone directory categories with information agents [Sigel 1998a], I also had the experience that we must expect (and deal with) a multitude of incompatible category systems because companies see their competitive advantage in creating such incompatibilities and idiosyncrasies. Hence the problem of arbitrary proliferation of uncontrolled KOSs and such categories used in subject metadata, against which a registry might constitute a (weak) countermeasure, recurs on a higher level: since anyone can open an independent registry, we must expect a proliferation of competing registries, raising the need for a registry of registries (a metaregistry), and so on.

Further requirements on such registries are notoriety/visibility, trustworthiness, persistence, and so on. The first means that providers of registries should be established and well-known entities in their field, and their registries should be widely known and respected. The second is necessary so that users searching for appropriate categories and relations can rely on the services. Both together allow a quality assurance and filtering concept based on a "seal of approval" (for example, people would trust a registry created by an important scientific society in the sought domain). Finally, persistence speaks to the fact that users would like to find the categories still existing three years after first using them.

KO and KR: Formal Semantics in KOSs

The essence of the subject as recognized or reconstructed by an interpreter in document and subject analysis has to be expressed somehow in a written symbolic form. In indexing, this is the function of a sophisticated indexing language (with syntax, semantics, and pragmatics). I recorded [Sigel 2000a] as an interim result the interrelation between indexing and KR: sophisticated indexing inevitably leads to KR. However, full KR might not be indicated for simpler retrieval tasks. By indexing, world knowledge only implied in a certain context is made explicit and represented. The basic relation between KO and KR is that KO (which is very interdisciplinary in nature but draws mainly from LIS, the humanities, and the social sciences) elaborates knowledge structures, and KR (part of computer science and mathematics, also of semiotics and linguistics) uses formal methods to code such knowledge structures (concepts, relations, and so on). KO thus sets KR requirements and applies KR methods. KR methods have to be adapted for KO purposes.

Conventional KOSs and indexing do not employ full semantic markup[72] to convey meaning but instead rely more on human interpretation. But it is to be expected that modern summarization products will increasingly do the former. In Chapter 3 Steven R. Newcomb makes the point that we need more formal languages and more

---

[72] Compare with the Knowledge Markup Language tutorial by Boley et al. [2000].

explicit markup such that computers can assist humans in dealing with knowledge structures. Ontologies are more formal (that is, explicit) than thesauri and the like, and KR languages are more formal than indexing languages. But the underlying intentions are the same: to carry semantics, to allow the reconstruction of meaning, and to draw inferences.

KO and KR. There are some typical overlap areas between the closely coupled fields of KO and KR. It is apparent in many KO publications how both fields are related.

- In an excellent paper, Kent [2000, p. 111] states, "Knowledge representation applies logic and ontology to knowledge organization."
- Dahlberg [1993, p. 211] points out that one aim of KO is "to show that the theoretical foundations developed in classification and thesaurus research during the past decades can well be used in all types of knowledge organization and for all kinds of general and special systems of knowledge organization and representation."

For KO, concept systems can be constructed by taking into account the characteristics of knowledge units (concepts). Likewise, the scope of the journal *KO* comprises concept theory, classification, indexing, and KR.

- The employment of AI methods in IRSs (and hence for reasoning in the Semantic Web) calls for more explicit KOSs. Thus thesauri and classifications are extended for computer reasoning purposes and become AI ontologies [Vickery 1997; Soergel 1999].[73]
- Ontology engineering draws from methods of designing and maintaining sound KOSs or vice versa. Ontology engineering methods help make good thesauri [Endres-Niggemeyer 2000].
- Frame-based indexing (which is, however, rarely applied in practice) is very close to KR [Green 1996b, 1997, 2000a].
- Once the subjects of a document have been determined in subject analysis through interpretation, they must be expressed in an appropriate form. Indiana University School of LIS course L505, called "Organization and Representation of Knowledge and Information,"[74] is an example of how representation naturally follows organization.

---

[73] See also Chapter 10, Artificial Intelligence and Classification, in Iyer [1995, pp. 163–176]. It briefly covers semantic networks, conceptual dependency and scripts, frames, and applications of knowledge-based indexing in LIS like Vickery's PLEXUS, the BIOSIS indexing system, and Susanne M. Humphrey's MedIndEx.

[74] See the Web page for this Indiana University School of Library and Information Science course at *http://www.slis.indiana.edu/jbradley/L505S98.html* (accessed in October 2001).

- Delgado [2000] is an example for KR on the Web within the context of ontologies for information agents.[75]
- Panyr [1988] wrote on thesauri and knowledge-based systems.

In sum, KO provides the intellectual tools, and KR adds the formalisms to express the results of conceptual analysis in a formal language as well as a calculus to reason with the results.

Formal Semantics in KO. For the purpose of sharing knowledge with others (and not forgetting it), we represent it outside our heads. Language itself is a structured KR form, although only formal languages allow formal reasoning, that is, without reference to interpretation of context. Jaenecke [1996, 2002], in discussing the Leibniz program, stated seven elementary principles for representing knowledge. Within representation principle 6 he defines formalization as "the process of representing knowledge in a formal language in such a way that syntax and semantics are identical" [Jaenecke 1996, p. 91].

Relevant here are his Section 3 on formal languages and Section 4 on representing and using knowledge in a formal language. Such formalization might ultimately be apt to implement a network of knowledge modules or building blocks [Jaenecke 2000b, 2001a]. Recently, a Human Markup Language was proposed in order to reduce human misunderstanding [Best 2001]. This seems to resemble the suggestion by Rost [1996] of a Discourse Markup Language (DML).

KOSs lack formal or axiomatic definition. Thesauri and classification schedules can be consulted, now also online, but their definitions are purely textual. The move from documentary thesauri and classifications to AI ontologies (to domain or indexing models) requires making more assumptions formally explicit, such that theorem provers in computers can reason upon them. Rahmstorf [2001] proposes a restricted language, Concept Language Formalism (CLF), to define concept spaces. Amann and colleagues [2000] already unite semantically rich but syntactically poor thesauri with ontologies (with complementing attributes). What we'd like to have with registries for KOSs entries is a way to attach one or more formal expressions from one or more formalisms that can be interpreted by machines, in addition to the textual definition found under the persistent URI for the entry.

A readable review on practical KR for the Web by van Harmelen and Fensel [1999] helps us to understand what formal semantics in practice means and which AI methods are promising on the route to the semantic Web. A semantic language consists of

---

[75]See particularly his Sections 2.5 and 2.6, where he cites work by various authors on, for example, thesaurus construction, thesaurus merging, SHOE, and RDF.

constructs such as variables, predicates, quantors, logical connectors, add so on. For the Web, there is not only the common KR tradeoff between expressiveness and tractability, that is, soundness and completeness versus computational complexity, but also the issue of marketing and common acceptance.

There exists a broad range of proposals for semantic markup in ontology engineering and KR, which are presumably applicable in KO, but it is sometimes difficult to see the wood for the trees. Below I point out some examples I regard as important.

We might start with early KL-ONE (Knowledge Language One) semantic networks (and successors) and subsumption systems [Brachmann and Schmolze 1985] (from which description or terminological logics sprang off). KL-ONE distinguished between the so-called T-Box (Terminological) and the A-Box (Assertional) [Katholische Universität Eichstätt 1998]. A KL-ONE descendant is a symbolic representation of knowledge for user modeling in BGP-MS (Belief, Goal, and Plan Maintenance System) [Kobsa and Pohl 1995]. The language TerminologyFramework by Rostek and Fischer, which models terminology systems, has been used to check WordNet for consistencies [Fischer 1998]. Dimitrov [2000] reviewed XML specifications for ontology exchange, and McEntire and colleagues [1999] reviewed several ontology exchange languages, including Conceptual Knowledge Markup Language (CKML). Kent [2000], in part also a KO researcher who proposed Ontology Markup Language (OML) and its extension CKML, demonstrated that ontology sharing is formalizable within K. Jon Barwise's knowledge model of information flow [Barwise and Seligman 1997]. Sowa formalized Peircean dependency graphs in Conceptual Graphs (CG). His recent book on KR [Sowa 2000a] is very readable. There was a whole international conference on CG and conceptual structures in general [Ganter and Mineau 2000; Stumme 2000] during which KR formalisms for IR were reviewed [Martin 2000] and at which Sowa presented a paper on ontology, metadata, and semiotics [Sowa 2000b]. There exists DAML+OIL, the most important proposal for a formal Semantic Web markup language.[76] Finally, RDF Schema (RDFS) [Connolly 2001][77] and XML Schema[78] are related to all this—but in ways yet to be determined.

---

[76] See *http://www.daml.org/2001/03/daml+oil-index.html*. See also the home page of OIL at *http://www.onto-knowledge.org/oil/* and a page on coordination points between RDF(S) and DAML+OIL at *http://lists.w3.org/Archives/Public/w3c-rdfcore-wg/2001Jul/att-0168/01-RDFS-DAML_OIL-coordination.html*. See also *http://www.daml.org/2000/10/daml-ont.html* about the initial release of the DAML ontology language specification and related discussion on W3C's mailing list on RDF logic at *http://lists.w3.org/Archives/Public/www-rdf-logic/*.

[77] RDFS is still only a *candidate* recommendation.

[78] See the approved 2001 W3C Recommendation at *http://www.w3.org/XML/Schema*. See also Martin Brian's 2001 proposed syntax using W3C XML Schema for ISO 13250 topic maps at *http://www.diffuse.org/TopicMaps/schema.html*.

In sum, it is possible to leverage KO with KR, ontology engineering, and semantic markup to a new quality for human intellectual progress. While this is a direction of increasing importance, it must be stressed that to this end epistemological questions in KO (typically neglected in mathematically oriented KR) are equally significant. Therefore, this effort needs experts from both fields.

Semantic Interoperability in KO and Some Bridging Approaches

Semantic heterogeneity (a bit more complicated than the homonymy and polysemy problem alone) has many causes but manifests itself ostentatiously in DLs. It is a violation of the collocation principle to have different classes and descriptors in different KOSs denoting the same meaning. This leads to scattering of the literature and impedes predictability for the searcher. But—particularly in the Web context—it is no longer possible to enforce centrally controlled vocabulary. Krause [1996] observed this prevailing trend and proposed a layered model of decentralized (meta-) information provision. Instead of normative authority we will have to live and cope with different layers of indexing quality and depth (among other attributes of heterogeneity). In addition to heterogeneity due to a multitude of independent actors, different domains and contexts require admission of different conceptualizations, which find their ways into KOSs and subject metadata.

Someone interested in a specialized topic or area who cross-searches many collections in order to increase recall will have to deal with categories originating from different schemata that may not even be interconnected. Therefore, we need transfer strategies that lessen such semantic gaps by building virtual bridges between them.

So, what basic approaches exist to aid semantic comparability and compatibility between entries in KOSs and associated metadata? First of all, arbitrary proliferation of the introduction of new terms should be avoided with an appropriate registry architecture. Most other approaches are empirical in nature (using training data/big corpora), for example, in machine learning, neural networks, corpus linguistics, and so on. Several projects work on strategies to transfer, map, and bridge between similar concepts and to merge them. Often, this results in pragmatic repair because one does not or cannot fix inadequate KO structures in principle. Although this is often neglected: in order to transparently switch and intermediate between diverging conceptualizations, it is necessary to work on the concept, not on the term level.

Nikolai and colleagues [1998] worked on Thesaurus Federations to flexibly integrate heterogeneous thesauri in the domain of environment data. Hunter [2001] proposed providing flexible semantic mappings via semantic knowledge bases (ontologies, thesauri). A metadata project directed by Buckland intended to provide search support for unfamiliar metadata.[79] Noy and Musen [1999a, 1999b] reported on SMART, an algorithm and tools to merge and align AI ontologies.

Krause [2000] names some basic strategies to treat semantic heterogeneity: cross-concordances, qualitative-deductive and statistical methods, and neural networks. As the literature had not substantially dealt with the question of which network model is most promising and whether neural networks will yield added informational value in the context of integrated specialized information systems at all, Mandl [2001] worked in his dissertation on improving a neural network approach to implement transfer modules between heterogeneous subject metadata. Krause draws consequences from Mandl's work for integrated information systems in the social sciences.[80]

After this lengthy encounter with problems and principles in KO, it has become high time for some practical KO examples!

KO in Practice

You are probably acquainted with abstracts, descriptors, and classes from metainformation on holdings in libraries. And you certainly have already practiced classification and KO many times, probably without noticing, since it is a basic activity of human intellect. We can classify mental concepts, ideas, or thoughts (for example, for a presentation, for organization of an article, or for better understanding); document-like objects; and physical entities (stamps, bottles of rare wine, and so on). Any time you add keywords to your e-mails with your favorite editor in order to find important stuff later with more ease, you are engaged in KO. To make a sophisticated index is to build a conceptual structure that can be used for understanding, navigation, and finding.

Universal KOSs for Organizing Internet Resources

A convenient way to familiarize yourself with the major KOSs is to visit CyberDewey[81] and the DDC Web pages by the Online Computer Library Center (OCLC).[82] You

---

[79]Several publications in the metadata research directed by Michael Buckland are available at *http://metadata. sims.berkeley.edu/papers/papers_bydate.html.* See also Bartolo and Trimble [2000] for related work on heterogeneous metadata, building on the work of Buckland and colleagues.

[80]In particular for the ongoing projects CARMEN and ViBSoz, in which transfer modules are employed.

[81]David A. Mundie began creating CyberDewey, a catalogue for the Web, in 1995. See the Web site at *http://www.anthus.com/CyberDewey/CyberDewey.html.*

[82]See *http://www.oclc.org/dewey/.*

may want to take the DDC tour,[83] have a look at OCLC's research in KO,[84] or check the projects Scorpion[85] and Wordsmith.[86]

If you have a look at question 0 in my former Mini-FAQ on KO on the Internet [Sigel 1996–2001], you will find classification applied to the document itself. Feeding the document text into Scorpion resulted (among other things) in the suggestion by automatic classification that DDC class 006.332 (Knowledge representation) was relevant. Since automatic indexing can never be perfect, I intellectually checked the schedules and added (among other things) DDC class 020 (Library and information sciences). One can do better: the former editor of the *KO* journal (Dahlberg), of course experienced in KO systems, published as scope of the *KO* journal the complex UDC class synthesized using syntactic features of the special KOS language: 025.4+168+001.4(05).

Have a look at the HTML source to see how this was encoded in 1997 as Dublin Core in HTML, with uncontrolled keywords together with DDC automatic and DDC and UDC intellectual indexing.

```
<META NAME="DC.subject.keyword" CONTENT="knowledge organization,
    classification, indexing, concept theory, knowledge
    representation, internet, retrieval, metadata">
  <LINK REL=SCHEMA.dc HREF=
    "http://purl.org/metadata/dublin_core_elements#subject">
  <META NAME="dc.subject" CONTENT=" (TYPE=x-scorpion)
      (SCHEME=DDC) 025.04">
  <META NAME="dc.subject" CONTENT="(TYPE=x-scorpion)
      (SCHEME=DDC) 025.06">
  <META NAME="dc.subject" CONTENT="(TYPE=x-scorpion)
      (SCHEME=DDC) 025.32">
  <META NAME="dc.subject" CONTENT="(TYPE=x-scorpion)
      (SCHEME=DDC) 025.524">
  <META NAME="dc.subject"
    CONTENT="(TYPE=x-scorpion)
      (SCHEME=DDC) 004.678">
  <META NAME="dc.subject" CONTENT="(TYPE=x-scorpion)
      (SCHEME=DDC) 006.332">
  <META NAME="dc.subject"
    CONTENT="(TYPE=x-scorpion)
      (SCHEME=DDC) 001.012">
```

---

[83] See OCLC's Dewey to the Rescue! A Multimedia Tour of the Dewey Decimal Classification at *http://www.oclc.org/dewey/about/ddctour.htm.*

[84] See OCLC's Knowledge Organization Research at *http://staff.oclc.org/~vizine/kor_ddc/.* Also, Mitchell and Vizine-Goetz [2000] reported on a taxonomy server for DDC.

[85] See the Scorpion project at *http://orc.rsch.oclc.org:6109/.*

[86] See the Wordsmith project at *http://orc.rsch.oclc.org:5061/.*

```
<META NAME="dc.subject" CONTENT="(SCHEME=DDC) 020">
<META NAME="dc.subject" CONTENT="(SCHEME=DDC) 111">
<LINK REL=SCHEMA.dc HREF=
    "http://purl.org/metadata/dublin_core_elements#subject">
<META NAME="dc.subject"
    CONTENT="(SCHEME=UDC) 025.4+168+001.4(05)">
<LINK REL=SCHEMA.dc HREF=
      "http://purl.org/metadata/dublin_core_elements#subject"418>
```

`DC.subject.keyword` contains uncontrolled terms. Seven DDC classes in `DC.subject` (generated with Scorpion), two more DDC classes, and one UDC class have been added. Note that although the classes are taken from controlled universal classification systems, this is not mandatory indexing (that is, it is not guaranteed that the most specific entry has been used).

The Value of Classification in Back-of-the-Book Indexing

While database indexing is typically a finding aid for several documents on the same subject from a larger collection, back-of-the-book indexing is a finding aid for occurrences of subjects on pages within one hopefully rather homogeneous book. So two differences are homogeneity and scope. The value of classification in back-of-the-book indexing lies in the provision of a proper syndetic structure. That means that cross-references are motivated by an underlying classification system. I can only recommend looking at a sophisticated back-of-the-book index. The alphabetical index should only be the lead in to a systematical index that is classified according to facets. Fugmann [1991, 1993, 1999] described and applied this principle at its best. The result is an extraordinary added value because of the index. However, since conceptual back-of-the-book indexes necessarily involve a high degree of interpretation and assignment, subjective idiosyncrasies are more difficult to avoid.

Intellectual versus Empirical Mappings between Elements of KOSs

A main challenge within KO is to interrelate different conceptual schemata to organize knowledge for user-oriented tasks. This section provides an example of mapping between entries in KOSs and lets you foretaste associated difficulties.

Let's say you are interested in Islamic fundamentalism in literature, and you even find this Library of Congress Subject Headings (LCSH) term, possibly by browsing the shelves and looking it up in the subject description of a relevant book. Now you go to a different library, one that is organized by DDC. Hmm. . . . You need a mapping between your LCSH entry and the nearest possible DDC classes. Typically, this is not a 1:1 mapping but an $n{:}m$ mapping, and even if there is a mapping it does not mean that both concepts are equivalent. Partial matches occur more frequently. For example, one concept may comprise only an aspect, the other several facets. This is a problem particularly within enumerative systems. For this reason, using faceted classification systems makes semantic mapping easier. You go to a KOS mapping service and get results like those shown in Table 15–1.

Now the problem is to find resources described by those suggested new Dewey Decimal Classification (DDC) headings. Often it is easier to search for the keyword in the title. For example, the online DDC catalog of Carnegie Mellon University lists books with "fundamentalism" in the title that seem relevant to Islam alone (as judged from the title) under the DDC categories shown in Table 15–2.

A pragmatic strategy for generating a parallel corpus for an automatic transfer strategy might thus be to write an information agent ("softbot" or software robot [Etzioni and Weld 1994]) that fetches details for all hits that have both "fundamentalism" and "Islam*" in the title and associates the corresponding classifications found with both the LCSH and the DDC 21 entries from Table 15–1. Thus we get mappings similar to those shown in Table 15–3.

Characteristics of the relations (for example, bidirectionality, transitivity) have to be defined. Now we can go on to use conceptual clustering, display results in networks, calculate similarities and distances, and so on.[87]

Although the resulting mappings may be somewhat useful for users (because the subjects have some pragmatic similarity), it is epistemologically crystal clear that Islamic

Table 15–1   Mapping between LCSH and Dewey Decimal Classification

LCSH	Dewey Decimal Classification 21st ed.
Islamic fundamentalism in literature	T3C--58
	T3C--3829709
	808.80358
	808.803829709

Source: *Mapping between Library of Congress Subject Headings/DDC Numbers of Current Interest at* http://www.oclc.org/dewey/updates/lcsh_ddc.htm, *accessed in July 2001. (Since this page is updated periodically, the term used in the example no longer appears.)*

---

[87] For similar mappings between business categories and industrial classifications from different classifications systems, see Sigel [1998a], Figures 3 and 4.

Table 15–2 Dewey Decimal Classification Categories for Books with "Fundamentalism" in the Title, Relevant to Islam

First Level	Second Level	Third Level	Fourth Level (Books)
200 Religion			
	290: Other and comparative religion		
		297 Islam and religions originating in it	
			297 297.09
300 Social Sciences			
	320: Political science/Politics		
		320: Political science/Politics	320.5 320.550917671

Source: *Compiled from DDC and information in the online DDC catalog of Carnegie Mellon University at* http://webcat. library.cmu.edu/, *accessed in July 2001.*

Table 15–3 Potential Mappings Resulting from a Heuristic, Pragmatic Transfer Strategy

Left Entry	Relation Type[a]	Relation Strength[b]	Right Entry
DC:297.09	Is_pragmatically_related_to	0.6	DC:320.550917671
DC:297.09	Is_pragmatically_related_to	0.6	LCSH: Islamic fundamentalism in literature
DC:297.09	Is_pragmatically_related_to	0.6	DC:808.80358

[a]The relation Is_pragmatically_related_to should be subtyped by the strategy employed.

[b]The relation strength is set equal for all, using a weight found to be useful by trial and error.

fundamentalism *in literature* is only very accidentally the same subject as Islam in religion or Islam in special political problems in the social sciences. In order to build reusable resources appropriate for sophisticated semantic retrieval, we should not create a multitude of weak interrelations without proper justification, but rather try to build semantic mappings on solid conceptual foundations.

Relational and Frame-Based Indexing and Semantic Retrieval

A paradigmatic example of frame-based indexing for semantic retrieval is the export of corn from the United States to Russia. Given that *export*, *corn*, and both *United States* and *Russia* are already descriptors, in flat indexing we get the unconnected entries EXPORT, CORN, UNITED STATES, and RUSSIA. Basic human knowledge immediately tells us that *United States* and *Russia* are countries, which are geopolitical entities; *corn* is an edible, which is a substance; and *export* is a process exhibiting several roles—importer (an actor), exporter, product, amount, price, supply, transport route, and so on.

No postcoordination (not even with proximity operators) can help later in always discerning hits on the subject of the United States exporting corn from hits on the subject of Russia exporting corn.

An improvement would be relational or frame-based indexing:

```
import/export relation:
:exporting_country_A [country]
:importing_country_B [country]
:transferred_product_G [product].
```

Let's say that in order to organize the relations, we'd like to subsume this import/export relation under a more abstract one (for example, a transfer relation, in which something is transferred from one location to another). We might want to add quantities, a negotiated price, and so on, to the transfer relation and relax the location constraint to also allow virtual locations. In the end, a query for relations below the transfer location might yield the relation not only on import/export but also on the transfer of electronic files (ftp) or even of spies. Green [1989] gives the example of an abstract way/path relation that can be employed for physical migration or the transposition of a work of music into a different key.

A big problem in relational indexing is the high cost associated with it and the larger effort needed to keep relations organized. Up to now, relational indexing did not prevail, but this may change with TMs.

User-Oriented Indexing Views: The Value of Viewpoints in Any Knowledge Repository

Views have become popular in targeted content presentation of Web pages. For example, a university may have differently focused portals for students, researchers, alumni, investors, and the press. Therefore, views should be of relevance in indexing, too.

Consider again the example of Islamic fundamentalism in literature. It is obvious that different cultures have different views on what constitutes *Islamic, fundamentalist*, and even *literature*. Can it be held that a critic of Islamism should be regarded in all contexts as a writer on Islamism? (Maybe he is denied competence in orthodox circles?) Can a book whose index[88] has only two page occurrences for "fundamentalism, Islamic" be said to be a critique of Islamic fundamentalism? (The obvious is often not indexed.) Can a work "on the index" (for example, the Index Purgatorius/the Index Librorum Prohibitorum) be said to be part of literature in all possible worldviews? (One way to censor a work is to deny it the status of literature.) Which part of the metadiscussion on this book[89] can be said to be part of the subject about Islamic fundamentalism in literature? Maybe we are better off if we, for indexing purposes, do not assume the existence of objective and absolute truth?

Lancaster [1998, Appendix 3] shows in an extended example (which follows the tradition of checklist indexing) how modular subject analysis leads to multiple views that can be adapted to user groups. Furthermore, he makes clear how several analyses of the same document from different viewpoints come closer to a document's epistemological potential than an abstract indexing for a hypothetical universal user.

Endres-Niggemeyer and colleagues [1994] show some flexible adaptation possibilities of a social science thesaurus: the view of a social worker regarding nicotine may be different than that of a tobacco manufacturer.

Finally, Hjørland provides two very instructive, even extreme examples for multiple viewpoints and interpretations, resulting from user-oriented indexing. He regards it as permissible to construct and represent the subject of a certain book for different target audiences alternatively, as, for example:

> Social history. Working-class women. Copenhagen, 1880–1920
>
> Psychohistory. The history of mentality
>
> Pornography [Hjørland 1997, p. 93ff]

---

[88] See Joel Kuortti's Satanic Verses Index, first mounted on March 12, 1997, and updated April 27, 1999, at *http://www.uta.fi/~fljoku/svindex2.htm*.

[89] See Paul Brians's Notes on Salman Rushdie (1996–2001): The On-line Study Guide to Salman Rushdie's novel *The Satanic Verses* at *http://www.wsu.edu/~brians/anglophone/satanic_verses/*.

I hold that the problem with view-based indexing is not how to represent the views but how to understand and analyze the variety of possible conceptualizations.

Let me synthesize the value of user- and group-oriented viewpoints in conceptual knowledge structures and apply it to KM. Take the project described by Burchill and colleagues [2000] as an example for such a knowledge repository in KM. Here, the main value created is represented in conceptual knowledge structures. The repository "can be accessed using the indexed logical format or queried to allow entry at user-defined points. The main topics are: Concept Dictionary, Research Definitions, Meta-Index, and Glossary" [Burchill et al. 2000].

Note that the vocabulary is controlled according to Medical Subject Headings (MeSH). In medicine, there exist natural views (for example, patient, relatives, nurse, pharmaceutical industry). In effect, collaboration is aided through provision of a corporate (or organizational) memory with a standardized but also user-oriented conceptual structure.

Views allow us to get closer to collective conceptualizations, that is, shared mental models. To know about views and to employ them in knowledge repositories is a competitive advantage. Wouldn't you admit that how your customers see your organization is different than how your production and sales forces see it? Instead of trying to make inadequate compromises, it seems to be better to separate contexts. This improves the chance that knowledge relevant to a specific context is accessible. Views should also have a positive effect on customer relationship management since knowing the needs of your customers better is always an important target.

KO as a Use Case for TMs

TMs and KO are natural partners because the invention of TMs was to a large extent driven by KO requirements. The original aim of TMs was to aid semantic integration of independently maintained back-of-the-book indexes in technical documentation, where the underlying corpora constantly changed. The constant change of corpora is what we now experience with living documents on the Web. That the indexes are independently maintained is in line with the trend in KO toward decentralized provision of information, where central control cannot be exerted any longer.

Semantic integration is about (re-) constructing shared conceptualizations (or mental models), about modeling structures in sophisticated finding aids, particularly about modeling community-dependent differences as views and contexts, and about relating and collocating like subjects. TM syntax helps us convey and exchange information about such models in explicit (and standardized, serialized) form. The receiver side must reconstruct the conceptual model from this flattened exchange syntax. One can say that KO is interested in the intellectual and social processes, and TMs provide a technology to model and exchange markup of the result of such processes. In this sense, *TMs are a new enabling technology for KO.* But keep also in mind: several important KO issues must necessarily recur with TMs!

KO: A Primary Use Case for TMs

To organize knowledge for specific purposes (a KO activity) is one of the primary use cases for which TMs were designed. Ann Wrightson [2000] prominently stated this overlap in the context of TM use cases: "The essence of the whole picture is captured for me by a phrase from one of Alexander Sigel's examples: *Interrelating different conceptual schemata to organize knowledge for user-oriented tasks.*"

Earlier I named two impact directions (KO on TMs and vice versa). In a certain sense, both directions are just two sides of the same coin.[90] They are to be seen interdependently. This is because the following use case relationship holds: On the one hand, practical KO experiences are directly relevant as TM requirements, and KO theory should inform TM design; on the other hand, working with TMs is an area in which new KO experiences are gained, which in the long run must affect any general KO theory. Therefore I invite KO researchers to include the case of TMs in their research.

Knowledge Networks in KM: A Typical KOxTM Use Case

Kamps [2000] has already managed to place the all-important TM catch phrases and sales pitch in a very understandable paper directed to a KM audience (without even mentioning TMs!).[91] It is interesting to note how typical KO issues (ontologies, conceptology, intellectual indexing) are naturally mentioned in a very attractive KM package. I summarize here his (admittedly commercial) view because this is nearly a paradigmatic example of a KO-related use case for TMs. The structure of the two figures in the article (about the European Union) will be familiar to TM people.

Kamps understands knowledge to signify the essence to which conversations and documents can be reduced. As a prerequisite to effective KM, knowledge is formalized to

---

[90] Similar to TM associations being nondirected but having different names, depending on the scope from which you are looking.

[91] Note that Kamps also supervises Andreas Faatz, who researches how to improve retrieval with ontologies in knowledge networks using TerminologyFramework (by Rostek and Fischer; compare with, for example, *http://www.darmstadt.gmd.de/publish/pave/term/term.html* or Fischer [1998]).

make it controllable by and operational for machines (that is, semantic markup). He defines a knowledge network to be a kind of long-term memory (corporate or organizational memory) whose basic units are concepts, interlinked with other concepts by semantic relations. Such knowledge networks act as networked metainformation, thus being suited for the subject representation of arbitrary documents. Automated indexing can exploit such knowledge networks, particularly if the terms and the concept levels are discernible, and can aid precise semantic retrieval. Knowledge models (or ontologies) underlying knowledge networks have a product value of their own. Kamps sees a special market for knowledge-based information portals. In his view, the main value of technologies for the interactive visualization of networks is to support exploratory search strategies in which the search target is not clearly defined in advance.

KO on Topic Map Core Concepts (the "T-A-O" and "I-F-S" of Topic Maps)

In this section, I use the TM mnemonics developed by Steve Pepper [2002; see also Rath and Pepper 2000]. Looking closer at the TAO of TMs, a KO expert will note that:

- **Topics** can hold terms.[92]
- **Associations** (whether binary or *n*-ary) allow for a complex indexing language grammar with semantic relations connecting concepts (relators, relational indexing). Associations also accommodate a powerful frame-based indexing language, which ultimately ends up in direct AI knowledge representation, since an unlimited number of relations can be associated with one concept.
- **Occurrence role types** allow modeling of quantitative relevance degrees using range topics (for example, the interval 0.1–0.2).

More interesting is the possibility to *qualitatively* model relevance reasons and to model several reasons for one occurrence. For this purpose, a multihierarchical classification of potential relevance reasons is needed. Because occurrences can be restricted to passages instead of full documents, it becomes possible to record why an evaluator deems a certain passage relevant. In order to obtain context-dependent reasons from a natural workflow, a TM indexing tool would have to be integrated into the software used.

---

[92] Not only descriptors, access vocabulary, nominal phrases, definitions, and explanations but also—and this is vital—concepts (although it is not yet fully clear to me how this works with complex concepts).

Considering the IFS mnemonic, notice that:

- **Identity** is important for registering PSIs, for referencing them, for merging subject data, and for mapping between KOSs.
- **Facet** (a feature no longer needed in XTM because scope is more general and associations can be generalized to handle the facet functionality) was used in ISO/IEC 13250 to attribute properties to occurrences, for example, the language a resource is in. It is important to note that sound KO is tied to the concept of KO facets.
- **Scope**, a very powerful concept that accounts for much of the multidimensionality of TMs, has at least three connections with KO.

    1. Scope is consistent with scope and scope note in thesauri, where scope indicates the domain (area) in which the term is used in this sense, for example, migration (social science) versus migration (information technology).
    2. Scoping allows multiple views on knowledge structures. Depending on the target group, resources indexed from various viewpoints can be presented differently, and structures can be filtered and adapted according to user profiles.
    3. Scoping is also strongly related to sound KO, which has developed several principles, and to KO facet.

You may have noticed that structural similarities exist between KOSs and structured link networks (which TMs are). Because KO provides some theoretical background on how to build such intellectual structures, it may be worthwhile to consider KO when designing TMs.

The Potential Value of TMs for KO

TMs are much more than just the online equivalent of introduced KO forms like indexes, glossaries, or thesauri. As Michel Biezunski put it in Chapter 2, TMs "provide a standard approach to creating and interchanging finding aids." KO is about the provision of such intellectual structures for accessing resources that fit given purposes. Because KM strives to maximize through proper management the business value of the knowledge assets implicitly present in such resources, KM is heavily interested in optimal access structures, that is, in applied KO plus TM technology. TMs allow such access structures to be explicitly modeled. We can independently superimpose views even on third-party resources—without having to agree on the multiple views taken by the authors or owners of those resources on how to organize them. And we can define arbitrarily complex knowledge structures and attribute them as metadata to information resources. TMs support the organization of knowledge according to semantic categories and aid both in the conceptual navigation of the underlying knowledge structures and in the information resources described with them. This is their potential value for KO: they provide methodological knowledge about building and maintaining pragmatically useful knowledge networks that basically consist of concepts (topics) interlinked via relations (associations) to form complex concepts. These knowledge networks can be used to describe resources (occurrences), for example, Web pages, regarded as relevant to the user.

Temporary Impediments to TM Adoption: KO Prejudices

Unfortunately, most KO researchers and practitioners have not yet had the chance to fully absorb the TM idea and its potential. It is therefore natural that they are still a bit reserved, which in turn limits the adoption of TMs. It is my hope that with the ripening of the TM standard and application and the diffusion of the basic concepts into other fields, prejudice will separate from qualified criticism. However, the TM community should consider whether, beneath misconceptions, there lies also some truth in statements such as the following.

- "Topic Maps? Ah, just another exchange format for my thesaurus."
- "I have been using RDF metadata since 1997. . . ."
- "What's specifically new with this approach? Haven't we gone through all this before, but without the necessary technology? After the hype is gone, my intellectual KO problems will remain."

Let's briefly examine these concerns.

Just Another KOS Format?

In Chapter 2 Michel Biezunski called the (boring) case where a topic has only one, not multiple, names "just another schema for encoding ontologies, indexes, or vocabularies." And that is how they are presently regarded in KO: as "just" a new (but powerful and exciting!) technical vehicle for expressing and interchanging intellectual knowledge structures of any type. In first approximation, TMs are "merely" a versatile exchange format for KOSs. On further reflection, it is also recognized that TMs can be used to capture assignments of metadata (bound to such KOSs) to arbitrary resources, that is, as an alternative to store and present indexing results for digital assets. TMs can support modeling and mapping not only on the terminological level but also—which is of utmost importance—on the conceptual level.

What about RDF?

Although TMs and RDF are making big progress in their (perhaps eventual) integration, up to now RDF for metadata is by far predominant in the library community, and many more tools are available for RDF (this is also true for KR with RDF). I have not yet seen real employment of TMs in the KO community. However, Eric Miller [2000a, 2000b] along with his colleagues at OCLC[93] [Godby et al. 1999] seem to have gotten close to this goal, and there are more signs of growing interest. Maybe people in DL metadata feel that RDF still works well for the purpose at hand. They may regard TMs as too new (experimental), or, at least for their tasks, they have not noted marked differences. I expect this to change with the progress of the closer intertwining between TMs and RDF[94] and with ongoing cooperation with W3C. For the success of TMs it is absolutely necessary that the joint efforts of TMs and RDF (which began visibly increasing around the Extreme Markup 2000 conference in Montreal) bear fruit. I am therefore happy about the recent posting by Steven R. Newcomb [2001] on the complimentary, interdependent nature of TMs and RDF.

Michel Biezunski wrote in Chapter 2 that the library community has agreed on fields, terms, and so on as a prerequisite for the metadata approach, but that this probably won't happen in general. I want to remark that even for DC the consensus is only on a minimal set of fields, and many special extensions exist. Furthermore, in the subject field of DC (DC.subject) you can employ any KOSs, so two sets of DC metadata will probably be semantically noninteroperable unless there exists a proper mapping. While Amann and Fundulaki [1999] use RDF to model conceptualizations in domains, Howarth [2000] and Heflin and Hendler [2000] are more critical about the value of RDF. Howarth explains why RDF is limited to supporting interoperability among diverse metadata schemata at the machine-understandable syntactic level, and Heflin and Hendler discuss why RDF is only a partial solution.

Nothing New Under the Sun?

A KO expert might be inclined to say that, apart from the special serialized interchange format, TMs don't appear to be very new. (Of course, this partially ignores the important work by Daniel Rivers-Moore on the conceptual model of TMs (former XTM-CMS subgroup deliverables), and of Newcomb and Biezunski [Newcomb and Biezunski 2001; TopicMaps.Org 2000] on the in-process ISO Reference Model for Topic Maps). For the purpose of conciseness I now slightly exaggerate such a fundamental but not fully justified position.

Though TM technology and tools may aid KO, we still need indexers and their expertise to design sound KOSs and to assign good subject access points (descriptors, classes) to resources. Since major challenges in indexing remain unsolved, the current enthusiasm of the "techies" is not fully warranted: we can only record and interchange

---

[93] Eric Miller is now with W3C.

[94] See, for example, Chapter 12 by Eric Freese.

in TMs the intellectual decisions made for the design of a certain indexing language and the interpretations made about resources. Similar to the criticisms made of certain IR tools: TMs are not magic. We are not freed from using our own brains, and we continue to stay within narrow epistemological limits.

Why should relational indexing of the 1960s and 1970s now become popular? We already had nodes and arcs, semantic and subsumption networks. Is this more than a revival of AI approaches, now properly marketed for the KM audience (for example, the marketing of DAML+OIL)?[95]

KO Challenges That Recur with TMs

Because TMs are tools to organize knowledge, KO challenges must inevitably continue to haunt us, even in their new TM disguise (like old wine in new bottles). Here is a (nonexhaustive) list of important recurring issues that also serves as an invitation to KO experts to include the case of TMs in their research.

- Which principles should aid the design of ontologies? How can we prepare today for the interoperability needed tomorrow?
- Which experiences from the construction (and, often enough, failure) of KOSs are relevant to the design of generally applicable ontologies?
- What set of basic concepts and relations should we use? Which types of concepts and relations shall be standardized as PSIs? Which should be agreed upon in application areas (in quality-controlled decentralized registries)? Who has the authority and is trusted to do so?
- What architecture would help prevent the arbitrary proliferation of topics?
- Which concepts help to map and merge, to bridge (where appropriate) between different KOSs and the associated heterogeneous subject metadata?
- Which KO concepts and TM features may help to cope with the growing trend toward decentralized provision of metadata?
- What effect does TM technology have on KO quality in general? In particular: Which areas might bring qualitative progress (for example, flexible indexing views, scope filtering, semantic retrieval)?

Since I am not able to answer those questions, in the next section I prefer to discuss examples of such KO issues that recur with TMs as far as I understand them.

---

[95]Nowadays everyone is jumping on the "Semantic Web" bandwagon. We already had experienced a comedown of AI and knowledge-based systems. Description logics and inferencing are fine technologies. Although realistic applications are still missing, they have a certain potential within indexing applications. But, of course, they don't advance the intellectual core of the indexing problem.

Examples of KO Issues That Recur with TMs

The Representation of Incomplete Knowledge

Both Newcomb (compare, for example, the end of Chapter 3) and Pepper (compare, for example, his postings to the xtm-wg e-mail discussion group on February 19, 2001, and April 26, 2001) have pointed out that it must be possible to express incomplete knowledge in TMs. This is also a KO requirement for two reasons.

1. When we organize knowledge in practice, we have only partial knowledge and continually refine it as we learn in natural working processes. We do not want to be forced to follow strict procedures.
2. The process of understanding and interpretation is epistemologically open.

Bottom-Up Construction of KOSs by Discourse Communities and the Balance Between Universal Order and Domains

The collaborative coding of knowledge in TMs is tied to a joint understanding process in which a shared conceptualization is developed and made explicit. Discourse communities should run their own PSI registries. A theory of sound KO (and thus of sound TM ontology design) must be grounded in knowledge construction in domains and their situatedness (a concept well-known in philosophy and other disciplines, here referring to Gadamer's dialectical hermeneutics). That the quality of a KOS depends on context factors set by different domains and situations makes evaluation very difficult. On the other hand, bottom-up construction of KOSs is the only way since strictly top-down approaches (on the conceptual level searching for a universally applicable order) are likely to fail. We have learned during the history of the construction of universal and special KOSs that the right balance is important. Since it is more likely that basic building blocks[96] are shared by a large number of people than specific conceptualizations are, I recommend that during the construction of upper ontologies[97] one should try hard to search for such building blocks.[98] Views can

---

[96]It can be argued that even universal building blocks are impossible, for example, because categories are innately fluid. Even the universality is to be understood in a relative sense: In a move from essentialism to moderate constructivism, the "universals" are the current best negotiation on abstract categories, not eternal entities. See also the discussion on universals versus fluid concepts in the context of conceptual knowledge organization [Dahlberg 1996b].

[97]For example, see the home page of the IEEE working group on a Standard Upper Ontology (SUO), *http://suo.ieee.org/*. See also information on the SUO workshop at IJCAI 2001, *http://reliant.teknowledge.com/IJCAI01/*.

[98]I think this is consistent with Dahlberg [1974, p. 198], in the context of universality—flexibility—compatibility.

accommodate different conceptualizations built from the same socially shared elements. I think both ingredients might make upper ontologies both more successful and generally applicable. Neither overly optimistic hopes nor the prediction of the complete failure of upper ontologies are appropriate. Chris Angus[99] has found the right words, commenting on the "natural symbiosis between ontologies and topic maps":

> Topic maps need published ontologies in order that topic maps may be well grounded, ontologies would benefit from being made available as topic maps so that they may be properly explained, understood and navigated, particularly over the web. I would therefore like to propose that we seriously consider the use [of] the topic map paradigm as the overarching mechanism for documenting the Standard Upper Ontology, both as it evolves (that is documenting the work in progress) and in its final form.

I am very much in agreement with Bernard Vatant, who in Chapter 5 emphasizes bottom-up construction, pragmatism,[100] and the grounding of shared understanding in conversations.

Sound KO Design: From Categories to Relations

One very interesting first step toward a methodology of how to build a consistent and meaningful TM is a recent paper by Bernard Vatant [2001]. Although this is a kind of ontological engineering/thesaurus building method, he does not make explicit reference to KO.

Recall that in KO it is mandatory to operate on the language-independent concept space, not on the name space, since there can be many paraphrases or lexicalizations for one concept.

When searching for the right granularity of typing and scoping topics, we enter the realm of appropriate KOS design. If done well, scoping results in a set of so-called basic categories that will be used to factorize any complex concept. The KO theory of categories and conceptology tells us what constitutes concepts, categories, and the like and how to find them. If we factorize (analyze) a concept into its independent basic constituents or synthesize a concept from such constituents, then we apply facet theory, the analytico-synthetic principle of sound KOS design most existing KO schedules now employ.

---

[99] See the posting on February 9, 2001, on standard-upper-ontology@ieee.org.

[100] See also Jacob [2000] on the legacy of pragmatism.

In facet theory, basic categories are used as building blocks to assemble complex concepts (themes). I am convinced that conceptology and facet classification are strongly related to scoping (in fact, facet theory is directly applicable to scoping). Facets allow perspectives and views, and TMs allow us to model them with scopes, hence providing complex scope-filtering capabilities. In Chapter 3 Steven R. Newcomb names scoping as one of the key distinguishing factors of TMs enabling incorporation of worldviews. Steve Pepper, who cites facet classification references in his haystacks and needles article [Pepper 1999], seems to have recognized this. I feel that both the paper on ontology analysis and design for TM applications [Wrightson 2001a] and the theory of scoping Steve Pepper is working on [Pepper and Grønmo 2001] are very close to a modern version of such KO design principles. It is necessary to think twice before publishing a new semantic relation type since an arbitrary proliferation of relations (their explosion) is more detrimental to semantic interoperability than the proliferation of concepts. Relations must be polyhierarchically organized because of the predictability principle in indexing languages. Of help can be services that show published similar relations, also in visual form, and a thorough human review system.

Export of KOSs as TMs, Ontology-Bound PSI Registries, and PSI Architecture

In DLs, many entries from KOSs (classes, descriptors, terms) are now employed as (in XTM speak) published subjects to describe Internet resources by subject. It is rather trivial to export existing KOSs, or relation sets like those by Rahmstorf [1983, 1994a, 1994b, 2001], or in RST. All of those relation sets are all well documented. TMs can model any such structure. As we will see a proliferation of incompatible metadata (not as published subjects), we will see a proliferation of entities registering published subjects or running their own independent registries.

A dynamically generated list of entries in a PSI is nice, but in the long run we need more. In the ISI-2000 Topic Map Tutorial [Sigel 2000a] I stated: "KO and TMs need closer cooperation, because without excellent registries of published subjects, TMs won't fully develop." I assume that an architecture for TM published subject registries will be necessarily decentralized since the common trend in KO goes from centrally controlled KOSs with normative authority to decentrally provided metadata. Maybe someone will even adapt a completely distributed system[101] to the needs of category brokering for TMs?[102]

---

[101] For example, peer-to-peer systems such as Napster, Gnutella, and Freenet.

[102] However, where in a peer-to-peer system would you point to when the user where your topic is registered switches off his or her computer? Would multilevel caching help at all?

Aboutness, Topicality, Relevance, and Relevance Reasons

Aboutness, or the subject ascribed to a resource, is an important concept in knowledge organization. It is difficult if not impossible to interpret what a document is about. With the typed occurrence relation, topic maps allow links between a statement about a subject (itself defined via a PSI) and an occurrence in a resource.

Michel Biezunski wrote in Chapter 2, "All occurrences of the same topic share the property of 'being about' the subject represented by that topic." Therefore, we can use occurrence role types for sophisticated aboutness modeling, including qualitative relevance reasons.

When designing the conceptual structure of TMs, we should take into account the high value of document-external usage contexts. I hold that different schools of thought and different communities require adequate representation of multiple and conflicting interpretations and views. A modern indexing tool must allow expression of different sources of contexts. The quality of KOSs and subject analysis can be better checked if the indexing tool facilitates the reconstruction of the interpretations that took place.

With TMs we should be able to qualitatively model indexing reasons, that is, why certain documents were estimated as relevant for whom and for which purposes. It is now possible to qualitatively model relevance reasons and inference rules on relevance.

In addition, occurrence role types allow us to distinguish between relevance reasons and to permit relevance weights.

Relational Indexing and Semantic Retrieval

Sam Hunting showed relational indexing in Chapter 6, where he refers to the roles of ingredient and dish in a recipe and the amount and process in a step. Relational indexing can be implemented with scoping, transitive relations, and maybe some inference rules. I am almost convinced that TMs can be used together with Green's approach of relational indexing [for example, Green 1997], but some extensions might be necessary.

Semantic retrieval, as it is going to be implemented in the Topic Map Query Language (TMQL) [Rath and Garshol 2001], is a major improvement over retrieval with flat lists of postcoordinated descriptors. In TMs and ontologies, the quality of the associations defined is critical for the quality of retrieval and inferencing. Thus I hope that TMs will boost relational indexing. Note, though, that the bottleneck here is not technology but the intellectual resources to build the necessary structures.

Toward Formal Semantics in TMs

In the interest of generality, TMs rightly do not prescribe the application semantics of the structured link network.[103] Stated differently, TMs are open to any formal semantics. In the words of Michel Biezunski in Chapter 2, "Topic maps were originally designed as neutral envelopes, hospitable to any existing or future schema for `knowledge representation`."

Since TMs are hospitable to almost anything, naturally KR folks are starting to give the TM skeleton flesh with variants of formal KR languages that have been developed in their domains. Ann Wrightson [2001b] makes some judgments on KR, Case-Based Reasoning, and ontologies. Unfortunately, the powerful association template mechanism was dropped from XTM 1.0.[104] I hope that some consensus on templates will be achieved soon. Holger Rath, in Chapter 14, and similarly Eric Freese [2000] (on conditions, rules, and constraints [Pepper 2001]) have shown that it is possible to attach formal semantics to TMs. How? What is needed to tie a KR formalism to TMs? You need to look at the elements of the KR formalism, and you have to ensure that both the single elements and the interpretation of any combination thereof can be expressed (emulated) with TM elements (and moderate extensions). In other words, you have to show that reasoning with the extended TM mechanism and with the native KR mechanism are homomorphic.

The trick is to model the elements providing the semantics required for KR (for example, Rath's TM schema) in the TM—that is, to have the control structure in the TM itself (hence TM "self-control"). Templates are a flexible mechanism. Note that something similar to T- and A-Box [Brachmann and Schmolze 1985] (and Penman's upper and lower models [Bateman 1990]) is introduced with the distinctions between ontology and domain model or between concepts and individuals.

What about predicates, variables, quantors? Well, the "ANY" quantor can be registered as a PSI. In general, we may attach formal semantics by extending registries, variant name parameters, special occurrences, and so on. Typical implementations return a textual description only when a PSI is resolved, but may this be accompanied by interpretable formulas?

Which KR language to choose? How might a KR tool like Protégé be used with TMs?[105] It won't be the case that one size fits them all. So we have to expect any

---

[103] Except typing semantics and the definition of a few basic published subjects in the XTM annex.

[104] See Newcomb and Biezunski [2001], TopicMaps.Org [2000], and *http://www.y12.doe.gov/sgml/document/0243.htm*. See also Chapter 4 by Sam Hunting in this book.

[105] See Chapter 7 by Leo Obrst and Howard Liu. See also Kal Ahmed's plugin TmTab at *http://www.techquila.com/news/tmtab-02.html*.

superimposed (compare, for example, Maier and Delcambre [1999]) semantic knowledge markup expression [Boley et al. 2000] in TMs, for example, DAML+OIL or TerminologyFramework [Fischer 1998]. The Unified Knowledge Language (UKL) has been suggested for use with TMs. It is a specification currently developed by the Knowledge Management Consortium International (KMCI) that will "specify the contextually rich language that can represent and transmit knowledge from one software program or device to another" [KMCI 2000]. TM-aware KM people[106] have discussed UKL on the KMCI mailing list; Dodds writes about it in his chapter on UKL and TMs in *Professional XML Meta Data* [Ahmed et al. 2001].[107]

I have discussed with Rahmstorf how to intertwine his CLF language with TMs.[108] A naive approach probably won't work since his language opens a concept space, such that topics are defined through their characteristics, expressed in composed CLF formulas, and the definition direction of his relations is independent from the hierarchical is-a relation dependency from the top down.

Semantic Interoperability and Merging of Like Subjects

What does the well-known obstacle in KO (and in epistemologically open knowledge systems in general)—the comparability and compatibility of heterogeneous subject organization schemata (KOSs)—mean in the TM context? The collocation principle demands that like subjects should be merged (or closely related). We could employ automatic classification, categorization, or clustering to this purpose [Koch and Ardö 2000]. Advances in KO still have to be transferred to the TM case. The widespread use of TM tools will not make this problem go away but will aggravate it if no countermeasures are taken. Bridging between KOSs starts with noting and registering semantic connections between schemata.[109]

Semantic interoperability problems can take various forms. Altheim [2001a] expects interoperability problems because a normative processing model is absent from the XTM specification as delivered by TopicMaps.org.

---

[106] For example, David Dodds, Joe Firestone, and Andrius Kulikauskas.

[107] See also the following of Dodd's e-mail postings on UKL: "UKL Unified Knowledge Language, notes," posted October 3, 2000, to the KMCI mailing list (*http://groups.yahoo.com/group/kmci/messages/38*), and "Topic maps and metadata," posted on September 30, 2001, to the topicmaps-comment mailing list (*http://lists.oasis-open.org/archives/topicmaps-comment/200109/msg00110.html*).

[108] See also the talks in the workshop by Rahmstorf and me at the ISKO's German Chapter's conference Wissensorganisation, March 2001, Berlin, available at *http://index.bonn.iz-soz.de/~sigel/veroeff/ISKO-2001/*.

[109] See the home page of the Semantic Web Agreement Group (SWAG), which states the site is "a third party index, where parties can register the semantic connections between schemata," at *http://purl.org/swag/*; also available at *http://swag.semanticweb.org/*.

There has been much debate about the topic naming constraint and merging. Topics can be merged on the basis of names (the same base name within the same scope) or of identities/subjects (for example, referring to the same PSI) [Newcomb and Biezunski 2001, their sections 7.0, 8.0, and glossary entry on "merging"]. Kal Ahmed wrote in his part of Chapter 10, "Merging requires that a topic exhibit its own *characteristics* (names, occurrences, and roles played in associations) plus the *characteristics* of all topics merged with it" (emphasis added). Albeit correct, this may (mis-) lead a KO expert to believe that TM merging is really based on characteristics of topics. However, *characteristic* is a somewhat different concept in KO and TMs.

In my opinion, Steven R. Newcomb stated it most clearly for TMs:[110] the topic characteristics (names, occurrences, and membership in user-defined associations) come into existence by having a node playing the member role at the member end of an association member arc. This means that a topic characteristic includes its name—which sounds very strange to a KO expert who knows the distinction in terminology between a concept's name (label) and its characteristic (related to language-independent predications) and who assumes topics to be bound to a concept, not to a name space. In terminology, one would join not concepts that have the same name but those that are about the same subject, that is, one would join concepts that share the same KO characteristics. The assignment of the metadata referencing the PSI can be made only after analysis has shown that the characteristics are the same (the likeness has been determined). Most functionally "like" topics cannot be automatically detected; they must be determined by intellectual analysis. Note that Newcomb and Biezunski [2001] explicitly state: "There are many situations in which a human being, on the basis of the human being's knowledge, must intervene in order to cause two nodes to be merged."

Although with TMs the name is a characteristic of a topic, the characteristic of a concept in KO is independent from its name. This leaves room for some confusion. As a KO researcher I am very much interested in how not-yet-existing heuristics operating on TMs might support humans in KO characteristic-based merging.

Just as a concept may have no name or no lexicalization,[111] a topic may have no name. From what Michel Biezunski writes in Chapter 2 ("Topic maps do not connect names together; instead, they connect topics that may have multiple names"), it is not fully clear to me if TMs are really in concept space[112] or if this is "just" a solution to synonymy/

---

[110] In his March 20, 2001, e-mail to topicmapmail@infoloom.com.

[111] For example, what do you call aquaplaning-like circumstances caused by milk? Lactoplaning?

[112] At least this is not necessarily so.

homonymy. Identity is not determined by sharing the same term (or name),[113] although the topic naming constraint and TM scoping help against homonymy.

Indexing Views and Decentralized Information Provision

A nice feature of TMs, as Michel Biezunski points out in Chapter 2, is that they do not require the whole world to use the same worldview for relating and merging. This is important in cooperative cataloguing, given the trend toward decentralized information and metadata provision. We also perceive this trend with TMs: we move from rather centralized control over KOSs and indexing procedures that describe fixed documents to the decentralized provision of KOSs and metadata (both in TM-related PSI registries and in TMs) by parties that have no formal training in KO (for example, authors). At the same time, collaborative KO processes (like collaborative indexing, cataloguing, and filtering) are on the rise.

The quality of decentrally provided KOSs and metadata may lead to not only a degradation in precision but also to a potential gain in recall as more material is indexed. We can no longer rely on predictable indexing of resources with certain controlled terms (and with a fixed set of relations) from one KOS—we must expect an open number of terms or relations from several KOSs of varying quality and coverage. TMs accelerate this trend, but groupware extensions can help us cope with this.

Illustrative Examples

To illustrate the previous theoretical discussion on KOxTM, this section assembles a broad range of KO forms, activities, and purposes of potential TM use cases (without a systematic order). Heterogeneous semantic metadata occurs in all of them. You still won't encounter TM markup since I depict here some directions I'd like to further explore while the discourse about this book is evolving. The section Toward a TM on KO Resources: First Experiences describes an already ongoing spare-time project that I hopefully can release soon.

---

[113] Except, of course, where the information author has intentionally chosen to structure his or her information to determine identity by sharing the same term or name.

Shorter Examples of Fruitful KO with TMs

Kinds of Innovative Indexing

Back-of-the-Book Indexing. Earlier in this chapter I wrote about Fugmann's innovation in back-of-the-book indexing [Fugmann 1991, 1993, 1999]. Such indexes of textbooks, proceedings volumes, or journals are a typical use case for TMs. Michel Biezunski has several navigational indexes for XML-related conferences online.[114] Although from a KO perspective their conceptual structure is not very sophisticated, they can be seen as a proof of concept.

Indexing of Repositories for Modules in Programming Languages. As can be seen from Eric Steven Raymond's cathedral versus bazaar metaphor (see, for example, *http:// www.tuxedo.org/~esr/writings/cathedral-bazaar/*), a multitude of open source programmers will always develop overlapping solutions. Even with a central repository, differently named modules often do the same things, and a lot of effort is wasted (in development and maintenance) because of a lack of sufficient organizational structure. The Comprehensive Perl Archive Network (CPAN) with its search engine[115] and a rough intellectual classification suffers from this, as does, for example, Sourceforge.[116] What about a collaboratively maintained TM index for CPAN?

Indexing of Threads in Academic Discussions. A recurring KO problem is high-volume academic (or technical) discussion mailing lists. The classical solutions are lists of frequently asked questions (FAQs). The bottleneck is the human end, where the resources have to be freed to provide the conceptual overview. Maybe TMs are apt support tools for FAQ-like indexing? With the suggested Discourse Markup Languages [Best 2001; Rost 1996] we may be able to interactively mark up such discussions and thus enhance human understanding. The idea of annotating scholarly discourse and enriching documents is also interesting. Relevant are several projects of the Knowledge Media Institute (KMI), but in particular I'd like to highlight ScholOnto.[117]

---

[114] See *http://www.infoloom.com.*

[115] See *http://www.cpan.org* and *http://search.cpan.org*, respectively. See *http://www.topicmapping.com/cpan. html* for a prototype.

[116] See *http://www.sourceforge.net.*

[117] See the home page of the Scholarly Ontologies Project at *http://kmi.open.ac.uk/projects/scholonto/*. Titles of papers at the site include ScholOnto: An Ontology-Based Digital Library Server for Research Documents and Discourse; Ontology-Driven Document Enrichment: Principles, Tools and Applications; Structuring Discourse for Collective Interpretation; and Scholarly Discourse as Computable Structure. See also other KMI projects at *http://kmi.open.ac.uk/projects/*.

Multiview Indexing of Knowledge Repositories. In his XML Europe 2000 Paris presentation, Kal Ahmed showed a TM improvement over an existing index to pharmaceuticals.[118] Meanwhile, a similar resource is available in Germany.[119] In addition to prescription information, extensive test reports or threads with advice are offered. A comparable resource is the index of the National Cancer Institute's CancerNet database.[120] TMs can aid in organizing such enormous resources more easily, and different viewpoints might improve indexing quality.

Indexing for Town Magazines and Innovative E-Journals. Some years ago, Gerhard Dirmoser and colleagues prototyped an index for articles that appeared in a town magazine.[121] Gerry McKiernan maintains a registry of innovative e-journals.[122] One innovative feature of such journals, compared with print journals or electronic journals that only resemble their print counterparts, is advanced indexing and searching, including automated indexing with self-organizing maps. A special case of innovative indexing is reader-designated hyperlinking in "eclectic" journals. This could be improved if readers provided not only links but also TMs; hence applications in electronic journals could be developed.

Coordinated Text Word Indexing, and Dictionaries, Glossaries, and Terminology Work in General. In philosophy, terminology is strongly bound to persons (Heidegger, Gadamer) and develops diachronically. A controlled vocabulary approach does not really work. Thus, Norbert Henrichs [1970; see also Stock [2000]) invented and applied the text word indexing method. It leads to word fields that searchers have to consult. In effect, the burden shifts from the indexer to the searcher. The success of this method critically depends on the overview a searcher can gain of the word field. In the following paragraph, I sketch the main ideas expressed by Stock [2000] in a recent description of the text word method.

Stock [2000, Figure 1, p. 312] shows the result of indexing with this method for "Meinong, Alexius". He graphically depicts [Figure 5, p. 317] a semantic network centered on "subject-matter" in the work of Meinong that was statistically calculated from such word fields. Stock shows it is possible to semiautomatically derive thesauri

---

[118]See *http://www.RxMed.com.*

[119]See *http://www.netzdoktor.de.*

[120]The CancerNet database, redistributed by the University of Bonn, Germany, is available at *http://www. meb.uni-bonn.de/cancernet/cancernet.html.*

[121]See Dirmoser's home page of the Hillinger Net, an online index of articles published in *Hillinger,* at *http://dose.servus.at/hillinger/netz/einstieg.html.* See the entry labeled "Das Fremde" (*http://dose.servus.at/ scripts/publikationen/information/info2.idc?bez=Das_Fremde*) (the foreign).

[122]See McKiernan's EJI: A Registry of Innovative E-Journal Features, Functionalities, and Content at *http://www.public.iastate.edu/~CYBERSTACKS/EJI.htm.*

from word fields. In his outlook, Stock envisages a further development of semantic networks based on text word indexing word fields to a statistical thesaurus, leading to a completely new form of graphical retrieval. Coincidence becomes the only relation, and the user decides, by choosing the coincidence value, which relations or themes are shown or searched. In TM terminology, this would be filtering with dynamic scopes!

In general, TMs can be applied to all kind of word fields.[123] TMs also might be apt for the exchange of terminological data. While subcommittee 3 of ISO's technical committee 37 (ISO TC 37 SC 3) has not yet very visibly made this link,[124] the SALT project[125] just evaluated TMs for this purpose [Schütz 2001]. A major deliverable of this project is XLT: XML representation of Lexicons and Terminologies, the primary member of the XLT family being DXLT (Default XLT Format).

The KO researcher Mario Barité published a bilingual (Spanish–English) dictionary of KO terms, now online, that employs a facet structure.[126] This excellent work would profit from TM technology. The people working on the glossary of the SWAG project[127] might consider using TMs. Finally, the cross-referencing of encyclopedia entries[128] is a prospective TM use case.

Export of KOSs as TMs, PSI Registries, Ontology Merging

What Biezunski describes in Chapter 2 as the import of KOSs as local TMs is a classic KOxTM application: make all thesauri and classifications available as TMs and publish their entries in PURL-safe PSI registries. I expect that in short time we will see referenceable TMs for every major KOS.

The J. Paul Getty Trust recently announced a relaunch of its controlled vocabulary aids.[129] This work is already a kind of PSI registry, albeit not yet in TM format. A

---

[123] See, for example, the graphs dynamically generated by Quasthoff et al. of Projekt Deutscher Wortschatz at *http://wortschatz.informatik.uni-leipzig.de/index_js.html*.

[124] See the Web site of the ISO subcommittee on computer applications in terminology at *http://korterm.or.kr/isotc37/sc3.htm*.

[125] Standards-based Access service to multilingual Lexicons and Terminologies. See the official SALT technical Web site at *http://www.loria.fr/projets/SALT/*. Additional resources on the SALT project from ttt.org (translation, theory, and technology) are available at *http://www.ttt.org/salt/*.

[126] See *http://www.eubca.edu.uy/diccionario/*.

[127] See *http://purl.org/swag* and *http://swag.semanticweb.org/*.

[128] As already exists at the sites *http://www.wissen.de* and *http://www.xrefer.com*.

[129] Including, for example, AAT (Art and Architecture Thesaurus), ULAN (The Union List of Artist Names), and TGN (The Getty List of Geographical Names). See *http://www.getty.edu/search/*. Try a search for "gothic" in the AAT or ULAN record #12899 with the alternative names for the topic "Leonardo da Vinci".

thesaurus example is German INFODATA,[130] with terms in information science, or its American equivalent, published by ASIS&T.[131]

Dahlberg [1982, 1996a][132] proposed ICC for the purpose of experimentally switching between KOSs. The major obstacles against converting this classification (which is already online[133]) into a TM are that currently no consortium exists and copyright issues would have to be settled.

Murray Altheim [2001b and personal communication] is working on the conversion of Upper CYC® with relations and LCC into XTM. SUO[134] might one day be available in TM format. Although not with TMs, Kiryakov and Simov [2000] have a demo on mapping Upper CYC® with upper EuroWordNet.

The first prototype PSI registries and services have been created. One example was Seruba's registry and the associated search engine with the lexicosaurus, both of which unfortunately are no longer available.[135]

Concept or Cognitive Mapping and Intellectual Juxtaposition of Ideas with Semantic Networks

A TM represents a formalism that can be seen to leverage work on concept and cognitive mapping. Consider the work by Gerhard Dirmoser [personal communication] resembling those approaches: the intellectual organization of cross-disciplinary ideas/concepts (and associated material) into a coherent whole in map format (called Knowledge Landscapes), often juxtapositioning ideas for the first time. It is outstanding how he organizes an exposition, an archive of a modern artist, or the historical developments and interdependencies of a special idea! Note that this level of indexing and overview can be achieved only through intellectual assignment and never through automated indexing. Others of Dirmoser's networks, all sized around 300–500 nodes, include French Philosophy, the Approach of Structuralism in Art and Science, and so on. Unfortunately, most exist only in handwriting. It would be a major achievement to have them in TM format. Because of the richness (he often employs very fine-grained

---

[130] See *http://www.iud.fh-darmstadt.de/iud/wwwmeth/publ/example/werkz/infodata/descrbd3.htm.*

[131] See *http://www.asis.org.*

[132] See also Dahlberg [1982a, pp. 115–132].

[133] See *http://index.bonn.iz-soz.de/~sigel/ISKO/ICC/.*

[134] See *http://reliant.teknowledge.com/IJCAI01/.*

[135] Algermissen announced the registry (*http://psi.seruba.com*, Web server no longer available) and the lexicosaurus (*http://www.lex4.com*, Web server no longer available) on February 16, 2001, on the xtm-wg e-mail discussion list; see *http://lists.oasis-open.org/archives/topicmaps-comment/200102/msg00143.html.*

semantic relations and adds faceted classification) and size of his large networks, they would also be critical test cases for TM technology (for example, in visualization).

"Kontext."[136] Together with Rainer Zendron, Gerhard Dirmoser developed an extremely rich semantic network that represents a conceptualization on how issues of context are treated in art and science. The network contains information about approximately 650 persons (335 artists, 105 art theoreticians, 190 scientists, and so on) and approximately 200 thematic nodes that are linked via more than 3,850 relations. In addition to its interesting content, this network can serve as an ideal KO use case for TMs because it employs typed topics and roles. Missing are explicitly typed and addressable occurrences (but they could be added, of course). A quick glance reveals several person roles (for example, curator of an exposition; invited, participant, or missing artist of an exposition; coauthor; representative or pupil of a school; and so on) and many semantic relations between people of high organizational value (for example, cooperation relations like teacher–pupil; discourse relations like comment upon, report on; influence relations like heard lecture, was impressed by, received hint by; and so on). The high value lies in the fact that two literatures not otherwise related can be explicitly connected. The value added by discovering unrelated literatures about a comparable subject (but possibly using differing terminologies) is stressed by its function according to the collocation principle. This was prominently investigated by Donald Swanson,[137] who, among other things, used ISI's citation index [Garfield 1994].

"Thinking."[138] This is a semantic network, available as a file with comma-separated values [Dirmoser, personal communication], with 10,000 relations on the concept of thinking (its definition, forms and schools of thinking, and so on). I recommend starting your exploration with the Plateau Philosophy concept or with concepts of thinking at Relevant for Art. To taste the pudding: Thinking at the Border of the Subject is

---

[136]See Studie: Kontextfragen in Kunst und Wissenschaft (Study: Context Issues in Art and Science) by Gerhard Dirmoser (author) and Rainer Zendron (artist) at *http://dose.servus.at/kontext/*. The context net was originally created on plates, approximately 2 m by 7 m, then photographed and published as three posters, which are available from OK Centrum für Gegenwartskunst, Dametzstr. 30, A-4020 Linz, Austria. Dirmoser has given lectures at Kunsthochschule Linz and Depot Wien. About 30 percent of the relations have been graphically implemented on the plates, and the content of each node was completely realized. With the aid of the plates the placement of the elements can be easily reconstructed. The plates originally exhibited pictures that are not contained in the Internet version. The classification of this work is available on a Web site with the title "Kontextualisierungsstrategien" (contextualization strategies); see *http://www.servus.at/kontext/KON_STU.HTM*.

[137]An easily readable summary is Swanson [2001]; see also his substantial works cited therein.

[138]See Dirmoser, Sichten auf das Denknetz at *http://dose.servus.at/denk/*; Plateau Philosophy at *http://dose.servus.at/scripts/kontext/information/info2.idc?bez=Philosophisches*; Relevant for Art at *http://dose.servus.at/scripts/kontext/information/allKunst.idc*; and Thinking at the Border of the Subject at *http://dose.servus.at/scripts/kontext/information/info2.idc?bez=am_Randes_des_Subjekts_denken*.

an art-relevant concept of thinking, which is at home on the plateau of psychoanalysis. At level 1 this is related to two expositions ("Real AIDS" and "Real Sex"), in which this concept was a theme, and to two concepts of thinking ("thinking at the border of the unthinkable" and "thinking related to sexuality"). At level 2 you find, for example, "Body-oriented thinking". "Analytic thinking" is one of the many concepts related at level 3. An exposition of this network is under preparation.

"Performance."[139] Dirmoser and Nieslony developed 32 views on the Performative Turn. They presented their work at the Performative Studies Conference [Dirmoser and Nieslony 2000, 2001], showing four colored posters on performance art. The posters depict a mental model, an imaginative theater of concepts. This could be one type of visual interface for TMs.

From Personal Note Taking to Corporate Knowledge Repositories

TMs could help organize any hypertext. After all, typed links are central to the hypertext model. Two prominent noncomputerized *Zettel* examples come to mind: Niklas Luhmann's famous *Zettelkasten*[140] and Arno Schmidt's [1970] *Zettel's Traum*. I have read that Luhmann's *Zettelkasten* would profit much from hypertext technology. Although Schmidt seems to have been unaware of hypertext, it has been shown that his work can be successfully converted to hypertext.[141] It is only a short way from Luhmann's *Zettelkasten* and Arno Schmidt's *Zettel's Traum* to Ted Nelson's Xanadu (see, for example, *http://xanadu.com/*). An example of a modern *Zettelkasten* is Beats Bibliotheksnetz.[142] On this Web site, the author tries to order and interconnect his thoughts, ideas, and the books and other sources he read. First steps toward groupware are visible, for example, reader-provided hyperlinks and annotations.

Interestingly, Daniel W. Connolly [1995], then with W3C, summarized the OHS paper by Engelbart [1990] as a measuring stick for collaborative systems. This brings me to the excellent work of the Bootstrap Institute[143] and to the role of intelligence in

---

[139] See Dirmoser and Nieslony, *http://dose.servus.at/kontext/kon450.htm* and *http://www.servus.at/kontext/KON_STU.HTM* (activity-related approaches).

[140] Please refer to Idensen et al., Odysseen des Wissens—Kollaborative Enzyklopädie, at *http://www.hyperdis.de/enzyklopaedie/*. On knowledge, in particular see Luhmann's *Zettelkasten* at *http://www.hyperdis.de/enzyklopaedie/odyssee_lexikon.html*. This is mainly based on a textual contribution by Markus Krajewski at *http://bscw.gmd.de/pub/german.cgi/d20798899/krajewski_zettel.rtf*. Note that Dirmoser also has an entry on Luhmann and his *Zettelkasten* in his context study at *http://dose.servus.at/kontext/kon390.htm*.

[141] In consequence, any literary hyperfiction could be held in TMs.

[142] See *http://beat.doebe.li/bibliothek/*.

[143] See *http://www.bootstrap.org*.

KO, as described by the Welch Company.[144] I am most impressed by the quality of KO visible in the diary entries there, for example, the June 5, 2000, entry by Rod Welch about a letter by Robert E. Kent on organizing information for "knowledge," which is discussed in the context of exchange with Jack Park.[145] This example is a mixture between personal note taking and building a public or corporate knowledge repository (or organizational memory).

Organization of Resources for Students, Vocational Training, and Life-Long Learning

Gerhard Knorz maintains a Web site with course material in information and documentation that exhibits an extraordinary degree of KO.[146] Have a look at the thematic search, which shows coordinated descriptors and occurrence types. Choose "Thesaurus" (27 hits at the time of this writing). The second and third columns in the results page further divide those hits by theme and form, respectively. Knorz [2001] is already TM-aware and is looking into how to use TM technology for his site.

Since Sowa's Conceptual Graphs are already employed in the Life-Long Learning (L3) project,[147] together with didactical ontologies to describe learning resources, TMs should be a natural complement in this application area. This has important implications both for courses in virtual universities and for business-internal training on the job.

Quality-Controlled Subject Gateways and Community-Oriented Webs (Portals)

The ability of TMs to associate addressable Internet and intranet resources with metadata makes them ideally suited for applications such as:

- Sophisticated bookmark management
- Quality-controlled subject gateways (or clearinghouses)[148]—an important TM case in KO
- Community-focused portals integrating content from various independent sources, maybe even from different viewpoints—a killer application in KM

---

[144] See *http://www.welchco.com*.

[145] See Welch's 10:47 A.M. diary entry on the letter from Robert Kent on organizing information for "knowledge" at *http://www.welchco.com/sd/08/00101/02/00/06/05/104726.HTM#0001*.

[146] See his Methodik Web site at *http://www.iud.fh-darmstadt.de/iud/wwmeth* and the thematic search at *http://www.iud.fh-darmstadt.de/iud/wwmeth/search/deskris.asp?des1*.

[147] See *http://www.l-3.de*.

[148] See Koch [2000] and the home pages of Koch (*http://www.lub.lu.se/netlab/staff/koch.html*) and the Renardus projects (*http://www.renardus.org/*).

One of the quality-controlled subject gateways maintained by the organization for which I work is on migration and ethnic minorities.[149] There is also a service of selective dissemination of information on the same topic, based on documentation of publications and research projects and intellectual postselection.[150] I envisioned how a virtual integration of both, together with the classification and the thesaurus, could be achieved.[151]

Business Category Brokering

Today I'd implement the concepts and relations in the bizzyB prototype for business category brokering [Sigel 1998a] with TM technology. The aim there was to interrelate business categories by a kind of "social indexing," in this case learning from the co-usage of terms in search profiles.

Research Fronts and Landscapes, Automated Domain Analysis

Research fronts can be detected by Citation Analysis and be visualized as maps. Pioneer work has been done by ISI with the (discontinued) *Atlas of Science* [Institute for Scientific Information 1981]. I imagine TMs to be of great value for the visualization of research fields through Citation Mapping [Small 1999] and for making the results of citation-based Automated Domain Analysis [White et al. 1998] (a perfect complement to intellectual domain analysis) navigable and searchable.

Interactive Annotated Bibliographies

A wonderful KOxTM project would be to improve ISKO's 10-year KO bibliography from paper [*KO* 1999] to an online TM version. Resource and copyright issues have prevented this so far. Bibliographic references are organized according to the Classification System for Knowledge Organization Literature,[152] itself subdivided by ICC.

Strategies embodied in information agents could use this bibliography as a starting point to find near-matching occurrences for the entries (for example, home pages, papers, publications, citations) and roughly classify them by the classifications the corresponding topics in the bibliography already have.

---

[149] See the Migration Clearinghouse at *http://www.bonn.iz-soz.de/themen/migration/*.

[150] See *http://www.gesis.org/Bestellen/IZ/index.htm?order/sofid.htm*.

[151] See the transparencies for Sigel [2000b].

[152] See *KO* 26(4):192–202 (1999).

Legal Evidence

Eduard Jacob [personal communication] made me aware that the process of finding truth in evidence law and in evidence-based medicine might be helped by organizing knowledge in TMs. (For example, which knowledge is produced by which question?) This seems to be related to the Issue-Based Information System (IBIS), which, according to Jack Park, can be implemented as TMs (see Chapter 17).

Toward a TM on KO Resources: First Experiences

I am currently working on a TM about relevant KO resources on the Web. In order to trace the usage of the term, in a first brute-force attempt I crawled all of the several thousand Web pages found by Google (*http://www.google.com*) for the search string "knowledge organization". I learned that KO is now also a term in KM, standing for an organization heavily dependent on knowledge (the "knowledge organization"). The next step will be to start from important directions in KO and also to trace the newer online citation context of influential publications in KO (for example, with Citeseer, *http://www.citeseer.com*), using the bibliography as a starter. But for the moment I defined an occurrence role "Web page" and threw in about 2,000 Web pages with their titles as topics and the URLs as their occurrences.

Then the laborious work began: to intellectually evaluate the pages one by one. After about 100 pages, I arrived at a rough mini-ontology of people, institutions, projects, conferences, publications, software, procedures, problems, processes, and so on, which allowed me (more or less) to qualitatively state why I evaluated a given resource as relevant (or not) for KO and to what degree. For relevance I use five labeled degrees, including nonrelevance, which is necessary to record resources already visited (for example, if someone suggests them again). The ontology naturally leads to relations like those listed below.

- A researcher participates in a conference.
- A researcher is a speaker at a conference.
- A researcher is affiliated with an institution.
- A researcher publishes a paper in a proceedings volume.
- A proceedings volume is the publication resulting from a conference.
- A researcher reports on a conference.
- A researcher reviews the work of other researchers.
- A conference is organized by an institution.
- A project is run by people at an institution.
- Software solves a problem or implements an algorithm.
- Problems are dealt with in research papers.

Absent access to a good visual ontology editor, I pinned the concepts and relations to a corkboard in order to maintain the overview of their polyhierarchy. This is very important for the semantic relations.

Now relevance of a resource can be (nonexhaustively) defined as relevance with respect to the ontology. A resource is relevant because:

- It is by a well-known KO researcher (published under his or her name in the literature or on his or her home page), or referenced by him or her, or about him or her.
- It is by a well-known institution in KO (ISKO or its chapters, or similar societies and working groups, for example, FID or ASIS&T's SIG/CR) or on its Web pages, or referenced by it, or about it.
- It is about a well-known KO issue (as determined by the classified bibliography or as taken from profiles on the home pages of other KO researchers).
- It is related to a well-known event in KO (for example, a conference).
- It is published in a well-known KO organ (for example, a journal or book series).
- It is referenced by a central resource (for example, a FAQ).

For example, the page *http://www.ischool.washington.edu/mai/* is a highly relevant KO resource because it is the home page of a renowned KO researcher, a KO teacher at a renowned KO institution, which links to relevant KO publications and relevant KO course material. Mai's research profile can be expressed as topics, linked to KO areas, and so on.

Thus I have created a more or less operational way to test whether a resource is relevant for this KO registry, why it is, and to what degree I think so, and a way to record the results of my decisions. This is a pragmatic solution to relevance and aboutness. Note that the effort to analyze each resource by multiple views (relevant as a researcher, relevant for publications, and so on) pays off later, for example, when it enables us to automatically link to other resources not yet crawled. I'd like to code heuristic relevance rules and inference rules directly into the TM, such that a special TM processor could calculate the centrality and semantic similarity of resources for a given topic, and a TM visualization engine could neatly display it, using the qualitative degrees and the calculated weights. In a meta–search engine project that implements heuristic strategies to determine the relevance of parts of Web pages about researchers, in 1999 my wife and I had used scoring points and rules of thumb with some success. This simple but powerful concept could also be useful in TM-based meta–search engines.

A Look into the Future: Toward Innovative TM-Based Information Services

Here I speculatively probe into the future of TMs. TMs and related technologies are instruments that make it easier to provide innovative KO services. I envision new strategies that achieve better semantic interoperability by exploiting TM networks. With TMs, search engines may group results and provide relevance reasons, for example, via occurrence roles, or filter according to user models that contain scope preferences. Users may organize search results into their pragmatic, context-dependent knowledge structures and make this added informational value public. This kind of "social indexing" (using co-usage contexts) may bootstrap mapping between concept spaces [Bartolo and Trimble 2000; Sigel 1998a]. Information agents may rework TMs and offer ontology-based inferencing, intermediating, and brokering. They may communicate with FIPA-sponsored ACL (see *http://www.fipa.org*), KIF/KQML, or IDL/CORBA (maybe also SOAP) performatives.

We need basic services to locate PSIs, their meanings, and occurrences described by them. (An early precursor of a PSI service was hosted by Seruba, mentioned earlier.)

Given the model of ISI's *Atlas of Science*, based on citation networks, I can imagine value-added TM services on top of bibliographic databases. One notable example of how such a potential information service might look is the earlier project AKCESS (Assistance by Knowledge-Based Context Evaluation in Social Science Information Retrieval) at the Social Science Information Centre in Bonn [Mutschke 1994, 1996, 1998, 2001; Mutschke and Quan-Haase 2001].

Here, various types of formal relationships among persons, institutions, documents, and projects and the respective roles played are analyzed and aggregated. From such network-like relations[153] research landscapes with social networks (cliques) of researchers can be inferred. Cooperation relations among scientists in a scientific community are semantically interpreted. Using network analysis, AKCESS calculates the social status (for example, centrality) of actors within such a scientific community. Moreover, it examines the relationships between co-occurrences of scientists and key words in bibliographic documents to generate thematic profiles under uncertainty (employing fuzzy matching). It seems natural to extend this approach with TMs. While already the input from the bibliographic databases could be in TM form, the resulting network of interlinked persons and themes would surely benefit from a graphical presentation as TM (Figure 15–1). With TMs going in and out, AKCESS would transform to a kind of "intelligent information agent" reworking TMs.

---

[153]For example, author—coauthor (or coeditor); project leader—project member; editor of a work—author of a publication in that work; and so on.

The person Claus Leggewie, central in Figure 15–1, is actor 317 in a collaboration network of 1,456 scientists of the field "German reunification" (Figure 15–2). Twelve authors related to Leggewie are listed in the standard AKCESS output; six of them are themselves central for the field studied, as shown in Figure 15–1. The keywords a coauthor shares with Leggewie are displayed. Furthermore, status measures are indicated, such as *closeness* centrality (the number of shortest paths of Leggewie to all other vertices in the graph), *betweenness* centrality (the ratio of shortest paths on which Leggewie lies), *hierarchy* (number of actors in equivalence classes "lower" than Leggewie's class; for directed graphs seen as a tree-like structure), and *relevance* as a summarizing index.

Resnik suggested at IJCAI 1995 a measure to evaluate semantic similarity in is a network that takes shared information content into account.[154] It would be possible to use this measure in TM search engines that locate subjects central to a theme or closely related subjects. One application could be to find experts on topics.[155]

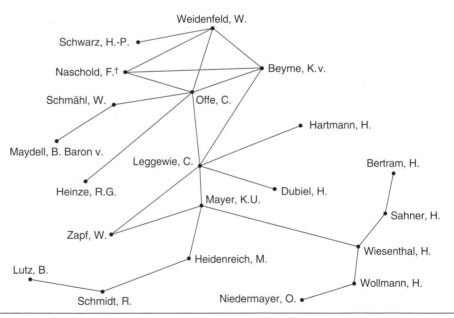

Figure 15–1   A coauthor network of central authors in the domain of German reunification (reprinted with permission from Mutschke [2000])

[154]An extended and more recent version is Resnik [1999].

[155]This is indeed the aim of Expert Locator described in Clark et al. [2000], who cite Resnik. Note that with AKCESS (and, in general, in any citation network) one can locate central experts.

AKCESS—Network Analysis

All actors: 5374
Connected actors: 3258
[...]

317. **Leggewie, Claus**
Occurrence (total): 5
Network (size, density): 1456, 0.000125
Ego-Network (number co-authors): 12
Centrality (closeness): 0.241895
Centrality (betweenness): 0.006594
Hierarchy: 0.995189
Relevance: 0.559717
connected with:

<u>Dubiel, Helmut:</u> DDR, Revolution, Zivilgesellschaft, Demokratie, Transformation, Totalitarismus, Sozialismus, Sozialstruktur, Konzeption

<u>Beyme, Klaus von:</u> politischer Wandel, Politikwissenschaft, Sozialwissenschaft, politische Theorie, sozialer Wandel, Wiedervereinigung, DDR, Bundesrepublik Deutschland, neue Bundesländer, realer Sozialismus

<u>Segert, Dieter:</u> politischer Wandel, Politikwissenschaft, Sozialwissenschaft, sozialer Wandel, Wiedervereinigung, DDR, Bundesrepublik Deutschland, neue Bundesländer

<u>Hartmann, Heinz:</u> politischer Wandel, Soziologie, Sozialwissenschaft, sozialer Wandel, Föderalismus, Wiedervereinigung, DDR, Bundesrepublik Deutschland, neue Bundesländer

<u>Lepsius, M. Rainer:</u> politischer Wandel, Soziologie, Sozialwissenschaft, sozialer Wandel, Wiedervereinigung, DDR, Bundesrepublik Deutschland, neue Bundesländer

<u>Weiß, Johannes:</u> politischer Wandel, Soziologie, Sozialwissenschaft, Marxismus-Leninismus, politische Linke, Wiedervereinigung, DDR, Bundesrepublik Deutschland, neue Bundesländer

<u>Meier, Artur:</u> politischer Wandel, Soziologie, Sozialwissenschaft, realer Sozialismus, Ständestaat, Wiedervereinigung, DDR, Bundesrepublik Deutschland, neue Bundesländer, sozialer Wandel

<u>Offe, Claus:</u> politischer Wandel, sozialer Wandel, Wertorientierung, Einstellung, Modernisierung, Wiedervereinigung, DDR, Bundesrepublik Deutschland, neue Bundesländer

<u>Mayer, Karl Ulrich:</u> soziale Ungleichheit, Lebenslauf, Institution, Ausbildung, Berufsstruktur, Arbeitsmarkt, Familie, Lebensweise, wirtschaftliche Lage, neue Bundesländer, Wiedervereinigung, soziale Folgen, Bundesrepublik Deutschland

<u>Weymann, Ansgar:</u> sozialer Wandel, Soziologie, Sozialwissenschaft, politischer Wandel, Wissenssoziologie, Wiedervereinigung, DDR, Bundesrepublik Deutschland, neue Bundesländer, Alltagswissen

<u>Zapf, Wolfgang:</u> politischer Wandel, Soziologie, Paradigma, Modernisierung, sozialer Wandel, Wiedervereinigung, DDR, Bundesrepublik Deutschland, neue Bundesländer

<u>Giesen, Bernhard:</u> politischer Wandel, Soziologie, Politikwissenschaft, Sozialwissenschaft, Wiedervereinigung, DDR, Bundesrepublik Deutschland, neue Bundesländer
[...]

Figure 15–2   Hypertext display for the author Claus Leggewie provided by AKCESS (adapted with permission from Mutschke [2000])

If users get their retrieval results from databases in the form of TMs, it would be possible to rework them and then store them as their search profiles (relevance models) on the server side. This structure is much more powerful than current profiles in selective dissemination of information and information filtering (or any personalized profile system). This in turn should allow us to explore the potential of TMs in user modeling: TM-structured user profiles allow better adaptation and filtering services. The semantic markup in TMs permits much more sophisticated heuristic searching and relevance ranking strategies. Personal agents (assistants) could aid in the adapted presentation of TMs.

Finally, summarizing agents (such as SummIT [Endres-Niggemeyer 2000]) working on conceptual structures might process the TM format in addition to low-level document markup.

Summary

In this quite lengthy chapter, I have looked into some aspects of KOxTM from both sides and have tried to depict KO as a use case for TMs from a theoretical and an (almost) practical side. Let me recapitulate here what we have gained. Both fields (as well as the KR community and the ontologists) have come much closer together since we discussed the idea of this book at XML Europe 2000 in Paris. I am already happy even if this chapter is useful only for the citations and joint discussion it provides.

The following questions formed the background of this exploration.

1. How can we, with principled KO, prepare for better semantic interoperability between independently authored TMs and between independently operated PSI registries?
2. How could TM-based services alleviate pressing KO problems, in particular, how to reorganize, enhance, and semantically integrate heterogeneous subject data? (And as a specialization of this question: Which effect does TM technology have on KO quality in general? In particular: Which areas might bring qualitative progress, for example, flexible indexing views, scope filtering, semantic retrieval?)

As a preliminary answer to the first question, I suggest research into conceptology, facet analysis, and ontology design (or thesaurus construction) since much fruitful knowledge is still hidden. Because scoping is so crucial for TMs, a scoping theory must take KO research into account. I also suggest searching for an appropriate PSI registry architecture to prevent an unnecessarily scattered multitude of entries (or even registries).

Concerning the second question: TM-based services are of high value where KO products are to be put to use in interactive online environments. Grounding in discourse and implementation of views and relevance reasons, together with sound ontological design, are key factors to semantic interoperability. Formal models can help us record our insights and draw certain conclusions. I see their application in consistency checking and relation mining. TMs can help improve the quality of KO products. While in principle a good knowledge structure is a prerequisite for a sensible TM visualization, I expect TM visualization[156] to have two positive effects: (1) users can search and browse with more ease in conceptual structures, thus we hopefully push the frontiers in conceptual navigation a bit farther [Veltman 1997]; and (2) TM-based visualization promises a better overview over the indexing language.[157] Such a visualization should increase indexing quality and consistency.

We are interested in building knowledge repositories to augment and propel human inquiry and understanding, based on the composition of knowledge units or building blocks (assumed to exist) into complex knowledge structures. If it is possible to accommodate sophisticated KR into TMs, then it should be possible to model knowledge in TMs.[158] It is clear that TMs cannot be the hammer for every nail, but they are an important step towards a "truly" semantic Web.

Acknowledgments

This chapter would not have been possible without the open exchange and inspiration I experienced in the TM and KO communities, where I was given the opportunity to learn much! Foremost I thank Steve Pepper for drawing me into this hospitable TM community. My encounters and exchanges with Jack Park have been invaluable. In addition to the suggestions from the reviewers, I received helpful comments from Michel Biezunski, Manfred Bonitz, Ingetraut Dahlberg, Gerhard Dirmoser, Elizabeth H. Dow, Robert Fugmann, Sam Hunting, Peter Jaenecke, Eduard Jacob, Gerry McKiernan, Peter Mutschke, Günther Neher, and Winfried Schmitz-Esser.

---

[156]A related field that might inspire TM cartography and visualization is conceptual Internet cartography. A prominent representative is Martin Dodge; see *http://www.cypergeography.org*, *http://www.mappingcyberspace.com*, and *http://www.casa.ucl.ac.uk/martin/isocnl/isoc_presentation.ppt*.

[157]See, for example, Ross [2000] on three-dimensional indexing and concept mapping, particularly Figure 3, and the innovative application of this concept for MacMillan's *Encyclopedia of Life Sciences*.

[158]In the sense of Jaenecke's idea [2001] to formulate scientific theories with building blocks.

Selected Abbreviations

ACL—Agent Communication Language

AI—artificial intelligence

ASIS&T—American Society for Information Science and Technology (*http://www.asis.org*)

BBK/LBC—Bibliothekarische-Bibliographische Klassifikation/Library-Bibliographical Classification

BIOSIS—not-for-profit organization, established in 1926; fosters the growth, communication, and use of biological knowledge for the common good (*http://www.biosis.org*)

Bliss—Bliss Classification

CG—Conceptual Graphs, by John F. Sowa (*http://www.jfsowa.com/cg/cgstand.htm*)

CKML—Conceptual Knowledge Markup Language

CLF—Concept Language Formalism, proposed by Prof. Gerhard Rahmstorf

Colon—Colon Classification, by S. R. Ranganathan and followers

DAML+OIL—DARPA Agent Markup Language + Ontology Inference Layer

DC—Dublin Core (metadata)

DDC—Dewey Decimal Classification, by Melvil Dewey, first published in 1876

DL—Digital Library

DML—Discourse Markup Language

DMOZ—DMOZ open directory project (*http://www.dmoz.org*)

DTD—Document Type Definition

ECAI— European Conference on Artificial Intelligence

FAQ—frequently asked and answered questions

FID—International Federation for Documentation (no longer exists)

HTML—Hypertext Markup Language

ICC—International (Information) Coding and Classification System, developed by Dr. Ingetraut Dahlberg

IDL/CORBA—Interface Definition Language/Common Object Request Broker Architecture

IEC—International Electrotechnical Commission (*http://www.iec.ch/*)

IFS—mnemonic for Identity, Facet, Scope [Pepper 2002; Rath and Pepper 2000]

IR—information retrieval

IRS—information retrieval system

IS—information science

ISKO—International Society for Knowledge Organization (*http://www.isko.org/*)

ISO—International Organization for Standardization (*http://www.iso.ch/*)

IT—information technology

KIF/KQML—Knowledge Interchange Format/Knowledge Query and Manipulation Language (*http://www.cs.umbc.edu/kqml/*)

KM—knowledge management

KO—knowledge organization

KO—Knowledge Organization journal (formerly *International Classification*); official quarterly journal of ISKO, devoted to concept theory, classification, indexing, and knowledge representation (*http://www.ergon-verlag.de/contents/06ainfobibl.htm*)

KOS—knowledge organization system (for example, classification schedule, thesaurus, ontology)

KOxTM—intellectual crossover between KO and TMs

KR—knowledge representation (AI area)

LCC—Library of Congress Classification

LCSH—Library of Congress Subject Headings

LIS—library and information science

MeSH—Medical Subject Headings

NKOS—Networked Knowledge Organization System(s)/Service(s)

OHS—Open Hypertext System

OIL—Ontology Inference Layer

OML—Ontology Markup Language

PMEST—citation order of facets in Colon Classification (Personality, Matter, Energy, Space, Time)

PSI—Published Subject Indicator in XTM; was Public Subject Identifier in ISO/IEC 13250 (see working group at *http://lists.oasis-open.org/archives/tm-pubsubj/*)

PURL—Persistent URL

RDF—Resource Description Framework

RDFS—Resource Description Framework Schema

RST—Rhetorical Structure Theory

RVK—Regensburger Verbundklassifikation (*http://www.bibliothek.uni-regensburg. de/Systematik/systemat.html*)

SHOE—Simple HTML Ontology Extension

SIG/CR—Special Interest Group on Classification Research (*http://www.asis. org/AboutASIS/asis-sigs.html#SIGCR*)

SOAP—Simple Object Access Protocol (*http://www.w3.org/TR/SOAP/*)

TAO—mnemonic for Topic, Association, Occurrence [Pepper 2002; Rath and Pepper 2000]

TM—topic map

TMCL—Topic Map Constraint Language

TMQL—Topic Map Query Language (see working group at *http://groups. yahoo.com/group/tmql-wg/*)

TREC—Text Retrieval Electronic Conference (*http://trec.nist.gov*)

UDC—Universal Decimal Classification (first published in 1899 by Otlet and Lafontaine)

UKL—Unified Knowledge Language

URI—Uniform Resource Identifier

URN—Uniform Resource Name

XML—Extensible Markup Language

XSLT—Extensible Stylesheet Language Transformations

XTM—XML Topic Maps (*http://www.topicmaps.org*)

References

Ahmed, Kal, et al. 2001. *Professional XML Meta Data*. Chicago: Wrox.

Aitchison, Jean. 1969. *Thesaurofacet: A Thesaurus and Faceted Classification for Engineering and Related Subjects*. Whetstone, Leicester, England: The English Electric Company, Ltd.

Aitchison, Jean, Alan Gilchrist, and David Bawden. 2001. *Thesaurus Construction and Use: A Practical Manual*. 4th ed. Chicago: Fitzroy Dearborn.

Albrechtsen, Hanne, and Örnager, Susanne, eds. 1994. *Knowledge Organization and Quality Management. Third International ISKO Conference, Copenhagen, Denmark, June 20–24, 1994*. Frankfurt, Germany: INDEKS.

Altheim, Murray. 2001a. E-mail on February 15 to xtm-wg discussion list. Accessed in October 2001 at *http://lists.oasis-open.org/archives/topicmaps-comment/200102/msg00137. html*.

———. 2001b. The Upper Cyc Ontology in XTM. Sun Microsystems Technical Report February 28 (a "work in progress"). Accessed in October 2001 at *http:// www.doctypes.org/cyc/cyc-xtm-20010227.html*.

Amann, Bernd, and Irini Fundulaki. 1999. Integrating Ontologies and Thesauri to Build RDF Schemas. In *Proceedings of the Third European Conference for Digital Libraries (ECDL) '99: Research and Advanced Technologies for Digital Libraries, Bibliotheque Nationale de France, Paris, France, September 1999*. Accessed in April 2002 at *http://cedric.cnam.fr/ PUBLIS/RC14.pdf*.

Amann, Bernd, Irini Fundulaki, and Michel Scholl. 2000. Integrating Ontologies and Thesauri for RDF Schema Creation and Metadata Querying. *International Journal of Digital Libraries* 3(3):221–236. Also available at *http://link.springer.de/link/service/ journals/00799/bibs/0003003/00030221.htm*.

Anderson, James D. 1997. Organization of Knowledge. In *International Encyclopedia of Information and Library Science*; John Feather and Paul Sturges, eds. New York: Routledge, pp. 336–353.

Barité, Mario. 2000a. *Diccionario de Organización y Representación del conocimiento: Clasificación, Indización, Terminología*. (Electronic edition of a book published in 1997, the first edition under the title *Glosario Sobre Organización y Representación del Conocimiento. Clasificación. Indización. Terminología*.) Accessed in April 2002 at *http:// www.eubca.edu.uy/diccionario/*.

———. 2000b. The Notion of "Category": Its Implications in Subject Analysis and in the Construction and Evaluation of Indexing Languages. *KO* 27(1–2):4–10.

Barth, R. 1996. 5000 Jahre Bibliotheken—eine Geschichte ihrer Benutzer, Bestände und Architektur [5,000 years of libraries, a history of their usage, holdings, and architecture, in German]. Lecture/course held October 24 through December 19, 1996. Accessed in October 2001 at *http://www.stub.unibe.ch/stub/vorl96/*.

Bartolo, Laura M., and Antonette M. Trimble. 2000. Heterogeneous Structures Project Database: Vocabulary Mapping within a Multidisciplinary, Multi-institutional Research Group. In *Dynamism and Stability in Knowledge Organization. Proceedings of the 6th International ISKO Conference, July 10–13, 2000, Toronto, Canada*; C. Beghtol et al., eds. Würzburg: Ergon, pp. 118–123.

Barwise, K. J., and J. Seligman. 1997. Information Flow: The Logic of Distributed Systems. Cambridge University Tracts in Theoretical Computer Science 44.

Bateman, J. A. 1990. Upper Modeling: Organizing Knowledge for Natural Language Processing. Paper presented at the 5th International Workshop on Natural Language Generation, June 3–6, 1990, Pittsburgh, PA. Accessed in May 2002 at *http://www.darmstadt.gmd.de/publish/komet/papers/general-description.ps*.

Beghtol, C., Lynne C. Howarth, and Nancy J. Williamson, eds. 2000. *Dynamism and Stability in Knowledge Organization. Proceedings of the 6th International ISKO Conference, July 10–13, 2000, Toronto, Canada*. Würzburg: Ergon.

Best, Karl F. 2001. Human Markup Language (HumanML). Message on February 7, 2001, to xml-dev@lists.xml.org containing the initial announcement and call for support for HumanML by Ranjeeth Kumar Thunga. For the discussion list, see *http://lists.oasis-open.org/archives/humanmarkup-comment*. For the HumanML home page, see *http://www.humanmarkup.org/*.

Blackler, Frank. 1995. (Abstract.) Knowledge, Knowledge Work and Organizations: An Overview and Interpretation. *Organization Studies* 16(6):1021–1046. Abstract accessed in October 2001 at *http://www.uts.edu.au/fac/hss/Departments/DIS/km/Papers.htm#Blackl95*. A version of the paper appears in *Strategic Management of Intellectual Capital and Organizational Knowledge*; Nick Bontis and Chun Wei Choo, eds. Oxford University Press, 2002.

Bliss, Henry Evelyn. 1933 (2nd ed. 1939). *The Organization of Knowledge in Libraries and the Subject Approach to Books*. New York: H.W. Wilson. Facsimile available from University Microfilms International (Ann Arbor, MI).

———. 1929. *The Organization of Knowledge and the System of the Sciences*. New York: Henry Holt.

Boley, Harold, Stefan Decker, and Michael Sintek. 2000. Tutorial on Knowledge Markup Techniques at ECAI 2000. Accessed in October 2001 at *http://www.semanticweb.org/knowmarktutorial/*.

Brachman, R. J., and J. G. Schmolze. 1985. An Overview of the KL-ONE Knowledge Representation System. *Cognitive Science* 9:171–216.

Bruza, P. D., and T. W. C. Huibers. 1996. A Study of Aboutness in Information Retrieval. *Artificial Intelligence Review* 10:1–27. (Special issue on AI and IR.)

Burchill, Charles, et al. 2000. Organizing the Present, Looking to the Future: An Online Knowledge Repository to Facilitate Collaboration. *Journal of Medical Internet Research (JMIR)* 2(2):e10. Also available at *http://www.jmir.org/2000/2/e10/*.

Campbell, Grant. 2000. The Relevance of Traditional Classification Principles to the Development and Use of Semantic Markup Languages for Electronic Text. In *Dynamism and Stability in Knowledge Organization. Proceedings of the 6th International ISKO Conference, July 10–13, 2000, Toronto, Canada;* C. Beghtol et al., eds. Würzburg: Ergon, pp. 345–351.

Capurro, Rafael. 2000a. Grundfragen des Wissensmanagements. Accessed in October 2001 at *http://v.hbi-stuttgart.de/WM/bausteine.htm*.

———. 2000b. Hermeneutics and the Phenomenon of Information. In *Metaphysics, Epistemology, and Technology* (Research in Philosophy and Technology, vol. 19); Carl Mitcham, ed. JAI/Elsevier, pp. 79–85.

———. 1997. Stable Knowledge. Paper presented at the workshop Knowledge for the Future—Wissen für die Zukunft, Brandenburgische Technische Universität Cottbus, Zentrum für Technik und Gesellschaft, March 19–21, 1997. Proceedings edited by K. Kornwachs; accessed in October 2001 at *http://www.capurro.de/cottbus.htm*.

———. 1986/1989. *Hermeneutik der Fachinformation.* Freiburg/München: Karl Alber, 1986. Also accepted as Habilitation Thesis at University of Stuttgart, 1989. See excerpts (in German) at *http://www.capurro.de/hermeneu.html*.

Clark, P., J. Thompson, H. Holmback, and L. Duncan. 2000. Exploiting a Thesaurus-Based Semantic Net for Knowledge-Based Search. In *Proceedings of the 12th Conference on Innovative Applications of AI (AAAI/IAAI '2000)*, pp. 988–995. Accessed in May 2002 at *http://www.cs.utexas.edu/users/pclark/papers/iaai00.pdf*, with slides at *http://www.cs.utexas.edu/users/pclark/presentations/iaai00/*.

Connolly, Daniel W. 2001. Building Ontologies with RDF and DAML+OIL. Paper presented at WWW10, May 2001, Hong Kong. Accessed in October 2001 at *http://www.w3.org/2001/Talks/05www10-swfig/all*.

———. 1995. Essential Elements of an Open Hyperdocument System. Accessed in October 2001 at *http://www.w3.org/People/Connolly/technologies/ioh.html*.

Cooper, William S. 1978. Indexing Documents by Gedanken Experimentation. *Journal of the American Society for Information Science* 29(3):107–119.

Corazzon, Raul, ed. 2000–2002. Descriptive and Formal Ontology. [The development of ontology from philosophy to knowledge engineering.] Accessed in April 2002 at *http://www.formalontology.it/*.

Craven, Timothy. 1997–2002. Introductory Tutorial on Thesaurus Construction. Accessed in April 2002 at *http://instruct.uwo.ca/gplis/677/thesaur/main00.htm*.

Dahlberg, Ingetraut. 1998. Wissenorganisation. In *Lexikon der Informatik und Daten-verarbeitung*, 4th updated and extended ed.; Hans-Jochen Schneider, ed. München: Oldenbourg, pp. 966–967.

———. 1996a. Library Catalogs in the Internet: Switching for Future Subject Access. In *Knowledge Organization and Change. Proceedings of the 4th International ISKO Conference, July 15–18, 1996, Washington, DC*; Rebecca Green, ed. Frankfurt/Main: INDEKS, pp. 155–164.

———. 1996b. Zur 'Begriffskultur' in den Sozialwissenschaften: Lassen sich ihre Probleme lösen? *Ethik und Sozialwissenschaften, Streitforum für Erwägungskultur* 7(1). See the table of contents for the journal at *http://iug.uni-paderborn.de/eus/Inhaltsverzeichnisse/Jahrgang07.html*.

———. 1995. Conceptual Structures and Systematization. *IFID Journal (International Forum on Information and Documentation)* 20(3):9–24.

———. 1994. Domain Interaction: Theory and Practice. In *Knowledge Organization and Quality Management. Third International ISKO Conference, Copenhagen, Denmark, June 20–24, 1994*; Hanne Albrechtsen and Susanne Örnager, eds. Frankfurt, Germany: INDEKS, pp. 60–71.

———. 1993. Knowledge Organization: Its Scope and Possibilities. *KO* 20(4):211–222.

———, comp. and ed. 1985. *Classification and Indexing Systems: Theory, Structure, Methodology; 1950–1982.* (International Classification and Indexing Bibliography, vol. 3.) Frankfurt/Main: INDEKS.

———, comp. and ed. 1984. *Reference Tools and Conferences in Classification and Indexing.* (International Classification and Indexing Bibliography, vol. 2.) Frankfurt/Main: INDEKS.

———, comp. 1982a. *Classification Systems and Thesauri: 1950–1982.* (International Classification and Indexing Bibliography, vol. 1.) Frankfurt/Main: INDEKS.

———. 1982b. ICC—Information Coding Classification—Principles, Structure and Application Possibilities. *International Classification* 9(2):87–93, 107–113.

———. 1978a. *Ontical Structures and Universal Classification.* Bangalore: Sarada Ranganathan Endowment for Library Science.

———. 1978b. A Referent-Oriented, Analytical Concept Theory for INTERCONCEPT. *International Classification* 5(3):142–151.

———. 1974. Grundlagen universaler Wissensordnung. Probleme und Möglichkeiten eines universalen Klassifikationssystems des Wissens. (DGD Schriftenreihe, vol. 3.) [Fundamentals of universal organization of knowledge. Problems of and possibilities for a universal classification system of knowledge, in German. For an English summary see her p. ix and x.] Pullach bei München: Verlag Dokumentation.

Delgado R., Joaquin A. 2000. Agent-Based Information Filtering and Recommender Systems on the Internet. Ph.D. thesis, Nagoya Institute of Technology, Department of Intelligence and Computer Science. March 2000. Accessed in October 2001 at *http://www-ishii.ics.nitech.ac.jp/~jdelgado/Thesis.pdf.*

Dimitrov, Marin. 2000. XML Standards for Ontology Exchange. Paper presented at OntoLex 2000: Ontologies and Lexical Knowledge Bases, Sozopol, September 8–10, 2000. Accessed in May 2002 at *http://www.sirma.bg/OntoText/publications/ontoxml.pdf.*

Dirmoser, Gerhard, and Boris Nieslony. 2001. Performative Ansätze in Kunst und Wissenschaft am Beispiel Performance Art. Presentation at 7th Performance Studies Conference PSI7, Mainz, Germany, March 29–April 1, 2001. Accessed in October 2001 at *http://www.nyu.edu/pages/psi/PSi7.html.*

————. 2000. 32 Sichten auf den "Performative Turn" [32 views upon the "performative turn," in German]. In *Kunst ohne Werk. Die Transformation der Kunst vom Werkhaften zum Performativen. Kunstforum International, Bd. 152, Okt.-Dez. 2000*; Paolo Bianchi, ed. Ruppichteroth: Kunstforum-Leserservice, pp. 64 ff. Also available at *http://www.kunstforum.de/zeitmodelle/archiv/iv/index152.htm.*

El Hadi, Widad Mustafa, Jacques Manize, and Steven A. Pollitt, eds. 1998. *Structures and Relations in Knowledge Organization. Proceedings of the 5th International ISKO Conference, Lille, France, 25–29 August 1998.* Würzburg: Ergon.

Endres-Niggemeyer, Brigitte. 2000. Empirical Methods for Ontology Engineering in Bone Marrow Transplantation. In *Globalisierung und Wissenorganisation: Neue Aspekte für Wissen, Wissenschaft und Informationssysteme*; H. Peter Ohly et al., eds. Würzburg: Ergon Verlag, pp. 335–341. See also the Summit-BMT (Summarize It in Bone Marrow Transplantation) Project home page at *http://summit-bmt.fh-hannover.de/.*

————. 1998. *Summarizing Information.* Berlin: Springer.

Endres-Niggemeyer, Brigitte, Kirsten Nax, and Michaela Storp. 1994. Ideenskizze eines dynamisch konfigurierbaren elektronischen Thesaurus am Beispiel der Sozialwissenschaften [Idea outline of a dynamically configurable electronic thesaurus, exemplified for the social sciences, in German]. In *Procs. Deutscher Dokumentartag 1994.*; Wolfram Neubauer, ed. Frankfurt/Main: DGD, pp. 327–337.

Engelbart, Douglas C. 1990. Knowledge-Domain Interoperability and an Open Hyperdocument System, June 1990. Accessed in October 2001 at *http://www.bootstrap.org/institute/augdocs/augment-132082.htm.*

Etzioni, Oren, and D. Weld. 1994. A Softbot-Based Interface to the Internet. *Communications of the ACM* 37(7):72–76. Also available at *http://www.cs.washington.edu/homes/etzioni/papers/cacm.pdf.*

Farradane, Jason. 1980. Relational Indexing (Parts I and II). *Journal of Information Science* 1(5):267–276, 313–324.

————. 1977. *String Indexing: Relational Indexing: Introduction and Indexing.* London, Ontario: School of Library and Information Science, University of Western Ontario.

————. 1967. Relational Indexing. *Information Storage and Retrieval* 3:296–314.

Fensel, Dieter, Jim Hendler, Henry Lieberman, and Wolfgang Wahlster. 2000. Dagstuhl-Seminar: Semantics for the WWW. Report accessed in October 2001 at *ftp://ftp.dagstuhl.de/pub/Reports/00/00121.pdf.gz.* See also seminar at Dagstuhl Castle, March 19–24, 2000, Seminar No. 00121, Report No. 269, at *http://www.aifb. uni-karlsruhe.de/WBS/dfe/dagstuhl.html.*

Fischer, Dietrich H. 1998. From Thesauri Towards Ontologies? In *Structures and Relations in Knowledge Organization. Proceedings of the 5th International ISKO Conference, Lille, France, 25–29 August 1998*; Widad Mustafa El Hadi et al., eds. Würzburg: Ergon, pp. 18–30.

Freese, Eric. 2000. Inferring Knowledge from Topic Map–Based Semantic Networks. *In XML 2000 Conference Proceedings, December 3–8, 2000.* Washington, DC: GCA.

Fugmann, Robert. 1999. *Inhaltserschließung durch Indexieren: Prinzipien und Praxis* [Subject analysis and representation by indexing: principles and practice, in German]. Frankfurt/Main: Deutsche Gesellschaft für Dokumentation (DGD).

————. 1993. *Subject Analysis and Indexing. Theoretical Foundation and Practical Advice.* (Textbooks for Knowledge Organization, vol. 1.) Frankfurt, Germany: INDEKS.

————. 1991. The Navigational Index. *International Classification* 19(2):122–132. (Published together with explanations. Unfortunately, this version is seriously flawed because of an indentation error. See correction sheet p. 127 and online version, *http://index.bonn.iz-soz.de/~sigel/ISKO/KO-Darmstadt90-Index/.*)

————, ed. 1990. *Proceedings of the 1st International ISKO Conference, Tools for Knowledge Organization and the Human Interface. Darmstadt, 14–17 August 1990.* Frankfurt/Main: INDEKS.

————. 1985. The Five-Axiom Theory of Indexing and Information Supply. *Journal of the American Society for Information Science* 36(2):116–129.

Ganter, B., and G. Mineau, eds. 2000. Conceptual Structures: Logical, Linguistic, and Computational Issues. Lecture Notes in Artificial Intelligence 1867. Berlin-Heidelberg: Springer.

Garfield, Eugene. 1994. Linking Literatures: An Intriguing Use of the Citation Index. *Current Contents* print editions May 23, 1994. Accessed in October 2001 at *http://www.isinet.com/isi/hot/essays/useofcitationdatabases/6.html.*

Gerick, Thomas. 2000. Topic Maps—der neue Standard für intelligentes Knowledge Retrieval. Wissensmanagement, Heft 2, März 2000. Accessed in October 2001 at *http://www.usu.de/Produkte/Download/uwe/Wissensmanagement.pdf.*

Godby, Jean, Eric Miller, and Ray Reighard. 1999. Automatically Generated Topic Maps of World Wide Web Resources. Demonstration in June 1999 at ACL 1999. Accessed in October 2001 at *http://orc.dev.oclc.org:5061/papers/acl_demo.html*.

Green, Rebecca. 2000a. Automated Identification of Frame Semantic Relational Structures. In *Dynamism and Stability in Knowledge Organization. Proceedings of the 6th International ISKO Conference, July 10–13, 2000, Toronto, Canada;* C. Beghtol et al., eds. Würzburg: Ergon, pp. 193–199.

———. 2000b. Two Recurring Themes: Universality and Clustering. *KO* 27(1–2): 55–58.

———. 1998. Personal communication, August 29. Based on a list of questions asked during the opening panel discussing the general theme Structures and Relations in Knowledge Organization at ISKO 1998.

———. 1997. The Role of Relational Structures in Indexing for the Humanities. *KO* 24(3):72–83.

———, ed. 1996a. *Knowledge Organization and Change. Proceedings of the 4th International ISKO Conference, July 15–18, 1996, Washington, DC.* Frankfurt/Main: INDEKS.

———. 1996b. A Relational Thesaurus: Modeling Semantic Relationships Using Frames. Accessed in October 2001 at *http://www.oclc.org/research/publications/arr/1996/green.htm*.

———. 1989. The Expression of Syntagmatic Relationships in Frame-Based Indexing. Ph.D. thesis for University of Maryland College Park. Accessed in April 2002 at *http://www.clis.umd.edu/students/dissertations/green.html*.

Greisdorf, Howard. 2000. Relevance: An Interdisciplinary and Information Science Perspective. *Informing Science* 3(2):67–72 (Special Issue on Information Science Research). Also available at *http://informingscience.com/Articles/Vol3/v3n2p67-72.pdf*.

Grey, Denham. 2001. Re: Working ontologies. E-mail posted February 9 to the e-mail discussion group *kmci-Virtual-Chapter@yahoogroups.com*, quoted by Bernard Vatant the same day in an e-mail to the e-mail discussion group

xtm-wg@yahoogroups.com. Archive accessed in April 2002 at *http://lists.oasis-open.org/archives/topicmaps-comment/200102/msg00098.html*.

Guarino, Nicola, and Chris Velty. 2000. Tutorial on Conceptual Modeling and Ontological Analysis. Presented at AAAI-2000. Accessed in October 2001 at *http://www.cs.vassar.edu/faculty/welty/aaai-2000/*.

Heflin, Jeff, and James Hendler. 2000. Semantic Interoperability on the Web. Presentation at Extreme Markup Languages, Montreal. Accessed in October 2001 at *http://www.cs.umd.edu/projects/plus/SHOE/pubs/extreme2000.pdf*. See also their Dynamic Ontologies on the Web at *http://www.cs.umd.edu/projects/plus/SHOE/pubs/aaai2000.ps*.

Henrichs, Norbert. 1970. Philosophische Dokumentation: Literatur-Dokumentation ohne strukturierten Thesaurus. *Nachrichten für Dokumentation* 21(1):20–25.

Hirsch, Sven. 2000. Aspekte der Entwicklung von Fachinformationssystemen auf der Basis von XML/RDF [Aspects of the development of information systems based on XML/RDF, in German]. *nfd Information—Wissenschaft und Praxis* 51(2):75–82.

Hjørland, Birger. 2001. Towards a Theory of Aboutness, Subject, Topicality, Theme, Domain, Field, Content . . . and Relevance. *Journal of the American Society for Information Science and Technology* 52(9):774–778.

———. 2000. Relevance Research: The Missing Perspective(s): "Non-Relevance" and "Epistemological Relevance." *Journal of the American Society for Information Science* 51(2):209–211 (letter to the editor).

———. 1997. *Information Seeking and Subject Representation: An Activity-Theoretical Approach to Information Science.* Westport, Connecticut: Greenwood.

———. 1994. Nine Principles of Knowledge Organization. In *Knowledge Organization and Quality Management. Third International ISKO Conference, Copenhagen, Denmark, June 20–24, 1994*; Hanne Albrechtsen and Susanne Örnager, eds. Frankfurt, Germany: INDEKS, pp. 91–100.

Hjørland, Birger, and Hanne Albrechtsen. 1995. Toward a New Horizon in Information Science: Domain Analysis. *Journal of the American Society for Information Science* 46(6):400–425. See also subsequent discussion in letters to the editor; table of contents available at *http://bubl.ac.uk/journals/lis/fj/jasis/v46n0695.htm*.

Hodge, Gail. 2000a. NKOS Group Reviews Draft DTD for Thesauri. *D-Lib Magazine* 6(12). Accessed in October 2001 at *http://www.dlib.org/dlib/december00/12inbrief.html#HODGE*.

———. 2000b. Systems of Knowledge Organization for Digital Libraries: Beyond Traditional Authority Files. Accessed in October 2001 at *http://www.clir.org/pubs/abstract/pub91abst.html*. See also *http://nkos.slis.kent.edu/KOS_taxonomy.htm*.

Hovy, E. H. 1990. Parsimonious and Profligate Approaches to the Question of Discourse Structure Relations. In *Proceedings of the 5th International Workshop on Natural Language Generation, Pittsburgh, PA*, pp. 128–136.

Howarth, Lynne C. 2000. Designing a "Human Understandable" Metalevel Ontology for Enhancing Resource Discovery in Knowledge Bases. In *Dynamism and Stability in Knowledge Organization. Proceedings of the 6th International ISKO Conference, July 10–13, 2000, Toronto, Canada*; C. Beghtol et al., eds. Würzburg: Ergon, pp. 391–397.

Hunter, Jane. 2001. MetaNet: A Metadata Term Thesaurus to Enable Semantic Interoperability between Metadata Domains. Accessed in October 2001 at *http://jodi.ecs.soton.ac.uk/Articles/v01/i08/Hunter/* and *http://archive.dstc.edu.au/RDU/staff/jane-hunter/harmony/jodi_article.html*. See also Results of the Harmony project at *http://www.*

ilrt.bris.ac.uk/discovery/harmony/project_results.htm and ABC draft (ABC: A Logical Model for Metadata Interoperability) at *http://www.ilrt.bris.ac.uk/discovery/harmony/docs/abc/abc_draft.html.*

IJCAI. 1999. IJCAI Workshop on Intelligent Information Integration (III'99). Accessed in October 2001 at *http://www.aifb.uni-karlsruhe.de/WBS/dfe/iii99.html.* Summary available at *ftp://ftp.aifb.uni-karlsruhe.de/pub/mike/dfe/spool/iii99.pdf.*

Institute for Scientific Information. 1981. *ISI Atlas of Science: Biochemistry and Molecular Biology.* Philadelphia, PA: Institute for Scientific Information. See also volumes on animal and plant sciences and immunology.

ISKO, Polish Librarians Association, and Society for Professional Information. 1996. *Compatibility and Integration of Order Systems. Proceedings of the Research Seminar TIP/ISKO Meeting, Warsaw, 13–15 September 1995.* Warszawa: SBP.

ISO. 1999. 01.140.20 Information Sciences: Including Documentation, Librarianship and Archive Systems. Accessed in April 2002 at *http://www.dfmg.com.tw/member/standard/iso/0114020.html.* (This page is a compilation of relevant standards in information science, part of a larger grouping of ISO standards by specialties/fields. See, for example, Standard 2788 of 1986 [ISO 2788:1986 Documentation—Guidelines for the Establishment and Development of Monolingual Thesauri] at *http://www.dfmg.com.tw/member/standard/iso/d7776.html#0* and Standard 5964 of 1985 [ISO 5964:1985 Documentation—Guidelines for the Establishment and Development of Multilingual Thesauri] at *http://www.dfmg.com.tw/member/standard/iso/d12159.html#0.*)

Iyer, Hemalata. 1995. *Classificatory Structures: Concepts, Relations and Representation.* (Textbooks for Knowledge Organization, vol. 2.) Frankfurt/Main: INDEKS.

Jacob, Elin K. 2000. The Legacy of Pragmatism: Implications for Knowledge Organization in a Pluralistic Universe. In *Dynamism and Stability in Knowledge Organization. Proceedings of the 6th International ISKO Conference, July 10–13, 2000, Toronto, Canada*; C. Beghtol et al., eds. Würzburg: Ergon, pp. 16–22.

Jaenecke, Peter. 2002. Wissensdarstellung bei Leibniz. In *Leibniz und die Gegenwart*; F. Hermanni and H. Breger, eds. München: Wilhelm Fink Verlag, pp. 89–118.

———. 2001. On the Structure of a Global Knowledge Space. Presentation at V Congreso ISKO, "Representación y Organización del Conocimiento: metodologías, modelos y aplicaciones" (in Spanish), April 25–27, 2001, Alcalá de Henares, Madrid, Spain. (Draft provided by personal communication.)

———. 2000a. Ist 'Wissen' ein definierbarer Begriff. In *Globalisierung und Wissenorganisation: Neue Aspekte für Wissen, Wissenschaft und Informationssysteme*; H. Peter Ohly et al., eds. Würzburg: Ergon Verlag, pp. 67–82.

———. 2000b. Wissensbausteine [Knowledge modules/building blocks, in German]. Presentation on September 25, 2000, at Mit Information zum Wissen—Durch Wissen zur Information. Symposion Wolfenbüttel, 25./26. September 2000. (Transparencies provided by personal communication.)

———. 1996. Elementary Principles for Representing Knowledge. *KO* 23(2):88–102 (Leibniz Special Issue).

———. 1994. To What End Knowledge Organization? *KO* 21(1):3–11. (English translation of the talk Wozu Wissensorganisation presented at ISKO Germany 3 Weilburg, 1993; see also *http://www.bonn.iz-soz.de/wiss-org/jaenecke0.htm.*)

Kamps, Thomas. 2000. Wissensnetze als Langzeitgedächtnis [Knowledge networks as long-term memory, in German]. Wissensmanagement, Heft 6, November 2000. Accessed in October 2001 at *http://www.wissensmanagement.net/online/archiv/2001/12_0101/wissensnetz.htm.* See also the Flash demos at *http://www.i-views.de/web/.*

Katholische Universität Eichstätt. 1998. Lehrstuhl für Angewandte Informatik. Skript zur Vorlesung Angewandte Informatik I. WS 1998/99. Abschnitt 7: Terminologische Logik (nach Nebel 1990, Mac Gregor 1991, Brachman et al. 1991). Accessed in October 2001 at *http://mathsrv.ku-eichstaett.de/MGF/informatik/angeinfo/terlog/terminlo.htm.*

Kent, Robert E. 2000. The Information Flow Foundation for Conceptual Knowledge Organization. In *Dynamism and Stability in Knowledge Organization. Proceedings of the 6th International ISKO Conference, July 10–13, 2000, Toronto, Canada;* C. Beghtol et al., eds. Würzburg: Ergon, pp. 111–117. Full paper available at *http://www.ontologos.org/Papers/ISKO6/ISKO6.pdf;* slides available at *http://www.ontologos.org/Papers/ISKO6/ISKO6.ppt.*

Kiel, Ewald. 1994. Knowledge Organization Needs Epistemological Openness. A Reply to Peter Jaenecke. *KO* 21(3):148–152.

Kiryakov, Atanas, and Kiril Iv. Simov. 2000. Demonstration: Mapping of EuroWordNet Top Ontology into Upper Cyc Ontology. Accessed in October 2001 at *http://demo.ontotext.com/.* Theoretical background: paper presented at the EKAW 2000 workshop Ontologies and Texts; see *http://www.ontotext.com/publications/kiryakovsimov_ekaw.ps.*

KMCI. 2000. KMCI page on standards, including UKL. Accessed in October 2001 at *http://www.kmci.org/Standards/standards.htm.*

Knorz, Gerhard. 2001. Visalisierung von Zusammenhängen. Von der Wissenskarte zur interaktiven graphischen Topic Map. Vortrag 10.5.2001 im Rahmen des 6. Archivwissenschaftlichen Kolloquiums: Online-Findbücher, Suchmaschinen und Portale. Internetanwendungen in Archiven. Marburg. Accessed in October 2001 at *http://www.iud.fh-darmstadt.de/iud/wwwmeth/Publ/vortrag/Marburg2001/paper1.htm.*

KO. 1999. Bibliography 10 Years International Society for Knowledge Organization. *KO* 26(4). See also *http://is.gseis.ucla.edu/orgs/isko/bib.html.*

Kobsa, A., and W. Pohl. 1995. The User Modeling Shell System BGP-MS. *User Modeling and User-Adapted Interaction* 4(2):59–106. Draft available at *http://www.ics.uci.edu/~kobsa/papers/1995-UMUAI-kobsa.ps.*

Koch, Traugott. 2000. Quality-Controlled Subject Gateways: Definitions, Typologies, Empirical Overview. *Online Information Review* 24(1) (Special Issue on Subject Gateways). Also available at *http://www.lub.lu.se/~traugott/OIR-SBIG.txt.*

Koch, Traugott, and Anders Ardö. 2000. Automatic Classification of Full-Text HTML-Documents from One Specific Subject Area. DESIRE II D3.6a, working paper 2. Accessed in October 2001 at *http://www.lub .lu.se/desire/DESIRE36a-WP2.htm.*

Krause, Jürgen. 2000. Integration von Ansätzen neuronaler Netzwerke in die Systemarchitektur von ViBSoz und CARMEN [Integration of neural network approaches into the system architecture of ViBSoz and CARMEN, in German]. IZ-Arbeitsbericht Nr. 21, Oktober 2000. Accessed in October 2001 at *http://www.gesis.org/Publikationen/Berichte/IZ_Arbeitsberichte/pdf/ab_21.pdf.*

———. 1996. Informationserschließung und -bereitstellung zwischen Deregulierung, Kommerzialisierung und weltweiter Vernetzung ("Schalenmodell") [The layered model of information provision, in German]. IZ-Arbeitsbericht Nr. 6, September 1996. Accessed in October 2001 at *http://www.gesis.org/Publikationen/Berichte/IZ_Arbeitsberichte/pdf/ab6.pdf.*

Lancaster, F. W. 1998. *Indexing and Abstracting in Theory and Practice.* University of Illinois Graduate School of Library and Information Science Publications Office.

Leidig, Thorsten. 2000. Technologische Aspekte didaktischer Ontologien [Technology aspects of didactic ontologies, in German]. In *Globalisierung und Wissenorganisation: Neue Aspekte für Wissen, Wissenschaft und Informationssysteme*; H. Peter Ohly et al., eds. Würzburg: Ergon Verlag, pp. 443–450.

Lykke Nielsen, Marianne. 2000. Domain Analysis, an Important Part of Thesaurus Construction. In *11th ASIS&T SIG/CR Classification Research Workshop, Chicago, IL, November 12, 2000*, pp. 9–50. Accessed in October 2001 at *http://uma.info-science.uiowa.edu/sigcr/papers/sigcr00lykke.pdf.*

Mädche, Alexander, and Steffen Staab. 1999. Seminar "Text Mining," Gruppe I: "Ontologiemodellierung und -akquisition." Universität Karlsruhe (TH), Institut für Angewandte Informatik und Formale Beschreibungsverfahren (AIFB), Prof. Dr. Studer. Accessed in October 2001 at *http://www.rz.uni-karlsruhe.de/~uaqk/.*

Mai, Jens-Erik. 2000a. Likeness: A Pragmatic Approach. In *Dynamism and Stability in Knowledge Organization. Proceedings of the 6th International ISKO Conference, July 10–13, 2000, Toronto, Canada*; C. Beghtol et al., eds. Würzburg: Ergon, pp. 23–27.

———. 2000b. Reflections on Papers at the 6th International ISKO Conference. *KO* 27(1–2):58–61.

————. 2000c. The Subject Indexing Process: An Investigation of Problems in Knowledge Representation. Ph.D. thesis at University of Texas, Austin, Graduate School of LIS, supervised by Francis Miksa. Thesis provided by personal communication. Abstract available at *http://www.ischool.washington.edu/mai/abstract.html*.

————. 1999. A Postmodern Theory of Knowledge Organization. In *Knowledge: Creation, Organization and Use. Proceedings of the 62nd ASIS Annual Meeting, October 31 through November 4, 1999.* Vol. 36. Medford, NJ: Information Today, Inc., pp. 547–556.

Maier, David, and Lois M. L. Delcambre. 1999. Superimposed Information for the Internet. WebDB (Informal Proceedings) 1999, pp. 1–9. Accessed in May 2002 at *http://www-rocq.inria.fr/~cluet/WEBDB/maier.pdf*.

Mandl, Thomas. 2001. *Tolerantes Information Retrieval: Neuronale Netze zur Erhöhung der Adaptivität und Flexibilität bei der Informationssuche.* Schriften zur Informationswissenschaft Bd. 399. Konstanz: Universitätsverlag. Abstract available at *http://www.uvk.de/db/detailk.asp?TITZIF=1287*.

Martin, P. 2000. Conventions and Notations for Knowledge Representation and Retrieval. Accessed in October 2001 at *http://meganesia.int.gu.edu.au/~phmartin/WebKB/doc/papers/iccs00/iccs00.ps*.

McEntire, Robin, et al. 1999. An Evaluation of Ontology Exchange Languages for Bioinformatics. Accessed in October 2001 at *ftp://smi.stanford.edu/pub/bio-ontology/OntologyExchange.doc*.

McInerney, Claire. 1997. An Interdisciplinary Perspective of Classification Structures. Accessed in October 2001 at *http://scils.rutgers.edu/~clairemc/classify.html*.

Meder, N., P. Jaenecke, and W. Schmitz-Esser, eds. 1995. *Konstruktion und Retrieval von Wissen. 3. Tagung der Deutschen Sektion der ISKO. Weilburg, 27.–29.10.1993.* Frankfurt/Main: INDEKS.

Miller, Eric. 2000a. RDF and Topic Maps. Presentation at Extreme Markup 2000, Montreal, August 17, 2000. Abstract accessed in October 2001 at *http://www.gca.org/attend/2000_conferences/Extreme_2000/thursday.htm*.

————. 2000b. RDF Topic Maps. Presentation at WWW9, Amsterdam, June 5, 2000. Accessed around June 2001 at *http://staff.oclc.org/~emiller/talks/emiller-w9dd-20000519/* (no longer available since Miller is now with W3C, *http://www.w3.org/People/EM/*).

Mitchell, Joan S., and Diana Vizine-Goetz. 2000. DDC Taxonomy Server. In *Dynamism and Stability in Knowledge Organization. Proceedings of the 6th International ISKO Conference, July 10–13, 2000, Toronto, Canada;* C. Beghtol et al., eds. Würzburg: Ergon, pp. 282–287.

Mizzaro, Stefano. 1998. How Many Relevances in Information Retrieval? *Interacting with Computers* 10(3):305–322. Full paper available at *http://www.dimi.uniud.it/~mizzaro/papers/IwC.ps.gz*.

————. 1997. Relevance: The Whole History. *Journal of the American Society for Information Science* 48(9):810–832. Republished with a short addendum as Relevance: The Whole History, in *Historical Studies in Information Science*, T. Bellardo Hahn and M. Buckland, eds., 1998, pp. 221–244.

Mutschke, P. 2001. Enhancing Information Retrieval in Federated Bibliographic Data Sources Using Author Network Based Stratagems. In *Research and Advanced Technology for Digital Libraries*; P. Constantopoulos et al., eds. (Lecture Notes in Computer Science 2163.) Berlin: Springer, pp. 287–299.

————. 2000. Kooperationsnetzwerke und Schwerpunktthemen im Forschungsfeld Wiedervereinigung. Eine Datenbankanalyse [Cooperation networks and focal themes in the research field reunification. A database analysis, in German]. In *Zehn Jahre deutsche Wiedervereinigung. Analysen und Deutungen. Eine Publikation des Instituts für Soziologie der Friedrich-Schiller-Universität Jena und des Informationszentrums Sozialwissenschaften (IZ) der Arbeitsgemeinschaft Sozialwissenschaftlicher Institute e.V., August 2000 (= Gesellschaft im FOKUS der Sozialwissenschaften)*; Heinrich Best, Hanjo Gergs, and Raj Kollmorgen, eds. Bonn: Informationszentrum Sozialwissenschaften, pp. 229–232.

————. 1998. Processing Network-Like Relationships in Bibliographic Social Science Databases. Presentation at the Special Session "New Technologies in Sociological Research, Documentation, Publishing and Teaching," World Congress of Sociology, Montreal, July 27, 1998. Abstract accessed in October 2001 at *http://web.ccr.jussieu.fr/bms/resources/New_Tech_Montreal*.

————. 1996. Uncertainty and Actor-Oriented Information Retrieval in μ-AKCESS. An Approach Based on Fuzzy Set Theory. In *Data Analysis and Information Systems. Statistical and Conceptual Approaches*; H. H. Bock et al., eds. Berlin-Heidelberg: Springer-Verlag, pp. 126–138.

————. 1994. Processing Scientific Networks in Bibliographic Databases. In *Information Systems and Data Analysis. Prospects—Foundations—Applications*; H. H. Bock et al., eds. Heidelberg-Berlin: Springer-Verlag, pp. 127–133.

Mutschke, P., and A. Quan-Haase. 2001. Collaboration and Cognitive Structures in Social Science Research Fields: Towards Socio-Cognitive Analysis in Information Systems. *Scientometrics* 52(3):487–502.

Neubauer, Wolfram, ed. 1994. *Procs. Deutscher Dokumentartag 1994*. Universität Trier. Frankfurt/Main: DGD.

Newcomb, Steven R. 2001a. E-mail with subject "[topicmapmail] Re: PMTM4 templates vs. TMCL (was: Re: [topicmaps-comment] RE: OASIS vs W3C)" sent October 2, 2001, to e-mail list topicmapmail (discussion of ISO/IEC 13250 topic maps by and for users and potential users of same). Accessed in April 2002 at *http://www.infoloom.com/pipermail/topicmapmail/2001q4/003361.html*.

————. 2001b. RDF/Topic Maps: Late/Lazy Reification vs. Early/Preemptive Reification. Accessed in October 2001 at *http://lists.oasis-open.org/archives/topicmaps-comment/200109/msg00093.html*.

Newcomb, Steven R., and Michel Biezunski. 2001. Topicmaps.net's Processing Model for XTM 1.0, version 1.0.2. A Processing Model for XML Topic Maps. Accessed in October 2001 at *http://www.topicmaps.net/pmtm4.htm*.

Nick, Nicholas. 1994. Parameters for Rhetorical Structure Theory Ontology. Abstract accessed in October 2001 at *http://www.linguistics.unimelb.edu.au/research/mplal/wpling15.html*.

Nikolai, Ralf, Andreas Traupe, and Ralf Kramer. 1998. Thesaurus Federations: A Framework for the Flexible Integration of Heterogeneous, Autonomous Thesauri. In *Proceedings of the Conference on Research and Technology Advances in Digital Libraries (ADL'98), Santa Barbara, USA, April 1998*, pp. 46–55. Abstract accessed in October 2001 at *http://www.fzi.de/dbs/people/abstracts/DBS-98nikolai98engl01.html*.

NKOS. 2001. Fourth NKOS Workshop at First ACM+IEEE Joint Conference on Digital Libraries (JCDL), June 28 in Roanoke, VA. Accessed in October 2001 at *http://nkos.slis.kent.edu/DL01workshop.htm*.

————. 2000. Initiatives and Projects in Europe, Options for Global Co-operation. Special Workshop at the 4th European Conference on Digital Libraries (ECDL2000), Lisbon, Portugal, September 18–20, 2000. Accessed in October 2001 at *http://nkos.slis.kent.edu/ECDL-NKOS-final.htm* and *http://www.bn.pt/org/agenda/ecdl2000/nkos.html*.

Noy, Natalya Fridman, and Mark A. Musen. 1999a. An Algorithm for Merging and Aligning Ontologies: Automation and Tool Support. SMI Report SMI-1999-0799. Presented at 16th National Conference on Artificial Intelligence (AAAI-99), Workshop on Ontology Management, Orlando, FL. Accessed in October 2001 at *http://smi-web.stanford.edu/pubs/SMI_Abstracts/SMI-1999-0799.html*.

————. 1999b. SMART: Automated Support for Ontology Merging and Alignment. Paper presented at Twelfth Banff Workshop on Knowledge Acquisition, Modeling, and Management, Banff, Alberta, Canada. Accessed in October 2001 at *http://smi-web.stanford.edu/pubs/SMI_Abstracts/SMI-1999-0813.html*.

Nuopponen, Anita. 2001. Bibliography of the Theory of Terminology Science. Accessed in April 2002 at *http://www.uwasa.fi/comm/termino/bibtheo1.html*.

Ohly, H. Peter, Gerhard Rahmstorf, and Alexander Sigel, eds. 2000. *Globalisierung und Wissensorganisation: Neue Aspekte für Wissen, Wissenschaft und Informationssysteme*. (Proceedings der 6. Tagung der Deutschen Sektion der Internationalen Gesellschaft für Wissensorganisation [ISKO], Hamburg, 23-25 September 1999.) Würzburg: Ergon Verlag.

Panyr, Jiri. 1988. Thesaurus und wissensbasierte Systeme—Thesauri und Wissensbasen. *Nachrichten für Dokumentation* 39:209–215.

Pathak, Lalit P. 2000. Concept-Term Relationship and a Classified Schedule of Isolates for the Term "Concept." *KO* 27(1–2):27–34.

Pepper, Steve. 2002. The TAO of Topic Maps: Finding the Way in the Age of Infoglut. Accessed in May 2002 at *http://www.ontopia.net/topicmaps/materials/tao.html*. (Revised version of a paper of the same name in *Conference Proceedings XML Europe 2000, 12–16 June 2000, Le Palais des Congrès de Paris, Paris, France*. GCA, pp. 167–180.)

———. 2001. Draft Requirements for TMCL. Accessed in October 2001 at *http://www.y12.doe.gov/sgml/sc34/document/0226.htm*.

———. 1999. Navigating Haystacks and Discovering Needles: Introducing the New Topic Map Standard. *Markup Languages: Theory and Practice* 1(4):41–68. Also available at *http://www.ontopia.net/topicmaps/materials/mlangart.pdf*.

Pepper, Steve, and Geir Ove Grønmo. 2001. Towards a General Theory of Scope. Paper presented at Extreme Markup 2001. Accessed in October 2001 at *http://www.ontopia.net/topicmaps/materials/scope.htm*.

Perreault, J. M. 1994. Categories and Relators: A New Schema. *KO* 21(4):189–198.

Priss, Uta, and Elin Jacob. 1999. Utilizing Faceted Structures for Information Systems Design. In *Knowledge, Creation, Organization and Use. Proceedings of the 62nd Annual Meeting (ASIS'99)*. Medford, NJ: Information Today, pp. 203–212.

Rahmstorf, Gerhard. 2001. Wortmodell und Begriffssprache als Basis des semantischen Retrievals [Word model and concept language as basis for semantic retrieval, in German]. In *Informationskompetenz—Basiskompetenz in der Informationsgesellschaft. Procs. 7. Int. Symposium für Informationswissenschaft*; Gerhard Knorz and Rainer Kuhlen, eds. Konstanz: UVK, pp. 71–87.

———. 1994a. A New Thesaurus Structure for Semantic Retrieval. In *Finding New Values and Uses of Information. Procs. 47th FID General Assembly, Tokyo, October 6–8, 1994*, pp. 114–121.

———. 1994b. Semantisches Information Retrieval. In *Procs. Deutscher Dokumentartag 1994*; Wolfram Neubauer, ed. Frankfurt/Main: DGD, pp. 237–260.

———. 1983. Die semantischen Relationen in nominalen Ausdrücken des Deutschen. Dissertation am Fachbereich 14 (Philologie II) der Universität Mainz (in German).

Ranganathan, S. R. 1989. *Prolegomena to Library Classification* (1937; 3rd ed. reprinted 1989). Bangalore: Sarada Ranganathan Endowment for Library Science.

———. 1965. *The Colon Classification*. (Rutgers Series on Systems for the Intellectual Organization of Information, vol. IV.) New Brunswick, NJ: Graduate School of Library Service, Rutgers University.

————. 1962. *Elements of Library Classification*. Bombay: Asia Publishing House.

Rath, Hans Holger. 1999. Mozart oder Kugel. Mit Topic Maps intelligente Informationsnetze aufbauen. Accessed in October 2001 at *http://www.empolis.de/deutsch/pdf/Mozart-und-Kugeln.pdf*.

Rath, Hans Holger, and Lars Maris Garshol. 2001. TMQL Requirements (0.8.2), Draft. Accessed in October 2001 at *http://www.y12.doe.gov/sgml/sc34/document/0227.htm*.

Rath, Hans Holger, and Steve Pepper. 2000. T10: Topic Maps Hands-on Workshop: Building Real World Applications. Preconference tutorial for XML Europe 2000, Paris, France, June 12, 2000. Accessed in October 2001 at *http://www.gca.org/attend/2000_conferences/europe_2000/tutorials.htm*.

Resnik, Philip. 1999. Semantic Similarity in a Taxonomy: An Information-Based Measure and Its Application to Problems of Ambiguity in Natural Language. *Journal of Artificial Intelligence Research (JAIR)* 11:95–130. Also available at *http://www.umiacs.umd.edu/~resnik/pubs.html*, *http://www.cs.washington.edu/research/jair/abstracts/resnik99a.html*, and *http://www.sims.berkeley.edu/courses/is296a-4/f99/papers/resnik99a.ps*.

Riggs, Fred W. 1996–1997. Onomantics and Terminology. Parts 1–4. *Knowledge Organization* 23(1):25–34, 23(3):156–168, 23(4):216–224, and 24(1):8–17. See also *http://www2.hawaii.edu/~fredr/welcome.htm#onoma*.

Ross, Jan. 2000. A New Way of Information Retrieval: 3-D Indexing and Concept Mapping. *Learned Publishing* 13(2):119–123. See also *http://cherubino.catchword.com/vl=30890218/cl=18/nw=1/rpsv/catchword/alpsp/09531513/v13n2/s9/p119*.

Rost, Martin. 1996. Vorschläge zur Entwicklung einer wissenschaftlichen Diskurs-Markup-Language [Proposals for the development of a scientific discourse markup language, in German]. In *Kursbuch Internet—Anschlüsse an Wirtschaft und Politik, Wissenschaft und Kultur*; Christiane Heibach and Stefan Bollmann, eds. See *http://www.netzservice.de/Home/mr/mr_dml.html*. English short summary by Michael Nentwich accessed in October 2001 at *http://www.oeaw.ac.at/ita/ebene5/dsk/APSA/discourse-markup-lan.htm* and *http://www.oeaw.ac.at/ita/ebene5/dsk/APSA/DML_details.htm#beginning*.

Schmidt, Arno. 1970. *Zettel's Traum*. Stuttgart: Stahlberg Verlag Stuttgart.

Schmidt, Christoph. 2001. Artificial Intelligence and Metaphysics. Accessed in October 2001 at *http://www.orga.uni-sb.de/lehre/mkm/Protagonisten/turing/Essay.htm*.

Schmidt, Ingrid, and Carolin Müller. 2000. Zaubernetz: Inhaltsstrukturen und Topic Maps als Potenzial neuer Informationstechnik. Accessed in October 2001 at *http://www.heise.de/ix/artikel/2000/11/100/*.

Schmitz-Esser, Winfried. Forthcoming. *Lines of Thought in Knowledge Organization. 10 Years Anniversary Festschrift. ISKO—International Society for Knowledge Organization 1989–1999*. Würzburg: Ergon.

————. 2000a. *EXPO-INFO 2000. Visuelles Besucherinformationssystem für Weltausstellungen* [Visual visitor information system for world expositions, in German]. Heidelberg: Springer.

————. 2000b. How to Cope with Dynamism in Ontologies. In *Dynamism and Stability in Knowledge Organization. Proceedings of the 6th International ISKO Conference, July 10–13, 2000, Toronto, Canada*; C. Beghtol et al., eds. Würzburg: Ergon, pp. 83–89.

————. 2000c. SERUBA. A New Search and Learning Technology for the Internet and Intranets. In *Proceedings of the 11th ASIS&T SIG/CR Classification Research Workshop, Chicago, IL, November 12, 2000*, pp. 91–102. Accessed in October 2001 at *http:// uma.info-science.uiowa.edu/sigcr/papers/sigcr00schmitz.pdf*.

————. 1999. Thesaurus and Beyond: An Advanced Formula for Linguistics Engineering and Information Retrieval. *KO* 26(1):10–22.

Schütz, Jörg. 2001. Ontologies in Terminology Work: Enabling Controlled Authoring. (Transparencies of a presentation at the SALT Workshop, Antwerp. See in particular slides 21–26.) Accessed in October 2001 at *http://www.loria.fr/projets/SALT/public/ TAMA/TAMA-pres/JS-WS-TAMA2001.pdf*.

Shute, Steven, and Philip J. Smith. 1993. Knowledge-Based Search Tactics. *Information Processing and Management* 29(1):29–45.

Sigel, Alexander. 2000a. Topic Maps for Knowledge Organization and Knowledge Management. An ISI-2000 Topic Map Tutorial (lead: Alexander Sigel) by Steve Pepper, Alexander Sigel, Ingrid Schmidt, and Carolin Müller. Dieburg, Germany, November 7, 2000. Accessed in October 2001 at *http://index.bonn.iz-soz.de/~sigel/ veroeff/ISI-2000/*.

————. 2000b. Towards Knowledge Organization with Topic Maps. In *Conference Proceedings XML Europe 2000, 12–16 June 2000, Le Palais des Congrès de Paris, Paris, France*. GCA, 2000, pp. 603–611. Full paper available at *http://www.gca.org/papers/ xmleurope2000/papers/s22-02.html*. Transparencies available at *http://index.bonn.iz-soz. de/~sigel/veroeff/XML-Europe2000/transparencies/index.htm*.

————. 2000c. Zum Wert multipler und adaptiver Indexierung mittels Konzeptrahmen für die Sozialwissenschaften [On the value of multiple and adaptive indexing with frames for the social sciences, in German]. In *Globalisierung und Wissenorganisation: Neue Aspekte für Wissen, Wissenschaft und Informationssysteme*; H. Peter Ohly et al., eds. Würzburg: Ergon Verlag, pp. 343–361. Full paper available at *http://index.bonn. iz-soz.de/~sigel/veroeff/ISKO-99/zum-wert.pdf*. Transparencies available at *http://index. bonn.iz-soz.de/~sigel/veroeff/ISKO-99/zum-wert-transparencies.pdf*.

————. 1999. Request for Discussion: Knowledge Organization and Management of Heterogeneous Subject Data with Topic Maps and Ontologies. Accessed in October 2001 at *http://index.bonn.iz-soz.de/~sigel/ISKO/topic-maps.html*.

————. 1998a. Long-Term Value Adding in an Open Category Network: An Informal Social Approach Towards Relating Order Systems on the Internet. In *Knowledge Management und Kommunikationssysteme. Workflow Management, Multimedia, Knowledge Transfer. Procs. 6. Int. Symposium für Informationswissenschaft (ISI'98), Praha, Nov. 3–7, 1998*; Harald H. Zimmermann and Volker Schramm, eds. Konstanz: UVK, pp. 296–305. Full paper available at *http://index.bonn.iz-soz.de/~sigel/veroeff/ISI-98/ isi98-dv-sigel-birlinghoven.rtf*. Transparencies available at *http://index.bonn.iz-soz.de/ ~sigel/veroeff/ISI-98/transparencies/index.htm*.

————. 1998b. Registry of (Registries of) Conceptual KO Schemata on the Internet. (Points to schemata useful for describing electronic resources that are freely available in machine-readable format.) Electronic publication through 2001 at *http://index. bonn.iz-soz.de/~sigel/ISKO/ko-schemata.html*, no longer updated.

————. 1996–2001. The Knowledge Organization on Internet Mini-FAQ. Electronic publication at *http://index.bonn.iz-soz.de/~sigel/ISKO/wiss-org.faq.html*, no longer updated.

Small, Henry G. 1999. Visualizing Science by Citation Mapping. *Journal of the American Society for Information Science* 50(9):799–813. Abstract available at *http://bubl.ac. uk/journals/lis/fj/jasis/v50n0999.htm*.

Soergel, Dagobert. 1999. The Rise of Ontologies or the Re-invention of Classification. *Journal of the American Society for Information Science* 50(12):1119–1120.

————. 1985. *Organizing Information: Principles of Data Base and Retrieval Systems*. Orlando, FL: Academic Press.

Solomon, Paul. 2000. Exploring Structuration in Knowledge Organization: Implications for Managing the Tension between Stability and Dynamism. In *Dynamism and Stability in Knowledge Organization. Proceedings of the 6th International ISKO Conference, July 10–13, 2000, Toronto, Canada*; C. Beghtol et al., eds. Würzburg: Ergon, pp. 254–260. Also available at *http://www.ils.unc.edu/~solomon/hp/pso.ako.7.pdf*.

Sowa, John F. 2000a. *Knowledge Representation: Logical, Philosophical, and Computational Foundations*. Pacific Grove, CA: Brooks Cole. Very useful metainformation and excerpts from the most important parts of the book available from the author at *http://www.jfsowa.com/krbook/index.htm*.

————. 2000b. Ontology, Metadata, and Semiotics. Paper presented at ICCS Darmstadt 2000. Accessed in October 2001 at *http://users.bestweb.net/~sowa/peirce/ ontometa.htm*.

Stock, Wolfgang G. 2000. Textwortmethode [Text word method, in German]. In *Auf dem Weg zur Informationskultur: Wa(h)re Information?* Thomas A. Schröder, ed., pp. 307–324. Accessed in October 2001 at *http://www.ulb.uni-duesseldorf.de/festschriften/ henrichs.html*.

Stuckenschmidt, H., K. C. Ranze, and O. Herzog. 1999. Entwicklungskonzepte für die Wiederverwendung unsicherer Wissensmodelle. Technologie-Zentrum Informatik, Universität Bremen. Accessed in October 2001 at *http://www.informatik. uni-bremen.de/~kcr/paper/TZI/tzi_report.html/*.

Stumme, G., ed. 2000. *Working with Conceptual Structures—Contributions to ICCS 2000*. Aachen, Germany: Shaker-Verlag.

Supper, Reinhard. 1978. *Neuere Methoden der intellektuellen Indexierung: Britische Systeme unter besonderer Berücksichtigung von PRECIS*. Beiträge zur Informations- und Dokumentationswissenschaft; Folge 11. München: Saur.

Svenonius, Elaine. 2001. The Epistemological Foundations of Knowledge Representations. Invited keynote address at Extreme Markup 2001, Montréal, Quebec, Canada, September 15, 2001. Abstract accessed in October 2001 at *http://www2. gca.org/extreme/2001/keynotes.htm*.

―――. 2000. *The Intellectual Foundation of Information Organization*. Cambridge, MA: MIT Press. A short review of this book is available at *http://www.library. ucsb.edu/istl/00-summer/review2.html*.

Swanson, Don R. 2001. On the Fragmentation of Knowledge, the Connection Explosion, and Assembling Other People's Ideas. ASIST Award of Merit Acceptance Speech. *Bulletin of the American Society for Information Science and Technology* 2001 (February/March):12–14. Also available at *http://www.asis.org/Bulletin/Mar-01/swanson. html*.

Teachware on Demand. 2000. The Content of Content: Metadaten zur Beschreibung von Lernmaterialien nach inhaltlichen und informationslogistischen Aspekten [Metadata for the description of learning materials by aspects of content and information logistics, in German]. Workshop, December 8, 2000, Fraunhofer ISST, Dortmund, Germany. Accessed in October 2001 at *http://www.informationslogistik. org/veranstaltungen/einladung-Metadaten-Ws.pdf*.

TopicMaps.Org. 2000. XML Topic Maps (XTM) Processing Model 1.0. TopicMaps. Org AG Review Specification, December 4, 2000. Accessed in October 2001 at *http://www.topicmaps.org/xtm/1.0/xtmp1.html*. (Note that this is a draft, superseded by TMPM4; see Newcomb and Biezunski [2001].)

van der Vet, Paul E., and N. J. I. Mars. 1999. CQE: A Query Engine for Coordinated Index Terms. *Journal of the American Society for Information Science* 50(6):485–492. Abstract available at *http://www.asis.org/Publications/JASIS/v50n699.html*.

van Harmelen, Frank, and Dieter Fensel. 1998. Practical Knowledge Representation for the Web. Paper presented at IJCAI 1999. Accessed in October 2001 at *http:// www.cs.vu.nl/~frankh/postscript/IJCAI99-III.html*.

Vatant, Bernard. 2001a. Managing Complex Environments with Topic Maps. Paper presented at Knowledge Technologies 2001. Accessed in October 2001 at *http://www.mondeca.com/site/products/bernard/a_managing_complex.html*.

————. 2001b. The Semantopic Map Project: *http://www.universimmedia.com/*. From Building Knowledge to Semantopic Universe. Personal communication via e-mail, February 16.

Veltman, Kim H. 1997. Frontiers in Conceptual Navigation. *KO* 24(4):225–245.

Vickery, B. C. 1997. Ontologies. *Journal of Information Science* 23(4):277–286. Abstract available at *http://www.bubl.ac.uk/journals/lis/fj/jinfsci/v23n0497.htm*.

————. 1965. *Faceted Classification*. New Brunswick: Rutgers University Press.

Viezzer, Manuela. 2000. ECAI 2000. Ontologies and Problem-Solving Methods and Ontology Learning. Accessed in October 2001 at *http://www.cs.bham.ac.uk/~mxv/onto_engineering/onto_engineering.html*. On ontologies in general, see *http://www.cs.bham.ac.uk/~mxv/onto_engineering/node1.html*.

Vizine-Goetz, Diane. 2001. Taxonomies and Indexing; A Technical Strategy. Paper presented at Knowledge Technologies 2001, Austin, TX.

von Foerster, Heinz, and Bernhard Pörksen. 2001. *Wahrheit ist die Erfindung eines Lügners: Gespräche für Skeptiker*. 4th ed. Heidelberg: Carl-Auer-Systeme.

von Glasersfeld, Ernst. 1998. Die radikal-konstruktivistische Wissenstheorie [The radical-constructivist knowledge theory, in German]. *Ethik und Sozialwissenschaften. Streitforum für Erwägungskultur* 9(4):503–511, 581–596 (in particular see the 37 critical replicas).

Wersig, Gernot, and Petra Schuck-Wersig. 1985. *Thesaurus-Leitfaden: Eine Einführung in das Thesaurus-Prinzip in Theorie und Praxis*. DGD-Schriftenreihe 8, 2nd amended ed. Frankfurt/Main: Deutsche Gesellschaft für Dokumentation (DGD).

White, Howard D., Xia Lin, and Katherine W. McCain. 1998. Two Modes of Automated Domain Analysis: Multidimensional Scaling vs. Kohonen Feature Mapping of Information Science. In *Structures and Relations in Knowledge Organization. Proceedings of the 5th International ISKO Conference, Lille, France, 25–29 August 1998*; Widad Mustafa El Hadi et al., eds. Würzburg: Ergon, pp. 57–61.

Wrightson, Ann. 2001a. Ontology Analysis and Design for Topic Map Applications. Paper presented at Knowledge Technologies 2001, Austin, TX. See announcement at *http://www.gca.org/attend/2001_conferences/kt_2001/mon.htm*.

————. 2001b. Topic Maps and Knowledge Representation. White paper. Accessed in October 2001 at *http://www.ontopia.net/topicmaps/materials/kr-tm.html*.

————. 2000. Grouped Use Cases as Preliminary Results of the XTM UC survey. Post to the xtm-wg discussion list, September 25. See also *http://index.bonn.iz-soz.de/~sigel/veroeff/ISI-2000/Perlpoint6/isi-tm-tutorial/page0045.html*.

Chapter 16

PREDICTION:
A PROFOUND PARADIGM SHIFT

KATHLEEN M. FISHER

Topic maps are included in a class of objects we refer to as *knowledge webs*. A knowledge web is an interconnected web of ideas that conveys in skeletal form not only a set of ideas but also how those ideas are organized and interrelated. The general term, knowledge web, includes but is not limited to concept maps, semantic networks, cluster maps, mind maps, circle diagrams, flow charts, and topic maps [Fisher et al. 2000]. Berners-Lee and colleagues [2001] recently wrote about the Semantic Web to make Internet technology smarter, and this is the goal of topic maps as well. Fisher and colleagues [2000] as well as many others are similarly interested in using semantic knowledge webs to make people smarter. Eventually, connections will be made between the knowledge webs created to make machines smarter and the knowledge webs created for human use. Presumably, topic maps and agents will be involved in making these connections.

This nontechnical chapter is relevant to this book in at least three ways. First, it predicts a profound paradigm shift in the ways in which humans communicate on the Web. Second, it considers the potential impacts of such a paradigm shift. And third, it describes some of what has been learned during half a century of research on the use of knowledge webs by humans. Topic map designers and implementers would do well to consider and learn from these ideas and experiences since topic maps are being created in the service of human users.

This chapter begins with a brief examination of the significance of language. It reviews several of the revolutions that have occurred as language has evolved. The goal is to share with you, the reader, a sense of the power of language. Vast and reverberating impacts have been associated with changes in the ways in which we use language. I propose that another change is occurring, one that will also have an enormous impact on what and how we think, how we build consensus, and how we solve problems. It is happening now, even as we resist.

The Lightness of Being section describes the manner of communication I imagine will become the standard on the Web. It describes the user interface, not the programming that underlies it (which is the subject of much of the rest of the book).

After that appears a brief history of knowledge mapping and education. (More complete treatments can be found in Wandersee [2000]; Fisher et al. [2000]; Mintzes et al. [1997]; and Novak [1998].) Next I contrast the ephemeral nature of many new ideas with what the research says about semantic networks and learning. Finally, I describe the paradigm shift that is under way, due entirely to our latest development in communication, the World Wide Web.

Language

Language is precious. Although we often take it for granted, it is one of our greatest riches. Further, it is clear that thought and language are inexplicably intertwined. Language exerts a powerful effect on the meanings that humans create, express, and transmit. It also influences human perceptions, understandings, feelings, and values. Language ultimately facilitates or impedes our chances of survival [Postman 1970].

Neil Postman is an author and media scholar, currently the head of the Culture and Communication Department at New York University and professor of Media Ecology. He has written 18 books and many articles on language, media, and culture. In one of his books [Postman 1982], he writes that changes in communication styles have three kinds of effects: (1) they alter our interests (the things that we think about); (2) they change the symbols (the things we think with); and (3) they change the community (the group among which thoughts develop). We can see evidence for these three types of changes as e-mail and the Web change the ways we think and interact with the world. Interestingly, Postman [1993] is quite pessimistic about the impact of these current and future technologies on the human race. I, on the other hand, tend to focus on the positive aspects of the new media.

Some scholars hypothesize that the advent of spoken language is responsible for humanity's "Great Leap Forward" between 100,000 and 50,000 years ago [Diamond 1999]. This may have involved perfection of the voice box or of the centers for language in the brain (or both). Gould [1977] suggests that our language capability is due primarily to neoteny, the slow rate of development in humans (compared to other primates) that presumably resulted from alterations in one or more biological regulatory systems. He suggests that it is the relatively slow rate of development of human babies that makes the emergence of language possible.

Language among humans gave rise to storytelling, singing, and other oral traditions. Talking and listening enabled the transmission of history, beliefs, and other cultural knowledge. It also nourished thought in astonishing new directions. While it is not intuitively obvious, research with the deaf has shown that, in the absence of language, "A human being is . . . confined, in effect, to an immediate and small world" [Sacks 1990, p. 40]. Without language, there is no access to imaginary beings or events, to abstract ideas, to yesterday and tomorrow, nor even to the concept of time itself [Sacks 1990]. Language dominates and transforms preverbal experiences. Language opens our horizons and possibilities onto vast new spaces.

Transmitting the Word

Historically, language has been transmitted through writing, printing, and dynamic visuals.

Writing. Within most cultures, at first there was a pictographic writing system. This was eventually replaced by the use of an alphabet. Prior to this change, readers and writers were required to learn and remember a very large number of images, a feat that could be achieved by only a small minority. This elite group of priests and scribes enjoyed a knowledge monopoly that gave them great power [Postman 1982]. With the advent of the alphabet, many more people had access to information, shifting the balance of power. Written material became more democratically available and a bit more comprehensible. At the same time, this was the beginning of the end of the pictographic writing system in Western cultures. In each step "forward," there are losses as well as gains.

Printing. *Galileo's Daughter* [Sobel 2000] provides historical insights into the difficulties involved in publishing after the advent of written language but before the invention of the printing press. To reproduce a book by hand was a tedious and time-consuming process. To make a thousand copies often took a year or more. Finally, Johann Gutenberg invented the printing press in about 1450, a time when there was a great demand for books [Hoe 1902; Peddie 1927]. Gutenberg put together all the essential elements of printing—type production, ink manufacture, paper supply, and the press—to create a coherent whole [Wells 1965]. Books are easy to use, and they increase the portability of and access to information—presumably these are some of the reasons why Gutenberg invented the press.

The printing press transformed the world, allowing humans to offload much of what they knew into permanent records, to share that information with people the authors would never meet, and to store the information for generations in vast vaults called libraries. Its effects were ultimately felt in every avenue of human activity. Interestingly, according to Postman [1982], the "book culture" of the sixteenth through twentieth centuries produced another unanticipated kind of knowledge monopoly. It gave adults the ability to protect children from knowledge deemed inappropriate, and in combination with other events it created a wonderful "age of innocence" for youngsters. Books also fostered the amazing growth of knowledge discovery and sharing.

Dynamic Visuals. When television came onto the stage, the separation between adults and children began to break down. "Television offers a fairly primitive but irresistible alternative to the linear and sequential logic of the printed word and tends to make the rigor of a literate education irrelevant" [Postman 1982, pp. 78–79]. According to Postman, TV levels the playing field between adults and children in at least three ways. First, no instruction is required to grasp its form. Second, it does not make complex cognitive or behavioral demands. And third, it does not segregate its audience.

Perhaps for the same reasons that television contributed to the disappearance of childhood, it is now drawing the world of humanity into a "global village." Thanks to CNN, sharing of knowledge, culture, and language is now more widespread than ever. And while we appear to be sinking to a relatively low common denominator via this medium, we experience another phenomenon: the attachment of a highly intrusive commercial message to each fragment of communication.

These examples illustrate, albeit briefly, that the medium does indeed affect the message. In addition, these examples demonstrate some of the ways in which the communication medium affects *what we think*, *how we think*, and *with whom we think*. The Internet is becoming the defining feature of the Information Age. What will its impacts be on our thinking habits?

Lightness of Being

The Web is creating another revolution in semantic communication. Linear text patterned after the spoken word is not well suited for rapid, just-in-time communication on the Internet. It is too dense, too cumbersome, too time-consuming, and too vague. It has the wrong shape for display on a monitor, and it is not attractive. Worse yet, it tends to be inefficient and unclear. The critical links between ideas that comprise the essence of meaning often remain implicit, buried in a barrage of linear semantics.

What is emerging is a form of semantic communication with a *lightness of being*, a skeletal knowledge structure that is concise, precise, and easily assimilated. This form is the Semantic Web, patterned after thought rather than speech. Like a great painting or the sign language used by deaf persons, the Semantic Web employs space as well as words to convey meaning. The open space also adds a sense of peace and order to the message.

The meanings captured in space are combined seamlessly with the meanings embedded in words. The links between ideas in this format are invariably explicit, present, and easily accessible. The information is often so clear and simple that it can be easily subsumed or taken in as a whole, as is known to occur with small clusters of numbers. Thus communication is efficient, meeting the demands of a world that is steadily speeding up.

In Laguna Beach, CA, each year there is the Pageant of the Masters festival in which great paintings are recreated with live actors and actresses on the stage. The living recreation of the painting is first presented to the audience as a whole, the participants in freeze-frame. Then the "painting" is dissembled piece by piece and examined from different perspectives so the audience can see how the illusion was created. Thus it is with this new communication form, which can be examined from many perspectives and at many levels.

The basic element of the Semantic Web is the *graphic frame*, a rectangular field that encodes meaning in space. In the center of the field of a graphic frame is the main idea, the *central concept*, shown in Figure 16–1 by a black oval. Ideas that are bigger than the central concept, such as what it is part of or what it is included in, go above the central idea. Mammal, for example, is a bigger idea than dog. A car is bigger than a tire. Ideas that are smaller than the central concept, such as its parts and characteristics, go below it. A dog has a tail. A dog has fur. A tire contains rubber. Thus, no matter what the topic, the reader looking at a graphic frame always knows to look up for the bigger ideas and down for the smaller ideas.

Temporal relations flow from left to right. Thus, what came before (signified by B in Figure 16–2) is shown on the left of the central concept, and what comes after (signified by A) is shown on the right. These ideas may be connected by links such as *caused by/causes, transformed from/transformed into,* or *follows/followed by.* What is lost in variability of expression is gained in elegance, simplicity, and consistency. The arrangement of information appears to be totally intuitive and easy for the reader to understand.

Family trees represented in a semantic network format use conventions like those shown in Figure 16–3. The previous generation (my parents) goes above me, the next generation (my children) go below me, my brothers and sisters (siblings) go on the

Figure 16–1   Placement of ideas and the central concept (*oval*) within a graphic frame

Figure 16–2   Temporal relations in a graphic frame; B = before, A = after

right, and my spouse (or significant other) goes on the left. The name that is placed on the link between me and the last generation (such as *has parent)* combines with the spatial location of that concept to doubly confirm that I am referring to the previous generation.

Each frame can be linked to many other frames. In my family tree, for example, there are 523 people. That means that there are 523 graphic frames, each following a similar format but containing different content and all of which are interconnected. There are only four people in my nuclear family, but my family tree knowledge web has grown to include all of my known blood relatives plus many of the families related by marriage.

Connectivity is the ultimate power of this elegant, light, streamlined knowledge format. In a web of ideas or interconnected frames, each idea is directly linked to a number of other ideas (Figure 16–4). It is quite like the brain itself, with its millions of synapses between dendrites and axons. Consider this example. In a knowledge web of 2,500 biology ideas, we identified (with the help of the computer) the shortest distance between many combinations of two distant ideas. The longest "shortest path" we were able to find was 11 nodes. Compare this to a linear list of 2,500 ideas, in

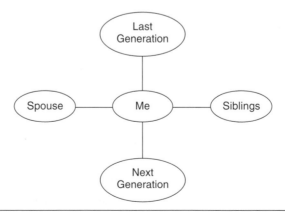

Figure 16–3   A portion of a family tree represented using semantic network elements

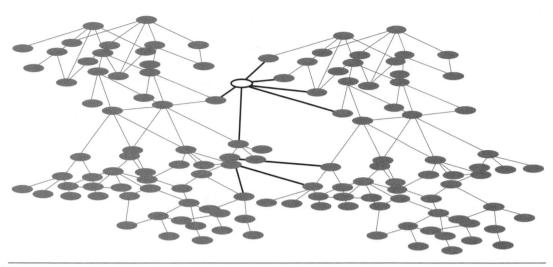

Figure 16–4   Portion of a semantic network

which the first and last idea are separated by 2,498 concepts. The increase of speed in moving through a web of knowledge compared to moving through a list of ideas is significant. Interconnected topic maps offer similar advantages.

Internet-based Semantic Webs provide an ideal format in which to embed knowledge objects. A knowledge object is ". . . a small, reusable digital component that can be selectively applied—alone or in combination—by computer software, learning facilitators or learners themselves, to meet individual needs for learning or performance support" [Shepherd 2001]. Every idea and every relation between ideas in a Semantic Web can be elaborated upon through links to one or more knowledge objects. The knowledge objects may be on your computer, or within your organization, or anywhere out there in cyberspace. Thus if you construct a knowledge web about freshwater streams, not only can you create a concise, precise representation of your knowledge about the topic, but you can also link that organizational structure to all the important sites you have found on the Web that describe that topic. You have created a super-organizer for freshwater streams.

When you realize the power this gives you, you will wonder why it took you so long to move from communication via speech (or linear discourse) to communication via thought (or Semantic Web). But it is understandable that such a paradigm shift would take time. A similar developmental period will likely be required before people feel confident about relying on agents working with invisible topic maps to solve their problems. The evolution typically involves both improvements in computer systems and gradual acceptance by human users. Yet using the new format is apparently relatively painless, as illustrated by 6,500 students who voluntarily enrolled in elective courses taught with this medium. (I'll discuss this more later in the chapter.)

Navigation is relatively easy in this emerging form of Web-based communication. With Web sites generated by the current Semantica 2.1 software, once you have entered a knowledge web, you can easily click through it. If you have forgotten the name of the concept, you can find it readily just by knowing some thing to which it is related, finding that related idea, and searching the vicinity. A Semantica 2.1 knowledge web can automatically generate its own index and its own list of ideas in order of importance. And you can see several overviews of the main ideas in the web.

Eventually, you will be able to extract hierarchies, temporal (sequential) flows of events, and other substructures from the knowledge web. You will be able to easily review your path through the knowledge web. You will be able to see the terrain of the knowledge structure in your neighborhood (that is, around whatever concept you are currently examining). And you will be able to open compressed nodes and enter entire subwebs. You will also be able to construct knowledge webs collaboratively with colleagues around the world.

I have moved from describing the past and present to visualizing the future. My visualization is likely to be incomplete in many ways, but it is a beginning. Semantic network theory was created by Quillian [1967, 1969] as a model of how we store information in long-term memory and how computers can mimic long-term memory. Semantic networks are probably the single most pervasive form of knowledge representation used today [Lehman and Rodin 1992]. There is a large body of research on semantic networks [for example, Sowa 1983, 1990, 1999; Brachman and Levesque 1985; Brachman et al. 1991; Jonassen et al. 1993] (see also Chapter 3). There is also extensive research on spreading activation theory, which describes the flow of signals in memory along the semantic network [for example, Collins and Loftus 1975]. In general, semantic networks are used to capture concept meanings concisely and precisely and to establish effective organizations of concepts in topical or psychological space. Semantic networks come in many variations, and they represent one of many types of knowledge webs. But let's return to history again to explore the link between knowledge representation and education.

A Brief History of Knowledge Representation and Education

Europeans spread the Western tradition of cartography everywhere, until mapmakers around the globe worked from the same set of methods and knowledge, speaking the common languages of mathematics, science, and geography.

—BOB SACHA [1998, P. 18]

A *knowledge map* is an external mirror of your own radiant thinking that gives you access to your vast powerhouse of thought [Buzan and Buzan 1993]. Knowledge mapping is an external extension of working memory that especially supports reflective thinking [Perkins 1993; McAleese 1998; McAleese et al. 1999]. Knowledge mapping is the representation of detailed, interconnected, nonlinear thought [Fisher and Kibby 1996].

Knowledge mapping is a much newer science than geographical mapping; the entire undertaking is still quite primitive. Methods for knowledge mapping have gradually evolved as variants have been explored [for example, Horn 1989; Woods 1985; Fisher and Kibby 1996; Heylighen 2000], but few conventions and standards have emerged. Consequently, the full power of knowledge mapping has yet to be realized. The standards and specifications being set forth for topic maps in this book represent an important step in this direction.

First within the field of knowledge mapping came the paper-based strategies: *cybernetic knowledge mapping, concept mapping,* and *conceptual graphing.* According to Brachman and Levesque [1985], knowledge representation began as a way to create artificial intelligence (AI) in computers in the 1950s. They define knowledge representation in the following way: "It simply has to do with writing down, in some language or communicative meaning, descriptions or pictures that correspond in some salient way to the world or the state of the world" [Brachman and Levesque 1985, p. xiii].

Gordon Pask [1976a, 1976b] developed *cybernetic knowledge mapping* during the 1950s through the 1970s. Pask was a visionary ahead of his time, a true believer in machine intelligence even though computers in his day were very stupid. His attitude is reflected by this sentence as well as any: "If cognitive processes can be realized in a general machine then it is possible to execute mental operations in artifacts that are not necessarily subject to the embarrassing spatio-temporal limitations and structural frailties of a biological processor" [Pask 1975, p. 2]. Pask devised large, complex, and interconnected paper-based knowledge representations. He also produced a computer-based tool called Thoughtsticker on an Apple II, software that was apparently sufficiently interesting to attract the attention of the American military, according to Ray McAleese [personal communication, 2001], who worked with Pask for about ten years, including work on Thoughtsticker. Heylighen [2000], Brooks [2000], and Wideman [2000] carry forth Pask's enthusiasm for what machines can do today.

In 1979, Novak and his students, Stewart, Van Kirk, and Rowell, invented *concept maps* as tools to help children think about and learn a subject [Stewart et al. 1979]. Wandersee [2000, p. 128] provides a nice definition of a concept map in the Novakian hierarchical style (below), although not all concept maps are hierarchical.

> A *concept map* is a two-dimensional, tree-like, hierarchical array of circumscribed concepts linked together by lines that are labeled with linking words. It can be read by starting with the top (superordinate) concept

and reading down the links and concepts of each branch of the map. Its hierarchical structure is intended to parallel the way the brain stores knowledge hierarchically. [Wandersee 2000, p. 128]

Conceptual graph structures use a formal conceptual graph syntax and were developed primarily for the purpose of eliciting knowledge from novices to experts [Gordon 1996]. With these knowledge structures, researchers can do such things as identify gaps or misunderstandings in an individual's knowledge, predict an individual's problem-solving performance, or use an individual's represented knowledge as a guide for instructional design purposes.

In 1980, microcomputers began to change the world. The transition to computer-based knowledge representation strategies in education began, and today concept mapping is available in multiple electronic forms (see the list assembled at my Web site, *http:// www.sci.sdsu.edu/CRMSE/kfisher_knowrep.html*). The AI community first produced various semantic networking programs on mainframe computers. Then in 1983, the SemNet Research Group began developing the SemNet semantic networking software for use in educational settings [Fisher et al. 1990]. The goal was to help college biology students make sense of ideas they were studying and to organize those ideas in meaningful ways.

Constructivism is the dominant paradigm in learning today. This theory basically holds that each individual must actively construct his or her own knowledge by connecting new ideas to known ideas. Personal knowledge constructs were first proposed by a psychoanalyst, George Kelly [1955]. The theory as applied to learning was developed by many people, including Ausubel [1963, 1968], Wittrock [1974a, 1974b], Pope [1982], Pope and Gilbert [1983], Resnick [1983, 1987a, 1987b], Vygotsky [1978], von Glasersfeld [1987a, 1987b, 1988, 1989, 1993], and Novak [1990, 1998].

The power of concept mapping and semantic networking as learning tools derives from the external support they provide for this internal process of knowledge building. Concept maps and semantic networks facilitate knowledge capture, knowledge construction, reflection on knowledge, knowledge refinement, knowledge communication, knowledge collaboration, and knowledge transfer. Knowledge webs can also promote *metacognition* or thinking about thinking [Gorodetsky and Fisher 1996].

High school and college students in various settings have been using the SemNet software as a knowledge construction tool since 1987. A major goal in using this tool is to counteract the tendency of students to engage in rote learning. One of the unanticipated benefits of the software is the way in which it lets instructors see how students are thinking and vice versa. One frame of a knowledge web that describes SemNet appears in Figure 16–5.

Semantic networks have been described in Chapters 7, 13, and 15 in this book from the perspectives of AI and metadata analysis. In contrast to these, a SemNet semantic

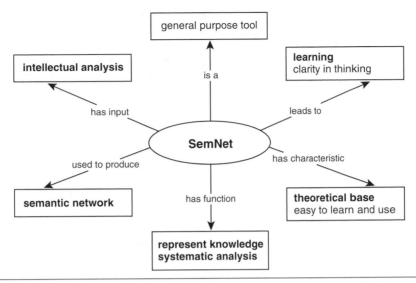

Figure 16–5   A single frame of a small knowledge web that contains a total of 126 concepts and 34 relations. The central concept in this frame, SemNet, is linked to 9 related concepts by 6 relations or links.

network consists of a computer-based web of related ideas (concepts) linked together by bidirectional relations. The main ideas are well developed with multiple links to other concepts. The information is displayed graphically and in other ways as well, with multiple (16–20) views available to the user. A SemNet semantic network may contain dozens or hundreds or thousands of ideas. It seems likely that if topic maps are used to represent knowledge as well as to identify documents, they will become as complex as the knowledge webs created by and for humans. The primary differences seem to be that knowledge webs for humans attend to visualization and are more free-form, while knowledge webs for computers can be written in linear code and follow more systematic rules in the effort to achieve standardization.

The Ephemeral Nature of Many New Ideas

How many times have you listened to a fascinating lecture and walked away feeling excited about all you learned—only to discover that you couldn't explain the topic in any satisfactory way later that day? Thinking often has this ephemeral quality—here one moment and gone the next. It is not unusual to listen and seemingly understand but then to be unable to retrieve or reproduce the very ideas you thought you understood.

Such events occur in part because humans often form vague associations between ideas rather than clear linkages. Students in biology, for example, can nearly always tell you that DNA, RNA, and genes are related to one another. But if you ask them to describe *how* they are related, they often don't have a clue. Yet the students harbor an illusion of understanding. This "fuzzy knowledge" consists of concept names connected by unnamed relations (that is, by associations).

However, not only are key relations often missed—many of the most common concepts have surprisingly elusive meanings. Logan [personal communication, 2001], for example, asked a class of about 60 students to define the concept *time*. None were able to define it to their own satisfaction or to the satisfaction of others in their groups. Likewise, a popular dictionary defines time as "a non-spatial continuum," ignoring Einstein's insights. Yet we use time every day of our lives. As another example, I once worked with 12 geneticists to produce a genetics course on television. These experts were absolutely unable to agree on the definition of a gene, the basic unit of their shared field of study.

These anecdotes reflect our abilities to live comfortably with vague understandings and our tendencies to hold tight to personal meanings. However, when students create a semantic network about ideas they are learning, they are able to transition from fuzzy knowledge to well-structured conceptual knowledge because they are required to think about and name ideas and the links between them.

What the Research Suggests about Knowledge Representation and Learning

Students Learn from Semantic Networks

Since 1998, 6,500 students voluntarily took elective Internet-based courses that use SemNet as a primary medium of instruction [Fisher and Logan 2001]. Students discovered the availability of these courses by hearing about them from other students or by independent exploration on the Internet. Among this entire student population, there was not a single student who asked, "How do I read this knowledge display?" This was true of both American and foreign students taking the courses. The sheer numbers of students suggest that knowledge web representations are intuitive, accessible, comprehensible, and self-evident, although some time may be required to adapt to them. It is a robust proof that semantic networks can serve as a viable means of communication on the Internet.

You can view information on seven of these Internet-based courses at the College Units.com Web site (*http://www.CollegeUnits.com/courses.html*). Some of the courses, such as Introduction to World Art (Art 100), use knowledge webs as if they were road maps. The webs lead the viewer to an organized series of knowledge objects that consist of texts and images. Other Internet-based courses, such as World Music in Contemporary Life (Music 300), employ a robust set of knowledge webs. For example, the world music course includes 11 rich knowledge webs that are interlinked with a course text. In courses using robust knowledge nets, the instructor shares with students his or her personal view of the ways in which knowledge about the subject can be effectively organized. Every relation as well as every concept is made explicit.

In addition, the world music course offers the same 11 knowledge webs with the central concepts masked (Figure 16–6). These serve as potential study tools for the students. The challenge is to identify the masked concept through its links to other concepts. There is no data, however, regarding how or if the Internet students actually use these masked webs.

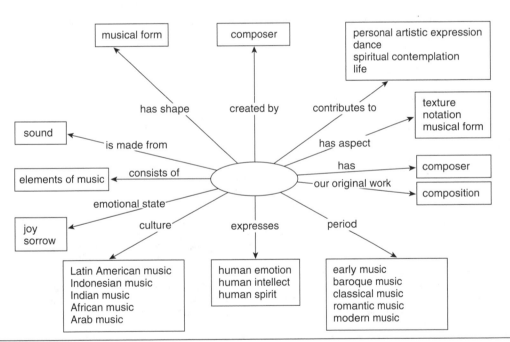

Figure 16–6   A graphic frame from an Internet-based world music knowledge web that has the central concept masked. Can you guess the identity of the masked concept?[1] (Figure reprinted with permission from Jack Logan, professor of the World Music in Contemporary Life course at CollegeUnits.com.)

---

[1] Music.

One of the things you quickly learn when you "peer into another person's mind" through a knowledge web is that there are many different ways to think about a topic—many correct ways and many incorrect ways.[1] Each frame of a knowledge web can be thought of as a meme, a captured unit of thought (Brodie [1966]; Blackmore & Dawkins [2000]). The webs reveal what we already know at some level: that thoughts in science classes are not readily transmitted from teacher to students, but rather are transformed in interesting ways by individuals.

As mentioned previously, knowledge webs on the Internet not only provide explicit connectivity among concepts but also can offer an ideal and coherent medium in which to embed knowledge objects. The world music course contains about a thousand such objects. The presence of a knowledge object is indicated by a capital "L" just below and to the right of the central concept, as in the two graphic frames about the periodic table shown in Figure 16–7.

These two graphic frames also illustrate another way of studying on the Internet. Native Spanish speakers find it helpful to open two browser windows side-by-side for displaying English–Spanish knowledge webs. They can then simultaneously

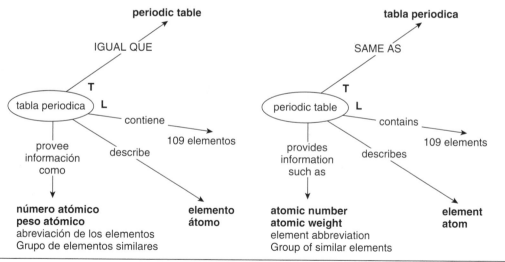

Figure 16–7   Two frames from an English–Spanish knowledge web (from my Web site at *http://www.BiologyLessons.sdsu.edu*)

---

[1]For this reason, any grading of semantic networks must be done like grading an essay, allowing for variation and individual ways of thinking. Thus you may feel dissatisfied with the description of the concept shown in Figure 16–6, but it reflects how this instructor thinks in the context of this course. If you think differently, I invite you to construct your own knowledge web.

click through the identical structures of the English and Spanish versions. Note that these side-by-side representations are not the same as incorporating in the English knowledge web *tabla periodica* as a synonym for *periodic table*. The strength of this dual representation lies in parallel descriptions of a single idea in two different languages. Such parallel descriptions are often but not always possible because of differences between languages.

The periodic table is itself an elegant map, but not one that most people can assimilate in its entirety. Learners still need to construct their own *conceptual map* about the many ideas represented in the periodic table.

A few of these unique features for knowledge displays on the Internet are shown to help you overcome the "horseless carriage" syndrome. When people think of courses on the Internet, their first image tends to be of texts and syllabi and problems transported from paper to electronic representations. This "horseless carriage" image is both evoked by and reflected in the names of some e-learning companies such as Blackboard.com and Chalkboard.com. The fact is, however, that the digital medium makes possible all sorts of new representations, many of which we have yet to imagine. It is not surprising that students are drawn to new forms of knowledge representation that make good use of digital technology—they do not have the same degree of vested interests in the old representations that so many faculty do.

Many of the students who completed one Internet-based course using the knowledge web format went on to take a second course and then a third in a similar format. It was apparently easy for students to transfer their learning skills from one topic to another. And judging by their numbers, it seems they enjoyed the learning experience.

Mastery learning is employed in these Internet courses. Mastery learning is a strategy that facilitates practice and reinforcement by allowing students to be tested as often as they wish, with immediate feedback. A meta-analysis of thousands of research studies concludes that mastery learning produces more than twice as much learning in the same period of time as compared with such strategies as computer-adaptive instruction or computer-assisted instruction [Ryan 1995]. One wonders if it might eventually be possible to use topic maps about the knowledge objects to generate test items.

Gilbert [2001] asserts that using time management skills and taking coursework seriously are keys to making the grade as on online student, since online, there's no teacher taking roll. At first students think they can take these courses in their pajamas, while keeping up with work, family, and school obligations. They soon find out that online courses require more responsibility and attention to detail than on-campus courses. A student has to be organized and must keep up with the work in order to master the subject within the allotted time. I suspect the clear course organization and content in these SemNet-based Internet courses assist students in these tasks.

Students' Models Become Increasingly Similar to Instructors' Models

Thro [1978] observed that over time, students' mental models in a college physics course became more and more like their instructor's mental model. In addition, the students' problem-solving abilities were directly related to their abilities to differentiate among the closely related items in their cognitive structures. One goal of teaching appears to be to bring students into the fold in such a way that they share the instructor's worldview and mental model of the field being studied [West and Pines 1985].

When instructors lecture, students have to work hard to infer the instructor's cognitive model. The clues are incomplete. However, when instructors construct and present robust semantic networks to their students, they are conveying their mental models of their domains to their students in a more direct and explicit manner. The error-prone step of inferencing is largely bypassed when thought-to-thought communication is employed. Previous research suggests that this direct approach should be both more efficient and more effective [Walberg 1991]. Whether instructors use semantic networks as lecture tools, as a medium for teaching across the Internet, or as study tools, they are explicitly sharing with their students not only their knowledge but also the ways in which they organize that knowledge. At the same time, each knowledge web represents one limited "slice" through an individual's knowledge, created at a specific point in time, in a particular context, and for a particular purpose. A knowledge representation is never complete, never all-purpose; it is always a work in progress.

Constructing Semantic Networks Alters the Ways We Think and Learn

Gorodetsky and Fisher [1996] compared prospective elementary school teachers in two sections of a capstone course in biology. Students in one section used SemNet as a study tool, while those in the other section studied by traditional means. Both groups responded to short essay questions at the end of the course. The SemNet students included significantly more (twice as many) relevant biology words in their responses, showing that they learned and were able to retrieve more biology ideas and organize them appropriately in the context of responding to an essay question (a transfer task). Further, the SemNet students wrote twice as many sentences, and their sentences were shorter and had greater clarity than those written by the traditional group. This shows that using SemNet has an impact on the way the user thinks, favoring short, concise propositions. Perhaps this is a Turing test in reverse, assessing the extent to which students can mimic the computer!

Anecdotal evidence also suggested that students were influenced toward SemNet-like thinking in other aspects of their lives. One student, for example, planned her entire wedding in the form of paper-based semantic networks sketched on napkins in a restaurant. Other students used the hardware and software provided in the computer lab to create semantic networks on other topics they were studying, including history, psychology, and literary analysis. This raises some questions: What long-term effects might result from the widespread use of knowledge webs as a means of communication? If humans and machines can communicate through topic maps, how will that affect human development?

Nonmajor biology students in an inquiry-based SemNet knowledge construction course achieved significantly higher scores than students in two teacher-centered, lecture-based, nonmajor biology courses that did not employ SemNet [Christianson and Fisher 1999]. The assessment was a two-tiered test for conceptual understanding of osmosis and diffusion. (The complete test can be reviewed in an appendix to Odom and Barrow [1995].) A two-tiered test consists of paired questions; the first item asks about factual content knowledge, and the second asks about underlying mechanisms. For example, one factual question asks students to choose between two options to make a true statement: "As the difference in concentration between two areas increases, the rate of diffusion (a) decreases or (b) increases." The related question about mechanism: "The reason for my answer is because (a) there is less room for the particles to move, (b) if the concentration is high enough, the particles will spread less and the rate will be slowed, (c) the molecules want to spread out, or (d) of the greater likelihood of random motion into other regions." The correct answers are (b) and (d), respectively.

Both groups did well on the content items, but the SemNet/inquiry group outperformed the comparison groups on the items that examined knowledge about the underlying mechanisms. This is consistent with findings from other studies—when students engage in carefully structured hands-on learning experiences combined with systematic knowledge representation, their content learning and meaningful understanding increase.

For example, Reader and Hammond [1994] compared two groups of students who were learning the same material but studying in different ways. One group of students was using a HyperCard-based knowledge mapping system, while a second group was using a computer-based notetaking strategy. At the end of the study, students took an achievement test that asked for both factual and relational information. The knowledge mapping group earned significantly higher post-test scores in both relational and factual knowledge.

In a similar vein, Chmielewski and Dansereau [1998] examined the performance of students who had been trained in concept mapping in the past. These students recalled more macro-level ideas from text passages than students who had not received such prior training. This occurred even in situations where concept mapping was not used, thus representing a transfer of learning from past concept mapping experiences to future tasks. Such transfer is generally difficult to achieve in education.

When students used SemNet, their abilities to discriminate between main and subordinate ideas increased significantly [Gorodetsky and Fisher 1996]. According to student self-reports, this enhanced ability to identify main ideas not only occurred in the course where SemNet was being used but transferred to other courses as well. As a consequence, students developed improved notetaking methods. This is an example of lateral transfer of skills.

All of these observations support the claim that constructing semantic networks alters the ways we think—and helps us learn! There is a much larger body of research with concept maps that I won't discuss here but that leads to similar conclusions [for example, Mintzes et al. 1997; Novak 1998].

Semantic Network–Based Courses Teach, Not Just Tell

"Telling is *not* teaching" is not in any way a new idea, but since it has not yet been heard by all teachers, it bears repeating. The basic message is that the lecture (also known as didactic instruction), which constitutes "telling," is not a highly effective method of instruction. The reform movement in science advocates maximizing learning through the use of active learning strategies including inquiry, problem solving, and open-ended questioning [American Association for the Advancement of Science 1990, 2000; National Research Council 1996; National Science Board Task Committee 1986; National Science Foundation and Department of Education 1980]. Science textbooks, like lectures, have been severely criticized. In fact, the American Association for the Advancement of Science [2000] recently concluded that big biology books simply fail to convey big biology ideas. Unfortunately, current textbooks as well as lectures tend to produce a mind-set that science is a compendium of facts to be memorized. Leaders in both science and education conclude that such one-way information transmission is outdated, ineffective, and long overdue for retirement—or at least significant modification.

Recent books on the effectiveness of teaching [Harlen 1999; Monk and Osborne 2000] don't even include the lecture. Active learning and inquiry methods are being widely promoted for science teaching because they have been shown to produce significantly better learning, deeper understanding, greater interest and motivation, and appreciation of the scientific process as well as knowledge of science [Minstrell and van Zee 2000; Mintzes et al. 1997]. The important goals are to engage students' minds, stimulate their curiosity, prompt their thinking deeply, and promote long-term understanding. Internet-based knowledge webs are highly interactive, with the student sitting in the driver's seat.

The best lecture teaching is not a total waste of time. Walberg [1991] reports that excellent lecturing (effect size 0.55) is about two-thirds as effective as active engagement (effect size 0.88) and half as effective as corrective feedback (effect size 0.94) and reinforcement (effect size 1.17). (Effect size is the average across all studies included in a meta-analysis of the difference between experimental and control groups in units of standard deviation.) The two most effective methods, corrective feedback and reinforcement, are two primary components in the mastery learning system mentioned previously as parts of the Internet-based knowledge web courses.

Why do people teach using less-than-optimum methods such as the lecture when significantly more effective, proven methods are available? The answers probably include familiarity, efficiency, and absence of rewards for putting greater effort into teaching. The human body has evolved with many suboptimal but usable features such as the knee, the lower back, and the prostate gland. Wandersee [personal communication, 2001] suggests that in a similar way, universities have evolved suboptimal but efficient methods of teaching.

Would you try to learn golf or sailing by sitting in on a series of lectures? Of course not. Some lectures may be useful, but you've got to get involved in the process to understand the challenges and acquire the skills. The same is true for science. Students who engage in inquiry, problem solving, and other aspects of science tend to develop a better understanding of the process of science and the nature of scientific thinking than those who don't.

As noted above, recognition of the importance of active learning grew out of the theory of constructivism. According to this theory, each individual actively *constructs* his or her own knowledge by linking one concept to another in meaningful ways. The richer the learning environment in which learners are immersed, the more information they have from which to construct their knowledge. The challenges presented to the students and the opportunities for interaction with the materials and with their peers guide and stimulate their learning—that is, their knowledge construction. Feedback helps students monitor their progress and correct wrong turns or misconceptions, and reinforcement allows students to acquire fluidity and competence in their thought processes. Practice, feedback, and reinforcement build skills, whether in golf or football or scientific thinking. Knowledge webs linked to suitable knowledge objects combined with frequent testing and instantaneous feedback can create this type of environment.

Learners in Internet-based knowledge web courses have many opportunities for exploring and playing with ideas, which Langer [1989, 1997] considers critical for mindful learning. The core information is presented in a manner that is parsimonious and thoughtfully structured. This follows Walberg's [1991, p. 37] advice: "To concentrate learners on essential points and to save time . . . remove elaborations and extraneous oral and written prose."

One of the travesties of standard science textbooks is that they present so many different concepts to students with so little information about each one that memorization is the only reasonable strategy for learning in the required time frame. And of course memorization results largely in short-term, temporary mastery, soon to be forgotten. Students are likely to recall or at least recognize the vocabulary, but not the meanings, of memorized science words.

Vygotsky [1978] emphasizes the two-way nature of teaching in the following way. Each learner has a *zone of proximal development* extending from what the learner can do independently to the maximum the learner can do with a teacher's help. Since learning involves connecting new ideas to preexisting ideas, an impasse is encountered when the new ideas are so far beyond one's experience that there is no obvious way to build these linkages. Teachers must interact regularly with their students to know whether or not their students are in those critical zones conducive to learning. The teacher then constructs scaffolding to help the students move along the path to higher understanding. The scaffolding can be in many forms including but not limited to inquiry, thought-provoking questioning, problem solving, exploration, prediction, reflection, feedback, and reinforcement. In autonomous, asynchronous learning environments, learners can theoretically guide themselves to comfortable learning zones, provided that the array of choices is sufficiently robust. It is conceivable that suitable agents with appropriate topic maps could assist in the process of identifying materials within the learner's zone of proximal development.

Understanding Relations *Is* Understanding

What are relations? The term has many different meanings, but in the context of this chapter, relations are the verbs and verb phrases that are used to link ideas together. Relations may also be referred to as *links* or *arcs*. Pask [1975, p. 553] understood the significance of relations, so much so that he defined a concept as "a procedure for bringing about a relation. *Not* a set of things." The English poet Ezra Pound (1885–1972) may have agreed with Pask because he once said that relations between things are more important than the things themselves. Even Plato spent a fair amount of time discussing the nature of relations.

In general, we can say that relations are challenging. Children find relations more difficult to understand than concepts, and they learn relations later than concepts [Gentner 1978, 1981a, 1981b, 1982]. Second-language learners similarly learn concepts before relations [Rosenthal 1996]. Since concepts are typically specified by nouns and relations are typically specified by verbs, this means that children and second-language learners learn nouns before verbs. Likewise, I have observed that when experts are trying to communicate from one domain to another, the usual impediments to understanding are the relations in the other field of study, which seem to present far more difficulties than the concepts.

What makes relations so difficult? For one thing, relational meanings are more fluid and less fixed than conceptual meanings. And relations are often implied rather than explicitly stated in text, lecture, and conversation. Thus inferencing is an important part of making sense in these settings. In addition, while concepts in a domain are typically represented by a highly standardized jargon, there is little standardization in the use of relation names. For example, is DNA *contained in* the nucleus or *part of* the nucleus or a *component of* the nucleus or *inside* the nucleus or *surrounded by* the nucleus? It could be any of the above. There is a high degree of consensus among experts on concept names, but relation names simply do not enjoy the same status. And as if this isn't enough, relations have tenses: past, present, and future. No wonder they are so elusive.

Below I summarize some conclusions about relations. For more extended discussions of these topics, see Fisher [1990], Fisher and Kibby [1996], Faletti and Fisher [1996], and Fisher et al. [2000].

- A relation is a specialized type of concept that explains the relationship between two other concepts [Sowa 1990].
- An association between two concepts is an unnamed relation; a link is perceived to exist, but its exact nature is not known or specified. (This is a very different definition than that used by most authors in this book and in the glossary; I find it a useful distinction in learning because students often have such unspecified links in their minds.)
- Relational meaning is context-dependent.
- Expression involves fewer relations than concepts, and the relations may be used again and again.
- The rich texture and meaning of a given knowledge domain is captured at least as much in its unique relations as in its unique concepts [Luoma-Overstreet 1990].
- Some relations are used much more frequently and are much less domain-specific than others; this is especially true of *whole/part, set/member,* and *characteristic* relations [Hoffman 1991].
- The quality of the relations one generates, the consistency with which these relations are used, and the ways in which ideas are organized with these relations are powerful determinants of whether or not one is learning meaningfully and whether one can efficiently retrieve and use information to solve problems.

- Many different names are possible for relations, and different people prefer different names; there is little standardization among science specialists about relation names, even though there is very strong consensus on concept names.
- Metaphors and analogies provide an entire template of relations with which to think about a new concept.
- The power of a scientific theory is that it explicates relations between things that haven't been perceived before. Darwin, for example, illuminated the relation, "is descended from" [Wandersee, personal communication, 1997].
- There is no universal, parsimonious set of relations for describing all knowledge, although people looked for such a set for many years.

In summary, relations are more difficult to understand than concepts, yet teachers organize their syllabi and lesson plans around concepts, not relations. Further, there is no standardized, agreed-upon jargon for most relations within a domain of knowledge. And in texts and other written materials, relations are often implicit rather than explicit. The fluidity of thought associated with relations in our thinking has yet to be satisfactorily explained, but given the very strong pattern we see, it seems likely that it is advantageous for our survival.

Clusters of concepts, often acquired as a first step in learning, have little meaning until they are connected by appropriate relations. Understanding relations and how to use them *is* indeed understanding. Creators of topic maps will face many of the same challenges as those encountered by creators of knowledge webs for humans.

A Paradigm Shift: Patterning Speech to Patterning Thought

Writing, since its inception in alphabet-based form and presumably even earlier, has been patterned after speech. With a shift to knowledge webs as a medium of written expression, we see writing being patterned after thought rather than after speech. This represents a profound paradigm shift for the human race. We can perceive its immediate implications, but the long-term implications of such a shift are impossible to fathom.

There are numerous benefits for learning and teaching. Being given not only the concepts but also the named bidirectional relations that describe a new domain provides a distinct advantage to learners. When learners construct their own knowledge webs as they learn, working with a tool that prompts generation not only of the concepts but also of the salient links between them helps learners develop meaningful as opposed to rote learning strategies. Making relations explicit and clearly evident is what learning is about.

Other advantages include chunking and dual coding. Chunking involves perceiving a complex set of information such as figures on a chess board (or a central concept with related concepts in a semantic network) as a single recognizable pattern and storing that pattern in memory [Chase and Simon 1973]. Human memory for images is impressive. Standing and colleagues [1970] found, for example, that a five-second exposure to each of a series of more than 2,500 pictures, followed by a recall test, produced more than 90 percent correct recall. Visuals are thus wonderful memory aids ("a picture is worth a thousand words"). For learning about a new science idea, a visual is often insufficient, however. Visuals in science typically require clear labels and supporting verbal explanations in order to be understood [Bottrill and Lock 1993]. A key advantage to such presentations is that the learner can encode information in two distinct information processing systems, one that represents information verbally (the internal semantic network) and one that represents information visually [Mayer and Sims 1994]. The images generated in the internal spatial processing system appear to be malleable but relatively long lasting [Shepard and Cooper 1982]. Thus dual coding both increases the amount of information available about an idea and facilitates recall of that idea by providing two separate storage and retrieval systems. The images that can be provided on the Web can be high quality, in color, and animated, which may further increase their comprehensibility and memorability (although this isn't necessarily guaranteed, as some research on textbook images has shown).

Semantic networks are primarily representations of "knowledge about." Can they possibly facilitate learning of procedural knowledge, or knowledge of "how to?" This in fact appears to be the case. There is evidence that 85–93 percent of procedural knowledge in many domains is grounded in semantic knowledge about that domain [Gordon and Gill 1989]. In addition, a semantic network representation that can be manipulated by the learner provides a concrete arena in which the learner can experiment with and manipulate verbal propositions—a sort of experimentation and playing with knowledge structures that can lead to their gradual refinement [Amlund et al. 1985; McAleese et al. 1999].

So there are many good reasons for leaving our "horseless carriage" syndrome behind and moving into a new millennium of thinking with the digital medium. As Peter Drucker, the organizational business guru, said, ". . . what these people [knowledge workers] were doing, and what most universities are still doing, was taking a conventional class lecture and basically putting it online. I was convinced from the beginning that a new distribution channel requires different forms" [GROK 2000, p. 36]. The president of Stanford University, John Hennessy, says: "Eventually this will lead to people taking courses whenever they want, in a completely asynchronous way, when they need to learn about a particular subject" [GROK 2000, p. 34]. The Internet has already become a major player in commerce, and many predict that online learning will produce a major shakedown in higher education in the coming years. The biggest schools (for example, Stanford, Harvard, University of Chicago, Wharton, Carnegie

Mellon) are hedging their bets by signing contracts with big e-learning companies [GROK 2000, p. 82], but many smaller schools are still doing nothing or doing the wrong thing (such as upholding their eighteenth-century standards with desperate vigor).

Summary

Hopefully, semantic networks will never replace linear text but rather will augment it. Text will continue to provide such things as detailed explanations and creative expressions. The major forms of knowledge representation, including visuals, semantic networks, and text, will be much more powerful than any single form alone.

I stand by my prediction that a profound paradigm shift will occur in the predominant mode of expression on the Internet. *The lightness of being is coming!* I believe that some form of semantic network representation will prevail as a primary organizing medium of the Web, although I don't know if the transition will take five years or fifty. The knowledge web format offers many advantages in terms of organizing and retrieving information, as emphasized in the rest of this book, and it offers many advantages in support of learning, as emphasized in this chapter. And with the Web at our fingertips, we are all becoming lifelong learners in need of easy, clear, efficient forms of communication. Hopefully, clever agents can build bridges between the topic maps and Semantic Webs of machines and the knowledge webs of humans.

Acknowledgments

I am grateful to Jack Logan for leading the way into the future and to Sunthar Visuvalingam, James Wandersee, Ray McAleese, and Sam Hunting for their helpful comments on this chapter.

References

American Association for the Advancement of Science. 1990. *Benchmarks for Science Literacy.* New York: Oxford University Press.

———. 2000. Big Biology Books Fail to Convey Big Ideas, Reports AAAS's Project 2061. Accessed in April 2002 at *http://www.project2061.org/newsinfo/press/rl000627.htm.*

Amlund, J. T., J. Gaffney, and R. W. Kulhavy. 1985. Map Feature Content and Text Recall of Good and Poor Readers. *Journal of Reading Behavior* 17:317–330.

Ausubel, D. P. 1963. *The Psychology of Meaningful Verbal Learning*. New York: Grune and Stratton.

———. 1968. *Educational Psychology: A Cognitive View*. San Francisco: Holt, Rinehart, and Winston.

Berners-Lee, T., J. Hendler, and O. Lassila. 2001. The Semantic Web. *Scientific American* (May). Accessed in April 2002 at *http://www.sciam.com/2001/0501issue/0501berners-lee.html*.

Blackmore, S., and R. Dawkins. 2000. *The Meme Machine*. Great Britain: Oxford University Press.

Bottrill, J., and R. Lock. 1993. Do Students Learn from Pictures or from Text? *Science Review* 74:109–112.

Brachman, R. J., and H. J. Levesque, eds. 1985. *Readings in Knowledge Representation*. Los Altos, CA: Morgan Kaufmann.

Brachman, R. J., H. J. Levesque, and R. Reiter, eds. 1991. Knowledge Representation: Special Issues of *Artificial Intelligence, an International Journal* (49), accessed in April 2002 at *http://www.elsevier.nl/inca/publications/store/5/2/1/1/4/0*.

Brady, R. 1996. *Virus of The Mind: The New Science of the Meme*. Seattle, WA: Integral Press.

Brooks, M. 2000. Global Brain. *New Scientist* (June 24). Accessed in April 2002 at *http://www.newscientist.com/hottopics/ai/globalbrain.jsp*.

Buzan, T., and B. Buzan. 1993. *The Mind Map Book: How to Use Radiant Thinking to Maximize Your Brain's Untapped Potential*. New York: Plume Books (Penguin).

Chase, W. G., and H. A. Simon. 1973. The Mind's Eye in Chess. In *Visual Information Processing: Proceedings*; W. G. Chase, ed. New York: Academic Press, pp. 215–281.

Chmielewski, T. L., and D. F. Dansereau. 1998. Enhancing the Recall of Text: Knowledge Mapping Training Promotes Implicit Transfer. *Journal of Educational Psychology* 90(3):407–413.

Christianson, R. G., and K. M. Fisher. 1999. Comparison of Student Learning about Diffusion and Osmosis in Constructivist and Traditional Classrooms. *International Journal of Science Education* 21(6):687–698.

Collins, A. M., and E. F. Loftus. 1975. A Spreading Activation Theory of Semantic Processing. *Psychological Review* (82):407–428.

Diamond, J. 1999. *Guns, Germs and Steel: The Fates of Human Societies*. New York: Norton.

Faletti, J., and K. M. Fisher. 1996. The Information in Relations in Biology, or the Unexamined Relation Is Not Worth Having. In *Knowledge Acquisition, Organization, and Use in Biology;* K. M. Fisher and M. R. Kibby, eds. New York: Springer Verlag, pp. 182–205.

Fisher, K. M. 1990. Semantic Networking: The New Kid on the Block. *Journal of Research in Science Teaching* (27):1001–1018.

Fisher, K. M., et al. 1990. Computer-Based Concept Mapping: SemNet® Software—A Tool for Describing Knowledge Networks. *Journal of College Science Teaching* (19):347–352.

Fisher, K. M., and M. Kibby, eds. 1996. *Knowledge Acquisition, Organization, and Use in Biology,* NATO ASI Series F, vol. 148. New York: Springer Verlag.

Fisher, K. M., and J. Logan. 2001. General Education Courses on the Internet: Why Do Students Love 'Em? Prepublication version posted on the Internet at *http:// t.collegeunits.com/Internet_Courses.html.*

Fisher, K. M., J. H. Wandersee, and D. Moody. 2000. *Mapping Biology Knowledge.* Boston, MA: Kluwer Academic Publishers.

Gentner, D. 1978. On Relational Meaning: The Acquisition of Verb Meaning. *Child Development* (49):988–998.

———. 1981a. Integrating Verb Meanings into Context. *Discourse Processes* (4): 349–375.

———. 1981b. Some Interesting Differences between Verbs and Nouns. *Cognition and Brain Theory* (4):161–178.

———. 1982. Why Nouns Are Learned before Verbs: Linguistic Relativity versus Natural Partitioning. In *Language Development: Language, Cognition, and Culture;* S. Kuczaj, ed. Hillsdale, NJ: Erlbaum, pp. 301–334.

Gilbert, S. D. 2001. How to Be a Successful Online Student. Reviewed by J. R. Young in *Chronicle of Higher Education* Feb. 2, 2001 (accessed in April 2002 at *http://chronicle. com/free/2001/02/2001020201u.htm.*

Gordon, S. E. 1996. Eliciting and Representing Biology Knowledge with Conceptual Graph Structures. In *Knowledge Acquisition, Organization, and Use in Biology;* K. M. Fisher and M. R. Kibby, eds. New York: Springer Verlag, pp. 206–225.

Gordon, S. E., and R. T. Gill. 1989. *The Formation and Use of Knowledge Structures in Problem Solving Domains.* Project Report. Moscow, ID: Psychology Department, University of Idaho.

Gorodetsky, M., and K. M. Fisher. 1996. Generating Connections and Learning in Biology. In *Knowledge Acquisition, Organization, and Use in Biology;* K. M. Fisher and M. R. Kibby, eds. New York: Springer Verlag, pp. 135–154.

Gould, S. J. 1977. *Ontogeny and Phylogeny.* Cambridge, MA: Harvard University Press.

GROK. 2000. *Special Reports on the Internet Economy.* San Francisco: The Industry Standard.

Harlen, W. 1999. *Effective Teaching of Science: A Review of Research.* Publication 142. Edinburgh, Scotland: Scottish Council of Research in Education.

Heylighen, F. 2000. Collective Web Intelligence and Its Implementation on the Web: Algorithms to Develop a Collective Mental Map. Accessed in April 2002 at *http:// pcp.lanl.gov/Papers/CollectiveWebIntelligence.pdf.*

Hoe, R. 1902. *A Short History of the Printing Press.* New York: Printed and published for Robert Hoe.

Hoffman, R. P. 1991. *Use of Relational Descriptors by Experienced Users of a Computer-Based Semantic Network.* Unpublished master's thesis. San Diego, CA: San Diego State University.

Horn, R. E. 1989. *Mapping Hypertext.* Lexington, MA: The Lexington Institute.

Jonassen, D. H., K. Beissner, and M. Yacci. 1993. *Structural Knowledge: Techniques for Representing, Conveying and Acquiring Structural Knowledge.* Hillsdale, NJ: Erlbaum.

Kelly, George A. 1955. *The Psychology of Personal Constructs: Volume I—A Theory of Personality.* New York: Norton.

Langer, Ellen J. 1989. *Mindfulness.* Menlo Park, CA: Addison-Wesley.

———. 1997. *The Power of Mindful Learning.* Menlo Park, CA: Addison-Wesley.

Lehman, F., and E. Y. Rodin. 1992. *Semantic Networks in Artificial Intelligence.* New York: Pergamon Press.

Luoma-Overstreet, K. 1990. SemNet® Journal: A Documentation of Progress over the Duration of the Final Assignment. Paper submitted to Dr. B. Allen for Cognitive Science 700 course, San Diego State University, San Diego, CA.

Mayer, R. E., and V. K. Sims. 1994. For Whom Is a Picture Worth a Thousand Words? Extensions of the Dual-Coding Theory of Multimedia Learning. *Journal of Educational Psychology* 46:389–401.

McAleese, R. 1998. The Knowledge Arena as an Extension to the Concept Map: Reflection in Action. *Interactive Learning Environments* 6:1–22.

McAleese, R., S. Grabinger, and K. Fisher. 1999. The Knowledge Arena: A Learning Environment That Underpins Concept Mapping. Paper presented at the annual meeting of the American Educational Research Association, Montreal, Canada, April 1999. Accessed in April 2002 at *http://www.cst.hw.ac.uk/~ray/McAleese.pdf.*

Minstrell, J., and E. H. van Zee, eds. 2000. *Teaching and Learning in an Inquiry-Based Science Classroom.* Washington, DC: American Association for the Advancement of Science.

Mintzes, J. J., J. H. Wandersee, and J. D. Novak. 1997. *Teaching Science for Understanding: A Human Constructivist View*. San Diego, CA: Academic Press.

Monk, M., and J. Osborne, eds. 2000. *Good Practice in Science Teaching: What Research Has to Say*. Buckingham, UK: Open University Press.

National Research Council. 1996. *National Science Education Standards*. Washington, DC: National Academy Press.

National Science Board Task Committee. 1986. *Undergraduate Science and Engineering Education*. Washington, DC: National Science Board.

National Science Foundation and Department of Education. 1980. *Science and Engineering Education for the 1980's and Beyond*. NSF Publication No. 80-78. Washington, DC: U.S. Government Printing Office.

Novak, J. D. 1990. Concept Maps and Vee Diagrams: Two Metacognitive Tools to Facilitate Meaningful Learning. *Instructional Science* 19:29–52.

———. 1998. *Learning, Creating and Using Knowledge: Concept Maps as Facilitative Tools in Schools and Corporations*. Mahwah, NJ: Erlbaum.

Odom, A. L., and L. H. Barrow. 1995. The Development and Application of a Two-Tiered Diagnostic Test Measuring College Biology Students' Understanding of Diffusion and Osmosis Following a Course of Instruction. *Journal of Research in Science Teaching* 32:45–61.

Pask, G. 1975. *Conversation, Cognition and Learning: A Cybernetic Theory and Methodology*. New York: Elsevier.

———. 1976a. Conversational Techniques in the Study and Practice of Education. *Journal of Educational Psychology* 46:12–25.

———. 1976b. Styles and Strategies of Learning. *Journal of Educational Psychology* 46:128–148.

Peddie, R. A. 1927. *Printing: A Short History of the Art*. London: Grafton and Co.

Perkins, D. N. 1993. Person-plus: A Distributed View of Thinking and Learning. In *Distributed Cognitions: Psychological and Educational Considerations*; G. Salomon, ed. New York: Cambridge University Press.

Pope, M. 1982. Personal Construction of Formal Knowledge. *Interchange on Educational Policy* 13(4):3–13.

Pope, M., and J. Gilbert. 1983. Conceptual Understanding and Science Learning: An Interpretation of Research within a Sources-of-Knowledge Framework. *Science Education* 70(5):583–604.

Postman, N. 1970. The Reformed English Curriculum. In *High School 1980: The Shape of the Future in American Secondary Education*; A. C. Eurich, ed. New York: Pitman, pp. 160–168.

———. 1982. *The Disappearance of Childhood.* New York: Delacorte.

———. 1993. *Technopoly: The Surrender of Culture to Technology.* New York: Vintage Books.

Quillian, M. R. 1967. Word Concepts: A Theory and Simulation of Some Basic Semantic Capabilities. *Behavioral Sciences* 12:410–430.

———. 1969. The Teachable Language Comprehender. *Communications of the Association for Computing Machinery* 12:459–475.

Reader, W., and N. Hammond. 1994. Computer-Based Tools to Support Learning from Hypertext: Concept Mapping Tools and Beyond. *Computers and Education* 22(1–2):99–106. Jan–Feb 1994

Resnick, L. B. 1983. Mathematics and Science Learning: A New Conception. *Science* 220:477–478.

———. 1987a. *Education and Learning to Think.* Washington, DC: National Academy Press.

———. 1987b. Learning in School and Out. *Educational Researcher* 16(9):13–20.

Rosenthal, J. W. 1996. *Teaching Science to Language Minority Students.* Bristol, PA: Multilingual Matters Ltd.

Ryan, D. W. 1995. Implementation of Mastery-Learning and Outcome-Based Education: A Review and Analysis of Lessons Learned, Research, Strategic Policy. First Internet Edition. Accessed in May 2002 at *http://www.hrdc-drhc.gc.ca/arb/publications/ research/abr-96-4e.shtml.*

Sacha, B. 1998. Revolution in Mapping. *National Geographic* 193(2):6–39.

Sacks, O. 1990. *Seeing Voices.* New York: Harper Collins.

Shepard, R. N., and L. A. Cooper. 1982. *Mental Images and Their Transformations.* Cambridge, MA: MIT Press.

Shepherd, C. 2001. Objects of Interest. Fastrack Consulting Limited. Accessed in April 2002 at *http://www.fastrak-consulting.co.uk/tactix/features/objects/objects.htm.*

Sobel, D. 2000. *Galileo's Daughter.* New York: Penguin Books.

Sowa, J., ed. 1983. Conceptual Structures: Information Processing in Mind and Machine. Menlo Park, CA: Addison-Wesley.

———, ed. 1990. *Principles of Semantic Networks: Explorations in the Representation of Knowledge.* San Francisco: Morgan Kaufmann.

———, ed. 1999. *Knowledge Representation: Logical, Philosophical, and Computational Foundations.* Pacific Grove, CA: PWS Publishing.

Standing, L., J. Conezio, and R. N. Haber. 1970. Perception and Memory for Pictures: Single Trial Learning of 2500 Visual Stimuli. *Psychonomic Science* 19:73–84.

Stewart, J., J. Van Kirk, and R. Rowell. 1979. Concept Maps: A Tool for Use in Biology Teaching. *The American Biology Teacher* (41):171–175.

Thro, M. P. 1978. Relationships between Associative and Content Structure in Physics. *Journal of Educational Psychology* (70):971–978.

von Glaserfeld, E. 1987a. Learning as a Constructive Activity. In *Problems of Representation in the Teaching and Learning of Mathematics;* Claude Janvier, ed. Hillsdale, NJ: Erlbaum, pp. 215–227.

———. 1987b. Learning as Constructive Activity. In *The Construction of Knowledge: Contributions to Conceptual Semantics.* The Systems Inquiry Series. Salinas, CA: Intersystems Publications.

———. 1988. Constructivism as a Scientific Method. *Scientific Reasoning Research Institute Newsletter* 3:8–9.

———. 1989. Cognition, Construction of Knowledge, and Teaching. *Synthese* 80(1): 121–140.

———. 1993. Questions and Answers about Radical Constructivism. In *The Practice of Constructivism in Science Education;* K. Tobin, ed. Washington, DC: American Association for the Advancement of Science Press.

Vygotsky, L. S. 1978. *Mind in Society: The Development of Higher Psychological Processes.* Cambridge, MA: Harvard University Press.

Walberg, H. J. 1991. Productive Teaching and Instruction: Assessing the Knowledge Base. In *Effective Teaching: Current Research;* H. C. Waxman and H. J. Walberg, eds. Berkeley, CA: McCutchan.

Wandersee, J. H. 2000. Using Concept Mapping as a Knowledge Mapping Tool. In *Mapping Biology Knowledge;* K. M. Fisher, J. H. Wandersee, and D. E. Moody, eds. Boston, MA: Kluwer Academic Publishers, p. 128 (paperback).

Wells, J. 1965. The History of Printing. In *Encyclopedia Britannica.* Chicago: William Benton.

West, L. H. T., and A. L. Pines. 1985. *Cognitive Structure and Conceptual Change.* New York: Academic Press.

Wideman, G. 2000. Evolution of the Human Relationship to Knowledge. Accessed in April 2002 at *http://www.wideman-one.com/gw/xm/concmod/humanrelknow.htm.*

Wittrock, M. C. 1974a. A Generative Model of Mathematics Learning. *Journal for Research in Mathematics Education* 5:181–196.

———. 1974b. Learning as a Generative Process. *Educational Psychologist* 11:87–95.

Woods, W. A. 1985. What's in a Link: Foundations for Semantic Networks. In *Readings in Knowledge Representation;* R. J. Brachman and H. J. Levesque, eds. Los Altos, CA: Morgan Kaufmann.

Chapter 17

TOPIC MAPS, THE SEMANTIC WEB, AND EDUCATION[1]

JACK PARK

Knowledge is information plus experience. Information can be bought, but knowledge must be found on your own gameboard of life.

— HARISH JOHARI [1998, p. xvi]

Topic maps are about knowledge representation.[2] Knowledge itself is a social construct; what we claim to know, we create in our own minds from interactions with our environment, and we learn from others by way of sharing processes. Topic maps are a way to represent aspects of what we know for the purpose of sharing. Verna Allee [1999] has this to say about knowledge: "If we have learned to appreciate one thing in the remarkable groundswell of interest in knowledge, it is that what we create arises from what we value, desire, believe, and conceptualize in the mysterious recesses of our hearts and minds."

I have a bias, which I happily admit. My bias is very strongly in favor of seeing that the World Wide Web becomes a tool that serves the purpose of amplifying human intellect. Kathleen Fisher's contribution to this book (Chapter 16) discusses topic maps in the classroom, and classrooms are finding ways to couple to the Web. This chapter continues the conversation on human intellect, what it is, how the Web figures into the picture, and how XTM serves as one of the tools in the Semantic Web. For that, let us consider three focus questions:

---

[1] Portions of this chapter involving discussions on constructivist learning and IBIS appeared in my talk "Bringing Knowledge Technologies to the Classroom" at Knowledge Technologies 2001, March 2001, Austin, Texas, GCA. Available on the Web at *http://www.thinkalong.com/JP/ParkKT2001.pdf*, accessed in April 2002.

[2] To say that topic maps are about navigation, information representation, even knowledge representation is to open a debate.

1. What is the Semantic Web?
2. How can topic maps play an important role in the Semantic Web?
3. What's next?

The goals of this chapter are to create a context with which to surround any further discussion on XTM and the Semantic Web and to animate discussions related to the future of the Web itself.

What Is the Semantic Web?

This question is important; if you are going to construct tools to participate in the Semantic Web, it's useful to know more about the activity. That's the tool builder's perspective. If you are going to use the Semantic Web, it is still useful to know more. Content owners fit into this discussion as well. In any case, break the phrase *Semantic Web* into its two constituent words, and *web* comes to mind fairly quickly. We think of spider webs, and, these days, neural networks and something called *semantic networks*. It seems that the meaning of *semantic* may not come to mind quite as easily.

Let's have some fun here. *Webster's Dictionary* defines *semantic* as "to **signify**, to **mean**." I emphasize these two words, *signify* and *mean*, because they will recur several ways during our search for meaning.[3] I would like to take a brief diversion from things "topic mappish" and search for meaning in the concept of a Semantic Web. Since I subscribe to the idea that meanings are social constructs, it might be interesting to see what others are saying about the Semantic Web and about things semantic.

When I started working on this chapter, Google got about 409,000 hits on the word *semantic*, and the Semantic Web Roadmap[4] was the first hit. Looking further, I saw that the National Library of Medicine [2001] has a fact sheet on the Unified Medical Language System (UMLS) Semantic Network that says:

> The Semantic Network serves as an authority for the semantic types that are assigned to concepts in the Metathesaurus and that are assigned to databases in the Information Source Map. The Network defines these types, both with textual descriptions and by means of the information inherent in its hierarchies.

---

[3] One of them, *mean*, just did.

[4] See *http://www.w3.org/DesignIssues/Semantic.html*. Actually, it's the third hit now that some time has passed since I first checked. And the hit count has fallen to around 369,000 as Google improves.

In that network, the nodes in the network represent the semantic types, and the links (or arcs) represent the relationships between the nodes.

A Semantic Web Technologies Workshop held during November 2000 in Luxembourg intended to "identify and discuss R&D priorities related to Semantic Web Technologies for applications, in, e.g., Knowledge Management, Web retrieval/navigation and e-Commerce" [Information Society Technologies Programme 2000].

Looking even further, I saw there exists something called Semantic Pragmatic Disorder,[5] which is defined with respect to children who have, among other things, specific semantic pragmatic language problems. These children have problems getting meanings out of words.

Webster's defines *mean* as "to have in the mind as a purpose, to show, **signify**, to have importance, to direct." Noticing the circularity here, I checked *signify*, which is defined as "to be a sign of, to **mean**, imply." We've gone circular again.

Eventually I landed on a Semantic Web home page where I found references to ontologies. Finally, I found a statement about the Semantic Web. "The Semantic Web is a vision: the idea of having data on the Web defined and linked in a way that it can be used by machines—not just for display purposes, but for using it in various applications" [SemanticWeb.Org 2002].

Consider the structure of the Semantic Web (also called Seweb), as described by Tim Berners-Lee [2000] in his XML 2000 talk. Figure 17–1 is a sketch of the salient features he envisions. We see that Unicode and URIs make up the foundation of readability and addressability in the Semantic Web initiative. Above that reside XML and namespaces, and we know that modern browsers are beginning to support XML. For older browsers, XML can be transformed, using XSL, to HTML for rendering as discussed in Chapter 9. Above those two levels, we enter the arena of *semantification* of the Web. I may not be the first to have coined that word, and my spelling checker really hates it, but the message is this: we need to put something called *semantics* into the Web. As I mentioned above, *Webster's Dictionary* defines *semantic* as "to signify, to mean." Let's accept the notion that we wish to put *meaning* into the Web. By using the word *meaning*, I am saying that if I mention some concept on my Web page, the minds of my readers should be triggered to experience or visualize the same concept that I experience or visualize when reading or describing the same page.

How can the Web be turned into an environment in which we share meanings? Start by imagining that we are looking at the RDF[6] level of Figure 17–1. Imagine popping

---

[5] See, for example, *http://www.hyperlexia.org/sp1.html*.

[6] Resource Description Framework, as discussed in Chapter 12 by Eric Freese.

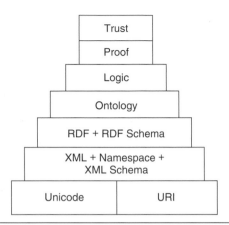

Figure 17–1   Semantic Web features (after Berners-Lee [2000, slide 10])

up to the next level, ontology, while keeping in mind RDF. Ontology is the study of being; its philosophical roots go way back. Today, we tend to think of ontologies as descriptions of things in our universe and the relationships that exist between those things. An ontology is a kind of vocabulary. If you have an ontology,[7] you may need a way to represent that vocabulary so that both computer programs and humans can read it. RDF coupled with RDF Schema (RDFS) supplies a structure well suited to this need. The suggestion has been made that XTM, the topic map specification, may satisfy this need as well. Indeed, there are discussions ongoing at this time to find the commonality between RDF and XTM [Berners-Lee 2000, slide 15]. In Chapter 12 in this book, Eric Freese discusses the similarities between XTM and the RDF being developed as part of the Semantic Web initiative. The XTM core deliverables document calls for the creation of Published Subject Indicators (PSIs),[8] some of which are mandatory to establish precise semantics of the XTM syntax and some of which are optional, serving as a kind of ontology for users of topic maps.

In summary, this chapter takes the view that, to be in a Semantic Web, we must develop ways to "put meaning" on the Web. If we accept that human knowledge is based on a collective, shared understanding of meanings, then it follows that the Semantic Web will need to evolve a mechanism by which these shared meanings can be represented and applied. This chapter centers on the notion that the XML topic maps initiative offers one such mechanism to satisfy at least part of that need. Consider, however,

---

[7]The mere fact that my word processor does not like the phrase "an ontology" reminds me that the use of the word *ontology* here is a fairly new one.

[8]See *http://www.topicmaps.org/xtm/1.0/core.html*. Chapter 5 in this book also talks about PSIs.

that, along with RDF, there are other ongoing developmental activities that aim to serve the same needs. The Ontology Inference Layer (OIL),[9] which is a particular example of the application of RDFS, began as a primarily European project to bring semantic information to the Web. DARPA Agent Markup Language (DAML)[10] is an American project that now includes a number of ontologies, such as the Universal Standard Products and Services Classification Code (UNSPSC),[11] created when the United Nations Development Program and Dunn & Bradstreet combined their separate commodity classification codes into a single open system.[12] DAML and OIL are essential input to the W3C's newly formed Web Ontology activity.[13]

How Can Topic Maps Play an Important Role in the Semantic Web?

Alexander Chislenko [1997] has this to say about the Web: "The Web is probably the richest information repository in human history, but most of its information is passive and unstructured."

"Passive and unstructured." What a concept! Let's imagine that a response to Chislenko's comment requires a look at mechanisms, which, at once, turn passive information into active experiences while adding structure to the information the Web provides. RDF was proposed to put structure into metadata, which is data *about* information. Metadata combined with topic maps, as discussed in this book, take care of adding structure. The opportunity to provide more structure combined with the activity of collaborative construction of knowledge lead us to think about discussion spaces. Let's turn now to discussion spaces and couple them to a learning environment with the goal of satisfying one of the Web's main use cases: education.

What's Next?

It is said that the tortoise never makes progress until the creature sticks its neck out.

—UNKNOWN

---

[9] See *http://www.ontoknowledge.org/oil/*.

[10] See *http://www.daml.org/*.

[11] See *http://eccma.org/unspsc/*.

[12] It should be noted that DAML and /OIL are far more important to the future of the Web than is suggested by the single paragraph here. Future books will cover these developments.

[13] See *http://www.w3.org/2001/SW/WebOnt*.

What's next? For me, the answer is simple: something I shall claim to be a *better* tool for education. My plan here is to discuss an opportunity that can be available only by way of the Semantic Web—the opportunity to implement *constructivist learning environments* that enable the development of world-class, critical thinking skills in all of humanity's children. This thinking seems completely in line with recent statements about the Semantic Web. For instance, Tim Berners-Lee, James Hendler, and Ora Lassila [2001] had this to say about the Semantic Web: "The Semantic Web is not 'merely' the tool for conducting individual tasks that we have discussed so far. In addition, if properly designed, the Semantic Web can assist the evolution of human knowledge as a whole."

Education on the Web

Let's follow the argument made recently by Douglas Engelbart [2000] that there is an "unfinished revolution" in the application of personal computing to the enhancement of human intellect in relation to finding solutions to complex, urgent problems. His Open Hyperdocument System[14] is a project intended to develop and exploit technologies that will work in harmony with the Semantic Web initiative started by Tim Berners-Lee [1998]. I believe that knowledge technologies growing out of initiatives like those of Engelbart and Berners-Lee will be of greatest value to the education of children.

Evolution of the Semantic Web provides the opportunity to examine the necessary tensions between many theories of learning. We are faced with a deluge of names for these learning theories, some of which are objectivist, interpretivist, constructivist, reductionist, developmental, and so forth. I will discuss one particular theory, constructivist, and its relations to critical thinking. I'll then connect that theory to its relations with the Semantic Web initiative.

David Schafersman [1991] says this of critical thinking: "Critical thinking means correct thinking in the pursuit of relevant and reliable knowledge about the world. Another way to describe it is reasonable, reflective, responsible, and skillful thinking that is focused on deciding what to believe or do."

Objectivist and reductionist theories assume that knowledge can be transferred by teachers or by interactions with technologies and therefore can be acquired by learners. Accumulation of facts and data here precedes critical thinking about them [Davis-Seaver et al. 2000]. Developmental theories withhold the exercise of critical thinking until certain levels of maturity are demonstrated. Constructivist theories assume that

---

[14]See *http://www.bootstrap.org/ohs/index.jsp*.

learners construct knowledge both individually and through social interactions. Indeed, in the constructivist view, critical thinking lies at the heart of the teaching and learning process [Davis-Seaver et al. 2000]. Kathleen Fisher, in Chapter 16, discusses topic maps in the light of constructivist thinking.

Each theory suggests different approaches to instructional design. This chapter focuses on those aspects of instructional design that couple the emerging technology of the Semantic Web with constructivist learning environments. In the next sections we'll examine the principles of constructivist epistemology and then discuss knowledge technologies useful in constructivist environments.

Constructivist Learning Theory

What biology shows us is that the uniqueness of being human lies exclusively in a social structural coupling that occurs through languaging, generating (a) the regularities proper to the human social dynamics, for example, individual identity and self-consciousness, and (b) the recursive social human dynamics that entails a reflection enabling us to see that as human beings we have only the world which we create with others—whether we like them or not.
                    —HUMBERTO R. MATURANA AND FRANCISCO J. VERALA [1987, p. 246]

Three names (although many others exist) come to mind in relation to the constructivist stance: Peirce, Piaget, and Vygotsky. Charles Sanders Peirce[15] established a foundation for pragmatism, the evolution of meanings negotiated within a social context. Jean Piaget[16] established an order in which children develop. Lev Semyonovich Vygotsky[17] argued with Piaget, holding that children, through social interactions (typically with adults), are able to achieve higher levels of knowing; development is enhanced by learning [Phillips 1997]. My plan here is to outline what can be mined from a base of literature established by these and other individuals and to connect that information to learning environments and the Semantic Web.

Principles of Constructivist Learning

The key points of constructivist learning theory discussed in Conceição-Runlee and Daley [1998] that apply to Web-based course design are listed below.

---

[15] See, for example, *http://www.peirce.org/*.

[16] See, for example, *http://www.piaget.org/*.

[17] See, for example, *http://www.psy.pdx.edu/PsiCafe/KeyTheorists/Vygotsky.htm*.

- Knowledge and beliefs are constructed within the learner. Learners both *create* and *own* their knowledge. The kind of ownership discussed here relates to pride of ownership; the learner's ability to learn is reinforced with each discovery.
- Knowledge formation involves constructing *meaning*. Learning must be self-regulating; the learner must take control of the process and progress at his or her own level of competence. The problem space must not be overprescribed; the learner must have the opportunity for discovery.
- Knowledge formation involves integration with prior knowledge. The integration process itself is rich in opportunities for new discoveries.
- Learning is a social process, greatly enhanced by shared experiences and shared memory.
- Learning involves reflection and metacognition. In order to form meanings, learners must reflect on their own methods of learning. Learners must also participate in the assessment of their own learning. Assessment must take into account alternative views and contexts.
- Learning outcomes are varied and often unpredictable. Individuals are likely to form meanings from experiences that are unique to and guided by their overall experience.

These points suggest use cases and eventual requirements involved in instructional design. Let's turn now to a view of constructivist learning environments.

Toward Constructivist Learning Environments

Children are natural mimics who act like their parents despite every effort to teach them good manners.   —UNKNOWN

Learners need an environment that supports both individual and collaborative projects intended to provide opportunities for discovery. Such environments are often designed around thematic projects that provide a uniform context for learning. Context includes features of the world expressed in the learning environment such as structural, political, social, and other features.

Equally important are the learner's own relationships with the environment. A goal in constructivist learning is the learner's ownership of new knowledge. The role of the instructional designer is less that of author of prescriptive lessons and more that of creator of environments that engage learners and that enable and require them to create meaningful knowledge.

A constructivist environment provides opportunities for critical thinking. Logical thinking is one of the mechanisms of critical thinking. Puzzles form a basis for the development of logical thinking. In an example puzzle, you are given a three-gallon can, a five-gallon can, and water; the objective is to load four gallons into the five-gallon can. I can still remember when that problem was hard!

Next to the logical thinking involved with solving puzzles are aspects of logical reasoning that permit one to participate in debate or argumentation. Students and teachers in classrooms around the world are quite used to conducting debates; I imagine that such debates could be taken online in such a fashion that debate skills will be honed against members of other cultures, leading to world-class thinking skills. In order to facilitate what Nikos Karacapilidis and Thomas Gordon [1995] call *Computational Dialectics*, the Issue-Based Information System (IBIS) [Toulmin 1958; Kuntz and Rittel 1970] provides computer support for responses to questions while tracking arguments both pro and con with respect to the responses. IBIS provides one of the tools I believe important to the evolution of constructivist environments.

A tool for tracking and visualizing the argument process is a required component in a constructivist environment. Some existing tools, for example, QuestMap[18] (Figure 17–2), offer visual presentations.

Graphical tools have a long history in the classroom, starting with concept-mapping tools [Novak 1998a; Fisher, Wandersee, and Wideman 2000; Fisher, Wandersee, and Moody 2000]. An instance of a classroom concept-mapping tool is SemNet,[19] which allows learners to construct concept maps (a kind of semantic network) graphically, as illustrated in Figure 17–3. Chapter 16 by Kathleen Fisher provides background discussion on this subject.

I believe that a combination of structured argumentation and visual representation of discourse will provide an important part of a constructivist learning environment. In the next sections we look a bit closer at these technologies. Earlier, the idea of generating discussion spaces was introduced as a tool for use in learning activities. Now I will relate discussion spaces to ideas of augmented discourse and facilitated argumentation. The approach taken is to apply IBISs as learning environments. Topic maps, with their XML syntax, and the XTM specification[20] can be applied to the task of providing both (1) a concept map–like graphical interface for visualizing the topics and their relationships as involved in argumentation and (2) a serialization scheme that supports comparison and merging of learning experiences. Topic maps, I think, can play an important role in implementations of IBIS discussion spaces on the Web. I will now sketch my ideas on how that may be so.

---

[18] See *http://www.gdss.com/wp/VIMS.html*, and for more information, see *http://www.cognexus.org/*.

[19] Available at *http://www.biologylessons.sdsu.edu/about/aboutsemnet.html*.

[20] See *http://www.topicmaps.org/xtm/index.html*.

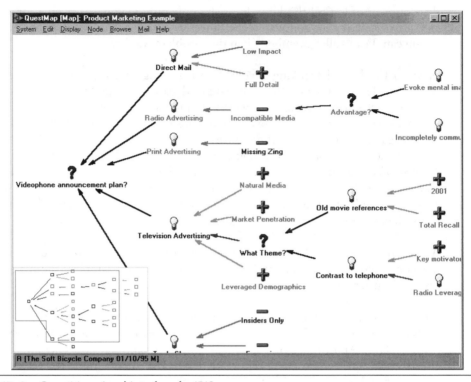

Figure 17–2   QuestMap visual interface for IBIS

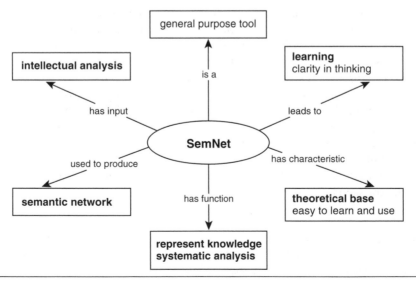

Figure 17–3   A SemNet semantic network (courtesy of Kathleen Fisher)

IBIS

Even in highly sophisticated modern knowledge organizations, the most valuable knowledge—the know-how in terms of what really gets results and what mistakes to avoid—often resides mainly in people's minds.

—STEVEN DENNING [2000]

Consider the issue of critical thinking. Joseph Novak [1998b] refers to the structure of knowledge expressed in any work as outlined by five questions proposed by D. B. Gowan:

1. What is the telling question?
2. What are the key concepts and conceptual structure?
3. What are the methods involved in answering the question?
4. What knowledge claims are made?
5. What value claims are made?

Figure 17–4 sketches Gowan's ideas in a flow chart. This chart was inspired by an illustration of Gowan's Knowledge "V" presented in Novak [1998b]. A question provokes the learner to apply a knowledge base to the task of creating a knowledge product in the form of knowledge claims and value claims. Cycles of review of those claims enable learning in the form of revisions and additions to the learner's knowledge base.

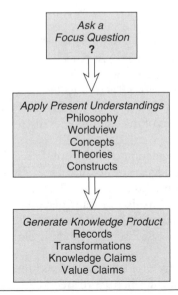

Figure 17–4   Knowledge activity according to Gowan

A key instrument in inquiry is a focus question. Learners are expected to apply the thinking skills described as present understandings in Figure 17–4 and are expected to perform operations required to generate the knowledge product: record (research), transform (responses to the question), summarize (make claims), and evaluate (discuss the value of the knowledge claims). A useful way to formalize this process is through the application of IBIS technology.

IBIS provides a tool that supports users in making statements, adducing reasons, inferring conclusions, and discussing exceptions. IBIS does this by:

- Managing the argument process
- Tracking issues that are raised and assumptions made
- Tracking reasons, counterarguments, and conclusions
- Tracking evaluation of justifications
- Enforcing the rules of argument

In an IBIS dialog, a question is posed. Each participating learner is expected to formulate a response, an *idea* in the terminology of the QuestMap manual [Group Decision Support Systems 2000]. Once responses are presented, the discussion begins. Learners formulate responses to the ideas. These can be in the form of *for* or *against* arguments, justifications for various responses, or just further commentary.

An IBIS discussion is a search for relevant and reliable knowledge, but IBIS, or any formalized interactive knowledge management tool, does not exist without open issues. Of particular note is the notion that formal systems tend to inhibit full participation among users. Shipman and Marshall [1999] discuss issues related to the use of formal systems from the perspectives of cognitive overhead, tacit knowledge, and prior structure. Indeed, cognitive overhead exists for any learner, and some of that overhead lends well to at least partial mitigation through appropriate user-interface design. Gaining tacit knowledge is what learning is all about, and just about everything constitutes prior structure to learners. I am suggesting that, with care, these issues need not interfere with classroom activities, though they certainly might interfere in applications of the technologies discussed here other than learning.

The basis for speculation that an issue-based discussion tool adds value to a learning environment is suggested in Figure 17–5. Two learning cycles are at work within the larger flow of information shown. There is first a *personal cycle* and second a *social cycle* requiring the participation of many personal cycles. The personal cycle occurs within the individual's personal knowledge base. The social cycle involves discourse, which can include IBIS-style discussion and the generation of a public knowledge base.

Generation of large discussion spaces within the public discourse creates many discussion threads, some of which are related to others. Topic maps offer tools appropriate to

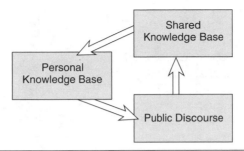

Figure 17–5   Personal comprehension in a collaborative environment (after Stahl [2000])

the representation of complex information spaces such as discussions. We turn now to thinking about combining topic maps with IBIS to create the tool this discussion seeks.

Topic Maps

The standard philosophical conception of knowledge defines knowledge as a *true well-justified belief* or *proposition*. Knowledge is achieved, at least in standard empiricist dogma, by some learning process, either through perception or through the adoption of such a tradition that contains previously gathered knowledge. In the tradition of EE [Evolutionary Epistemology] followed here, an analogy between evolutionary *adaptation* through natural selection and the increase in *environmental knowledge* is emphasized. More specifically, this knowledge is not simply about the environment, but rather about the relationships between the knower (e.g., organism) and its environment.

— TOMMI VEHKAVAARA [1998, p. 208]

In the beginning, there was the concept map. Later, there was the topic map. Now, there is XTM, an XML language for expression and serialization of topics, associations, and scopes. Concept maps have their roots in pedagogy, while topic maps have their roots in the HyTime and the bibliographic communities. Topic maps find application in, among other things, indexing documents, as, for example, InfoLoom's indexing of IDEAlliance (formerly GCA) conferences since 1996.[21] The Mondeca Topic Navigator[22] (Figure 17–6) is an example of a topic map engine that provides graphical representation of its contents.

---

[21] See *http://www.infoloom.com/tmweb.htm*.

[22] See *http://www.mondeca.com/*.

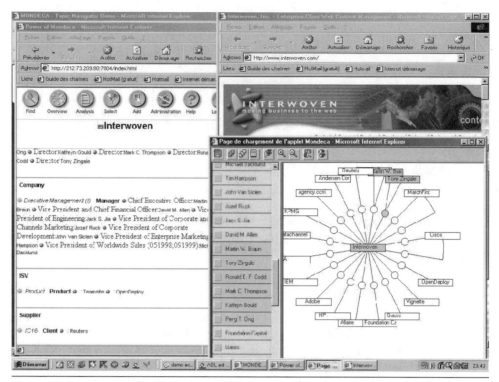

Figure 17–6   Mondeca Topic Navigator (thumbnail image courtesy of Jean Delahousse)

An application that both concept maps and topic maps are well suited for is that of knowledge representation (KR). There remains the open question whether XTM can serve as a primary KR system; XTM was most certainly not designed with intentions of serving as a KR system, but recent work (for example, Freese [2000] and Rath [2000]) and the chapters by Eric Freese and Holger Rath in this book indicate that semantic networks and inference capabilities can be implemented within the XTM specification.

Given that concept maps and topic maps are capable of serving the same purposes, it seems reasonable to call for a migration of concept map technology toward the XTM specification. This move will provide the capability of concept map interchange. I further believe that topic maps (when applied to the representation of argumentation developed in IBIS dialogs) combined with collaborative projects on the Web will, in turn, create a constructivist environment conducive to the evolution of world-class thinkers.

Learners of all ages, including those at the post-doctorate and professional levels, can participate. Such participation encourages each learner to stretch beyond native abilities to enter discussions with others. I believe that XTM, when coupled with many of the candidate use cases it can serve, offers a kind of *source code for the Web*, as suggested by Nikita Ogievetsky in Chapter 9.

Toward an Implementation

Albert Sevlin and his colleagues [2001] listed three challenges in managing knowledge (quoted here from the paper):

> Improving communication between disparate communities tackling ill-structured problems
>
> Real-time capture and integration of hybrid material (both predictable/formal and unexpected/informal) into a reusable group memory
>
> Transforming the resulting resource into the right representational formats for different stakeholders[23]

These points emerged after more than 10 years of experience with the Compendium Project,[24] in which many of the technologies discussed here have been developed. The key points they associate with managing knowledge are the same as those associated with knowledge formation. What we discuss here is a methodology with which we can combine XML topic maps with the conversational technologies suggested in the IBIS system. This discussion takes advantage of the fact that XTM documents can be transformed (as discussed, for example, in Chapter 9) using XSL style sheets into any representational system appropriate to a particular stakeholder.

Turning now to the issue of mapping IBIS events into XTM, consider the notion of implementing a Web-based learning center. Such a site would offer several tools, including the discussion and navigation tools discussed here. How might this all come together? Let's begin by sketching the format of an IBIS session (Figure 17–7).

IBIS is about argumentation, particularly about logical methodology associated with argumentation. An argument can be started by means of a *claim*. A claim (or *idea*, as suggested above) may be offered alone or as a response to a *question*.

A claim is made through an inference process associated with a coupling of *data* and *warrants*. Warrants are supported with *backing*. Once a claim is made, *rebuttals* may exist. Warrants are like rules within the space of discussion. Backing provides further support for the warrants.

---

[23] A stakeholder is a participant in the knowledge event.

[24] See *http://www.compendiuminstitute.org*.

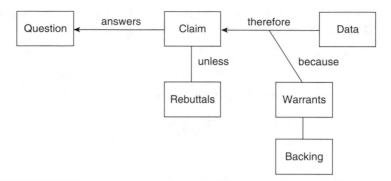

Figure 17–7   Format of an IBIS session

Within the space of logic and argumentation, think of data as providing evidence for a *minor premise* and a warrant providing a *major premise*. Those, by an inference process, lead to the claim. For example, consider this data: *Socrates is a man.*

Within that space of discourse, an appropriate warrant is: *All men are mortal.* We logically conclude that *Socrates is mortal.* Viewed another way, we can claim that Socrates is mortal because he is a man and all men are mortal. Unless, of course, Socrates is . . . well, let's not go there. All of that to answer the question "Is Socrates mortal?"

How do IBIS sessions run? Consider Figure 17–8, which illustrates the anatomy of an argument. A question can spawn either claims or further questions raised to narrow the main question and start threads of discourse. A claim can spawn arguments or other questions (not illustrated).

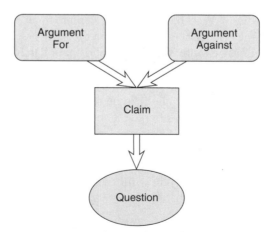

Figure 17–8   Anatomy of an IBIS session

We now must ask if there is a mechanism by which IBIS and XTM can be combined. Our approach to a response to this question is to establish visual vocabularies by which we can compare and combine the two technologies. Figure 17–7 presents a kind of visual vocabulary for thinking about IBIS; let's establish a visual vocabulary for thinking about XTM. Figure 17–9 presents a visual representation of a fragment of the structure of a topic map, showing one way to represent the following classes in XTM:

- Topic
- Association
- Occurrence
- Role

There can be many other classes, but those illustrated here get us started. We are now ready to cast IBIS within the constraints of the XTM specification. Figure 17–10 does just that.

Questions, claims, premises, warrants, and so forth are represented by `<topic>` elements. Each topic is connected to one or more `<occurrence>` elements, which are the statements themselves. Topics are connected by `<association>` elements according to the IBIS relationships established in Figure 17–7. Figure 17–10 suggests one way to map IBIS into XTM. No doubt there are other such maps, perhaps better.

How do we package all of these ideas? We must think in terms of a small group of software packages that provide the necessary functionality. In my section of Chapter 10, I presented a view of a project I call Nexist, which includes a topic map engine written in Java. In case you're wondering how a user interface for participation in IBIS discussions might look, Figure 17–11 shows a simple prototype of an IBIS interface in the Nexist project.

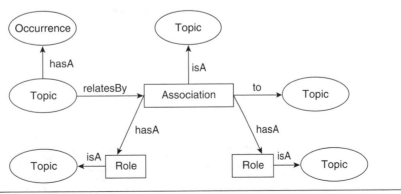

Figure 17–9   Visual structure of a topic map

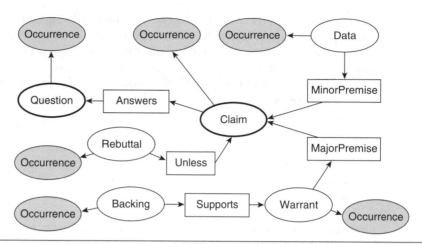

Figure 17–10   Visual structure of IBIS in XTM (the topic map illustrated uses the ontology of Toulmin [1958]). White ovals are `<topic>` elements, shaded ovals are `<occurrence>` elements, and rectangles are `<association>` elements.

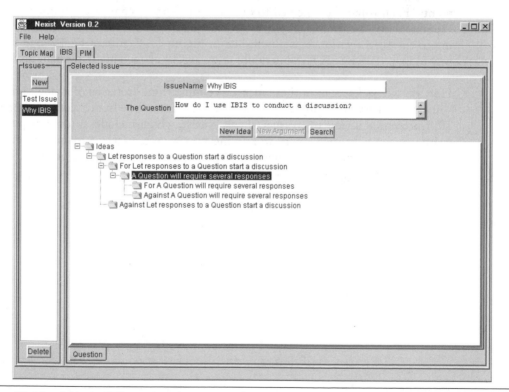

Figure 17–11   A Nexist IBIS user interface

A user creates a new issue and then begins the discussion.[25] Clicking on the New Idea button starts the process of responding to the question. Clicking on an idea allows the user to click the New Argument button and begin the process of making statements in support of or against the selected idea. All of these actions generate a lot of new information, which must be captured and stored as occurrences in a topic map created around the new issue.

A sketch of the software architecture needed to satisfy all the requirements for this system is presented in Figure 17–12. This is the architecture of the Nexist project.

In this architecture, Content represents the collection of information resources generated by participants in discussions, other Web pages, and other documents. Context represents the user experience: the user interfaces, user models, and so forth. For instance, Figure 17–11 illustrates one user interface component of Context.

The Knowledge space represents an important contribution to learning environments: here, we propose to mine the Content layer looking for knowledge structures that form the ontologies discussed in other chapters of this book. These knowledge structures form a kind of link database that ties bits of information floating about in Content, rendering a graph structure much more detailed than XTM topic maps are capable of providing,[26] and providing views to Context such that users can browse this Knowledge space. In effect, knowledge grows as users contribute more information to the Content space by way of user interfaces in Context. By placing a topic map interface and an IBIS interface in Context and constructing a Content space that uses XTM as a language for transporting information between Context and Content, this architecture offers one approach to the implementation of a constructivist Web-based learning environment.

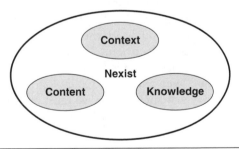

Figure 17–12   The Nexist architecture (diagram from suggestions by Lee Iverson and Charlie Ortize, both at SRI, *http://www.sri.com*)

---

[25] Discussions are typically started in search of consensus.

[26] Although the semantic networks described by Eric Freese (Chapter 13) move XTM documents in the direction of detailed knowledge structures, I envision applying DAML/OIL to the Knowledge layer.

An Application

To make sense of all this, I am proposing to take the project documented in Chapter 8, written by two members of my family, to the Web itself. In that project we envision a Web site that is constructed and navigated as a series of topic maps. These topic maps are arranged in a drill-down fashion, with higher levels used for navigation to more detailed levels. An instance of a drill-down topic map Web site has already been created by Robert Barta at Bond University, near Brisbane, Australia,[27] and we think this approach will allow learners of all ages to navigate within a Web space devoted to the life sciences, contributing to the topic maps that are growing there.

To augment this activity, I am further proposing to mount an IBIS discussion forum at the Web site such that each node in any topic map is hyperlinked to a discussion specific to that node.

I envision this Web site as a kind of proof of concept for applying topic maps to constructivist learning environments on a global scale. I believe that this represents a sound (though not the only) approach to the evolution of world-class critical thinkers.

Closing Salvo

We are smart enough to realize we are stupid, and stupid enough to make the problem of becoming smarter hard.
                                                                    —ANDERS SANDBERG

You already saw that quote before, back in my opening salvo in Chapter 1. I happen to like it enough to bring it back. Douglas Engelbart is right: we do have tough problems to solve. It is time to take on the "stupid enough" part of the quote; Engelbart's notion of augmented collective intelligence lies as a key to collective improvement. I believe that the case has been made in this book that XML topic maps, when coupled with the Semantic Web and other technologies, offer a powerful set of tools in the great collaborative armamentarium we must construct in order to solve those tough problems. Steve Newcomb's quest for a global knowledge interchange is indeed the right quest for these times.

The rest is up to us.

---

[27] See *http://topicmaps.bond.edu.au/deployment/*.

References

Allee, Verna. 1999. The Art and Practice of Being a Revolutionary. Accessed in April 2002 at *http://www.vernaallee.com/in%20the%20Library/articles/Art&Practice.pdf*.

Berners-Lee, Tim. 1998. Semantic Web Road Map. Accessed in April 2002 at *http://www.w3.org/DesignIssues/Semantic.html*.

———. 2000. Semantic Web—XML 2000. Talk presented at XML 2000, Washington, DC, GCA. Slides accessed in April 2002 at *http://www.w3.org/2000/Talks/1206-xml2k-tbl/slide1-0.html*; audio/video of the same talk accessed in April 2002 at *http://www.technetcast.com/tnc_play_stream.html?stream_id=459*.

Berners-Lee, Tim, James Hendler, and Ora Lassila. 2001. The Semantic Web. *Scientific American* (May). Accessed in April 2002 at *http://www.sciam.com/2001/0501issue/0501berners-lee.html*.

Chislenko, Alexander. 1997. Semantic Web Vision Paper. Accessed in April 2002 at *http://www.lucifer.com/~sasha/articles/SemanticWeb.html*.

Conceição-Runlee, Simone, and Barbara J. Daley. 1998. Constructivist Learning Theory to Web-Based Course Design: An Instructional Design Approach. Accessed in April 2002 at *http://www.bsu.edu/teachers/departments/edld/conf/constructionism.html*.

Davis-Seaver, Jane, Tom Smith, and Dorothy Leflore. 2000. Constructivism: A Path to Critical Thinking in Early Childhood. *International Journal of Scholarly Academic Intellectual Diversity* 4(1). Accessed in April 2002 at *http://www.nationalforum.com/ijsaidcurrent.htm*.

Denning, Steven. 2000. History of Knowledge Management. Accessed in April 2002 at *http://www.stevedenning.com/history_knowledge_management.html*.

Engelbart, Douglas. 2000. Unrev-II Colloquium. Webcast accessed in April 2002 from a link at the Bootstrap Institute Web site at *http://www.bootstrap.org/colloquium/index.jsp*.

Fisher, Kathleen M., James H. Wandersee, and David E. Moody. 2000. *Mapping Biology Knowledge*. Boston, MA: Kluwer Academic Publishers.

Fisher, Kathleen M., James H. Wandersee, and Graham Wideman. 2000. Enhancing Cognitive Skills for Meaningful Understanding of Domain Specific Knowledge. Paper presented at AAAS Annual Meeting, Washington DC, February 2000. Accessed in April 2002 at *http://www.sci.sdsu.edu/CRMSE/Fisher_aaas2000.html*.

Freese, Eric. 2000. Inferring Knowledge from Topic Map–Based Semantic Networks. In *XML 2000 Conference Proceedings, December 3–8, 2000, Washington, DC*; GCA.

Gaines, Brian R., and Mildred L. G. Shaw. 1995. Concept Maps as Hypermedia Components. Accessed in April 2002 at *http://ksi.cpsc.ucalgary.ca/articles/ConceptMaps/CM.html*.

Group Decision Support Systems. 2000. *IBIS Manual*. Accessed in April 2002 at *http://www.gdss.com/wp/IBIS.htm*.

Information Society Technologies Programme. 2000. Semantic Web Technologies Workshop, Luxembourg, November 2000. Information accessed in April 2002 at *http://www.cordis.lu/ist/ka3/iaf/swt_presentations/swt_presentations.htm*.

Johari, Harish. 1998. *Dhanwantari: A Complete Guide to the Ayurvedic Life*. Rochester, NY: Healing Arts Press.

Karacapilidis, Nikos, and Thomas Gordon. 1995. Dialectical Planning. In *Proceedings of IAI-95 Workshop on Intelligent Manufacturing Systems, Montreal, Canada, 1995*. Accessed in April 2002 at *http://ais.gmd.de/MS/zeno/papers/karacapilidis1995a.pdf*.

Kuntz, Werner, and Horst W. J. Rittel. 1970. Issues as Elements of Information Systems. Accessed in April 2002 at *http://www-iurd.ced.berkeley.edu/pub/WP-131.pdf*.

Maturana, Humberto R., and Francisco J. Verala. 1987. *The Tree of Knowledge: The Biological Roots of Human Understanding*. Boston, MA: New Science Library.

National Library of Medicine. 2001. Fact Sheet on the UMLS Semantic Network. Accessed in April 2002 at *http://www.nlm.nih.gov/pubs/factsheets/umlssemn.html*.

Norman, Donald. 1980. Cognitive Engineering and Education. In *Problem Solving and Education: Issues in Teaching and Research;* D. T. Tuna and F. Reif, eds. Mahwah, NJ: Erlbaum.

Novak, Joseph D. 1998a. *Learning, Creating and Using Knowledge: Concept Maps™ as Facilitative Tools in Schools and Corporations*. Mahwah, NJ: Erlbaum.

————. 1998b. The Pursuit of a Dream: Education Can Be Improved. In *Teaching Science for Understanding: A Human Constructivist View;* Joel J. Mintzes, James H. Wandersee, and Joseph D. Novak, eds. San Diego, CA: Academic Press.

Phillips, Laurie. 1997. EM 600 Vygotsky: From a Primer on Topics Related to Instructional Design. Accessed in April 2002 at *http://www.auburn.edu/academic/education/eflt/vyg.html*.

Rath, Hans Holger. 2000. Topic Maps Self-Control. In *Extreme Markup Languages 2000 Conference Proceedings, Montreal, Canada, 2000*. Accessed in April 2002 at *http://www.gca.org/attend/2000_conferences/Extreme_2000/Papers/Rath/tom-hhr.PDF*.

Schafersman, Steven D. 1991. An Introduction to Critical Thinking. Accessed in April 2002 at *http://www.freeinquiry.com/critical-thinking.html*.

SemanticWeb.Org. 2002. Welcome page. Accessed in April 2002 at *http://www.semanticweb.org/introduction.html*.

Sevlin, Albert, et al. 2001. Compendium: Making Meetings into Knowledge Events. Paper presented at Knowledge Technologies 2001, March 4–7, Austin, TX. Accessed in April 2002 at *http://kmi.open.ac.uk/publications/tr.cfm?trnumber=103* .

Shipman, Frank M., III, and Catherine C. Marshall. 1999. Formality Considered Harmful: Experiences, Emerging Themes, and Directions on the Use of Formal Representations in Interactive Systems. *Computer-Supported Cooperative Work* 8(4): 333–352. Also available at *http://bush.cs.tamu.edu/~shipman/cscw.pdf*.

Sowa, John F. 2000. *Knowledge Representation: Logical, Philosophical, and Computational Foundations*. Pacific Grove, CA: Brooks/Cole.

Stahl, G. 2000. A Model of Collaborative Knowledge-Building. In *Proceedings of the Fourth International Conference of the Learning Sciences*; B. Fishman and S. O'Connor-Divelbiss, eds. Mahwah, NJ: Erlbaum, pp. 70–77. Also available at *http://orgwis.gmd. de/~gerry/publications/conferences/2000/icls/icls.pdf*.

Toulmin, Stephen, ed. 1958. *The Uses of Argument*. Cambridge, UK: Cambridge University Press.

Vehkavaara, Tommi. 1998. Extended Concept of Knowledge for Evolutionary Epistemology and for Biosemiotics. In *Emergence, Complexity, Hierarchy, Organization. Selected and Edited Papers from ECHO III Conference*. Mathematics, Computing and Management in Engineering Series No. 91; Georg L. Farre and Tarkko Oksala, eds. Espoo, Finland: Acta Polytechnica Scandinavica, pp. 207–216. Also available at *http://www.uta.fi/~attove/vehka-f.htm*.

GLOSSARY

The following glossary presents some conceptual definitions for terms used in the topic map community. When element tag names are mentioned, they are the tag names used in the XTM 2000–2002 syntax.

addressable information resource

(Synonym: *resource*.) An information resource that is retrievable by some systematic means, using one or more addresses expressed in one or more formal addressing schemes. An online copy of a document, or an addressable portion of that document, are examples of addressable information resources.

Every addressable information resource can be regarded as a subject of a topic. If it is, it is called an addressable subject or, synonymously, a subject-constituting resource or a resource constituting a subject.

Implementations of the topic maps paradigm should determine, to the maximum extent possible, whether two addressable information resources are the same or different.[1]

Implementations should be able, at a minimum, to compare two addresses of information resources (for example, two URIs) and determine whether the addresses are identical. The ability to recognize that nonidentical addressing expressions are in fact equivalent, in that they address the same resource, is highly desirable but necessarily optional.[2]

---

[1] That is, whether they both have the same addressing context. When two URIs are identical, it's easy (and always correct) to infer that they address exactly the same addressable information resource. If two resources, when retrieved, return different data, they are definitely not the same resource. However, in the general case, if two resources, when retrieved, return the same data, that, in itself, cannot serve as an indication that they are the same resource. For example, in one addressing context the resource "603" might be the number of an aircraft subassembly, in a second the Dewey Decimal Code for some set of books, and in a third the order number for an item in a catalog. However, because two resources cannot occupy the same place at the same time, testing for addressing context equivalence would always be sufficient to determine whether two resources are identical.

[2] However, it's sometimes true that two different addressing expressions can be known to address exactly the same information resource. For example, because the case of Internet domain names is not significant, the URIs *http://www.TOPICMAPS.org* and *http://www.topicmaps.org* address the same resource.

addressable subject

(Synonym: *subject-constituting resource*.) See also *addressable information resource*.

assertion

See *association*. In most contexts, and in the chapters of this book, the terms *assertion* and *association* are almost synonymous. When they appear in the same context (for example, in the discussion of the draft Reference Model for topic maps in Chapter 4) *association* is limited to an XTM tag name used to represent relationships syntactically, whereas *assertion* includes expressions of relationships that appear in ready-to-use topic maps, regardless of the means used to represent them.

association

An association asserts a relationship between subjects, where each of the subjects is represented as a topic. Associations have *roles*; the topics that play those roles are called the *role players* or *members* of the association. Roles and role players may be constrained by *association templates*.

Associations can always be regarded as topics because, as with all topics, they represent a specific subject; the subject of an association is always the relationship that it represents.

association member role

The role played in an association by a topic that is a role player (member) of that association.

association template

A topic whose subject is a type of association, and that specifies the roles played in the association type and that may declare the constraints on the role players of each role. Applications may specify such constraints using a language like TMCL (see Chapter 4). Applications may use association templates to validate instances of a given association type. (Compare with *topic map template*.)

association type

A class of associations; one of the classes of associations of which a particular association is an instance; a topic whose subject is a class of association.

base name

A base name characteristic of a topic. (See also *topic–base name association.*) Informally, a string of characters specified as a name of a topic using a `<baseNameString>` element in the XTM syntax.

base name topic

The topic that plays the base name role in a topic–base name association.

characteristic

See *topic characteristic.*

class–instance association

An assertion that one topic (the topic playing the class role) has, as its subject, the class of subjects of which another topic (the topic playing the instance role) is an instance. Like any association, this type of association has scope.

In the XTM syntax, an association of this type can be expressed as a member `<association>` that is an instance of the class–instance association type, where the topic whose subject is the class plays the class role, and the member topic whose subject is an instance of the class plays the instance role.

Alternatively, the XTM syntax allows this same association type to be expressed using the less verbose `<occurrence>` element type.

Again in XTM syntax, this same association type can be expressed using the less verbose `<instanceOf>` element type, where the class topic is derived from the child of the `<instanceOf>` element and the instance topic is derived from the parent of the `<instanceOf>` element, although this syntax does not permit scope to be specified.

class topic

The topic that plays the class role in a class–instance association.

deserialization

The process of reading an instance of some *interchange syntax* and creating a ready-to-use topic map. (See also *serialization.*)

identity point

See *subject identity point.*

instance topic

The topic that plays the instance role in a class–instance association.

interchange syntax

The grammar used to interchange a particular kind of information, for example, topic map information. XTM 1.0 and ISO 13250 specify two interchange syntaxes for topic map information, one for SGML (and "Web SGML" or XML), called *HyTM,* and the other, for XML Topic Maps, called *XTM* or *XTM 1.0.*

For example, the XTM syntax specifies that an interchangeable topic map consists of a `<topicMap>` element, including all of the `<topic>`, `<association>`, and other elements that can appear in its content. (Compare with *ready-to-use topic map.*)

member

See *role player.*

merging

There are two kinds of merging: *topic merging* and *topic map merging.*

Topic merging begins with two or more topics and ends with one topic, whose topic characteristics are the union of the topic characteristics of the original topics.[3] The resulting topic has the union of the set of subject identity points of the formerly separate topics. The integrity and usefulness of a ready-to-use topic map depends on the existence of a one-to-one correspondence between topics and subjects; this is why topic merging is necessary and required. There are two rules that trigger topic merging: the topic naming constraint-based merging rule and the subject-based merging.

Topic map merging begins with two or more topic maps and ends with a single ready-to-use topic map. Topics from all of the topic maps are merged as the topic naming constraint-based rule and the subject-based merging rule are applied. When instances of the XTM syntax are processed, topic map merging occurs automatically when a `<topicMap>` element contains a `<mergeMap>` element that references a `<topicMap>`.

---

[3] Because it is possible for associations to be regarded as topics, topics and associations may merge.

nonaddressable subject

A subject that is not an addressable information resource. Non-addressable subjects can (and should) be "indicated" by addressable resources. Such resources, called *subject-indicating resources*, are subject identity points. (Compare with *subject-constituting resource*.) Examples of nonaddressable subjects include the notion of love, the Statue of Liberty, a memorable dinner at La Guadriole in Montréal, and all Platonic forms.[4]

occurrence

Information (an addressable subject) that is specified as relevant to a given subject. An occurrence characteristic of a topic. (See *topic occurrence*.)

occurrence topic

The topic that plays the occurrence role in a topic–occurrence association.

occurrence type

A class of topic occurrence; a topic whose subject is a class of topic occurrence; a sub-type of the topic–occurrence association type.

Published Subject Indicator (PSI)

A subject indicator that is maintained at an advertised address to serve as a subject identity point for topics in topic maps created by anyone. PSIs should indicate their subjects unambiguously and compellingly. To maximize the return on investment of topic maps that use them, PSI addresses should remain stable.

ready-to-use topic map

The application-internal form of a topic map, after the interchangeable form has been parsed and processed. There is an unbounded number of ways to implement and use ready-to-use topic maps. (Compare with *interchange syntax*.)

reify

To make a subject the subject of a topic. (Subjects may exist in themselves without having been reified as topics. See Chapter 3.)

---

[4]See generally Plato's *Republic*.

resource

See *addressable information resource.*

resource constituting a subject

See *subject-constituting resource.*

resource indicating a subject

See *subject-indicating resource.*

role

The rule that a subject plays as a member of an association; the nature of a subject's participation in an association.

role player

One of the set of subjects related by an association.

scope

The set of topics that determines the extent of the validity of an association (and its topic characteristic assignments). Scope provides a context in which a name or an occurrence is assigned to a given topic, or a context in which topics are related through associations. Every association has scope. (See also *unconstrained scope.*)

scoping topic

A topic that is a member of a scope. Any topic can potentially be used as a member of a scope. (But see *topic map template.*)

serialization

The process of converting a ready-to-use topic map into an instance of some interchange syntax (for example, into a topic map document). (See also *deserialization.*)

set

A collection of things that are distinguishable (that is, not identical) and in which no thing appears more than once. If every thing in set A is contained in set B, and set A is not equal to set B, then set A is a subset of set B, and set B is a superset of set A.

subject

The organizing principle or essence of a topic; a "subject of conversation." Every topic reifies exactly one subject: the idea or notion that the topic represents. Humans are the ultimate authorities for determining the subjects of topics. (See also *subject identity point.*)

subject constituter

See *subject constituting resource.*

subject-based merging rule

The subject-based merging rule requires that, in ready-to-use topic maps, all pairs of topics that have the same subject be merged into single topics. Subject identity points (SIPs)—that is, subject-indicating resources (SIRs) and subject-constituting resources (SCRs)—control merging behavior. This means that:

1. All topics that regard the same addressable information resource as their SCR are always merged by topic map applications because they all have the same subject.
2. Similarly, all topics that regard the same addressable information resource as an SIR are always merged by topic map applications, again because they all have the same subject.
3. However, if one topic regards a resource as an SCR and another topic regards the same resource as an SIR, and not an SCR, the two topics are not merged because the two topics do not have the same subject. (See also *subject; merging.*)

subject-constituting resource (SCR)

(Synonyms: *addressable subject; resource constituting a subject.*) An addressable information resource, considered as a subject regardless of any subject that it may discuss, describe, or otherwise indicate. Such a resource is a subject identity point for any topic that regards it as its subject constituter. No topic may have more than one SCR, and many (perhaps most) topics have none, because their subjects are not pieces of information. (Compare with *subject-indicating resource.*)

subject identity

A subject as distinguished from all other subjects. Every topic has exactly one subject, and every subject has a unique identity, regardless of how (or in how many different ways) it may be defined, expressed, or otherwise indicated (that is, regardless of how many SIPs the topic may have). Humans are the ultimate authorities for determining subject identity, even (or perhaps especially) in automated systems.[5]

subject identity point (SIP)

(Synonym: *identity point.*) An addressable information resource, when, with respect to a topic, it is regarded as either the subject-constituting resource (SCR) or as a subject-indicating resource (SIR). A single subject when reified must have at least one SIP, including zero or one SCRs, and any number of SIRs, each of which is capable of independently establishing the unique identity of the subject.

In the XTM syntax, the values of the `-xlink:href-` attributes of the children of the `<subjectIdentity>` element are the addresses of the following kinds of SIPs, depending on the element types of the children of the `<subjectIdentity>` element:

- A `<subjectIndicatorRef>` refers to an SIR.
- A `<topicRef>` refers to an SIR.
- A `<resourceRef>` refers to an SCR.

SIPs control merging behavior under the subject-based merging rule.

subject-indicating resource (SIR)

(Synonyms: *subject indicator; resource indicating a subject.*) A resource used to describe, define, or otherwise express a subject. Such a resource is a subject identity point for any topic that regards it as a subject indicator.[6] A given topic may have zero or more subject indicating resources. (Compare with *subject-constituting resource.*)

subject indicator

See *subject-indicating resource.*

---

[5] All this holds whether one takes a constructivist or a Platonic view on the ultimate reality of the subject. Here again, topic maps function as a "neutral envelope," as Michel Biezunski calls them in Chapter 2.

[6] Normally, the indicated subject is a nonaddressable subject. If the subject were addressable, that is, if the subject were itself an addressable information resource, it could be addressed directly as a subject-constituting resource. This is easier and more reliable than using a subject-indicating resource to indicate the subject. It is not an error to use a subject-indicating resource to indicate an addressable subject; it is, however, hard to justify the use of an intermediary subject indicator to indicate it since the subject indicator itself must be examined, only to discover that the subject could have been addressed directly.

subtype topic

The topic that plays the subtype role in a supertype–subtype association.

supertype–subtype association

An association between a supertype topic and a subtype topic. Like any association, this type of association has scope.

Using XTM syntax, an association of this type can be expressed by means of an `<association>` that is an instance of the supertype-subtype association type, where the member of the topic whose subject is the subtype plays the subtype role.

supertype topic

The topic that plays the supertype role in a supertype–subtype association.

topic

The computer representation (proxy, surrogate, reification) of a subject. The integrity of a ready-to-use topic map depends on the existence of a one-to-one correspondence between topics and subjects.

In XTM 1.0, topics can be interchanged as `<topic>` elements. The representation of topics in ready-to-use (that is, application-internal) topic maps is not standardized, but it is still true that, regardless of how topics are represented, they reify (that is, serve as surrogates for) their subjects.

topic–base name association

An assertion that one topic (the topic playing the topic role) has, as one of its names, the name that is the subject of another topic (the topic playing the base name role— the base name topic). Like any association, this type of association has scope.

In the XTM syntax, an association of this type can be expressed as an `<association>` that is an instance of the topic–base name association type, where the member topic that is being given a name plays the topic role, and the base name member topic's subject is the name.

Alternatively, the XTM 1.0 syntax allows this same association type to be expressed using the less verbose `<baseName>` element type. The base name topic's subject is indicated by the content of the `<baseNameString>` element in the content of the `<baseName>`; the topic playing the topic role is derived from the topic specified by the containing `<topic>` that contains the `<baseName>`.

topic characteristic

Topic characteristic are assertions about topics. There are three kinds of topic characteristics:

1. Names (name characteristics)
2. Occurrences (occurrence characteristics)
3. Roles played in associations

In terms of the Standard Application Model, name characteristics are topic–base name associations, and occurrence characteristics are topic–occurrence associations.

topic characteristic assignment

The fact that a specific topic plays a specific role in a specific association. All associations have scopes, therefore topic characteristic assignments are scoped.

topic map

A topic map is a set of topics and associations between them. A topic map may exist in either interchangeable syntax and/or ready-to-use form.[7]

The creators of topic maps determine the subjects of topics. For each topic, they assert some set of topic characteristics (in other words, they create associations in which topics play roles).

topic map merging

See *merging*.

---

[7] When a topic map exists in the serialized form of interchange syntax, it is entirely possible for redundant elements (for example, XTM `<topic>` elements) to interchange the same subject. However, when the topic map is in ready-to-use form, topic merging should take place, and one topic should represent one and only one subject.

topic map template

A topic map used as a starting point for the creation of other, larger topic maps, all of which will contain (that is, be merged with) the topic map template. A topic map template generally specifies association types (including association templates and their supporting role topics and role player constraint topics), topic class topics, role topics, scoping topics, and so on; see Chapter 14. (Compare with *association template*.)

topic maps paradigm

The topic maps paradigm enables global federated knowledge interchange by using computer constructs, called topics, to represent subjects, such that everything that is known about a given subject is attached to the one and only topic that corresponds to the subject.

topic merging

See *merging*.

topic name

See *base name*.

topic namespace

A set of base names of one or more topics, each of which is unique and all of which are the names of their respective topics within a single, common scope. Variant names are not members of a topic namespace.

topic naming constraint

The constraint, imposed by the topic maps paradigm, that no two subjects can have corresponding topics that have the same base name within the same scope (that is, the same topic namespace).

topic naming constraint-based merging rule

By this rule, two different topics with at least one name characteristic in the same scope will be merged. The rule maintains the integrity of topic namespaces, so that any topic can be unambiguously addressed by means of its name within some topic namespace. (See also *merging*.)

topic occurrence

See *occurrence*.

topic–occurrence association

An assertion that one topic (the topic playing the topic role) has, as one of its occurrences, the addressable subject of another topic (the topic playing the occurrences role—the occurrence topic). Like any association, this type of association has scope.

In the XTM syntax, an assertion of this type can be expressed as an `<association>` that is an instance of the topic–occurrence association type, where the member topic for which an occurrence is being specified plays the topic role, and the occurrence member topic's subject is the addressable information resource that is the occurrence.

Alternatively, the XTM syntax allows this same association type to be expressed using the less verbose `<occurrence>` element type. Unlike `<instanceOf>` elements, `<occurrence>` elements can contain `<scope>` elements that allow the scope of the topic–occurrence assertion to be explicitly specified. The topic playing the topic role is the topic specified by the `<topic>` that contains the `<occurrence>`, while the topic playing the occurrence role is the topic implicitly specified by the `<resourceRef>` or the `<resourceData>` in the content of the `<occurrence>`.

topic type

A class of topics; a topic whose subject is a class of topic. (See also *class topic* and *instance topic*.)

unconstrained scope

The scope comprised of the null set of topics. In the XTM and HyTM syntaxes, when no scoping topics are explicitly specified as governing an association, the scope within which the association is made defaults to the unconstrained scope.

variant

See *variant name*.

variant name

(Synonym: *variant*.) An alternative form of a base name, intended for use in a particular processing context, like sorting or display (perhaps via some specific kind of display technology).

TOMATOES TOPIC MAP

This appendix contains the complete topic map created in Chapter 6.

```
<?xml version="1.0"?>
<!DOCTYPE topicMap SYSTEM "xtm1.dtd">

<topicMap xmlns="http://www.topicmaps.org/xtm/1.0/"
xmlns:xlink="http://www.w3.org/1999/xlink">

<!-- utility topics -->
<topic id="EN">
<subjectIdentity>
<subjectIndicatorRef
xlink:href="http://www.topicmaps.org/xtm/1.0/language.xtm#en"/>
</subjectIdentity>
</topic>
<topic id="FR">
<subjectIdentity>
<subjectIndicatorRef
xlink:href="http://www.topicmaps.org/xtm/1.0/language.xtm#fr"/>
</subjectIdentity>
</topic>

<!-- the main ingredient -->
<topic id="myTomato">
<subjectIdentity>
<subjectIndicatorRef
xlink:href="www.fed.gov/usda/doc/tomato.htm#gradeA"/>
</subjectIdentity>
<baseName>
<scope>
<topicRef xlink:href="#EN"/>
</scope>
<baseNameString>
tomato
</baseNameString>
</baseName>
<baseName>
<scope>
<topicRef xlink:href="#FR"/>
</scope>
```

```
<baseNameString>
tomate
</baseNameString>
</baseName>
<baseName>
<baseNameString>
tomato
</baseNameString>
<variant>
<variantName>
<resourceData>
TMT
</resourceData>
</variantName>
<parameters>
<topicRef xlink:href="#cell_phone"/>
</parameters>
</variant>
</baseName>
<occurrence>
<resourceRef xlink:href="tomato.gif"/>
</occurrence>
</topic>

<!-- the dessert -->
<topic id="myConfite">
<instanceOf>
<topicRef xlink:href="#dessert"/>
</instanceOf>
<baseName>
<baseNameString>
tomate confite farcie aux douze saveurs
</baseNameString>
</baseName>
</topic>

<!-- association between an ingredient and dessert -->
<association id="tomato_confite_association">
<instanceOf>
<topicRef xlink:href="#ingredient_of"/>
</instanceOf>
<member>
<roleSpec>
<topicRef xlink:href="#anIngredient"/>
</roleSpec>
<topicRef xlink:href="#myTomato"/>
</member>
<member>
<roleSpec>
<topicRef xlink:href="#aDish"/>
</roleSpec>
<topicRef xlink:href="#myConfite"/>
```

```xml
</member>
</association>
<topic id="aDish"/>

<!-- another association between an ingredient and dessert -->
<association id="caramels_confite">
<instanceOf>
<topicRef xlink:href="#ingredient_of"/>
</instanceOf>
<member>
<roleSpec>
<topicRef xlink:href="#anIngredient"/>
</roleSpec>
<topicRef xlink:href="#myCaramel"/>
</member>
<member>
<roleSpec>
<topicRef xlink:href="#aDish"/>
</roleSpec>
<topicRef xlink:href="#myConfite"/>
</member>
</association>
<topic id="myCaramel"/>

<!-- A menu associates an entree and a dessert. -->
<association id="entree_dessert">
<instanceOf>
<topicRef xlink:href="#menu"/>
</instanceOf>
<member>
<roleSpec>
<topicRef xlink:href="#dessert"/>
</roleSpec>
<topicRef xlink:href="#myConfite"/>
</member>
<member>
<roleSpec>
<topicRef xlink:href="#entrees"/>
</roleSpec>
<topicRef xlink:href="#myFoieGras"/>
</member>
</association>

<topic id="menu"/>
<topic id="dessert"/>
<topic id="entrees"/>
<topic id="myFoieGras"/>
<topic id="cell_phone"/>
</topicMap>
```

Appendix B
TOPIC MAP FOR CHAPTER 9

This appendix contains the topic map discussed in Chapter 9.

```xml
<?xml version="1.0" encoding="iso-8859-1"?>
<!-DOCTYPE topicMap SYSTEM "xtm1.dtd"->
<topicMap id="map"
  xmlns:xlink="http://www.w3.org/1999/xlink">
  <topic id="default">
    <subjectIdentity>
      <subjectIndicatorRef xlink:href="#map"/>
    </subjectIdentity>
    <baseName>
      <baseNameString>
        Long Island Seashore Creatures
      </baseNameString>
    </baseName>
    <occurrence>
      <instanceOf>
        <topicRef xlink:href="#description"/>
      </instanceOf>
      <resourceData>Long Island Seashore is rich with various forms of
        life.
      As a beginning scuba diver, I shot some pictures during my
          dives, learned some new information while talking with
          experienced scuba divers, and then went to a local library and
          collected more information from encyclopedias. All these sources
          of information I am accumulating and organizing in a topic map.
          This topic map will contain a representation of my knowledge
          about seashore creatures, my interpretation of the received
          information. The next step will be to create XSLT style sheets
          in order to share this knowledge with people via a Web site.
      </resourceData>
    </occurrence>
    <occurrence>
      <instanceOf>
        <topicRef xlink:href="#landsc-img"/>
      </instanceOf>
      <scope>
        <topicRef xlink:href="#nikita"/>
      </scope>
      <resourceRef xlink:href="ocean5.jpg"/>
```

```
        </occurrence>
        <occurrence>
          <instanceOf>
            <topicRef xlink:href="#landsc-img"/>
          </instanceOf>
          <scope>
            <topicRef xlink:href="#nikita"/>
          </scope>
          <resourceRef xlink:href="ocean14.jpg"/>
        </occurrence>
        <!occurrence>
          <instanceOf>
              <topicRef xlink:href="#landsc-img"/>
          </instanceOf>
          <scope><topicRef xlink:href="#nikita"/></scope>
          <resourceRef xlink:href="ocean2.jpg"/>
        </occurrence>
        <occurrence>
          <instanceOf>
              <topicRef xlink:href="#landsc-img"/>
          </instanceOf>
          <scope><topicRef xlink:href="#nikita"/></scope>
          <resourceRef xlink:href="ocean3.jpg"/>
        </occurrence>
        <occurrence>
          <instanceOf>
              <topicRef xlink:href="#landsc-img"/>
          </instanceOf>
          <scope><topicRef xlink:href="#nikita"/></scope>
          <resourceRef xlink:href="ocean11.jpg"/>
        </occurrence>
        <occurrence>
          <instanceOf>
              <topicRef xlink:href="#landsc-img"/>
          </instanceOf>
          <scope><topicRef xlink:href="#nikita"/></scope>
          <resourceRef xlink:href="ocean12.jpg"/>
        </occurrence>
        <occurrence>
          <instanceOf>
              <topicRef xlink:href="#landsc-img"/>
          </instanceOf>
          <scope><topicRef xlink:href="#nikita"/></scope>
          <resourceRef xlink:href="ocean17.jpg"/>
        </occurrence>
        <occurrence>
          <instanceOf>
              <topicRef xlink:href="#landsc-img"/>
          </instanceOf>
          <scope><topicRef xlink:href="#nikita"/></scope>
          <resourceRef xlink:href="ocean18.jpg"/>
        </occurrence>
```

```
        <occurrence>
          <instanceOf>
            <topicRef xlink:href="#landsc-img"/>
          </instanceOf>
          <scope><topicRef xlink:href="#nikita"/></scope>
          <resourceRef xlink:href="ocean19.jpg"/>
        </occurrence>
        <occurrence>
          <instanceOf>
              <topicRef xlink:href="#landsc-img"/>
          </instanceOf>
          <scope><topicRef xlink:href="#nikita"/></scope>
          <resourceRef xlink:href="ocean22.jpg"/>
        </occurrence->
      </topic>
      <topic id="animal-kingdom"/>
      <topic id="class-subclass">
        <subjectIdentity>
          <subjectIndicatorRef xlink:href="http://www.topicmaps.org/xtm/1.0/
psi1.xtm#at-superclass-subclass"/>
        </subjectIdentity>
      </topic>
      <topic id="class">
        <subjectIdentity>
          <subjectIndicatorRef xlink:href="http://www.topicmaps.org/xtm/1.0/
psi1.xtm#role-superclass"/>
        </subjectIdentity>
      </topic>
      <topic id="sub-class">
        <subjectIdentity>
          <subjectIndicatorRef xlink:href="http://www.topicmaps.org/xtm/1.0/
psi1.xtm#role-subclass"/>
        </subjectIdentity>
      </topic>
      <association>
        <instanceOf>
          <topicRef xlink:href="#class-subclass"/>
        </instanceOf>
        <scope>
          <topicRef xlink:href="#animal-taxonomy"/>
        </scope>
        <member>
          <roleSpec>
            <topicRef xlink:href="#class"/>
          </roleSpec>
          <topicRef xlink:href="#animal-kingdom"/>
        </member>
        <member>
          <roleSpec>
            <topicRef xlink:href="#sub-class"/>
          </roleSpec>
          <topicRef xlink:href="#arthropods"/>
```

```
    <topicRef xlink:href="#echinoderma"/>
  </member>
</association>
<association>
  <instanceOf>
    <topicRef xlink:href="#class-subclass"/>
  </instanceOf>
  <scope>
    <topicRef xlink:href="#animal-taxonomy"/>
  </scope>
  <member>
    <roleSpec>
      <topicRef xlink:href="#class"/>
    </roleSpec>
    <topicRef xlink:href="#arthropods"/>
  </member>
  <member>
    <roleSpec>
      <topicRef xlink:href="#sub-class"/>
    </roleSpec>
    <topicRef xlink:href="#merostomata"/>
    <topicRef xlink:href="#crustacea"/>
    <topicRef xlink:href="#sea-spiders"/>
  </member>
</association>
<association>
  <instanceOf>
    <topicRef xlink:href="#class-subclass"/>
  </instanceOf>
  <scope>
    <topicRef xlink:href="#animal-taxonomy"/>
  </scope>
  <member>
    <roleSpec>
      <topicRef xlink:href="#class"/>
    </roleSpec>
    <topicRef xlink:href="#echinoderma"/>
  </member>
  <member>
    <roleSpec>
      <topicRef xlink:href="#sub-class"/>
    </roleSpec>
    <topicRef xlink:href="#sea-star"/>
    <topicRef xlink:href="#brittle-stars"/>
    <topicRef xlink:href="#sea-urchine"/>
  </member>
</association>
<topic id="sea-star">
  <instanceOf>
    <topicRef xlink:href="#animal-class"/>
  </instanceOf>
```

```
<baseName>
  <scope>
    <topicRef xlink:href="#taxon"/>
  </scope>
  <baseNameString>Asteroidea</baseNameString>
</baseName>
<baseName>
  <baseNameString>sea-star</baseNameString>
</baseName>
<baseName>
  <scope>
    <topicRef xlink:href="#also-known-as"/>
  </scope>
  <baseNameString>starfish</baseNameString>
</baseName>
<occurrence>
  <instanceOf>
    <topicRef xlink:href="#landsc-img"/>
  </instanceOf>
  <scope>
    <topicRef xlink:href="#nikita"/>
  </scope>
  <resourceRef xlink:href="ocean6.jpg"/>
</occurrence>
<occurrence>
  <instanceOf>
    <topicRef xlink:href="#landsc-img"/>
  </instanceOf>
  <scope>
    <topicRef xlink:href="#john"/>
  </scope>
  <resourceRef xlink:href="ocean8.jpg"/>
</occurrence>
<occurrence>
  <instanceOf>
    <topicRef xlink:href="#definition"/>
  </instanceOf>
  <scope>
    <topicRef xlink:href="#audubon"/>
  </scope>
  <resourceData> The asteroid body has the form of a somewhat
    flattened star with arms (rays) usually numbering 5 or a multiple
    of 5, rarely 6 or some other number, each in contact with adjacent
    arms where it joins the central disk. The surface of the central
    disk has the anus in the center, the sieve plate near the junction
    of 2 arms, and opening of sex ducts at each juncture of adjacent
    arms. The upper surface of each arm has the spines and other
    features of the species, and the eyespot, usually red at the tip.
    The underside of a sea star has the mouth in the middle of the
    central disk and an open groove from the mouth to the tip of
    each arm; 2 or 4 crowded rows of tube feet lie in each groove.
```

```
        In some sea stars there is a special skeletal structure for
        pinching small objects, a modification of 2 or 3 spines.
    </resourceData>
  </occurrence>
  <occurrence>
    <instanceOf>
      <topicRef xlink:href="#definition"/>
    </instanceOf>
    <scope>
      <topicRef xlink:href="#audubon"/>
    </scope>
    <resourceData> The stars can regenerate lost arms. When an arm is
        damaged, it is shed at a point close to the central disk, even
        though the damage may be near the tip, a process called autotomy.
        In most species, after autotomy the cut surface heals over,
        regeneration of a new arm begins, and the autotomized limb dies.
  However, there are a few sea stars in which autotomy is spontaneous;
        not only does the star regenerate a limb, but the limb regenerates
        the star.
    </resourceData>
  </occurrence>
</topic>
<topic id="brittle-stars">
  <instanceOf>
    <topicRef xlink:href="#animal-class"/>
  </instanceOf>
  <baseName>
    <scope>
      <topicRef xlink:href="#taxon"/>
    </scope>
    <baseNameString>Ophiuroidea</baseNameString>
  </baseName>
  <baseName>
    <baseNameString>brittle-star</baseNameString>
  </baseName>
  <baseName>
    <scope>
      <topicRef xlink:href="#also-known-as"/>
    </scope>
    <baseNameString>snake-star</baseNameString>
  </baseName>
  <occurrence>
    <instanceOf>
      <topicRef xlink:href="#definition"/>
    </instanceOf>
    <scope>
      <topicRef xlink:href="#aherd"/>
    </scope>
    <resourceData>Any of various marine organisms of the class
        Ophiuroidea, related to and resembling the starfish but having
        long, slender arms.</resourceData>
```

```
      </occurrence>
      <occurrence>
        <instanceOf>
          <topicRef xlink:href="#portr-img"/>
        </instanceOf>
        <scope>
          <topicRef xlink:href="#nikita"/>
        </scope>
        <resourceRef xlink:href="521706.jpg"/>
      </occurrence>
  </topic>
  <topic id="sea-urchine">
    <instanceOf>
      <topicRef xlink:href="#animal-class"/>
    </instanceOf>
    <baseName>
      <scope>
        <topicRef xlink:href="#taxon"/>
      </scope>
      <baseNameString>Echinoidea</baseNameString>
    </baseName>
    <baseName>
      <baseNameString>sea-urchin</baseNameString>
    </baseName>
    <occurrence>
      <instanceOf>
        <topicRef xlink:href="#definition"/>
      </instanceOf>
      <scope>
        <topicRef xlink:href="#aherd"/>
      </scope>
      <resourceData>Any of various echinoderms of the class Echinoidea,
          having a soft body enclosed in a round, symmetrical, calcareous
          shell covered with long spines.</resourceData>
    </occurrence>
    <occurrence>
      <instanceOf>
        <topicRef xlink:href="#landsc-img"/>
      </instanceOf>
      <scope>
        <topicRef xlink:href="#nikita"/>
      </scope>
      <resourceRef xlink:href="ocean4.jpg"/>
    </occurrence>
    <occurrence>
      <instanceOf>
        <topicRef xlink:href="#landsc-img"/>
      </instanceOf>
      <scope>
        <topicRef xlink:href="#nikita"/>
      </scope>
```

```
        <resourceRef xlink:href="ocean13.jpg"/>
      </occurrence>
      <occurrence>
        <instanceOf>
          <topicRef xlink:href="#definition"/>
        </instanceOf>
        <scope>
          <topicRef xlink:href="#audubon"/>
        </scope>
        <resourceData> Unlike sea stars or brittle stars, these creatures
          do not have arms or rays. The skeleton, called a test, consists
          of rows of radially arranged plates immovably joined to each
          other. Movable spines, each with a concave base, fit on
          correspondingly convex bumps on each plate. Muscle fibers
          attached to each spine enable it to swing about in any
          direction.
        </resourceData>
      </occurrence>
    </topic>
    <topic id="echinoderma">
      <instanceOf>
        <topicRef xlink:href="#phylum"/>
      </instanceOf>
      <baseName>
        <baseNameString>Echinoderm</baseNameString>
      </baseName>
      <baseName>
        <scope>
          <topicRef xlink:href="#taxon"/>
        </scope>
        <baseNameString>Echinodermata</baseNameString>
      </baseName>
      <occurrence>
        <instanceOf>
          <topicRef xlink:href="#definition"/>
        </instanceOf>
        <scope>
          <topicRef xlink:href="#aherd"/>
        </scope>
        <resourceData>Any of numerous radially symmetrical marine
          invertebrates of the phylum Echinodermata, which includes
          the starfishes, sea urchins, and sea cucumbers, having an
          internal calcareous skeleton and often covered with
          spines.</resourceData>
      </occurrence>
      <occurrence>
        <instanceOf>
          <topicRef xlink:href="#definition"/>
        </instanceOf>
        <scope>
          <topicRef xlink:href="#fb-seashore-life"/>
        </scope>
```

```
        <resourceData>The word Echinoderma is derived from two Greek words,
    echino, a hedgehog, and derma, meaning skin.
This refers to the fact that their skeleton consists of calcareous plates
    with projecting spines imbedded in the skin.
Another distinctive characteristic is the possession of a radial symmetry
    or starlike pattern, instead of the bilateral or elongate symmetry of
    all other animals above the Coelentera.</resourceData>
      </occurrence>
  </topic>
  <topic id="arthropods">
    <instanceOf>
      <topicRef xlink:href="#phylum""/>
    </instanceOf>
    <baseName>
      <scope>
        <topicRef xlink:href="#taxon"/>
      </scope>
      <baseNameString>Arthropoda</baseNameString>
    </baseName>
    <baseName>
      <baseNameString>Arthropods</baseNameString>
    </baseName>
    <occurrence>
      <instanceOf>
        <topicRef xlink:href="#definition"/>
      </instanceOf>
      <scope>
        <topicRef xlink:href="#aherd"/>
      </scope>
      <resourceData>Any of numerous invertebrate animals of the phylum
          Arthropoda, including the insects, crustaceans, arachnids, and
          myriapods, that are characterized by a chitinous exoskeleton and
          a segmented body to which jointed appendages are articulated in
          pairs.</resourceData>
    </occurrence>
    <occurrence>
      <instanceOf>
        <topicRef xlink:href="#definition"/>
      </instanceOf>
      <scope>
        <topicRef xlink:href="#audubon"/>
      </scope>
      <resourceData>An arthropod's most obvious characteristic is the
          tough encasement of armor, or exoskeleton. This armor is made
          principally of a substance called chitin, secreted by the
          underlying epidermal cells.
The exoskeleton has joints, regions where chitin is thin and flexible,
    permitting movements.
Such joints are particularly obvious on the legs and give the phylum its
    name, Arthropoda, which means "jointed foot" in Greek. Movement is
    achieved by muscles attached inside the skeleton, rather than on the
    outside as in human beings.</resourceData>
```

```
      </occurrence>
    </topic>
    <topic id="merostomata">
      <instanceOf>
        <topicRef xlink:href="#animal-class"/>
      </instanceOf>
      <baseName>
        <scope>
          <topicRef xlink:href="#taxon"/>
        </scope>
        <baseNameString>Merostomata</baseNameString>
      </baseName>
      <baseName>
        <baseNameString>Horseshoe Crab</baseNameString>
      </baseName>
      <baseName>
        <scope>
          <topicRef xlink:href="#also-known-as"/>
        </scope>
        <baseNameString>king crab</baseNameString>
      </baseName>
      <baseName>
        <scope>
          <topicRef xlink:href="#also-known-as"/>
        </scope>
        <baseNameString>limulus</baseNameString>
      </baseName>
      <occurrence>
        <instanceOf>
          <topicRef xlink:href="#landsc-img"/>
        </instanceOf>
        <scope>
          <topicRef xlink:href="#nikita"/>
        </scope>
        <resourceRef xlink:href="ocean10.jpg"/>
      </occurrence>
      <occurrence>
        <instanceOf>
          <topicRef xlink:href="#definition"/>
        </instanceOf>
        <scope>
          <topicRef xlink:href="#aherd"/>
        </scope>
        <resourceData>Any of various marine arthropods of the class
            Merostomata, especially Limulus polyphemus or Xiphosura
            polyphemus of eastern North America, having a large, rounded
            body and a stiff, pointed tail.</resourceData>
      </occurrence>
      <occurrence>
        <instanceOf>
          <topicRef xlink:href="#definition"/>
        </instanceOf>
```

```
    <scope>
      <topicRef xlink:href="#audubon"/>
    </scope>
    <resourceData> Horseshoe Crab's body consists of a convex forepart
      covered with a carapace (cephalothorax or prosoma), a rear part
      (abdomen orcopistosoma), and a long, spinelike tail (telson).
    </resourceData>
  </occurrence>
</topic>
<topic id="crustacea">
  <instanceOf>
    <topicRef xlink:href="#animal-class"/>
  </instanceOf>
  <baseName>
    <baseNameString>Crustacea</baseNameString>
  </baseName>
  <occurrence>
    <instanceOf>
      <topicRef xlink:href="#landsc-img"/>
    </instanceOf>
    <scope>
      <topicRef xlink:href="#nikita"/>
    </scope>
    <resourceRef xlink:href="ocean11.jpg"/>
  </occurrence>
  <occurrence>
    <instanceOf>
      <topicRef xlink:href="#landsc-img"/>
    </instanceOf>
    <scope>
      <topicRef xlink:href="#nikita"/>
    </scope>
    <resourceRef xlink:href="ocean20.jpg"/>
  </occurrence>
  <occurrence>
    <instanceOf>
      <topicRef xlink:href="#landsc-img"/>
    </instanceOf>
    <scope>
      <topicRef xlink:href="#nikita"/>
    </scope>
    <resourceRef xlink:href="ocean1.jpg"/>
  </occurrence>
  <occurrence>
    <instanceOf>
      <topicRef xlink:href="#definition"/>
    </instanceOf>
    <scope>
      <topicRef xlink:href="#aherd"/>
    </scope>
    <resourceData>Any of various predominantly aquatic arthropods
        of the class Crustacea, including lobsters, crabs, shrimps,
```

```
          and barnacles, characteristically having a segmented body, a
          chitinous exoskeleton, and paired, jointed limbs.</resourceData>
      </occurrence>
      <occurrence>
        <instanceOf>
          <topicRef xlink:href="#definition"/>
        </instanceOf>
        <scope>
          <topicRef xlink:href="#audubon"/>
        </scope>
        <resourceData> A crustacean is an arthropod with 5 pairs of
          appendages on 6 segments: 2 pairs of antennae, a pair of jaws,
          or mandibles, 1 on each side of the mouth, and 2 pairs of
          manipulatory mouthparts. The number of segments in the body
          varies, depending on the group. In some forms the body may
          simply be a trunk.
In more advanced types it may be divided into a thorax and abdomen.
    The thorax has a maximum of 8 segments, and the abdomen, 6. . . .
Reproduction is almost entirely sexual, fertilization is usually
    internal, and the eggs are attached to the body of the
    female.</resourceData>
      </occurrence>
    </topic>
    <topic id="sea-spiders">
      <instanceOf>
        <topicRef xlink:href="#animal-class"/>
      </instanceOf>
      <baseName>
        <scope>
          <topicRef xlink:href="#taxon"/>
        </scope>
        <baseNameString>Pycnogonida</baseNameString>
      </baseName>
      <baseName>
        <baseNameString>sea-spiders</baseNameString>
      </baseName>
      <occurrence>
        <instanceOf>
          <topicRef xlink:href="#definition"/>
        </instanceOf>
        <scope>
          <topicRef xlink:href="#audubon"/>
        </scope>
        <resourceData>The pycnogonids, or sea spiders, are a strange group
          of small-bodied, long-legged marine arthropods.
Though they walk on 8 legs, they are not spiders, which belong to a quite
    different group of arthropods. . . .
Pycnogonids feed by sucking the body fluids and soft tissues of hydroids,
    sea anemones, soft corals, sponges, or bryozoans.</resourceData>
      </occurrence>
      <occurrence>
        <instanceOf>
```

```
        <topicRef xlink:href="#portr-img"/>
      </instanceOf>
      <scope>
        <topicRef xlink:href="#nikita"/>
      </scope>
      <resourceRef xlink:href="284337.jpg"/>
    </occurrence>
  </topic>
  <topic id="fb-seashore-life">
    <subjectIdentity>
      <subjectIndicatorRef xlink:href="urn:ISBN:0399102930"/>
    </subjectIdentity>
    <baseName>
      <baseNameString>
      Field Book of Seashore Life
      </baseNameString>
    </baseName>
  </topic>
  <topic id="audubon">
    <subjectIdentity>
      <subjectIndicatorRef xlink:href="urn:ISBN:0394519930"/>
    </subjectIdentity>
    <baseName>
      <baseNameString>
      National Audubon Society Field Guide of North American Seashore
          Creatures.
      </baseNameString>
    </baseName>
  </topic>
  <topic id="img">
    <instanceOf>
      <topicRef xlink:href="#orole"/>
    </instanceOf>
  </topic>
  <topic id="scuba-diver">
    <instanceOf>
      <topicRef xlink:href="#person"/>
    </instanceOf>
  </topic>
  <topic id="person">
    <instanceOf>
      <topicRef xlink:href="#animal"/>
    </instanceOf>
  </topic>
  <topic id="phylum">
    <instanceOf>
      <topicRef xlink:href="#taxon"/>
    </instanceOf>
    <baseName>
      <baseNameString>Phylum</baseNameString>
    </baseName>
  </topic>
```

```
<topic id="taxon">
  <baseName>
    <baseNameString>taxon</baseNameString>
  </baseName>
  <occurrence>
    <instanceOf>
      <topicRef xlink:href="#definition"/>
    </instanceOf>
    <resourceData>Level or grouping in the animal
  hierarchy.</resourceData>
  </occurrence>
</topic>
<topic id="animal-class">
  <instanceOf>
    <topicRef xlink:href="#taxon"/>
  </instanceOf>
  <baseName>
    <baseNameString>Class</baseNameString>
  </baseName>
</topic>
<topic id="landsc-img">
  <instanceOf>
    <topicRef xlink:href="#img"/>
  </instanceOf>
</topic>
<topic id="portr-img">
  <instanceOf>
    <topicRef xlink:href="#img"/>
  </instanceOf>
</topic>
<topic id="nikita">
  <instanceOf>
    <topicRef xlink:href="#scuba-diver"/>
  </instanceOf>
  <subjectIdentity>
    <subjectIndicatorRef xlink:href=
      "urn:padi-diver-no:9907571524"/>
  </subjectIdentity>
  <baseName>
    <baseNameString>Nikita</baseNameString>
  </baseName>
</topic>
<topic id="john">
  <instanceOf>
    <topicRef xlink:href="#scuba-diver"/>
  </instanceOf>
  <subjectIdentity>
    <subjectIndicatorRef xlink:href=
      "urn:padi-diver-no:9999999999"/>
  </subjectIdentity>
  <baseName>
    <baseNameString>John</baseNameString>
```

```
      </baseName>
    </topic>
    <topic id="definition">
      <instanceOf>
        <topicRef xlink:href="#orole"/>
      </instanceOf>
    </topic>
    <topic id="description">
      <instanceOf>
        <topicRef xlink:href="#orole"/>
      </instanceOf>
    </topic>
    <topic id="aherd">
      <baseName>
        <baseNameString>American Heritage Dictionary</baseNameString>
      </baseName>
    </topic>
    <topic id="orole">
      <subjectIdentity>
        <subjectIndicatorRef xlink:href=
            "http://www.topicmaps.org/xtm/1.0/psi1.xtm#associaton-role"/>
      </subjectIdentity>
    </topic>
  </topicMap>
```

Appendix C

XSLT Style Sheet for Chapter 9

Appendix C is the XSLT style sheet used to process the topic map presented in Chapter 9 and in Appendix B. The result of applying an XSLT style sheet to an XML document is an HTML document to be displayed as a Web page.

```
<xsl:stylesheet
  xmlns:xlink="http://www.w3.org/1999/xlink"
  xmlns:xsl="http://www.w3.org/1999/XSL/Transform"
    xmlns:lxslt="http://xml.apache.org/xslt"
    xmlns:redirect="org.apache.xalan.xslt.extensions.Redirect"
    extension-element-prefixes="redirect"
    version="1.0">
  <xsl:output method="html"  indent="yes" />

<xsl:key
  name = "topic"
  match = "topic"
  use = "concat('#',@id)" />

<xsl:key
  name = "instance"
  match = "topic"
  use = "instanceOf/topicRef/@xlink:href" />

<xsl:key
  name = "subjectIndicator"
  match = "topic"
  use = "subjectIdentity/subjectIndicatorRef/@xlink:href" />

<xsl:key
  name = "classAssoc"
  match = "association[instanceOf/topicRef/@xlink:href=
          '#class-subclass']"
  use = "member[roleSpec/topicRef/@xlink:href=
        '#class']/topicRef/@xlink:href" />

<xsl:param name="out"/>
<xsl:variable name="out-dir" select="concat($out,'/')"/>
<xsl:variable name="root"
    select="key('subjectIndicator',concat('#',/topicMap/@id))"/>
```

```
<xsl:template match="/">
===Welcome to sample Cogitative Topic Map Web Site Generator===
  <xsl:for-each select="/topicMap/topic">
  <redirect:write select="concat($out-dir,@id,'.html')">
    <html>
      <header>
        <title></title>
        <style>
        A  {
               color: #cc6600;
               font-family: sans serif;
               font-size: 11pt;
               font-weight: bold;
          text-decoration : none;
        }
        .A {
               color: #0066cc;
               font-family: sans serif;
               font-size: 11pt;
               font-weight: bold;
        }
        .h1 {  .
          font-size: 26pt;
          color: #0066cc;
        }
        .bibitem {
               font-family: sans serif;
               font-size: 8pt;
        }
        </style>
      </header>
      <body>
      <a href="default.html" class="h1">
        <xsl:call-template name="name">
          <xsl:with-param name="topic" select="$root"/>
        </xsl:call-template>
      </a>
      <hr/>
      <table width="800"><tr>
        <td valign="top" width="200">
          <xsl:call-template name="sitemap">
            <xsl:with-param name="classRef"
                            select="'#animal-kingdom'"/>
            <xsl:with-param name="current" select="."/>
          </xsl:call-template>
        </td>
        <td valign="top"><xsl:call-template name="page-layout"/>
        </td>
      </tr></table>
      </body>
    </html>
  </redirect:write>
```

```
    </xsl:for-each>
</xsl:template>

<xsl:template name="sitemap">
  <xsl:param name="classRef"/>
  <xsl:param name="current"/>
  <xsl:variable name="topic" select="key('topic',$classRef)"/>
  <xsl:choose>
    <xsl:when test="$topic=$current">
      <xsl:apply-templates select="$topic" mode="label"/>
    </xsl:when>
    <xsl:otherwise>
      <xsl:apply-templates select="$topic" mode="link"/>
    </xsl:otherwise>
  </xsl:choose>
  <xsl:variable name="aref" select="key('classAssoc',$classRef)"/>

  <xsl:if test="$aref">
    <ul>
      <xsl:for-each
        select="$aref/member[roleSpec/topicRef/@xlink:href=
                '#sub-class']/topicRef">
        <li>
        <xsl:call-template name="sitemap">
          <xsl:with-param name="classRef" select="@xlink:href"/>
          <xsl:with-param name="current" select="$current"/>
        </xsl:call-template>
        </li>
      </xsl:for-each>
    </ul>
  </xsl:if>
</xsl:template>


<xsl:template name="page-layout">
<!--determine type of context topic-->
  <xsl:variable name="taxon">
    <xsl:call-template name="getTopicRef">
      <xsl:with-param name="topic" select="."/>
      <xsl:with-param name="ref">#taxon</xsl:with-param>
    </xsl:call-template>
  </xsl:variable>
  <xsl:choose>
  <xsl:when test="normalize-space($taxon)='#phylum'">
    <xsl:call-template name="phylum-page-layout"/>
  </xsl:when>
  <xsl:when test="normalize-space($taxon)='#animal-class'">
    <xsl:call-template name="class-page-layout"/>
  </xsl:when>
  <xsl:otherwise>
    <xsl:call-template name="generic-page-layout"/>
  </xsl:otherwise>
```

```
    </xsl:choose>
  </xsl:template>

  <xsl:template name="class-page-layout">
    <h1><xsl:call-template name="name"/></h1>
    <h3>
      Class
      <xsl:call-template name="name">
        <xsl:with-param name="scope">taxon</xsl:with-param>
      </xsl:call-template>
    </h3>
    [
      <xsl:call-template name="name">
        <xsl:with-param name="scope">also-known-as</xsl:with-param>
      </xsl:call-template>
    ]<hr/>
    <table align="right"><tr><td align="right">
      <xsl:apply-templates
        select="occurrence[instanceOf/topicRef/@xlink:href =
                '#landsc-img']"/>
      <xsl:apply-templates
          select="occurrence[instanceOf/topicRef/@xlink:href =
                '#portr-img']"/>
    </td></tr></table>
    <xsl:apply-templates
        select="occurrence[instanceOf/topicRef/@xlink:href =
                '#definition']"/>
  </xsl:template>
  <xsl:template name="phylum-page-layout">
    <h1><xsl:call-template name="name"/></h1>
    <h2>Phylum
      <xsl:call-template name="name">
        <xsl:with-param name="scope">taxon</xsl:with-param>
      </xsl:call-template>
    </h2>
    <hr/>
    <xsl:apply-templates select="occurrence"/>
    <hr/>
    Classes of Phylum <xsl:call-template name="sitemap">
      <xsl:with-param name="classRef" select="concat('#',@id)"/>
      <xsl:with-param name="current" select="."/>
    </xsl:call-template>
  </xsl:template>
  <xsl:template name="generic-page-layout">
    <table align="right"><tr><td align="right">
      <xsl:apply-templates
          select="occurrence[instanceOf/topicRef/@xlink:href =
                '#landsc-img']"/>
      <xsl:apply-templates
          select="occurrence[instanceOf/topicRef/@xlink:href =
                '#portr-img']"/>
```

```
      </td></tr></table>
      <xsl:apply-templates
          select="occurrence[instanceOf/topicRef/@xlink:href =
              '#description']"/>
</xsl:template>

<xsl:template name="name">
  <xsl:param name="topic" select="."/>
  <xsl:param name="scope"/>
    <xsl:choose>
    <xsl:when
        test="$topic/baseName/scope/topicRef/@xlink:href=
            concat('#',$scope)">
      <xsl:value-of
        select="$topic/baseName[scope/topicRef/@xlink:href=
            concat('#',$scope)]/baseNameString"/>
    </xsl:when>
    <xsl:otherwise>
      <xsl:value-of
          select="$topic/baseName[not(scope)]/baseNameString"/>
    </xsl:otherwise>
    </xsl:choose>
</xsl:template>
<xsl:template name="link">
  <xsl:param name="topic" select="."/>
  <xsl:param name="scope"/>
  <a href="{@id}.html">
    <xsl:call-template name="name">
      <xsl:with-param name="topic" select="$topic"/>
      <xsl:with-param name="scope" select="$scope"/>
    </xsl:call-template>
  </a>
</xsl:template>

<xsl:template match="topic" mode="link">
  <a href="{@id}.html"><xsl:call-template name="name"/></a>
</xsl:template>
<xsl:template match="topic" mode="label">
  <span class="A"><xsl:call-template name="name"/></span>
</xsl:template>

<xsl:template match="occurrence">
  <xsl:variable name="scope-name">
    <xsl:call-template name="name">
      <xsl:with-param name="topic"
          select="key('topic',scope/topicRef/@xlink:href)"/>
    </xsl:call-template>
  </xsl:variable>
  <xsl:choose>
    <xsl:when
      test="instanceOf/topicRef/@xlink:href = '#landsc-img'">
```

```
                <table border="1" bgcolor="#ffffde"><tr><td>
                    <img src=../images/{resourceRef/@xlink:href}
                         width="130"/>
            </td></tr><tr><td>
              <font size="-1">Photo by : <i>
              <b><xsl:value-of select="$scope-name"/></b></i></font>
            </td></tr></table>
          </xsl:when>
          <xsl:when test="instanceOf/topicRef/@xlink:href =
                '#portr-img'">
              <table border="1" bgcolor="#ffffde"><tr><td>
                <img src=../images/{resourceRef/@xlink:href}
                       width="100"/>
            </td><td>
              <font size="-1">Photo by :<br/>
              <i><b><xsl:value-of select="$scope-name"/></b></i></font>
            </td></tr></table>
          </xsl:when>
          <xsl:when test="instanceOf/topicRef/@xlink:href =
                 '#definition'">
            <i><xsl:value-of select="resourceData"/></i>
            <p class="bibitem">[<xsl:value-of select="$scope-name"/>]</p>
          </xsl:when>
          <xsl:when test="instanceOf/topicRef/@xlink:href =
                 '#description'">
            <font size="+1"><b>
            <xsl:value-of select="resourceData"/></b></font>
          </xsl:when>
        </xsl:choose>
      <br/>
  </xsl:template>

  <xsl:template name="getTopicRef">
  <xsl:param name="topic"/>
  <xsl:param name="ref"/>
  <xsl:choose>
   <xsl:when test="$topic/instanceOf/topicRef/@xlink:href=$ref">
     #<xsl:value-of select="$topic/@id"/>
   </xsl:when>
   <xsl:otherwise>
     <xsl:for-each
         select="key('topic',$topic/instanceOf/topicRef/
                  @xlink:href)">
       <xsl:call-template name="getTopicRef">
       <xsl:with-param name="topic" select="."/>
       <xsl:with-param name="ref" select="$ref"/>
       </xsl:call-template>
     </xsl:for-each>
   </xsl:otherwise>
   </xsl:choose>
  </xsl:template>
  </xsl:stylesheet>
```

Appendix D

GENEALOGICAL TOPIC MAP

ERIC FREESE

This appendix contains the entire topic map for the genealogy chart example presented in Chapter 13. This topic map develops the <association> element as it is used in constructing taxonomies. Many of the taxonomic ideas expressed here are useful in similar projects, such as the biology project discussed in Chapter 8.

```xml
<?xml version="1.0"?>
<!DOCTYPE topicMap SYSTEM "xtm1.dtd">
<topicMap xmlns="http://www.topicmaps.org/xtm/1.0/"
    xmlns:xlink="http://www.w3.org/1999/xlink">
 <topic id="association.property">
  <instanceOf>
   <topicRef xlink:href=
      "http://www.semantext.com/psi/occurrence-class"/>
  </instanceOf>
  <subjectIdentity>
   <subjectIndicatorRef xlink:href=
      "http://www.semantext.com/psi/association-property"/>
  </subjectIdentity>
  <baseName>
   <baseNameString>association property</baseNameString>
  </baseName>
 </topic>
 <topic id="transitive">
  <instanceOf>
   <topicRef xlink:href="#association.property"/>
  </instanceOf>
  <subjectIdentity>
   <subjectIndicatorRef xlink:href=
      "http://www.semantext.com/psi/transitive-association"/>
  </subjectIdentity>
  <baseName>
   <baseNameString>transitive association</baseNameString>
  </baseName>
 </topic>
 <topic id="reflexive">
  <instanceOf>
   <topicRef xlink:href="#association.property"/>
  </instanceOf>
```

```xml
    <subjectIdentity>
     <subjectIndicatorRef xlink:href=
        "http://www.semantext.com/psi/reflexive-association"/>
    </subjectIdentity>
    <baseName>
     <baseNameString>reflexive association</baseNameString>
    </baseName>
   </topic>
   <topic id="symmetrical">
    <instanceOf>
     <topicRef xlink:href="#association.property"/>
    </instanceOf>
    <subjectIdentity>
     <subjectIndicatorRef xlink:href=
        "http://www.semantext.com/psi/symmetrical-association"/>
    </subjectIdentity>
    <baseName>
     <baseNameString>symmetrical association</baseNameString>
    </baseName>
   </topic>
   <topic id="person">
    <instanceOf>
     <topicRef xlink:href="#topic.class"/>
    </instanceOf>
    <baseName>
     <baseNameString>Person</baseNameString>
    </baseName>
   </topic>

   <topic id="male">
    <instanceOf>
     <topicRef xlink:href="#topic.class"/>
    </instanceOf>
    <baseName>
     <baseNameString>Male</baseNameString>
    </baseName>
   </topic>

   <topic id="female">
    <instanceOf>
     <topicRef xlink:href="#topic.class"/>
    </instanceOf>
    <baseName>
     <baseNameString>Female</baseNameString>
    </baseName>
   </topic>

   <topic id="parent">
    <instanceOf>
     <topicRef xlink:href="#topic.class"/>
    </instanceOf>
    <baseName>
```

```xml
    <baseNameString>Parent</baseNameString>
   </baseName>
 </topic>

 <topic id="mother">
  <instanceOf>
   <topicRef xlink:href="#topic.class"/>
  </instanceOf>
  <baseName>
   <baseNameString>Mother</baseNameString>
  </baseName>
 </topic>

 <topic id="father">
  <instanceOf>
   <topicRef xlink:href="#topic.class"/>
  </instanceOf>
  <baseName>
   <baseNameString>Father</baseNameString>
  </baseName>
 </topic>

 <topic id="spouse">
  <instanceOf>
   <topicRef xlink:href="#topic.class"/>
  </instanceOf>
  <baseName>
   <baseNameString>Spouse</baseNameString>
  </baseName>
 </topic>

 <topic id="wife">
  <instanceOf>
   <topicRef xlink:href="#topic.class"/>
  </instanceOf>
  <baseName>
   <baseNameString>Wife</baseNameString>
  </baseName>
 </topic>

 <topic id="husband">
  <instanceOf>
   <topicRef xlink:href="#topic.class"/>
  </instanceOf>
  <baseName>
   <baseNameString>Husband</baseNameString>
  </baseName>
 </topic>

 <topic id="child">
  <instanceOf>
   <topicRef xlink:href="#topic.class"/>
```

```
 </instanceOf>
 <baseName>
  <baseNameString>Child</baseNameString>
 </baseName>
</topic>

<topic id="daughter">
 <instanceOf>
  <topicRef xlink:href="#topic.class"/>
 </instanceOf>
 <baseName>
  <baseNameString>Daughter</baseNameString>
 </baseName>
</topic>

<topic id="son">
 <instanceOf>
  <topicRef xlink:href="#topic.class"/>
 </instanceOf>
 <baseName>
  <baseNameString>Son</baseNameString>
 </baseName>
</topic>

<topic id="sibling">
 <instanceOf>
  <topicRef xlink:href="#topic.class"/>
 </instanceOf>
 <baseName>
  <baseNameString>Sibling</baseNameString>
 </baseName>
</topic>

<topic id="sister">
 <instanceOf>
  <topicRef xlink:href="#topic.class"/>
 </instanceOf>
 <baseName>
  <baseNameString>Sister</baseNameString>
 </baseName>
</topic>

<topic id="brother">
 <instanceOf>
  <topicRef xlink:href="#topic.class"/>
 </instanceOf>
 <baseName>
  <baseNameString>Brother</baseNameString>
 </baseName>
</topic>

<topic id="cousin">
 <instanceOf>
```

```
    <topicRef xlink:href="#topic.class"/>
   </instanceOf>
   <baseName>
    <baseNameString>Cousin</baseNameString>
   </baseName>
  </topic>

  <topic id="uncle">
   <instanceOf>
    <topicRef xlink:href="#topic.class"/>
   </instanceOf>
   <baseName>
    <baseNameString>Uncle</baseNameString>
   </baseName>
  </topic>

  <topic id="aunt">
   <instanceOf>
    <topicRef xlink:href="#topic.class"/>
   </instanceOf>
   <baseName>
    <baseNameString>Aunt</baseNameString>
   </baseName>
  </topic>

  <association>
   <instanceOf>
    <subjectIndicatorRef xlink:href=
       "http://www.topicmaps.org/xtm/1.0/
       core.xtm#superclass-subclass"/>
   </instanceOf>
   <member>
    <roleSpec>
     <subjectIndicatorRef xlink:href=
       "http://www.topicmaps.org/xtm/1.0/core.xtm#superclass"/>
    </roleSpec>
    <topicRef xlink:href="#parent"/>
   </member>
   <member>
    <roleSpec>
     <subjectIndicatorRef xlink:href=
       "http://www.topicmaps.org/xtm/1.0/core.xtm#subclass"/>
    </roleSpec>
    <topicRef xlink:href="#mother"/>
    <topicRef xlink:href="#father"/>
   </member>
  </association>

 <association>
   <instanceOf>
    <subjectIndicatorRef xlink:href=
       "http://www.topicmaps.org/xtm/1.0/
       core.xtm#superclass-subclass"/>
```

```
 </instanceOf>
 <member>
  <roleSpec>
   <subjectIndicatorRef xlink:href=
     "http://www.topicmaps.org/xtm/1.0/core.xtm#superclass"/>
  </roleSpec>
  <topicRef xlink:href="#spouse"/>
 </member>
 <member>
  <roleSpec>
   <subjectIndicatorRef xlink:href=
     "http://www.topicmaps.org/xtm/1.0/core.xtm#subclass"/>
  </roleSpec>
  <topicRef xlink:href="#husband"/>
  <topicRef xlink:href="#wife"/>
 </member>
</association>

<association>
 <instanceOf>
  <subjectIndicatorRef xlink:href=
    "http://www.topicmaps.org/xtm/1.0/
    core.xtm#superclass-subclass"/>
 </instanceOf>
 <member>
  <roleSpec>
   <subjectIndicatorRef xlink:href=
     "http://www.topicmaps.org/xtm/1.0/core.xtm#superclass"/>
  </roleSpec>
  <topicRef xlink:href="#child"/>
 </member>
 <member>
  <roleSpec>
   <subjectIndicatorRef xlink:href=
     "http://www.topicmaps.org/xtm/1.0/core.xtm#subclass"/>
  </roleSpec>
  <topicRef xlink:href="#daughter"/>
  <topicRef xlink:href="#son"/>
 </member>
</association>

<association>
 <instanceOf>
  <subjectIndicatorRef xlink:href=
    "http://www.topicmaps.org/xtm/1.0/
    core.xtm#superclass-subclass"/>
 </instanceOf>
 <member>
  <roleSpec>
   <subjectIndicatorRef xlink:href=
     "http://www.topicmaps.org/xtm/1.0/core.xtm#superclass"/>
  </roleSpec>
```

```
    <topicRef xlink:href="#sibling"/>
   </member>
   <member>
    <roleSpec>
     <subjectIndicatorRef xlink:href=
       "http://www.topicmaps.org/xtm/1.0/core.xtm#subclass"/>
    </roleSpec>
    <topicRef xlink:href="#brother"/>
    <topicRef xlink:href="#sister"/>
   </member>
</association>

<association>
 <instanceOf>
  <subjectIndicatorRef xlink:href=
    "http://www.topicmaps.org/xtm/1.0/core.xtm#class-instance"/>
 </instanceOf>
 <member>
  <roleSpec>
   <subjectIndicatorRef xlink:href=
     "http://www.topicmaps.org/xtm/1.0/core.xtm#class"/>
  </roleSpec>
  <topicRef xlink:href="#female"/>
 </member>
 <member>
  <roleSpec>
   <subjectIndicatorRef xlink:href=
     "http://www.topicmaps.org/xtm/1.0/core.xtm#instance"/>
  </roleSpec>
  <topicRef xlink:href="#wife"/>
  <topicRef xlink:href="#mother"/>
  <topicRef xlink:href="#sister"/>
  <topicRef xlink:href="#daughter"/>
 </member>
</association>

<association>
 <instanceOf>
  <subjectIndicatorRef xlink:href=
    "http://www.topicmaps.org/xtm/1.0/core.xtm#class-instance"/>
 </instanceOf>
 <member>
  <roleSpec>
   <subjectIndicatorRef xlink:href=
     "http://www.topicmaps.org/xtm/1.0/core.xtm#class"/>
  </roleSpec>
  <topicRef xlink:href="#male"/>
 </member>
 <member>
  <roleSpec>
   <subjectIndicatorRef xlink:href=
     "http://www.topicmaps.org/xtm/1.0/core.xtm#instance"/>
```

```
      </roleSpec>
      <topicRef xlink:href="#husband"/>
      <topicRef xlink:href="#father"/>
      <topicRef xlink:href="#brother"/>
      <topicRef xlink:href="#son"/>
     </member>
    </association>


    <topic id="is-married-to">
     <instanceOf>
      <topicRef xlink:href="#association.class"/>
     </instanceOf>
     <baseName>
      <baseNameString>is married to</baseNameString>
     </baseName>
    </topic>
    <topic id="is-parent-of">
     <instanceOf>
      <topicRef xlink:href="#association.class"/>
     </instanceOf>
     <baseName>
      <baseNameString>is the parent of</baseNameString>
     </baseName>
    </topic>
    <topic id="is-child-of">
     <instanceOf>
      <topicRef xlink:href="#association.class"/>
     </instanceOf>
     <baseName>
      <baseNameString>is the child of</baseNameString>
     </baseName>
    </topic>
    <topic id="is-sibling-of">
     <instanceOf>
      <topicRef xlink:href="#association.class"/>
     </instanceOf>
     <baseName>
      <baseNameString>is a sibling of</baseNameString>
     </baseName>
    </topic>
    <topic id="is-cousin-of">
     <instanceOf>
      <topicRef xlink:href="#association.class"/>
     </instanceOf>
     <baseName>
      <baseNameString>is a cousin of</baseNameString>
     </baseName>
    </topic>
    <topic id="date-of-birth">
     <instanceOf>
      <topicRef xlink:href="#occurrence.class"/>
```

```xml
  </instanceOf>
  <baseName>
   <baseNameString>Date of Birth</baseNameString>
  </baseName>
 </topic>
 <topic id="date-of-death">
  <instanceOf>
   <topicRef xlink:href="#occurrence.class"/>
  </instanceOf>
  <baseName>
   <baseNameString>Date of Death</baseNameString>
  </baseName>
 </topic>
 <topic id="place-of-birth">
  <instanceOf>
   <topicRef xlink:href="#occurrence.class"/>
  </instanceOf>
  <baseName>
   <baseNameString>Place of Birth</baseNameString>
  </baseName>
 </topic>
 <topic id="place-of-death">
  <instanceOf>
   <topicRef xlink:href="#occurrence.class"/>
  </instanceOf>
  <baseName>
   <baseNameString>Place of Death</baseNameString>
  </baseName>
 </topic>
 <topic id="website">
  <instanceOf>
   <topicRef xlink:href="#occurrence.class"/>
  </instanceOf>
  <baseName>
   <baseNameString>Web site</baseNameString>
  </baseName>
 </topic>
 <topic id="email">
  <instanceOf>
   <topicRef xlink:href="#occurrence.class"/>
  </instanceOf>
  <baseName>
   <baseNameString>E-mail address</baseNameString>
  </baseName>
 </topic>
 <topic id="george">
  <instanceOf>
   <topicRef xlink:href="#male"/>
  </instanceOf>
  <instanceOf>
   <topicRef xlink:href="#person"/>
  </instanceOf>
```

```
<baseName>
 <baseNameString>George</baseNameString>
</baseName>
<occurrence>
 <instanceOf>
   <topicRef xlink:href="#date-of-birth" />
 </instanceOf>
 <resourceData>19400625</resourceData>
</occurrence>
</topic>
<topic id="cara">
 <instanceOf>
  <topicRef xlink:href="#female"/>
 </instanceOf>
 <instanceOf>
  <topicRef xlink:href="#person"/>
 </instanceOf>
 <baseName>
  <baseNameString>Cara</baseNameString>
 </baseName>
 <occurrence>
  <instanceOf>
    <topicRef xlink:href="#date-of-birth" />
  </instanceOf>
  <resourceData>19420503</resourceData>
 </occurrence>
</topic>
<topic id="eric">
 <instanceOf>
  <topicRef xlink:href="#male"/>
 </instanceOf>
 <instanceOf>
  <topicRef xlink:href="#person"/>
 </instanceOf>
 <subjectIdentity>
  <subjectIndicatorRef xlink:href=
     "http://semantext.com/genealogy/eric.freese"/>
 </subjectIdentity>
 <baseName>
  <baseNameString>Eric</baseNameString>
  <variant>
   <parameters>
    <topicRef xlink:href=
     "http://www.topicmaps.org/xtm/1.0/#psi-display"/>
   </parameters>
   <variantName>
    <resourceData id="N1C5-N1C8">Eric Freese</resourceData>
   </variantName>
  </variant>
  <variant>
   <parameters>
    <topicRef xlink:href=
```

```
        "http://www.topicmaps.org/xtm/1.0/#psi-sort"/>
    </parameters>
    <variantName>
     <resourceData id="N1C5-N1CB">FREESE,ERIC,DEAN</resourceData>
    </variantName>
   </variant>
  </baseName>
  <occurrence>
   <instanceOf>
    <topicRef xlink:href="#website"/>
   </instanceOf>
   <resourceRef xlink:href="http://www.datafoundry.com/eric.htm"/>
  </occurrence>
  <occurrence>
   <instanceOf>
    <topicRef xlink:href="#date-of-birth" />
   </instanceOf>
   <resourceData>19630507</resourceData>
  </occurrence>
 </topic>
 <topic id="becky">
  <instanceOf>
   <topicRef xlink:href="#female"/>
  </instanceOf>
  <instanceOf>
   <topicRef xlink:href="#person"/>
  </instanceOf>
  <baseName>
   <baseNameString>Becky</baseNameString>
  </baseName>
  <occurrence>
   <instanceOf>
    <topicRef xlink:href="#date-of-birth"/>
   </instanceOf>
   <resourceData>19660404</resourceData>
  </occurrence>
 </topic>
 <topic id="dawn">
  <instanceOf>
   <topicRef xlink:href="#female"/>
  </instanceOf>
  <instanceOf>
   <topicRef xlink:href="#person"/>
  </instanceOf>
  <baseName>
   <baseNameString>Dawn</baseNameString>
  </baseName>
  <occurrence>
   <instanceOf>
    <topicRef xlink:href="#date-of-birth" />
   </instanceOf>
   <resourceData>19690224</resourceData>
```

```xml
    </occurrence>
   </topic>
   <topic id="rita">
    <instanceOf>
     <topicRef xlink:href="#female"/>
    </instanceOf>
    <instanceOf>
     <topicRef xlink:href="#person"/>
    </instanceOf>
    <baseName>
     <baseNameString>Rita</baseNameString>
    </baseName>
    <occurrence>
     <instanceOf>
      <topicRef xlink:href="#website"/>
     </instanceOf>
     <resourceRef xlink:href=""/>
    </occurrence>
    <occurrence>
     <instanceOf>
      <topicRef xlink:href="#date-of-birth"/>
     </instanceOf>
     <resourceData>19630110</resourceData>
    </occurrence>
   </topic>
   <topic id="todd">
    <instanceOf>
     <topicRef xlink:href="#male"/>
    </instanceOf>
    <instanceOf>
     <topicRef xlink:href="#person"/>
    </instanceOf>
    <baseName>
     <baseNameString>Todd</baseNameString>
    </baseName>
   </topic>
   <topic id="scott">
    <instanceOf>
     <topicRef xlink:href="#male"/>
    </instanceOf>
    <instanceOf>
     <topicRef xlink:href="#person"/>
    </instanceOf>
    <baseName>
     <baseNameString>Scott</baseNameString>
    </baseName>
   </topic>
   <topic id="olivia">
    <instanceOf>
     <topicRef xlink:href="#female"/>
    </instanceOf>
```

```xml
  <instanceOf>
   <topicRef xlink:href="#person"/>
  </instanceOf>
  <baseName>
   <baseNameString>Olivia</baseNameString>
  </baseName>
 </topic>
 <topic id="jordan">
  <instanceOf>
   <topicRef xlink:href="#male"/>
  </instanceOf>
  <instanceOf>
   <topicRef xlink:href="#person"/>
  </instanceOf>
  <baseName>
   <baseNameString>Jordan</baseNameString>
  </baseName>
 </topic>
 <topic id="keri">
  <instanceOf>
   <topicRef xlink:href="#female"/>
  </instanceOf>
  <instanceOf>
   <topicRef xlink:href="#person"/>
  </instanceOf>
  <baseName>
   <baseNameString>Keri</baseNameString>
  </baseName>
 </topic>
 <topic id="tiffani">
  <instanceOf>
   <topicRef xlink:href="#female"/>
  </instanceOf>
  <instanceOf>
   <topicRef xlink:href="#person"/>
  </instanceOf>
  <baseName>
   <baseNameString>Tiffani</baseNameString>
  </baseName>
 </topic>
 <topic id="carmen">
  <instanceOf>
   <topicRef xlink:href="#female"/>
  </instanceOf>
  <instanceOf>
   <topicRef xlink:href="#person"/>
  </instanceOf>
  <baseName>
   <baseNameString>Carmen</baseNameString>
  </baseName>
 </topic>
```

```
<association id="N233">
 <instanceOf>
  <topicRef xlink:href="#is-married-to"/>
 </instanceOf>
 <member>
 <roleSpec>
  <topicRef xlink:href="#husband"/>
 </roleSpec>
 <topicRef xlink:href="#george"/>
 </member>
 <member>
  <roleSpec>
   <topicRef xlink:href="#wife"/>
  </roleSpec>
  <topicRef xlink:href="#cara"/>
 </member>
</association>

<association id="N23F">
 <instanceOf>
  <topicRef xlink:href="#is-married-to"/>
 </instanceOf>
 <member>
  <roleSpec>
   <topicRef xlink:href="#wife"/>
  </roleSpec>
  <topicRef xlink:href="#rita"/>
 </member>
 <member>
  <roleSpec>
   <topicRef xlink:href="#husband"/>
  </roleSpec>
  <topicRef xlink:href="#eric"/>
 </member>
</association>

<association id="N24B">
 <instanceOf>
  <topicRef xlink:href="#is-married-to"/>
 </instanceOf>
 <member>
  <roleSpec>
   <topicRef xlink:href="#wife"/>
  </roleSpec>
  <topicRef xlink:href="#becky"/>
 </member>
 <member>
  <roleSpec>
   <topicRef xlink:href="#husband"/>
  </roleSpec>
  <topicRef xlink:href="#todd"/>
```

```
    </member>
  </association>

  <association id="N257">
   <instanceOf>
    <topicRef xlink:href="#is-married-to"/>
   </instanceOf>
   <member>
    <roleSpec>
     <topicRef xlink:href="#wife"/>
    </roleSpec>
    <topicRef xlink:href="#dawn"/>
   </member>
   <member>
    <roleSpec>
     <topicRef xlink:href="#husband"/>
    </roleSpec>
    <topicRef xlink:href="#scott"/>
   </member>
  </association>

  <association id="N265">
   <instanceOf>
    <topicRef xlink:href="#is-parent-of"/>
   </instanceOf>
   <member>
    <roleSpec>
     <topicRef xlink:href="#parent"/>
    </roleSpec>
    <topicRef xlink:href="#george"/>
    <topicRef xlink:href="#cara"/>
   </member>
   <member>
    <roleSpec>
     <topicRef xlink:href="#child"/>
    </roleSpec>
    <topicRef xlink:href="#eric"/>
    <topicRef xlink:href="#becky"/>
    <topicRef xlink:href="#dawn"/>
   </member>
  </association>

  <association id="N271">
   <instanceOf>
    <topicRef xlink:href="#is-parent-of"/>
   </instanceOf>
   <member>
    <roleSpec>
     <topicRef xlink:href="#parent"/>
    </roleSpec>
    <topicRef xlink:href="#eric"/>
    <topicRef xlink:href="#rita"/>
```

```
    </member>
    <member>
     <roleSpec>
      <topicRef xlink:href="#child"/>
     </roleSpec>
     <topicRef xlink:href="#olivia"/>
     <topicRef xlink:href="#jordan"/>
    </member>
  </association>

  <association id="N27D">
   <instanceOf>
    <topicRef xlink:href="#is-parent-of"/>
   </instanceOf>
   <member>
    <roleSpec>
     <topicRef xlink:href="#parent"/>
    </roleSpec>
    <topicRef xlink:href="#todd"/>
    <topicRef xlink:href="#becky"/>
   </member>
   <member>
    <roleSpec>
     <topicRef xlink:href="#child"/>
    </roleSpec>
    <topicRef xlink:href="#keri"/>
    <topicRef xlink:href="#tiffani"/>
    <topicRef xlink:href="#carmen"/>
   </member>
  </association>
</topicMap>
```

INDEX

Page numbers followed by *f* and *t* indicate figures and tables, respectively.

A

about capability, in RDF, 305–307

aboutness, in knowledge organization, 403–404, 434

A-Box, in description logics, 117

academic discussion threads, indexing of, 439

academic resources, organization of, with KOxTM, 445

AC arcs, in dRM, 58

active database systems, influence of expert systems on, 116

Adams, Douglas, 1*n*

addressable information resource. *See* resource(s)

addressing, in topic map standards and specifications, 25–26

advertising, on Internet, interchange structure of, 47

aggregation, in RDF, 316–319

aggregation systems, definition of, 167*n*

algorithm development, in logic programming, 118

Alt container, in RDF, 303–305

AM arc, in TMPM4, 57–58

ambiguity
in subject identity, 68
in topic maps, 18

Animalia kingdom, 152–155
phyla of, 153, 153*t*

Animalia topic, construction of, 159–160, 161*f*

Animalia topic map, construction of, 156–157, 158*f*

AnimaliaTopicMap topic, construction of, 159, 160*f*

animals, definition of, 152–153

annotated bibliographies, interactive, topic maps for, 446

a-nodes (association nodes), 29
in TMPM4, 57

AP arcs, in dRM, 58

application(s)
in dRM, 57
for information interpretation, 17
for markup, sequential, 46
in TMP3, 229–230
architecture of, 230–231, 231*f*
extension of, 243–244
processing function of, 231–232

and topic maps, independence of, 18
for topic maps (*See* topic map applications)

application programming interface (API)
DOM as, 46–47
in TM4J, 211–213
advanced features of, 223–225
basic features of, 213–218
vs. topic map interchange systems, 47

applied knowledge organization, purpose of, 401

arc(s)
in dRM, 57–58
in TMPM4, 57
in topic map processing, 29

architectural forms
vs. DTD, 53
in ISO 13250, 26, 39

ART-Enterprise (Brightware), 112

artificial intelligence
expert systems and, effect on, 113
information repurposing with, xxi
logic programming in, 117–118

AS arc, in TMPM4, 57
assertion(s). *See also* association(s)
  vs. association, 59
  components of, 58, 58*f*
  definition of, 53, 57
  in dRM, 59*f*
  typing mechanism in, 60–62,
    61*f*
assertionPattern-role-
    rolePlayerConstraints
    assertion type, 58–59
assertion types, 58–59
  semantics of, privileging, 62
association(s), 88–90. *See also*
    assertion(s)
  as a-nodes in topic map graph,
    29
  vs. assertion, 59
  class-instance relationship as,
    364–365
  in concept map, 4, 4*f*
  control over, 93
  creation of, in SemanText,
    206, 206*f*
  in CTW generation, 169
  defining, 19
  definition of, 19, 532
  in early drafts of ISO 13250
    standard, 38
  enumeration of, in TM4J,
    216
  ID generation for, in TM4J,
    216
  inferring, 352
  instances of, in knowledge
    representation example,
    359
  in knowledge organization use
    case, 426
  querying and displaying,
    195–197
  in RDF, 301–303, 305–307
  resolving, and a-nodes, 29
  roleSpec in, 90
  in semantic networks, 338–339
  sitemap controlled by,
    195–196

source of, scope for indicating,
    175
  superclass-subclass
    relationship as,
    363–364
  for TMP3
    creation of, 240–242
    defining, 228, 229*f*
  visualization of, 269
  in XTM specification, 54
association classes
  constraints on, 375–377
  PSIs for, 361, 361*t*
association member role,
    definition of, 532
associationMembership handler,
    in GooseWorks Toolkit,
    262
association properties
  in knowledge representation,
    359, 365–366
  for semantic networks,
    332–333
association role classes, PSIs for,
    361, 361*t*
associationScoping handler,
    in GooseWorks Toolkit,
    262
association template, definition
    of, 532
associationTemplating handler,
    in GooseWorks Toolkit,
    262
association types. *See also*
    instanceOf
  definition of, 532
  in knowledge representation
    example, 358
  in semantic networks, 334–335
assumptions, within book, xxii
AT&T/Lucent, CLASSIC,
    111
attributes, *vs.* element types, 27
attitude, topic maps, 48–50
authority, in PSIs, 75, 76
Automated Domain Analysis,
    topic maps for, 446

avatars, in visualizations, 279,
    279*f*
AX arc, in TMPM4, 57
axiomatic systems, in ontological
    engineering, 122

B
BACK, 117
back-end layer, of XSLT style
    sheets in CTW, 182
backward chaining, in expert
    systems, 114
bag structure, in RDF, 303–305,
    309–311
base name, 84–85
  in CTW generation, 169,
    184
  definition of, 533
  querying and displaying, in
    CTW framework,
    190–191
  and scope, 87–88
baseNameString, 84–85
base name topic, definition of,
    532
Berkeley, Mercury Prolog, 118
Berners-Lee, Tim, World Wide
    Web design of, 39
bibliographic databases, topic
    maps in, 449–452, 450*f*,
    451*f*
bibliographies, annotated,
    interactive, topic maps
    for, 446
Biezunski's Principle, 38–39
binary relations, in semantic
    networks, 329–330
Bosak, Jon, on money as
    document, 33
boundaries, foundational
    theories for, ontological,
    119
bounded object sets, in HyTime
    addressing, 26
Bravo (Global Wisdom), 65
Brightware, ART-Enterprise,
    112

business category brokering, topic maps for, 446

C
canonical syntax, constructs for, documentation for, 62
CApH (Conventions for the Application of HyTime), 38
categories
 knowledge as, 399
 in knowledge organization, 395, 397, 404–405
  sound design of, 432–433
  theory of, 398
C code, in logic programming, 118
central concept, in Semantic Web, 481, 481f
channels, use of, 188
CHIP, 118
Chordata phylum, 154, 154f
chunking, 499
city metaphor, for visualizations, 279–280, 280f, 281f
civilization, global knowledge interchange and, importance of, 48
class
 definition of, 92, 533
 vs. instance, 334
 as instance of other classes, 189–190
 PSIs, 361, 361t
class hierarchies
 constraints on, 379–380
 in knowledge representation, 359, 362–365
CLASSIC (AT&T/Lucent), 111, 117
classification, history of, 150
class-instance relationship
 definition of, 533
 in knowledge representation, 362
  as association, 364–365
  PSIs for, 364t

CLIPS (NASA), 112
Cogitative Topic Map Websites framework. *See* CTW framework
collocation, of subjects, in knowledge organization, 403–404
communication
 changes in style of, 478
 symbolic nature of, 43–44, 48–49
communities
 KOS construction in, 431–432
 PSIs in, 75–76
complexity, in standards, and simplicity, relation of, 24
compositional modeling, for ontology encoding, 120
Computational Logic, Inc., 111
concept(s)
 in knowledge organization, 395, 397, 405
 understanding, and learning, 496–498
concept map
 in education, 519–520
 history of, 485–486
 as topic map, 3–4, 4f, 442–443
 XTM document for, 5–7
conceptual graphs, history of, 486
conceptualization, definition of, 124
conceptual model, as ontology, 125, 126f
concurrent constraint logic programming, 118
connectivity, in Semantic Web, 482–483, 483f
constraint(s)
 on class hierarchies, 379–380
 in knowledge representation, 359, 373–374
  example of, 375–379
  PSIs for, 375t
 in topic maps, 339–340

constraint patterns, for knowledge representation, 374–375
constraint programming, 117–119
 companies in, 111
 in Web-based technologies, 119
constraints and queries layer, of road map of forthcoming ISO topic maps standards, 63–64
constructivist learning
 collaboration in, 518, 519f
 dominance of, 486
 environments for, 514–515, 516f
 principles of, 513–514
 in Semantic Web, 512–513
 theory of, 495, 513
 topic maps in, 13, 14–15
constructivist viewpoint, of subject identity, 68
contexts/microtheories method, for ontology encoding, 120
Conventions for the Application of HyTime (CApH), 38
conversation
 subject emergence through, 68–69
 subjects of
  addressability of, 49
  and symbolic communication, 43–44, 49, 78
Converter modules, in TMP3, 230
CR arcs, in dRM, 58
critical thinking
 definition of, 512
 structure of, 517, 517f
CTW (Cogitative Topic Map Websites) framework
 content in, as structured cognitive system, 169
 design in, 169, 172–173
 information styled in, 172

CTW (*cont.*)
layers of, 168
maintaining source code with,
168–169
merging in, 174
resolution levels in, 188
source code generated with,
for Web sites, 171–173,
177–178, 179*f*
C*x* arcs, in dRM, 58
CyberDewey, 417–419
cybernetic knowledge mapping,
history of, 485
Cyc (Cycorp), 111, 119

D
DARPA, Knowledge Sharing
Effort, 120
DARPA Agent Markup
Language (DAML), 22,
120, 124
for knowledge organization
semantics, 415
data
annotation of, for computer-
assisted interpretation,
107
definition of, 104
and documents, relation
of, 22
and knowledge, relation of,
105
vs. metadata, 40
subject-centric view of, 42–45
use of term, 104
database(s)
relationships in, 125
vs. topic maps, 17–18
database(s), deductive, logic
programming in, 118
database(s), relational
as documents, 46
information of, on Internet,
106
purpose of, 106
SQL in, 250–251

database systems, active, expert
systems and, influence on,
116
data models, *vs.* ontologies, 125
Davenport Group, in topic maps
history, 37
declarative domain knowledge,
encoding of, 119–120,
122
deductive databases, logic
programming in, 118
deep knowledge management,
107
description
in knowledge organization,
396
in RDF, 286, 286*f*
description logics, 116–117
deserialization, definition of, 533
Dewey Decimal Classification,
mapping to Library of
Congress Subject
Headings, 419–422,
420*t*, 421*t*
dimensions of knowledge,
400–401
display names (ISO), 20
vs. variant names, 27, 54
diversity, in topic maps
paradigm, 48
DOCTYPE line, in topic maps,
98
document(s)
connotation of term, 46
and data, relation of, 22
money as, 33
relational databases as, 46
document() function, use of,
193–194
Document Object Model
(DOM), disadvantages of,
46–47
document type definition. *See*
DTD
DOM. *See* Document Object
Model

domain(s), Linnaean, 152*n*, 154,
154*f*
domain theory
encoding of, 122
logical, as ontology, 125, 126*f*
in ontologies, 122
DOMXIncluder, 194
draft Reference Model. *See* dRM
drill-down topic maps, 12, 155,
157*f*
dRM (draft Reference Model).
See also RM
arc types in, 58
assertion types in, 58–59
patterns for, 60–62, 61*f*
assertion *vs.* association in, 59
compliance with, in
GooseWorks Toolkit, 263
construction rules for, 58
in GooseWorks Toolkit,
260–265
implementation of, traversing,
59–60, 59*f*
querying of, in GooseWorks
Toolkit, 264–265
role player constraints in, 62
serialization of, syntaxes for,
262–263
TMPM4 superseded by, 57
DTD (document type definition)
vs. SGML architectures, 53
in syntax layer, in road map of
forthcoming ISO topic
map standards, 62
for XTM specification,
26, 55
mapping of, to TM4J
interfaces, 213, 214*t*
dual coding, 499
Dublin Core, 23
metadata items from, in RDF,
307–308, 321–325,
410–411
dynamic visuals, language
transmitted through,
480

E
ECLiPSe, 118
education
knowledge mapping in,
485–487
semantic networks in,
486–487, 488–498, 489*f*,
490*f*
on Semantic Web, 512–513
topic maps in, 12, 14–15
(*See also* IBIS)
e-journals, indexing of, 440
element(s)
of documents, 22
in XML, 81
element types
vs. attributes, 27
meaning of, 47–48
empolis K42, 64, 270, 272*f*
emptiness, PSI for, 78
EMYCIN, 114
Enterprise JavaBeans (EJB), in
Nexist, 251
epistemology, in knowledge
organization, 397
error handling, in TM4J, 217,
217*t*
ET-Maps, for visualization, 275,
276*f*
Eukarya domain, 154, 154*f*
events, foundational theories for,
ontological, 119
exception classes, in TM4J, 217,
217*t*
expertise, in PSIs, 75, 76
expert systems, 113–116
and artificial intelligence,
effect on, 113
backward chaining in, 114
benefits of, 115
capabilities of, 114
deficiencies of, 115–116
forward chaining in, 114
influence of, on active database
systems, 116
knowledge bases based on, 112

knowledge representation
tools based on, 111
rules in, 114
semantic networks for
modeling, 329
single-level nature of, 113, 122
explicit referencing
constraint on, in STWOL,
181
in XTM, 28–29

F
facet(s)
creation of, in SemanText,
206, 207*f*
in early drafts of ISO 13250
standard, 38
in knowledge organization use
case, 427
vs. RDF, 293
and XTM specification, lack
of, 29, 54
facet analysis, in knowledge
organization, 398,
405–406
family tree
as RDF illustration, 283–284,
283*f*
in semantic network, 481–482,
482*f*
topic map from, 327, 327*f*
filtering. *See also* facet(s)
of information, on Web, 41
finding aids, for information
location, 17
five kingdoms, Linnaean, 150,
151–152, 152*t*
FiveKingdoms topic map, construction of, 156–157, 158*f*
f-logic, in On2broker and
Ontobroker, 124
formal languages. *See also*
semantic(s)
computing, 34–35
in knowledge representation,
109–110

in KOSs, 412–414
on World Wide Web, 35*n*
formatting conventions, for
XML in this book, 15
forward chaining, in expert
systems, 114
frame-based indexing, in
knowledge organization,
407–408, 422
functional equivalence, in
knowledge organization,
403–404

G
G2 (Gensym), 112
Galen (Generalised Architecture
for Languages,
Encylopaedias and
Nomenclatures in
medicine) project, reuse
of, in ontology-driven
topic maps, 130
GCARI (Graphic Communi-
cations Association
Research Institute),
CApH hosted by, 38
general interest information,
PSIs and, usefulness of,
76–77
generic markup. *See* SGML
Gensym, G2, 112
global knowledge interchange
abstractions of, 32
SGML and, 36
importance of, in civilization,
48
increased understanding
of, 49
infoglut and, problem of, 49
technological contributions
to, 49
XML and, 36
XTM for, 10–11
Global Wisdom, Bravo, 65
glyphs, in interpretation, 105
GML, 36. *See also* SGML

GooseWorks Toolkit, 260–265
  current tools of, 265
  design of, 261–262
  ISO 13250 compliance in, 263
  and other software,
    comparison of, 200
  serialization of dRM in,
    syntaxes for, 262–263
  use cases for, 263
Gowan's Knowledge, 517, 517f
Graph. *See* RM
Graphic Communications
    Association Research
    Institute (GCARI),
    CApH hosted by, 38
graphic frame, in Semantic Web,
    481, 481f
  temporal relations in, 481, 482f
GraphMaker, 247f
  in Nexist development, 245
  use cases for, 246–247
graph visualization, 271–275
GraphVisualizer 3D (Nvision),
    274, 275f
grove
  definition of, 201n
  implementation of, in
    SemanText, 209

H
hacking software, 13
hermeneutics
  and knowledge, 399
  in knowledge organization,
    397
High Performance Knowledge
    Base (HPKB) Project,
    120, 121
HTML (Hypertext Markup
    Language)
  rendering of
    in CTW generation, 169
    sequential nature of, 46
  SGML in, 35
  topic map elements rendered
    in, 173, 173t
  XML transformation to, 7

from XSLT style sheets, 184
  topic-specific, 184–186,
    187f
HTML editors, *vs.* topic maps,
    for Web site maintenance,
    170, 170f
HTML links, as topics, 19–20
HTTP (Hypertext Transport
    Protocol), formal
    language in, 35n
humans
  languages of, development of,
    478–479
  in Linnaean system, 150, 151f
  stupidity of, 1
hybrid information, management
    of, 36–37
hyperbolic geometry, for
    visualization, 273, 274f
hyperedge, in TMPM4, 58
HypersonicSQL, in Nexist
    database engine, 245,
    249–251
Hypertext Transport Protocol
    (HTTP), formal language
    in, 35n
HyTime
  inheritance in, 26
  in ISO 13250 addressing,
    25–26
  links in, 27
  for master indexes, 38
  origin of, 45n
HyTM. *See* ISO 13250

I
IBIS, 517–519
  implementation of, 521–525,
    522f
  with topic maps, 523–525,
    523f, 524f, 525f
  with XML, 523–525
ID
  generation of, in TM4J, 216
  in knowledge organization use
    case, 427
  in Nexist, 259, 260f

for TMP3, 228, 229t, 243
  in topic, 84
  requirements for, 84
ID property, in TM4J, in
    TopicMapObject
    interface, 214
IFF (Information Flow
    Framework), 124
ILOG, 111
implicit topics, creation of, in
    TM4J, 220–221
indexes, master, maintenance of,
    37–38
indexing
  back-of-the-book, classifi-
    cation in, 419
  frame-based, 407–408
  interpretive nature of,
    402–403
  KOxTM use cases in, 439–441
  relational, 407–408
  semantic markup in, 412–414
  views-based, 408, 423–424
inference rules
  developing, in SemanText,
    208–209, 209f
  in knowledge representation,
    359, 366–367
    example of, 367–373
  relevance in, 434
  in semantic networks, 343–352
infoglut, problem of, 40, 49
information
  accessing, dimensions of, 17
  categorization of, conflicts in,
    42
  definition of, 105
  general interest, PSIs and,
    usefulness of, 76–77
  hiding, imperative of, 41
  hybrid, management of, 36–37
  locating, finding aids for, 17
  money as, 33
  and reality, relation of, 32–34,
    42–45
  styling of, in CTW, 172
  use of term, 104

information continuum. *See* interpretation continuum
information economy, 33
information exchange, within communities, PSIs for, 75–76
Information Flow Framework (IFF), 124
information overlays. *See* topic map(s)
information presentation
    approaches to, simplicity *vs.* complexity, 24
    topic maps for, 17
information repurposing, with artificial intelligence, xxi
information resource(s)
    as subject, 44
    as surrogate for reality, 44–45
Information Retrieval System (IRS)
    function of, 403
    knowledge organization in, 397
information structure, 34
    vs. interchange structure
        in DOM, 45–46
        in topic maps, 47, 49
    requirements for, conflicting, 46
information structuring, 22. *See also* structured information; Web navigation
    metadata for, 22–23
    topic maps for, 23
Information Systems Institute/University of Southern California
    LOOM, 111
    PowerLOOM, 111
inheritance hierarchies, semantic networks for modeling, 329
inheritance mechanism, in ISO 13250, 26

initialization function, in TMP3 classes, 232–236
inquiry, in XTM specification, 11
instance(s)
    vs. class, 334
    in knowledge representation example, 358–359
    in several classes, 182, 188
    in XSLT templates, 190
instanceOf, 27, 90–93
instance topic, definition of, 534
IntelliCorp, KEE, 112
interchange structure, *vs.* information structure
    in DOM, 45–46
    in topic maps, 47, 49
interchange syntax, definition of, 534
interpretation. *See also* semantic(s)
    automation of, 106–107
    computer-assisted, 107
    and databases, relation of, 106
    definition of, 105
    knowledge as, 104
    in knowledge organization structures, 402–403
interpretation continuum, 104, 105f
    annotated, 107, 108f
    structured information in, 104
intuition, in symbolic communication, 44
IRS (Information Retrieval System)
    function of, 403
    knowledge organization in, 397
ISO 10744. *See* HyTime
ISO 13250 (topic maps standard), 11
    addressing in, 25–26
    architectural forms in, 26
    definition of, 39
    development of, 25, 38–39
    disabilities of, 53

layered approach of standards development process, 51, 52f
    names in, 20
    seminal character of, 51, 52f
    simplification of, 23, 24f
    syntax of, 39
    vs. XTM specification, 53–54
ISO topic maps standards (forthcoming)
    layers in road map of, 55
    relationships among, 55, 56f

J
Java APIs, in TM4J, 211
    advanced features of, 223–225
    basic features of, 213–218
Java packages, in TM4J, 211–213
Jext, 246f
    in Nexist development, 245
    use cases for, 246–247

K
KEE (IntelliCorp), 112
key() function, in XSLT, 194–195, 196
KIF (Knowledge Interchange Format), 120
kingdoms, Linnaean, 150, 151–152, 152t
KL-ONE, 116–117
    for knowledge organization semantics, 415
knowledge
    component-based languages for, 120
    for ontology encoding, 120
    and data, relation of, 105
    definition of, 104, 398–399, 507
    dimensions of, 400–401
    and hermeneutics, 399
    as interpretation, 104

knowledge (*cont.*)
  sharing of, techniques for,
    for component-based
    knowledge represen-
    tation, 120
  use of term, 104
knowledge acquisition tools,
    domain-specific,
    ontological engineering
    as basis for, 121
knowledge assets, federation of,
    and evolution of, 50
knowledge availability, 49
knowledge bases
  definition of, 112
  existing, topic maps for, 171
  intermediate, for Web site
    maintenance, 170, 171*f*
knowledge bottleneck, in expert
    systems, 115
knowledge construction, within
    communities, PSIs for,
    75–76
knowledge engineering
  definition of, 112
  issues in, 113
  questions for, 112
  research threads in, 123, 123*f*
  XML topic maps in, 12
knowledge fusion, definition of,
    110–111
Knowledge Interchange Format
    (KIF), 120
knowledge languages, for
    component-based
    knowledge representa-
    tion, 120
knowledge management
  definition of, 107
  semantic interpretation in,
    110
  topic maps for, 353–354
    vs. HTML editors, 170,
    170*f*
  XTM as API for, 252
Knowledge Manager (Mondeca),
    64

knowledge mapping, history of,
    485–487
knowledge networks
  in KOxTM use case, 425–426
  semantic interoperability in,
    387–388
  topic maps for management of,
    17–18
knowledge organization (KO),
    389–390
  abbreviations in, 474–476
  aboutness in, 403–404
  applied, purpose of, 401
  categories in, 395, 397,
    404–405
    theory of, 398
  collocation in, of subjects,
    403–404
  concepts in, 395, 397, 405
  context-dependency of,
    400–401
  definition of, 385, 392–393
  facet analysis in, 398, 405–406
  formal semantics in, 414–416
  frame-based indexing in,
    407–408, 422
  functional equivalence in,
    403–404
  history of, 391
  inquiry aided by, 386
  in IRSs, 397
  and knowledge representation,
    relation of, 412–414
  knowledge structures in,
    385–386, 399
  metadata in, 410–412
  and ontological engineering,
    408–410
  ontologies in, 408–410
  postmodern theory of,
    399–400
  principles of, 389–390,
    397–398
  problems in, 390–391, 397–398
  in PSI architecture, 387
  purpose of, 384, 385–386,
    393–394

relational indexing in,
    407–408, 422
  relations in, 395, 397, 406–407
  relevance in, 403–404
  resources on, topic map of,
    447–448
  semantic interoperability in,
    416–417
  semantic retrieval in,
    395, 408
  sound design of, 432–433
  theory of, 394–395
  and topic maps
    future of, 449–452
    impediments to adoption of,
      428–430
    merging in, 436–438
    overlap between (KOxTM),
      384–385, 386–391
    potential value of, 427–428
    recurring challenges in,
      430–438
    relation of, 386
    uses of, 439–447
  as topic map use case, 424–438
  views-based indexing in, 408
knowledge organization systems
    (KOS), 387. *See also*
    ontology(ies)
  construction of, within
    communities,
    431–432
  decentralized, 438
  elements of, mapping between,
    419–422, 420*t*
  export of, to topic maps, 433,
    441–442
  form of, 401
  quality assurance for, 389–390
  registry for, for metadata
    usage, 410–412
  semantic markup in, 412–414
  vs. topic maps, 428
  universal, 401–402
    vs. domains, 431–432
    for internet resources,
      417–419

knowledge repositories
  multiview indexing of, 440
  topic maps in, 443–444
knowledge representation (KR)
  association properties in,
    365–366
  basic concepts of, 359–360
  class hierarchies in, 362–365
  class-instance relationship in,
    as association, 364–365
  constraint patterns for,
    374–375
  constraints in, 374–375
    example of, 375–379
    PSIs for, 375*t*
  design issues in, 111–112
  example of, 357–359
  general issues in, 110–111
  inference rules in, 366–367
    example of, 367–373
    PSIs for, 373*t*
  and knowledge organization,
    relation of, 412–414
  levels of, classification of,
    109–110, 110*t*
  questions for, 109
  research threads in, 123,
    123*f*
  semantic interoperability in,
    388
  software for, 111, 127
  superclass-subclass
    relationship in, as
    association, 363–364
  in topic maps, 507, 520
  topic map templates in,
    360–362
Knowledge Sharing Effort
  (DARPA), 120
knowledge structures
  in knowledge organization,
    385–386, 397, 399
  semantic interoperability in,
    388
Knowledge Suite (Ontopia), 64
knowledge technologies, premise
  of, 119

knowledge web, topic maps as,
  477
KO. *See* knowledge organization
  (KO)
Kontext semantic network, 443
KOS. *See* knowledge organiza-
  tion systems
KOxTM. *See* knowledge
  organization (KO), and
  topic maps
KR. *See* knowledge represen-
  tation
Krypton, 117

L
language. *See* formal languages;
  natural language
layout layer, of XSLT style sheets
  in CTW, 182–187
legal evidence, topic maps for,
  447
Leggewie, Claus, 450, 450*f*,
  451*f*
Library of Congress Subject
  Headings, mapping to
  Dewey Decimal
  Classification, 419–422,
  420*t*, 421*t*
LIFE, 118
life sciences, topic map of,
  purpose of, 149
likeness. *See* functional
  equivalence
link(s), in semantic networks,
  328, 328*f*
link information, management
  of, with topic maps,
  19–20
Linnaean system of classification,
  kingdoms in, 150
Linnaeus, Carlous, classification
  system of, 150
Linux, open source status of,
  200
liquids, foundational theories for,
  ontological, 119
literature, *vs.* science, xxi

logical domain theory, as
  ontology, 125, 126*f*
logic programming, 117–119
  in artificial intelligence field,
    117–118
  C code in, 118
  in database technology,
    118
  multiparadigm languages for,
    118
  synthesis languages for, 118
  systems for, 111
  WAM-based, 118
  in Web-based technologies,
    119
LOOM (Information Systems
  Institute/University of
  Southern California),
  111, 117
Lucid Fried Eggs, 202

M
M.4 (Teknowledge), 112
magazines, indexing for, 440
MAK (Mind Map and
  Knowledge Manage-
  ment), 201, 201*f*
map(s)
  vs. territory, 2
  usefulness of, 2
Mapper modules, in TMP3,
  230
map visualization, 275–278
markup applications, sequential,
  46
master indexes, maintenance of,
  37–38
MDF (metadata processing
  framework), 230
member, 89–90
  control over, 93
Mercury Prolog (Berkeley),
  118
mereotopology, foundational
  theories for, ontological,
  119
mergeMap, 93–97

merging. *See also* name-based
   merging rule; subject-
   based merging rule
   benefit of, 96
   of CTW-based Web sites,
      174
   definition of, 534
   of ontologies, 120, 130
   processing in, 47
   in topic maps, and knowledge
      organization, 436–438
   of topic maps, 20–21
   in SemanText, 207
   of topics
      with scopes, 20–21
      in TM4J, 223–224
metadata
   vs. data, 40
   decentralized, 438
   description of, need for, 50
   from Dublin Core, in RDF,
      307–308, 321–325,
      410–411
   maintenance of, 171
   in ontologies, 122
   and Platonic forms, 42
   resource-centric view of, 43,
      49
   from SGML, 36
   structure of, RDF for,
      284–285
   for Web navigation, 22–23
metadata processing framework
   (MDF), 230
metalevel dialogue, subject
   emergence through,
      68–69
metaproperties, foundational
   theories for, ontological,
      120
Mind Map and Knowledge
   Management, MAK, 201,
      201*f*
modeling layer, of road map for
   forthcoming ISO topic
   maps standards, 55. *See
   also* RM; SAM

modules, in metadata processing
   framework, 230
Mondeca
   Knowledge Manager, 64
   Topic Navigator, 270, 272*f*
money
   as document, 33
   as information class, 33
multiparadigm languages, for
   logic programming, 118
multivalued properties, in TM4J,
      227
music, abstract representation of,
      45–46
MYCIN, 114

N
naïve viewpoint, of subject
   identity, 67–68
name(s)
   absence of, 19–20
   in CTW generation, 169
   merging, and knowledge
      organization, 436–438
   number of, 19–20
   vs. PSIs, for subject identity,
      74
name-based merging rule, 21
   definition of, 541
   mergeMap in, 95
   and subject-based merging,
      interaction of, 96–97
   in TM4J, 223
namespaces
   declaration of, in XSLT,
      186–187
   definition of, 21, 541
   in RDF, 288–290, 289*f*, 290*f*
   in topicMap, 98
   naming constraint, topic,
      definition of, 541
NASA, CLIPS, 112
natural language, 478–479
   in knowledge representation,
      109–110
   marked-up, 45*n*
   structure of, 34

in topic maps, scope for, 82
   transmission of, 479–480
natural language generated
   (NLG) text fragments,
      173*n*
natural language input interface,
   in SemanText, 210
navigation requirement, for
   visualization, 268,
      269–270
   in graphs and trees, 273–275
   in virtual worlds, 280
network address handling, in
   TM4J, 218
Newcomb, Peter J., and
   Victoria T. Newcomb,
   Whataburger model for
   topic maps by, 38
Nexist
   design requirements for, 249
   development of, 245
   early stages of, 248*f*
   future plans for, use cases for,
      249
   HypersonicSQL in, 245
   and other software,
      comparison of, 200
   persistent storage in, 245
   use cases for, 248
   SemanText in, 245
   use cases for, 245–249
   user interface for, 254–259
   Web site address for, xxii
   XTM specification in, use
      cases for, 248
NicheWorks, for visualization,
   275, 276*f*
NLG (natural language
   generated) text fragments,
      173*n*
node(s)
   in dRM, 57
   in semantic networks, 328,
      328*f*
   in topic map processing, 29
nonaddressable subject,
   definition of, 535

notations, in interpretation, 105
Nvision, GraphVisualizer 3D, 274, 275*f*

O

OASIS (Organization for the Advancement of Structured Information Standards), 55
occurrence(s), 84–85
    construction of, 160, 161*f*, 162*f*, 163, 163*f*
    creation of
        in Nexist, 257–259, 259*f*
        in SemanText, 206, 207*f*
        in CTW generation, 169, 186
    definition of, 18, 535
    querying and displaying, 192–195
    role types for
        formatting for, 192
        in knowledge organization use case, 426
    for TMP3, creation of, 240–242
    of topic characteristics, 188–189
occurrence classes
    in knowledge representation example, 358
    PSIs for, 361, 361*t*
occurrence type, definition of, 535
OIL (Ontology Inference Layer), 120–121, 124
    for knowledge organization semantics, 415
OKBC (Open Knowledge Base Connectivity) language, 120
OML/CKML (Ontology Markup Language/ Conceptual Knowledge Markup Language), 124
    for knowledge organization semantics, 415

omnigator (Ontopia Navigator), 270, 271*f*
Ontobroker, 124
On2broker, 124
Ontolingua/Chimaera (Stanford University Knowledge Systems Laboratory), 111, 120
ontological engineering
    applications of, and Web, 124
    definition of, 107*n*, 120, 121*f*
    and domain-specific knowledge acquisition tools, basis for, 121
    and knowledge organization, 408–410
    multilevel nature of, 122
    ontologies defined in, 122
    requirements in, 119
    topic maps in, 12
ontology(ies)
    building, 126–129
    coding of, with XTM, 127–128
    components of, 125
    composition of, technologies for, 120
    convergence of, PSIs in, 75
    vs. other data models, 125
    definition of, 122, 124–125, 409–410
    design consideration for, 127
    domain theory in, 122
    encoding, 120
    existing, reuse of, 130
    in knowledge organization, 408–410
    merging of, 130
        technologies for, 120
    metadata in, 122
    multiple uses of, 130
    relationships in, 125, 127
    spectrum of, 125, 126*f*
    and topic maps, comparison of, 125–126
    topics of (*See* topic map templates)

universe of discourse for, 127
    of Web sites, design of, 171
ontology-driven topic map(s), 129
    advantages of, 129–131
    future of, 131–132
    knowledge reuse with, 130
Ontology Inference Layer (OIL), 120–121, 124
    for knowledge organization semantics, 415
Ontology Markup Language/ Conceptual Knowledge Markup Language (OML/CKML), 124
    for knowledge organization semantics, 415
Ontopia, Knowledge Suite, 64
Ontopia Navigator, omnigator, 270, 271*f*
OntoSeek, 124
Open Knowledge Base Connectivity (OKBC) language, 120
Open Knowledge Systems series, purpose of, xxii
open source software
    about, 199–200
    for topic maps, 13
OPS5, 114
order-sorted unification, in logic programming, 118
Organization for the Advancement of Structured Information Standards (OASIS), 55
Oz, 118

P

parallel constraint logic programming, 118
parallel logic programming, 118
parameters element type, 98
PARKA (University of Maryland), 111
PARLOG, 118

patterns, for typing assertions, in dRM, 60–62, 61*f*
Performance semantic network, 443–444
persistent storage
in Nexist, 245, 249–251
and SQL, 250–251
use cases for, 248
in TM4J, 211, 212
persistent XTM engine, in Nexist, 249–251, 252*f*, 253*f*
phyla
of Animalia kingdom, 153, 153*t*
number of, 152
physical objects, foundational theories for, ontological, 119
PITs (Populated Information Terrains), for visualization, 279, 279*f*
"planet"
meaning of, 69–73, 70*f*, 71*f*, 73*f*
PSI for, 77–78, 78*f*
Planet 9 Studios, visualization developed by, 279, 280*f*
Platonic forms, and metadata, 42
polynomial, definition of, 150*n*
Populated Information Terrains (PITs), for visualization, 279, 279*f*
PowerLOOM (Information Systems Institute/ University of Southern California), 111
presentation layer, of XSLT style sheets in CTW, 182
principled knowledge organization, 389–390
printing, language transmitted through, 479–480
problem-solving methods, encoding of, 119
procedural markup, *vs.* generic markup, 36

processing model, for XTM specification, 29
Producer modules, in TMP3, 230
programming modules, repository for, indexing of, 439
Prolog, 117–118
properties, foundational theories for, ontological, 120
property change listeners, in TM4J, 225–227, 225*t*–226*t*
property types, in RDF, 285
disambiguating, 288–290, 289*f*, 290*f*
Protégé-2000 (Stanford University Medical Informatics Laboratory), 111, 121, 127
pseudodescriptors, in knowledge organization, 396
PSIs (Published Subject Indicators)
best practices for, development of, 55
changing nature of, 77–78
context for, necessity of, 76–77
definition of, 73, 535
for inference rules, in semantic networks, 343
for inquiry disambiguation, 11
knowledge organization applied to, 387
in knowledge representation, 360
for classes, 361, 361*t*
for class-instance relationship, 364*t*
for constraints, 375*t*
for inference rules, 373*t*
for superclass-subclass relationship, 363, 363*t*
for transitive relationships, 365*t*
vs. names, for subject identity, 74
in Nexist, 256, 258*f*

for nonaddressable subjects, 49
quality requirements for, 75
registries for, 441–442, 449
ontology-bound, 433
semantics assigned from, 331–332
in TMP3, subjects defined by, 236–240
for topic maps, Web address for, 77
for TopicMap topic, 158, 159*f*
updating, 88
and variant names, relation of, 54
Published Subject Indicators. *See* PSIs
published subjects
for Web navigation, 23
in XTM specification, 29

Q
QuestMap, 515, 516*f*
Quintus, 111

R
Rapid Knowledge Formation (RKF), 120, 121
RDF (Resource Description Framework)
about capability in, 305–307
aggregation in, 316–319
Alt container in, 303–305
associations in, 301–303, 305–307
bag structure in, 303–305
data model of, 285–288
deployment of, 428–429
description in, 286, 286*f*
extensibility of, 292–293
vs. facets, 293
family tree as illustration of, 283–284, 283*f*
markup of, *vs.* XTM, 297, 299–300
metadata in, from Dublin Core, 307–308, 321–325, 410–411

for metadata structure, 284–285
in On2broker and Ontobroker, 124
property types in
  definition of, 285
  disambiguating, 288
reification in
  of statements, 311–314
  of topics, 300–301
relational data structures in, 320–321
resources in, definition of, 285
scope and, 294–295
and semantic interoperability, 388
and semantic networks, comparison of, 330
semantic networks built with, 293
in Semantic Web, 17–18
Sequence container in, 303–305
sorted data structures in, 315–316
statements in, 286–287, 287*f*
  multiple, 307–309
  RDF statements about, 311–314
and topic maps
  combination of, 295–296
  comparison of, 292–293, 294–295, 330
  relation of, 18
values in, 285–286
XML in, 285, 288–291
  namespaces in, 288–290, 289*f*, 290*f*
and XTM specification, 14
RDFS (RDF Schema), 291–292
vs. topics, 293
ready-to-use topic map, definition of, 535
reality
  and information, relation of, 32–34, 42–45

information resource as surrogate for, 44–45
symbolic representation of, 43–44, 48–49
redundancy-elimination, in topic map processing, 47
reference merge, in SemanText, 207
Reference Model (RM), 55–62. *See also* dRM
purpose of, 56
referencing, explicit
  constraint on, in STWOL, 181
  in XTM, 28–29
reflexive relationships, in semantic networks, 328–329
reification, 67
  definition of, 28, 535
  of occurrences, 159
  of statements, in RDF, 311–314
  of topic maps, by root topic, 174
  of topics, in RDF, 300–301
relation(s)
  in knowledge organization, 395, 397, 406–407
    sound design of, 432–433
  understanding, and learning, 496–498
relational data structures, in RDF, 320–321
relational indexing
  in knowledge organization, 407–408, 422
  topic maps in, 434
relevance
  in knowledge organization, 403–404
  topic maps in, 434
representation
  dual, in Semantic Web, 490–491, 490*f*
  of incomplete knowledge, in topic maps, 431
  in subject construction, 68

representation requirement, for visualization, 268–269
  in graphs and trees, 271–273
  in maps, 275–278
  in virtual worlds, 279–280
research fronts, topic maps for, 446
resolution levels, in CTW framework, 188
resolution principle, 117
resource(s)
  definition of, 19, 531
  interchangeable, structure of (*See* interchange structure)
  subject-indicating *vs.* subject-constituting, 19, 28–29, 53
  as topics, 27–28
resource(s), RDF, 289–290
  definition of, 285
  description of, RDF Schema for, 291–292
  with multiple statements, 307–309
  sharing, 315–316
  unique identifiers for, 287
resourceData, 98
  in XSLT templates in CTW, 193
Resource Description Framework. *See* RDF
resourceID property, in TM4J, 214–215
resourceRef
  in explicit referencing, 28
  inside member element, 89*n*
  and resourceData, use of, 98
  for subject identification, 86
  vs. subjectIdentity, 86
  in XSLT templates, 193
Rete algorithm, production systems based on, 114
reusable knowledge components, for ontology encoding, 120
RKF (Rapid Knowledge Formation), 120, 121

RM (Reference Model), 55–62.
  See also dRM
  purpose of, 56
role(s)
  definition of, 536
  topics for, 89–90
role player, definition of, 536
roleSpec, 89–90
  control over, 93
root topic in CTW
  source code for, 175, 176*f*
  topic map reified by, 174
  Web page generation for,
    174–175
Rubinsky, Yuri, SGML video
    by, 31
rule(s)
  in expert systems, 114
  for inference (*See* inference
    rules)

S
SAM (Standard Application
    Model), 56–57, 62
Sandberg, Anders, on human
    stupidity, 1
SC arc, in TMPM4, 57–58
science, role of, in daily life, xxi
scope, 87–88
  association source indicated in,
    179–180
  definition of, 20, 536
  in early drafts of ISO 13250
    standard, 38
  in knowledge organization use
    case, 427
  merging topics with, 20–21
  for natural languages, 82
  occurrence source indicated in,
    186
  in RDF, *vs.* topic maps,
    294–295
  and s-nodes, 29
  in TM4J, 224–225
  for TMP3, 228
  unconstrained (*See*
    unconstrained scope)

uses of, 20–21
  for association source, 175
  visualization of, 269
scopic, definition of, for CTW,
    190–191
scoping topic(s)
  definition of, 536
  function of, in STWOL, 177
  multiple, 195
scoping topic classes, PSIs for,
    361, 361*t*
search engines
  disorganization of, 41
  semantic interpretation and,
    103
sea-star topic element, source
    code for, 177–178, 179*f*
self-organizing map (SOM)
    algorithm, for
    visualization, 275–277,
    277*f*
SemanText
  function of, 204
  future plans for, 209–210
  inference rules in, developing,
    208–209, 209*f*
  in Nexist, 245
    use cases for, 248
  and other software,
    comparison of, 200
  output formats of, 210
  topic map creation in,
    204–207, 206*f*
  topic map merging in, 207
  Web address of, 210
semantic(s). *See also* formal
    languages; interpretation
  definition of, 508
  formal
    in knowledge organization,
      414–416
    in KOSs, 412–414
    in topic maps, 435–436
  interpretation of, in
    knowledge management,
    110
  from PSIs, 331–332

statistics for inference of,
    106–107
  in topic map architecture, 18,
    25
semantic heterogeneity, 416
semantic indexing, in knowledge
    organization, 395
semantic interoperability
  in knowledge networks,
    387–388
  in knowledge organization,
    416–417
  through ontologies, 125–126
  in topic maps, 436–438
semantic networks, 328–330
  association properties for,
    332–333
  binary relations in, 329–330
  connectivity in, 482–483, 483*f*
  constraints in, 339–340
  construction of, and learning
    process, 492–494
  creation of
    with RDF, 293
    in SemanText, 204
    with topic maps, 293
  definition of, 328, 508–509
  in education, 486–487,
    488–498, 489*f*, 490*f*
  family tree in, 481–482, 482*f*
  formalization of, 116–117
  inference rules in, 343–352
  information extraction from,
    353
  in KOxTM use cases, 442–444
  modeling with, 329
  for procedural knowledge, 499
  and RDF, comparison of, 330
  reflexive relationships in,
    328–329
  symmetric relationships in,
    329
  teaching with, 494–496
  and topic maps, comparison of,
    330
  transitive relationships in, 328,
    337

validation in, 340
weightings in, in SemanText, 210
semantic retrieval
in knowledge organization, 395, 408, 422
topic maps in, 434
Semantic Web
connectivity in, 482–483, 483*f*
definition of, 508–511
development of, 480–484
dual representations of, 490–491, 490*f*
education on, 512–513
languages in, 124
meanings shared on, 507, 509–510
navigation on, 484
RDF in, 17–18
structure of, 509
subject identity in, 74
systems in, 124
topic maps in, 2, 17–18, 511
SemNet, 486–487, 487*f*, 515, 516*f*
Sequence container, in RDF, 303–305
serialization
definition of, 536
of dRM, syntaxes for, 262–263
server, for Nexist, user interface for, 254, 254*f*, 255*f*
set, definition of, 536
SGML (Standard Generalized Markup Language)
description of, need for, 50
evolution of, 45
flexibility of, 49
in HTML, 35
on Internet, 53
metadata from, 36
in origin of XML, 23, 24*f*
problems with, 36
vs. procedural markup, 36
purpose of, 31, 35–36

topic maps built from parsing, 206–207, 208*f*
for Web, 35
shell topic maps, in drill-down technique, 156
SHOE (Simple HTML Ontology Extension), 124
and semantic interoperability, 388
simplicity, in standards, and complexity, relation of, 24
site map, of Web sites, control of, with association, 195–196
Sixtus, 111
s-nodes (scope nodes), 29
in TMPM4, 57
SOFABED (Standard Open Formal Architecture for Browsable Electronic Documents), 38
software, open source. *See* open source software
software applications. *See* application(s)
SOM (self-organizing map) algorithm, for visualization, 275–277, 277*f*
sorted data structures, in RDF, 315–316
sort key names (ISO), 20
vs. variant names, 27, 54
Sourceforge, projects hosted by, 200
space, foundational theories for, ontological, 119
Special Topic Map Website Ontology Layer. *See* STWOL
stability, in PSIs, 75
Standard Application Model (SAM), 56–57, 62
Standard Generalized Markup Language. *See* SGML
Standard Open Formal Architecture for Browsable Electronic Documents (SOFABED), 38

standards, creation of, 24–25
Stanford University Knowledge Systems Laboratory, Ontolingua/Chimaera, 111
Stanford University Medical Informatics Laboratory, Protégé-2000, 111
start tag, definition of, 36
statements, in RDF, 286–287, 287*f*, 291–292
multiple, 307–309
RDF statements about, 311–314
reification of, 311–314
resources shared between, 315–316
stochastic methods, for interpretation automation, 106–107
structured information
in interpretation continuum, 104
vs. unstructured information, 34
student resources, organization of, with KOxTM, 445
STWOL (Special Topic Map Website Ontology Layer), 176–182
concept of, 176–177
topics in, 176
as instance of several classes, 182
layout function of, 177
referential constraint on, 182
source code for, 180–181
subject(s) of conversation
addressability of, 49
and symbolic communication, 43–44, 49, 78
subject(s) of topics
computer access to, 43
construction of, representations in, 68
defining, viewpoints on, 67–68

subject(s) of topics (*cont.*)
definition of, 19, 537
emergence of, in natural
conversation, 68–69,
69–73, 70*f*, 71*f*, 73*f*
identity of (*See also*
subjectIdentity)
ambiguity in, 68, 74
duplicating, 86
viewpoints on, 67–68
information resource as, 44
merging, and knowledge
organization, 434
nonaddressable, definition of,
535
and resources, relation of, 19,
28–29
as t-node in topic map graphs,
29
subject-based merging rule, 21
definition of, 537
mergeMap in, 95
and name-based merging,
interaction of, 96–97
in TM4J, 223–224
in XTM processing model, 29
subject-based Topic Map Query
Language (sTMQL), in
GooseWorks Toolkit,
264–265
subject-centric view, of data,
42–45
subject-constituting resource
definition of, 537
vs. subject-indicating, 19,
28–29, 53
subjectEquilvalence handler, in
GooseWorks Toolkit, 262
subject gateways, quality-
controlled, topic maps
for, 445–446
subject identity, 85–87
definition of, 537–538
empty, 98–99
vs. resourceRef, 86
subject identity point, definition
of, 538

subject-indicating resource
definition of, 538
vs. subject-constituting
resource, 19, 28–29, 53
subjectIndicatorRef
in explicit referencing, 28
inside member element, 89*n*
subphyla, Linnaean, 152*n*
subtype topic, definition of, 539
superclass-subclass relationship
in knowledge representation,
359, 362
as association, 363–364
PSIs for, 363, 363*t*
in semantic networks, 334, 336
supertype-subtype association,
definition of, 539
supertype topic, definition of,
539
SWAGs, 2
symbol(s), interpretation of, 105
symbolic communication, 43–44,
48–49
symmetric relationships, in
semantic networks, 329
syndication systems, definition
of, 167*n*
syntactic interoperability, through
topic maps, 125–126
syntax
canonical, constructs for,
documentation for, in
syntax layer, 62
serialization of, in dRM,
262–263
syntax layer, in road map of
forthcoming ISO topic
map standards, 62
synthesis languages, for logic
programming, 118
Systematifier, 392

T
tag names
length of, in XTM
specification, 54
meaning of, 47–48

TalvaStudio, 194
TAO (topics, associations, and
occurrences), 65
taxonomy, as ontology, 125, 126*f*
T-Box, in description logics,
117
teaching, with semantic
networks, 494–496
technology, role of, in daily life,
xxi
Teknowledge, M.4, 112
telephone numbers, as formal
languages, 34–35
television, language transmitted
through, 480
template, definition of, 361
temporal relations, in Semantic
Web, 481, 482*f*
terminological logics. *See*
description logics
territory, *vs.* map, 2
text word indexing, 440–441
ThemeScape, for visualization,
277–278, 278*f*
Thinking semantic network,
443–444
thought
ephemeral nature of, 487–488
writing pattered after, 498
time, foundational theories for,
ontological, 119
TM4J
distribution of, organization
of, 211, 212*f*
error handling in, 217, 217*t*
export process of, 221, 221*f*
extensions of, 244
implicit topics in, 220–221
Java APIs of, 211–213
advanced features of,
223–225
basic features of, 213–218
element types of XTM
DTD mapped to, 213,
214*t*
network address handling in,
218

object properties in, *225t–226t*
and other software,
    comparison of, 200
property change listeners in,
    225–227, *225t–226t*
scope in, 224–225
TopicMapObject interface of,
    214–215
topic maps in
    creation of, 215
    loading, 218–220
    saving, 221–223
topic merging in, 223–224
unconstrained scope in,
    224–225
utilities in, 215–217
TMCL (Topic Map Constraint
    Language)
development of, 340
user requirements for, 63–64
TMP3
applications in, 229–230
    architecture of, 230–231,
        231*f*
    extension of, 243–244
    processing function of,
        231–232
classes in, initialization
    function in, 232–236
ontology for, 228–229
TMPM4 (topicmaps.net
    Processing Model)
nodes in, 57
replacement of, 57
TMQL (Topic Map Query
    Language), user
    requirements for, 63
t-nodes (in topic nodes), 29
in TMPM4, 57
topic(s), 84–85
and aboutness, in knowledge
    organization, 434
in concept map, 4, 4*f*
creation of, 67, 158–165
    in Nexist, 256, 257*f*
    in SemanText, 204–207,
        206*f*

CTW generated from, 174
definition of, 18, 539
in early drafts of ISO 13250
    standard, 38
empty, 98–99
enumeration of, in TM4J, 216
ID generation for, in TM4J,
    216
implicit, creation of, in TM4J,
    220–221
instances of
    in several classes, 182, 188
    in XSLT templates, 190
in knowledge organization use
    case, 426
in knowledge representation
    example, 358
merging, with scopes, 20–21
processing of, merging in, 47
vs. RDFS, 293
regular, *vs.* ontology, 360
representation of, in topic map
    applications, 47–48
resources as, 27–28
in STWOL, 176
    as instance of several classes,
        182
    layout function of, 177
    referential constraint on,
        182
    source code for, 180–181
for TMP3
    creation of, 236–240
    defining, 228, 229*f*
in topic map syntax, 39
in XTM, as instance of several
    classes, 188
topic-base name association,
    definition of, 539
topic characteristic(s). *See also*
    association(s); member;
    name(s); occurrences
definition of, 540
scope applied to, in TM4J,
    224
for Web page content and
    rendering, 171–173

topic characteristic assignment
definition of, 540
occurrences example, 188–189
topic classes, PSIs for, 361, 361*t*
topic hierarchy, defining, in
    semantic networks, 338
topic map(s), 17–18
vs. API, 47
applications for (*See* topic map
    applications)
attitude 48–50
in bibliographic databases,
    449–452, 450*f*, 451*f*
browsing, in SemanText, 204,
    205*f*
changes to, automatic
    detection of, through
    TM4J, 225–227
completeness of, 49
complexity of, 13
components of, 23–24
concept map as, 3–4, 4*f*,
    442–443
content model of, 98–99
constraints on, 339–340
    example of, 375–377
in constructivist learning, 13,
    14–15
in corporate knowledge
    repositories, 443–444
creation of, 155–165, 164*f*
    in Nexist, 256, 257*f*
    in SemanText, 204–207,
        206*f*
    in TM4J, 215
vs. databases, 17–18
definition of, 3, 540
drill-down (*See* drill-down
    topic maps)
in education, 12, 14–15,
    519–521, 520*f* (*See also*
    IBIS)
element 98–99
elements of
    HTML rendering of, 173,
        173*t*
    in TM4J APIs, 213–215

topic map(s) (*cont.*)
    empty, 98–99
    extensibility of, 292–293
    extraction of information
        from, 353
    formal semantics in, 435–436
    future of, 66, 449–452
    in GooseWorks Toolkit,
        261–262
    with IBIS, 523–525, 523*f*,
        524*f*, 525*f*
    and indexing views, 438
    information and reality in,
        33
    for information presentation,
        17
    innovation of, 429–430
    for knowledge bases, existing,
        171
    for knowledge management,
        353–354
    vs. HTML editors, 170,
        170*f*
    and knowledge organization
        future of, 449–452
        impediments to adoption of,
            428–430
        overlap between (KOxTM),
            384–385, 386–391
        potential value of, 427–428
        recurring challenges in,
            430–438
        relation of, 386
        uses of, 439–447
    vs. knowledge organization
        systems, 428
    knowledge organization
        systems exported to, 433,
        441–442
    for knowledge representation,
        507
    as knowledge webs, 477
    for life sciences, purpose of,
        149
    limited deployment of,
        428–429
    loading, in TM4J, 218–220

    merging, 20–21
        in SemanText, 207
    merging in, and knowledge
        organization, 436–438
    for MP3 collection (*See*
        TMP3)
    neutrality of, 18, 25
    in Nexist, as container,
        249–251
    and ontologies, comparison of,
        125–126
    ontology-driven (*See*
        ontology-driven
        topic map(s))
    origins of, 17–18, 37–40, 65
    perspectives for, 9
    purpose of, 82
    and RDF
        combination of, 295–296
        comparison of, 292–293,
            294–295, 330
        relation of, 18
    ready-to-use, definition of,
        535
    reification of, by root topic,
        174
    in relational indexing, 434
    and relevance, 434
    representation in, of
        incomplete knowledge,
        431
    saving, in TM4J, 221–223
    and semantic networks, 293
        comparison of, 330
        in SemanText, 204
    in semantic retrieval, 434
    in Semantic Web, 2, 17–18,
        511
    and software applications,
        independence from, 18
    standards and specifications
        for, 11
    and SQL, for persistent
        storage, 250–251
    subject-centric nature of, 43
    for TMP3, extension of,
        243–244

    use cases for, knowledge
        organization as, 424–438
    usefulness of, 3
    uses of, 268
    validation in, in semantic
        networks, 340
    view construction for, 4–5
    visualization of (*See*
        visualization)
    for Web navigation, 23, 171
    Web site references for, 7
    and XSLT, benefits of, 167
topic map applications
    from GooseWorks, 261
    topics represented in, 47–48
topic map concepts, expression
    of, in ISO 13250, 26
Topic Map Constraint Language
    (TMCL)
        development of, 340
        user requirements for,
            63–64
TopicMapObject interface, of
    TM4J, 214–215
topic map objects, creation of, in
    TM4J, 215
topic map paradigm
    definition of, 541
    evolution of, 65
    future of, 66
    philosophy inherent in,
        48–50
Topic Map Query Language
    (TMQL), user
    requirements for, 63
topic map schema, in knowledge
    representation, 359–360
topicmaps.net Processing Model
    (TMPM4)
        nodes in, 57
        replacement of, 57
topic map software, 64–65
    open source, 13
    proliferation of, 51, 52*f*
    Web site references for, 9
TopicMaps.Org, 39–40, 51, 52*f*,
    53

topic map templates
    definition of, 541
    in knowledge representation,
        359, 360–362
TopicMap topic, construction of
    in CTW, 158, 159*f*
Topic Navigator (Mondeca), 270,
    272*f*, 519, 520*f*
topic-occurrence association,
    definition of, 542
topicRef, 27
    for explicit referencing, 28
    in member elements, 89–90,
        89*n*
    in scope, 87–88
    for subject identification,
        86–87
topic-subjectIndicator assertion
    type, 58
topic types
    definition of, 542
    filtering for, 195
    semantics of, in XTM
        specification, 25
    in XSLT templates, 177
    querying, 188–190
TouchGraph, 202–203, 202*f*,
    203*f*
transitive relationships
    in knowledge representation,
        365
        PSIs for, 365*t*
    in semantic networks, 328,
        337
Translator modules, in TMP3,
    230
tree visualization, 271–275
trust
    building, for PSIs, 76
    in PSIs, 75
type. *See* class
type hierarchies, in semantic
    networks, 334–339

U
UML (Unified Modeling
    Language), 62

UMLS (Unified Medical
    Language System),
    project, reuse of, in
    ontology-driven topic
    maps, 130
unconstrained scope
    in CTW implementation, 174
    definition of, 542
    in TM4J, 224–225
unification, in logic program-
    ming, 118
Uniform Resource Indicators
    (URIs)
    in Nexist, 259, 259*f*
    in XTM addressing, 25, 54
Universal Interactive
    Visualization Tool
    (UNIVIT), 270, 273*f*
universal knowledge organiza-
    tion systems, 401–402
    vs. domains, 431–432
    for internet resources,
        417–419
universe of discourse, defining,
    for ontologies, 127
University of Maryland, PARKA,
    111
UNIVIT (Universal Interactive
    Visualization Tool), 270,
    273*f*
unstructured information
    definition of, 104*n*
    vs. structured information, 34
URIs (Uniform Resource
    Indicators)
    in Nexist, 259, 259*f*
    in XTM addressing, 25, 54

V
validation, in topic maps, in
    semantic networks, 340
values, in RDF, 285–286
variant element type, 97–98
variant names (XTM), 20,
    97–98
    in CTW generation, 169
    definition of, 98, 542

vs. display name/sort name, 27,
    54
    nesting of, 27
varlink, *vs.* xlink, 27
view, construction of, for XTM
    document, 4–5, 7
views-based indexing, 423–424
    in knowledge organization,
        408
virtual cities, for visualizations,
    279–280, 280*f*, 281*f*
virtual reality, for visualization,
    279, 279*f*
viruses, classification of, 154–155
visual(s), dynamic, language
    transmitted through, 480
visual data-mining tools, for
    visualization, 278–280
visualization
    current, 270
    graphs and trees for, 271–275
    hyperbolic geometry for, 273,
        274*f*
    maps for, 275–278
    navigation requirement for,
        268, 269–270
    in graphs and trees, 273–275
    in virtual worlds, 280
    representation requirement
        for, 268–269
    in graphs and trees, 271–273
    in maps, 275–278
    in virtual worlds, 279–280
    usefulness of, 267
    virtual reality for, 279, 279*f*
    visual data-mining tools for,
        278–280
vocabulary, as ontology, 125,
    126*f*

W
Warren Abstract Machine
    (WAM), 118
Web browsers, use of, 103
Web navigation
    metadata for, 22–23
    topic maps for, 23, 171

Web portal
  maintenance of, 167
  topic maps for, 445–446
WebSGML, correspondence to
    XML, 35
Web site
  CTW-based
    design of, 169, 172–173
    maintenance of, 168–169
    merging of, 174
    source code for, 177–178,
      179f
  definition of, 167
  maintenance of, HTML
    editors *vs.* topic maps for,
      170, 170f
  ontology of, design of, 171
  sitemap for, control of, with
    association, 195–196
  source code for, XTM as,
    171–173
Web site references
  for topic map, general, 8
  for topic map software, 9
  updating of, xxii
weightings, in SemanText, 210
Weinberger, David, on the Web,
    nature of, 1
Whataburger model for topic
    maps, 38
Whittaker, R. H., 151
Wiki Web sites, 68
World Wide Web. *See also* Web
  design of, by Tim Berners-
    Lee, 39
  finding information on, 41
  formal languages in, 35n
  information on, from
    relational databases,
    106
  logic and constraint
    programming on, 119
  meanings shared on, 507,
    509–510
  ontological engineering
    applications and, 124
  purpose of, 507

semantic communication and,
    revolution in (*See*
    Semantic Web)
  as social realm, 1
World Wide Web Consortium,
    web address of, 35n
writing
  language transmitted through,
    479
  paradigm shift in, 498

X

xinclude:include, 193–194
xlink, in XTM specification, 27,
    54
xlink:href attribute
  constraint imposed by, in
    STWOL, 181
  function of, 85
XML (eXtensible Markup
    Language)
  angle brackets used in, 81
  content-based tagging in, 353
  elements in, 81
  formatting conventions for, 15
  function of, 22
  and HTML, transformation
    into, 7 (*See also* XTM
    document, and Web
    pages)
  with IBIS, 523–525
  ontological extensions to, 124
  for ontologies, 120–121
  in RDF, 285, 288–291
    namespaces in, 288–290,
      289f, 290f
  for relational databases, 46
  semantic extensions to, 124
  and semantic interoperability,
    388
  syntax of, 39
  topic maps built from parsing,
    206–207, 208f
  WebSGML in, 35
XML InfoSet, 46n, 62
xml declaration line, in topic
    maps, 98

XML Ontology Exchange
    Language (XOL), 120,
    124
XML topic map specification. *See*
    XTM specification
XSLT layers in CTW, 182–183
XSLT style sheets in CTW
  back-end layer of, 182
  HTML from, 184
    topic-specific, 184–186,
      187f
  layout layer of, 182–187
  namespace declaration in,
    186–187
  presentation layer of, 182
XSLT technology
  and topic maps, benefits of,
    167
  uses of, 168
  for XML to HTML
    transformation, 7
XSLT templates in CTW,
    183–184
  for occurrences, 192–193
  topic instances determined by,
    190
  topic-specific, 184–186, 187f
  topic types for, 177
    querying, 188–190
XTM Authoring Group, xxii, 26
XTM document
  of concept map, 5–7
  view for, 7
  and Web pages, transforma-
    tion into, 13 (*See also*
    XML, and HTML)
XTM elements, number of, 83
XTM engine
  as API, for knowledge
    management, 252
  in Nexist, 251–254, 252f, 253f
XTM framework. *See* CTW
    (Creative Topic Map
    Websites) framework
XTM specification
  addressing in, 25–26
  conceptual model for, 26

constructs for, documentation for, in syntax layer, 62
creation of, 39–40
design of, 23–25
DTD for, 26, 55
element types in, 27
evolution of, xxii
facets and, lack of, 29
future of, 66
history of, 10, 23, 24*f*, 53
vs. ISO 13250, 53–54
markup of, *vs.* RDF, 297

in Nexist, use cases for, 248
ontologies coded with, 127–128
ontology-driven topic maps in, 129–130
philosophical perspective of, 10–11
processing model for, 29
published subjects in, 29
purpose of, 39
and RDF, 14
referencing in, explicit, 28–29

reification in, of topics, 27–28
release of, 53–54
semantics in, 25
support for, in SemanText, 204, 209
variant names in, 27
varlinks in, 27
XTM technology, conception of, xxii

Y
Yahoo, topical organization of, 41

Also Available from Addison-Wesley

0-201-74852-5

0-201-73063-4

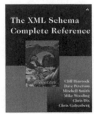

0-201-65796-1

0-672-32374-5

0-201-70914-7

0-201-67487-4

0-201-77059-8

0-201-70915-5

0-201-77641-3

0-201-77006-7

0-201-75605-6

0-201-71103-6

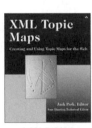

0-201-72920-2

0-672-32354-0

0-201-77004-0

0-201-75081-3

0-201-74960-2

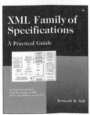

0-201-70359-9

0-201-65764-3

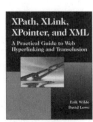

0-201-74095-8

0-201-70344-0

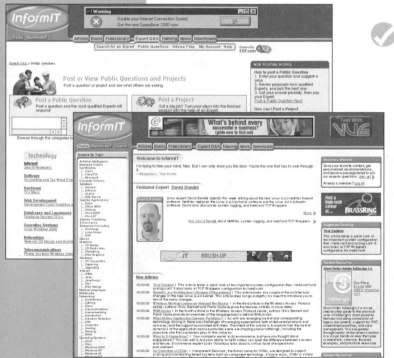

Register
Your Book
at www.aw.com/cseng/register

You may be eligible to receive:

- Advance notice of forthcoming editions of the book
- Related book recommendations
- Chapter excerpts and supplements of forthcoming titles
- Information about special contests and promotions throughout the year
- Notices and reminders about author appearances, tradeshows, and online chats with special guests

Contact us

If you are interested in writing a book or reviewing manuscripts prior to publication, please write to us at:

Editorial Department
Addison-Wesley Professional
75 Arlington Street, Suite 300
Boston, MA 02116 USA
Email: AWPro@aw.com

Addison-Wesley

Visit us on the Web: http://www.aw.com/cseng